ATLAS OF HAWAII

SECOND EDITION

Atlas of Hawaii

Department of Geography
University of Hawaii

 UNIVERSITY OF HAWAII PRESS   Honolulu

Copyright © 1983 by the University of Hawaii Press
Copyright © 1973 by The University Press of Hawaii
First edition 1973
Second edition 1983
Manufactured in the United States of America

Library of Congress Cataloging in Publication Data

University of Hawaii (Honolulu). Dept. of
  Geography.
  Atlas of Hawaii.

  Bibliography: p.
  1. Hawaii—Maps. I. Armstrong, R. Warwick.
II. Bier, James Allen. III. Title.
G1534.20.U5 1983   912'.969   82-675462
ISBN 0-8248-0837-1

Editor and Project Director: R. Warwick Armstrong
Professor of Public Health and Geography, University of Hawaii at
Manoa, Honolulu.

Cartographer: James A. Bier
Cartographer, Department of Geography, University
of Illinois at Urbana-Champaign.

Deputy Project Director: Joseph R. Morgan
Assistant Professor of Geography, University of Hawaii at
Manoa, Honolulu.

STAFF

Cartographic Drafting: George W. Hall III, Karen T. Fukushima
Department of Geography, University of Hawaii at Manoa,
Honolulu.

Cover Design and Photo-cartographic Specialist: Everett A. Wingert
Associate Professor of Geography, University of Hawaii at Manoa, Honolulu.

Place Name Authority: Samuel H. Elbert
Professor Emeritus of Pacific Languages and Linguistics,
University of Hawaii at Manoa, Honolulu.

Secretary: Monica Y. Okido
Department of Geography, University of Hawaii at Manoa, Honolulu.

Technical Assistants: Rebecca Brown • Mary Dee •
Christopher Galik • Lee S. Motteler •
Patricia A. Pennywell • Tokiko Sato

CARTOGRAPHIC ASSISTANCE

Samuel Aea • Michael W. Armstrong • Paul Bacon •
Jeff Bejach • John Briel • E. H. Bryan, Jr. • Thomas A. Burch •
Bobbie Camaro •Jen-hu Chang • P. Kalani Chong •
Julie Chun • Roxanne M. Chun • Charlie Daley •
Paul C. Ekern, Jr. • Susan Ezawa • Gary A. Fuller • Pam Gring •
Kathryn Gibbs • Chandra Gurung • Stanly E. Harter •
Nathan Higashida • Barbara Hopp • Lorie Koba •
Jeri Kuwada •Jack Leishman • Linda Lembeck •
Kathy McBryde • Donald Martin • Ryland Moore •
Lauren Nagata • Blake Nakamura • Patricia-Ann Otsuka •
Christopher Peterson • Ilima Piianaia • Paul Schwind •
Iris Shinohara • John M. Street • Katie Y. Takeshita •
Eileen Tamaru • Ross Togashi • George H. Tokuyama

THE COVER

This map of the Hawaiian Islands is a three-dimensional cartographic depiction viewed from a point east of the island of Hawaii and along the chain to the northeast. It shows the landforms under the ocean as well as above, and the great bulk of Mauna Loa and Mauna Kea rising six miles above the bottom of the Hawaiian Deep is clearly apparent. The vertical exaggeration of the drafting is over eight times, and the horizontal scale in the foreground is 1:1,000,000. The map is constructed by plotting a series of profiles from contour and bathymetric maps. These profiles produce a distorted grid similar to a fishnet which is then used as a base for the final drawing. The underwater area was prepared with an airbrush to give a softened effect, and the above-water area with pencil to produce a land texture.

ATLAS COMMITTEE

Roland J. Fuchs, Chairman, Department of Geography, University of Hawaii at
  Manoa, Honolulu.
Robert W. Sparks, Director, University of Hawaii Press, Honolulu.
R. Warwick Armstrong • Joseph R. Morgan • Brian J. Murton •
Abraham Piianaia • Everett A. Wingert

CONTRIBUTING AUTHORS AND COMPILERS

Agatin T. Abbott*, Professor of Geology, University of Hawaii at Manoa, Honolulu.

Harold L. Baker, Specialist, Agricultural Economics, University of Hawaii at Manoa, Honolulu.

Andrew J. Berger, Professor of Zoology, University of Hawaii at Manoa, Honolulu.

David Bess, Professor of Transportation, University of Hawaii at Manoa, Honolulu.

Robert T. Bobilin, Professor of Religion, University of Hawaii at Manoa, Honolulu.

Edith H. Chave, Marine Programs, University of Hawaii at Manoa, Honolulu.

Michaelyn P. Chou, Head of Public Services, Special Collections, Hamilton Library, University of Hawaii at Manoa, Honolulu.

Anders P. Daniels, Associate Professor of Meteorology, University of Hawaii at Manoa, Honolulu.

Gavan Daws, Professor of History, Australian National University, Canberra.

Bryce G. Decker, Assistant Professor of Geography, University of Hawaii at Manoa, Honolulu.

Donald W. Fryer, Professor of Geography, University of Hawaii at Manoa, Honolulu.

P. Bion Griffin, Associate Professor of Anthropology, University of Hawaii at Manoa, Honolulu.

D. Elmo Hardy, Senior Professor of Entomology, University of Hawaii at Manoa, Honolulu.

John R. Healy, Professor of Geography, University of Hawaii at Hilo, Hilo.

Paul F. Hooper, Associate Professor of American Studies, University of Hawaii at Manoa, Honolulu.

E. Alison Kay, Professor of Zoology, University of Hawaii at Manoa, Honolulu.

Sarah S. King, Professor of Communication, University of Hawaii at Manoa, Honolulu.

Edgar C. Knowlton, Jr., Professor of European Languages, University of Hawaii at Manoa, Honolulu.

David H. Kornhauser, Professor of Geography, University of Hawaii at Manoa, Honolulu.

Charles H. Lamoureux, Professor of Botany, University of Hawaii at Manoa, Honolulu.

L. Stephen Lau, Director, Water Resources Research Center, University of Hawaii at Manoa, Honolulu.

Nancy D. Lewis, Assistant Professor of Geography, University of Hawaii at Manoa, Honolulu.

Gordon A. Macdonald*, Senior Professor of Geology and Geophysics, University of Hawaii at Manoa, Honolulu.

Ralph M. Moberly, Professor of Geology, University of Hawaii at Manoa, Honolulu.

Sally W. Morgan, Pearl City Regional Library, State of Hawaii.

Hal F. Olson, Department of Geography, University of Hawaii at Manoa, Honolulu.

Abraham Piianaia, Director, Hawaiian Studies Program, University of Hawaii at Manoa, Honolulu.

Saul Price, Regional Climatologist, National Weather Service, Pacific Region, National Oceanic and Atmospheric Administration, Honolulu.

Mark J. Rauzon, Department of Geography, University of Hawaii at Manoa, Honolulu.

Robert C. Schmitt, State Statistician, Department of Planning and Economic Development, State of Hawaii, Honolulu.

Yung C. Shang, Associate Professor of Agricultural Economics, University of Hawaii at Manoa, Honolulu.

Ralph K. Stueber, Professor of Education, University of Hawaii at Manoa, Honolulu.

P. Quentin Tomich, Animal Ecologist, Department of Health, State of Hawaii, Honokaa.

Daniel W. Tuttle, Jr., Specialist, Educational Administration, University of Hawaii at Manoa, Honolulu.

Goro Uehara, Professor of Soil Science, University of Hawaii at Manoa, Honolulu.

Lyndon L. Wester, Associate Professor of Geography, University of Hawaii at Manoa, Honolulu.

Ramon D. Wolstencroft, Astronomer, Royal Observatory, Edinburgh.

*deceased

ACKNOWLEDGEMENTS

It is not possible to acknowledge individually the help received from a large number of people in the University of Hawaii, government agencies, and private industry, and from many private individuals. Specific contributions to text, maps, and illustrations are acknowledged on the page where they appear in the Atlas.

Special recognition is due authors and cartographic assistants who volunteered their time and talents to the Atlas without remuneration. Their generosity and cooperation made it possible for the small staff to produce the Atlas within the constraining limits of time and money available. The second edition of the Atlas of Hawaii was compiled and drafted in twelve months.

Many government and private organizations contributed information through official publications and personal correspondence. They are listed on this page. Special mention is made of the State Department of Planning and Economic Development which provided a substantial portion of the statistical data. Its staff gave much valuable assistance with clarification of questions on statistics, boundaries, and geographic names.

The coastlines, geodesy, and most of the place names for Atlas maps were taken from maps of the U.S. Geological Survey and National Ocean Survey. The chief reference was the Geological Survey 7.5-minute quadrangle topographic map series, scale 1:24,000.

Since the publication of the first edition in 1973, many people have pointed out errors or made suggestions for improvements. Their help is greatly appreciated and wherever possible the suggestions have been incorporated into the second edition.

The Atlas project (second edition) was financed primarily by a grant from the University of Hawaii to the Department of Geography for cartography and drafting.

Publication was financed by the University of Hawaii Press.

CONTRIBUTING ORGANIZATIONS

United States Government. Bureau of Sport Fisheries and Wildlife, Forest Service (Institute of Pacific Islands Forestry), Geological Survey, National Ocean Survey, National Park Service, National Weather Service, Postal Service, Soil Conservation Service.

State of Hawaii. Department of Agriculture, Department of Defense, Department of Education, Department of Health, Department of Land and Natural Resources, Department of Planning and Economic Development, Department of Regulatory Agencies, Department of Social Services and Housing, Department of Taxation, Department of Transportation, Hawaii Cooperative Health Statistics System, Hawaii Public Television, Office of the Lieutenant Governor, State Archives, State Foundation on Culture and the Arts, The Judiciary, University of Hawaii.

City and County of Honolulu. Board of Water Supply, Civil Defense Agency, Department of General Planning, Fire Department, Department of Parks and Recreation, Department of Public Works, Police Department.

County of Hawaii. Civil Defense Agency, Planning Department, Research and Development Department.

County of Kauai. Civil Defense Agency, Fire Department, Department of Public Works, Department of Water.

County of Maui. Civil Defense Agency, Parks Department, Planning Department, Department of Water Supply.

Private Organizations. Bank of Hawaii (Department of Business Research), Bernice P. Bishop Museum (Pacific Scientific Information Center), Chamber of Commerce of Hawaii, Hawaii Audubon Society, Hawaii Visitors Bureau, Hawaiian Electric Company, Hawaiian Sugar Planters' Association, Hawaiian Telephone Company, Kauai Electric Company, Pineapple Growers Association of Hawaii.

CONTENTS

5

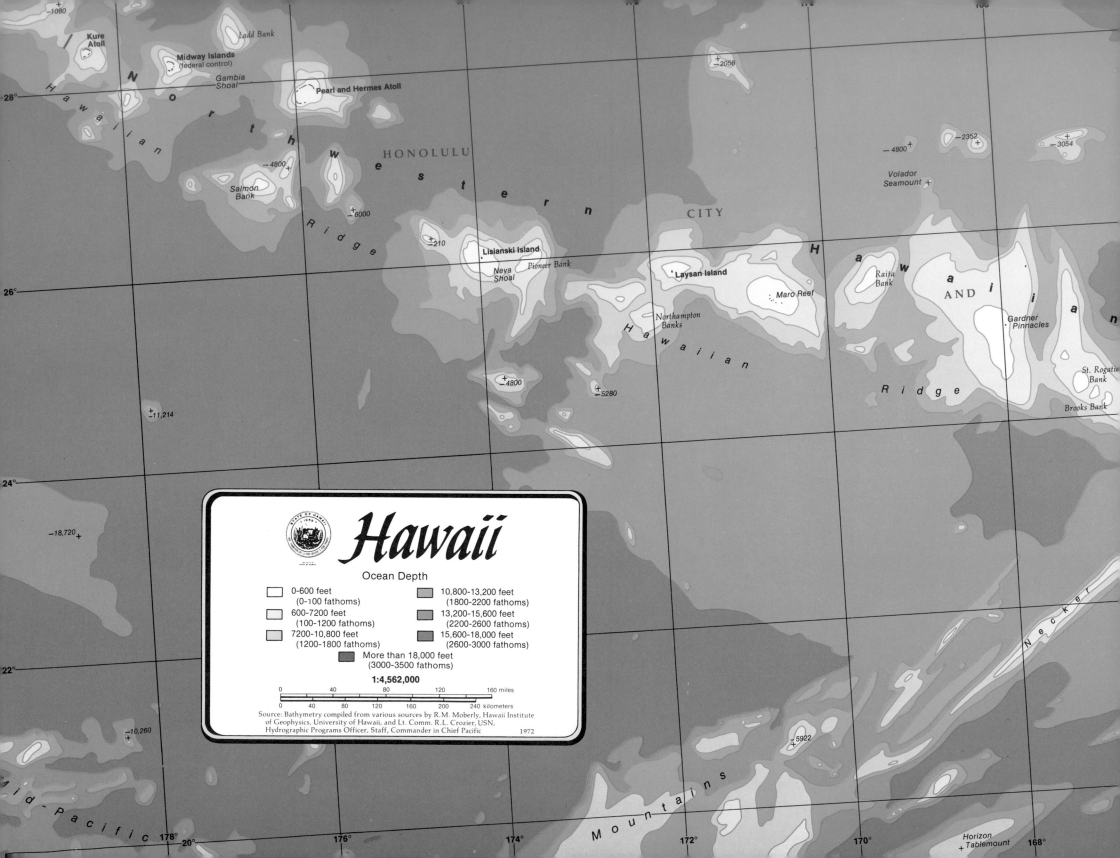

Hawaii

Ocean Depth

0-600 feet (0-100 fathoms)		10,800-13,200 feet (1800-2200 fathoms)
600-7200 feet (100-1200 fathoms)		13,200-15,600 feet (2200-2600 fathoms)
7200-10,800 feet (1200-1800 fathoms)		15,600-18,000 feet (2600-3000 fathoms)

More than 18,000 feet
(3000-3500 fathoms)

1:4,562,000

0   40   80   120   160 miles

0   40   80   160   200   240 kilometers

Source: Bathymetry compiled from various sources by R.M. Moberly, Hawaii Institute
of Geophysics, University of Hawaii, and Lt. Comm. R.L. Crozier, USN,
Hydrographic Programs Officer, Staff, Commander in Chief Pacific   1972

Kure Atoll
Ladd Bank
Midway Islands (federal control)
Gambia Shoal
Pearl and Hermes Atoll
−1080
−2056
Salmon Bank
−4800
−6000
−210
Lisianski Island
Neva Shoal
Pioneer Bank
Northampton Banks
Laysan Island
Maro Reef
−2352
−3054
−4800
Volador Seamount
Raita Bank
Gardner Pinnacles
St. Rogatie Bank
Brooks Bank
−4800
−5280
−11,214
−18,720
−10,260
−5922
Necker
Horizon Tablemount
HONOLULU
North
west
ern
CITY
H
a
w
a
i
i
a
n
Hawaiian
Ridge
Ha
waiian
Ridge
Mid-Pacific
Mountains

28°
26°
24°
22°
20°

178°   176°   174°   172°   170°   168°

City of Refuge · Hawaii

Puuhonua o Honaunau National
Historical Park, Hawaii Island.
National Parks Centennial airmail stamp,
3 May, 1972.

INTRODUCTION

Like the first edition, the second edition of the *Atlas of Hawaii* is a general thematic atlas which treats the State of Hawaii as a whole rather than emphasizing a particular island or area. Since 1825, when the first United States state atlas appeared, for South Carolina, many states have prepared atlases to serve the needs of general reference, resource inventory, education, or promotion. Although the *Atlas of Hawaii* is primarily a general reference work, it serves these other functions as well. For instance, the first edition has been used in Hawaii as a textbook in college and university geography courses. The information is presented primarily in the form of maps, graphs, and other illustrations, supplemented by short text discussions. Because of Hawaii's diversity of peoples, cultures, and environments, several topics not usually found in a state atlas, such as languages and religions, are included here.

The Atlas is arranged in five parts. The first contains the reference maps with 3,224 place names for towns, mountains, bays, harbors, and other features; a geographical description of the State and each of the main islands; and a text on place names.

The second part deals with aspects of the natural environment. Here, the special character of island and marine environments is demonstrated, with special note of the unique assemblages of plant and animal life in Hawaii and some of the implications of the impact of human activities on the natural environment.

The third part considers the people. The diversity of the State's cultures is treated in sections on history and demography as well as archaeology, languages, religions, and the arts. These topics inevitably overlap those in the fourth part of the Atlas, which treats elements of the economy and additional topics of the social environment.

The fifth part comprises a statistical supplement, bibliography, and the gazetteer for the reference maps. The statistical supplement includes tables of geographical and climatic data, and conversion factors. The bibliography, in which the entries are arranged by section, is intended as a guide for further reading. It also contains references cited in the text.

All maps in the second edition have been revised and updated and the text for most sections has been rewritten. The sections appear in different (and, it is thought, more logical) order, and some were retitled. Three new sections were added: land snails, astronomy, and government and politics.

All place names in the Atlas have been checked with official listings of the Advisory Committee on Geographic Names, State Department of Planning and Economic Development, and with existing maps and gazetteers. The pronunciation of all Hawaiian names in the reference map section and gazetteer is clarified by the inclusion of diacritical marks.

Page references in the text refer the reader to related materials elsewhere in the Atlas.

In keeping with the effort to introduce metric measurement in the United States, metric measures are added in parentheses where appropriate after the English measures in text, and conversion diagrams are included on maps, diagrams and graphs. Complete conversion was not practicable nor prudent at this time.

Every effort was made to ensure accuracy and consistency of information throughout the Atlas. Coverage and treatment necessarily vary somewhat due to resource limitations; that is, certain topics are not developed as thoroughly as they could have been or as fully as was initially hoped. Again, as a state atlas the prime objective was to examine Hawaii as a whole. This meant that as far as possible information had to be prepared and presented at levels of generalization appropriate for the State. All maps in the Atlas show the main islands at the same scale, which permits geographical comparisons, especially of areal densities. This helps to illustrate, for example, the true proportion of population and cultural activity concentrated on Oahu in comparison with other islands. On the other hand, special attention was not given to Oahu or Honolulu despite their relative importance in many respects. While enlarged inset maps of the Honolulu area are employed for clarification of detail, the scale of the maps used is appropriate for a state atlas rather than for a city or island atlas.

Data used in compilation of the second edition were the most recent available until going to press. A major source of information was the 1980 U.S. Census of Population; most state and county data are for 1981. The State of Hawaii, *Data Book, 1981;* and Bank of Hawaii, *Annual Economic Review, 1981,* were used as sources for data on population, economics, and society. All maps and diagrams give the source and date of information. In design the Atlas aims for a balance between maps and text. The cartography emphasizes the insular, oceanic setting, with colors suggesting the bright, natural hues of the islands.

HAWAII
THE FIFTIETH STATE

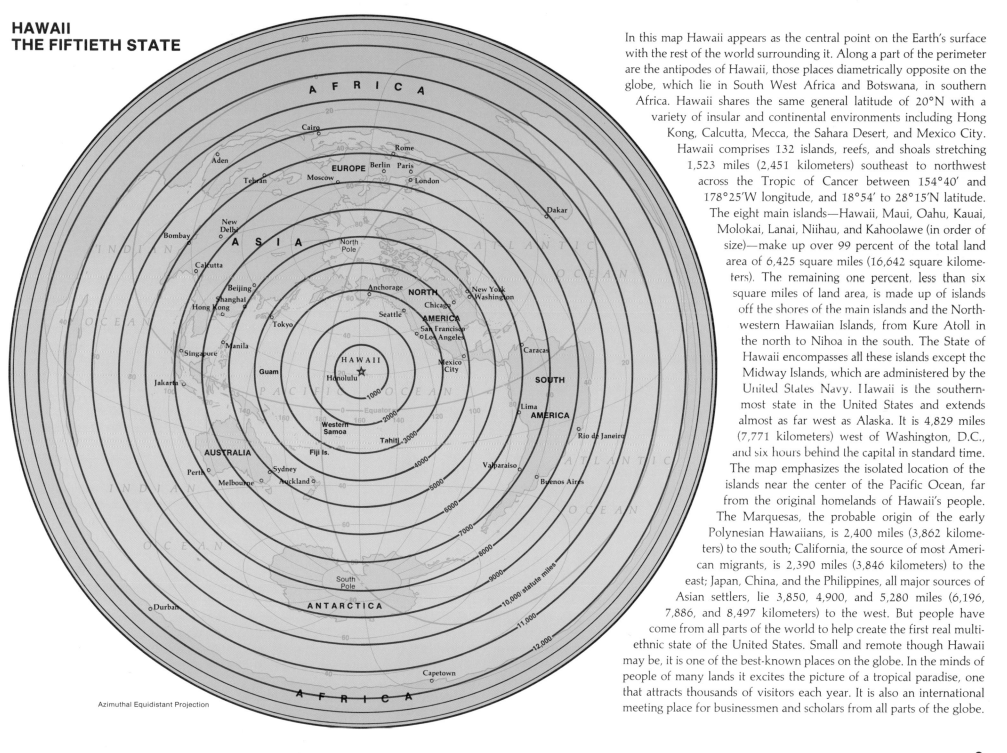

Azimuthal Equidistant Projection

In this map Hawaii appears as the central point on the Earth's surface with the rest of the world surrounding it. Along a part of the perimeter are the antipodes of Hawaii, those places diametrically opposite on the globe, which lie in South West Africa and Botswana, in southern Africa. Hawaii shares the same general latitude of 20°N with a variety of insular and continental environments including Hong Kong, Calcutta, Mecca, the Sahara Desert, and Mexico City. Hawaii comprises 132 islands, reefs, and shoals stretching 1,523 miles (2,451 kilometers) southeast to northwest across the Tropic of Cancer between 154°40' and 178°25'W longitude, and 18°54' to 28°15'N latitude. The eight main islands—Hawaii, Maui, Oahu, Kauai, Molokai, Lanai, Niihau, and Kahoolawe (in order of size)—make up over 99 percent of the total land area of 6,425 square miles (16,642 square kilometers). The remaining one percent, less than six square miles of land area, is made up of islands off the shores of the main islands and the Northwestern Hawaiian Islands, from Kure Atoll in the north to Nihoa in the south. The State of Hawaii encompasses all these islands except the Midway Islands, which are administered by the United States Navy. Hawaii is the southernmost state in the United States and extends almost as far west as Alaska. It is 4,829 miles (7,771 kilometers) west of Washington, D.C., and six hours behind the capital in standard time. The map emphasizes the isolated location of the islands near the center of the Pacific Ocean, far from the original homelands of Hawaii's people. The Marquesas, the probable origin of the early Polynesian Hawaiians, is 2,400 miles (3,862 kilometers) to the south; California, the source of most American migrants, is 2,390 miles (3,846 kilometers) to the east; Japan, China, and the Philippines, all major sources of Asian settlers, lie 3,850, 4,900, and 5,280 miles (6,196, 7,886, and 8,497 kilometers) to the west. But people have come from all parts of the world to help create the first real multiethnic state of the United States. Small and remote though Hawaii may be, it is one of the best-known places on the globe. In the minds of people of many lands it excites the picture of a tropical paradise, one that attracts thousands of visitors each year. It is also an international meeting place for businessmen and scholars from all parts of the globe.

Na Pali Coast, Kauai.

Drawing by John A. Dixon

GEOGRAPHIC OVERVIEW

Hawaii is the only state of the United States which is not located on the North American continent. The land mass that makes up the Hawaiian Islands is comprised almost entirely of basaltic rock, not the granitic material characteristic of continental locations, and Hawaii's marine location influences other aspects of the physical and cultural geography of the state.

The Hawaiian Islands form an archipelago, which, like similar island groups, extends over a vast area of the Pacific Ocean, but has little actual land area. Yet Hawaii is by no means the smallest state of the Union; three others—Rhode Island, Connecticut, and Delaware—are smaller, and the largest of Hawaii's islands, the island of Hawaii, is more than three times as large as the state of Rhode Island. To sustain a population, islands need good transportation and communication connections with other regions; modern shipping and air transport between Hawaii and the U.S. mainland are both vital and efficient. Hawaii also depends on interisland transportation of people and goods to an extent that is unique in the nation (page 180).

Although there are volcanoes in other states, no other state has a physical landscape so dominated by volcanic landforms as Hawaii. Kilauea, on the island of Hawaii, is the most continuously active volcano in the world, and volcanic features such as giant shields or domes, cinder and tuff cones, and black sand beaches are prominent on several of the islands. Loihi Seamount, now an undersea volcano southeast of Hawaii Island, may eventually emerge as a new Hawaiian island, a process that may take thousands of years. Stream erosion, resulting from the State's copious rainfall, and the constant erosional action of the sea, have carved the spectacular amphitheater-headed valleys, canyons, and great sea cliffs for which Hawaii is famous (page 35).

Hawaii's climate is one of surprising diversity. There are examples of tropical rainforests and deserts in close proximity; rainfall on the same island can vary from less than 10 inches to more than 400 inches per year (page 59).

Hawaii's climate, volcanic soils, and—most important—isolation in the central Pacific Ocean, resulted in the development of a unique endemic flora and fauna before the arrival of humans; many species of plants, birds, insects, and snails are found here and nowhere else in the world. On the other hand, humans have been instrumental in the introduction of many plants, mammals, birds, and insects common to tropical locations in Oceania, America, Africa, and Asia (pages 69–86).

Hawaii is one of a few states in which sugarcane is grown, and it is the only state where coffee, macadamia nuts, and pineapples are grown commercially. Other tropical fruit and flower products, as well as vegetables, mostly for local consumption, are a part of the state's diversified agriculture (page 154).

Tourism has become the leading industry in Hawaii—not surprisingly, in view of the islands' undeniable attractions: a year-round pleasant climate, superb beaches, the balmy Pacific Ocean, beautiful scenery, a unique blended culture, and friendly local residents (page 173). Hawaii's strategic location in the Pacific and as the state nearest to Asia, has led to the establishment of a number of military bases, which occupy a sizeable percentage of the land of the State (page 179). Military activities (the islands' second largest "industry") provide substantial civilian employment, and federal government expenditures to maintain military establishments in the islands constitute a major source of revenue (page 144). Plantation agriculture, for sugar and pineapple, is the third largest industry. Smaller industries include food processing, oil refining, and garment and textile manufacture.

The islands are by no means self sufficient, and most materials required to sustain a high standard of living must be imported from elsewhere. Transportation charges and distance from markets add to the high cost of living in the islands. Other contributing factors are a shortage of land and a strong desire to live in Hawaii. Costs of housing and food are the highest in the United States.

Hawaii's multi-ethnic population is the basis of one of the most interesting culture aspects of the State. From the time of European contact, intermarriage between Polynesians, Caucasians, Chinese, Japanese, Filipinos, Koreans, and others has always been frequent. Today there is no majority group, and Hawaii's society reflects the influence of many cultures, such as in the diversity of languages, religions, and architectural styles (page 113).

Evidences of the original Polynesian culture can be found in the form of petroglyphs, ruins of ancient temples (heiau), fishponds, burial sites, and house sites (page 95). The early Caucasian influences are seen in missionary churches dating back to the early years of the nineteenth century, while Oriental influences can be seen in Buddhist temples, Shinto shrines, and a number of Christian churches in distinctive Oriental architectural styles.

Throughout the islands several languages are regularly spoken, there is a great variety of cuisines, and distinctive cultural festivals are held. At least partially as a result of the Chinese influence, Hawaii celebrates both the Western and Chinese New Years, as well as the Fourth of July, with noisy, smokey fireworks displays.

With a total area of only 6,450 square miles (10,380 square kilometers), land is precious in Hawaii. Almost half of it is zoned as conservation, partly because of the steep slopes but also the need to preserve watersheds, while agricultural uses, plantation agriculture and cattle ranching, utilize one third. Urban uses range from modern Honolulu, with its high-rise downtown area and Waikiki, to small towns and villages, many evolved from plantation "camps" (page 147).

Land use is a controversial topic in Hawaii. On the one hand there is pressure to conserve agricultural land, and on the other, to develop land for tourism and to house a rapidly increasing population. The controversies are most severe on Oahu, the third largest but by far the most populous of the islands. Sprawling suburban communities, such as Hawaii Kai in southeastern Oahu and Mililani Town in the central part of the island, have replaced thousands of acres of farmland (page 126). Resort development, sometimes at the expense of land reserved for state and county parks, has been a controversial issue on several islands.

The political geography of the State is unique in several respects. Because of the nature of the island geography and the relatively small population and land area there are only four counties, and the mayors are not mayors of cities but of the counties. The governmental structure is distinctly different in some respects from typical mainland states. For example, there is a unified statewide school system, but no state police force (page 140). There are, of course, no land connections with other states or even between counties, yet there are two Interstate Highways.

Hawaii is still largely dependent on imported crude oil to supply fuel for electrical energy, as well as gasoline for automobiles, which are the most numerous per capita of any state. However, some electrical power is generated by burning sugarcane waste (bagasse), and there are prospects for development of energy from wind and from geothermal and ocean thermal sources (page 164). Meanwhile, electric power is very costly because of the need to import large quantities of crude oil, mostly from Southeast Asia.

Abundant rainfall in the State and a well-developed water supply system on the principal islands has thus far been able to provide for the water needs of both agriculture and urban settlements. However, there are signs of strain, as population and per capita use have increased, and on Oahu it has become necessary to regulate water use (page 48).

Hawaii gained population at a rate greater than that for the rest of the nation between 1970 and 1980 (page 107). Most of the increase in population came from immigration from the U.S. mainland, a trend which, if continued, will inevitably change the ethnic makeup of the State. The increase in population places special strains on housing and water supply, and creates additional problems in apportioning land among the competing uses.

Both sugar and pineapples are finding it hard to compete with foreign and mainland sources of the same products. In 1980, the visitor industry showed a drop in number of tourists for the first time, although the trend reversed again in 1982. Inevitably, Hawaii's future fortunes are increasingly influenced by events on the U.S. mainland. The economy, cultural diversity, and the very appearance of the islands are changing. Political decisions in Hawaii can moderate the rate of change, but they cannot prevent it.

J.R.M.

Iao Needle, West Maui.

Drawing by John A. Dixon

Downtown Honolulu and waterfront in 1982. Aloha Tower is in the center foreground.

Container ships form the mainstay of Hawaii's interstate highway to the U.S. mainland. Modern Hawaii depends on sea transport for most of its supply of food, energy, and consumer goods.

Photographs by J. R. Morgan

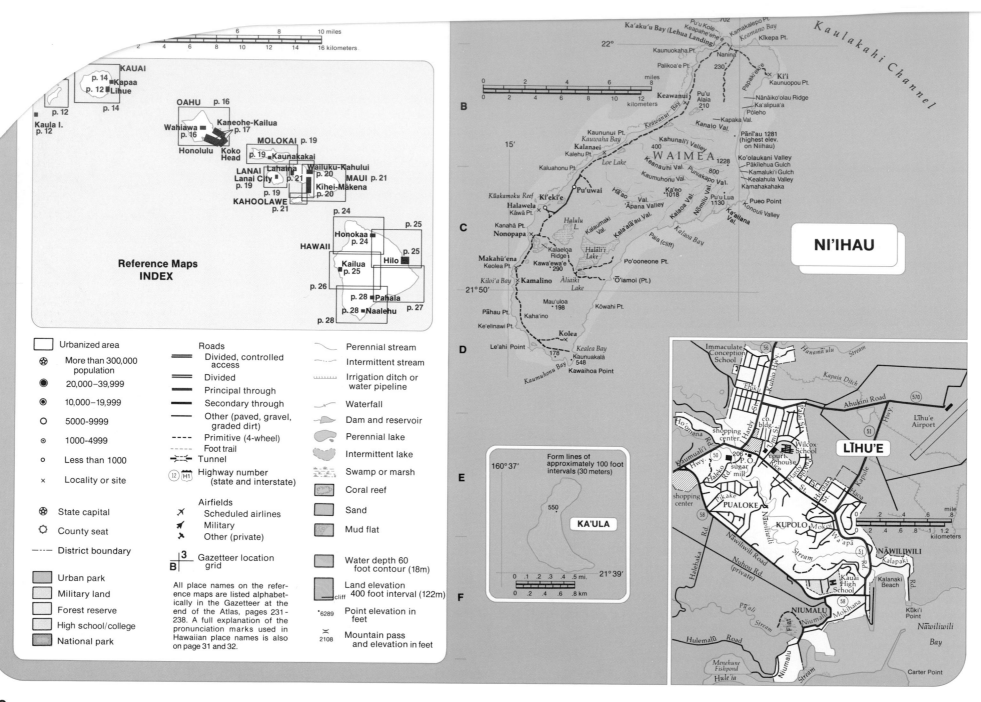

Reference Maps INDEX

KAUAI
- p. 14 — Kapaa
- p. 12 — Lihue
- p. 14
- p. 12
- Kaula I. p. 12

OAHU p. 16
- Wahiawa p. 16 — Kaneohe-Kailua p. 17
- Honolulu — Koko Head

MOLOKAI p. 19
- p. 19 — Kaunakakai

LANAI
- Lanai City p. 19 — Lahaina p. 19 — Wailuku-Kahului p. 20 — MAUI p. 21
- Kihei-Makena p. 20

KAHOOLAWE p. 21

HAWAII
- Honokaa p. 24 — p. 24 — p. 25
- Kailua p. 25 — Hilo p. 25
- p. 26
- p. 28 — Pahala
- p. 28 — Naalehu p. 27
- p. 28

Legend

Urbanized area

Population:
- ⊛ More than 300,000 population
- ◉ 20,000–39,999
- ◉ 10,000–19,999
- ○ 5000–9999
- ⊙ 1000–4999
- ∘ Less than 1000
- × Locality or site

- ⊛ State capital
- ⬡ County seat
- --·--· District boundary

Land types:
- Urban park
- Military land
- Forest reserve
- High school/college
- National park

Roads
- ═══ Divided, controlled access
- ═══ Divided
- ━━━ Principal through
- ━━ Secondary through
- ─── Other (paved, gravel, graded dirt)
- ---- Primitive (4-wheel)
- ····· Foot trail
- ═⊏⊐═ Tunnel
- (12) (H1) Highway number (state and interstate)

Airfields
- ✈ Scheduled airlines
- ✈ Military
- ✈ Other (private)

- Gazetteer location grid

All place names on the reference maps are listed alphabetically in the Gazetteer at the end of the Atlas, pages 231–238. A full explanation of the pronunciation marks used in Hawaiian place names is also on page 31 and 32.

- Perennial stream
- Intermittent stream
- Irrigation ditch or water pipeline
- Waterfall
- Dam and reservoir
- Perennial lake
- Intermittent lake
- Swamp or marsh
- Coral reef
- Sand
- Mud flat
- Water depth 60 foot contour (18m)
- Land elevation 400 foot interval (122m) — cliff
- •6289 Point elevation in feet
- ⤬ 2108 Mountain pass and elevation in feet

NI'IHAU

WAIMEA

Ka'aku'u Bay (Lehua Landing)
Keapahe'ehe'e
Kaunuokaha Pt.
Palikoa'e Pt.
Nanina — 230
Kamakalepo Pt.
Kamoano Bay
Kikepa Pt.
Ki'i
Kaunuopou Pt.
Keawanui — Pu'u Alaia 210
Nanaiko'olau Ridge
Ka'alipua'a
Poleho
Kapaka Val.
Kaununui Pt.
Kauwaha Bay
Kalanaei — 400
Kalehu Pt.
Kahunali'i Valley 400
Pani'au 1281 (highest elev. on Niihau)
Ko'olaukani Valley
Pakilehua Gulch
Keanauhi Val. — 1228
Kamaluki'i Gulch
Kealahula Valley
Kamahakahaka
Kaluahonu Pt.
Loe Lake
Kaumuhonu Val.
Punakapo Val. 800
Ka'eo 1018
Apana Valley
Kalaoa Val.
Nomilu Val.
Pu'u Lua 1130
Ka'ailana Val.
Kuakamoku Reef — Ki'eki'e
Pu'uwai
Ha'ao Val.
Pueo Point
Konouli Valley
Halawela — Kawa Pt.
Halulu L.
Kalaumaki Val.
Kala'ala'au Val.
Paia (cliff)
Kanaha Pt.
Nonopapa
Kalaeloa Ridge
Halali'i Lake
Po'ooneone Pt.
Makahu'ena — Keolea Pt.
Kawa'ewa'e 290
Aliaiki Lake
O'iamoi (Pt.)
Kiloi'a Bay — Kamalino
Pahau Pt.
Mau'uloa •198
Kowahi Pt.
Ke'elinawi Pt.
Kaha'ino
Kolea
Le'ahi Point — 178
Kealea Bay
Kaunuakala •548
Kawaihoa Point
Kaumuhonu Bay

Kaulakahi Channel

KA'ULA

160° 37'
Form lines of approximately 100 foot intervals (30 meters)
550
21° 39'
0 .1 .2 .3 .4 .5 mi.
0 .2 .4 .6 .8 km

LIHU'E

Immaculate Conception School
Hanama'ulu Stream
Kapaia Ditch
Ho'omana Rd.
Kuhio Hwy.
Ehiku St.
shopping center — Hardy
co. bldg.
Ahukini Road (570)
Lihu'e Airport
Kaumuali'i Hwy. (50)
Wilcox School
P.O. — 206 sugar mill — courthouse
Kapule Hwy. (51)
LIHU'E
Kalena St.
Haleko
shopping center — Ulukake Rd.
PUALOKE
Nawiliwili Rd.
Kupolo — Moko
'Iwa'apa
NAWILIWILI
Kalapaki
Nawiliwili Road (private)
Nuhou Rd.
Kalanaki Beach
Halehaka Rd.
Ka'uai High School
Kuki'i Point
Pa'ali
Nawiliwili Bay
NIUMALU
Niumalu — Mokihana
Hulemalu Road
Menehune Fishpond
Hule'ia Stream
Carter Point

miles / kilometers scale:
6 8 10 miles
2 4 6 8 10 12 14 16 kilometers

1 2 3 4 5 6 7 8 9

A B C D E F

159°45' 159°30' 159°15' 22°15' 22°

10 miles
16 kilometers
0 2 4 6 8 10 12 14

KAUA'I

Na Pali Coast / North Shore

Hā'ena Pt. Ka'īlio Pt. Hā'ena Lae'oka'ōnohi (pt.) Kanonui Pt. Hale Ho'omaha
Kepuhi Pt. Kolokolo Honono Pt. Anini Beach Kalihi Kai Honono Pt.
Waihuakua Bch. Hanakoa Pt. caves Makana 1280 Mauna Pulu'ō 1766 Kulanalilia
Makahoa Pt. Princeville Kalihiwai Crater Hill 568
Waiʻoli Bay Hanalei Bay Ka Manu Pu'u 690 Kīlauea Kīlauea Point Mōkōlea Bay
Kīlauea Rock Makapili Rock Ke'ilu Pt. Kepuhi Pt. Kulikoa Pt. Pākalā
Kalae'āmana (pt.) Moloa'a Bay

Hanalei Pu'oku Kalihi Wai Pu'ohenui Waiakalua Str. Pu'u Au'au Pāpa'a Bay

Hanakāpī'ai Bch. Kalalau Str. Pōnākea 3355 Pali 'Ele'ele 3225 HANALEI
Hihīmanu 2262 1272 Pu'u Pane Kamoku Kahala Point Laeokaili'u (pt.) Kua'ehu Pt.
Kalalau Beach Coast Guard Ni'ani'au 3558 Hono'onāpali Kilohana 4030 Pu'u 'Iliahi 3390
Māmalahoa 3745 3204 Kapaka Haleone 2007 Kahili 2561 Kaho'opulu Pu'u Ehu 1946
Anahola Bay Anahola

Keawanui Alapi'i Pt. Makuaiki Pt. Puanaiea Pt. Ni'ani'au 3330 Keanapuka 4080
Kamakeanu Kaliko Ho'opouli Falls Kekōiki 2814 Mālamalamaiki 2010 Konanae 1433
Anahola Pōhakuloa Pt. Anapālau Pt. 'Ahihi Pt. Lae Lipoa Lae o Paliku (pt.)

Mākole Miloli'i Kawai ulu Val. 3880 Pu'u Manu Kaliko 4200 Nāmolokama Mtn. 4421
Pu'u Kamaha 4016 Kawailena 3300 Kualapa 2128 Maheo 2155 Makaleha Mtns. 3255
Wēkiu 2592 Keiwa Rg. Kamāhuna 1726 Kumukumu Keālia

Mākaha Point Mākaha Ridge Kahalua Valley Pu'u o Hua 4160 Pu'u Lā'au 3504
Mōhihi Falls Awini Falls Pōhakupili Maiaki 2750 Kapa'a Str. Kawaihau

Mākole Kauhao Kauhao Rg. Kā'aweiki Val. Polihale Sacred Spr. Waipo'o Falls 800
Kohua Hīnalele Falls 280 Kapakanui Falls Kamāli'i Rg. Pōhaki'iki Moalepe
Pōhaku Pele Kamalomalo'o Str.

WAIMEA Ha'ele'ele Ka'ula'ula Kolo 'Ōhai'ula Ridge Pāpa'alai 2003 Kawai Iki Rg.
Wai'alae 4000 Keana'āwi Falls Kapa'a Nounou Mountain (Sleeping Giant) 1124
Waianuenue Waipouli Alakukui Pt.

Nohili Pt. Saki Māna Kahelunui Haleiele Valley Ka'aha 2922 Wai'ale Leli
Hihinui Falls Nakanukapo Ridge Ka'āpua Kawaikini 5243 (highest elev. on Kauai)
Wai'ale'ale 5148 North Fork Wailua Res. 'Opaeka'a Falls 'Ōpaeka'a Str. WAILUA
Hanahanapuni 910 Wailua River 'Ōpaeka'a Wailua Bay

Mānā Point Barking Sands Pacific Missile Range Māna Niu Rg. Pu'u 'Ōpae 2144
Kukui 3005 'O'opulele Falls Kipole Make'ōpihi 2980 Mauna Kapu Fern Grotto
' Aʻahoaka 1802 683 Kokomo 707

Waiokapua Kekaha Kōke'e Hwy. Kaumuali'i Mānā Pu'u Kī 1662 Kāhililoa 1872
Olokele Pālehua 4315 Ka'āpua 4451 'Ili'ili 2637 Mauna LIHU'E Kapaia Kalepa 710
Kawailoa Kapaia Res. Kilohana Crater 1134

Kaulakahi Channel Wainea 'O'oma'o Pt. Mokhana Pu'u Kī Waiānuenue Falls Kīhua
3975 'Iole 2637 Haʻiki Str. Kalaluanahelehela Kapaia Kapaia Crater Hanamā'ulu
Hanamā'ulu Bay

Kiki'a Ola Harbor Waimea Bay Lā'au'ōkala Pt. Po'o 'O'oma 2030 Kauhoko
Pe'ape'a 3059 Kapalaoa 3310 Kamo 'oloa Kilohana Halemanahu Res. Puhi Līhu'e
Līhu'e Airport Ahukini Point Kamilo Point

Nu Hale o Ko'u Kahili 3089 Mānā Wai puna Falls 280 Kanaele Swamp 2200
Kalualea 1845 Knudsen 1234 Omoe Kōki'i 1509 Ho'inakaunalehua Str. Keōpāweo
779 Kalanipu'u Carter Pt. Kawai Pt. Nāwiliwili Nīnini Pt.

'O'oniano Pt. Kauhoko Mahinauli Gul. A'awela 1963 A'aka Lani 1429
Āhua'eliku 1222 Pōhākea Res. Papapaholahola Lā'aukahi Kahuamoa Koa'e
1167 Hā'upu (Hoary Head) Range 2297 Hōkūnui Menehune Fishpond 1666 Nohiu Bay

Pākalā (Makaweli) Kaluapuhi Kaki Pt. Hoaka Pt. Mānienie'ula Kapaka 'Papa'i
KOLOA 'Oma'o Kahuamoa Māhaulele 'Oma'o Str. Kapa Kai Kapa Kai Kuahonu Pt.
Kuahunu Pt. Nāluakapohu Waita Reservoir Pu'u Pihakapu 733 Kawelikoa Pt.

Kaumakani 'Ele'ele Wahiawa Kalāheo Lāwa'i Kōloa Keke Hā'ula Pao'o Pt.
Kawailoa Bay

Port Allen Numila 'Iole'au Manuhonohono 499 Kamala Pt.

Hanapēpē Hts. Hanapēpē Kukui'ula Kōloa Landing Makawehi Bluff Koloa

Ku'unaka'iole Pt. Pu'olo Pt. Kapeku West Bay Kōheo Pt. Nahunakuea Pt.
Nōmilu Fishpond Maka o Kaha'i Pt. Manoloa Lāwa'i ula Bay Kaisekiki Spouting Horn
Natumū Bay Kīhouna Laeokamilo Nukumoi Pt. Po'ipū Kemiloa Bay Makahū'ena Point

PRONUNCIATION MARKS
The glottal stop, ', is similar to the stopping of sound between the oh's in English oh-oh! The macrons, ā, ē, ī, ō, ū, denote long, stressed vowels.

KAPA'A (inset)

0 .1 .2 mile
0 1 2 3 kilometer

Kawaihau Road Hau'a'ala Kapa'a Keālia Kapa'a Str. Laipo Rd.
St. Catherine's Church & School Kapa'a High School Hau'a'ala Rd. Mā'ikeha Canal
Kanaele 'Apopo Rd. court house Kūhiō Hwy. Olohena Rd. Mailihuna Rd.
Lehua St. Kahau St. Kapa'a Beach Park 'Ulu St. Waika'ea Canal
Panihi Rd. Mākaha Rd. Moanakakai Rd. Keaka Rd. shopping center

KAPA'A

Hanalei Valley, Kauai.

Drawing by John A. Dixon

NIIHAU • KAUAI

Kauai. The single shield volcano which is the island of Kauai has been eroded over millions of years into some truly spectacular landforms. Waimea Canyon and the Na Pali Coast, with its awesome cliffs, are products of the rain that falls on Kawaikini (5,243 feet or 1,598 meters) and Waialeale (5,148 feet or 1,569 meters), twin peaks at the summit of the old volcano. Rainfall at the latter has been measured at more than 450 inches per year. The Alakai Swamp, extending almost 10 miles (16 kilometers) northwest of the summit peaks, is accessible only to experienced hikers. It is the home of a number of species of rare endemic plants and birds. The southeastern part of the island has been eroded into almost flat tableland, now planted to extensive fields of sugarcane. Kauai has a total area of 627 square miles (1,624 square kilometers).

Sugar and tourism are the principal industries. The first successful sugar plantation in the islands was established in 1835 at Koloa, in southeastern Kauai, and the same land is still producing sugar. Extensive fields of cane are also found along much of the south and southwest coasts. The visitor industry is centered around Poipu Beach in the southeast, and near Kapaa on the east coast, with some lesser hotel development on the north shore, near Hanalei.

There are two ports, at Nawiliwili (near Lihue) and Port Allen (near Hanapepe). The island's raw sugar is shipped from Nawiliwili, the larger of the two ports, while Port Allen receives most of the island's petroleum products. General cargo, which arrives on a small interisland container ship or by tug and barge, is usually received at Nawiliwili.

The chief airport, near Lihue, has regularly scheduled flights, and there are smaller airfields at Princeville on the north shore, and at Barking Sands on the west coast. The latter serves a small U.S. Navy facility, the Barking Sands Pacific Missile Range.

In 1980 the population of the island was 38,856. Kapaa (4,467) and Lihue (4,000), the seat of Kauai County, are the largest towns. Other towns of note are: Kekaha (3,260), Hanamaulu (3,227), Kalaheo (2,500), Wailua (1,587), Waimea (1,569), Koloa (1,457), and Hanapepe (1,417). It was at Waimea that Captain James Cook made his first landing in the Hawaiian Islands in January 1778.

Geologically, Kauai is the oldest of the main Hawaiian Islands and has extensive beaches, many of them popular with surfers, and offshore coral reefs. No description of the island's geography should fail to mention the well-known Lumahai Beach on the north shore and the beautiful beach and spectacular Kalalau Valley on the Na Pali Coast. But it is Poipu Beach in the southeast that is the most extensively developed tourist site. The nearby Spouting Horn, a blowhole, is one of the tourist attractions of the area.

Kauai's heavy rainfall, many streams, and extensive areas of lush vegetation give to many parts of the island the image of a green, tropical "paradise." Hanalei Valley on the north coast, where taro is still extensively grown, is renowned for scenic beauty, and the tiny town of Hanalei (483) remains little affected by the developments elsewhere on the island. West of Hanalei on the north shore there is little development. In marked contrast to the wet areas are the dry coastal plains of the southwest where tussock, cacti, and sand cover much of the area.

Niihau. The island of Niihau is privately owned by the Robinson family of Kauai, who operate it as a sheep and cattle ranch. Thus its population of 226 is entirely rural. There has been little development on the island since it was acquired by its owners in the 1870s; it still has no community electricity supply. Private generators and batteries power some radio and television sets, refrigerators, and other appliances. The language of instruction in the single elementary school is English, but Hawaiian is regularly spoken by the residents, 95 percent of whom are of Hawaiian ethnicity, the other 5 percent being Japanese.

World War II-type landing craft make trips from Kauai, bringing supplies to the island residents and taking off the livestock. There are no port facilities, but landings are almost always possible at Kii or Lehua Landing, though dependent on prevailing weather conditions. Residents are free to leave Niihau, but visitors are not welcome unless specifically invited.

The 73 square miles (189 square kilometers) of Niihau comprise a single eroded shield volcano, with a maximum elevation of 1,281 feet (390 meters), at Paniau. An unusual feature of the island's physical geography is the presence of two large playa lakes, Halalii and Halulu. Rainfall on the island is slight, due to its location in the lee of Kauai, which shields it from trade wind rains, and its modest elevation. The ranch lands have less than 30 inches of rain per year.

J.R.M.

OAHU

With only 607.7 square miles (1,574 square kilometers) of land area, Oahu is the third largest of the Hawaiian Islands. Yet it houses almost 80 percent of the State's people and is the center of government and industry.

Geologically, the island is made up of two old, greatly eroded shield volcanoes, the Waianae and the Koolau mountains. Lava flows from both have joined to create a central plain, the Leilehua Plateau, and a raised coral reef forms the south shore of the island and parts of the remaining coast. In both mountain ranges are amphitheater-headed valleys and spectacular cliffs. At the same time there are a number of rainshadow areas on the island where precipitation is light and the landscape a semi-desert. The Koolau is the younger and the wetter remnant of the two old volcanoes.

Some of the island's most well known volcanic features were formed late in the geological history of the island, in a post-erosional sequence of eruptions. Prominent tuff cones, of which Diamond Head, Punchbowl, and Koko Head are the best known examples, are located in the southeastern portion of the island. At the southeastern and northwestern extremities of the island are rugged sea coasts.

Oahu's coastline is studded with beaches; the best known is Waikiki, the center of the State's tourist industry. Waikiki had 29,000 hotel and other rooms for visitors in 1982, half the total for the State, which accommodated on the average 75,000 visitors daily. Almost as well known are the north shore beaches, famous for their massive surf each winter, and thus the site for international surfing contests.

Honolulu, on the southeastern coast of Oahu, is the largest and most populous city in the State, the State capital, the county seat, and the headquarters for virtually all major commercial and industrial activities in Hawaii. Other urbanized areas have grown up as suburbs of Honolulu, or as small towns in their own right. In contrast to the considerable urban growth, there remain a number of small plantation communities, such as Ewa, Kunia, and Poamoho.

Sugar and pineapple plantations occupy much of the Leilehua Plateau and extend north to Waialua and south to Ewa. Industrial parks are centered around Honolulu and Pearl Harbor and at Barbers Point. The major industries are food processing, oil refining, garment and textile manufacture, and manufacture of concrete products.

Military bases and training areas occupy 26 percent of Oahu's land. The best known are Pearl Harbor, Schofield Barracks, and Hickam Air Force Base; in addition other large areas are used by the military for live-firing and training and for the storage of ammunition.

Honolulu's fine harbor is capable of handling large container ships, which bring to Hawaii most of its consumer goods. Crude oil tankers, however, moor offshore near Barbers Point and discharge their cargoes into pipelines extending to the two oil refineries at Campbell Industrial Park. Honolulu International Airport is one of the nation's busiest. Since 1979, the planes landing there have brought to Oahu more than 5 million visitors each year, and interisland air traffic is thriving. Pearl Harbor, the largest and best natural harbor in Hawaii, is the site of a naval base and is used only by navy ships or by vessels bringing supplies to military bases.

With no subway in Honolulu or rapid transit system anywhere on the island, Oahu is completely dependent on automobile and bus transportation. There are two interstate highways, H-1 connecting the leeward side of the island to downtown Honolulu and beyond, and H-2 which links Honolulu with central Oahu and terminates at Schofield Barracks. In general, the highway system is adequate, but traffic slowdowns are a feature of life for commuters to and within Honolulu.

Oahu is the center for most of the educational, artistic, and social activities of the State. On this island are the University of Hawaii at Manoa, four community colleges, and several other small universities, as well as a large number of public and private primary and secondary schools. Most of the libraries, art galleries, museums, and theaters are located in Honolulu, as well as a great variety of restaurants and evening entertainments. The island is also the site of frequent major festivals and sporting events.

J.R.M.

Kawaiahao Church, Oahu.

Drawing by John A. Dixon

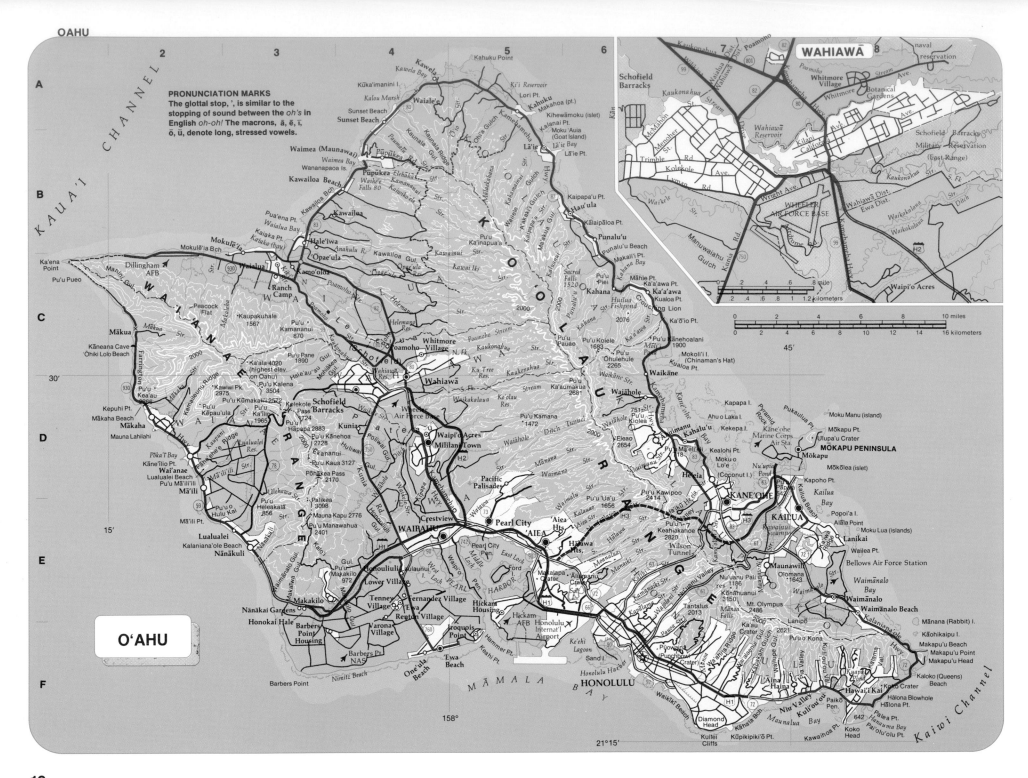

PRONUNCIATION MARKS

The glottal stop, ', is similar to the stopping of sound between the *oh's* in English *oh-oh!* The macrons, ā, ē, ī, ō, ū, denote long, stressed vowels.

O'AHU

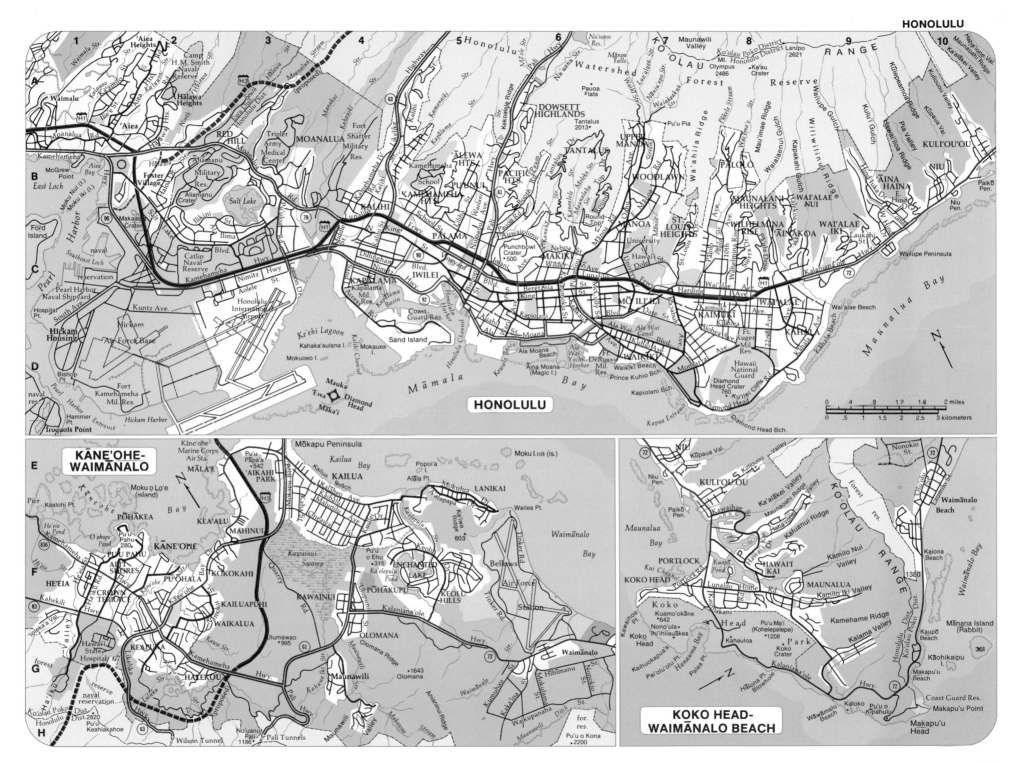

HONOLULU

KĀNE'OHE-WAIMĀNALO

KOKO HEAD-WAIMĀNALO BEACH

Congregational Church, Halawa Valley, Molokai.
Drawing by John A. Dixon

Lanai City, Lanai.
Drawing by John A. Dixon

MOLOKAI • LANAI

Molokai. Despite its small population and area (261 square miles or 676 square kilometers), Molokai is an island of surprising diversity. Three separate shield volcanoes make up its natural landforms. Eastern Molokai, with a maximum elevation of 4,970 feet (1,813 meters), receives ample rainfall and its streams and waterfalls have cut the deep valleys and the rugged topography typical of the more moist areas of the State. West Molokai, which rises to only 1,381 feet (503 meters), is much drier and consists for the most part of rolling hills and plateaus. Along the northeast shore of the island steep sea cliffs drop into the ocean, while the south shore is generally a plain with a fringing coral reef. Late in the geological history of the island, a third small volcano emerged to form what is now Kalaupapa Peninsula. A steep, virtually perpendicular cliff separates the peninsula from the rest of Molokai, isolating the small settlements of Kalawao and Kalaupapa, which since 1865 have served as colony and hospital for victims of Hansen's disease.

In 1980, Molokai had a population of 6,049 showing modest growth since 1970. However, the largest town, Kaunakakai, more than doubled in population, from 1,070 to 2,231. The second largest community, Maunaloa, has but 633 residents, a decline from the 1970 population of 872 due to the closing of a major pineapple plantation (Dole Co.), which had employed many residents. Kualapuu, with 502 residents, is third in population. It has grown, however, since 1970 and is a thriving community for employees of the remaining pineapple plantation (Del Monte Co.).

The sparsely populated west end of the island, which has some fine white sand beaches, is being developed as a tourist destination. A major hotel in that area provides employment for Molokai residents and attracts visitors from the U.S. mainland and other Hawaiian islands. Kaunakakai also has two small tourist hotels. A pineapple plantation, extensive cattle ranch lands, and a large area set aside as Hawaiian homestead lands make up the remainder of west Molokai. There is some diversified agriculture, but yields are not high. The produce reaches Honolulu markets by a twice-weekly tug and barge service, which also brings manufactured goods from Oahu. With the exception of a cattle ranch which occupies more than 14,000 acres, there is little in the way of agriculture.

Halawa Valley, a spectacular broad, deep valley with two waterfalls at its head, is the only part of the north coast that is accessible by automobile. The magnificent sea cliffs for which the coast is noted can be reached only by strenuous hiking, or from the sea. The Kalaupapa peninsula, now the Kalaupapa National Historical Park, can be reached by air, sea, or via a steep trail down the formidable cliff.

Lanai. With 139.5 square miles (361 square kilometers), Lanai is little more than half the size of Molokai. It was formed by a single shield volcano, which still shows the classic rounded form. Lying in the lee of the West Maui Mountains, Lanai receives only sparse rainfall, but it is an ideal area for growing pineapples which require relatively little moisture.

The island is privately owned by Castle & Cook Inc. through a subsidiary (Dole Co.), which operates a 16,000-acre pineapple plantation on lands at about 500-meter elevation. Lanai City was built by the island's owners and is said to be the most sophisticated plantation camp in existence. Its population is 2,092, and all but 27 of the island's residents live there.

The population of Lanai increases greatly in the summer months when temporary workers (usually high school age youths from the U.S. mainland and other islands) augment the regular labor force on the pineapple plantations. The temporary workers are housed in barracks. A variety of generally modest homes exist for the permanent island residents.

A small port at Kaumalapau has been developed on the southwest coast, providing facilities for shipping out the pineapple crop and receiving goods from Oahu. There is an airport with scheduled flights from Honolulu and other islands. One 12-room hotel serves local visitors, but there are no special facilities for tourists.

Life is quiet on the island, but all the necessities and most modern amenities are available to the residents. There is, for example, a golf course, as well as stores, a bank, post office, hospital, churches, public library, and schools. The hotel provides a restaurant for both local residents and visitors.

Paved roads are few on Lanai, but four-wheel drive vehicles can take hunters, fishermen, and other venturers to rugged coastal areas.

J.R.M.

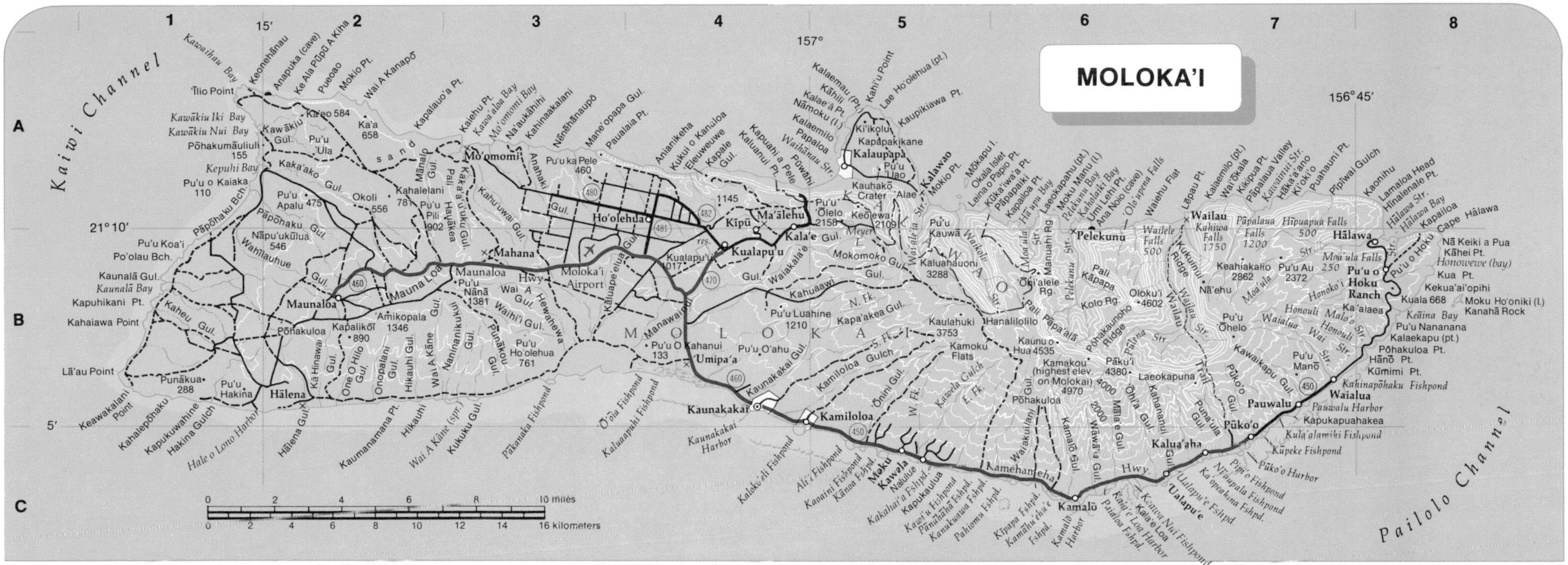
MOLOKA'I
Kaiwi Channel
Pailolo Channel
Kalaupapa
Kalawao
Ho'olehua
Kualapu'u
Kala'e
Kipū
Ma'alehu
Mahana
Maunaloa
Molokai Airport
Hālena
Kaunakakai
Kaunakakai Harbor
Kamiloloa
Kawela
Kamalō
Kalua'aha
Pūko'o
Pauwalu
Waialua
Pelekunu
Wailau
Hālawa
Pu'u o Hoku Ranch
Kamakou (highest elev. on Molokai) 4970
Mo'omomi
Lā'au Point
'Īlio Point
Cape Hālawa
Mokio Pt.
Pu'u Nānā 1381
Kaunakakai Harbor
21°10'
157°
156°45'
15'
5'
0 2 4 6 8 10 miles
0 2 4 6 8 10 12 14 16 kilometers

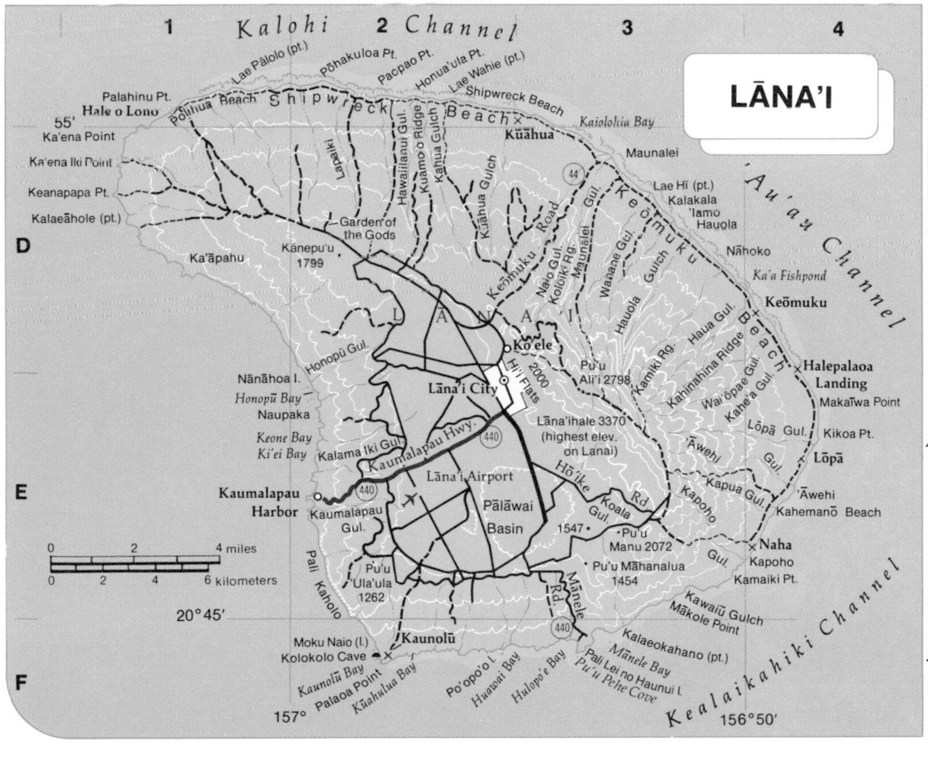
LĀNA'I
Kalohi Channel
'Au'au Channel
Kealaikahiki Channel
Shipwreck Beach
Lāna'i City
Kō'ele
Lāna'i Airport
Pālāwai Basin
Kaumalapau Harbor
Kaunolū
Keōmuku
Halepalaoa Landing
Naha
Lōpā
Maunalei
Garden of the Gods
Lāna'ihale 3370 (highest elev. on Lanai)
Kānepu'u 1799
Kaumalapau Hwy.
Keōmuku Road
Hale o Lono
Ka'ena Point
Palaoa Point
Mānele Bay
Hulopo'e Bay
20°45'
157°
156°50'
55'
0 2 4 miles
0 2 4 6 kilometers

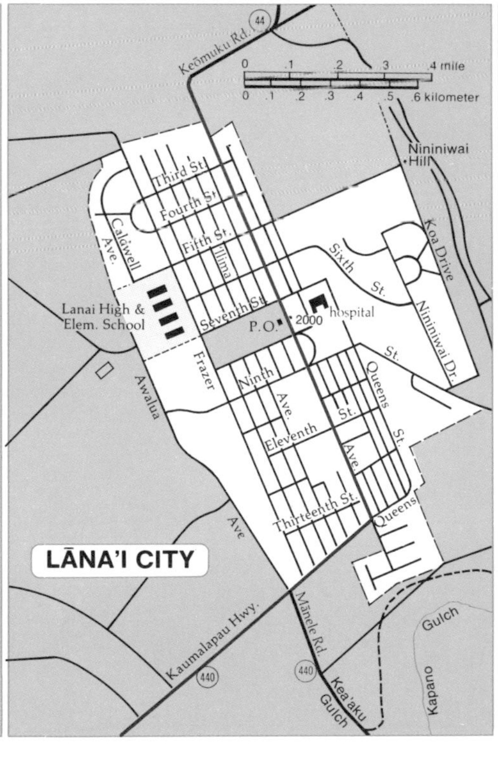
LĀNA'I CITY
Keōmuku Rd.
Kaumalapau Hwy.
Mānele Rd.
Third St.
Fourth St.
Fifth St.
Sixth St.
Seventh St.
Ninth
Eleventh
Thirteenth St.
Queens St.
Fraser Ave.
Lanai High & Elem. School
P.O.
hospital
Ninininiwai Hill
Koa Drive
0 .1 .2 .3 .4 mile
0 .1 .2 .3 .4 .5 .6 kilometer

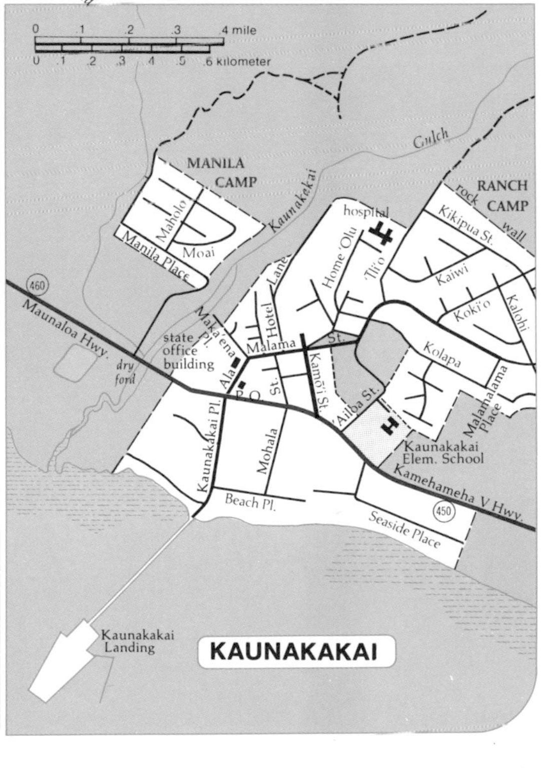
KAUNAKAKAI
MANILA CAMP
RANCH CAMP
Maunaloa Hwy.
Kamehameha V Hwy.
hospital
state office building
Kaunakakai Elem. School
Kaunakakai Landing
Beach Pl.
Seaside Place
Ala Malama
Kaunakakai Pl.
Mohala
Ailoa St.
Manila Place
0 .1 .2 .3 .4 mile
0 .1 .2 .3 .4 .5 .6 kilometer

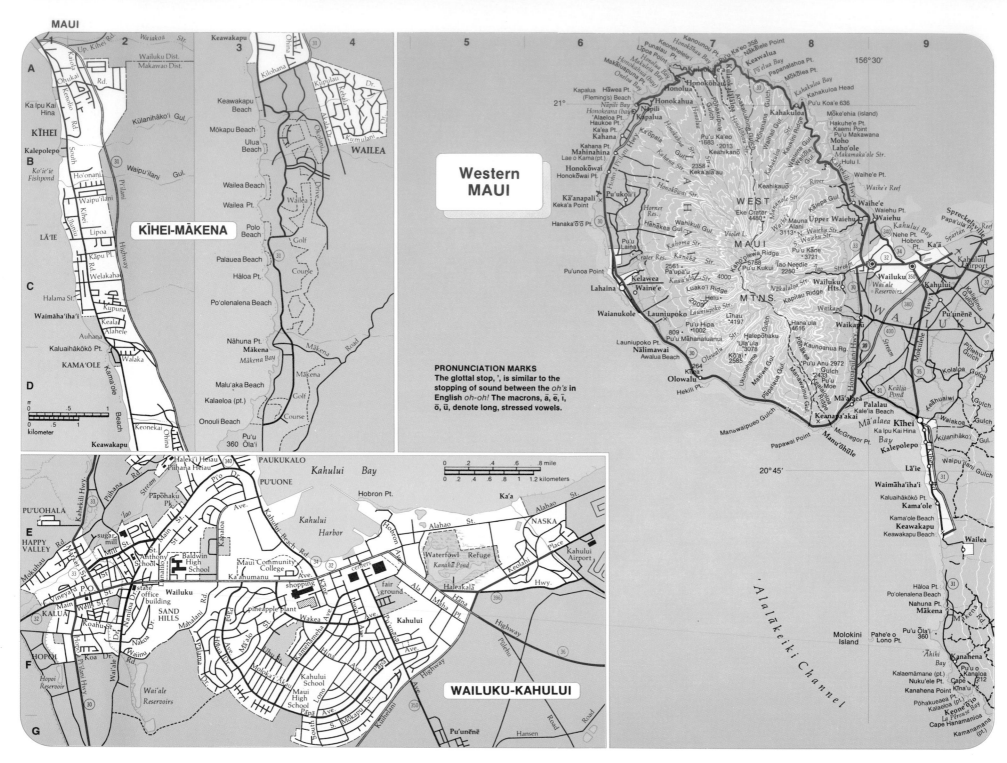

KĪHEI-MĀKENA

Western MAUI

PRONUNCIATION MARKS
The glottal stop, ', is similar to the stopping of sound between the *oh's* in English *oh-oh!* The macrons, ā, ē, ī, ō, ū, denote long, stressed vowels.

WAILUKU-KAHULUI

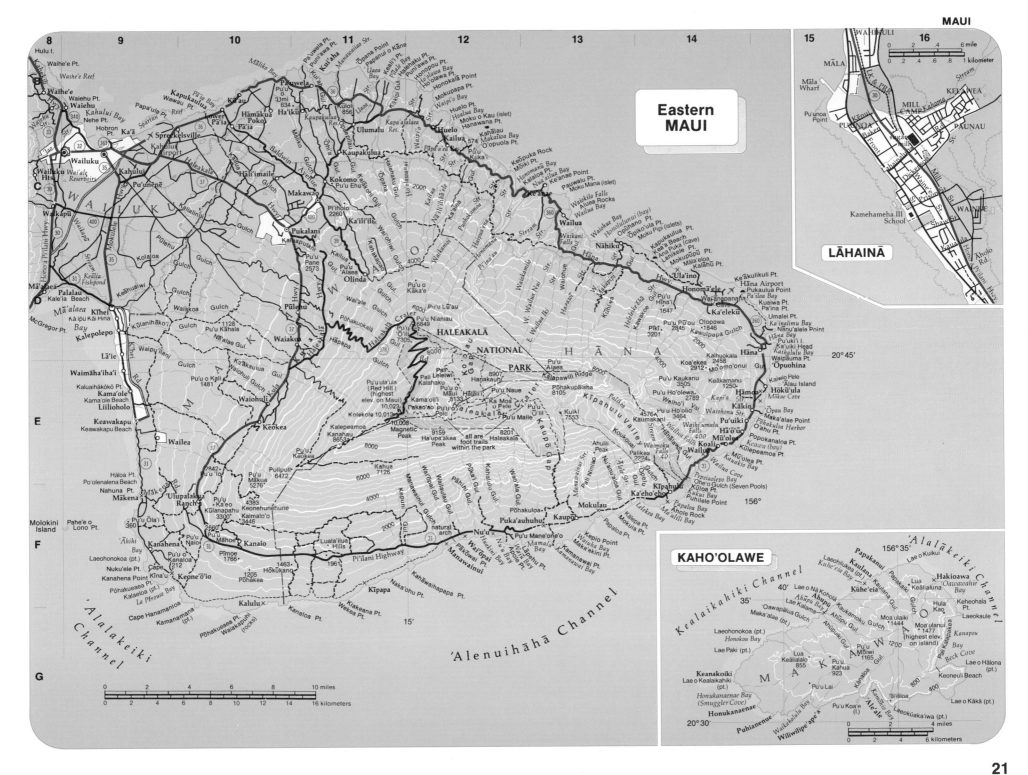

Eastern MAUI

LĀHAINĀ

KAHO'OLAWE

Pioneer Inn, Lahaina, Maui.

Drawing by John A. Dixon

MAUI • KAHOOLAWE

Maui. Two shield volcanoes with a connecting isthmus make up Maui, the second largest of the Hawaiian Islands, with an area of 728.8 square miles (1,887 square kilometers). The older of the shields, now the West Maui Mountains, has been intricately carved, chiefly by stream erosion, into numerous valleys and peaks. The highest point is Puu Kukui, at 5,788 feet (1,764 meters). The tip of Iao Needle, an erosional remnant in Iao Valley State Park, is 2,250 feet (686 meters) above the level of the valley floor.

Haleakala, the other volcano, is a giant dome, much younger than West Maui, and still showing the classic rounded form of the typical shield. Its crater can be viewed from the Haleakala National Park Visitors Center lookout at Puu Ulaula, 10,023 feet (3,055 meters) above sea level. The crater, several kilometers across, is a gigantic erosional feature in which a number of prominent cinder cones are evidence of eruptions that took place after a long period of erosion. The volcano last erupted in about 1790.

Lava flows from the two volcanoes have formed the isthmus between them. Here are some of the island's most fertile and productive soils, as well as its largest concentration of population, in the contiguous towns of Kahului and Wailuku, having a combined population of more than 23,000. Wailuku is the seat for Maui County, which includes the islands of Maui, Molokai, Lanai, and Kahoolawe.

Other urbanized areas are Pukalani and Makawao, upslope from Kahului on the Haleakala shield, with populations of 3,950 and 2,900 respectively, which serve as residential communities for many who work in Kahului or Wailuku; and Lahaina, Kihei, and Napili-Honokowai, which have grown rapidly in the last decade as tourist centers. The Kihei community hardly existed in 1970, but by the 1980 census it had a population of 5,644, while Lahaina grew from 3,718 to 6,095 persons in the same period. Both areas are ideal for tourists, located as they are in the rain shadows of Haleakala and the West Maui Mountains. Except for Wailea (1,124), also a prime tourist location, and Lower Paia (1,500), on the northern slope of Haleakala, no other communities on the island exceed 1,000 in population. Among the smaller communities, Hana, at the extreme eastern end of the island, is best known, undoubtedly for its scenic location and idyllic isolation.

Rainfall is high on the windward slopes of both volcanoes. It exceeds 350 inches per year on the slopes of Haleakala and reaches 400 inches annually at the summit of West Maui.

Tourism is the prime industry, and in the decade 1970/1980 helped substantially to improve the general economy of the island. A construction boom associated with new hotels and condominiums has created employment opportunities and encouraged investment. Construction and its associated demand for imported building materials led to expansion of the island's main port at Kahului to accommodate roll-on/roll-off container ships. Another, smaller port at Maalaea, at the southern end of the isthmus, serves as a harbor for pleasure boats and a fishing fleet.

Both sugar and pineapples are grown on Maui, mostly on the isthmus, on the northern slopes of Haleakala, and on the leeward side of the West Maui Mountains. There are three sugar mills and one pineapple cannery. Cattle ranching and diversified farming are also important.

There are numerous archaeological and historic sites on the island. The town of Lahaina is especially notable for its missionary heritage, as the former center and port for the whaling industry, and the fact that it was once the capital of the Hawaiian Kingdom.

Kahoolawe. Kahoolawe is small (45 square miles or 116 square kilometers) and dry. Its location in the rainshadow of the massive bulk of Haleakala accounts for its low annual precipitation, estimated to be no more than 25 inches per year anywhere on the island. The island's maximum elevation is 1,477 feet (450 meters).

Although a number of archaeological sites indicate ancient Hawaiian habitation, it has been difficult to put the land to economic use in historical times. Various agricultural pursuits, including most recently cattle ranching, have been attempted with little commercial success. The island is currently under control of the federal government and is administered by the U.S. Navy. It is used by the military as a target for live-firing and bombing exercises. Use of the island for military purposes is controversial, with the military maintaining that its use is justified due to the need for live-firing areas, and a community group of largely Hawaiian ancestry contending that the island should be returned to the State for civilian use, as a historical park.

J.R.M.

HAWAII

Hawaii. With an area of 4,038 square miles (10,458 square kilometers), Hawaii Island makes up almost two thirds of the land area of the entire State; hence, its popular name "Big Island" is appropriate. Five large shield volcanoes form its land mass; the highest is Mauna Kea, which rises 13,796 feet (4,205 meters) above the sea. The other volcanoes are Mauna Loa (13,677 feet or 4,169 meters), Hualalai (8,271 feet or 2,521 meters), Kohala (5,480 feet or 1,670 meters), and Kilauea (4,093 feet or 1,248 meters). Kilauea and Mauna Loa are active volcanoes; their summit craters and portions of their slopes are contained within Hawaii Volcanoes National Park. Mauna Kea and Kohala mountain have not erupted for at least many hundreds of years, but Hualalai, which erupted in about 1800, must be considered dormant if not actually active.

The size of the island and the range of elevations contribute to a climate of great diversity. The windward slopes of Mauna Loa are wet, with rainfall exceeding 300 inches annually in some areas. The leeward, or Kona, coast, on the other hand, is shielded by the mountains from the rain of the prevailing tradewinds; in some areas this coast is dry enough to be classed as true desert. Snow falls at the summits of Mauna Kea and Mauna Loa each year.

Most of the agricultural land is used for sugarcane and cattle production. Much of the sugar is grown in the wet Hamakua Coast district and requires no irrigation. The Parker Ranch, which controls about 120,000 acres (486 square kilometers), is the second largest landowner in the State and one of the largest cattle ranches in the United States. Papayas, macadamia nuts, flowers, and coffee are also important agricultural products.

The island is subject to a number of natural hazards, including volcanic eruptions, earthquakes, floods, and tsunamis. Tsunamis have caused loss of life on seven known occasions. The eruptions, earthquakes, and floods have caused property damage in the last fifty years but fortunately no human casualties.

Much of the island's population of 92,053 is concentrated in the city of Hilo (35,269). Kailua with 4,751 residents and Captain Cook with 2,008 are the next largest communities. Both are on the dryer, sunnier Kona Coast, which has been experiencing a tourist industry "boom" during the last decade. Honokaa, Kealakekua, Naalehu, Pahala, Papaikou, and Waimea, the only other communities with populations of more than 1,000, are typical of the small towns of the island.

The principal deep-water ports are at Hilo and Kawaihae. Kawaihae has seen little activity since 1972 when the sugar plantation it was constructed to serve closed down, but Hilo receives virtually all of the island's incoming cargoes and is the main port for shipment of Hawaii's sugar crop to California for refining. It is equipped for roll-on/roll-off container ships as well as other types of vessels, including tankers which bring gasoline and other refined petroleum products. The visitor industry is concentrated in Hilo, from which tourists can visit the Kilauea volcano area on short tours, and, more especially, on the Kona Coast, which has the desirable attributes of sunny weather and good beaches.

Each of the island's nine districts has its own distinctive character. South Hilo, on the eastern slopes of Mauna Loa and Mauna Kea, is dominated by the town of Hilo. Lava flows from Mauna Loa menaced the town in 1942 and could do so again. North Hilo contains the southern part of the Hamakua Coast with its sugarcane fields and small villages. Hamakua extends inland from the northern portion of the Hamakua Coast to the summit of Mauna Kea; it includes Waipio Valley and much of the rugged sea coast of which it is a part. The largest settlement in North Kohala is the village of Hawi, surrounded by the cane fields of a once-thriving plantation. Its land mass is made up of the Kohala volcano, the oldest on the island. South Kohala includes the port of Kawaihae, extensive cattle ranch land, and the northern portion of the Kona Coast tourist strip. The tourist developments continue into North Kona, where they are centered around the main town of Kailua-Kona, and served by an airport near Keahole Point. In South Kona are the Puuhonua o Honaunau National Historical Park and Kealakekua Bay, site of Captain Cook's death. Kau is noted for Ka Lae (South Point), the southernmost point of the United States, the Kau Desert (a barren landscape on the southwest rift of Kilauea volcano), and the communities of Naalehu and Pahala, former plantation towns. Hawaii Volcanoes National Park lies partly in Kau and partly in Puna District. The chief towns of Puna are Keaau and Pahoa. Notable features are the famous Black Sand Beach at Kaimu, papaya groves, anthurium and orchid farms, and an experimental geothermal power station.

J.R.M.

Pahoa, Hawaii.   Drawing by John A. Dixon

Kohala-Hāmākua HAWAI'I

PRONUNCIATION MARKS
The glottal stop, ', is similar to the stopping of sound between the oh's in English oh-oh! The macrons, ā, ē, ī, ō, ū, denote long, stressed vowels.

HONOKA'A

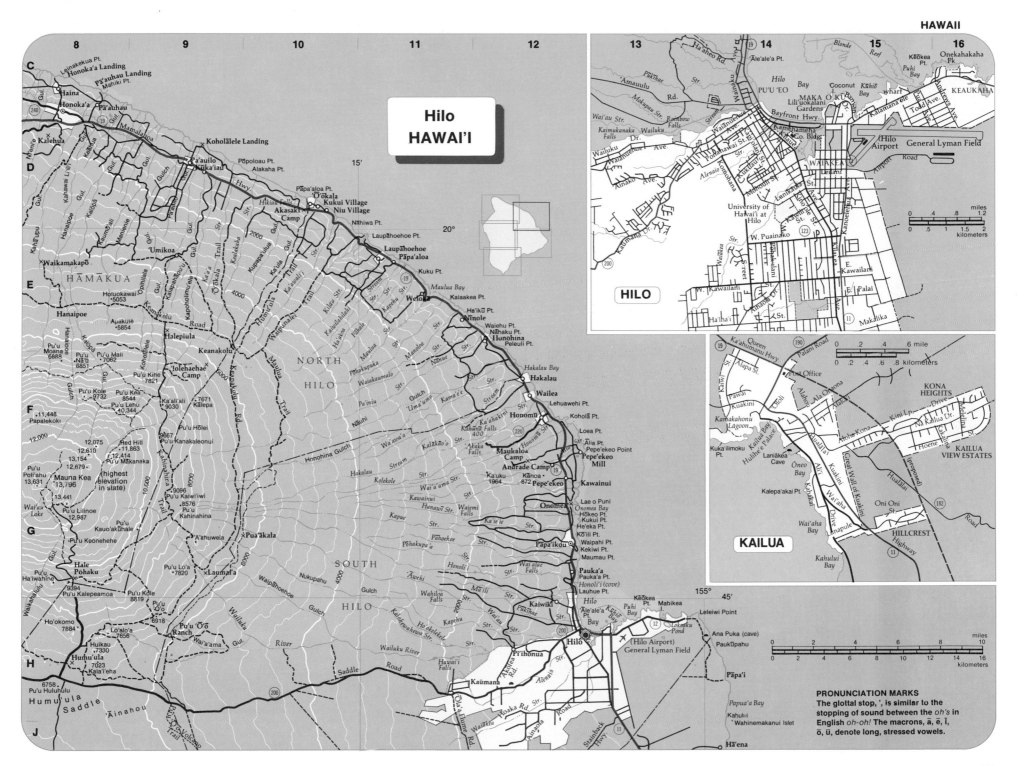

Hilo
HAWAI'I

HILO

KAILUA

PRONUNCIATION MARKS
The glottal stop, ', is similar to the stopping of sound between the oh's in English oh-oh! The macrons, ā, ē, ī, ō, ū, denote long, stressed vowels.

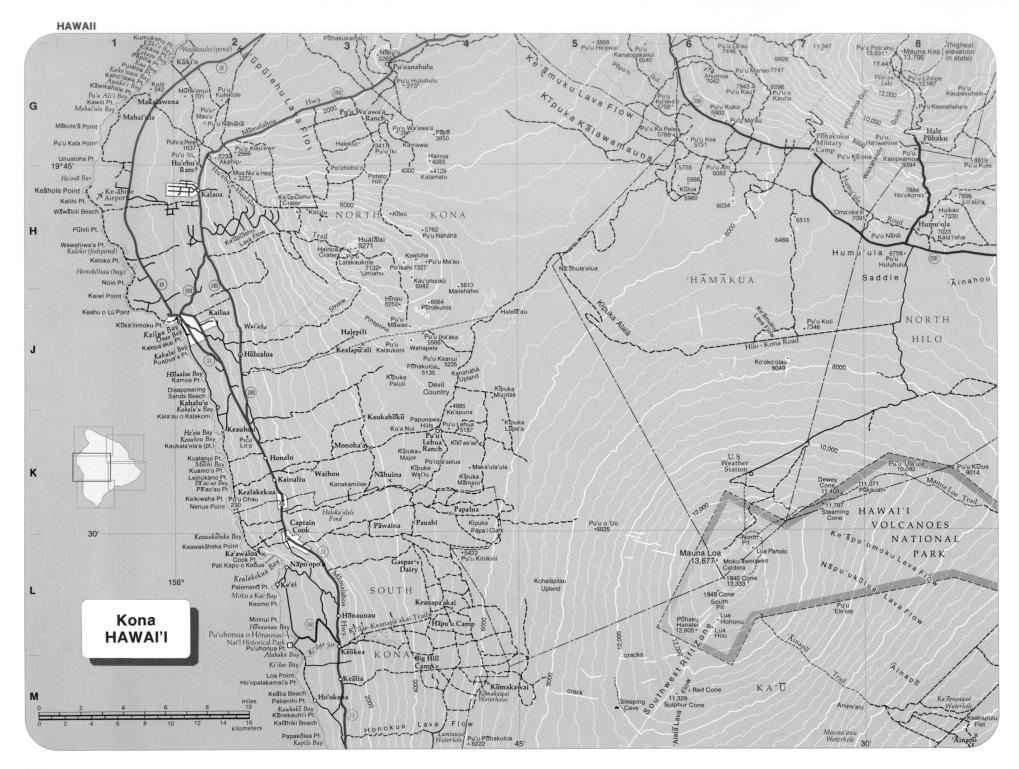

Kona
HAWAI'I

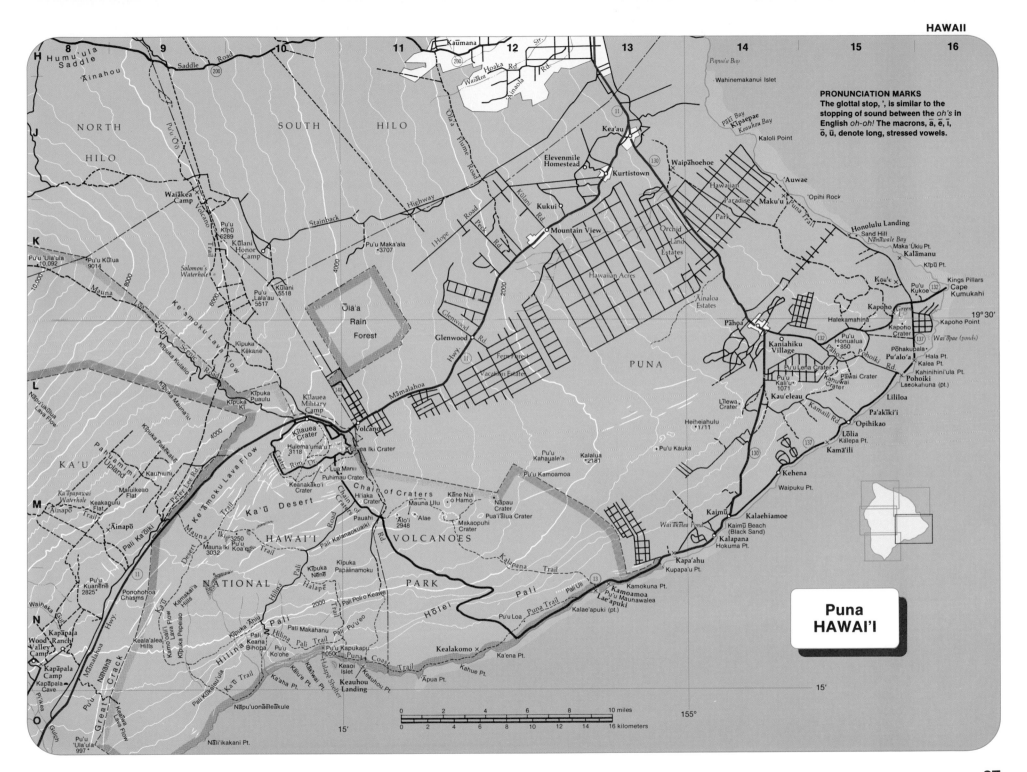

**Puna
HAWAI'I**

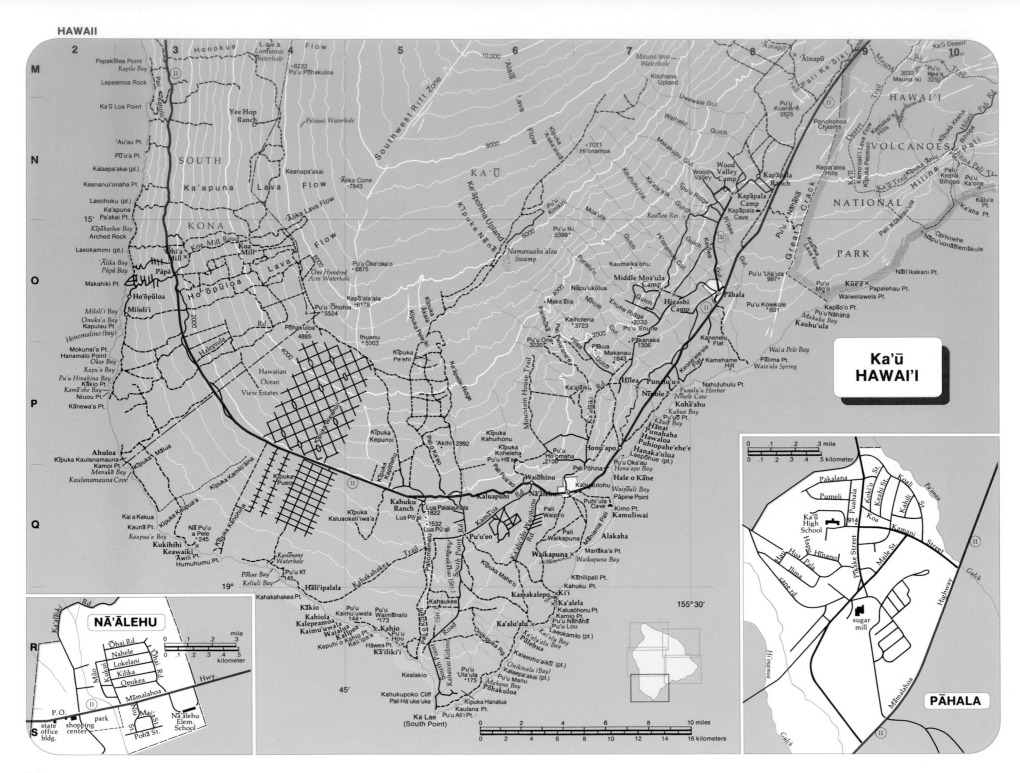

Ka'ū
HAWAI'I

NĀ'ĀLEHU

PĀHALA

NORTHWESTERN HAWAIIAN ISLANDS

The Northwestern Hawaiian Islands, extending in a long chain northwest from Kauai, are a little-known part of the State. With the exception of the Midway Islands, all the islands are included in the City and County of Honolulu. The Midway Islands are under control of the federal government and are not part of the State of Hawaii. In 1909, President Theodore Roosevelt established the Hawaiian Islands National Wildlife Refuge under Executive Order No. 1019. The refuge includes all the islands and reefs from Nihoa Island to Pearl and Hermes Reef and places them under the management of the Fish and Wildlife Service, U.S. Department of the Interior. The boundaries are currently disputed by the State.

Geographically, the archipelago begins at Nihoa and extends 1,091 miles (1,756 kilometers) to Kure Atoll. A series of submarine peaks, the Emperor Seamounts, extends beyond Kure to the Aleutian Islands. Collectively, the Northwestern Hawaiian Islands comprise 3,328 acres (13.5 square kilometers) of emerged land. The largest group of islands are the Midway Islands having a total land area of 1,280 acres (about 5 square kilometers). Some of the submerged reefs rival the main islands in size. The islands receive 20 to 30 inches of rain per year, and annual average temperatures vary between 50° and 90°F. Although most of the vegetation is typical of pantropical strand communities, unique terrestrial and marine ecological communities comprise the last near-pristine environments in Hawaii. Eighteen species of seabirds breed on the islands, with a total estimated population of 10 million birds. There are also three endemic species of land birds, and the endangered Hawaiian monk seal and the threatened green sea turtle breed onshore.

The islands have a history of exploitation by guano miners, feather hunters, mother-of-pearl divers, sealers, and fishermen. Laysan Island was completely denuded by introduced rabbits in 1913. The Midway Islands have been vastly altered by introduced vegetation and rats. Despite these disruptions to wildlife habitats, extensive seabird rookeries exist on both islands. Only the relatively inaccessible island of Nihoa retains much of its endemic biota in spite of extensive terracing by ancient Polynesian settlers. A Tahitian-like culture, isolated from the rest of Hawaii, once existed on Nihoa and the Necker Islands.

Most of the Northwestern Hawaiian Islands were discovered by accident. French Frigate, Maro, Pearl and Hermes, Lisianski, and Kure are names of ships or captains of ships that grounded on the treacherous reefs. Frequent shipwrecks testify to the continuing hazard posed to modern navigation.

Currently, three of these islands or island groups are inhabited: French Frigate Shoals has a U.S. Fish and Wildlife field station on Tern Island; Midway Islands, with a Naval Air Station, had a military and civilian population of 468 in 1980; and a U.S. Coast Guard LORAN-C base on Kure Atoll is manned by about 20 persons. Researchers and fishermen visit the area with increasing frequency. Permission to land on any of the islands must be obtained from federal and state regulatory agencies.

The Northwestern Hawaiian Islands are unique natural laboratories ideal for the study of island and reef biogeography and ecology. The relatively undisturbed biotic populations recall an earlier period when Hawaii was less affected by human development. Pressures to harvest the marine resources need to be kept in check with continued wildlife management and research to insure that these fragile environments are conserved.

M.J.R.

Nihoa Island with an elevation of 910 feet is the highest of the Northwestern Hawaiian Islands.

Drawing by John A. Dixon

Northwestern Hawaiian Islands

Island	Area (acres)	Area (hectares)	Elevation (feet)	Elevation (meters)	Western Date of Discovery	Notes
Nihoa	190.7	77.2	910	277.4	1789	Southernmost of the NWHI, settled by Polynesians in prehistoric times.
Necker	58.2	23.6	277	84.4	1786	Settled by Polynesians in prehistoric times; has extensive *heiau*.
French Frigate Shoals	56.3	22.8	135	41.2	1786	Twelve islets; has the largest monk seal population in NWHI.
Gardner Pinnacles	2.6	1.0	190	57.9	1820	Volcanic plug.
Maro Reef	awash	awash	awash	awash	1820	Partially submerged.
Laysan	981.1	397.0	35	10.7	1828	Largest seabird population in NWHI.
Lisianski	432.0	174.8	20	6.1	1805	Emerged atoll.
Pearl and Hermes Atoll	78.1	31.6	10	3.3	1822	Classic atoll with seven islets.
Midway Islands	1280.0	518.0	12	3.7	1859	Not part of the NWHI: under federal government control; U.S. Navy air base.
Kure Atoll	237.4	96.1	20	6.1	1823	Northernmost of the NWHI; U.S. Coast Guard Base.

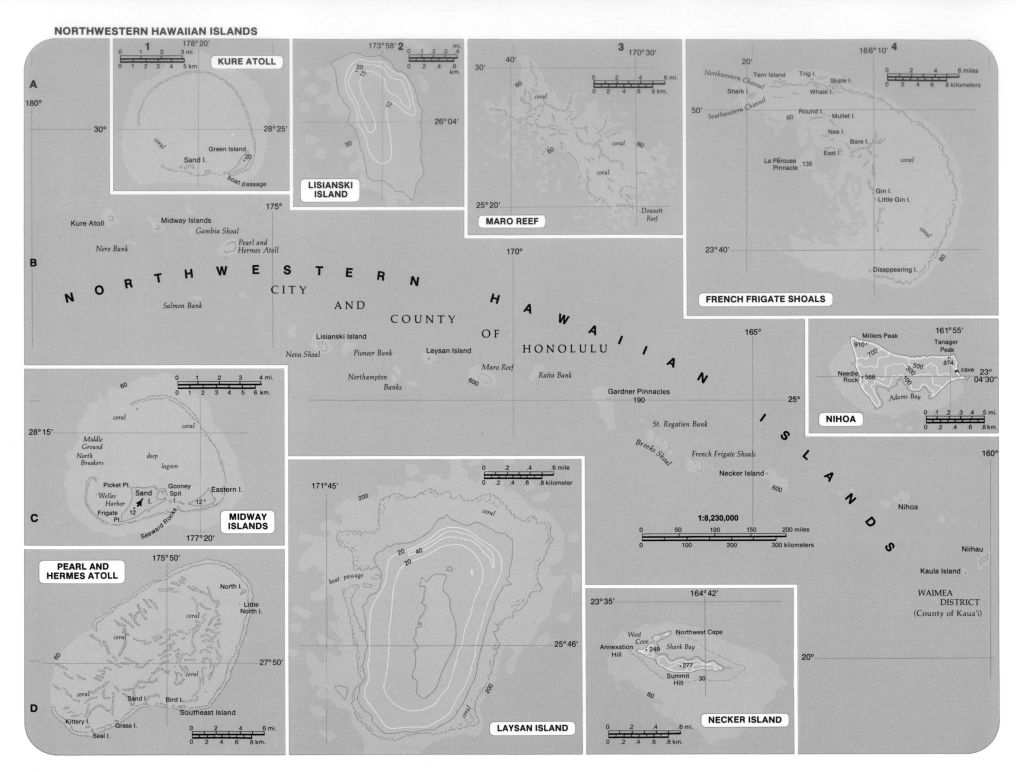

1 KURE ATOLL
178°20'
Green Island
Sand I.
coral
boat passage
28°25'
30°
180°

2 LISIANSKI ISLAND
173°58'
20
15
10
30
26°04'

3 MARO REEF
170°30'
30'
40'
coral
60
60
coral
coral
coral
25°20'
Dowsett Reef

4 FRENCH FRIGATE SHOALS
166°10'
20'
Northwestern Channel
Tern Island
Trig I.
Skate I.
Shark I.
Whale I.
Southwestern Channel
50'
60
Round I.
Mullet I.
Nea I.
Bare I.
La Pérouse Pinnacle .135
East I.
coral
Gin I.
Little Gin I.
coral
23°40'
Disappearing I.
80

MIDWAY ISLANDS
177°20'
28°15'
60
coral
coral
Middle Ground
North Breakers
deep
lagoon
coral
Picket Pt.
Gooney Spit
Eastern I.
Welles Harbor
Sand I.
12
Frigate Pt.
12
Seaward Rocks

PEARL AND HERMES ATOLL
175°50'
60
North I.
Little North I.
coral
coral
coral
coral
coral
Sand I.
Bird I.
Kittery I.
Grass I.
Seal I.
Southeast Island
27°50'

LAYSAN ISLAND
171°45'
200
coral
20
40
20
boat passage
200
25°46'

NIHOA
161°55'
Millers Peak
910
700
Tanager Peak
874
500
300
100
Needle Rock .568
cave
23°04'30"
Adams Bay

NECKER ISLAND
164°42'
23°35'
West Cove
Northwest Cape
Annexation Hill
.249
Shark Bay
.277
Summit Hill
30
60

Main map labels:
NORTHWESTERN
CITY
AND
COUNTY
OF
HONOLULU
HAWAIIAN ISLANDS
Kure Atoll
Midway Islands
Gambia Shoal
Nero Bank
Pearl and Hermes Atoll
Salmon Bank
Lisianski Island
Laysan Island
Neva Shoal
Pioneer Bank
Northampton Banks
Maro Reef
Raita Bank
600
Gardner Pinnacles
190
St. Rogatien Bank
Brooks Shoal
French Frigate Shoals
Necker Island
600
25°
Nihoa
Niihau
Kaula Island
WAIMEA DISTRICT (County of Kaua'i)
20°
165°
160°
170°
175°
180°
30°
1:8,230,000
0   50   100   150   200 miles
0   100   200   300 kilometers

THE PLACE NAMES

The spelling used on the reference maps and in the gazetteer of the Atlas differs from that used on the U.S. Geological Survey maps in that the glottal stops in Hawaiian place names are shown by reversed apostrophes, and macrons are placed over long, stressed vowels. This is done to help persons not familiar with the places to pronounce their names correctly. As the number of speakers of Hawaiian as a mother tongue has steadily decreased, the pronunciation has become more and more anglicized. Fortunately, young people of Hawaiian ancestry are showing increased interest in the language of their forefathers, and a great number of other islanders are also concerned. Such persons, if they are to pronounce the names correctly, need these two symbols. Otherwise, how are they to know that the Moloka'i town Kala'e and the southernmost point in the United States, Ka Lae, do not rhyme? How are they to know that 'Ala'ē on Hawai'i ends with a long and stressed final -'ē, but that the crater 'Alae on the same island ends with final lae? Furthermore, unless the pronunciation is known, translation of a name is impossible.

Consultants on spellings and pronunciations of place names in the Atlas have been Mrs. Mary Kawena Pukui, associate in Hawaiian culture, emeritus, Bernice P. Bishop Museum, and Dr. Samuel H. Elbert, professor emeritus of Pacific languages and linguistics, University of Hawaii. For the second edition, the Pacific Scientific Information Center, B. P. Bishop Museum, provided more than 50 additional place names for the islands of Kahoolawe and Niihau.

Some names are marked with asterisks, an indication that their pronunciations were not known to the compilers. It is hoped that persons with knowledge of these names will inform the editors so that corrections can be made in future printings.

Once the pronunciation is known, translation of Hawaiian place names is in general easier, for example, than translation of American Indian names, which come from languages belonging to numerous families with complex sound systems. The Hawaiian names, in contrast, come from a single language that, although at least a thousand years old, has a historic past of less than 200 years. The sound system is simple, but as a result many words that sound alike have different meanings. *Hau*, for example, means 'dew' in Honokōhau (bay draining dew), the tree *Hibiscus tiliaceus* in Hau'ula (red *hau* tree), and 'strike' in Hauko'i (strike adze). *Mo'o* is 'lizard' in Kamo'oali'i (the royal lizard) and 'mountain range' in Kamo'oho'opulu (the wet range). Lua is 'pit' in Kalua o Pele (the pit of Pele), a type of free-for-all fighting in Kalua 'ōlohe (the skilled fighter), and 'two' in Kailua (two seas). (*Lua* meaning 'toilet' has not been recorded in any place name.)

Word division, too, causes difficulties. The name commonly spelled Honuapo is not *honua-pō* 'night land' but Honu-'apo (catch turtle). The black sand beach spelled Kaimu is not *ka-imu* 'the oven' but Kai-mū (sea crowded [with surf watchers]).

Whereas English words have about two consonants for every vowel, the proportion is reversed in Hawaiian. Many vowels are separated by glottal stops, as in Ka'a'awa, but some are not, as in *heiau* 'temple', *awaawa* 'valley', and Nu'uanu 'cool height'.

Most mainland place names are composed of single words (Illinois, Chicago, Miami). About half of all Hawaiian place names are composed of two or more words, and many of them contain grammatical particles —for example, the articles *ka* and *ke*, as in Ka'a'awa (the 'a'awa fish) and Kekaha (the place), and the possessive prepositions *a* and *o*, as in Haleakalā (house of the sun) and Pu'u o Pele (hill of Pele). The most common prefixes are *hana-* and *hono-*, both meaning 'bay', as in Hanalei (*lei* bay) and Honolulu (sheltered bay).

Topographic terms commonly used in the place names follow:

wai 'stream, river, pond, fresh water', as in Waikīkī (spouting water)
pu'u 'hill, mound', as in Pu'unēnē (goose hill)
moku 'island, district', as in Mokumanu (bird island)
lua 'pit, crater', as in Kaluako'i (the adze pit)
lae 'cape, point, forehead' as in Ka Lae (the point)
mauna 'mountain, peak' as in Mauna Kea (white mountain) and Mauna Loa (long Mountain)
kai 'sea', as in Kailua (two seas)

A few adjectives occur frequently: *loa* 'long', *nui* 'large', *iki* 'small', and *'ula* 'red' (by far the most common color found in the place names—which is not surprising, since red was the sacred Polynesian color and a symbol of royalty).

Puuhonua o Honaunau (City of Refuge), Hawaii Island.

Drawing by John A. Dixon

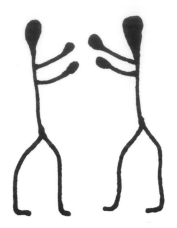

Petroglyph: boxers, Kalailinui, Maui.

The place names may be classified as descriptive, legendary, cultural, transferred, and newly coined:

Descriptive names include the previously mentioned Honolulu, Mauna Kea, Mauna Loa, and Nu'uanu, as well as Kawailoa (the long stream), Pu'u 'Ula'ula (red hill), and many more.

Names with legendary associations include the names of gods and demigods of old, as Nā iwi o Pele (the bones of Pele) and Wai a Kāne (water of Kāne). On each island was a *heiau* called Hale o Lono, dedicated to worship of Lono, god of clouds, the sea, agriculture, and fertility. The island of Maui was named for the culture hero, Māui, who snared the sun in the crater of Haleakalā to lengthen the day so that his mother, Hina, would have time to dry her tapa. The island name must once have been Māui, but during the centuries it has been shortened to present-day Maui.

Kohelepelepe (fringed vagina) is an old name for Koko Crater. Kamapua'a, the pig god, attempted to ravish Pele at Kapoho, Hawai'i. Pele's sister, Kapo, had a flying vagina that she could send where she willed. She sent it to entice Kamapua'a, who straightway forgot Pele and followed the flying object to Koko Crater, O'ahu, where it landed, left an imprint, and then flew away to Kalihi.

Names that show the cultural interests of the Hawaiians include words for objects of material culture and the names of plants and animals. We find *hale* 'house', *pā* 'fence, enclosure', *wa'a* 'canoe', *lei* 'garland', *lama* 'torch', and *ko'i* 'adze'.

Plant names, especially *kukui* 'candlenut' and *hau* 'Hibiscus tiliaceus', are extremely common: on each of the major islands is a place called Kukui. The kukui is the State tree, a symbol of enlightenment and wisdom because its nuts were used for small oil lamps. Other plants named frequently are *niu* 'coconut', *hala* 'pandanus', the *maile* vine, and the *lehua* flower. In all, at least 153 plant names have been noted.

Names of fish and other sealife are less common. They include *manō* 'shark', *puhi* 'eel', and such well-known fish as *'ahi, 'ama, 'anae, awa, kala, kūmū, uhu,* and *ulua.* Land animals named are *pua'a* 'pig', *'īlio* 'dog', *'iole* 'rat', and the birds *pueo* 'owl', *'alae* 'mudhen', *'alalā* 'crow', and *'elepaio* 'flycatcher', as well as *manu* 'bird'.

Names brought from the homeland in the original Hawaiian migrations may have been numerous, but only a few survive that are definitely known as place names elsewhere. Hawai'i, Ka'ū, 'Upolu, and Manu'a are cognate (that is, derived from a single source) with Savai'i, Ta'ū, and 'Upolu, all of them names of islands or island groups in Samoa. Cognates of Ko'olau (windward) and Kona (leeward) occur in most parts of Polynesia—for example, the Tokelau Islands, north of Samoa, and the Kingdom of Tonga, far to the south. Kahiki-nui on East Maui is cognate with Tahitinui in Tahiti and Tawhitinui in New Zealand. Except for Ko'olau and Kona, these names have no meanings in Hawaiian. Other important names without meanings and for which cognates have not been found in the South Sea islands include Kaua'i and Moloka'i.

Place names are continually being coined, especially by developers, who, in seeking names for their developments and new streets, unfortunately do not look for the old Hawaiian names, or endeavor to discover who were the original owners of the land. The area once known as Ka'elepulu (the wet blackness) is now Enchanted Lake. Kokokahi (one blood) was the name given by Theodore Richards for an interracial camp. The name Lanikai is probably a mistake for Kailani (heavenly sea)—why would the area have been named 'marine heaven', the literal translation of Lanikai?

Hawaiian place names, then, hold other attractions than their pleasant and mellifluous sounds, for they describe the Hawaiians, the deeds of their culture heroes, the close relationship of Hawaiians to their Polynesian cousins to the south, and the kinship that Hawaiians have always felt with the natural forces that surround them, physically and spiritually.

S.H.E.

THE NATURAL ENVIRONMENT

Kahoolawe Island. Smallest of the eight main Hawaiian Islands, Kahoolawe displays vertical sea cliffs on its southern side. The island is waterless, parched, windswept, dusty, desolate, deserted. It serves as a bombing target for the U.S. Navy. In the distance the shield shape of West Maui volcano shows beneath the clouds.   *Hawaii Institute of Geophysics photograph by A.T. Abbott*

Lehua Island and Niihau. Lehua Island, in the foreground, is a breached tuff cone which was built during a late stage of volcanic activity. Behind it, on Niihau, the dry Kiekie volcanic plain belongs to the same period, whereas the Paniau upland, in the background, is an erosional remnant of the much older Niihau shield volcano.   *Hawaii Institute of Geophysics photograph by A.T. Abbott*

Napali Cliffs, Kauai. The steep slopes of Kalalau Valley, in the foreground, display spectacular erosional effects of running water which has incised the prominent vertical grooves in the face of the palis. Wave erosion is biting deep into the volcanic shield to form the majestic Napali coastline.
Hawaii Institute of Geophysics photograph by A.T. Abbott

The Mana plain, Kauai. The arid Mana plain, formed by marine erosion at higher stands of the sea and covered by alluvium and sedimentary debris, clings to the southwest corner of Kauai. A former sea cliff cut into the Kauai volcanic shield rises sharply above the plain.
Hawaii Institute of Geophysics photographs by A.T. Abbott

Haleakala Crater, Maui. Seven miles across to the opposite wall, two miles wide, and one-half mile deep, Haleakala Crater, at an elevation of nearly 10,000 feet, is an erosional depression that was partly filled by lava and cinders extruded during a period of renewed volcanic activity. The highest cinder cone rises about 800 feet above its base.
Hawaii Institute of Geophysics photographs by A.T. Abbott

LANDFORMS

The major relief features in Hawaii are the result of building by volcanoes (page 42). Even the lowest of the islands, Niihau, is a volcanic mountain rising more than 3,700 meters above its base on the ocean floor. The tops of the highest mountains, Mauna Kea and Mauna Loa, on the island of Hawaii, are about 10 kilometers above the bottom of the Hawaiian Deep, just to the northeast (page 55).

Relief features of intermediate size are partly constructional, and partly the result of erosion. Cinder cones and tuff cones, built by moderately explosive volcanic eruptions, reach heights of 100 to 200 meters above their surroundings. For instance, Puu Makanaka, on Mauna Kea, is a cinder cone about 200 meters high; and Diamond Head, in Honolulu, is a tuff cone nearly 245 meters high above its base, which lies a little below sea level.

Valleys may be eroded deeper than 600 meters by streams. The upper part of Waimea Canyon, on Kauai, is as much as 790 meters deep. Waterfalls along the streams commonly are several hundred meters high. Hiilawe Falls, in Waipio Valley on Hawaii Island, with a vertical drop of about 300 meters is one of the highest free falls in the world.

Sea cliffs, cut by waves, range in height from a few to several hundred meters. The cliffs of the Napali Coast, on Kauai, are 90 to 600 meters high; and the sea cliff on the north side of East Molokai, one of the highest in the world, is 600 to 1,100 meters high.

On the island of Hawaii the Kahuku Pali is a fault scarp (cliff) as much as 200 meters high; and the Hilina Pali is a series of fault scarps, mostly veneered with later lava flows, that rise more than 610 meters above the adjacent ocean. Kilauea Crater (a caldera) is bounded on its west side by a fault scarp 120 meters high; and Mokuaweoweo Caldera, on Mauna Loa, has a boundary scarp 180 meters high, also on its west side.

Landforms in Hawaii are the result of construction by volcanoes, living organisms, and sedimentary processes, and of destruction by erosion.

The major constructional landform is the typical, broadly rounded shield volcano built by innumerable thin lava flows. Commonly it has at its summit a large crater (caldera) formed by collapse of the mountain-top. Similar smaller craters (pit craters) may form on its flanks. Smaller volcanic constructional forms are spatter cones and ramparts, seldom as much as 15 meters high, built where fluid lava erupts at the surface; larger cinder cones, up to 200 meters high, built by more explosive eruptions; and steep-sided hills (domes) formed by viscous lava piling up over the vent. Cinder cones are well seen on Mauna Kea and Haleakala; domes, on West Maui.

Stream erosion first cuts small V-shaped gulches, and eventually great canyons, into the volcanoes. The most characteristic stream-eroded landform is the amphitheater-headed valley, with its steep walls and rounded head. Examples are Manoa Valley on Oahu, Halawa on Molokai, Manawainui on Maui, and Waipio on Hawaii. As adjacent valleys grow larger, their steep walls meet in knife ridges, and sharp-pointed peaks such as Olomana, on Oahu, are formed. Triangular segments of the original shield surface (planezes) may be left between the lower ends of the valleys. The Pali, on windward Oahu, has been formed largely by coalescence of a series of amphitheater-headed valleys. Wave erosion cuts back the edges of the islands and forms sea cliffs (page 34). Waves also erode sea caves and arches, and where the roof of the cave is perforated, a spouting horn ("blowhole") may result.

Corals and algae build fringing reefs, and where sea level has later dropped in relation to the land, the reef surface may form a plain. Deposition of detrital material by streams forms flat alluvial floors in valleys; and the gravel, sand, and silt may be dropped where mountain streams emerge onto flatter land, building alluvial fans, or be spread over the marginal reef plains, or deposited along the shore to form beaches. Locally, the wind has built sand dunes, especially where beach sand has been blown inland.

G.A.M.

State tree, *kukui* (candlenut).

Source: Hawaii State Archives

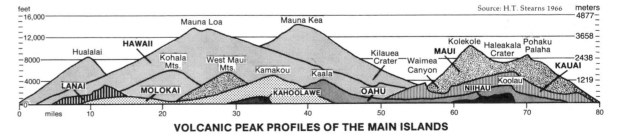

VOLCANIC PEAK PROFILES OF THE MAIN ISLANDS

Source: H.T. Stearns 1966

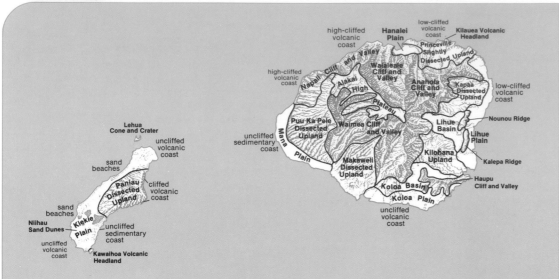

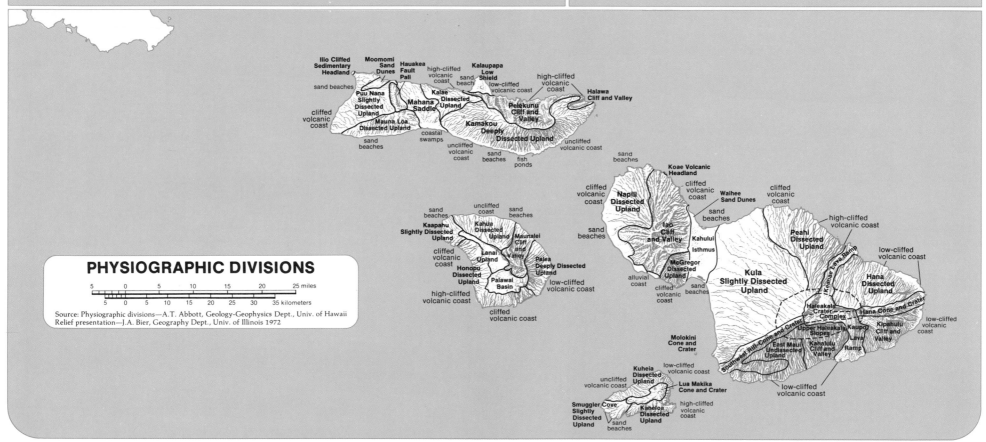

Lehua Cone and Crater
uncliffed volcanic coast
sand beaches
Paniau Dissected Upland
cliffed volcanic coast
sand beaches
Niihau Sand Dunes
Kiekie Plain
uncliffed sedimentary coast
uncliffed volcanic coast
Kawaihoa Volcanic Headland
high-cliffed volcanic coast
Hanalei Plain
low-cliffed volcanic coast
Kilauea Volcanic Headland
Princeville Slightly Dissected Upland
high-cliffed volcanic coast
Napali Cliff and Valley
Waialeale Cliff and Valley
Alakai High Plateau
Anahola Cliff and Valley
Kapaa Dissected Upland
low-cliffed volcanic coast
Puu Ka Pele Dissected Upland
Waimea Cliff and Valley
Lihue Basin
Nounou Ridge
Lihue Plain
uncliffed sedimentary coast
Mana Plain
Makaweli Dissected Upland
Kilohana Upland
Kalepa Ridge
Haupu Cliff and Valley
Koloa Basin
Koloa Plain
uncliffed volcanic coast
Kahuku Plain
uncliffed sedimentary coast
Laie Dunes
sand beaches
Mokuleia Deeply Dissected Upland
uncliffed sedimentary coast
sand beaches
Kaena Dunes
Waialua Plain
Kawailoa Deeply Dissected Upland
sand beaches
cliffed volcanic coast
cliffed volcanic coast
Waianae Cliff and Valley
Schofield Saddle
uncliffed sedimentary coast
Kaala High Plateau
Lualualei Plain
Palikea Deeply Dissected Upland
Kaneohe Bay Plain
mud flats
Ulupau Cone and Crater
sand beaches
sand beaches
Kailua Plain
Makakilo Slightly Dissected Upland
Pearl Harbor Plain
Kaolau Cliff and Valley
Waimanalo Plain
sand beaches
Ewa Plain
Makapuu Headland
uncliffed sedimentary coast
Honolulu Plain
cliffed volcanic coast
Diamond Head Cone and Crater
Kahala Plain
Koko Cone and Crater
Ilio Cliffed Sedimentary Headland
Moomomi Sand Dunes
Hauakea Fault Pali
high-cliffed volcanic coast
Kalaupapa Low Shield
sand beach
low-cliffed volcanic coast
high-cliffed volcanic coast
Halawa Cliff and Valley
sand beaches
Puu Nana Slightly Dissected Upland
Mahana Saddle
Kalae Dissected Upland
Pelekunu Cliff and Valley
cliffed volcanic coast
Mauna Loa Dissected Upland
Kamakou Deeply Dissected Upland
sand beaches
coastal swamps
uncliffed volcanic coast
sand beaches
fish ponds
uncliffed volcanic coast
sand beaches
Koae Volcanic Headland
cliffed volcanic coast
Napili Dissected Upland
cliffed volcanic coast
Waihee Sand Dunes
cliffed volcanic coast
sand beaches
uncliffed coast
sand beaches
sand beaches
Kaapahu Slightly Dissected Upland
Kahua Dissected Upland
Maunalei Cliff and Valley
sand beaches
Iao Cliff and Valley
Kahului Isthmus
high-cliffed volcanic coast
Peahi Dissected Upland
cliffed volcanic coast
Lanai Upland
Palea Deeply Dissected Upland
Honopu Dissected Upland
McGregor Dissected Upland
low-cliffed volcanic coast
Palawai Basin
low-cliffed volcanic coast
alluvial coast
cliffed volcanic coast
sand beaches
Kula Slightly Dissected Upland
Keanae Lava Ramp
Hana Dissected Upland
high-cliffed volcanic coast
cliffed volcanic coast
Haleakala Crater Complex
Hana Cone and Crater
Upper Haleakala Slopes
Kaupo Lava Ramp
Kipahulu Cliff and Valley
low-cliffed volcanic coast
Southwest Rift Cone and Crater
East Maui Undissected Upland
Kahalulu Cliff and Valley
Molokini Cone and Crater
Kuheia Dissected Upland
low-cliffed volcanic coast
uncliffed volcanic coast
Lua Makika Cone and Crater
low-cliffed volcanic coast
Smuggler Cove Slightly Dissected Upland
Kanaloa Dissected Upland
high-cliffed volcanic coast
sand beaches
5 0 5 10 15 20 25 miles
5 0 5 10 15 20 25 30 35 kilometers

PHYSIOGRAPHIC DIVISIONS

Source: Physiographic divisions—A.T. Abbott, Geology-Geophysics Dept., Univ. of Hawaii
Relief presentation—J.A. Bier, Geography Dept., Univ. of Illinois 1972

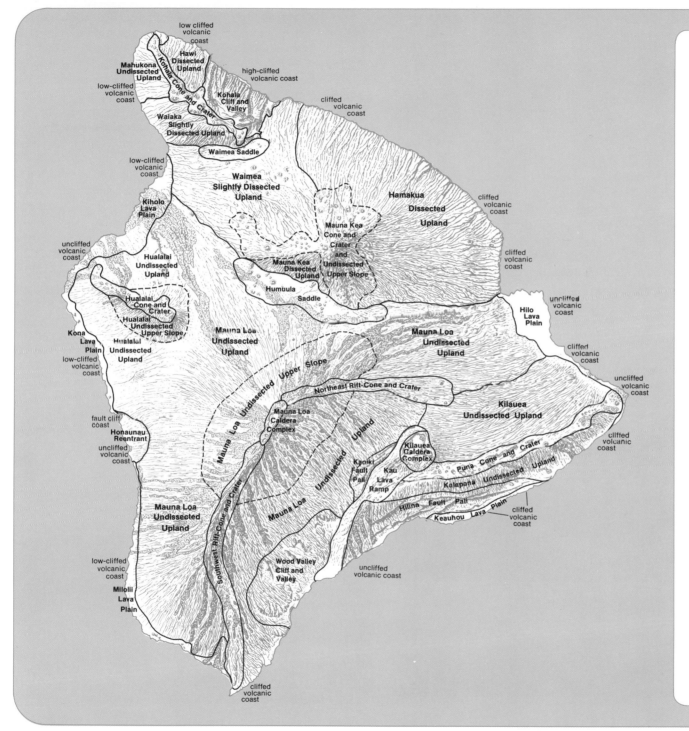

Physiographic Types

Caldera complex. Area having features associated with calderas including craters, cones, bounding faults, fissures, slump blocks, talus heaps, caldera-filling lavas.

Cliff and valley. Area showing little evidence of former slope; with high, nearly vertical cliffs and amphitheater-headed valleys; some valley floors may be gently sloping.

Uncliffed coast. Coastline with little or no cliff along the shoreline.

Low cliffed coast. Coastline with wave-cut cliff—average height about 20 feet.

Cliffed coast. A more mature cliffed coastline—average height about 100 feet.

High cliffed coast. Coast with extreme cliff development up to 2,000 feet in height.

Cone and crater. Volcanic cones and craters of diverse origins, common along volcanic rift zones.

Fault palis. Cliffs resulting from displacement along faults.

Headland. A particularly prominent coastal cliff or promontory.

Isthmus. A low land link between former islands

Lava ramp. A distinctive linear incline formed by lava flows.

Plain. A large area of low relief.

Saddle. Subdued divide between two volcanoes formed where lavas meet or impinge.

Sand dunes. Dunes of loose and/or lithified, wind-blown sand.

Sandy beach. Strips of sand of varying widths at the water's edge.

Undissected upland. Slopes with little or no established surface drainage.

Slightly dissected upland. Slopes cut by widely spaced erosional gullies.

Dissected upland. Slopes cut by numerous major valleys; master drainage patterns established.

Deeply dissected upland. Slopes incised by large, deep valleys; some ridge crests may reflect former slope. Transitional toward the cliff-and-valley type.

Upper slope. A zone above the uplands found only on the highest volcanic shields; characterized by little or no vegetation, late lavas, and barren, rocky terrain.

Malina, sisal, *Agave sisalana*. Introduced as a crop plant and used to make modern hula skirts.

Bishop Museum drawing from Neal (1965:225)

GEOLOGY

The Hawaiian Islands are almost wholly volcanic. Sedimentary rocks form only a narrow fringe around the edges. The vast majority of the volcanic rocks are *lava flows,* formed by outpouring of liquid *magma.* Only a few percent are *pyroclastic* rocks, formed of fragments thrown out by volcanic explosions.

The volcanoes were built along a line, probably a series of cracks, extending in a northwest-southeast direction across the ocean floor. Starting at the northwest end, at Kure Island, about 30 million years ago, the centers of eruption gradually shifted, until today only the volcanoes at the southeastern end of the chain are still active. The shifting

of the eruptive centers may have resulted from a slow northwestward movement of the earth's upper layer across a point of magma generation in the region beneath, at or near the present island of Hawaii.

The general history of formation of the islands is illustrated by the accompanying figure. Quiet eruptions of very fluid lava on the sea floor gradually built up a broad turtle-backed mountain called a *shield volcano.* As the mountaintop neared the surface, some steam explosions occurred, but as it built above sea level quiet eruptions resumed. Eventually, toward the end of growth of the shield, the top of the volcano sank in to form a big crater called a *caldera.* Continued eruptions gradually filled the caldera.

Then, late in the volcano's history, the frequency of eruption decreased, the composition of the magma changed, and its gas content increased. The lavas became more viscous, the flows were shorter and thicker, and more-explosive eruptions formed larger amounts of pyroclastic rocks. A steep-sided, bumpy cap was built on top of the shield.

As the late-stage eruptions gradually died out, erosion was able to take ever greater bites out of the volcanic mountain. Waves cut high sea cliffs, and streams cut deep valleys, gradually transforming the rounded shield volcano into a jagged range of mountains, such as the Koolau Range on Oahu. The gravel, sand, and clay formed by weathering and erosion were washed down, some into the neighboring ocean, but some deposited on the floors of the valleys and in shallow water around the edge of the island. At the same time colonial corals and algae started to build fringing reefs around the island.

Meanwhile sea level repeatedly rose and fell, at least in part because of changes in the volume of ice on the continents during the glacial period. Glaciation also affected Hawaii more directly, a series of small glaciers occupying the summit of Mauna Kea. At times sea level was as much as 100 meters lower, and at others 30 meters or possibly higher, than now. During a stand 8 meters above present level, a broad coral reef was built along the south side of Oahu, forming the present Honolulu and Ewa plains. During later lower sea levels, streams cut valleys into the reef, and as sea level rose again the mouths of the valleys were flooded to form Pearl Harbor.

Finally, after a long period of quiet, volcanic activity resumed, sending lava flows down the valleys and building cones such as Diamond Head and Tantalus. On Haleakala eruptions partly refilled a great cavity carved by streams into the heart of the volcano and formed the present floor of Haleakala Crater.

G.A.M.

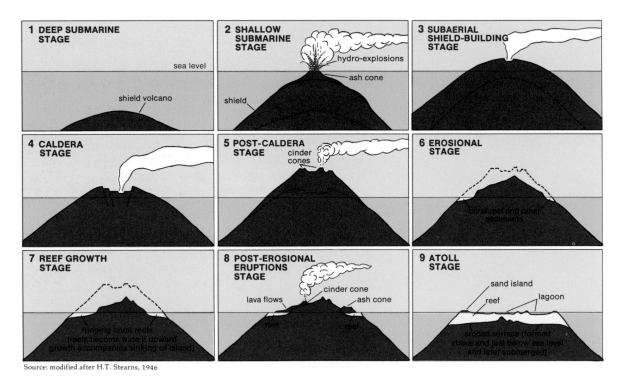

Source: modified after H.T. Stearns, 1946

LIFE HISTORY OF A TYPICAL MID-PACIFIC ISLAND

The Pali, Oahu. The Pali is a continuous line of sheer cliffs resulting from the headward erosion and coalescence of westward migrating valley heads which have reached a common extent at about the same time. The V-shaped gaps of Nuuanu Valley on the left and Kalihi Valley on the right were cut by large streams flowing westward from the former Koolau summit area, which has since been destroyed by erosion.

Hawaii Institute of Geophysics photograph by A.T. Abbott

Maunalei Valley, Lanai. Hidden from casual view, Maunalei Valley slices deep into the east side of Lanai. The steep, deeply grooved slopes and amphitheater head typify Hawaiian valley development. A freshwater well and pump house are located on the floor of the valley.

Hawaii Institute of Geophysics photograph by A.T. Abbott

Waipio Valley, Hawaii, is a great flat-floored chasm cut into the upland of the Kohala shield volcano. Hiilawe Falls cascades a thousand feet over the lip of the precipitous stubby tributary on the left. Note the greater amount of erosional dissection on older Kohala lavas to the right of Waipio Valley as compared with that on the younger Mauna Kea flows to the left.

Hawaii Institute of Geophysics photograph by A.T. Abbott

Mauna Kea, Hawaii. The summit of Mauna Kea is surrounded by a light-colored ridge of glacial moraine. In the foreground is the head of Pohakuloa Gulch, on the south side of the mountain.

Hawaii Institute of Geophysics photograph by A.T. Abbott

Mauna Kea, Hawaii. The summit of Mauna Kea, shown here, reaches an elevation of 13,796 feet above sea level. Numerous andesitic cinder cones characterize the summit area, which is often snow covered for several months in winter. Lake Waiau, in the foreground, is about 100 yards in diameter and is the highest lake in the United States, with an altitude of 13,020 feet. The astronomical observatory occupies the top of the Summit Cone.

Hawaii Institute of Geophysics photograph by A.T. Abbott

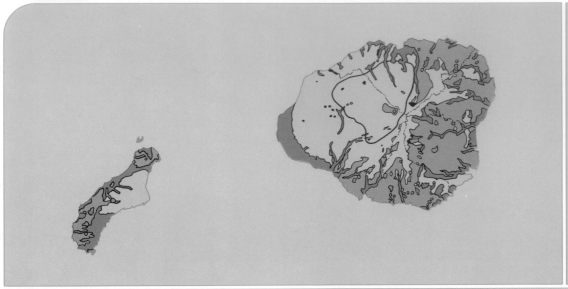

GEOLOGY
IGNEOUS ROCKS

- Historic lava flows (since 1750)
- Post-erosional lavas
- Cones at vents of post-erosional lavas
- Late stage lavas
  - Trachyte flow from Puu Waawaa, Hawaii
- Cones at vents of late stage and main lavas
  (includes small intrusive masses on Maui)
- Lavas of main shield-building stage
  - Separate lavas of Niihau, Kauai, Lanai and Kahoolawe

Oahu
- Koolau Volcano
- Waianae Volcano

Molokai
- West Molokai Volcano
- East Molokai Volcano

Maui
- West Maui Volcano
- East Maui Volcano

Hawaii
- Mauna Loa lavas with thick ash cover
- Mauna Loa lavas with little ash cover
- Mauna Kea
- Kilauea
- Kohala Mountain and Ninole Volcano
- Caldera boundary (dashed where approximate)
- Fault (hachures on downthrown side)

SEDIMENTARY ROCKS

- Alluvium, dune sand, colluvium, mudflow deposits,
  lagoonal deposits
- Coral reef

5 0 5 10 15 20 25 miles

5 0 5 10 15 20 25 30 35 kilometers

Source: Dept. of Geology, Univ. of Hawaii   1982

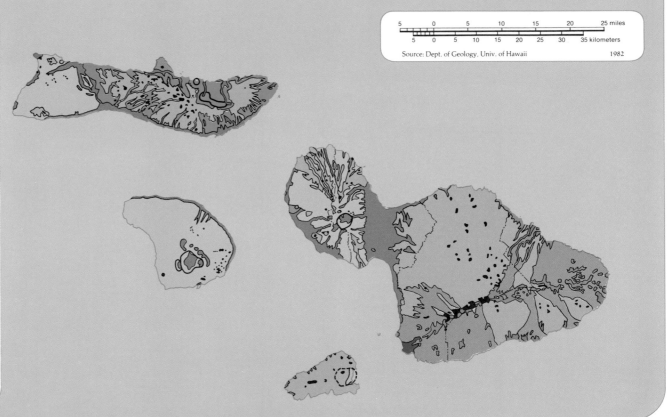

The rocks of the main shield-building stage are **tholeiitic basalts,** rich in magnesium and iron and poor in alkalies (sodium and potassium). Many of them contain visible crystals of green glassy olivine. The matrix is fine grained and stony in appearance. White crystals of feldspar occasionally are visible, but black crystals of pyroxene are rare. Some rocks **(oceanites)** contain as much as 50 percent olivine. Many of the rocks of the late stage also are basalts, but they contain more alkalies than the earlier rocks and are known as **alkalic basalts.** Olivine crystals commonly are visible, and often are accompanied by crystals of the black pyroxene, augite. Feldspar crystals may also be present. Large augite and olivine crystals make up more than half of some rocks **(ankaramites).** Along with the alkalic basalts are other rocks that contain less iron and magnesium and more alkalies. These rocks are **hawaiite** and **mugearite,** the latter being the richer in alkalies. Still richer in alkalies is the rock **trachyte.** On some volcanoes, such as Mauna Kea and Haleakala, the late-stage lavas consist very largely of alkalic basalt and hawaiite; on others, such as Kohala and West Maui, they are mugearite and trachyte. Those of Hualalai are all alkalic basalt except for the trachyte pumice cone of Puu Waawaa and the lava flow from it. The post-erosional lavas are partly alkalic basalt, richer in alkalies and somewhat poorer in silicon than those of the late stage, and partly other rocks still poorer in silicon and richer in alkalies, calcium and magnesium, in which the place of feldspar is taken in part or entirely by nepheline **(basanites** and **nephelinites).** The post-erosional lavas of Niihau, Kauai, and Oahu include alkalic basalts, basanites, and nephelinites; that of Kalaupapa Peninsula on Molokai is alkalic basalt; those of West Maui are basanites; and those of Haleakala (the Hana Volcanic Series) are largely alkalic basalts. Not shown on the map are small post-erosional flows of alkalic basalt in Kolekole Pass, Oahu, and at Kanapou Bay on Kahoolawe.

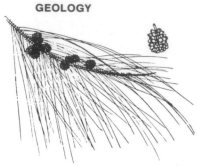

Ironwood, *Casuarina equisetifolia*; needle-like branches and female cones. An introduced tree commonly used for coastal windbreaks.
Bishop Museum drawing from Neal (1965:289)

Volcanism

The main shield-building stage of Hawaiian volcanoes is characterized by gentle eruptions of very fluid lava containing little gas. At the vents, fountains of liquid lava may reach heights of more than 500 meters, but there is little true explosion, and pyroclastic materials amount to less than one percent. Most of the magma forms thin lava flows that spread freely, often to distances of several kilometers.

The lava flows are of two types. *Pahoehoe* has a smooth surface that is often wrinkled by dragging of the still-plastic crust by movement of liquid lava beneath it. The flow quickly crusts over, and as it gradually freezes inward from the edges the moving liquid portion becomes narrower until only a stream a few meters across continues to flow through a sort of pipe with solidified walls. At the end of the eruption, part or all of the liquid may drain away, leaving a lava tube. Most lava tubes are less than a meter across, but a few are as much as 15 meters.

As pahoehoe advances downhill, it commonly changes to *aa*, which has a rough surface of jagged fragments of clinker. Some flows start as aa. Usually aa flows are fed by open rivers, and at the end of the eruption the liquid in the river may drain away leaving a trench-like channel a meter or so deep and about 1 to 15 meters wide. Aa flows usually have layers of clinker at both top and bottom, and a center of massive lava. Both pahoehoe and aa contain many small holes (vesicles) formed by gas bubbles in the liquid lava.

Hawaiian lava flows are more voluminous than those of most other parts of the world. Areas and volumes of flows formed during a few recent eruptions are as follows:

DATE	VOLCANO	AREA OF FLOWS (square kilometers)	VOLUME OF FLOWS (cubic meters)
1790	Haleakala	5.7	27,000,000
1801	Hualalai	45.8	315,000,000
1840	Kilauea	17.1	215,000,000
1859	Mauna Loa	84.7	450,000,000+
1942	Mauna Loa	27.4	75,000,000
1950	Mauna Loa	90.6	450,000,000+
1955	Kilauea	15.8	92,000,000
1960	Kilauea	10.6	118,000,000
1975	Mauna Loa	13.5	17,000,000
1977	Kilauea	5.2	21,000,000

The lava of 1859 flowed more than 55 kilometers from its vent on Mauna Loa into the sea. Speeds of advance of lava flows may be greater than 8 kilometers an hour, but are usually between 3 and 300 meters an hour.

During historic times Mauna Loa has been active 6.2 percent of the time, erupting, on an average, once every 3.7 years, and has poured out more than 2.9 cubic kilometers of lava. Kilauea has been active 62 percent of the time, but most of the activity was confined to the inner crater, Halemaumau. Eruptions outside the caldera have occurred, on the average, once every 7.2 years, and have poured out about 0.8 cubic kilometer of lava. During most of the time from 1823 to 1924, a lake of molten lava existed in Halemaumau. In 1924 a splitting open of the mountain allowed the lava lake to drain away and water from the surrounding rocks to enter the hot lava conduits below the surface, resulting in one of the rare explosive eruptions of the volcano as the water was rapidly transformed into steam. Rock fragments weighing as much as 14 tons were thrown over a large part of the caldera floor.

The July 5–6, 1975, eruption at the summit of Mauna Loa and the September 13–October 1, 1977, eruption on Kilauea's southeast rift zone were of moderate size by Hawaiian standards.

Observations of fresh lava by scientists in a submersible vehicle that dived on Loihi Seamount southeast of Hawaii, and swarms of earthquakes there, indicate that Loihi is a site of active volcanism.

The late-stage eruptions of Hawaiian volcanoes are more explosive than those of the shield-building stage, because the magma is more viscous and contains more gas. Instead of the small mounds and cones of spatter built around the vents in the earlier stage, late-stage eruptions build cinder cones, some of which are several hundred meters high and as much as a kilometer across. Most of the flows are of aa type, and are shorter and thicker than those of the earlier stage.

Where the rising magma encounters water, the generation of steam brings about explosions which tear the liquid lava into tiny bits and throw them into the air, where they solidify to fragments mostly of sand size, known as *ash*. Most of the ash piles up around the vent to form a cone, and becomes cemented together to form the solid rock called *tuff*. This may happen during any stage, but it was particularly common during the post-erosional eruptions on Oahu. Punchbowl, Diamond Head, Koko Crater, Koko Head, Hanauma Bay, and Ulupau Head are tuff cones. Others are Kilauea Cone on Kauai, Lehua Island near Niihau, Molokini Island near Maui, and Kapoho Cone on Hawaii.

G.A.M.

Mauna Loa and Kilauea, Hawaii. In the distance Mauna Loa, a classic example of a shield volcano, rises gently and majestically to an elevation of 13,677 feet. Kilauea's summit at 4,090 feet is marked by a large caldera within which lies Halemaumau Crater, known as the fire pit. On the near side of Kilauea caldera lies Kilauea Iki pit crater, the scene of a spectacular eruption in 1959 which formed a lava lake 365 feet in depth. The thickness of the crust on the lake (in mid-1972) is about 100 feet.

Hawaii Institute of Geophysics photograph by A.T. Abbott

Kilauea eruption. The floor of Halemaumau fire pit is the site of this eruption in November 1967. Small lava fountains in the center of the pit are putting forth a flood of fluid lava which glows through cracks in its cooling crust.

Hawaii Institute of Geophysics photograph by A.T. Abbott

Lava fountain about 300 feet high, with a cinder cone at its base, on the east flank of Kilauea volcano during the eruption of 1955.

U.S. Geological Survey photograph by G.A. Macdonald

A spatter cone in the Puna district forming during the 1955 eruption of Kilauea. Spatter is molten blobs of lava that congeal and weld themselves to the earlier ejecta thus building a steep-sided cone around the volcanic throat.

U.S. Geological Survey photograph by G.A. Macdonald

Front of an aa lava flow, 10 to 15 feet high, advancing across cleared land on the east flank of Kilauea volcano. The flow was advancing about 1,000 feet per hour. Flames along the edge of the flow are from burning vegetation.

U.S. Geological Survey photograph by G.A. Macdonald

Some pahoehoe lava flows can be recognized by the twisted, ropy, billowy, or drapery-like patterns that develop on the crust during final moments of congealing of the fluid lava.

Photograph by C.K. Wentworth

Koa, *Acacia koa;* true and false leaves, flower heads, pods. Known as Hawaiian mahogany, koa wood is valued for furniture, ukuleles, and carvings.

Bishop Museum drawing from Neal (1965:410)

Earthquakes and Tsunamis

Volcanic eruptions on the island of Hawaii commonly are preceded and accompanied by thousands of earthquakes, but only a few of them are strong enough to be felt, and still fewer do any damage. The quakes result from shifting of segments of the volcano as the mountain swells before eruptions, due to inflation of a shallow magma reservoir beneath, or shrinks during the eruption as magma is drained away. In terms of origin, they are volcanic earthquakes.

Tectonic activity, in the sense of crustal deformation such as that which causes most earthquakes in continental regions, is nearly absent in Hawaii. The entire Hawaiian region is tilting slightly to the southeast, with Hawaii Island going down at a rate of about 0.3 meter per century. The islands are partly surrounded by a deep that appears to be the result of sinking of the adjacent ocean floor, probably because of the load of the volcanoes resting on it. Minor basins have been formed by sagging of some caldera floors over shallow magma chambers, and some faults pass into monoclines, but no other folding is present.

Major earthquakes, here as elsewhere, are the result of faulting. Some of the faults are on, and probably genetically associated with, the volcanoes. Others are on the ocean floor near the islands. Since 1925, 11 earthquakes with magnitude greater than 5.3 have occurred in the Hawaiian region. Of these, seven originated on Hawaii Island and four on faults on the ocean floor. In 1951 a magnitude 6.8 earthquake originated on the Kealakekua fault, just off the Kona Coast of Hawaii. The Maui earthquake of 1938 (magnitude 6.75) had its epicenter about 40 kilometers north of Pauwela Point on the north shore of Maui, probably on one of the strands of the Molokai fracture zone, a great system of sea-floor faults that trends nearly westward from Baja California to Hawaii. The magnitude 7.2 earthquake of 29 November 1975 was centered at the Puna coast southeast of Kilauea caldera.

The greatest Hawaiian earthquake of historic time occurred in April 1868. It was accompanied, and probably was caused, by movements on faults both on- and offshore near the south end of the island of Hawaii. The road near Waiohinu was broken and offset about 4 meters by one of the faults. It is reported that every European-style building in the Kau district was destroyed. The magnitude of the quake was probably around 8.0. In Wood Valley the shaking set off a great mud flow which buried about 500 animals and a village with 31 persons.

The offshore fault movements during the 1868 earthquake caused a huge water wave—a tsunami—which is reported to have come in over the tops of the coconut trees on the south shore of Hawaii. However, most tsunamis that affect the Hawaiian Islands come from sources in the zone of mountain building that borders the Pacific Ocean. Since 1820, nine tsunamis have caused moderate to severe damage or deaths on Hawaiian shores, but only those of 1868 and 1975 were of local origin. Five came from South America, one from Kamchatka, and one from the Aleutian Islands. Six others, including one of local origin, did a little damage. The Aleutian tsunami of 1946 drove water to heights as great as 17 meters above sea level at some places in Hawaii. At Hilo, where the water reached 10 meters above sea level, 83 lives were lost. The Chilean tsunami of 1960 created a bore in Hilo Bay which struck shore with a speed of 65 kilometers an hour, drove water to heights as great as 11 meters, and killed 61 persons (page 58).

G.A.M.

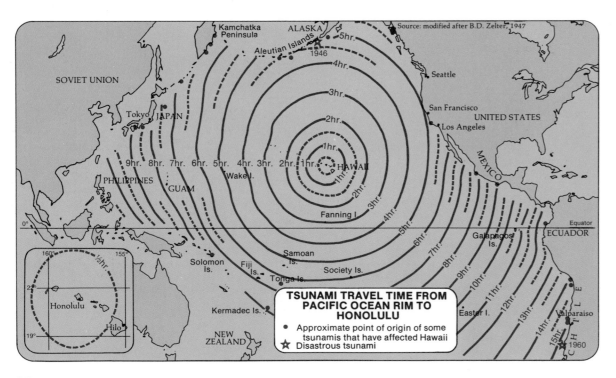

TSUNAMI TRAVEL TIME FROM PACIFIC OCEAN RIM TO HONOLULU
• Approximate point of origin of some tsunamis that have affected Hawaii
★ Disastrous tsunami

vice, 1960). Hawaii was the first state in the Union to complete a survey of its soil based on this system. The report appeared in two parts, one for the island of Hawaii (Sato et al., 1972), and the other for the remaining islands (Foote et al., 1972).

In this new system there are ten Orders of soils at the highest level of classification. Lower categories are the Suborder, Great Group, Subgroup, Family, and Series. Hawaii is the only state in which all ten Orders are found. There are 190 soil series in Hawaii. The classification of the Wahiawa series, the dominant soil of the Wahiawa-Schofield area of Oahu, is an example:

Papaya, *Carica papaya.* A common lowland fruit tree.

Bishop Museum drawing from Neal (1965.000)

Order: Oxisol
Suborder: Ustox
Great Group: Eutrustox
Subgroup: Tropeptic Eutrustox
Family: clayey, kaolinitic, isohyperthermic, Tropeptic Eutrustox
Series: Wahiawa

SOILS

Just as there are many different species of plants or animals, there are many different types of soil. Soils differ because of differences in (1) the length of time to which they have been exposed to weathering, (2) the materials from which they have been formed, (3) drainage conditions, (4) the kinds and number of plants and animals that live in and on them, and (5) temperature and rainfall conditions to which the soils are exposed.

It is not surprising then that the soils on the island of Kauai are different from those on the island of Hawaii, for the soils of Kauai have been exposed to weathering for a longer period of time. One would also expect soils that form from alluvium to be different from soils developed from lava rock, and that both would differ from soils developed from volcanic cinders. One need only to compare the soil on valley bottoms with those on adjacent ridge-tops to discover that differences in drainage can cause soil variations. Soils on the windward side of an island differ markedly from those found on the leeward side because climate and vegetation are not the same.

Soils are similar if the factors that contribute to their formation are similar. There are no two identical soils, just as there are no two identical human beings. However, soils are considered to be of the same type if all their measurable and visible properties are alike, that is, if they respond and behave alike. Thus two soils of the same classification, occurring in widely separated parts of the world, could be expected to behave in similar ways.

The soils of Hawaii have been classified and mapped twice in the last 25 years. Field work for the first survey was completed before World War II, but the report was not published until 1955 (Cline, 1955). In that report soils were classified according to the now obsolete Great Soil Group system. In 1960 the Soil Conservation Service of the United States Department of Agriculture published the 7th Approximation to a new comprehensive system of soil classification (Soil Conservation Ser-

A person unacquainted with Hawaii's soil but familiar with the classification scheme would find in this summary a wealth of information about this particular soil. For example, he knows that Oxisols are oxide-rich soils normally found in the tropics. They are the soils which historically have been called lateritic soils or latosols. The designation at the Suborder level indicates that the Wahiawa soil occurs in an area with relatively low rainfall but where the rains coincide with the plant-growing season. The Great Group category provides additional information, which in this case points to the relatively high fertility of this soil. The Subgroup designation suggests that this soil has one or more features not unlike those of soils belonging to the Order Inceptisol. The most useful information from the point of view of management of the Wahiawa soil is found at the Family level. Here one finds information on size distribution of soil particles, the mineral make-up of the soil particles, and soil temperature. The soil series name corresponds to the locality where this soil was first identified.

The table provides details of the land area occupied by the different soil Orders in Hawaii. The two Orders that occur most extensively—the Histosols and Inceptisols, which together comprise almost 40 percent of the area of the State—are largely confined to the island of Hawaii. The remaining eight Orders occupy about 15 percent of the land area. Forty-six percent of Hawaii's land area is classified as "miscellaneous land types"—areas covered by lava or cinders, rough mountainous land, coral outcrops, beaches, and fill-land.

G.U.

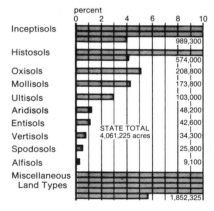

ACREAGE OF STATE SOIL ORDERS

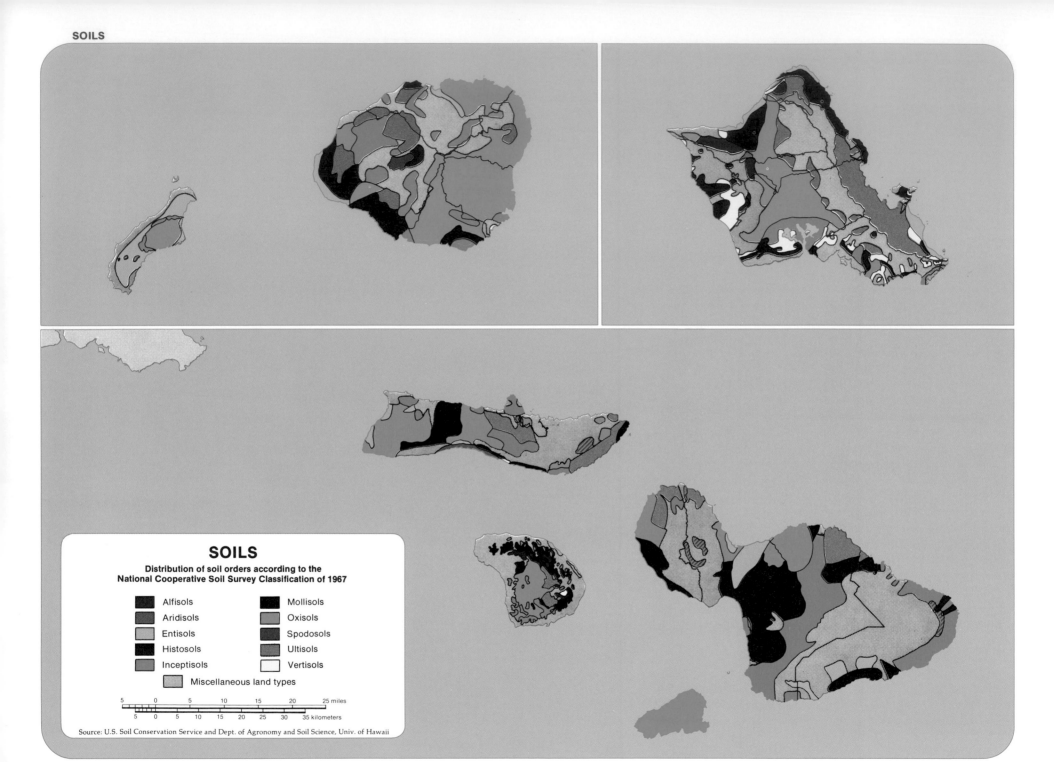

SOILS

Distribution of soil orders according to the
National Cooperative Soil Survey Classification of 1967

Alfisols		Mollisols
Aridisols		Oxisols
Entisols		Spodosols
Histosols		Ultisols
Inceptisols		Vertisols

Miscellaneous land types

5 0 5 10 15 20 25 miles
5 0 5 10 15 20 25 30 35 kilometers

Source: U.S. Soil Conservation Service and Dept. of Agronomy and Soil Science, Univ. of Hawaii

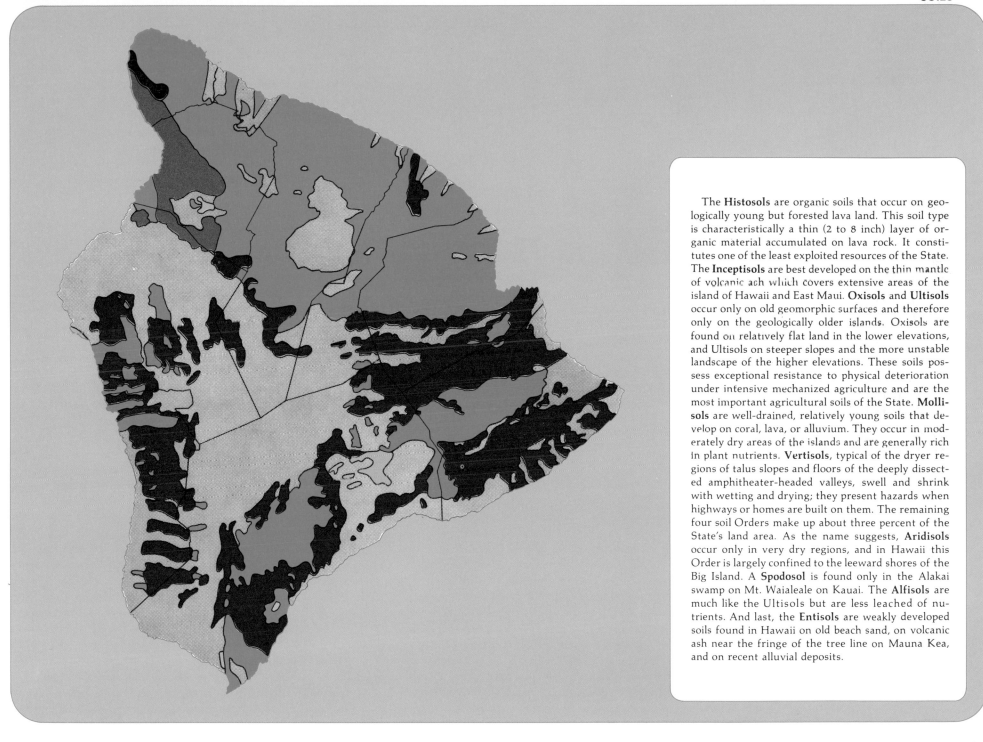

The **Histosols** are organic soils that occur on geologically young but forested lava land. This soil type is characteristically a thin (2 to 8 inch) layer of organic material accumulated on lava rock. It constitutes one of the least exploited resources of the State. The **Inceptisols** are best developed on the thin mantle of volcanic ash which covers extensive areas of the island of Hawaii and East Maui. **Oxisols** and **Ultisols** occur only on old geomorphic surfaces and therefore only on the geologically older islands. Oxisols are found on relatively flat land in the lower elevations, and Ultisols on steeper slopes and the more unstable landscape of the higher elevations. These soils possess exceptional resistance to physical deterioration under intensive mechanized agriculture and are the most important agricultural soils of the State. **Mollisols** are well-drained, relatively young soils that develop on coral, lava, or alluvium. They occur in moderately dry areas of the islands and are generally rich in plant nutrients. **Vertisols**, typical of the dryer regions of talus slopes and floors of the deeply dissected amphitheater-headed valleys, swell and shrink with wetting and drying; they present hazards when highways or homes are built on them. The remaining four soil Orders make up about three percent of the State's land area. As the name suggests, **Aridisols** occur only in very dry regions, and in Hawaii this Order is largely confined to the leeward shores of the Big Island. A **Spodosol** is found only in the Alakai swamp on Mt. Waialeale on Kauai. The **Alfisols** are much like the Ultisols but are less leached of nutrients. And last, the **Entisols** are weakly developed soils found in Hawaii on old beach sand, on volcanic ash near the fringe of the tree line on Mauna Kea, and on recent alluvial deposits.

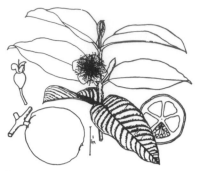

Guava, *Psidium guajava;* flower, bud, leaves, young fruit, ripe fruit. Introduced tree common along roadsides and in waste areas; the fruit is popular and useful.

Bishop Museum drawing from Neal (1965:632)

WATER

Hawaii's water resources are remarkably diverse. There are perennial streams and flashy streams, rain forests and cactus deserts, and groundwater tunnels high in the mountains and low near sea level. The complex nature of Hawaii's water control and development can be understood only in the context of the climate and geology of the islands (pages 38 and 59).

A continuous cycle of water can be easily traced on small oceanic islands (page 49). Its pattern will vary at different times and places according to variations in geology, landforms, soils, and rainfall. The cycle is also modified by human activities, such as diverting mountain stream water for irrigation, pumping groundwater, changing infiltration by resurfacing the land, altering evapotranspiration and runoff patterns by agricultural and urban development, and disposing of sewage effluent into the ocean.

Hydrology. The principal geologic feature of great hydrologic importance is the presence of thousands of thin-bedded (3 meters or less), gently sloping (3–10°), basaltic extrusive lava flows that comprise the bulk of the island volcanoes. The structural features associated with these flows, such as an abundance of clinker sections, voids between flow surfaces, shrinkage joints and fractures, and lava tubes and gas vesicles, make these rocks porous and highly permeable—and thus, principal aquifers. In the rift zones on the flanks of Hawaiian volcanoes, molten lava intrudes and remains in the fissures as dikes. Unlike the flow basalt, the dikes are dense, poorly permeable, thin and nearly vertical sheets of basaltic rock. When dikes make up 10 percent or more of the total rock volume and cut into the permeable basalt flows to form water storage compartments, they are called dike complexes. These are generally located at high elevations and impound rain-fed percolating water 60 to 90 meters above sea level. Natural discharges from the compartments are via high-level springs and from streams.

The principal aquifers in Hawaii, however, are the basaltic flows in which fresh water can accumulate in large lens-shaped bodies (commonly known as the Ghyben-Herzberg lens). The lens is maintained by direct recharge by rain water and by discharges from the high-level, dike-impounded water. At the time when an island is newly emerged above the ocean, the only groundwater in the rock would be salt water from the ocean and its surface would be at ocean level. A freshwater lens develops as fresh water percolates down to the salt water and, because of its lower density, floats on the underlying salt water. The freshwater lens gradually expands in thickness and depresses the interface between the fresh water and the salt water to some depth below sea level. At the interface, the salt water and fresh water mix to form a "zone of transition" whose thickness varies from about 3 meters in a relatively undisturbed lens to as much as 305 meters in parts of southern Oahu.

On the older islands, especially Kauai and Oahu, the coastal margins of the volcanic mountains covered by sediments of alluvial and marine origin, called caprock. The sediments act as barriers that retard the seaward escape of groundwater and cause the basal freshwater lens to thicken and to become artesian. The freshwater lenses in southern Oahu are of this type, with heads that are presently 6–8 meters above sea level, and with total thicknesses of about 250–312 meters. In other permeable basalt regions that lack an effective caprock, the lenses are thin (15–30 meters).

The landforms of surface water drainage basins reflect the geologic age and rainfall in different parts of the Hawaiian Islands and watersheds are typically small. Of the streams gauged on Oahu, 80 percent have drainage areas smaller than 13 square kilometers. The relief of the watershed land and the stream channel is steep, especially in the headwaters. Stream channels are short and lack storage, and at times of heavy rain they are liable to flash floods. The November 1930 peak flow of Kalihi Stream of 52 cubic meters per second per square kilometer is a U.S. record. Since 1920, floods have caused serious damage on Oahu, principally in Honolulu and in other urbanized areas.

Many streams are nearly perennial in mountainous areas where orographic rain occurs daily, producing constant overland flow and interflow, and where high-level springs discharge perched and dike-impounded groundwater. Streams that traverse dry lowland and coastal plains tend to lose water from channel infiltration. Only two streams, the Wailuku River on Hawaii, and the Hanalei River on Kauai, have average discharges reaching 150 to 185 million gallons per day (mgd) (6.6 to 8.1 cubic meters per second). Most of the other streams have average discharges of less than 50 mgd (2.2 cubic meters per second).

Water Quality. The quality of Hawaii's fresh water from a basaltic aquifer is excellent: the water is soft, low in mineral content, and potable without disinfection. During its passage to the basaltic aquifer, the infiltrated rainwater acquires silica, calcium, and magnesium from basalt; bicarbonate from the biological cycle; and sodium, chloride and sulfate from the encroaching seawater. The only serious source of contamination of the basal freshwater lens is the underlying seawater, indicated by a rise in the concentration of chloride. Another concern is the sugarcane-culture return-irrigation water, which accumulates in the uppermost layer of the basal water and which contains high concentrations of chloride, nitrate, and sulfate. The fresh water from basaltic aquifers is free of coliform bacteria and meets U.S. drinking water standards. Sewage-borne coliform bacteria and pathogenic enteric viruses are effectively removed by the passage of water through a meter of Oxisol, a common soils order found on all major islands except Hawaii Island (page 46).

Stream water quality is generally lower than that of groundwater in terms of turbidity, nutrients, and coliforms, especially during wet weather periods; however, the water is still soft and low in mineral content. Outside the forest reserve headwater areas, urban and agricultural activities introduce pollutants such as traces of pesticides and heavy metals. Depletion of dissolved oxygen in stream water is seldom a problem.

Because urban development in Hawaii parallels the coastline, rather than river courses, the impact of land use and urban activities is mostly on the coastal water, affecting its quality and its ecosystem, rather than on streams. However, the coastal water is of high quality because the former practice of ocean disposal of municipal, agricultural, and industrial wastes has been much improved or eliminated by land treatment and water-reuse practices.

Water Resources. Water budget estimates for Hawaii indicate the rainwater is dispensed as 39 percent evapotranspiration, 31 percent surface water runoff, and 30 percent groundwater recharge. However, these percentages differ considerably from island to island (page 49). Not all of the surface water and groundwater indicated in the water budget is available for human use. The sustainable yield of groundwater for Oahu is estimated to be in the range of 480–630 mgd (21 to 28 cubic meters per second), which is somewhat less than the groundwater recharge. Surface water flow quantity is subject to great seasonal variability and it is easily contaminated. However, increased use of surface water and construction of more surface water treatment plants will have to be considered in the near future. A minor source of water supply is rainwater catchment, which is practiced in rainy areas and especially in rural areas on islands other than Oahu.

Water Uses. The early Hawaiians developed a water supply system based on streams, springs, and dug wells for subsistence and agriculture. They built low, stone dams in streambeds to raise the level of water, which could then be diverted to flow into ditches for the irrigation of taro fields. In the second half of the nineteenth century, long ditches were built for the sugarcane plantations, to carry stream water

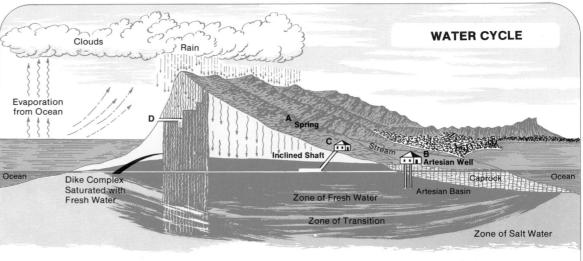

WATER CYCLE

The water cycle illustrates a typical island water system, such as for Oahu. Evaporation from the ocean off the windward coast forms clouds, at left. As the clouds rise over the mountains and cool, condensation occurs and rain pours on the uplands. Some of the water filters down through the watertight dike complex; much of the rest trickles through the mass of rock into the zone of fresh water underlying the island. Below this zone is salt water. A small amount goes into springs at A, and into surface streams. A blanket of caprock thickens the fresh-water zone. Some of this pure fresh water is drawn off by means of artesian wells drilled through the caprock at B. More is taken from well shafts and skimming tunnels at C. Small but important amounts of water are tapped from the dike complex at D. The water is brought to the surface, used and returned to the sea through ocean outfalls. Some of the rainwater runs over land surfaces into streams and returns also to the sea.

Modified from Board of Water Supply, City and County of Honolulu.

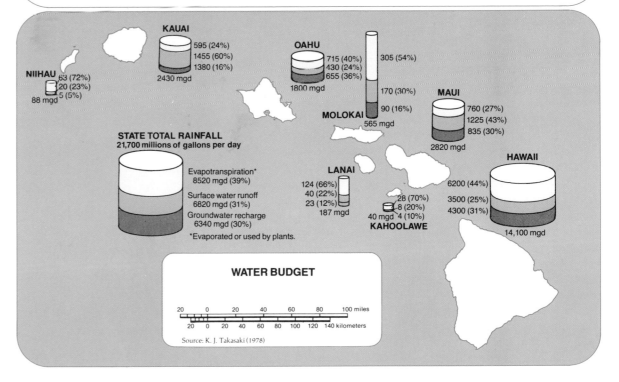

KAUAI
595 (24%)
1455 (60%)
1380 (16%)
2430 mgd

OAHU
715 (40%)
430 (24%)
655 (36%)
1800 mgd

305 (54%)
170 (30%)
90 (16%)
MOLOKAI
565 mgd

MAUI
760 (27%)
1225 (43%)
835 (30%)
2820 mgd

NIIHAU
63 (72%)
20 (23%)
5 (5%)
88 mgd

STATE TOTAL RAINFALL
21,700 millions of gallons per day

Evapotranspiration*
8520 mgd (39%)

Surface water runoff
6820 mgd (31%)

Groundwater recharge
6340 mgd (30%)

*Evaporated or used by plants.

LANAI
124 (66%)
40 (22%)
23 (12%)
187 mgd

28 (70%)
8 (20%)
40 mgd 4 (10%)
KAHOOLAWE

HAWAII
6200 (44%)
3500 (25%)
4300 (31%)
14,100 mgd

WATER BUDGET

20   0   20   40   60   80   100 miles
20   0   20   40   60   80   100 120 140 kilometers

Source: K. J. Takasaki (1978)

to dry, leeward areas for large-scale farming. The first irrigation ditch was built for Lihue Plantation on Kauai in 1857. An outstanding example is the Hamakua Ditch, completed in 1878, which runs 27.4 kilometers along the mountain slopes of eastern Maui delivering up to 60 mgd of water. Hawaii's first drilled well, completed in 1879 near Ewa, Oahu, struck artesian water, and the secret of the vast groundwater resources in southern Oahu became quickly known.

Agricultural enterprises require the greatest amounts of water, principally for sugarcane irrigation. However, the need for potable water for municipal use is rapidly increasing on Oahu, where 85 percent of the state population resides, and on parts of Maui. Industry, the military, and others consume much smaller amounts.

On the island of Oahu in 1975, total use of fresh water amounted to 470 mgd (20.6 cubic meters per second), of which 400 mgd, or 85 percent, was drawn from groundwater sources. Oahu's municipal water supply is virtually 100 percent dependent on groundwater sources. However, stream water is again regarded as an important alternative source for areas where groundwater sources, such as the Pearl Harbor aquifer, are nearing full exploitation. For the entire island of Oahu, the present 400-mgd (17.5 cubic meters per second) draft from groundwater approaches the sustainable yield from this source of 480–630 mgd (21 to 28 cubic meters per second), a situation that indicates a potential water shortage by the year 2000.

On Maui and Kauai, by far the greatest use of water is for irrigation of sugarcane, but there is less dependence on groundwater. In localized areas on Maui, such as the tourist center of Lahaina, municipal water demand has already exceeded the developed sources, and water must be imported. Water withdrawn for various uses in 1975 is shown on page 51.

In-stream uses of water in Hawaii include a modest amount of hydroelectric power generation on some islands to meet the energy demands of the sugar industry, localized recreational use and aesthetic enjoyment, and maintenance of indigenous fish and aquatic life. Navigable freshwater channels are insignificant, with a total 72.4 kilometers.

Important uses of Hawaii's coastal waters include use as a wastewater receptacle, which, if done improperly, can have an adverse impact on recreational waters and beaches. Further, marine conservation and preservation zones, as well as fisheries, are continually affected by coastal land and water uses and management practices. The 1970s have seen considerable research, planning, regulation, and improvement in wastewater management, with the result that coastal waters and marshes are now better protected than formerly.

The basal groundwater is tapped by pumped wells and infiltration galleries. Infiltration galleries known as Maui wells throughout the world are nearly horizontal tunnels of great length drilled just below

At an elevation of about 700 feet in the dike zone of windward Oahu, groundwater emerges as springs to become the headwaters of streams. A tributary of Waihee stream starts as a 75-foot high waterfall.

Photograph by Honolulu Board of Water Supply

Vertical dikes exposed on Puu Papaa near Kaneohe. Dikes control the movement of groundwater in windward Oahu.

Photograph by Frank L. Peterson

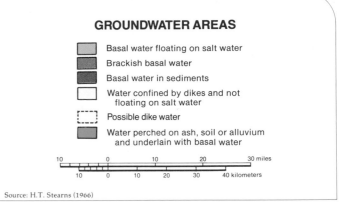

GROUNDWATER AREAS

- Basal water floating on salt water
- Brackish basal water
- Basal water in sediments
- Water confined by dikes and not floating on salt water
- Possible dike water
- Water perched on ash, soil or alluvium and underlain with basal water

10   0   10   20   30 miles
10   0   10   20   30   40 kilometers

Source: H.T. Stearns (1966)

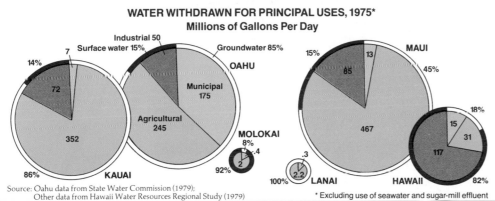

WATER WITHDRAWN FOR PRINCIPAL USES, 1975*
Millions of Gallons Per Day

Industrial 50
Surface water 15%
7
14%
72
352
86%   KAUAI

Groundwater 85%
OAHU
Municipal 175
Agricultural 245
92%

MOLOKAI
8%
.4
2

MAUI
15%   13
85   45%
467

LANAI
.3
2.2
100%

HAWAII
18%
15
31
117
82%

Source: Oahu data from State Water Commission (1979);
Other data from Hawaii Water Resources Regional Study (1979)

* Excluding use of seawater and sugar-mill effluent

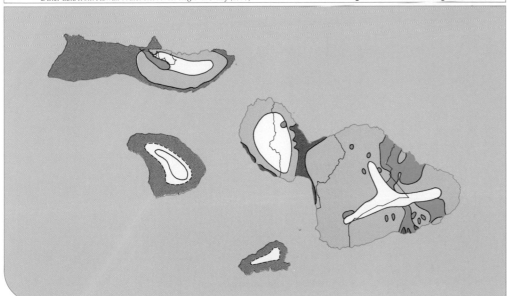

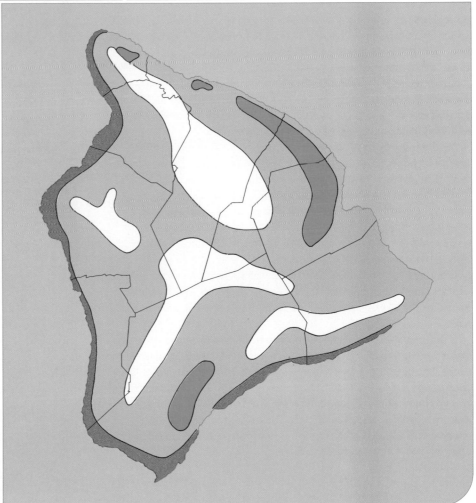

the water table; theoretically, they skim the top of the basal lens water. Dike water is collected by piercing a tunnel through several dike compartments at high elevations from which the water drains by gravity. Approximately 54 mgd (2.4 cubic meters per second) is drawn from dike compartments on Oahu. Stream water is usually tapped by diversion in rainy headwater areas and transported long distances from the watershed. Impounding reservoirs in Hawaii are few, but holding reservoirs for irrigation supply are numerous.

On sugar and pineapple plantations, irrigation methods are rapidly changing from furrow and ridge systems to drip irrigation, thus increasing the potential efficiency by greater uniformity of water distribution. In addition to the average 24 inches of water obtained from rainfall, sugarcane actually, uses only 48 inches of the 108 inches of water usually applied each year by furrow irrigation. Cane can recover those needed 48 inches of additional water from only 60 inches added by drip irrigation. In contrast to sugarcane, pineapple needs only 12–18 inches of rainfall and requires less than 6 inches of irrigation in a year. However, much of the planted acreage is in moderately high rainfall areas of 60 inches or more and requires no irrigation. For example, of 220,000 acres planted in sugarcane, only about one-half of the cultivated areas is irrigated. Secondary treated sewage effluent is successfully used today for irrigation of sugarcane, golf courses and grazing land.

Water Problems. Whether there will be an adequate water supply for the island of Oahu beyond the year 2000 is a major concern. By the turn of the century, water demand on Oahu could exceed the total sustainable yield of all of the island's water sources developed by conventional methods. Potential and alternative water sources will have to be determined, including greater use of dike and stream waters, use of sewage effluent for irrigation, the exchange of low quality water for high quality water now used for irrigation, blending brackish water with fresh water, and desalting brackish water. On other islands too, for example in the Lahaina-Kaanapali area of Maui and Kekaha-Mana on Kauai, water use is rapidly approaching sustainable yields from basal lenses.

The State Water Commission has recommended a number of policies, some of which are presently being implemented: regulating the Pearl Harbor groundwater resources, establishing a state water code, stabilizing or reducing per capita consumption of municipal water, and encouraging the development of new and alternative water resources.

In addition to water supply, three general groupings of water problems need continued attention: water quality protection and enhancement, in-stream uses of water and their values, and a water allocation system.

L.S.L.

Kahana Valley, Oahu, looking toward the crest of the Koolau Range. The average annual rainfall at the head of the valley is 250 inches.
Photograph by Henry K. Gee

Halawa underground water development tunnel excavation exposes basalt rock and groundwater discharging into a sump.
Photograph by Honolulu Board of Water Supply

THE OCEAN

Regional. The Hawaiian Islands, along with numerous banks, guyots, and seamounts, rise from a linear swell of the Pacific sea floor, the Hawaiian Ridge (see maps pages 6–7). Thus they resemble the Society, Line, Samoan, and several other linear chains in the Central Pacific. The islands and seamounts are volcanoes, or volcanoes now capped by coralline limestone. Volcanism appears to have been localized where the trend of the ridge has crossed branches of great east trending fractures. From the junction of the Emperor Seamount chain and the Hawaiian Ridge, volcanism progressed 2,600 kilometers southeastward past Midway Islands, active about 28,000,000 years ago, to Mauna Loa and Kilauea, active today. The suboceanic lithosphere subsides under the mass of the volcanoes, so that a moat, the Hawaiian Deep, extends part of the way around the islands. Beyond the Deep the elastic lithosphere is flexed gently upward as the Hawaiian Arch.

Northeast trade winds generate the dominant waves in the region around Hawaii and also drive surface currents generally westward at 0.4 to 0.6 knots (20 to 30 cm sec^{-1}). Patterns of the currents, as well as characteristics of waves, salinity, and water temperature in this part of the North Pacific gyre, vary moderately with the seasons, as the cyclonic storms of the Northern Hemisphere move closer to the Hawaiian Islands in winter (page 54).

Nearshore. The original volcanic slopes of the islands have been modified by subaerial erosion of canyons and valleys, by the shaping of terraces near sea level by littoral processes including reef building, and by later episodes of volcanism. Many of these geomorphic features were drowned as the islands sank, and they now characterize the bathymetry (page 55). Submarine canyons are best developed north of Molokai, northeast of Oahu, and northwest of Maui. The deepest and most extensive terrace, named the Waho Shelf, is tilted to the north and ranges between 900 and 1,100 meters in depth. Muds washed as detritus from the islands, and calcareous sands, muds, and gravel of shallow-water origin, are the principal sediments near the islands, whereas pelagic brown clays cover most of the deep-sea floor (page 56).

Surface currents are modified by the shapes of the islands and, very close to shore, by the tides as well (page 57). Eddies in the lee of islands, especially west of Hawaii, are common and probably result from high winds funneled between Maui and Hawaii. Waves near the islands have sources in sea and swell which vary seasonally and which affect different exposures of the coasts. Tsunami waves are rare but may be devastating (page 58). Hawaii has a mixed tide with a low range. Spring tides nowhere exceed 1 meter.

Economic Aspects. The ocean-formed, nonliving resource of greatest value to Hawaii is its shoreline and in particular its beaches. Generally, beaches are larger on older islands, and on a given island they are larger on coasts exposed to the North Pacific swell (page 55). Precious coral has been discovered at various localities along the Hawaiian Archipelago at depths between 300 and 500 meters, ferromanganese deposits are common on old terraces below 400 meters, and a few billion cubic meters of sand are present at depths shallower than 30 meters. These are the principal potential offshore mineral deposits of the Hawaiian Islands (page 56).

R.M.M.

Swamp mahogany, *Eucalyptus robusta*; leaves, fruit, bark. Introduced tree important in Hawaiian forestry.

Bishop Museum drawing from Neal (1965:639)

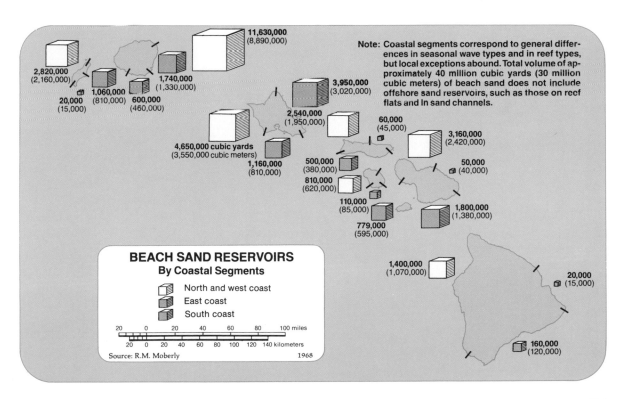

Note: Coastal segments correspond to general differences in seasonal wave types and in reef types, but local exceptions abound. Total volume of approximately 40 million cubic yards (30 million cubic meters) of beach sand does not include offshore sand reservoirs, such as those on reef flats and in sand channels.

BEACH SAND RESERVOIRS
By Coastal Segments

- North and west coast
- East coast
- South coast

Source: R.M. Moberly   1968

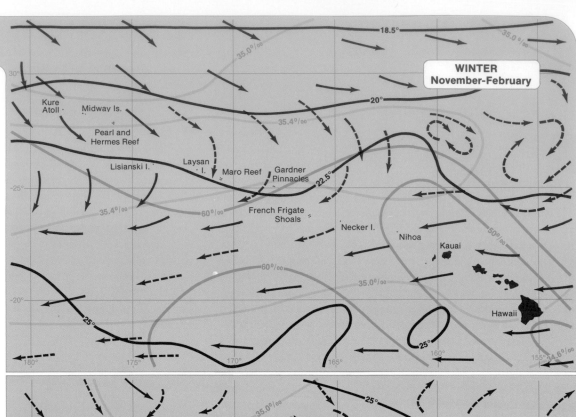

WINTER
November–February

PHYSICAL OCEANOGRAPHY
OF THE NORTH CENTRAL PACIFIC

Average surface currents
0.3–0.5 knots
0.5–0.8 knots
0.8–1.0 knots

waves, percent frequency
5 feet or higher

Surface temperature: isotherms at
intervals of 2.5 degrees Celsius

Surface salinity: isolines at intervals
of 0.4 per mille (per thousand)

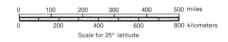

Scale for 25° latitude

Source: U.S. Bureau of Commercial Fisheries and U.S. Navy Oceanographic Office   1972

TYPES AND SOURCES OF HAWAIIAN WAVES

2. NORTH PACIFIC SWELL
—Winter and early spring
—Generated by winter storms
   in the North Pacific
—Heights 8–14 feet
—Periods 10–17 seconds

1. TRADE WIND WAVES
—Possibly present all year
—Largest late spring through
   late autumn
   —Generated by northeast
      trade winds
   —Heights 4–12 feet
   —Periods 5–8 seconds

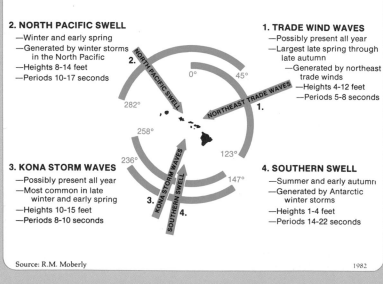

3. KONA STORM WAVES
—Possibly present all year
—Most common in late
   winter and early spring
—Heights 10–15 feet
—Periods 8–10 seconds

4. SOUTHERN SWELL
—Summer and early autumn
—Generated by Antarctic
   winter storms
—Heights 1–4 feet
—Periods 14–22 seconds

Source: R.M. Moberly   1982

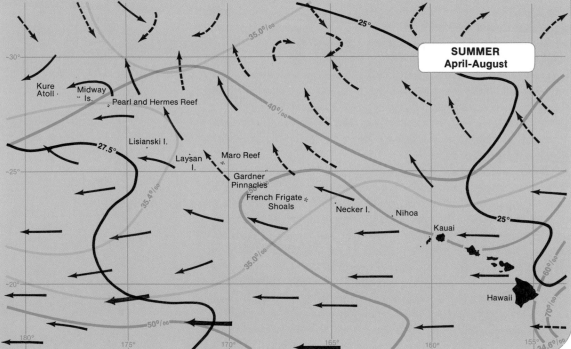

SUMMER
April–August

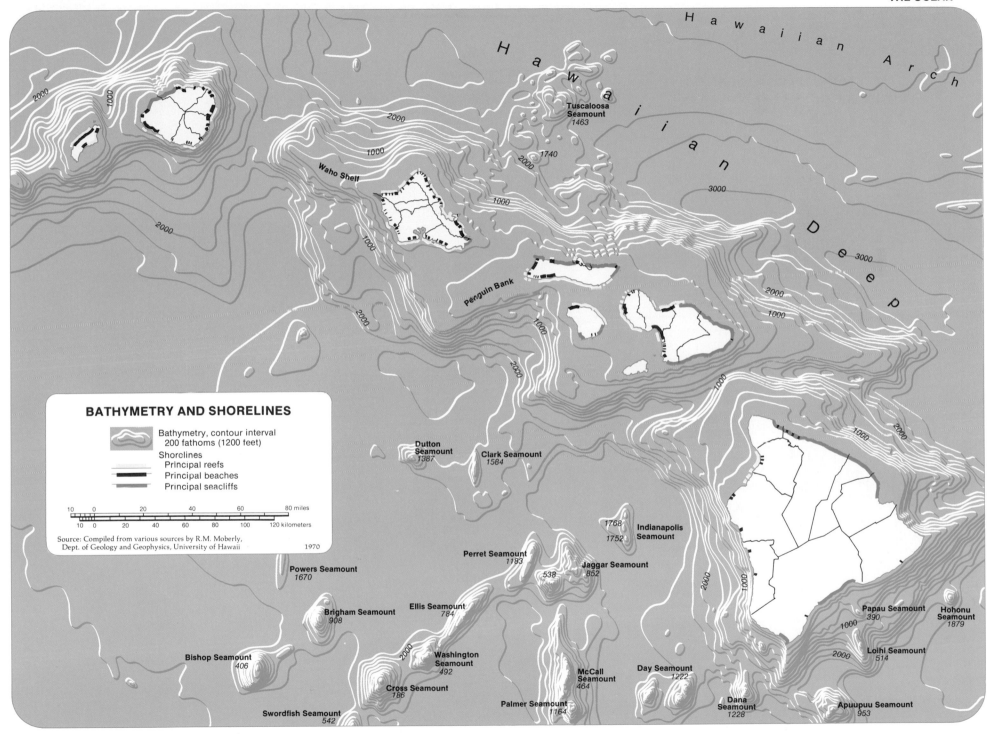

BATHYMETRY AND SHORELINES

Bathymetry, contour interval
200 fathoms (1200 feet)

Shorelines
Principal reefs
Principal beaches
Principal seacliffs

10 0   20   40   60   80 miles
10 0   20   40   60   80   100   120 kilometers

Source: Compiled from various sources by R.M. Moberly,
Dept. of Geology and Geophysics, University of Hawaii   1970

Hawaiian Arch

Hawaiian Deep

Tuscaloosa
Seamount
1463

1740

Waho Shelf

Penguin Bank

Dutton
Seamount
1387

Clark Seamount
1584

1768
1752

Indianapolis
Seamount

Perret Seamount
1183

538

Jaggar Seamount
852

Powers Seamount
1670

Brigham Seamount
908

Ellis Seamount
784

Papau Seamount
390

Hohonu
Seamount
1879

Bishop Seamount
406

Washington
Seamount
492

McCall
Seamount
464

Day Seamount
1222

Loihi Seamount
514

Cross Seamount
186

Dana
Seamount
1228

Apuupuu Seamount
953

Swordfish Seamount
542

Palmer Seamount
1164

SEDIMENTS AND POTENTIAL MINERAL RESOURCES

Minerals of potential economic significance

▨	Ferromanganese crust
⬤⬤	Pink coral
⬤⬤	Black coral
⬤⬤	Shallow water sand bodies

Other sediments

▨	Shallow and intermediate depth carbonate and detritus
▨	Foraminiferal ooze
▨	Diatom ooze
▨	Pelagic brown clay

```
10        0        10        20       30 miles
10     0      10     20     30    40 kilometers
```

Source: Fan and Grunwald (1971), and Sea Grant Program, University of Hawaii 1982

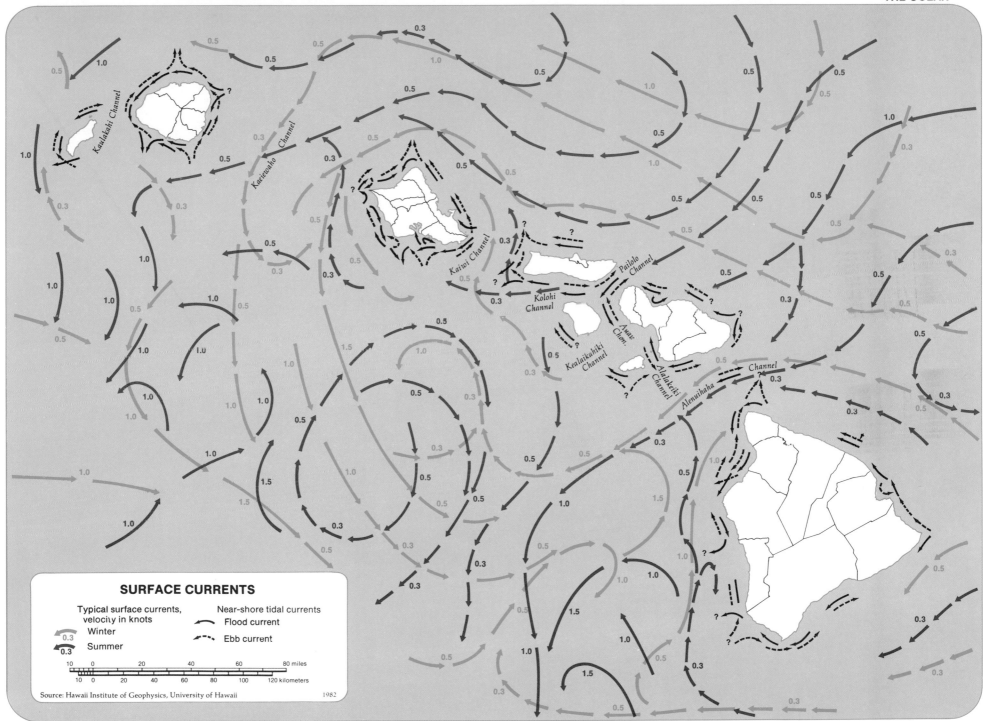

SURFACE CURRENTS

Typical surface currents,
velocity in knots

Near-shore tidal currents

0.3   Winter

0.3   Summer

Flood current

Ebb current

10   0   20   40   60   80 miles

10   0   20   40   60   80   100   120 kilometers

Source: Hawaii Institute of Geophysics, University of Hawaii   1982

Kaulakahi Channel

Kaieiewaho Channel

Kaiwi Channel

Pailolo Channel

Kolohi Channel

Awau Chan.

Kealaikahiki Channel

Alalakeiki Channel

Alenuihaha Channel

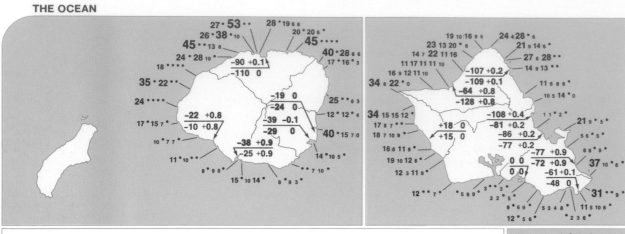

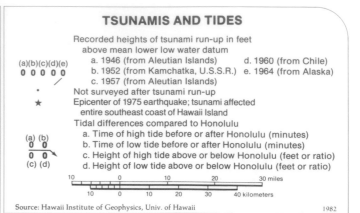

TSUNAMIS AND TIDES

Recorded heights of tsunami run-up in feet
above mean lower low water datum

(a)(b)(c)(d)(e)
0 0 0 0 0

a. 1946 (from Aleutian Islands) d. 1960 (from Chile)
b. 1952 (from Kamchatka, U.S.S.R.) e. 1964 (from Alaska)
c. 1957 (from Aleutian Islands)

• Not surveyed after tsunami run-up
★ Epicenter of 1975 earthquake; tsunami affected
entire southeast coast of Hawaii Island

Tidal differences compared to Honolulu

(a)   (b)
0   0
0   0
(c)   (d)

a. Time of high tide before or after Honolulu (minutes)
b. Time of low tide before or after Honolulu (minutes)
c. Height of high tide above or below Honolulu (feet or ratio)
d. Height of low tide above or below Honolulu (feet or ratio)

10   0   10   20   30 miles
10   0   10   20   30   40 kilometers

Source: Hawaii Institute of Geophysics, Univ. of Hawaii   1982

HONOLULU TIDE CURVE

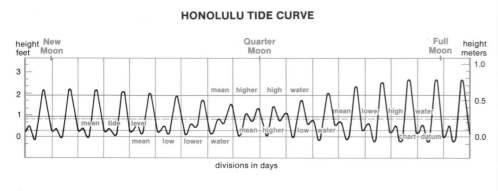

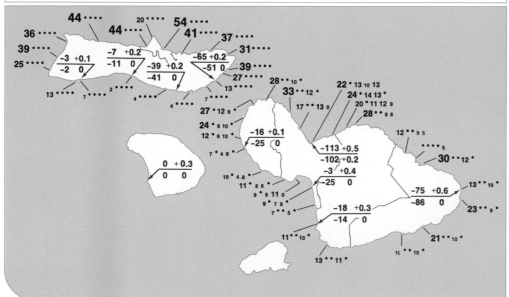

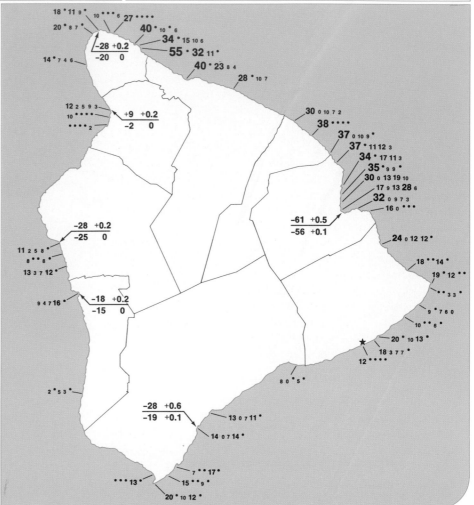

again in late July, as it returns south.

Uniform day lengths and sun angles result in correspondingly small seasonal variations in incoming solar radiation. Level ground in Hawaii receives at least two-thirds as much solar energy between sunrise and sunset of a clear winter's day as on a clear day in summer, while at latitude 40° the ratio is only one-third, and at latitude 50°, only one-fifth. Owing to the clarity of Hawaii's atmosphere, nearly three-fourths of the incident solar energy penetrates to sea level on a clear day.

The Surrounding Ocean. The ocean supplies moisture to the air and acts as a giant thermostat, since its own temperature varies little compared with that of large land masses. The seasonal range of sea surface temperature near Hawaii is only about 6°, from a low of 73° or 74° between late February and March to a high near 80° in late September or early October. The variation from day to night is only one or two degrees.

Because Hawaii is more than 2,000 miles from the nearest continental land mass, air that reaches it, regardless of its source, spends enough time over the equable ocean to moderate the harsher properties with which it may have begun its journey. In fact, Arctic air reaching Hawaii during the winter is sometimes warmed by as much as 100°F during its passage over the waters of the North Pacific. Hawaii's warmest months are not June and July, when the sun is highest, but August and September; and its coolest month, not December, when the sun is farthest south and days are shortest, but February and March—reflecting the seasonal lag in the ocean's temperature.

Storm Tracks and the Pacific Anticyclone. The so-called storm tracks, the paths taken by eastward-migrating high- and low-pressure areas, generally lie between 35°N and 65°N, and so these are the latitudes of changeable weather. But to the south, and particularly over the subtropical oceans, we often find a different breed of atmospheric eddy, one that changes its position so little that it is referred to as "semi-stationary" and lasts so long that it is called "quasi-permanent."

These relatively well anchored eddies include the large subtropical high pressure systems or anticyclones, and places in their vicinity can expect to have correspondingly stable weather. One of these—the Pacific High or anticyclone—generally lies northeast of Hawaii, so that the air moving outward from it streams past the islands as a northeasterly wind. This is in fact the northeasterly trade wind, whose persistence directly reflects that of the Pacific High from which it comes.

Together with the storm tracks, the Pacific High follows the seasonal shift of the sun, moving northward in summer, southward in winter, and tends to be stronger and more persistent in summer than in winter. So in winter, with the weakening and occasional absence of the Pacific High and the closer approach of the storm tracks, the trade winds may be interrupted for days or even weeks at a time by the inva-

Kou, *Cordia subcordata*; leaf, flowers, fruit. The wood was used by the early Hawaiians for making cups, dishes, and calabashes.
Bishop Museum drawing from Neal (1965:714)

CLIMATE

The climate of an area can best be thought of as a composite or frequency distribution of the various kinds of weather that occur there. The outstanding features of Hawaii's climate include mild and equable temperatures the year round, moderate humidities, persistence of northeasterly trade winds, remarkable differences in rainfall within short distances, and infrequency of severe storms.

In most of Hawaii there are only two seasons: "summer," between about May and October, when the sun is more nearly overhead, the weather warmer and drier, and the trade winds most persistent; and "winter," between about October and April, when the sun is in the south, the weather cooler, and the trade winds more often interrupted by other winds and by intervals of widespread cloud and rain.

Hawaii's climate reflects chiefly the interplay of four factors: latitude, the surrounding ocean, Hawaii's location relative to the storm tracks and the Pacific anticyclone, and terrain.

Latitude. Hawaii is well within the tropics, which accounts for the relative uniformity throughout the year in length of day and received solar energy, and hence in temperature.

Hawaii's longest and shortest days are about 13½ and 11 hours, respectively, as compared with 14½ and 10 hours for Southern California, and 15½ and 8½ hours for Maine. The sun at noon is never more than 45° from the zenith and is directly overhead twice during the year—toward the end of May, as it travels to its farthest north, and

sion of the fronts or migratory cyclones of more northerly latitudes and by Kona storms forming nearer by. Hence, winter in Hawaii is the season of more frequent cloudiness and rainstorms, and of southerly and westerly winds replacing the trades for shorter or longer periods.

Terrain. Hawaii's mountains profoundly influence every aspect of its weather and climate. Their endless variety of peaks, valleys, ridges, and broad slopes, each presenting a different aspect to the wind, not only give Hawaii as a whole a climate in some respects markedly different from that of the surrounding ocean, but create within the small compass of the islands a climatic variety that would not exist here if these were flat islands of the same size.

The mountains obstruct, deflect, and accelerate the flow of air. Where the warm, moist winds are forced to rise over windward coasts and slopes, cloudiness and rainfall are much greater than over the nearby open sea; while leeward areas, where the air descends, tend to be sunny and dry. In places sheltered by terrain, local air movements arise quite at variance with winds in exposed localities. And since temperature decreases with elevation by about 3° per thousand feet, Hawaii's mountains, which extend from sea level to nearly 14,000 feet, encompass a climatic range from the tropic to the sub-Arctic.

The climate of Hawaii is defined not only by what it has but by what it seems to lack: the extremes of winter cold and snow on the one hand and summer heat waves, hurricanes, and hailstorms on the other. Yet Hawaii's tallest peaks do get their share of winter blizzards, ice, and snow; highest temperatures reach into the 90s; and thunderstorms, lightning, hail, floods, and droughts—and even hurricanes and tornadoes—are not unknown. But usually these are on a minor scale, less frequent and less severe than their counterparts in continental regions.

Rainfall. Over the open sea near Hawaii, rainfall averages between 25 to 30 inches a year. Yet the islands themselves receive up to 15 times this amount in some places and less than one-third of it in others. The cause of this remarkable variability, and of yearly totals which rival the greatest on earth, is principally the "orographic" (mountain-caused) rains which form within the moist trade-wind air as it moves in from the sea and overrides the steep and high terrain of the islands. Over the lower islands the resulting average rainfall distribution resembles closely the topographic contours: amounts are greatest over upper slopes and crests and least in the leeward lowlands. On the higher mountains the belt of maximum rainfall lies at only 2,000 to 3,000 feet, and amounts drop off rapidly with further elevation, so that the highest slopes are relatively dry.

Another source of rainfall is the towering cumulus clouds that build up over mountains and interiors on sunny calm afternoons. Although such convective showers may be intense, they are usually brief and localized.

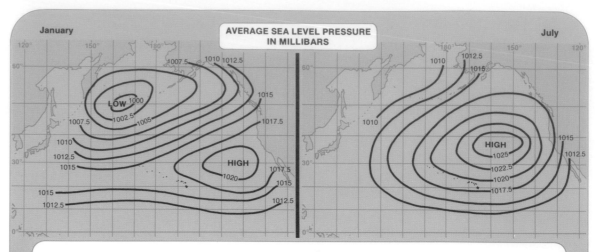

The average location and configuration of the Pacific anticyclone is shown for January and for July, the months in which it attains its greatest and least magnitudes, respectively, and its furthest north and south positions. Air streaming outward in a clockwise direction from the southern portions of this extensive region of high pressure moves across the eastern and central Pacific Ocean as a broad current of northeasterly winds. This is the trade wind, whose persistence reflects that of the Pacific High itself, and which constitutes one of the outstanding features of Hawaii's climate. These winds reaching Hawaii are only moderately warm and humid since their approach lies over the cooler waters to the northeast of the islands. What is regarded as typical Hawaiian weather is that associated with the trade winds: sunny days, breezy and warm, but not sultry, with clouds and showers confined mainly to the mountain areas.

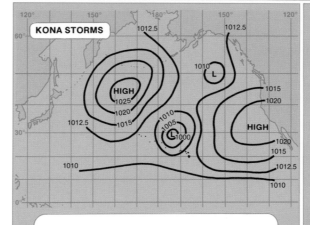

Kona storms are low pressure areas (cyclones) of subtropical origin which usually develop northwest of Hawaii in winter and move slowly eastward, accompanied by southerly winds from whose direction the storm derives its name (*kona* means 'leeward' in Hawaiian) and by the clouds and rain that have made Kona storms synonymous with bad weather in Hawaii. Kona storms vary in number from year to year. Some winters have had none, others five or more.

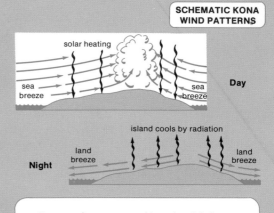

Kona weather is warm and humid with light, variable winds; it occurs when trade winds or other large-scale weather systems are absent from Hawaii. It is less frequent in summer, but also more sultry then, owing to the higher temperatures. Diurnal heating and cooling of the islands relative to the surrounding ocean generates sea breezes during the day and land breezes at night. Afternoon heating often leads to cloudiness and showers over mountains and interiors.

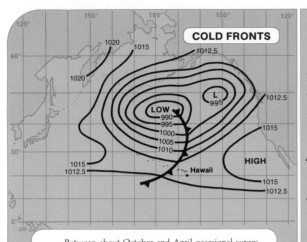

COLD FRONTS

Between about October and April occasional surges of cold air invade the Hawaiian area from the north. The cold fronts, which mark the leading edges of these cold air masses, are frequently accompanied by widespread cloud, heavy rain, and thunderstorms. Severe fronts may be preceded by strong southwest winds and followed by gusty northerly winds. As many as 20 fronts may reach Kauai in a winter, but only about half progress as far as Hawaii Island.

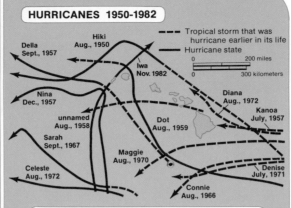

HURRICANES 1950-1982

- - - Tropical storm that was hurricane earlier in its life
——— Hurricane state

Hurricanes (called typhoons west of 180°) are uncommon in Hawaii. Hurricane Dot's winds and rain in 1959 caused $6 million damage to property and crops, chiefly on Kauai; and Hurricane Iwa's winds and surf in 1982 caused over $200 million damage, chiefly on Niihau, Kauai, and Oahu. The hurricanes and lesser tropical cyclones that affect Hawaii usually originate off Mexico or Central America, but almost always they dissipate before reaching the islands or pass westward to the south.

SEASONAL RAINFALL
Percentage of Mean Annual Rainfall at Selected Stations

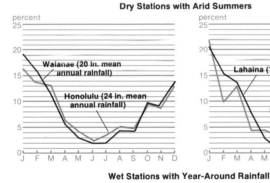

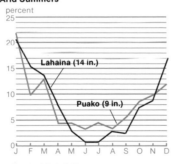

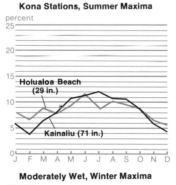

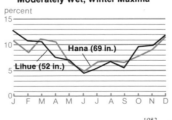

Source: National Weather Service, Pacific Region

1982

Hawaii's heaviest rains are brought by winter storms during the October-to-April season. While the effects of terrain on storm rainfall are not as pronounced as on trade-wind showers, large differences over small distances do occur, due both to topography and to the location of the rain clouds; but these differences vary from storm to storm.

Frequently, the heaviest storm rains do not occur in localities having the greatest average rainfall; nor is it uncommon during such storms for relatively dry areas to receive within a day, or even a few hours, totals exceeding half their mean annual rainfall. For example, downtown Honolulu, with an average yearly rainfall of only 24 inches, has had more than 17 inches in a single day. During storms, 3 inches or more may fall in a single hour, and Hawaii's record rains—more than 11 inches in an hour and nearly 40 inches in 24 hours—rank near the world's greatest.

Since the lowland lees and other dry areas obtain their rainfall chiefly from a few winter storms, and only negligibly from tradewind showers, their rainfall is strongly seasonal, their summers being arid. In the wetter regions, on the other hand, where rainfall comes from both winter storms and year-round trade-wind showers, seasonal differences are much smaller.

At the opposite extreme, drought is not unknown in Hawaii, although it rarely affects even an entire island at one time. Drought may occur when either the winter storms or the trade winds fail. If the winter storms fail, the normally dry leeward areas are hardest hit; and two successive dry winters, with the intervening normally dry summer, can have serious effects. The failure of the trades most affects windward and upland regions, which receive a smaller proportion of their rain from winter storms.

S.P.

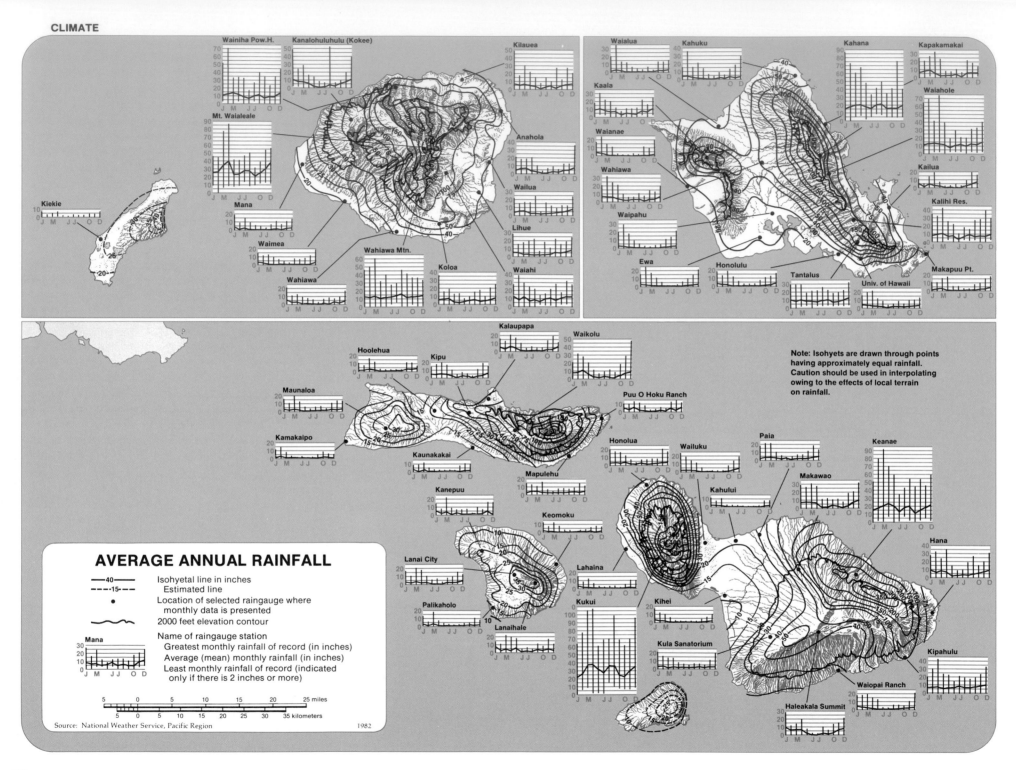

AVERAGE ANNUAL RAINFALL

——40—— Isohyetal line in inches
--15-- Estimated line
• Location of selected raingauge where
monthly data is presented
～～～ 2000 feet elevation contour

Name of raingauge station
Greatest monthly rainfall of record (in inches)
Average (mean) monthly rainfall (in inches)
Least monthly rainfall of record (indicated
only if there is 2 inches or more)

Note: Isohyets are drawn through points
having approximately equal rainfall.
Caution should be used in interpolating
owing to the effects of local terrain
on rainfall.

Source: National Weather Service, Pacific Region   1982

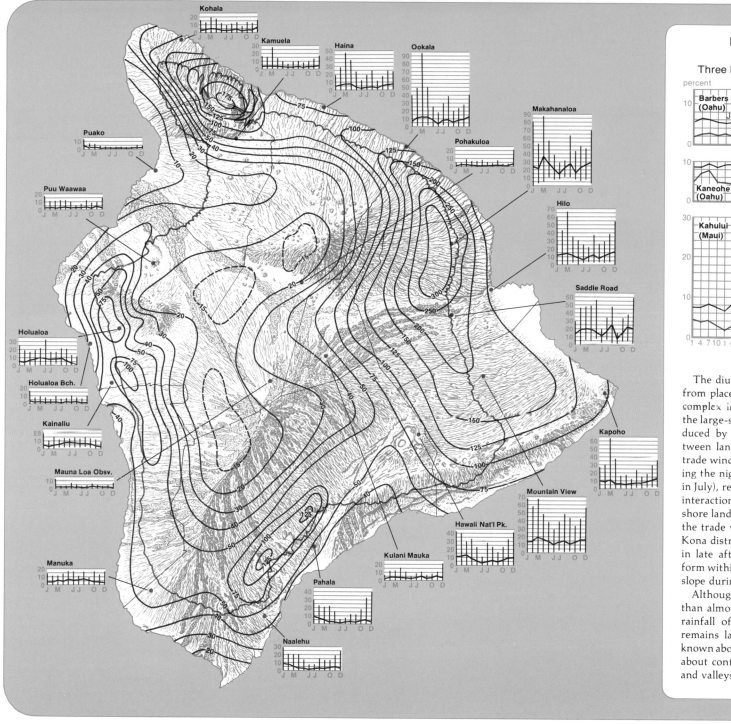

RAINFALL FREQUENCY BY HOUR OF DAY
Three Hour Intervals Centered at Hour Shown

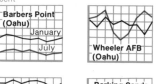
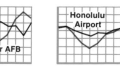

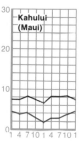
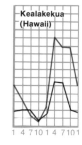

The diurnal variation in rainfall frequency differs from place to place in Hawaii, since it represents a complex interplay between terrain and wind—both the large-scale flow and the local air movements produced by day-to-night temperature contrasts between land and sea. In places well exposed to the trade winds, showers are usually more frequent during the night and early morning (for example, Lihue in July), reflecting conditions over the open sea or an interaction between the trades and nocturnal offshore land breezes. In contrast, areas sheltered from the trade winds (like Kealakekua, in Hawaii Island's Kona district) tend to have their rainfall maximums in late afternoon and evening, from showers that form within sea breezes which move onshore and upslope during the day.

Although Hawaii has considerably more gages than almost any other area of comparable size, the rainfall of its inaccessible or uninhabited regions remains largely conjectural. Nor is nearly enough known about the effects of smaller terrain features or about contrasts in rainfall between adjoining ridges and valleys.

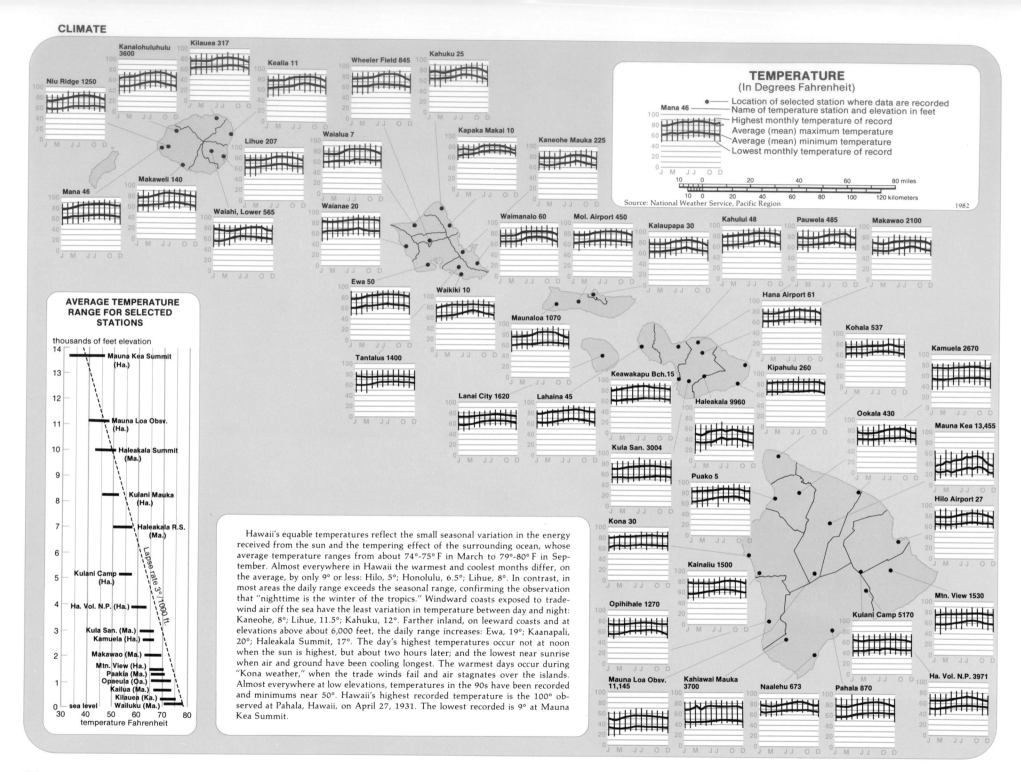

TEMPERATURE
(In Degrees Fahrenheit)

● Location of selected station where data are recorded
Name of temperature station and elevation in feet
Highest monthly temperature of record
Average (mean) maximum temperature
Average (mean) minimum temperature
Lowest monthly temperature of record

Mana 46

Source: National Weather Service, Pacific Region

1982

AVERAGE TEMPERATURE RANGE FOR SELECTED STATIONS

thousands of feet elevation

Mauna Kea Summit (Ha.)

Mauna Loa Obsv. (Ha.)

Haleakala Summit (Ma.)

Kulani Mauka (Ha.)

Haleakala R.S. (Ma.)

Kulani Camp (Ha.)

Ha. Vol. N.P. (Ha.)

Kula San. (Ma.)
Kamuela (Ha.)

Makawao (Ma.)

Mtn. View (Ha.)
Paakia (Ha.)
Opaeula (Oa.)
Kailua (Ha.)
Kilauea (Ka.)
Wailuku (Ma.)

sea level

temperature Fahrenheit

Lapse rate 3°/1000 ft.

Hawaii's equable temperatures reflect the small seasonal variation in the energy received from the sun and the tempering effect of the surrounding ocean, whose average temperature ranges from about 74°-75° F in March to 79°-80° F in September. Almost everywhere in Hawaii the warmest and coolest months differ, on the average, by only 9° or less: Hilo, 5°; Honolulu, 6.5°; Lihue, 8°. In contrast, in most areas the daily range exceeds the seasonal range, confirming the observation that "nighttime is the winter of the tropics." Windward coasts exposed to trade-wind air off the sea have the least variation in temperature between day and night: Kaneohe, 8°; Lihue, 11.5°; Kahuku, 12°. Farther inland, on leeward coasts and at elevations above about 6,000 feet, the daily range increases: Ewa, 19°; Kaanapali, 20°; Haleakala Summit, 17°. The day's highest temperatures occur not at noon when the sun is highest, but about two hours later; and the lowest near sunrise when air and ground have been cooling longest. The warmest days occur during "Kona weather," when the trade winds fail and air stagnates over the islands. Almost everywhere at low elevations, temperatures in the 90s have been recorded and minimums near 50°. Hawaii's highest recorded temperature is the 100° observed at Pahala, Hawaii, on April 27, 1931. The lowest recorded is 9° at Mauna Kea Summit.

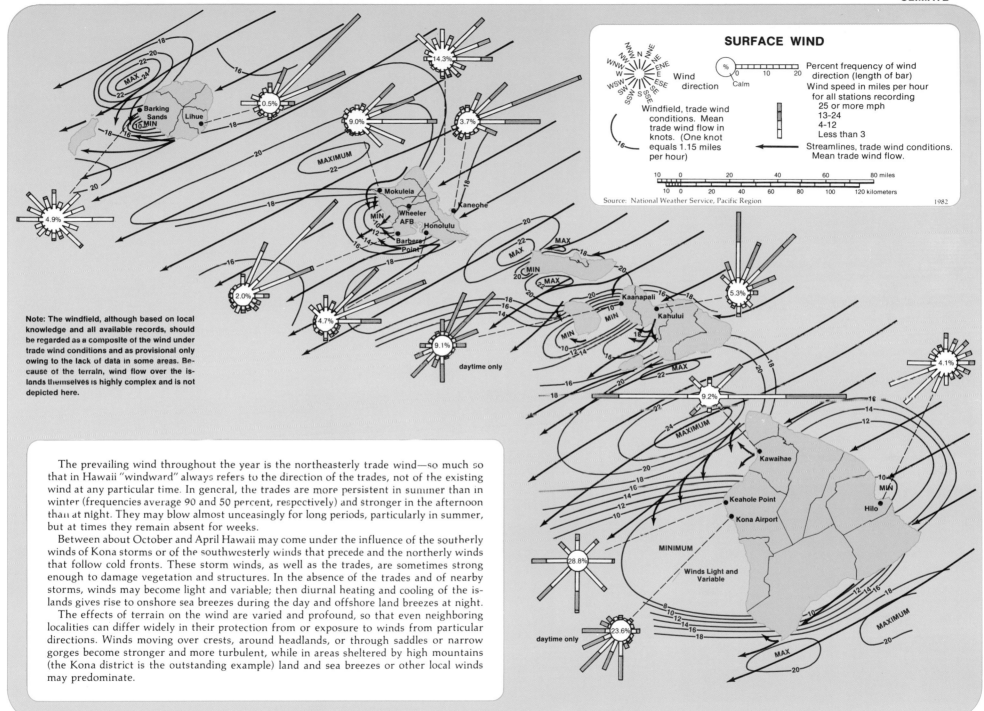

SURFACE WIND

Wind direction

% Calm

Percent frequency of wind direction (length of bar)

Wind speed in miles per hour for all stations recording
25 or more mph
13-24
4-12
Less than 3

Windfield, trade wind conditions. Mean trade wind flow in knots. (One knot equals 1.15 miles per hour)

Streamlines, trade wind conditions. Mean trade wind flow.

Source: National Weather Service, Pacific Region

1982

Note: The windfield, although based on local knowledge and all available records, should be regarded as a composite of the wind under trade wind conditions and as provisional only owing to the lack of data in some areas. Because of the terrain, wind flow over the islands themselves is highly complex and is not depicted here.

The prevailing wind throughout the year is the northeasterly trade wind—so much so that in Hawaii "windward" always refers to the direction of the trades, not of the existing wind at any particular time. In general, the trades are more persistent in summer than in winter (frequencies average 90 and 50 percent, respectively) and stronger in the afternoon than at night. They may blow almost unceasingly for long periods, particularly in summer, but at times they remain absent for weeks.

Between about October and April Hawaii may come under the influence of the southerly winds of Kona storms or of the southwesterly winds that precede and the northerly winds that follow cold fronts. These storm winds, as well as the trades, are sometimes strong enough to damage vegetation and structures. In the absence of the trades and of nearby storms, winds may become light and variable; then diurnal heating and cooling of the islands gives rise to onshore sea breezes during the day and offshore land breezes at night.

The effects of terrain on the wind are varied and profound, so that even neighboring localities can differ widely in their protection from or exposure to winds from particular directions. Winds moving over crests, around headlands, or through saddles or narrow gorges become stronger and more turbulent, while in areas sheltered by high mountains (the Kona district is the outstanding example) land and sea breezes or other local winds may predominate.

SEASONAL AND DIURNAL WIND DIRECTION AND PERCENT FREQUENCY

At Four Selected Stations

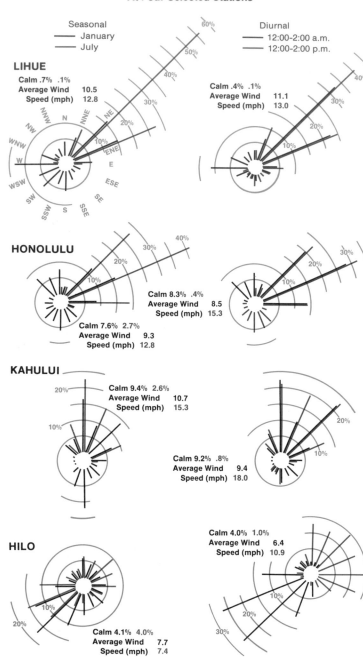

Seasonal
— January
— July

Diurnal
— 12:00-2:00 a.m.
— 12:00-2:00 p.m.

LIHUE
Calm .7% .1%
Average Wind 10.5
Speed (mph) 12.8

Calm .4% .1%
Average Wind 11.1
Speed (mph) 13.0

HONOLULU
Calm 8.3% .4%
Average Wind 8.5
Speed (mph) 15.3

Calm 7.6% 2.7%
Average Wind 9.3
Speed (mph) 12.8

KAHULUI
Calm 9.4% 2.6%
Average Wind 10.7
Speed (mph) 15.3

Calm 9.2% .8%
Average Wind 9.4
Speed (mph) 18.0

HILO
Calm 4.0% 1.0%
Average Wind 6.4
Speed (mph) 10.9

Calm 4.1% 4.0%
Average Wind 7.7
Speed (mph) 7.4

Source: National Weather Service, Pacific Region 1982

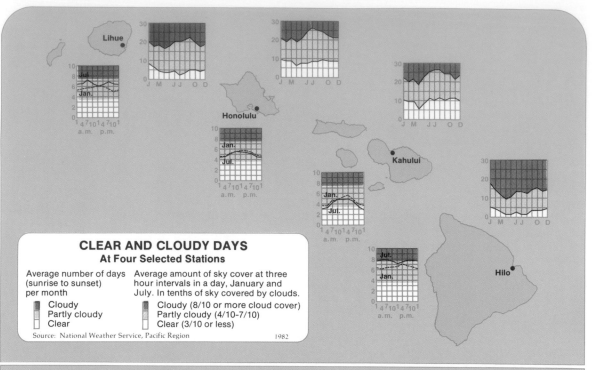

CLEAR AND CLOUDY DAYS
At Four Selected Stations

Average number of days (sunrise to sunset) per month
- Cloudy
- Partly cloudy
- Clear

Average amount of sky cover at three hour intervals in a day, January and July. In tenths of sky covered by clouds.
- Cloudy (8/10 or more cloud cover)
- Partly cloudy (4/10-7/10)
- Clear (3/10 or less)

Source: National Weather Service, Pacific Region 1982

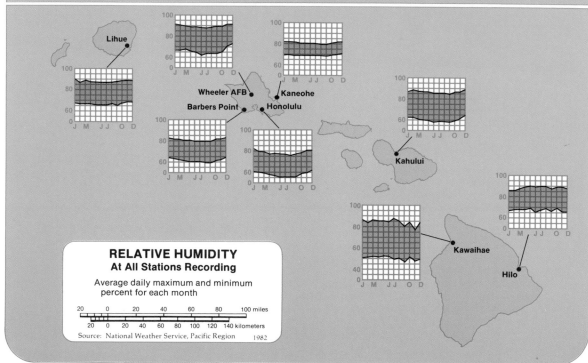

RELATIVE HUMIDITY
At All Stations Recording

Average daily maximum and minimum percent for each month

20 0 20 40 60 80 100 miles
20 0 20 40 60 80 100 120 140 kilometers

Source: National Weather Service, Pacific Region 1982

AIR QUALITY

While the air over Hawaii in general is relatively clean and low in pollution, conditions in certain areas give cause for serious concern. Chief among them is the urban area of Honolulu where large numbers of motor vehicles (page 181) daily pour tons of exhaust gases and particulates into the air. Industrial air pollution is comparatively minor. Natural pollution from volcanic action can be severe under certain wind conditions, but it is a rare occurrence. Many physical and meteorological factors combine to allow motor vehicle pollutants to concentrate at high levels in certain parts of the city. These include: the site of the city in the lee of the trade winds and occasional long periods of light and variable wind flow; modified local air circulation due to tall buildings and higher surface temperatures caused by buildings, pavements, and traffic; and large amounts of sunshine.

Some air pollutants, such as suspended particulates, can be measured directly in order to forecast spatial and temporal patterns over a city. Other pollutants, such as carbon monoxide, which are more difficult to measure directly on a mobile continuous basis, are best forecast through a meteorological diffusion model.

The maps on this page present data for suspended particulates. The measurements were made with an integrating nephelometer, an instrument which can be attached to a car or aircraft to give instantaneous recordings of air quality at any location. It measures concentrations of particles in the small size range of 0.1 to 1.0 micrometers, a range critical to human respiratory health.

For the purpose of sampling suspended particulates, the Honolulu urban area was subdivided into 3,500 squares of 250 × 250 meters each. The mobile sampling was conducted from 6 A.M. to noon on one day, and from noon to 6 P.M. on the following day, from July through September 1971. During the six-hour sampling periods, which covered some 120 miles and produced some 40 feet of chart paper with continuous data, it was arranged that as many squares as possible were sampled during different two-hour time periods. About 20 six-hour sampling runs were made. Thus each two-hour sampling run is based on about 1,000 data, and each 12-hour sampling map is constructed from about 6,000 data. This constitutes one of the most detailed monitorings of an air pollutant conducted in any urban area. However, the maps reflect only trade-wind conditions, which produce the best dispersion conditions for pollutants in Hawaii.

The first map on this page shows the lowest concentrations of suspended particulates recorded during any of the 20 separate runs, which can be taken as indicative of Honolulu's background pollution levels. The lowest values are characteristically found on the exposed residential hilltops of St. Louis Heights and Maunalani Heights. The highest values are found in congested downtown areas and along Moanalua Road.

The second map depicts maximum suspended particulate concentrations averaged for each grid square from vehicular sources only. It is important to note that vehicular emission can raise the suspended particulate levels more than ten times above the 12-hour average background level to 228 micrograms per cubic meter. Again, the busy intersection of Moanalua Road and Hale Street, the Nuuanu Pali Highway, and congested streets in Waikiki stand out as the most polluted areas.

The third map shows the morning rush-hour conditions from 6 A.M. to 8 A.M. Since this map includes data for suspended particulates from all sources during the

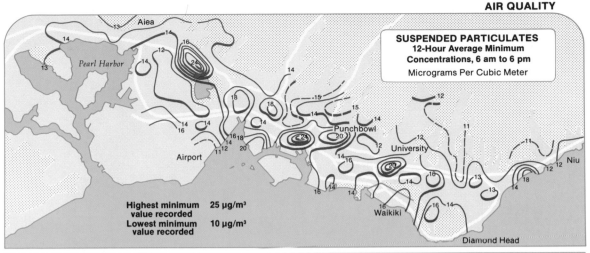

SUSPENDED PARTICULATES
12-Hour Average Minimum
Concentrations, 6 am to 6 pm
Micrograms Per Cubic Meter

Highest minimum value recorded   25 µg/m³
Lowest minimum value recorded   10 µg/m³

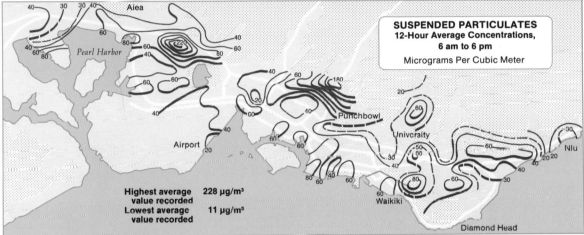

SUSPENDED PARTICULATES
12-Hour Average Concentrations,
6 am to 6 pm
Micrograms Per Cubic Meter

Highest average value recorded   228 µg/m³
Lowest average value recorded   11 µg/m³

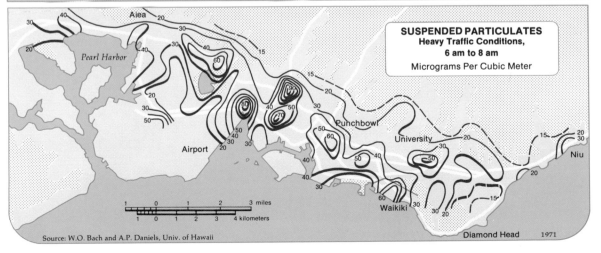

SUSPENDED PARTICULATES
Heavy Traffic Conditions,
6 am to 8 am
Micrograms Per Cubic Meter

Source: W.O. Bach and A.P. Daniels, Univ. of Hawaii   1971

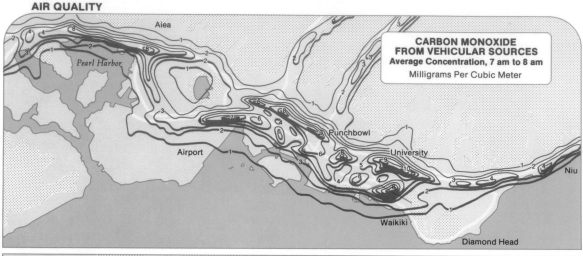

CARBON MONOXIDE FROM VEHICULAR SOURCES
Average Concentration, 7 am to 8 am
Milligrams Per Cubic Meter

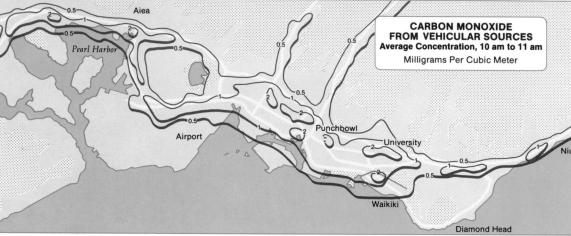

CARBON MONOXIDE FROM VEHICULAR SOURCES
Average Concentration, 10 am to 11 am
Milligrams Per Cubic Meter

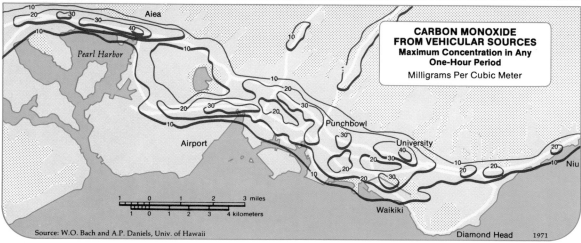

CARBON MONOXIDE FROM VEHICULAR SOURCES
Maximum Concentration in Any One-Hour Period
Milligrams Per Cubic Meter

Source: W.O. Bach and A.P. Daniels, Univ. of Hawaii

rush-hour period, including any background values, the mean values are somewhat lower than those reflecting maximum average concentrations produced by vehicular sources only. Again it is clear that the highest concentrations cluster around the busiest intersections. It is now generally accepted that particles of a size range that penetrate deeply into the lungs are produced in cities by automobile exhausts, tire wear, and turbulent dust-blowing enhanced by the moving vehicles.

Meteorological Diffusion Models. Because of the current technical difficulties in direct measurement of certain gases, meteorological diffusion models can make the most realistic assessment of air quality in urban areas where there is a combination of fixed and mobile sources of air pollution.

Results of diffusion modeling for carbon monoxide (CO) in Honolulu are shown in maps on this page. Data for the model for the 1970–1971 period included sample measurements of CO, estimated emissions from motor vehicles, traffic densities, and street lengths. The first map shows the average concentration of CO for the morning rush-hour period. The CO-concentration patterns coincide closely with those of traffic and highway density. The second map shows the average CO concentration two hours later. Increased ventilation and decreased traffic density produce in some areas as much as a five-fold reduction in CO concentration.

Since the Hawaii Air Quality Control Region, like most other control regions, does not attempt to control average concentrations, but rather the frequency of occurrence of a selected maximum concentration, such maxima are presented in the third map. The one-hour maximum air quality standard for CO has been set at 10 mg/m³ for Hawaii. This standard is already exceeded in Honolulu and surrounding urban areas. In some areas the magnitude of the standard is exceeded almost five times.

The graph below shows annual mean CO concentrations at the Department of Health Building on Punchbowl Street from the first complete year of sampling (1972) to the last one (1979). This was the only continuously operating CO sampler in the State during these years. In 1979 the sampler was moved to Leahi Hospital on Kilauea Avenue. Concentrations at this site have been very low, for example, 0.6 mg/m³ as an average for 1980. In 1981 a second sampler was installed on Kalakaua Avenue in Waikiki. This sampler shows higher concentrations than at the previous sites. The CO concentration trend at the Health Department Building shows significantly improved air quality which, however, could partly be a result of a changed traffic pattern. The number of times the state air quality standard was exceeded at this location decreased from more than fifty in 1972 to ten in 1979, and the annual maximum value showed a similar trend, dropping from over 40 mg/m³ in 1971 to between 20 mg/m³ in 1979.

A.P.D.

milligrams per cubic meter

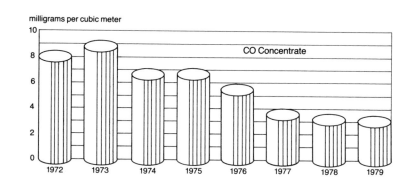

PLANTS

Hawaii has a fascinating and unique collection of plant life. There are more than 2,500 kinds of higher plants that occur only in the Hawaiian Islands and nowhere else. Yet most visitors and many residents of the State are not aware of these unique plants and see very few of them. The coconuts, orchids, sugarcane, and pineapples of the tourist advertisements are recent immigrants to Hawaii, neither native nor unique. The native plants are common today only in such remote places as the headwalls of deep valleys, on steep cliffs, and on mountain ridges and peaks.

A brief review of the history of Hawaii's plant life will help us understand why this is so. When the Hawaiian Islands first reached above the surface of the sea they were without land plants. Gradually, over long periods of time, living seeds and spores of plants from elsewhere reached the islands, borne by winds, drifting on the sea, or carried by birds. Each time a different seed or spore happened to land in a place where the young plant developing from it could survive, grow, and produce a new crop of seeds or spores, then another kind of plant had become established in Hawaii. Through time, gradual changes have occurred in these isolated Hawaiian populations, and many have evolved to a point at which they differ enough from all other plants that they can be classified as distinct species or varieties.

The plant geographer uses the term *native* to refer to a plant, the ancestors of which reached the area where it now grows by natural means without help from man. He distinguishes between native and

introduced (or *exotic*) species—those plants that reached a given geographic area only with the assistance of man, whether such assistance was intentional or inadvertent. The term *endemic* is applied to a group of organisms native to a single small geographic area. Thus a species endemic to the Hawaiian Islands is one that occurs naturally only in this group of islands. An *indigenous* organism is one that is native to a larger geographic area—thus a species which is native to Hawaii, the Society Islands, the Marquesas, Samoa, and Fiji would be described as indigenous to Hawaii, but not endemic.

The most recent compilation of Hawaiian plants (St. John, 1972) lists 1,381 native species of flowering plants, of which 96.6 percent are endemic and 3.4 percent indigenous. When subspecies, varieties, and forms are included, there are 2,656 recognized taxonomic groups of which 99.1 percent are endemic. Other work has indicated that all of these plants have evolved from about 275 species of successful natural immigrants which have arrived in Hawaii on the average of once every 70,000 years or so since the time when the islands emerged from the sea. Most of these orginal immigrants seem to have come from the Indo-Pacific area to the south and west of Hawaii, but about 20 percent probably came from the east, from the Americas.

The isolation of the Hawaiian island chain from other land masses, the isolation between the separate islands in the chain, the equable but variable climate, the topography which leads to isolation of small populations in deep valleys or separate mountain peaks, and isolation brought about by lava flows and formation of kipukas are all factors which have permitted evolution to occur at an especially rapid rate.

The products of these evolutionary processes as we can observe them in Hawaii today include a series of botanical novelties. There are several groups that have woody species in Hawaii although they are members of a family which elsewhere in the world consists mostly of small herbs. Such woodiness occurs in violets (*Viola, Isodendrion*), lobelias (*Lobelia, Trematolobelia, Cyanea, Clermontia, Delissea, Rollandia,* and *Brighamia*), plantains (*Plantago*), amaranths (*Charpentiera*), and chenopods (*Chenopodium*). In some families, adaptive radiation has occurred—several species and genera have evolved from a common ancestor and now occupy a series of different ecological niches. Examples can be found among the lobelias, but perhaps the most striking example is a group of members of the sunflower family closely related to the tarweeds of western North America. In this group are several species of *Dubautia* ranging from small rain-forest trees to shrubs of open dry lava flows, species of *Argyroxiphium* (the silverswords and greenswords), and species of *Wilkesia* (the iliau or Kauai greenswords). While some otherwise herbaceous plants seem to have developed the woody habit in Hawaii, others are giant herbs such as the apeape (*Gunnera*) with circular leaves up to 2 meters in diameter.

Silversword or hinahina, *Argyroxiphium sandvicense*. A spectacular plant from Haleakala, Maui.
Photograph by C.H. Lamoureux

Mao or Hawaiian cotton, *Gossypium sandvicense*. A rare plant from dry coastal regions.
Photograph by C.H. Lamoureux

Ohai, *Sesbania tomentosa*. A small shrub from coastal areas that is becoming very rare.
Photograph by C.H. Lamoureux

Mamane, *Sophora chrysophylla*. A dominant tree in drier forests at high elevations.
Photograph by C.H. Lamoureux

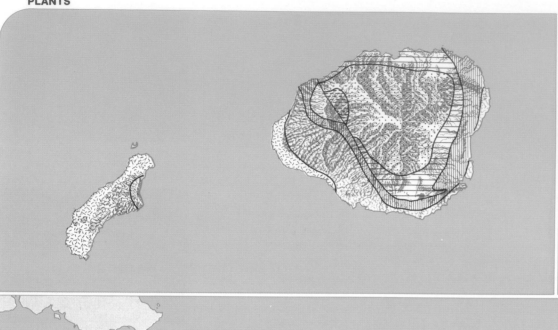

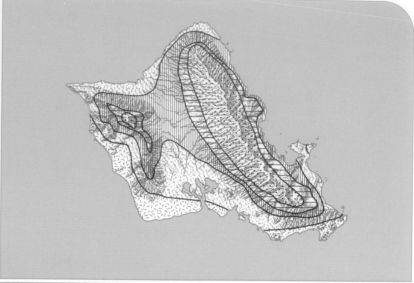

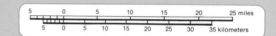

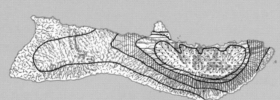

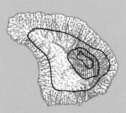

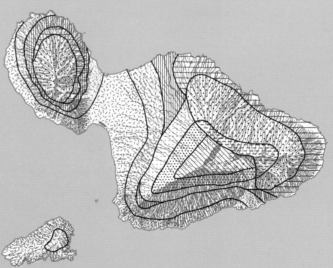

VEGETATION ZONES

	ZONE	ALTITUDE	RAINFALL (in./yr.)	CHARACTERISTIC PLANTS (Native Hawaiian species in **bold** type)
	Kiawe and lowland shrubs	Below 1000	Less than 20	Kiawe, koa haole, finger grass, **pili grass**
	Lantana-koa haole shrubs	Below 3000	20-40	Lantana, koa haole, klu, panini, **ilima**, Natal redtop grass
	Open guava forest with shrubs	Below 2500	40-60	Guava, koa haole, lantana, Spanish clover, Bermuda grass
	Mixed open forest	2500-4000	40-60	**Ohia lehua, koa,** Spanish clover, Bermuda grass
	Closed guava forest with shrubs	Below 1500	60 or more	Guava, Boston fern, Hilo grass, basket grass, **false staghorn fern,** kukui, **hala**
	Closed ohia lehua rainforest	1500-7000	60-400	**Ohia lehua, hapuu tree, olapa**
	Open koa forest	4000-7000	60 or more	**Koa, ohia lehua,** rattail grass, **hue pueo grass**
	Open koa forest with mamane	4000-7000	Less than 50	Koa, **mamane,** heu pueo grass, **pukiawe, aalii**
	Open mamane-naio forest with subalpine shrubs	7000-10,000	Less than 50	**Mamane, naio, pukiawe, aalii, ohelo**
	Alpine stone desert	Above 10,000	Less than 20	**Scattered mosses, silversword, Hawaiian bent grass**

Source: After J.C. Ripperton and E.Y. Hosaka (1942); C.H. Lamoureux, Botany Dept., Univ. of Hawaii   1982

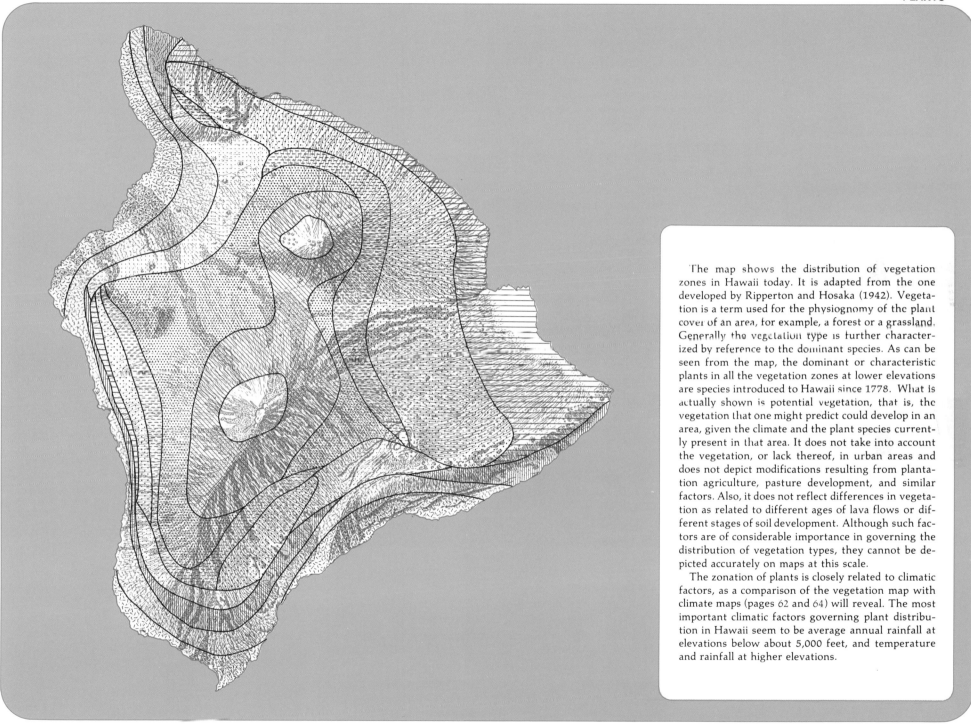

The map shows the distribution of vegetation zones in Hawaii today. It is adapted from the one developed by Ripperton and Hosaka (1942). Vegetation is a term used for the physiognomy of the plant cover of an area, for example, a forest or a grassland. Generally the vegetation type is further characterized by reference to the dominant species. As can be seen from the map, the dominant or characteristic plants in all the vegetation zones at lower elevations are species introduced to Hawaii since 1778. What is actually shown is potential vegetation, that is, the vegetation that one might predict could develop in an area, given the climate and the plant species currently present in that area. It does not take into account the vegetation, or lack thereof, in urban areas and does not depict modifications resulting from plantation agriculture, pasture development, and similar factors. Also, it does not reflect differences in vegetation as related to different ages of lava flows or different stages of soil development. Although such factors are of considerable importance in governing the distribution of vegetation types, they cannot be depicted accurately on maps at this scale.

The zonation of plants is closely related to climatic factors, as a comparison of the vegetation map with climate maps (pages 62 and 64) will reveal. The most important climatic factors governing plant distribution in Hawaii seem to be average annual rainfall at elevations below about 5,000 feet, and temperature and rainfall at higher elevations.

Ohia lehua. *Metrosideros collina* subsp. *polymorpha*. The most common and most widely distributed native Hawaiian tree.

Night-blooming cereus, *Hylocereus undatus*. This cactus, introduced from Mexico, has been widely planted in Hawaii.

Kolea lau nui, *Myrsine lessertiana*. An endemic tree, found frequently as an understory tree in rain forests.

Uluhe, *Dicranopteris linearis*. A fern that forms dense tangled patches in forest openings at lower elevations.

Photographs by C.H. Lamoureux

Very few native plants have spines or thorns, even those whose continental ancestors probably possessed them. The akala or Hawaiian raspberry (*Rubus*) is usually almost without prickles although some individuals do exhibit them. This lack of spininess can probably be explained by the fact that the native plants evolved in Hawaii when there were no grazing or browsing mammals present. Therefore there was no evolutionary pressure resulting in retention or development of such protective mechanisms as spines or thorns.

As a consequence of the isolation of the islands, several major groups of plants did not become successfully established in Hawaii until they were brought in by man. For example, Hawaii has no native conifers, no native mangroves, no native aroids, and no native banyans or figs, although all these groups are native throughout most of the tropics.

Other large groups of plants are poorly represented in the native flora. There is only one native genus of palms, the loulu (*Pritchardia*). There are only four native species of orchids—the lowest number of native orchids in any of the 50 states. Of the hundreds of species of palms and orchids grown in Hawaii today, essentially all have been introduced by man since 1800 from tropical parts of America, Africa, and Asia and from other Pacific islands.

The intentional introduction of plants to Hawaii was begun by early Polynesian voyagers, who brought with them about 25 species of plants used for food, fiber, shelter, and medicine. Among these plants were taro (*Colocasia*), coconut (*Cocos*), wauke (*Broussonetia*), kukui (*Aleurites*), breadfruit (*Artocarpus*), sugarcane (*Saccharum*), yams (*Dioscorea*), and ti (*Cordyline*). The Polynesians also brought the pig, the first herbivorous mammal to be introduced, as well as the dog, the jungle fowl, and the rat. This was the beginning of a series of ecological and environmental changes in Hawaii which continue at an ever-accelerating rate today. Land was cleared, crops were planted, native species of plants were replaced with introduced species. It is probable that some species of native plants became extinct, especially in the lowlands where the Hawaiians had the greatest environmental impact. There are no records, of course, to help modern scientists determine exactly what plants may have become extinct in the period between initial Polynesian colonization and the arrival of Captain Cook in 1778, but it is doubtful that the number was very great in comparison with the number which have become extinct since that time.

Cook released goats in Hawaii, and shortly thereafter other European explorers brought sheep, cattle, and horses. These hoofed, grazing, and browsing mammals had an especially severe impact on Hawaiian plants, which had no effective defenses against being either eaten or trampled by the animals. While the native plants were disappearing from large areas, new waves of European immigrants were busily introducing potentially useful plants. Some of these did prove useful,

others escaped from cultivation and eventually became pests; still other weedy plants were unintentionally introduced along with the desirable species. As land was cleared for plantations and ranches, as sandalwood (*Santalum*) forests were destroyed for commercial purposes, and as other areas were stripped of native plants by feral animals, many of the newly introduced plants were able to spread into these areas and quickly became established. Some of these, such as klu (*Acacia farnesiana*), panini (*Opuntia megacantha*), and lantana (*Lantana camara*), possessed spines or thorns and were thus less susceptible to destruction by feral mammals.

By 1900 the native plant cover below about 450 meters elevation had been almost completely destroyed and replaced by a plant cover consisting largely of introduced species. At higher elevations, in some areas, larger numbers of native species persist but they are declining in numbers and being replaced by introduced competitors. The plants one sees in Honolulu today are the same popular ornamental species to be found in any city in the tropics—monkeypods (*Samanea*) and jacarandas (*Jacaranda*) from tropical America, tulip trees (*Spathodea*) and sausage trees (*Kigelia*) from tropical Africa, royal poincianas (*Delonix*) from Madagascar, and shower trees (*Cassia*) from India and tropical Asia.

C. H. L.

Amaumau, *Sadleria cyatheoides*. The young fronds of this fern are frequently reddish; they become green as they mature.

Photograph by C.H. Lamoureux

Poinsettia, *Euphorbia pulcherrima*. A shrub, introduced from Mexico, which produces masses of brightly colored floral bracts during the winter months.

Photograph by C.H. Lamoureux

years. Our bat is a small reddish form, distinct at the subspecies level from its larger, grizzled brown continental relatives. There are two continental populations, one in North America and one in South America. The hoary bat is strongly migratory and regularly reaches the Farallon Islands off California, the Galápagos, and the Bermudas. Specimens have been captured in Iceland, and there is one probable record for the Orkney Islands, near Scotland. Thus the hoary bat of Hawaii is from a hardy stock with a proved potential for dispersal. Long flights must depend on adequate supplies of fuel, in the form of fat, for sustained energy. Even now, the resident bat of Hawaii lays in a reserve of body fat late in summer, although its migratory instincts are suppressed. The principal breeding population is on the island of Hawaii, but another exists on Kauai. Bats are reported occasionally on Oahu and on Maui, but it is not known whether they are resident there or whether bats move regularly between the islands.

Hoary bat from Hawaii Island.

Photograph by P. Q. Tomich

Seal. The seal of Hawaii is one of the monk seals (*Monachus*). It is a relict species that became isolated from close relatives in the Caribbean and Mediterranean when the Isthmus of Panama was formed some 200,000 years ago. The Hawaiian monk seal somehow made its way to the Hawaiian Archipelago, and very possibly it was the first mammal to live on these shores. It is now endemic to Hawaii; that is, it is found nowhere else in the world. The principal breeding population frequents the region from French Frigate Shoals to Kure Atoll. Although this monk seal ranges at sea, it is typically a creature of sandy beaches and adjacent shallows. Rarely, one is seen in the vicinity of the main islands. The ancient Hawaiians probably did not regularly hunt the monk seal. By about 1900, however, it was near extinction as a result of exploitation by explorers and other seafarers who killed the animals for food and perhaps for their skins and oil. Remarkably, it was unknown to science until 1905. In spite of careful protection in the Hawaiian Islands National Wildlife Refuge, it leads a precarious existence with the current population probably of fewer than a thousand animals.

Rat. The Polynesian rat (*Rattus*) that accompanied the colonizers of Hawaii some 1,000 to 1,500 years ago is widely distributed in the Pacific wherever Polynesian peoples settled. Like them, it originated in Southeast Asia. Because of its minor importance in Hawaiian culture, the Polynesian rat is generally supposed to have come as an accidental stowaway and not as an intentional introduction. It was not eaten in Hawaii, as it was in New Zealand, although it was used in a formalized contest or sport in which rats were placed in an arena and shot with bows and arrows. This singular pastime is authenticated only for Hawaii. The Polynesian rat in Hawaii is justly referred to as a native rat; it has evolved into an assemblage of populations distinct from those in other regions of the Pacific, and is considered a separate subspecies or geographic race.

MAMMALS

Because Hawaii is far from any continent and because geologically the present islands are very young, few land mammals have arrived through natural dispersal and become established. It is likely that truly marine mammals, the whales and dolphins, have been numerous in Hawaiian waters since very early times inasmuch as they are widely distributed in the oceans and are of ancient origin. When the seafaring Polynesians first came to Hawaii the only mammals associated with the land were a seal and a small bat. The domestic dog and pig and a commensal rat accompanied the Polynesians.

Most of the impressive variety of land mammals found in the Hawaiian Islands today have arrived since the rediscovery of the group by Cook in 1778. These aggressive introduced species have had a pronounced effect on the face of Hawaii—its vegetation, its birds, and in one way or another on all terrestrial life of the islands. However, this brief discussion will summarize only what is known of the mammals of earlier periods and their place in the island ecosystem, as a background to more familiar present-day conditions.

Bat. The most remarkable example of a land-based mammal reaching Hawaii under its own power is the hoary bat (*Lasiurus*). Flights that brought bats to Hawaii may have been rare, and the local population probably has been isolated from its parent stock for tens of thousands of

Hawaiian monk seal at Laysan Island.

Photograph by William G. Gilmartin

Tamed feral piglet. Traces of wild-type coat stripings are evident.

Photograph by P. Q. Tomich

Rodents in modern Hawaii, including the Polynesian rat, have been a serious problem in wildlife conservation, in the economy, and in public health. A specific example of wildlife predation is the direct extinction of the Laysan rail (*Porzanula*) when the roof rat invaded its last refuge at Midway Islands in World War II. We may never know the toll that rats have taken of birdlife on the larger islands, and it is remarkable that forest-inhabiting native birds survive at all in the presence of these rodents. Sugarcane and other crops are damaged by rats in the fields, and annual losses are estimated in millions of dollars. Rats have been reservoirs of bubonic plague in Hawaii for more than half a century, from 1899 until at least 1957, but this fearsome disease of man has disappeared from the islands. Intensive research in Hawaii during the past 20 years has helped find means to alleviate many problems inflicted on humans by rodents.

Dog. The domestic dog (*Canis*), like the domestic pig, was important in Polynesian cultures as a pet, for food, for barter, in religious ritual, and as a source of raw materials for arts and crafts. Both animals were available, fully domesticated, in an earlier Asian homeland of the Polynesians, and they would certainly have been brought to Hawaii eventually by voyagers who intended to settle in the islands. Dogs were a staple item of food; they were kept in pens and reared on a vegetable diet. At large feasts in the early 1800s as many as 200 to 400 dogs would be served. The Polynesian dog was evidently a small, dull-witted, and unaggressive beast that most likely did not survive away from the villages. There is no evidence that it developed a predator-prey relationship with the pigs that may have roamed in the forests. Rather, it was probably dependent on man for both care and shelter and was not man's companion nor a protector of the home, as is the dog of Western cultures. The original Hawaiian breeds of dogs have been gradually submerged by repeated crossings with those brought from other regions of the world. The introduction of suitable prey species made it possible for these new aggressive strains to live in the wild. Domestic and feral sheep have been the most important food of feral dogs, and such dogs are still found in outlying areas where they are a menace to poultry, wild birds, game mammals, and livestock. Dogs breed in the wild on all the major islands, but packs of uniform character seldom are formed because of the frequent infusion of new blood from strays. Dogs reared in the wild recognize humans as potential prey rather than as either friend or foe, and are prone to attack them on sight.

Pig. It is probable that pigs (*Sus*) lived free in the mountains before European times in Hawaii, but the evidence is indirect and scanty. Certainly, the omnivorous pig should have had no difficulty making its living in the lush forests, much as it does today. However, there is no tradition which suggests that the Hawaiians were hunters or that they made use of forest animals other than birds. Captain Cook made the pointed remark that he could get no pigs larger than 50 to 60 pounds when he bartered for them as provender for his ships in 1779. Total impact of pigs on the indigenous vegetation may have been slight. The pig of early times has been modified or perhaps totally replaced by more recently imported domestic breeds that readily took to the wild. After many generations, these feral pigs have selectively reverted to types that resemble the European wild boar and are generally large in size. This newer stock of pigs certainly has placed its mark on native forest vegetation through direct damage to the forest floor and by the spread of exotic plants, to an extent that is only now being assessed.

It can be inferred that the early Polynesians lived in harmony with the community of mammals then established in Hawaii, and with the natural ecosystem. Their technology was poorly developed; they had no large, hoofed mammals; and they depended heavily on the resources of the sea. It is no credit to European explorers and those who followed to Hawaii that several introduced land mammals were permitted to revert to nature and to form uncontrolled feral populations (e.g., cattle, goats, and sheep), or came as uninvited immigrants on their ships (a mouse and additional species of rats), or were unwise introductions in the first place (mongoose, axis deer). The fragile terrestrial ecosystems of Hawaii, with assemblages of plants, birds, and insects that are unique in the world, have suffered accordingly. Today there are encouraging signs that more considerate action will prevail in perpetuating our invaluable biological assets. The keys to the problem are long-term research programs, community education toward better understanding of the natural environment, and vigilant preservation of significant natural habitats. Great effort must be made to halt unwise exploitation of land resources for short-term gain, and to enforce strict control of the browsers, the tramplers, and other predators on natural plant and animal communities.

P.Q.T.

MAMMALS CLASSED ACCORDING TO PERIOD OF ARRIVAL, MEANS OF ARRIVAL, AND CULTURAL SIGNIFICANCE

Marine mammals that may have ranged into the area before the islands arose, and are currently found in Hawaiian waters

Minke whale	*Balaenoptera acutorostrata*
Bryde's whale	*Balaenoptera edeni*
Fin whale	*Balaenoptera physalus*
Humpback whale	*Megaptera novaeangliae*
Right whale	*Eubalaena glacialis*
Rough-toothed dolphin	*Steno bredanensis*
Bottlenose dolphin	*Tursiops truncatus*
Spinner dolphin	*Stenella longirostris*
Bridled dolphin	*Stenella attenuata*
Striped dolphin	*Stenella coeruleoalba*
Risso's dolphin	*Grampus griseus*
Melon-headed whale	*Peponocephala electra*
Pygmy killer whale	*Feresa attenuata*
False killer whale	*Pseudorca crassidens*
Shortfin pilot whale	*Globicephala macrorhynchus*
Killer whale	*Orcinus orca*
Sperm whale	*Physeter macrocephalus*
Pygmy sperm whale	*Kogia breviceps*
Cuvier's beaked whale	*Ziphius cavirostris*
Blaineville's whale	*Mesoplodon densirostris*

Land-based mammals with specialized abilities for reaching Hawaii from continental shores before the arrival of man in Hawaii

Hoary bat	*Lasiurus cinereus*
Hawaiian monk seal	*Monachus schauinslandi*

Species that accompanied the Polynesian peoples and were associated with their cultures

Polynesian rat	*Rattus exulans*
Domestic dog	*Canis familiaris*
Pig	*Sus scrofa*

Immigrant species that arrived accidentally with shipping and developed commensal and wild populations

Roof rat	*Rattus rattus*
Norway rat	*Rattus norvegicus*
House mouse	*Mus musculus*

Domesticated mammals brought by man in post-contact times and developed significant feral populations

European rabbit	*Oryctolagus cuniculus*
Domestic dog	*Canis familiaris*
House cat	*Felis catus*
Domestic horse	*Equus caballus*
Donkey	*Equus asinus*
Pig	*Sus scrofa*
Domestic cattle	*Bos taurus*
Domestic goat	*Capra hircus*
Domestic sheep	*Ovis aries*

Bat
Cattle
Deer, mule
Dog
Goat
Horse
Pig

Pig
Rabbit (Lehua Island only)

Bat
Deer, axis
Dog
Goat
Mongoose
Pig
Rabbit (Manana Island only)
Wallaby

Cattle
Deer, axis
Dog
Goat
Mongoose
Pig

Generally Found on all Eight Main Islands
Cat
Mouse
Rat, Norway
Rat, Polynesian
Rat, roof

Bat
Deer, axis
Dog
Goat
Mongoose
Pig

Antelope, pronghorn
Deer, axis
Dog
Goat
Mouflon

Goat

Bat
Cattle
Dog
Donkey
Goat
Mongoose
Mouflon
Pig
Sheep

On Hawaiian Islands
National Wildlife Refuge
(Northwestern Hawaiian Islands)
Mouse, (Midway Is. only)
Rat, roof (Midway Is. only)
Rat, Polynesian (Kure Atoll only)
Seal, monk

In Hawaiian Waters
Twenty species of whales and dolphins

WILD AND FERAL MAMMALS

Source: P.Q. Tomich, State Dept. of Health   1982

Wild mammals brought for zoo display, rat control or sport hunting, and which produced stable free-ranging populations

Brush-tailed rock-wallaby	*Petrogale penicillata*
Small Indian mongoose	*Herpestes auropunctatus*
Axis deer	*Axis axis*
Mule (black-tail) deer	*Odocoileus hemionus*
Pronghorn antelope	*Antilocapra americana*
Mouflon sheep	*Ovis musimon*

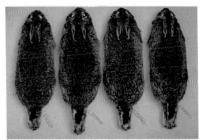

Rabbits from a population established on Manana Island.

Feral goats rounded up in Hawaii Volcanoes National Park. The Park is now virtually free of goats.

Petroglyph figure of a cat from Hawaii Island (chalked for contrast).

Photographs by P. Q. Tomich

Koloa or Hawaiian duck, *Anas wyvilliana*.
Photograph by E. Kridler

Io or Hawaiian hawk, *Buteo solitarius*.
Illustration from Wilson and Evans (1890-1899)

Omao or Hawaiian thrush, *Phaeornis obscurus*.
Illustration from Wilson and Evans (1890-1899)

BIRDS

Native Hawaiian Birds. Hawaii's isolated location in the middle of the Pacific Ocean, far from the continental land masses of North America and Asia, has made possible the evolution of many unique Hawaiian land birds. Ten families of world birds have representatives on the Hawaiian Islands, and one family is found only in Hawaii.

Some of Hawaii's native birds are adapted for spending most of their lives in the vicinity of streams, ponds, marshes, or tidal flats. These include the koloa or Hawaiian duck (*Anas wyvilliana*), Laysan duck (*Anas laysanensis*), gallinule (*Gallinula chloropus sandvicensis*), coot (*Fulica americana alai*), and the black-necked stilt (*Himantopus mexicanus knudseni*).

Nene or Hawaiian goose, *Branta sandvicensis*.
Photograph by E. Kridler

The State bird of Hawaii is the nene or Hawaiian goose (*Branta sandvicensis*). Unlike its relatives in other parts of the world, the nene has become adapted to life on rugged lava flows far removed from either standing or running water. The nene carries on its nesting activities at elevations between about 1,500 and 2,400 meters on Mauna Loa on the island of Hawaii. The State Division of Fish and Game released more than 475 pen-reared nene in Haleakala Crater, Maui, between 1962 and 1978. Reproductive success of these birds has been exceedingly low, however, and a maximum of three young birds were known to have been raised to independence as of 1972.

The largest number of Hawaii's native birds inhabit dense forests, but three species usually are found in pastures, scrubland, and cutover forests. Two of these are found only on the island of Hawaii—the Hawaiian hawk or io (*Buteo solitarius*) and the Hawaiian crow or alala (*Corvus tropicus*). The Hawaiian short-eared owl or pueo (*Asio flammeus sandwichensis*) is a permanent resident on all of the main inhabited islands; it is found in open grassland, pastures, and forests, on lava flows and in residential areas. The true forest birds of the main islands belong to four different bird families, and a fifth family (Sylviidae, Old World warblers) is represented by the Nihoa millerbird (*Acrocephalus familiaris kingi*), whose total world range is confined to the 156-acre (63 hectare) volcanic remnant called Nihoa Island.

The Hawaiian thrush or omao (*Phaeornis obscurus*) is a common inhabitant of the relatively undisturbed native forests on Hawaii and Kauai. The small Kauai thrush (*Phaeornis palmeri*) lives only in the Alakai Swamp on Kauai.

The elepaio (*Chasiempis sandwichensis*), an important bird in Hawaiian mythology, is found on Kauai, Oahu, and Hawaii. The elepaio has been the most adaptable of all the native land birds, and on Oahu it can be found in some areas (such as upper Manoa Valley and Moanalua Valley) where nearly all of the vegetation is composed of introduced plants. It also inhabits the very wet native ohia forests and the relatively dry mamani-naio forests on Mauna Kea. The elepaio is a member of a large family (Muscicapidae) consisting of Old World flycatchers. Another Old World family contains birds called honeyeaters (Meliphagidae). The center of abundance of this family is Australia and New Guinea, but five species once lived in Hawaii. Separate species of oo (genus *Moho*) occurred on the islands of Hawaii, Kauai, Oahu, and Molokai as recently as the 1890s, but all are now thought to be extinct except for the Kauai oo (*Moho braccatus*). This rare species is to be found only in the depths of the Alakai Swamp.

Hawaii is best known among ornithologists around the world for the endemic family of Hawaiian honeycreepers (Drepanididae). From a single ancestral species that reached the Hawaiian Islands in the remote past, 28 species and 18 subspecies or geographical races evolved on the various islands of the chain. This family of birds demonstrates better than any other bird family the evolutionary process of adaptive radiation. The bills of the several species vary from extremely heavy, seed-crushing and wood-tearing bills to long, decurved bills suited for obtaining the nectar from lobelia flowers and short, delicate bills that can be used either for catching insects or sipping nectar. In fact, so diverse in their bill structure are the honeycreepers that the first European ornithologists who studied them placed different species in several different bird families. In plumage pattern, the many species vary from the brilliant, vermilion-colored iiwi (*Vestiaria coccinea*), with black wings and tail, to the yellow and yellowish green anianiau (*Hemignathus parvus*).

Some species of honeycreeper were confined to a single island—for example, the anianiau to Kauai, and the akiapolaau (*Hemignathus wilsoni*) and the mamo (*Drepanis pacifica*) to Hawaii. By contrast, the apapane (*Himatione sanguinea*) was found on all of the inhabited islands, and a subspecies inhabited Laysan Island.

Unfortunately, of the 67 different kinds of unique Hawaiian land birds that were known during the nineteenth century, about 40 percent are thought to be extinct, and another 40 percent are considered to be rare and endangered. These endangered Hawaiian birds account for more than *one-half* of all the birds listed by the United States Bureau of Sport Fisheries and Wildlife in the Red Book of rare and endangered species! In fact, four times as many birds have become extinct in Hawaii as in the entire North American continent, or any other area of the world with the possible exception of the Mascarene Islands.

Indigenous Hawaiian Birds. These are birds that are native to Hawaii but also to a much wider geographical area. The black-crowned night heron (*Nycticorax nycticorax hoactli*), for example, has inhabited the main Hawaiian Islands for an unknown, but very long, period of time. However, this heron is not considered to be an endemic species because ornithologists do not recognize it as having any distinctive characteristics that would justify separating it from the continental subspecies, which has a breeding range extending from Washington and Oregon southward to northern Chile and Argentina.

The black-crowned night heron occurs on all of the main islands, where it inhabits ponds, marshes, and lagoons. It feeds on aquatic insects, fish, frogs, and mice. The birds roost and nest in trees. The future of this species in Hawaii is completely dependent upon the preservation of suitable feeding habitat. With the rapid expansion of Hawaii's population and the consequent demand for housing and commercial buildings, the marshland habitat required by the heron, coot, and gallinule has been reduced drastically in recent years, and these birds are classified as endangered species.

The so-called seabirds or oceanic birds comprise the largest group of indigenous birds. Twenty-two different species belonging to six

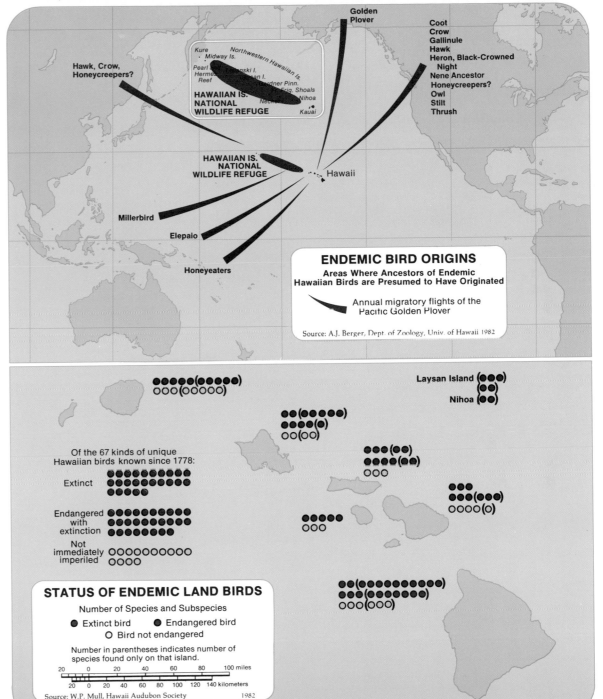

ENDEMIC BIRD ORIGINS
Areas Where Ancestors of Endemic
Hawaiian Birds are Presumed to Have Originated

Annual migratory flights of the Pacific Golden Plover

Source: A.J. Berger, Dept. of Zoology, Univ. of Hawaii 1982

Of the 67 kinds of unique Hawaiian birds known since 1778:

Extinct

Endangered with extinction

Not immediately imperiled

STATUS OF ENDEMIC LAND BIRDS
Number of Species and Subspecies

● Extinct bird   ● Endangered bird
○ Bird not endangered

Number in parentheses indicates number of species found only on that island.

Source: W.P. Mull, Hawaii Audubon Society   1982

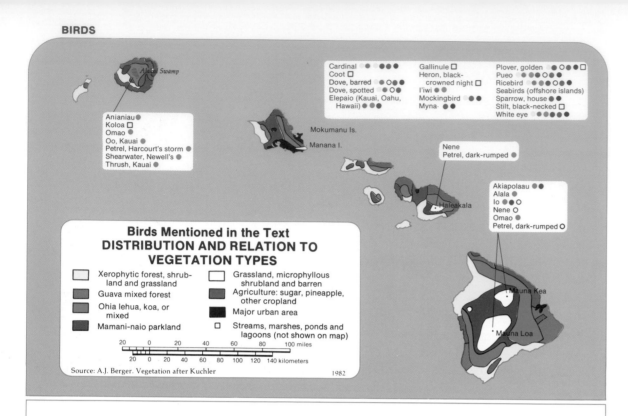

Birds Mentioned in the Text
DISTRIBUTION AND RELATION TO VEGETATION TYPES

☐ Xerophytic forest, shrubland and grassland
☐ Grassland, microphyllous shrubland and barren
Guava mixed forest
Agriculture: sugar, pineapple, other cropland
Ohia lehua, koa, or mixed
Major urban area
Mamani-naio parkland
☐ Streams, marshes, ponds and lagoons (not shown on map)

20 0 20 40 60 80 100 miles
20 0 20 40 60 80 100 120 140 kilometers

Source: A.J. Berger. Vegetation after Kuchler.   1982

Cardinal ● ● ● ● ●
Coot ☐
Dove, barred ● ● ● ● ●
Dove, spotted ● ○ ●
Elepaio (Kauai, Oahu, Hawaii) ● ● ●
Gallinule ☐
Heron, black-crowned night ☐
I'iwi ●
Mockingbird ● ●
Myna· ● ● ●
Plover, golden ● ○ ● ● ☐
Pueo ● ● ● ● ●
Ricebird ● ● ● ○ ●
Seabirds (offshore islands)
Sparrow, house ● ●
Stilt, black-necked ☐
White eye ● ● ● ● ●

Anianiau ●
Koloa ☐
Omao ☐
Oo, Kauai ●
Petrel, Harcourt's storm ●
Shearwater, Newell's ●
Thrush, Kauai ●

Mokumanu Is.
Manana I.

Nene
Petrel, dark-rumped ●

Akiapolaau ● ●
Alala ●
Io ● ● ○
Nene ○
Omao ○
Petrel, dark-rumped ○

Haleakala

Mauna Kea
Mauna Loa

EXTINCT HAWAIIAN BIRDS

FULL SPECIES:

Rail, Hawaiian
Rail, Laysan
Akialoa (Oahu, Lanai, Hawaii)
Oo, Oahu
Mamo, black (Molokai)
Oo, Molokai
Amakihi, greater (Hawaii)
Finch, greater koa (Hawaii)
Finch, grosbeak (Hawaii)
Finch, lesser koa (Hawaii)
Kioea (Hawaii)
Mamo (Hawaii)
Oo, Hawaii
Ula-ai-hawene (Hawaii)

SUBSPECIES:

Honeycreeper, Laysan
Millerbird, Laysan
Akepa, Oahu
Nukupuu, Oahu
Thrush, Oahu
Creeper, Lanai
Thrush, Lanai

EXTINCT ISLAND POPULATION OF SPECIES SURVIVING ON OTHER ISLANDS

Honeycreeper, crested (Molokai)
Iiwi, Lanai
Ou (Oahu, Molokai, Lanai)

RARE AND ENDANGERED HONEYCREEPERS

Finch, Laysan
Finch, Nihoa
Millerbird, Nihoa
Akialoa, Kauai
Nukupuu, Kauai
Oo, Kauai
Creeper, Oahu
Iiwi, Oahu
Creeper, Molokai
Iiwi, Molokai
Amakihi, Lanai
Apapane, Lanai
Honeycreeper, Maui crested
Nukupuu, Maui
Ou, Maui
Parrotbill, Maui
Poouli, Maui
Akepa, Hawaii
Akiapolaau (Hawaii)
Creeper, Hawaii
Ou, Hawaii
Palila (Hawaii)

families and three orders of birds return to the Hawaiian Islands each year to carry on their nesting activities. Many of these species spend the nonbreeding season flying over the open ocean, obtaining their food (fish and squid) from the ocean and resting on its surface. Some species, such as the sooty tern (*Sterna fuscata*), however, are thought to fly continuously for months at a time during the nonbreeding season, not once alighting on land or on the surface of the ocean to rest.

The majority of seabirds in Hawaii nest on the Northwestern Hawaiian Islands. All of these islands, except Midway and Kure, form the Hawaiian Islands National Wildlife Refuge. Several million seabirds nest on these tiny islands where the only mammalian predator is man himself. Three small passerine birds also live out their lives on two of these islands: the Laysan finch (*Telespyza cantans*) and Nihoa finch (*Telespyza ultima*), both finch-billed honeycreepers, and the Nihoa millerbird, an Old World warbler.

Some of the offshore islands of the main chain also provide suitable nesting areas for seabirds. Two of the most important are Mokumanu and Manana Island off the coast of Oahu. Twelve different species are known to have nested on Mokumanu in recent years and four species on Manana Island. Sooty terns and common noddies (*Anous stolidus*) nest on Manana Island by the tens of thousands.

Some species of seabirds probably nested on all of the high inhabited islands, and it is known that the Hawaiians used both the adults and the fat nestlings for food. Two species are believed now to nest only the remote mountains of Kauai: Newell's shearwater (*Puffinus puffinus newelli*), whose nesting grounds were not discovered until 1967, and Harcourt's storm petrel (*Oceanodroma castro cryptoleucura*), whose nesting grounds still had not been discovered as of 1981. The dark-rumped petrel (*Pterodroma phaeopygia sandwichensis*) nests in Haleakala Crater, Maui, and, in much smaller numbers, on Mauna Loa and Mauna Kea on the island of Hawaii, and on Lanai.

Also included in the category of indigenous birds is a group of migratory species that spend the nonbreeding season on the Hawaiian Islands but nest 2,000 or more miles (3,200 kilometers) north of the islands in Alaska or Siberia. The best known of these is the Pacific golden plover (*Pluvialis dominica fulva*), a shorebird that is a common winter resident on all of the islands. It inhabits the lawns and golf courses of residential areas and also is found at elevations up to about 3,000 meters on the mountains of Hawaii. Other species of shorebirds and ducks also migrate to Hawaii at the end of their breeding seasons in northern areas.

Introduced Birds. There is no way of being certain what kind of vegetation covered the lowlands of the main Hawaiian Islands when the first Polynesians landed. Whatever the vegetation had been, it was largely replaced by the introduced plants that the Hawaiians used for food and fiber. We do know that the naturalists who accompanied Captain Cook found some native birds at no great elevation above sea level. Cook and later visitors unintentionally caused the destruction of much of the native flora by releasing cattle, goats, pigs, sheep, and other grazing animals (page 73). Protected by a kapu declared by Kamehameha the Great, and in the absence of any of their normal predators, these feral animals multiplied exceedingly fast. They destroyed many native forests by trampling the ground and by eating the seedlings of the trees. Being dependent upon the endemic plants for food, shelter, and nesting sites, the native birds either had to move or perish, and many perished. As a result, when foreigners from many lands made a new home in Hawaii during the nineteenth century, there were no songbirds in the lowlands. It was natural that the settlers should want to import familiar birds from their homelands, and, when sugarcane, pineapple, and cattle became important economically, an effort was made to introduce birds that would feed upon the insect pests of the crops and cattle.

Records of foreign bird introductions in Hawaii have always been scanty, but we know that a minimum of 170 different kinds of exotic birds had gained their freedom in the Hawaiian Islands between 1796, when the first pigeons or rock doves (*Columba livia*) were released, and 1981. We know that other species were released, but, if any records at all were made, they consisted only of a common name in a newspaper article.

Available evidence suggests that, of the 170 foreign introductions, 110 failed to survive and 60 species are now established as breeding populations. The most familiar of the established species are the common myna (*Acridotheres tristis*), white-eye (*Zosterops japonicus*), cardinal (*Cardinalis cardinalis*), red-crested cardinal (*Paroaria coronata*), mockingbird (*Mimus polyglottos*), house sparrow (*Passer domesticus*), barred dove (*Geopelia striata*), and spotted dove (*Streptopelia chinensis*). These exotic species were brought to Hawaii from many parts of the world: North America, South America, Africa, Japan, India, China, and other parts of Asia.

A.J.B.

Elepaio, *Chasiempis sandwichensis*.
Illustration from Rothschild (1893-1900)

Blue-faced booby, *Sula dactylatra*
Photograph by E. Kridler
U.S. Sport Fisheries and Wildlife

Mamo, *Drepanis pacifica*.
Illustration from Wilson and Evans (1890-1899)

Kauai Oo, *Moho braccatus*.
Illustration from Rothschild (1893-1900)

Laysan albatross, *Diomedea immutabilis*
Photograph by E. Kridler
U.S. Sport Fisheries and Wildlife

Apapane, *Himatione sanguinea*.
Illustration from Wilson and Evans (1890-1899)

Iiwi, *Vestiaria coccinea*.
Illustration from Wilson and Evans (1890-1899)

Kauai Akialoa, *Hemignathus procerus*.
Illustration from Rothschild (1893-1900)

Akohekohe, crested honeycreeper,
Palmeria dolei.
Illustration from Wilson and Evans (1890-1899)

Fig. 1. Kamehameha butterfly, *Vanessa tameamea* Eschscholtz.

Photograph by Ron Mau

Fig. 2. Blackburn's butterfly, *Vaga blackburni* (Tuely).

Photograph by W. Gagne

Fig. 3. The coconut leafroller, *Hedylepta blackburni* (Butler).

Photograph by Ron Mau

Fig. 4. The "fabulous green sphinx of Kauai," *Tinostoma smaragditis* (Meyrick).

Photograph by Robin Rice

INSECTS

Insects were probably the first terrestrial animals to reach the Hawaiian Islands. Long before man came, there were many thousands of insect species established.

When the Hawaiians first arrived there were no pestiferous forms present and no insects which would damage plants used as human food. But the situation changed rapidly as the early immigrants brought body lice, some domestic flies, and probably fleas. The first published reference to Hawaiian insects was made by William Ellis (1783:156), the assistant surgeon on Cook's voyage of 1778, when he indicated that house flies were troublesome to the natives. He reported that flyflaps, or brushes, made of a bunch of feathers fixed to the end of a thin piece of polished wood or bone, were used to brush away flies. The kahilis, as the brushes were called, gradually became symbols of rank among the Hawaiians, and kahili bearers usually accompanied royalty. The flyflaps evolved into the immense symbolic kahilis which were used at funerals and royal occasions, and which are still seen at special Hawaiian ceremonies.

With the arrival of Europeans came mosquitoes, cockroaches, ticks, termites, flies, ants, grasshoppers, bugs, and other destructive and pestiferous insects. As transport became faster and as more people ar-rived in the islands, the number of new immigrant insects increased rapidly. In spite of strict quarantine measures over the past 30 years an average of 18 new insect species have become established each year, but fortunately relatively few of these have been injurious species. Nevertheless, in the past few years Hawaii has received one new mosquito, several whiteflies, scale insects, sap sucking bugs, defoliating caterpillars, leaf hoppers, thrips, stem mining flies, weevils, earwigs, ants, and mites. The public is well aware of the havoc caused by just one of these in 1981—the spiraling whitefly. The constant influx of new insects creates a threat to the local economy, and the State needs to be prepared to combat dangerous species as soon as they are discovered.

These invasions of insects from other areas over the years and the tremendous changes brought about by man—urbanization, destruction of the forests, depredation by introduced deer, goats, pigs, cattle, sheep, and rats—have caused the native Hawaiian insects, almost without exception, to disappear from the lowland areas, as is the case with the native plants, birds, and land snails. The endemic forms are now found only at higher elevations, in deep valleys, and in areas where native plants are still found. The native flora and fauna are closely associated and interdependent; as one or more species of plants disappear the associated species of animals soon follow.

One of the most unusual features of the Hawaiian Islands is the remarkable fauna of insects—as well as of birds and land snails—which has evolved. Probably nowhere else in the world has such a profusion of different forms and unusual adaptations developed in such a short period of geological time. Hawaii is indeed one of the most ideal places in the world for evolutionary studies. Compared with those of continental areas, the biotic factors affecting speciation, or change, are rather simple in oceanic situations, and research technics now being used should begin to explain why evolution has proceeded at such a rapid pace, how and why animals evolve, and how long a period is required for speciation to occur. But the islands are changing rapidly, and many native species have already been lost and many others are endangered; it is vital that the unusual opportunities for research on this remarkable fauna be exploited as rapidly as possible.

It appears evident that nearly 10,000 species of insects occur throughout Hawaii of which about 98 percent are found nowhere else in the world. It has been estimated that this total fauna probably originated from as few as 150 ancestral species. The 10,000 estimated species are divided roughly into the following groups: approximately 3,000 beetles; 1,500 flies; 1,250–1,500 wasps and bees; 1,250–1,500 moths and butterflies; 1,000 bugs; 750–1,000 leafhoppers and scale insects; and nearly 1,000 grasshoppers, crickets, lacewings, bark lice; and miscellaneous groups of insects. It is apparent that many thousands of new species remain to be discovered, named, and described.

The layman is usually unaware of Hawaii's remarkable biota, especially its insects. The native species are mostly confined to areas relatively unmolested by man and are seldom encountered except by the biologist. For the most part, they are cryptic, often small, well camouflaged, and inconspicuous; they are often found in only certain types of habitats.

The Hawaiian insect fauna is described by biologists as disharmonic—that is, many major groups which would be found in continental areas are completely lacking in Hawaii, and their places are taken by forms that evolved in the islands. The ancestral types were mostly small species carried to Hawaii by cyclonic winds or perhaps in the jet stream; others may have been carried on the feet or bodies of migratory birds; and still others may have traversed the ocean on driftwood. For instance, the Emperor Seamounts, north of Kure Atoll, were once high islands and an earlier portion of the Hawaiian chain that would have supported a flora and fauna. The seamounts are at least 70 million years old and no doubt provided habitats for a developing biota, and served as stepping stones for the present-day flora and fauna. Allowing 20 million years for the establishment of a basic flora, this means that the ancestors of the present-day Hawaiian insects arrived at the rate of one every 300,000+ years. In this time span the "impossible" feat of a gravid female insect, usually small and fragile, being carried by wind or some other means over the ocean for great distance, arriving on an island and depositing its eggs in a suitable medium, obviously did occur many times. The majority of the immigrants came from Asia and the southwest Pacific. The founder species found ample unoccupied habitats in which to live, with little or no competition, predation, or parasitism, plenty of food plants, and a favorable climate. Nevertheless, tremendous adaptations had to be made to enable them to fit into this new environment. One of the unusual features is that many of the species which developed in Hawaii took over completely different habitats and ways of life from those of related forms in other parts of the world. Deviations from the usual are common in all orders.

Some visitors to the islands are disappointed not to find large, showy butterflies and other "exotic" insects in evidence. The butterfly fauna is sparse; there are only eleven species, of which only two are native. One is rather large, brightly colored, orange-red and black marked (Fig. 1). It feeds on mamaki (*Pipturus*) and related plants in the mountains. This species was named for King Kamehameha. The other, a small hairstreak, blue-brown above (Fig. 2) and bright green on the underside of the wings, feeds on leaves of koa. Well over a thousand species of moths have developed throughout the islands. Most are small, rather nondescript (Fig. 3), rarely seen creatures associated with a wide assortment of native plants. The hawk, or sphinx, moths, however, are large, showy insects, some having a wingspread of 4 inches

and marked with bright colors. One has been referred to as "the fabulous green Sphinx" or "the elusive green Sphinx of Kauai" (Fig. 4). It is apparently the only green species of these large moths known in the world, and few specimens have been collected. It seems to be confined to the tops of ohia trees in the Kokee region of Kauai.

Most people are acquainted with *Drosophila* (pomace flies, or vinegar gnats), the small flies attracted to overripe or fermenting fruits, or to vinegar. These flies are used widely throughout the world in the study of genetics, and until about 1950 a large portion of the knowledge of this field was based on laboratory studies of these animals. An astonishing number of species of drosophilids occur in Hawaii, and more than 500 species have now been described. It is estimated that the total number of species will reach 750. This is the greatest concentration of species known in the world, and the flies exhibit many modifications of structures and habits not found in other areas. Since 1963 a major research project at the University of Hawaii has been the study of their evolution and genetics.

The Hawaiian drosophilid flies are ideal for studies of evolution and genetics since many of them are gigantic in size, many times larger than normal. They have giant chromosomes from the study of which a great deal of evolutionary information can be obtained. Many can be reared in artificial media for study and manipulation under laboratory conditions. Conspicuous markings over the wings characterize many species (Figs. 5–8), and most exhibit extraordinary sexual dimorphism, including, in the males, unusual structural developments on the legs and other parts of the body. Courtship and mating behavior is most elaborate. Each species has its distinctive behavior, and relationships and evolutionary trends can be determined by studying the courtship and mating patterns. From studies of the chromosomes, behavior, morphology, and ecology, the relationships and evolution of approximately 100 of the picture-winged species have been ascertained. The degrees of relationship have been narrowed until it is now possible to identify newly formed species and incipient species. Some that can be demonstrated to be valid biological species cannot be differentiated by morphological characters.

It is evident that approximately 97 percent of the species are restricted to single islands, and most are plant specific. The representatives of ancestral types have been traced to Kauai, and the typical route of distribution has been shown to be from Kauai directly to Maui, bypassing Oahu in most cases. At least in the case of drosophilid flies, it seems apparent that Maui has been the main center of diversification— that this is the area where the greatest number of species have developed. It has been clearly demonstrated that many major species groups arose on Maui and spread from there to the other Hawaiian Islands, although only rarely have they gone back to Kauai.

Fig. 5. Native *Drosophila* with common "garbage can" species, *Drosophila nigrofacies* (Hardy) and *D. simulans* Sturtevant.
Photograph by D.E. Hardy

Fig. 6. Aggressive behavior, Native *Drosophilia, D. heteroneura* Perkins.
Photograph by Karen E. Loeblich

Fig. 7. Native *Drosophila, D. conspicua* Grimshaw.
Photograph by W. P. Mull

Fig. 8. *Drosophila grimshawi* Bryan.
Photograph by W. P. Mull

Fig. 9. Native longhorned beetle, *Plagithmysus bilineatus* (Sharp).

Photograph by D.E. Hardy

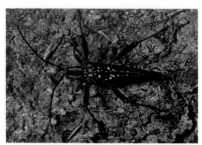

Fig. 10. Native longhorned beetle, *Plagithmysus vitticollis* Sharp.

Photograph by D.E. Hardy

Fig. 11. Native damselfly, *Megalagrion* sp?

Photograph by W. P. Mull

Fig. 12. Flightless hemerobiid, *Pseudosectra swezeyi* Zimmerman.

Photograph by W. Gagne

Beetles are the most abundant group of Hawaiian insects. This is a vast assemblage of highly diversified animals which in most parts of the world are among the most common and conspicuous of insects. In Hawaii, however, the native species are secretive and not readily seen. They are predominantly small creatures living in and under bark, as borers in wood of native trees, in mosses, and in ground litter and decaying plant materials. The largest and most ornate are the longhorned beetles (Figs. 9–10). These are wood borers which are highly host specific, and each different type is usually restricted to a certain species of native tree or woody shrub. More than 100 species have been described, and there are apparently many new species still to be discovered. Even though these beetles are large and often brightly marked—they often measure 7 or more cm in length with the antennae (feelers) extended—the adults are rarely seen, even by entomologists. The specialist working on these insects collects them by searching through the forests, finding trees or shrubs that have been damaged by the boring of the larvae; he cuts off these twigs and branches and brings them into the laboratory to rear the adult beetles.

Perhaps the most obvious of the native Hawaiian insects are the dragonflies and damselflies. The former are commonly seen all the way from sea level to the mountaintops; they are very strong fliers and represent one of the few groups whose ancestors probably reached Hawaii on their own power. The damselflies (Fig. 11) are among the most unusual in the world. In Hawaii they have evolved from aquatic to terrestrial animals; in other parts of the world the nymph stage of these insects lives in ponds and slow-moving streams. Twenty-seven species are known in Hawaii, many living in the leaf axils of certain forest plants, and one in the ground litter under dense fern growth.

Flightlessness has developed in a number of cases; certain insects, which have evolved from winged, actively flying ancestors, have lost their power of flight and have developed entirely different habits from those of relatives in other areas. Several lacewings have lost their ability to fly and have become rather bizarre creatures. Zimmerman (1957:80) referred to one of these (Fig. 12) as "one of the marvels of creation." A group of small predaceous flies have also lost their wings, except for a narrow strip along each front margin. They hop about like fleas on ground litter in the forest.

A recent discovery of immense biological importance is the presence of cave-dwelling insects and related animals in Hawaii. Howarth (1980), of the Bishop Museum, found an entirely new fauna living in lava tubes. About 35 forms have been discovered which have lost most of the attributes that are normally essential for life on the surface, such as eyes, wings, pigmentation, and jumping powers. From an evolutionary standpoint this is an exciting discovery since, in terms of geological time, these adaptations must have occurred very recently;

these insects may provide rather precise data concerning the time required for new forms of animals to evolve. An eyeless and flightless planthopper lives on tree roots that dangle in the caves and apparently finds its food by means of refined senses of touch and smell. Two kinds of crickets walk on the floors and walls instead of jumping, as their surface relatives do. Their antennae are greatly elongated, three times longer than their bodies. Another specialized member of the community is a water-treading bug. Unlike its surface relatives which live near or on water, it lives on the damp walls and preys on worms and fly larvae. A tiny beetle captures the springtails and mites that scurry on the walls, and the larger insects are preyed on by a large, blind wolf spider. It is probable that many other animals, still to be discovered, live in the total darkness of island caves.

The same pattern of profuse speciation and unusual adaptation occurs in many other different groups of Hawaiian insects (Figs. 13,14). The brief space available here has allowed discussion of only a few examples of a truly remarkable fauna. To date, 14 volumes of the series *Insects of Hawaii* have been published dealing with the major orders except for Coleoptera (beetles) and Hymenoptera (wasps and bees).

D.E.H.

Fig. 13. The Koa bug, *Coleotichus blackburniae* White.

Photograph by Ron Mau

Fig. 14. Unique ambushing inchworm, *Eupithecia orichloris* Meyrick, eats picture-winged *Drosophila* prey.

Photograph by R. W. Western and S. L. Montgomery

LAND SNAILS

Early in the nineteenth century F. J. F. Meyen, a young German explorer-naturalist who during his travels around the world had encountered "horrible amphibians and numberless insects" in tropical forests, wrote that on Oahu "if you shake the trees, instead of insects falling off, there are prettily shaped, often brightly colored snails." The snails to which Meyen referred were the achatinellids (Family Achatinellidae), the tree snails. Tree snails, however, comprise only about 100 species of the more than 1,000 species of native land mollusks which constitute what scientists have come to regard as the most remarkable land snail fauna in the world.

Ancestral species of nine land snail families reached Hawaii millions of years ago and, from an estimated 22 to 24 colonizations, gave rise to the more than 1,000 species of endemic land snails. The colonizers represented families with small shells which are amenable to dispersal at infrequent intervals. The ancestral achatinellids exploited the trees of Oahu, Maui, Molokai, and Lanai, evolving into the relatively large (2.5 to 3 cm), colorful tree snails collected by the thousands by early explorers and residents of the islands during the nineteenth century. The ancestors of another group, the ground-dwelling amastrids (Family Amastridae) were apparently most successful on Kauai (which lacks achatinellids), where representatives of *Carelia,* the largest of the Hawaiian land snails, may be more than 7 cm long. The amastrids diverged so far from their ancestors that the entire group is considered a family endemic to the Hawaiian Islands. Other successful land snails in Hawaii include the succinids (Family Succineidae) and the endodontids (Family Endodontidae). The succinids have a reduced shell and sluglike body. Elsewhere they are associated with marshes and wetlands; in Hawaii they have radiated away from wetlands to trees and shrubs.

Land snails are hermaphroditic but not usually self-fertilizing. The Hawaiian land snails reproduce by laying eggs and by producing living young. In *Achatinella mustellina* only one young snail is produced at a time, growth is very slow, on the order of 2 mm a year, and the snails are nearly seven years old before they first reproduce. They have a potential life span of at least nine years and on the average produce 0.4 living young a year.

Most people are familiar with garden snails and slugs but unaware that most of them are exotics in Hawaii; that is, they are introduced either accidentally or on purpose from other places. Many of the commonly encountered land snails in the lowlands today were introduced accidentally. These introduced snails are sometimes called "tropical tramps" because they are widespread in the Pacific in cultivated or otherwise ecologically altered areas, wherever people, whether migrating Polynesians or other travelers, have touched the shores of an island. Prominent among them are the familiar garden snails *Bradybaena similaris* and *Subulina octona,* and the slugs *Deroceras laeve* and *Veronicella alte.*

Other land snails were brought in for a purpose. The best known of these introductions is the giant African snail, *Achatina fulica,* brought to Hawaii from Japan and released in a garden in 1936. It is extremely prolific, capable of producing more than a billion eggs a year, and it is a serious agricultural pest. Efforts to eradicate the snail failed, and in 1957 carnivorous snails were introduced in an attempt at biological control. One of these introductions, *Euglandina rosea,* which in its native habitat in Florida lives with tree snails, has multiplied beyond count and moved from the lowlands into the native forests where it is now a serious threat to the tree-dwelling achatinellids.

The advent of urbanization, the destruction of lowland forests and the reproductive success of introductions— not only snails, but also rats and ants—have all taken their toll of Hawaii's native land snails. The achatinellids on Oahu are now designated an endangered species, and more than 600 of the native land snail species may now be extinct.

E.A.K.

Fig. 1. *Achatinella mustelina* on olopua, Kunia Trail, Oahu, is endemic to the Waianae Mountains.
Photograph by R. J. Western

Fig. 2. *Achatinella soworbyana* on the Poamoho Trail, Oahu, is endemic to the Koolau Mountains.
Photograph by R. J. Western

Fig. 3. *Achatinella lila* on the Waikane Trail, Oahu, is endemic to the Koolau Mountains.
Photograph by R. J. Western

Fig. 5. *Succinea* sp. from the Saddle Road area, Hawaii. In these snails the shell is reduced and the body is sluglike.
Photograph by Charles Van Riper

Fig. 4. *Philonesia* sp. on the Konahuanui Trail, Oahu.
Photograph by R. J. Western

Fig. 1. Claw of the Star II about to harvest a living specimen of precious coral at a depth of 1,200 feet off Makapuu, Oahu.

Photograph by R. Grigg

REEF AND SHORE COMMUNITIES

Communities of colorful seaweeds, fishes, and corals and other invertebrates occur throughout the Hawaiian Islands. In the deep blue waters offshore, pelagic fishes such as tuna and mahimahi roam the open sea, feeding on smaller fishes. At depths of 100 meters and more, precious corals (Fig. 1) and the bivalve *Pinna* are bottom-dwelling forms which live where there is little or no light and which maintain themselves on detritus and plankton falling through the water column. Island coastlines are ringed with rocky shores and tide pools, calcareous benches, fringing and subtidal coral reefs, and sandy beaches.

There are about 700 species of fishes, 400 seaweeds (algae), 1,000 mollusks, and 1,350 other kinds of invertebrates in the shallow waters around the islands. Most of these organisms are representatives of species distributed through the tropical Indian and Pacific oceans from the east coast of Africa to Hawaii. The ancestors of these Hawaiian marine organisms must have arrived from elsewhere. Most are related to forms found to the west of Hawaii. Many of these animals have free-swimming larval stages which could have reached the islands in currents that flow past the island chain.

Although Hawaii's marine animals and plants bear the indelible stamp of their Indo-Pacific origin, they are distinguished by several features which may be associated with the isolation of the islands. One of the most noticeable features is that there are fewer species in Hawaii than are usually associated with tropical Pacific islands. Several well-known mollusks, for example, do not occur in Hawaii today (although they may be represented in the fossil record), among them the giant clam *Tridacna*, the spider shells *Lambis*, and the cuttlefish. Some families of well-known tropical Indo-Pacific animals have fewer species in Hawaii than are found elsewhere in the tropical Pacific: there are only about 35 species of cowries in Hawaii compared with 60 in the Marianas islands. About 20 percent of Hawaii's marine organisms are distinguished from those found elsewhere: some are valid species, others are just larger than they are elsewhere or have unique identifying marks, such as the sickle-shaped bar on the pectoral fin of the manini. Whether endemic or widespread, each plays a role in the ecosystems of the shore and sea.

High rocky shorelines, reached only by spray, are inhabited by relatively few species; they are dull gray or black in color and can withstand long periods without water. The littorines (pupu kolea) among the mollusks, and the scuttling black grapsid crab (a'ama) are the most con-spicuous members of this community, but in shallow, sun-warmed pools there may also be a species of blenny and a goby. Seaward of the littorines and the crab, but still above the reach of the tide, are the black nerite (pipipi) and, in a narrow band, a pulmonate limpet, *Siphonaria*.

Seaward of the spray zone the variety of animals and plants increases. Much of the surf-swept lava coast is painted pink by the alga *Porolithon* and studded with the dark, dome-shaped shingle urchin *Colobocentrotus* (Fig. 2) and the opihi (*Cellana* spp.). Subtidally, surf-swept cliffs are inhabited by other rather dark-colored and heavy-shelled animals, such as the muricids *Thais* and *Drupa* on the surface of the substrate, and the brown and white cowries *Cypraea mauritiana* and *C. maculifera* in crevices. Fishes in these areas are strong swimmers and often dark in color like the Achilles tang shown in Figure 3.

Tide pools are most conspicuous and best developed on sea-level lava shorelines. The substrate is matted with green and brown seaweeds in which are cone shells, miters, and some of the smaller cowries. There is often a tangle of spaghetti-like tentacles of the worm *Terebellum* (Fig. 4), and the bottom of the pools may be littered with sea cucumbers (loli). The common fish of tide pools are young silver perch (aholehole), damselfish (kupipi), surgeonfish (manini), and small blennies.

Along many areas of the shorelines of Kauai, Oahu, and Maui, water-leveled calcareous benches jut 30 meters or more from the shore into the sea. The flat surface of the benches is turfed with a thick algal mat in which are found at least eight species of cone shells, two or three miters, the small snakehead cowry, and a black *Morula*. Common algae forming this mat include *Sargassum*, *Laurencia*, and *Halimeda*. *Codium* and *Gracillaria*, the limu we eat, may also be present. The wave-pounded frontal ramparts of the benches are studded with the short-spined sea urchin *Echinometra*, and in the crevices there are often small drupes and morulas among the mollusks and xanthid crabs. At high tide surgeonfishes (manini and palani), parrotfishes (uhu), and wrasses (hinalea) feed on the algae or on the invertebrates of these benches (Fig. 5).

Along the shoreline, usually back of fringing reefs, are sandy beaches. Ghost crabs (*Ocypode*) run along the water line and excavate their burrows in beach sand, and auger shells (*Terebra* spp.) burrow where the waves wash up the beach. Subtidally, a variety of organisms is found over or in the sand. Razorfishes hover over it, diving into it when disturbed, and goatfishes (weke) stir up the sand with their barbles. The kona crab, helmet shell, and some of the cones, miters, and auger shells are other sand-dwelling forms that occur in these areas of depths of 1 to 20 meters and more.

The most conspicuous, diverse, and colorful of the shallow-water communities are those of the corals which form both fringing and subtidal reefs. Coral communities are variously developed in the island chain: to the north, Kure, Midway, and Pearl and Hermes Reef are com-

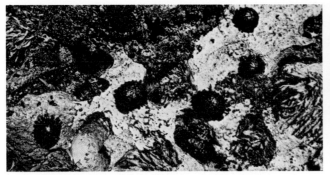

Fig. 2. Opihi (*Cellana*) and the shingle urchin (*Colobocentrotus*) on the wave-beaten face of a rocky coastline.

Photograph by E. A. Kay

Fig. 3. Achilles tang among basalt boulders at Mahukona, Hawaii.

Photograph by J. A. Maciolek

Fig. 4. Tide pool at Honaunau, Hawaii, with manini and the tentacles of the worm *Terebellum*.

Photograph by E. A. Kay

Fig. 5. Manini feeding on filamentous algae near Palaau, Molokai.

Photograph by J. A. Maciolek

Fig. 6. Fringing reef off Diamond Head, Oahu.

Photograph by E. A. Kay

Fig. 7. *Pocillopora* heads with the yellow coral *Porites* and a slate-pencil sea urchin at Kealakekua Bay, Hawaii.

Photograph by E. H. Chave

Fig. 8. Lobster under a rock encrusted with *Porites* and sponges at Pearl and Hermes Reef.

Photograph by J. A. Maciolek

Fig. 9. Four butterflyfishes and a surgeonfish near a well-developed head of *Porites* at Pearl and Hermes Reef.

Photograph by J. A. Maciolek

Fig. 10. Moorish idol and striped wrasse in lava and coral rubble at Pokai Bay, Oahu.

Photograph by E. H. Chave

Triphora triticea.
×14

Kogomea sandwicensis.
×7

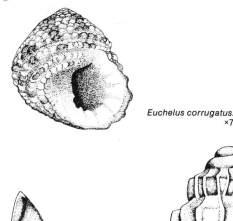

Euchelus corrugatus.
×7

plex calcareous structures capping volcanoes which may have been above the sea more than 20 million years ago; farther south, Kauai, Oahu, Maui, Molokai, and Lanai are partially ringed by fringing reefs (Fig. 6). The island of Hawaii has no fringing reef, but extensively developed subtidal reefs occur off the Kona Coast. Reef growth in Hawaii may be slower than elsewhere, perhaps because the water surrounding the islands is cooler than that of other Pacific reefs. *Porites* and *Pocillopora* are the most common reef-building corals in the major islands of the Hawaiian chain, where the main reef-building coral of the Pacific, *Acropora*, is absent.

Although the most conspicuous members of coral communities are the corals themselves, reefs are intricate structures comprised of many other invertebrates, fishes, and plants. Indeed, living corals comprise only a small part of the mass of the reef itself in Hawaiian waters where calcareous algae exceed the corals in reef composition. Even the brilliant colors of the corals are due in large part to the minute algae which live symbiotically in the tissues of coral polyps.

Coral reefs are unique in that they have the ability to construct and maintain shore habitats where none existed previously. Fringing reefs are topographically and biologically complex structures. The active, growing part of the reef is the seaward edge where most of the live corals are found. Just shoreward of this front there is a ridge which may rise above sea level; it is comprised largely of pink calcareous algae and is termed the algal ridge. Shoreward of the algal ridge is the most extensive part of the reef—the reef flat—sand covered, channeled, some-

times showing masses of the frondose brown alga *Sargassum*, and studded with rubble; only an occasional live coral head is seen on the reef flat. The reef includes many distinctive biological communities. At the seaward edge where there is much living coral are the sea urchins, especially the slate-pencil urchin (Fig. 7), and long-spined urchins (wana). Here too are some of the cowries and cones and the coral-eating mollusk, *Coralliophila*. Among the reef fishes frequenting this area are the brilliantly hued butterflyfishes, parrotfishes, wrasses, and surgeonfishes. Many of these forms feed on coral polyps. On the algal ridge there are a number of mollusks, especially reef-building forms such as vermetid or worm-shells, and the limpet-like *Hipponix*. On the reef flat, damselfishes and wrasses predominate among the fishes. And in crevices and caves are octopus (he'e), the spiny lobster (Fig. 8), and squirrelfishes (menpachi and u'u).

Subtidal reefs exhibit an even greater diversity of animal life than do fringing reefs, for here are found most of Hawaii's more spectacular shells, the tiger cowry, *Cypraea tigris*, many of the endemic Hawaiian cowries, miters, cones, and triton shells. Studded among the brilliant colors and diverse shapes of the corals are sea urchins such as the slate-pencil and long-spined wana, and nibbling on the coral polyps are the brilliantly colored butterflyfishes and the tangs (Figs. 9 and 10). Many of the fishes of this community are yellow, matching the coloration of the reef corals.

E.A.K. and E.H.C.

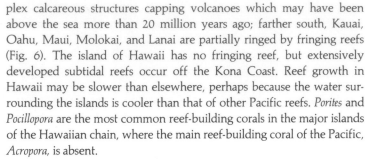

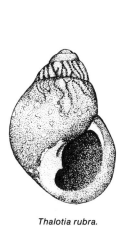

Strebloceros annulata.
×7

Parashiela beetsi.
×14

Seminella varia.
×16

Merelina sp.
×14

Lienardia crassicostata.
×3

Thalotia rubra.
×14

Bittium zebrum.
×7

Drawings by Dept. of General Science, University of Hawaii

A SELECTION OF MICROMOLLUSKS FROM HAWAIIAN WATERS

Hanauma Bay

Hanauma is a unique crater bay on Oahu's southeastern tip. It is both a state park and a marine conservation district. The latter designation was awarded in 1967 to protect the bay's diverse marine life from excessive exploitation. Restrictions prohibiting the taking of any plants, animals, or substrate materials were imposed at that time, allowing marine life to be only viewed and photographed. With this protection, fishes, corals, and other animals have flourished.

Hanauma Bay has become a popular recreational area because of its natural attributes and nearness to Honolulu (a 20-minute drive from Waikiki). Its clear, blue waters lie deep within a double, steep-sided volcanic crater that opens southeasterly to the sea. The inner edge of the bay is bordered by an attractive sandy beach. Beach park facilities are provided and lifeguards are on duty daily.

Although it is only a hundred or so acres in area, the bay contains a variety of habitats, ranging from a protective barrier reef and calm-water swimming areas at the inner end, through submerged, coral-studded lava ledges and sand patches to a depth of nearly 100 feet (30 meters) at its mouth. Seaweeds, fishes, corals, urchins, and many other organisms abound. At least 90 species of fishes have been recorded in the bay. They appear to have increased in numbers and tameness since protective restrictions were imposed. Among the common ones are parrotfishes (uhu), surgeonfishes (manini, palani, kole, etc.), and goatfishes (weke, kumu, etc.). Colorful butterflyfishes (kikakapu) and wrasses (hinalea) are easily approached and photographed with an underwater camera.

The novice snorkler or diver may find many species of seaweeds, fishes, and invertebrate animals in nearshore swimming areas and pools in the barrier reef. Proficient, properly equipped divers desiring to explore deeper waters usually follow an underwater cable which passes through the barrier reef and out into deeper water (see map). Swimmers and divers should avoid those areas indicated on the map as hazardous because of currents, eddies, and large waves. Attractive corals and fishes are more abundant in the center of the bay, away from these danger zones.

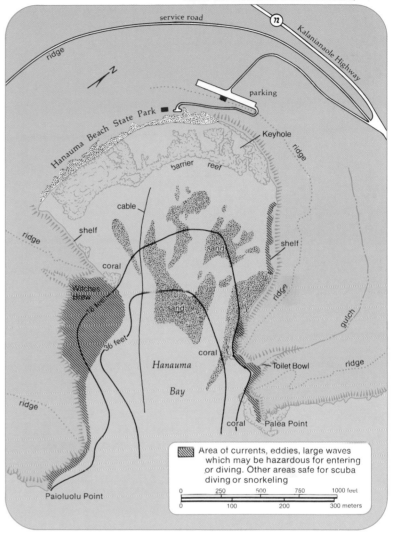

Area of currents, eddies, large waves which may be hazardous for entering or diving. Other areas safe for scuba diving or snorkeling

HANAUMA BAY. View across the entrance to the bay looking northwest to Maunalua Bay and the residential suburbs of Portlock, Hawaii Kai and Kuliouou. Koko Head is to the left (out of the photograph).
Photograph by Agatin T. Abbott, Hawaii Institute of Geophysics; map and text by Edith H. Chave and John A. Maciolek, Marine Programs, University of Hawaii.

Hokulea, double-hulled Hawaiian canoe.
Drawing by John A. Dixon

ASTRONOMY

With its favorable latitude and equable climate, Hawaii is an excellent place to view and study the stars. During the course of the year the entire northern sky and more than 90 percent of the southern sky can be seen at the 20° North latitude of Hawaii; this includes essentially all of the southern Milky Way. The warm evenings and generally clear skies experienced in the leeward areas of the islands encourage a wide public interest in astronomy.

The interests of professional astronomers were first attracted in the early 1960s to the excellent conditions for astronomy on the highest mountains of Hawaii, notably Haleakala and Mauna Kea, whose summits extend above the tropical inversion layer. This layer is normally between 2,000 and 3,000 meters altitude, and although cumulus cloud is often found during the day near the 4,200 m summit of Mauna Kea, rapid cooling of the volcanic cinder cone at sunset results in downslip winds that quickly dissipate these clouds and bring in dry air from above. The atmosphere around and above Mauna Kea is extremely dry, and because water vapor is the principal source of atmospheric opacity at infrared and submillimeter wavelengths (about 1 micron to 1 millimeter), this makes Mauna Kea an excellent site for the relatively new and exciting fields of infrared and submillimeter astronomy. There are a number of atmospheric "windows," that is, wavelength bands of usefully high atmospheric transmission; these lie at wavelengths (a) between 1 and 35 microns, and (b) longward of 0.35 millimeters. Observations from an airborne observatory are used to fill the wavelength gap between the two bands. It is widely acknowledged that these "windows" are, on average, "cleaner" and usable on a greater fraction of nights at Mauna Kea than at any other observatory site in the world. This is especially true at the longer wavelengths. Another value of this site is its excellent seeing quality. The constant turbulence of the air as the starlight passes through the atmosphere results in small varying changes in direction of the beam which produce a blurred stellar image. The best seeing occurs when the image diameter is smallest: this allows fainter stars to be seen more readily against the low, but not zero, brightness of the night sky background, as well as showing up fine detail in extended objects such as planets or galaxies. At Mauna Kea under average seeing conditions the image diameter at visible wavelengths is about 1 arc second; occasionally it falls to less than 0.5 arc second, a level of seeing rarely found at other observatories. (An arc second is 1/3600th of a degree).

These superb observational conditions and other factors have led to the development of a major international observatory at the summit of Mauna Kea that seeks to exploit the unique qualities of the site. There are currently four major telescopes operating at Mauna Kea: the University of Hawaii's 2.2-meter telescope (which began regular operation in 1970); the 3.8-meter United Kingdom Infrared Telescope (1979); NASA's 3.0-meter Infrared Telescope Facility (1979); and the 3.6-meter Canada-France-Hawaii Telescope (1980). Other telescopes are planned for the site, including a 10-meter optical telescope and two telescopes for millimeter and submillimeter studies.

Infrared and submillimeter astronomy, fields actively pursued at the Mauna Kea Observatory, may be thought of as the astronomy of cool and cold objects with temperatures between about 3°K and 3,000°K. (The Kelvin, or K, scale of absolute temperature has degree intervals equal to those of the Celsius scale in which 0° equals −273.16° Celsius.) The source of radiation is very often thermally emitting dust, which may, for example, be heated by nearby stars to temperatures typically between several 100°K and about 1,000°K, or may be in dense, cool (about 20°K) interstellar clouds protected from starlight. It is widely believed that new stars can form in such dense, cool regions, which are usually found in giant molecular clouds about 200 light-years across. The low temperatures in these clouds make possible the formation of molecules, and up to 50 percent of the gas is believed to be in the form of molecules, the most abundant being the hydrogen molecule and the most readily observed being the asymmetric molecule carbon monoxide. Study of the spectral line emission from molecules provides important information on the physical conditions in these clouds. The search for protostars, which are stars in the process of formation, and studies aimed at understanding the physical processes involved in star formation is a major program being actively pursued in Hawaii and elsewhere.

R.D.W.

With the recent application of sophisticated imaging devices having electronic readout to astronomy, the exploitation of the excellent seeing conditions at Mauna Kea has become a major scientific activity. The especially dark skies at Mauna Kea make the imaging of faint, distant galaxies and quasars a rewarding study. Such investigations are leading, for example, to information about the nature of the galaxies in which quasars are embedded and to the discovery of gravitationally lensed quasars. At present the new imaging devices are small (less than 3 cm diameter), so that for objects of large angular size, the photographic plate is still an important tool. Two examples of extended objects photographed in sub arc second seeing conditions are shown below. The great advantages of high angular resolution astronomy provide the overriding justification for the Space Telescope, a 2.4-meter telescope to be placed in orbit by NASA's Space Shuttle in the mid 1980s. The diameter of its stellar images, limited only by diffraction in the telescope optics, will be between 0.1 and 0.2 arc seconds at near ultraviolet and visible wavelengths. This will permit astronomers to observe objects about 50 times fainter than the faintest objects measured from ground-based observatories, that is, objects about 7 times more distant. Exciting new discoveries with the telescope are firmly predicted!

● Kokee Tracking Station, NASA
● Palehua Solar Observatory, USAF

Bishop Museum Planetarium ● ● Institute for Astronomy,
University of Hawaii, at Manoa

Mees Solar Observatory,
University of Hawaii
Haleakala

—University of Hawaii
—United Kingdom
—Canada, France,
   Hawaii
—NASA

Mauna
Kea

ASTRONOMICAL OBSERVATORIES AND INSTITUTES

20   0   20   40   60   80   100 miles
20   0   20   40   60   80   100   120   140 kilometers

Source: Univ. of Hawaii Institute for Astronomy   1982

Crab Nebula, produced as the result of a supernova explosion that was witnessed by Chinese astronomers in the year 1054. The whitish emission is synchrotron radiation produced by very rapidly moving electrons. Spectral line emission from ionized hydrogen gas is the source of the red filaments. The remnant of the explosion, a rapidly spinning neutron star, is still visible at the center of the nebula. Photographed with the Canada-France-Hawaii Telescope in sub arc second seeing conditions (30 minute exposure on baked Ektachrome 400 film).

Photograph by Laird Thompson

M51 spiral galaxy. The spiral arms are the site of young stars and ionized gas. The object at the end of the faint outer arm is believed to be another galaxy which is interacting gravitationally with M51. Photographed with the Canada-France-Hawaii Telescope (1 hour exposure on baked Ektachrome 400 film).

Photograph by Laird Thompson

Astronomical observatories on the summit of Mauna Kea. From left to right: the 3.6m Canada-France-Hawaii Telescope, the 2.2m University of Hawaii Telescope, the 3.8m United Kingdom Infrared Telescope, and NASA's 3.0m Infrared Telescope.

Photograph by Duncan Chesley

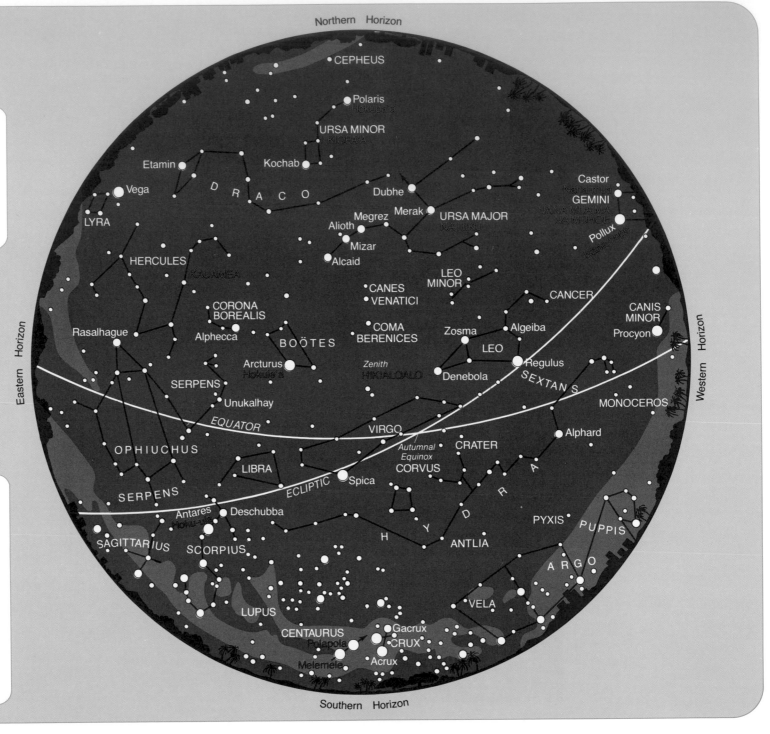

Northern Horizon

STAR CHART
June

○ 1st Magnitude
○ 2nd Magnitude
○ 3rd Magnitude
○ 4th Magnitude
▨ Limit of Milky Way

Observed on:
June 1 at 8:20 pm
June 6 at 8:00 pm
June 11 at 7:40 pm
June 16 at 7:20 pm
June 21 at 7:00 pm
June 26 at 6:40 pm

Hawaiian names of some of the brightest stars are given in red.

Source: E. H. Bryan, Jr. (1977)

CEPHEUS
Polaris
Hokupa'a
URSA MINOR
KIOPA'A
Kochab
Etamin
D R A C O
Dubhe
Castor
GEMINI
NANA MUA
Vega
Megrez
Merak
URSA MAJOR
NA HIKU
Pollux
LYRA
Alioth
Mizar
Alcaid
LEO MINOR
HERCULES
KAUAMEA
CANES VENATICI
CANCER
CORONA BOREALIS
COMA BERENICES
Zosma
Algeiba
CANIS MINOR
Alphecca
BOÖTES
LEO
Procyon
Rasalhague
Arcturus
Hokule'a
Zenith
HIKIALOALO
Regulus
SERPENS
Denebola
SEXTANS
Unukalhay
MONOCEROS
EQUATOR
VIRGO
Alphard
OPHIUCHUS
Autumnal Equinox
CRATER
LIBRA
CORVUS
H Y D R A
SERPENS
ECLIPTIC
Spica
Antares
Deschubba
ANTLIA
Hoku'ula
PYXIS
PUPPIS
SAGITTARIUS
SCORPIUS
A R G O
LUPUS
VELA
CENTAURUS
Gacrux
Polapola
CRUX
Acrux
Melemele
Eastern Horizon

Western Horizon

USING THE CHARTS

The two star maps represent the night sky as seen from the latitude of Hawaii in the early evening of June and December, respectively. For intervening months the north-south orientation will be different and the maps will need to be turned slightly. Each map is drawn to represent the stars as you look up at them. Thus the map should be held so that you look up at it as well. When you face south, hold the map upright in front of you with the lower edge labeled "Southern Horizon" down, toward the south. If you face north, tip the map upside down and hold its upper "Northern Horizon" toward north. If you face east, or west, hold the left or right hand side of the map, respectively, downward toward the horizon.

Southern Horizon

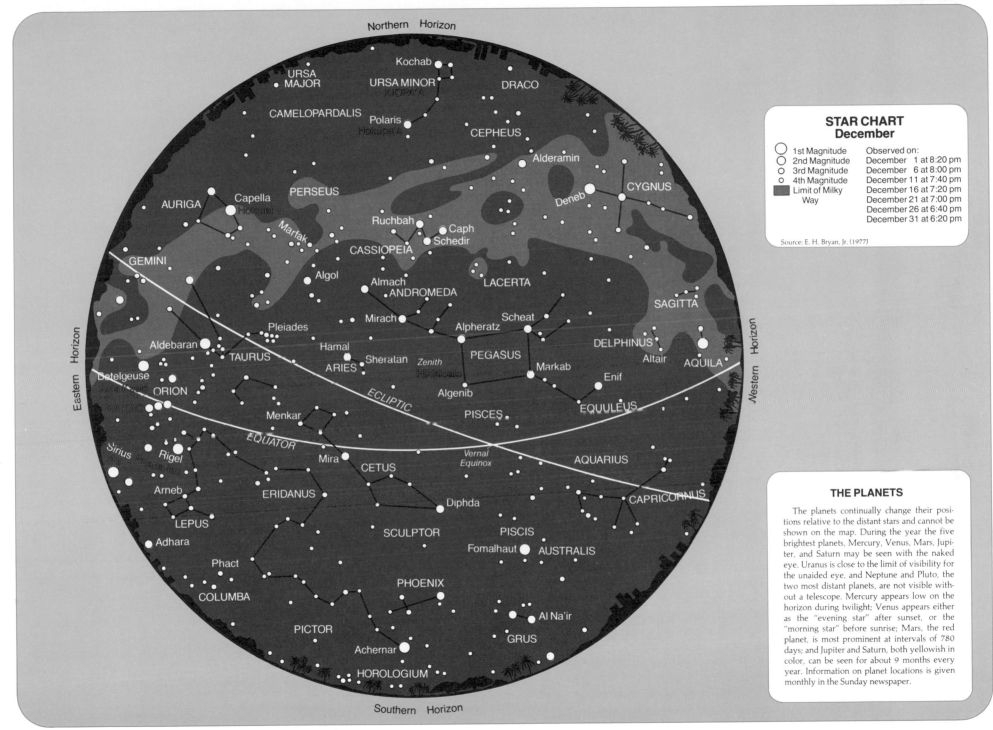

Northern Horizon

URSA MAJOR
URSA MINOR
KIOPAPA
DRACO
Kochab
CAMELOPARDALIS
Polaris
Hokupaa
CEPHEUS
Alderamin
CYGNUS
PERSEUS
Deneb
Marfak
Ruchbah
Caph
Schedir
CASSIOPEIA
AURIGA
Capella
Hokulei
Algol
Almach
Mirach
ANDROMEDA
LACERTA
SAGITTA
GEMINI
Pleiades
Scheat
Alpheratz
Hamal
Sheratan
PEGASUS
DELPHINUS
Aldebaran
TAURUS
ARIES
Zenith
Hikianalia
Markab
Altair
AQUILA
Betelgeuse
ORION
Mira
Enif
Algenib
EQUULEUS
Menkar
ECLIPTIC
PISCES
NA KAO
Sirius
A'a
Rigel
EQUATOR
CETUS
Vernal Equinox
AQUARIUS
Arneb
ERIDANUS
Diphda
CAPRICORNUS
LEPUS
Adhara
SCULPTOR
PISCIS
Phact
Fomalhaut
AUSTRALIS
COLUMBA
PHOENIX
Al Na'ir
PICTOR
GRUS
Achernar
HOROLOGIUM

Eastern Horizon
Western Horizon

Southern Horizon

Source: E. H. Bryan, Jr. (1977)

STAR CHART
December

○ 1st Magnitude
○ 2nd Magnitude
○ 3rd Magnitude
○ 4th Magnitude
■ Limit of Milky Way

Observed on:
December 1 at 8:20 pm
December 6 at 8:00 pm
December 11 at 7:40 pm
December 16 at 7:20 pm
December 21 at 7:00 pm
December 26 at 6:40 pm
December 31 at 6:20 pm

THE PLANETS

The planets continually change their positions relative to the distant stars and cannot be shown on the map. During the year the five brightest planets, Mercury, Venus, Mars, Jupiter, and Saturn may be seen with the naked eye. Uranus is close to the limit of visibility for the unaided eye, and Neptune and Pluto, the two most distant planets, are not visible without a telescope. Mercury appears low on the horizon during twilight; Venus appears either as the "evening star" after sunset, or the "morning star" before sunrise; Mars, the red planet, is most prominent at intervals of 780 days; and Jupiter and Saturn, both yellowish in color, can be seen for about 9 months every year. Information on planet locations is given monthly in the Sunday newspaper.

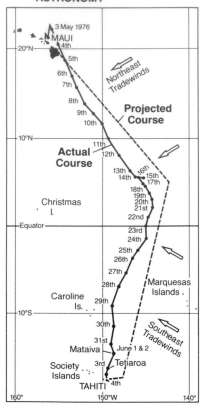

VOYAGE OF THE HOKULEʻA 1976
Voyage of the Hawaiian double-hulled canoe
Hokuleʻa from Honolua Bay, Maui, to Papeete,
Tahiti, 1 May to 4 June 1976.

Map from Finney (1977)

Polynesian Navigation

The eastward migration into the Pacific of the ancestors of the Polynesians probably began about 40,000 years ago with ocean voyages from the islands of Asia, such as Indonesia, to New Guinea, Australia, and Melanesia. About 3,000 years ago they had migrated as far as Samoa and Tonga in western Polynesia. The main period of Polynesian exploration was relatively short, beginning in about A.D. 300 with the settlement of the Marquesas Islands and ending when Hawaii and New Zealand were reached in about A.D. 800 to 900. There are some intriguing questions concerning the discovery and colonization of these islands whose answers hinge on the navigational abilities of the Polynesians. For example, given the large distances between the island groups and the prevailing directions of the trade winds and ocean currents, which generally opposed the directions of migration, is it likely that discoveries of new islands were the result of voyagers being blown off course during storms, or was an element of systematic searching involved? And following a discovery could the voyagers return to their home island to organize a colonizing expedition?

The skills of the Polynesian navigators were passed on orally from generation to generation, often in the form of navigational chants. Although much of the knowledge has now been lost, some has survived among the handful of Pacific Island navigators alive today, and recently some has also been rediscovered as a result of the voyages of the double-hulled canoe *Hokuleʻa* between Hawaii and Tahiti in 1976 and 1980. Besides his familiarity with basic astronomy, the navigator depended greatly on his knowledge of the winds and the ocean swells in setting and steering his course. During periods of cloudiness when the stars were obscured, he would rely heavily on these non-astronomical skills. The presence of land birds near islands, the build-up of high cloud over distant islands, the likely presence of neighboring islands, wave patterns, and other clues assisted the navigator in making landfall when he knew land was near. The canoe's course would be maintained at night using a number of known stars when they were close to the horizon, and also during the day by using the sun's position. A sequence of

guiding stars for the chosen course and season were probably incorporated into chants before the voyage. On the voyage between Hawaii and Tahiti two especially important stars were the bright stars Arcturus or Hokulea (Star of Happiness) and Sirius or Aʻa (Glowing Star), which pass through the zenith in Hawaii and Tahiti respectively. On this journey the navigator would probably sail close to the wind (at right angles to it), until the appropriate star was overhead, and then sail downwind until land was sighted (latitude sailing). An alternative and more precise method may also have been used, namely that of looking for the simultaneous rising or setting of two bright stars which occurs at the desired latitude (for example, Sirius and Pollux when setting in Tahiti, Hokulea and Spica when rising in Hawaii). A further clue to the latitude of Hawaii that may also have been used is the position of the Southern Cross: at this latitude, when the constellation is at its highest point above the horizon, the bottom star, Acrux, is midway between the horizon and the top star, Gacrux.

R.D.W.

Early Polynesian voyagers made practical use of the stars in sailing the Pacific Ocean. Without navigational instruments they reached tiny islands over thousands of miles of open sea. The sailing instructions were contained in chants, carefully memorized and passed from one generation of voyagers to the next.

Illustration from Kyselka and Lanterman (1976)

THE CULTURAL ENVIRONMENT

Hawaiian arts and crafts: temple image with carved headdress.

Bishop Museum drawing from Te Rangi Hiroa (1964:493)

ARCHAEOLOGY

Archaeology in Hawaii has two foci: the preservation and enhancement of Hawaii's cultural heritage by studying and reporting to the public the places, events, and changes in Hawaiian culture, particularly of the precontact (A.D. 1778) period; and, like anthropology, the goal of understanding the how and why of processes of change in Hawaiian culture. A brief discussion of several recent projects will illustrate the aims and products of archaeological study. The results of the research will become more available to the public through park development, site restorations, and publications.

The district of Kohala on the island of Hawaii is one of the richest in historical, archaeological, and legendary materials in the State. The dry leeward coast, just south of Mahukona, has been the site of University of Hawaii archaeological investigations into colonization, population growth, subsistence activities, and general culture change before A.D. 1800. In the *ahupuaa* (a native territorial unit) of Lapakahi, three years' work has indicated that Koaie hamlet, on the coast, was founded about A.D. 1300. A small group of fishermen lived in houses built on the bare ground and supported by large posts. About A.D. 1500 the hamlet changed in character: the houses were built on stone platforms with fine pebble floors, and perhaps a high-status residential area was set off by a huge stone wall. At the same time people moved upland and began growing sweet potatoes and building small C-shaped dwellings or shelters. Eventually, the uplands were intensively cultivated, and the lowland coastal area became a strip of nearly continuous clusters of family-sized residential units. Between A.D. 1700 and 1778 or 1800, a maximum number of people may have been fully exploiting all available food resources and may have united into a district-based political and economic network. Lapakahi State Park today contains the archaeological evidence of these changes. (See Newman, 1970; and Tuggle and Griffin, 1973.)

Windward Kohala begins with Pololu Valley and extends through steep and high sea cliffs, waterfalls, and isolated valleys into northern Hamakua and the famous valley of Waipio. In the early 1970s the University of Hawaii conducted archaeological studies along this rugged seacoast. The research centered on the valley settlement, population expansion, and agricultural system change. The wet valleys seem to have been initially occupied at about A.D. 1500, and to have rapidly attained maximum population density and agricultural productivity. It now seems that Kohala Hawaiians may have shifted to the wet valleys generations after farming the leeward slopes and coast. (See Tuggle, 1979; and Tuggle and Tomonari-Tuggle, 1980.)

Kohala is also the land of Kamehameha I. His "birth site," near Upolu Point, and above Hapuu Bay is, reputedly, his family *heiau*. Mookini *heiau*, famous in history and legend, was rededicated by Kamehameha. Other important *heiau* are the "un-Hawaiian" looking Kukuipahu, with its dressed stone, and Kupalaha *heiau*. Just to the south near Kawaihae are the imposing *heiau* Puu Kohola and Mailekini (page 95), and the recently excavated John Young house.

South along the dry coast extending from Kawaihae, Kohala, into Kona, are two important Bishop Museum excavations seeking to gain knowledge concerning Hawaiian adaptation to arid coastal environments—at Kalahuipuaa and Anaehoomalu. (See Kirch, 1979.) In Kona, is the famous Honokohau settlement, known for prehistoric and historic occupation, and for its fishponds and *heiau*. Research suggests large populations in pre-historical time, and use by high *alii* into the 1800s. Along the same coast are the Puako and Anaehoomalu petroglyphs and nearby Kuualii fishpond. The Puu Honua o Honaunau National Historical Park at Honaunau is the most striking and best restored of all Hawaiian site complexes. Once a place of sanctuary for refugees and the location of several *heiau*, it has been rebuilt to approximate its early historic appearance. *Holua*, or slides, are also present. At the villages of Napoopoo and Kaawaloa, *heiau* and burial caves can still be seen, as well as extensive agricultural fields above the cliffs.

In Kau, around the South Point area, archaeologists from the Bishop Museum have excavated several sites that suggest occupation as early as A.D. 700 for these fishing stations, shelters, *heiau*, salt pans, and canoe mooring holes. Handy and Pukui (1958) describe the historic Hawaiian culture in Kau.

At the summit of Mauna Kea is a basalt quarry which furnished the raw material for adzes, basic wood-working tools of the Hawaiians.

Of all the islands, Oahu has seen the destruction of the greatest number of sites, but several locales are important in terms of archaeological knowledge and cultural heritage. Makaha Valley in Leeward Oahu has undergone excavation by the Bishop Museum. While much of the lower valley has been altered, middle and upper portions con-

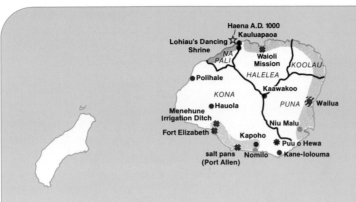

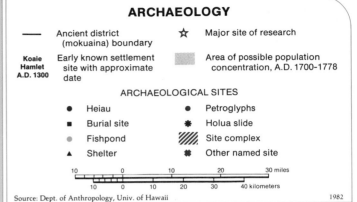

ARCHAEOLOGY

— Ancient district (mokuaina) boundary

☆ Major site of research

Koaie Hamlet A.D. 1300 — Early known settlement site with approximate date

▨ Area of possible population concentration, A.D. 1700-1778

ARCHAEOLOGICAL SITES

● Heiau
■ Burial site
● Fishpond
▲ Shelter
● Petroglyphs
✳ Holua slide
▨ Site complex
✳ Other named site

Source: Dept. of Anthropology, Univ. of Hawaii   1982

The map locates many of the important, better known, or accessible archaeological sites. The selections have been made with a wide range of audience interests in mind, and exemplify all the types of surface structures and complexes now available. They do not, however, comprise all the remains of prehistoric Hawaiian culture that exist. All the islands are rich in unmapped or unstudied hamlets, *heiau*, agricultural fields, and fishponds, with great need for preservation. Several of the sites on the map are in out-of-the-way places, but most are marked and accessible. Some are on private land. At none of the sites should anything be disturbed or removed, since the more remain to be seen, the better the picture of the past. A poi

pounder tells little by itself, but in context the whole activity of poi production may be seen. The ancient district (*mokuaina* or *mokuoloko*) boundaries are shown as they probably were around A.D. 1778. At some previous time the *ahupuaa* (narrow bands of land extending from sea to mountains) were overlain with the district organization. Maui has one area which is not a district but four *ilikupono*, smaller units of land but different from the *ahupuaa*. The possible population concentrations as of A.D. 1700, like the dates of some earlier sites, must be considered tentative; archaeologists have acquired only a fraction of the wealth of information awaiting excavation.

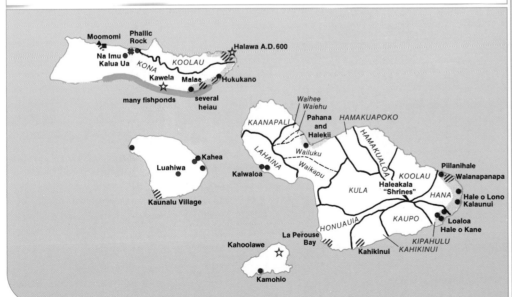

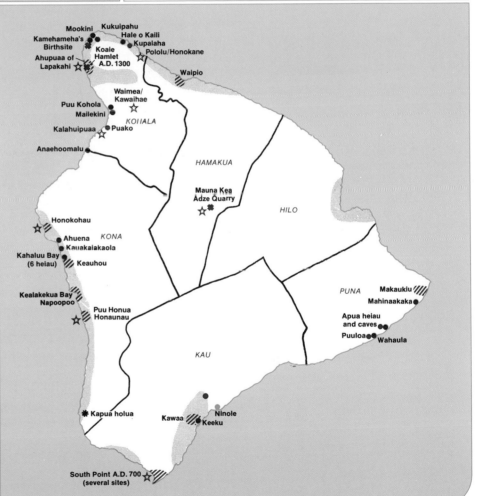

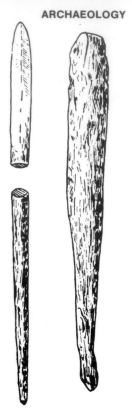

Hawaiian arts and crafts: digging sticks.
Bishop Museum drawing from Te Rangi Hiroa (1964:12)

tained the remains of agricultural systems, residences, and Kaneaki *heiau*. The latter is now restored and topped by a thatched house. On the windward side, Kahana Valley, the site of a state park, is fronted by Huilua fishpond, a beautiful example of the once-numerous man-made fishponds in Oahu. Other fishponds to the south on the windward coast are at Molii, Kahaluu, Heeia, and Mokapu.

Kualoa Beach Park, a City and County park, is one of the more important site complexes on Oahu. While little is to be seen on the surface, there are extensive deposits of well-preserved, water-logged artifacts and living residues. The City and County of Honolulu has acted to ensure preservation of the area, and Kualoa is on the National Register of Historic Places.

Kawainui Marsh, in Kailua, has seen recent archaeological investigations, with occupation dates of A.D. 700–900 likely. Ulupo *heiau* is beside the marsh and accessible by road. Bellows Beach in Waimanalo is one of the earliest sites in the State. Excavated by the University of Hawaii, it contained residences on top of old sand dunes, and burials within. A date of approximately A.D. 600 reinforces the hypothesis that the early colonists, upon reaching Hawaii, settled in wet environments where both fishing and agriculture could best be pursued. At Maunalua Bay, southeast Oahu, Kuliouou and Makaniou shelters were two of the first sites excavated in the State.

An important and easily seen *heiau* on Oahu is Puu o Mahuka, a gigantic site on a bluff above Waimea Bay. Malaekahana near Laie, is a new state park that underwent extensive archaeological research as a part of park development. Intensive excavations at Barbers Point have turned up unusual findings concerning Oahu archaeology. Hawaiian adaptation to this arid locale seems tied to major modification of the flora and fauna of the coastal area, and to perhaps have coincided with the extinction of various birds.

Molokai is rich in sites. Most notable may be the numerous fishponds along the south coast, the phallic rock, the *heiau* of Hokukano (Iliiliopae is very striking), and the settlement complex in Halawa Valley. Archaeologically, Halawa is one of our best known valleys. A sand dune fishing hamlet was established as early as A.D. 600. With population growth, a gradual movement into the valley occurred, wet taro terraces were built, and dry taro was grown wherever possible. Residential clusters appeared along each side of the valley on ridges extending down the valley sides. Two major *heiau*, Mana and Papa, as well as lesser shrines, were also built on the valley sides. Most of these sites are observable today. In fact, the whole "East End" of Molokai is so rich in archaeological sites that it is now designated the Southeast Molokai Archaeological District.

Maui has undergone little recent excavation. Among its impressive *heiau* are Loaloa, near Kaupo, and Piilanihale near Hana. The latter is the largest *heiau* in Hawaii and is in good condition although difficult to reach. Waianapanapa State Park, also near Hana, contains several small sites ranging from caves to shrines and burial mounds. The Kahikinui complex is a large, well-preserved series of hamlets and sites.

Kauai has several excavated and unexcavated sites of importance, as well as areas of considerable potential for future excavation. The Wailua complex of *heiau* includes a place of refuge, Puuhonua Hikina-akala, and associated *heiau*. The Menehune Irrigation Ditch by the Waimea River is a remnant example of dressed-stone masonry and a reminder of the complex water-movement systems built before 1778.

Like Maui, Kauai has abundant remains available for the casual observer. Na Pali State Park is one of the best in the State. At Haena State Park we find an early, complex, and extensive archaeological site. Lohiau's Dancing Platform and Ka ulu a Paoa *heiau* overlook Kee beach. Kee itself is a sand dune site with beginning dates in the early A.D. 1200s. Nualolo Kai valley, next to Milolii, has been studied by the Bishop Museum. Russian Fort Elizabeth is another Kauai state park, and an unusual and easily visited archaeological structure of great importance, though only preliminary excavations have yet been undertaken.

Lanai is best represented by Kaunolu, a well-preserved village complex of numerous house platforms, pens, and other stone features. Halulu *heiau*, canoe sheds, petroglyphs, and burial mounds complete this example of an early historic fishing village. The islands of Niihau, Nihoa, Necker, and Kahoolawe all contain archaeological sites, but all except Kahoolawe are fully closed to the public.

Kahoolawe is an "Archaeological District." The coastal areas and several upland localities have abundant and important sites, including houses, shrines, *heiau*, and agricultural features. Access to the island is limited.

Several museums in the State display artifacts and reconstructions of Hawaiian life. The displays at the Bishop Museum in Honolulu are outstanding, complementing the archaeological sites located throughout the islands. The famous sites such as Puu Kohola *heiau* on Hawaii and the "complexes" indicated on page 95 are especially valuable. "Complexes" are groups of sites of many kinds—for example, a village with its houses, *heiau*, canoe sheds, *holua* slide, fields for crops, and burial mounds. Each year archaeological excavations are conducted at various locations throughout the islands. The excavation teams are generally hospitable to interested visitors and, when field conditions permit, will discuss their research. The Bishop Museum's department of anthropology and authorities at several campuses of the University of Hawaii should be consulted for information concerning the whereabouts of work in progress.

P.B.G.

HISTORY

The Post-Contact Period, 1778 to 1982

The discovery of the Hawaiian Islands by Europeans, a thousand years or more after the original settlement by Polynesians, was the work of the English naval captain James Cook, certainly the greatest explorer of his century, perhaps the greatest in the history of Western expansion. In the course of his third major voyage in the Pacific, Cook was taking his two ships, HMS *Resolution* and HMS *Discovery*, from the South Pacific to the northwest coast of America when, on January 18, 1778, he sighted the island of Oahu. On January 20 his ships anchored off Waimea, Kauai, and Cook and his men spent several days there and at Niihau, leaving on February 2.

Making his way south again from the American coast late in 1778, Cook sighted Maui on November 25, and Hawaii on November 30. He needed a safe anchorage where he could refit the ships, take on supplies, and allow his men some relaxation. In search of such a place, he took the *Resolution* and the *Discovery* along the north and east coasts of Hawaii, around the southern point, and up the west coast as far as Kealakekua Bay, where on January 18, 1779, the ships dropped anchor.

By chance, Cook's two visits—to Kauai and Niihau in 1778 and Hawaii in 1779—occurred at the time of an annual religious festival in honor of the Hawaiian god Lono. The priests of Lono's cult at Kealakekua Bay honored Cook in a way that identified him with Lono, and on this basis the men of the expedition were treated with great respect and hospitality for the more than two weeks of their stay.

Cook left Kealakekua Bay on February 4 but was forced to return on February 11, when the *Resolution's* foremast was damaged in a storm. For whatever reason, the white men had evidently outstayed their welcome, and the protection and sponsorship of the priests of Lono were at an end. On the night of February 13, some Hawaiians stole a ship's boat from the *Discovery*. Next morning, Cook went ashore with a party of marines, about a dozen armed men in all, to take a chief hostage against the return of the boat. This was a strategy that Cook had used to good effect in other island groups, but here it misfired, fatally for him. Things went wrong on the shore at Kaawaloa village, and in fighting that flared up too suddenly to be comprehended, Cook was killed, along with some of his men.

Violence and tragedy were enough to cloud somewhat among Europeans the initial reputation of the Hawaiian Islands. No Western ship put in again for several years. Just the same, Cook's discovery was of great potential usefulness. In all the Pacific north of the equator, there was no other island group so well placed to serve as a way station in the developing commerce between Asia and the west coast of the American continent. Contact was reestablished in 1785, and merchantmen trading between Canton and the American northwest began wintering at the Hawaiian Islands. At the turn of the nineteenth century sandalwood, in demand at Canton, was discovered, first on Kauai and then on the other islands, and this made the Hawaiian group even more attractive to ships' captains.

The Hawaiian high chiefs, on their side, had a use for Westerners—as suppliers of firearms. In the generations before Cook's appearance, power among the chiefs had evidently become concentrated among the regional rulers of the two biggest islands, Maui and Hawaii. At no time, though, were all the islands under a single ruler. For one thing, the agriculture of the islands did not produce a big enough surplus to allow chiefs to take men away from the taro patches to fight their wars indefinitely on islands separated by wide channels. Furthermore, in a war technology of nothing but spears, clubs, daggers, and slingshots, no chief had the weight of arms to impose convincing and permanent defeat upon his competitors for power.

Within one generation of Cook's appearance, however, the islands were united by means of war. It is hard to escape the conclusion that the introduction of Western arms was one important element in making unification possible. It is equally hard to escape the conclusion that the unifying chief, Kamehameha, was a remarkable man. The west coast of the island of Hawaii, where he emerged as a leader to be reckoned with, was frequented by Western ships, and thus he had the chance to make an early assessment of the usefulness of guns. But then, so did all the other chiefs of his time and place. All traded for firearms when they could; each used them in his own interest. It was Kamehameha who fought his way to supremacy, first on Hawaii, then on the other islands. The Battle of Nuuanu, fought on Oahu in the spring of 1795, made him ruler of all the islands except Kauai and Niihau, and these came under his control by an agreement made in 1810.

Kamehameha consolidated his power by keeping a monopoly of trade, so that he would always have a decisive edge in the use of resources. Chiefs who might challenge him were brought to live under his surveillance, away from their lands and followers; and each island was put under the administration of a governor appointed by and responsi-

Coat of Arms of the Hawaiian Monarchy. The motto *Ua mau ke ea o ka aina i ka pono* means "The life of the land is perpetuated in righteousness." It is now the State Motto.

Source: Hawaii State Archives

MONARCHS

Kamehameha I (Kamehameha the Great)	1795–1819
Kamehameha II (Liholiho)	1819–1824
Kamehameha III (Kauikeaouli)	1825–1854
Kamehameha IV (Alexander Liholiho)	1854–1863
Kamehameha V (Lot Kamehameha)	1863–1872
William C. Lunalilo	1873–1874
(David) Kalakaua	1874–1891
Liliuokalani	1891–1893

Queen Liliuokalani statue, Honolulu.

Drawing by John A. Dixon

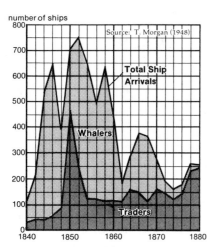

**EARLY SHIP ARRIVALS IN HAWAII
WHALERS AND TRADERS**

ble to Kamehameha. Kamehameha was extremely quick, as well, to learn how to handle white men. Before the conquest, he had a number of them working for him as gunners and ship handlers; afterward, the most competent became his governors, harbormasters, and political advisers.

Kamehameha's power remained essentially unchallenged from the Battle of Nuuanu in 1795 until his death at Kailua, Hawaii, in May 1819; he was in his sixties. The dynasty he founded survived his death, but in altered form. The kapu system, upon whose maintenance he insisted all his life, was deliberately discarded six months after his death by two of his surviving wives, Kaahumanu and Keopuolani, and his successor as king, his son Liholiho, who reigned as Kamehameha II (1819–1824).

The abolition of the kapu, four decades after Cook's death, has been variously explained. One likely interpretation of events is that with the coming of the white man the sources of power in the Hawaiian world changed, and governing systems changed accordingly. Before the white man's arrival, high chiefs ruled on the basis of their claim to closeness to divinity. The kapu operated as a constant reaffirmation of this claim. That is to say, power was ritually defined, expressed, and maintained. The obviously powerful white man drew his power from sources other than the kapu, and some of the instruments of this power—ships, guns, metal, money—could be acquired by chiefs in trade. A dynasty basing its right to rule on an accumulation of power of a Western sort did not need the kapu. Indeed, the old religion, involving a numerous and unproductive priesthood, the practice of rituals which consumed time and resources, including the maintenance of large, laboriously constructed temples, might be nothing more than a drain on the strength of the dynasty. Then, too, female chiefs of whatever exalted rank were ritually excluded from the making of the highest political decisions. Once the kapu was gone, however, women like Kaahumanu could use their great personal influence directly in the ruling politics of the nation.

The 1820s opened a new era in more ways than one. The Pacific whaling industry was moving into the northern oceans, and whalers, principally American ships from New England ports, began putting in at the islands twice a year, spring and fall, in ever-increasing numbers. At the same time, the islands came within the orbit of Christian missionary work, also directed from Protestant New England.

This New England influence—more broadly, American influence—became the outstanding fact of Hawaii's experience with the outside world. To be sure, nations other than the United States had interests in the Pacific. From the late 1820s to the 1850s, France pushed its powers and privileges in Hawaii. For six months in 1843, the islands were under the British flag as the result of a hasty annexation by a naval captain (an

action later countermanded by the British Foreign Office). At no time in the nineteenth century, in fact, was Hawaii's independence secure; and if arms were the test, a single warship of a foreign power could command the situation, as the 1843 annexation showed. Hawaii retained its political independence through the mingled forbearance and mutual suspicion of the great powers. In the meantime, American commercial and social influence created ties between the islands and the United States which made it next to inevitable that, if and when annexation came, it would be American annexation.

Whaling, in its effect on Hawaii, far outstripped the earlier trade in sandalwood and ships' supplies. In general terms, it urbanized the islands. Honolulu on Oahu, with its protected deep water harbor, and Lahaina on Maui, with its open but usable roadstead, became port towns, centers of commercial exchange and social change, attracting by mid-nineteenth century between a quarter and a third of all Hawaiians as more or less permanent residents. Lahaina all but died with the whaling industry in the 1870s. Honolulu, named the capital in 1850, continued to grow relative to all the other towns during the nineteenth century and into the twentieth. It was true enough throughout that period to say that what happened in rural Oahu and on the outer islands might have nothing but local significance; what happened in Honolulu might very well affect all Hawaii.

Honolulu was the place where the white population was concentrated: transients, like sailors off merchant ships and whalers; sojourners, like the earliest traders; residents, like the established businessmen and the missionaries. The most concentrated attempt to bring Hawaiians into some sort of long-range working relationship with the West was organized by the Protestant missionaries from New England, beginning with the arrival of the first contingent in March 1820. They were joined—or, rather, challenged—in 1827 by French Roman Catholics of the Congregation of the Sacred Hearts of Jesus and Mary. Then Mormons appeared in 1850 and Anglicans in 1862. But without question it was the Protestant influence that was decisive. From the beginning, they made it their business to be close to the chiefs. Within a few years they were rewarded with converts among the *alii*. In the reign of Kauikeaouli, Kamehameha III (1824–1854), all but a very few of the important chiefs became church members. In the late 1830s a religious "awakening" among the commoners brought new members by the thousand. In terms of statistics, the Hawaiian mission was certainly the most successful of its era in the Pacific. And in terms of influence on national policy, the most important white men of that era were certainly men who came to the islands with the mission. Hiram Bingham, the mission leader of the 1820s and 1830s, was the unofficial but constant adviser of the chiefs, from Kaahumanu on; and when in the 1840s the kingdom modernized its government along constitutional lines, a

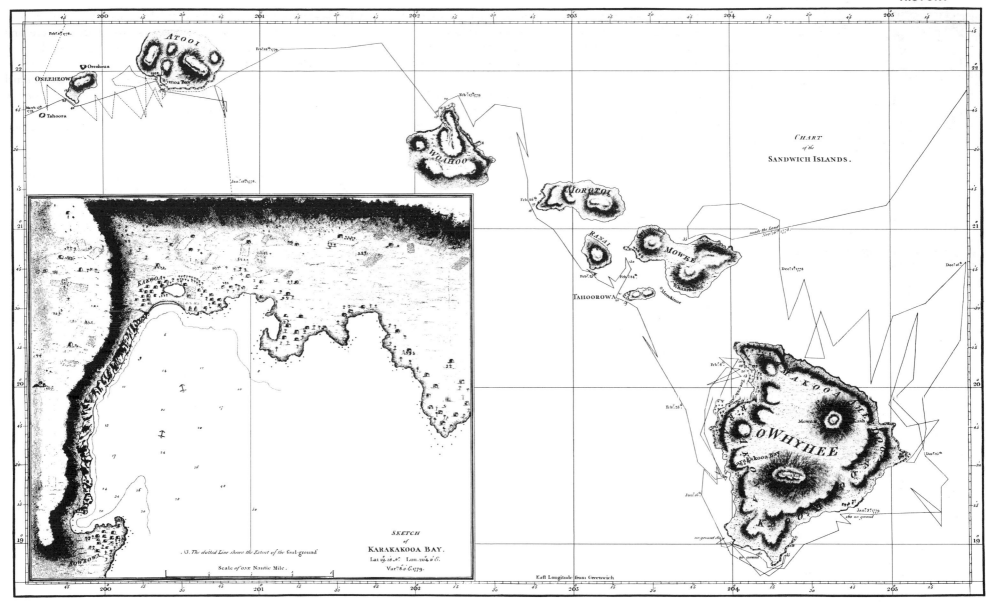

This reproduction of Captain James Cook's map of the Sandwich Islands—as he called them—is the earliest historic map of Hawaii. The dashed line traces Cook's first arrival, in January 1778 from Tahiti, and his landing at Waimea, Kauai. The solid line marks his course on the return visit in November 1778 from North America. Cook's ships cruised off Maui and Hawaii for seven weeks before landing on January 18, 1779 at Kealakekua Bay (inset map). The spelling of names on the map is the navigator's transliteration of local pronunciation and does not conform to modern spelling.

Original map in the Special Collection of the Suzzallo Library, University of Washington, Seattle
Photograph by Robert P. Campbell

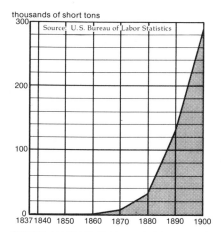

Seal of the Provisional Government, 1893–1894.
Source: Hawaii State Archives

thousands of short tons

EARLY HAWAII SUGAR PRODUCTION

handful of men left the mission to take up cabinet appointments or judicial posts—William Richards, Richard Armstrong, Lorrin Andrews, and Gerrit P. Judd, the last of whom was preeminent in policy making until 1853.

The Protestant view of the ideal Hawaii involved the following elements: an independent nation governed according to a constitution which would embody as much American republicanism as was compatible with the continuance of monarchy; a people literate, Westernized in culture, politically well-informed, enjoying the modest fruits of honest labor on the land, and living in the Protestant faith. The actual Hawaiian came some of the way to meeting these specifications, but by no means all the way. The missionary accomplishment was impressive by the standards of the time, sufficient for the governing body in Boston to phase the mission out of existence in the 1850s and 1860s in favor of an independent Hawaiian church. At the same time, other influences of a broad cosmopolitan nature among both whites and Hawaiian commoners served to dilute the attempted strict Puritanism of the early mission days, and there was a drift away from American Protestantism toward Anglicanism in the ruling house under Alexander Liholiho, Kamehameha IV (1854–1863). For the rest of the nineteenth century, American Protestantism as a strictly religious force declined in strength, until by 1900 Protestants among the Hawaiians were far outnumbered by Catholics and Mormons.

By the 1860s, whaling, which for 40 years had been the basis of the money economy of Hawaii, was in decline. At its height it had brought 500 or more ships to Hawaii a year, put thousands of crewmen on leave on the streets of Honolulu and Lahaina in the spring and fall seasons, and left $1,000,000 or more at a time to circulate in the islands. Then in 1859 petroleum came into production in the United States, and the demand for whale oil lessened. The Civil War disrupted seagoing commerce, and the whaling industry recovered somewhat, only to be virtually ended in 1871 by a disaster which trapped a good part of the American fleet in the Arctic ice.

Sugar succeeded whaling as the economic mainstay of the islands. As early as 1802 attempts had been made to boil sugar from wild cane. In 1835 the first Western-style plantation was established, on Kauai. Small cargoes of sugar were shipped to California as part of the increasing agricultural export trade that peaked with the gold rushes. The Civil War, which kept the American whaling fleet away from Hawaii, at the same time allowed Hawaiian sugar into the mainland market in quantity, as a replacement for sugar no longer produced in the wartime South. The year 1869 was significant: thanks to sugar, Hawaii achieved, for the first time, a favorable balance of trade.

Once it became clear that sugar could do for the economy what other products could not (coffee, silk, wheat, indigo, and beef were among the many tried), the great aim of economic policy became the guaranteeing of the American market. This was accomplished in 1875–1876, when a treaty of commercial reciprocity was negotiated. It provided for the duty-free entry of Hawaiian sugar to the United States, giving the islands a great advantage over other foreign producers competing in that market.

In political terms, reciprocity bound Hawaii's general interests more closely still to the United States. Domestically, reciprocity turned Hawaii into a plantation society, which it remained in substance until well into the twentieth century.

For sugar, the large plantation was the logical producing unit. The idea of Hawaii as a nation of small independent farmers became obsolete without ever having been realized. Changes in land ownership inaugurated in the 1840s (the Great Mahele) introduced the idea of land held in fee simple. In 1850 a new law permitted foreigners to buy and sell land. This was the beginning of the era of large estates in Western hands. Sugar made big landholdings necessary; the reciprocity treaty made them, with good management, highly profitable. Just before the reciprocity treaty was passed, Hawaii was exporting about 25 million pounds of sugar; by 1890, 250 million pounds. By 1900, Hawaii was supplying 10 percent of the United States sugar market.

This process of accumulation and exploitation of land for sugar set the course of politics as well as commerce, and in addition transformed society at large. One part of the transformation was directly observable in human terms. The cultivation of sugar demanded a large labor force. The Hawaiians themselves would certainly not supply it. Disease had made terrible inroads among them. The Hawaiian population at the time of Cook was between 200,000 and 300,000. A century later, at the time of reciprocity, it was less then 60,000. According to one estimate made in the 1870s there were no more, than 5,000 able-bodied Hawaiian men available for plantation work.

A good part of the ingenuity of government and private enterprise was directed toward ensuring a steady supply of labor. Two lines of thought, not always compatible, emerged. First, the plantations had to be served. Second, it would be good if the population of Hawaii could somehow be replenished at the same time. Pacific islanders were tried, briefly and unsuccessfully, as laborers. Inquiries were made about India as a possible source of supply. Malaysia was discussed. Periodically, the argument was made that the islands would be better off with more white men; but it was generally acknowledged (and unsuccessful experiments bore it out) that plantation labor was not suitable work for imported whites, except perhaps for Mediterranean types such as Portuguese, some thousands of whom were recruited.

Out of all this, in the end, grew the practical consensus that first China and then Japan would have to be the sources of labor. The first

Chinese under contract arrived in 1852. By the mid-1860s there were more Chinese males in the islands than white males. The first group of Japanese arrived in 1868, but not until 1887 did the large-scale, continuous importation of laborers from the southern provinces of Japan begin. Recruitment of Japanese stemmed, in fact, from the planters' dissatisfaction with Chinese. Contracts ran for several years; at the end of the term, a good many Chinese chose not to renew their work agreements. Unable in most cases to pay their way back to China, they went to the towns, especially Honolulu, looking for work. The Japanese in their turn followed much the same pattern of movement. Among neither the Chinese nor the Japanese in the nineteenth century was there a good balance between men and women—it was in the interest of the planters to recruit young single men as laborers—and so the question of population as against labor supply remained unsettled.

The establishment of the sugar industry—more exactly, the emergence of a white planter class with its affiliates of businessmen and professional men in Honolulu—began to work changes in the mood of Hawaiian politics from the 1860s on. In crude terms, the influential white man in the islands was finding less and less of worth and usefulness in the native Hawaiian. Earlier in the century, missionary orthodoxy held that the Hawaiian possessed many good qualities, and that with Christian help he could very likely be saved from himself. The orthodoxy of the sugar planter, the businessman, the lawyer, and the white civil servant of the prosperous reciprocity era was that Western industry and ingenuity produced all that was good in the islands. Hawaiians, by contrast, could not sustain themselves—as workers, as taxpayers, as useful citizens, even as a people: they appeared, indeed, to be dying out. Toward the end of the nineteenth century, the rationale of social Darwinist thinking began to be applied in the islands: perhaps the Hawaiians were unfit to survive, biologically, culturally, and historically; perhaps the whites were fated to rule.

The fifth and last of the Kamehamehas, Lot (1863–1872), died without an heir. His successor, William Lunalilo (1872–1873), chosen in a royal election, was a bachelor. On his early death, a new election returned as king David Kalakaua (1874–1891). In his reign, which spanned almost exactly the years of reciprocity under the kingdom, the question of the political control of the islands became acute, and as often as not the question was put in racial terms.

The planters had a point. It was their productivity that kept the kingdom going. The Hawaiians had a point, too. They were, they felt, being pushed off the land by whites. Kalakaua reigned over a polarized citizenry, white and brown (for political purposes, the alien Orientals, though increasing in numbers, were negligible). He emerged more and more, in white eyes at least, as a champion of brown against white. He was, in addition, a king of expensive tastes and strong monarchical principles, or at least practices.

For several years, Kalakaua and his leading adviser Walter Murray Gibson were allied with the wealthy sugar grower, steamship owner, and financier, Claus Spreckels, who had made his millions in California and used his money to get a toehold, then a foothold, then a near stranglehold on the political economy of Hawaii. The majority of the planters, and especially those descended from Protestant missionary families, regarded Spreckels as a dangerous interloper, and Gibson and Kalakaua together as the embodiment of the irresponsible government.

Throughout the 1880s, the political situation became more and more unstable. Eventually, the rule of Kalakaua and Gibson became intolerable to the leading taxpayers of the kingdom and their adherents. On June 30, 1887, in a bloodless revolution involving a few hundred men under arms but no shots fired in anger, Gibson was ousted and Kalakaua was compelled to assent to a new constitution, which reduced him to not much more than ceremonial status. Legislative, executive, and judicial power were lodged with the propertied (largely white) minority, and the vote was denied to about two-thirds of the native population.

From this time on, talk of annexation of Hawaii by the United States was heard more and more openly. The year of the revolution, 1887, was also the year of the renewal of the reciprocity treaty. The

Seal of the Republic, 1894–1900.

Source: Hawaii State Archives

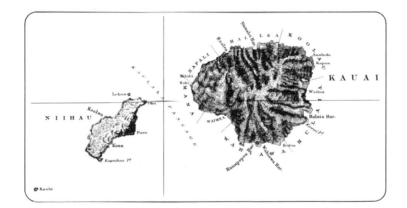

This map of the island of Kauai, dated 1841, is reproduced from a map of the Hawaiian Islands prepared by the U.S. Exploring Expedition of 1838–1841, led by Charles Wilkes. Other portions of the map appear on pages 102 and 105.

Photograph by Robert P. Campbell

revolutionary Reform Party negotiated, along with the renewal, an agreement by which the United States would have exclusive rights to the use of Pearl Harbor as a naval station. In July 1889, an abortive counterrevolution took place at Honolulu. A part-Hawaiian named Robert Wilcox and several dozen followers occupied Iolani Palace briefly and had to be driven out by gunfire and explosives. Wilcox's politics were by no means clear, but he was certainly anti-Reform. In 1890 the United States revised its tariff policy, to the great detriment of the Hawaiian sugar industry, and in the depression that followed in the

Seal of the Territory, 1900–1959.
Source: Hawaii State Archives

Hawaiian Islands from Oahu to Maui. Part of
Wilkes' map of 1841 (see page 101).
Photograph by Robert P. Campbell

islands, the arguments for annexation were renewed.

Kalakaua did not live to see the outcome. He died in February 1891, in the course of a visit to California. His successor was his sister Liliuokalani (1891–1893), first queen of Hawaii in her own right and last ruler of the monarchy. Liliuokalani, even more than Kalakaua, was insistent that the reigning monarch should control the kingdom on behalf of the Hawaiian people. For this purpose, the Reform constitution was an unsuitable instrument. The queen's views were well known among her enemies, and for them this was a powerful political reason to be added to their economic reasons for wanting annexation to the United States. Early in 1892 Lorrin Thurston, one of the leading revolutionaries of 1887, formed a secret Annexation Club.

Between mid-1892 and early 1893, legislative affairs were more than ordinarily confused, with four changes of cabinet and innumerable arguments over two pieces of legislation favored by the queen as means to improve the revenues of the crown—a national lottery and a scheme to license the sale of opium.

On Saturday, January 14, 1893, the queen prorogued the legislature and prepared to make public her new constitution. Lorrin Thurston and the other annexationists formed themselves into a revolutionary Committee of Safety. They consulted United States Minister to Hawaii John L. Stevens and the commander of USS *Boston*, a warship stationed at Honolulu, and composed a proclamation announcing the end of the monarchy and the formation of a provisional government, with the aim of annexation.

The revolutionaries armed themselves and took to the streets of Honolulu on Tuesday, January 17, to secure the government buildings. American troops from the *Boston* were ashore; Minister Stevens was more than ready to recognize the revolutionary regime. The proclamation was read. Resistance was minimal: the only casualty was one man shot in the shoulder. By nightfall on Tuesday the revolution was over; the queen had surrendered, as she put it, to superior force, under protest, and in the expectation that the United States Congress would not countenance the support given the revolutionaries by Minister Stevens.

The provisional government immediately proposed the joining of Hawaii and the United States by annexation. Unfortunately for the revolutionaries, at Washington the Republican administration of Benjamin Harrison was being succeeded at that moment by the Democratic administration of Grover Cleveland. Investigations were ordered by Cleveland, and the report convinced him that the monarchy would not have been overthrown without the aid of Minister Stevens. On this basis, Cleveland found the revolutionaries' offer of annexation unacceptable and directed that the monarchy be restored.

The revolutionaries refused to retrace their steps. They repeated their wish for annexation and, while waiting for a change of heart at Washington, brought into being their own republic under the presidency of Sanford B. Dole, a highly regarded politician descended from a Protestant missionary family. The new regime was inaugurated on July 4, 1894.

The royalists, regarding themselves as unjustly abandoned by the Cleveland administration, plotted a counterrevolution. For ten days following a shooting on January 6, 1895, Honolulu was under arms again. The royalists were easily defeated and their leaders tried for treason. Liliuokalani, under house arrest, signed a document of abdication and was sentenced, in her married name of Mrs. John O. Dominis, to five years at hard labor and a fine of $5,000. The sentence was later reduced. By November 1896 she was free, a citizen with full rights once more.

By then, too, the prospects for annexation were better. At Washington, Cleveland was being succeeded by the Republican William McKinley, whose administration was sure to be cordial to the acquisition of the islands. The United States Senate discussed an annexation treaty, and when it appeared as though a majority favored it, but not the essential two-thirds majority, the idea of a joint resolution of annexation by simple majority in each house of Congress was substituted.

Arguments against acquiring Hawaii centered on the idea that the United States was traditionally a continental power, without noncontiguous territories. Then, too, it was pointed out that the racially mixed population of Hawaii, where whites of American origin were a small (if powerful) minority, was not traditionally regarded as the best raw material for American politics and society.

It would take some powerful arguments to overcome these negative propositions. In the end, annexation was one product of war between the United States and Spain in 1898. The United States went to war with Spain over Cuba, then a Spanish holding in the Caribbean. Part of the United States' broad strategy was to embarrass the Spanish empire in its Pacific holdings, particularly the Philippines. The spectacular success of the United States Navy in this arena brought into national prominence for the first time the possibility that the United States could enter the twentieth century as a great Pacific power, with territories spread across the ocean all the way to Asia. In this reading of the "manifest destiny" of the American people, Hawaii assumed a strategic and geopolitical importance outweighing its demographic doubtfulness. The joint resolution of annexation, which had been hanging fire, quickly passed both houses of Congress, and President McKinley signed it on July 7. The transfer of sovereignty took place on August 12 in Honolulu. Under organic legislation which took effect in 1900, Hawaii became a territory of the United States.

The revolutionaries of 1887 and 1893 and the annexationists of the period up to 1898 could congratulate themselves. They would always have said that, in opposing and then overthrowing the monarchy, they were basing their actions on American ideas of what was good in government. The planters as well could be pleased, in one sense at least. Now that Hawaii was a domestic rather than a foreign producer of sugar, the great industry of the islands was no longer at the mercy of changes in American tariff policy. From the point of view of labor supply, however, annexation might mean difficulty for the sugar men. The United States, late in the nineteenth and early in the twentieth century, was moving toward ending the admission of Oriental immigrants. Once Hawaii became part of the nation, this policy would apply in the islands as on the mainland. In practice, at annexation, Chinese were already barred from immigrating. The likelihood was that Japanese in their turn would be excluded: no more new migrants would be permitted.

The planters responded by bringing in as many Japanese workers as possible before any ban might take effect, more than 70,000 between 1896 and 1907. Even this was not enough to supply the still-expanding sugar industry (and the relatively new pineapple industry, which at its height later in the twentieth century would provide about 75 percent of the world's canned pineapple). Looking for yet another source of cheap field labor, the planters turned to the Philippines—a highly suitable place, since it had fallen under the American flag in the war with Spain in 1898, and thus no problems existed in bringing in Filipinos. Between 1907 and 1946, some 120,000 Filipino workers were recruited.

The idea put forward at times in the nineteenth century that "cognate races" could be found, similar to the Hawaiian, to strengthen the native element of the population, seemed merely strange by the twentieth century. Chinese married Hawaiians in some numbers; so did Filipinos in their turn; Japanese too, but in fewer numbers. The result of this, together with the growth of a second generation of Orientals, children of migrants, was a distinctively local population; but the simple days of a population composed only of Hawaiians and whites were gone forever.

As for the Hawaiian proper, his fate was still very much in doubt. The population figures of the twentieth century showed a diminishing pure Hawaiian group, an increasing part-Hawaiian group. For a variety of reasons, it was felt that special provision should be made for those who identified themselves as Hawaiians. One expression of this feeling was the establishment of the Kamehameha Schools, begun in 1887, lavishly endowed from the revenues of the Bishop Estate, whose landholdings, the most extensive in the islands, were derived from the former estates of the Kamehameha dynasty. Another program designed especially for Hawaiians came into being with the Hawaiian Homes Commission Act of 1920. It was intended to rehabilitate Hawaiians disadvantaged by urban society, by giving them the chance to farm on homesteads held on long leases at nominal rents.

Whatever directions the various ethnic groups took in the early decades of the twentieth century, political, economic, and social leadership remained very much in the hands of the men who had engineered revolution and annexation, together with their associates and descendants. The era of reciprocity had centralized the sugar industry greatly. The twentieth century carried centralization further, until a complex of firms, popularly known as the Big Five, emerged with almost total control. These five—Castle and Cooke, Alexander and Baldwin, C. Brewer, Theo. H. Davies, and American Factors—produced and marketed 75 percent of the sugar crop in 1910, 96 percent in 1933. They also controlled, by stock ownership and interlocking directorates, the bulk of the territory's banking, insurance, utilities, wholesale and retail commerce, and transportation.

Inevitably, they controlled politics as well. Their brand of business conservatism was stamped on the policies of every gubernatorial administration from annexation to World War II. Eight out of every ten legislators elected during the same period were Republicans.

As paternalistic societies went, Hawaii was sufficiently enlightened. Agricultural workers were paid, on the average, more than many unskilled industrial workers on the mainland. Management was ready to make some concessions in matters of health and welfare (largely, of course, in order to turn aside attempts at labor organization). Public education up to a certain level was available to the children of im-

Seal of the State, 1959.

Source: Hawaii State Archives

103

State Flag.

Source: Hawaii State Archives

TERRITORIAL GOVERNORS

Sanford B. Dole	1900–1903
George R. Carter	1903–1907
Walter F. Frear	1907–1913
Lucius E. Pinkham	1913–1918
Charles J. McCarthy	1918–1921
Wallace R. Farrington	1921–1929
Lawrence M. Judd	1929–1934
Joseph B. Poindexter	1934–1942
Ingram M. Stainback	1942–1951
Oren E. Long	1951–1953
Samuel W. King	1953–1957
William F. Quinn	1957–1959

migrant laborers. Still, until World War II the territory could by no means be described as an open society. The plantation was the model for all other institutions, and its hierarchies of power were ethnically determined.

Some extremely serious long-term issues could not be damped down by such a society. If Hawaiians, perforce, accepted in large numbers their position as clients of the ruling white minority, Orientals in larger numbers did not. As, increasingly, the immigrant laboring population was supplemented by a second generation of Orientals born in the islands and thus American by citizenship, the prospect of basic social change became apparent. It could be seen in the population figures, census period by census period.

The issue was essentially simple. The original Oriental plantation laborer was not expected to be a full member of society. The second generation, citizens by birth, could not constitutionally be denied full membership in that society. If the Orientals came into their own politically, this would mean the end of the era of unchallenged control by the Big Five. By 1936 one out of every four voters was Japanese.

Increasingly, the Japanese population became the focus of the problem. First, it was by far the biggest single element in the Oriental population. Second, its percentage of the total population kept growing because of births in the islands, even after immigration from Japan was halted, and this meant that the proportion of citizen Japanese to alien Japanese was growing. Third, and this was a great complication, Japan and the United States, by mid-thirties, were headed toward war.

The Japanese attack on Pearl Harbor at 7:55 a.m. on Sunday, December 7, 1941, opened another era in Hawaii's history. The damage to the Pacific Fleet at Pearl Harbor and to airplanes on the ground at nearby bases constituted the worst military disaster in American history. Martial law was declared immediately, and the islands remained under curfew and blackout restrictions until close to the end of the war.

Military courts took over law enforcement, and though their legality was challenged periodically, it was not until 1946 that the United States Supreme Court ruled against the military in this respect.

The apparent justification for the harshness of the military government was, of course, the presence of such a large population of Japanese, citizen and alien. They were too numerous by far to be interned, as were California's Japanese, and at the same time their loyalty was regarded as so problematic that martial law seemed necessary. Among Japanese of military age there were very few aliens. It was this group that settled, actually and symbolically, the question of loyalty. A volunteer fighting force composed of Nisei, or Americans of Japanese ancestry (AJAs), was formed, called the 100th Battalion, later incorporated in the 442nd Regimental Combat Team. This unit distinguished itself greatly in the European theater, becoming the most highly decorated unit in the armed forces of the United States.

The veterans of the 442nd, many of them with law degrees earned under the GI Bill of Rights, became the nucleus of the postwar Democratic Party, challenging and finally—in 1954—dislodging from power the long-entrenched Republican Party. In the territorial legislature of that year, one out of every two members was an AJA.

This was one great victory in the general postwar emancipation of the Oriental. Another great change, associated with the political victory, was the rise of an extremely powerful labor movement. There had in fact been strikes against sugar and pineapple management since early in the century, some of them involving violence, and one, in 1924 on Kauai, resulting in the deaths of sixteen strikers by gunfire. As late, almost, as World War II, the general basis of labor organization had been ethnic identity; thus there had been Japanese strikes or Filipino strikes, often limited to a handful of plantations. Ethnic divisions in the labor force made it easier for management to break strikes. Not until class solidarity was substituted for ethnic identity as an organizing principle did the labor movement succeed. This substitution was accomplished within the framework of federal labor legislation of the New Deal period. The union leader of note during this period, indeed from the late thirties to the late sixties, was Jack Hall of the ILWU. His union, considered as a political and economic force, came to equal the Big Five in influence. With more than 30,000 members in a total population of 500,000 in the late forties, it had decisive strength, as was shown by a paralyzing dock strike in 1949.

At the height of the cold war, during the McCarthy period of American politics, the ILWU was regarded as being the instrument of a Communist conspiracy in Hawaii. On the basis of congressional hearings held by the House Un-American Activities Committee, Jack Hall and six others, most of them with union connections, were charged under the Smith Act with conspiring to teach the overthrow of the United States government by force and violence. They were convicted in 1953. Their appeals were eventually sustained in 1958, by which time the issue of Communism within the United States was generally rather less heated than it had been earlier in the fifties.

The Communist issue in Hawaii became embroiled with the issue of statehood, which assumed greater importance every year in the postwar period. The islands had been American soil since 1898, with territorial status. The question of statehood for Hawaii began to be raised seriously before World War II, with congressional hearings in the islands in 1935 and 1937. That the question was not resolved in Hawaii's favor until 1959 can be attributed to the issue of Communism as much as to anything else (except, perhaps a residual distrust of Hawaii's multi-racialism, manifesting itself among some Southern senators).

There was never anything in the exhaustive public record to show that the problem of Communism in Hawaii was more serious than that on the mainland at the same time. In itself, then, if logic had prevailed, the problem should not have interfered with Hawaii's progress toward statehood. It was such a powerful emotional issue, however, that it tended to obscure other considerations put forward in Hawaii's favor.

At the time of annexation, no arrangements were made for Hawaii's ultimate transition from territory to state. This in itself was somewhat unusual: in the past, new areas had been acquired on the assumption that they would become states. Hawaii, though, was such an unusual acquisition that past practices apparently did not hold. Thus, even as Hawaii met one test after another regarding statehood, there was a lingering reluctance on the part of Congress to grant the islands equal status with the mainland states.

Territorial status carried with it certain disabilities. American citizens in Hawaii, for example, could not vote in presidential elections. Hawaii had an elected delegate to Congress, but he had no vote. Hawaii thus had virtually no formal voice at Washington, no bargaining power, no way of ensuring (to take one case which mattered) that Hawaii got its reasonable share of federal tax disbursements. Washington controlled Hawaii's local affairs more closely than it did those of sovereign states. Governors of Hawaii were appointed by the president; so were high court judges. The basis of all this was the organic legislation framed for Hawaii by Congress after annexation. This organic law itself could be altered at any time by Congress.

Two episodes in the thirties, each in its own way, prompted reconsideration of Hawaii's status. First, the Massie case of 1931, involving the alleged rape of a Navy officer's wife by five young men of nonwhite ancestry and the subsequent killing of one of the men by the woman's family, was given nationwide publicity. Hawaii was portrayed in the sensational press as uncivilized, unsafe, unfit for self-determination. Congressional committees for a time discussed putting the islands under a naval commission, which would have been a retrograde step from territorial status. Second, in 1934, Congress passed the Jones-Costagan Act, under which Hawaii was classed for sugar importation purposes with offshore and foreign producers. Hawaii's share of the mainland market was cut, and it was made vulnerable to future cuts. The Big Five, up to this time, had considered territorial status generally satisfactory: with a powerful lobby at Washington, big business had been able to protect its interests, have a voice in presidential appointments to Hawaii, and so on. From the time of the Jones-Costagan Act onward, some businessmen, and more as time went on, argued that the only real guarantee for the sugar industry would be statehood—indisputable equality of status.

World War II gave the supporters of statehood positive evidence of Hawaii's readiness. Hawaii suffered Pearl Harbor, bore martial law, and supplied some of the best fighting men on the Allied side. These arguments were marshalled by the Hawaii Statehood Commission, together with more prosaic figures about population, literacy, earning power, and tax contributions to the federal treasury, all showing that Hawaii ranked with a number of already established states.

Not until the middle fifties was a strategy developed that would give the islands a better than even chance of admission. This involved linking Hawaii with Alaska, another candidate for statehood. In the end, Alaska was admitted before Hawaii, in 1958. This was a disappointment for Hawaii in a sense, but it also made further delays over Hawaii next to indefensible. The Senate finally passed a Hawaii statehood bill on March 11, 1959, and the House passed it on March 12. On June 27 a plebiscite in the islands ratified the congressional vote by a margin of 17 to one, indicating overwhelming approval. Admission day was set for August 21, and Hawaii became the fiftieth state.

In the years following statehood, Hawaii experienced tremendous change. In 1960, Honolulu's skyline was dominated by the ten-story Aloha Tower, and most of the 296,517 tourists who visited the Islands found accommodations in a scattering of Waikiki hotels that seldom rose above palm tree level. There were no resort facilities of note

Governor's Flag.

Source: Hawaii State Archives

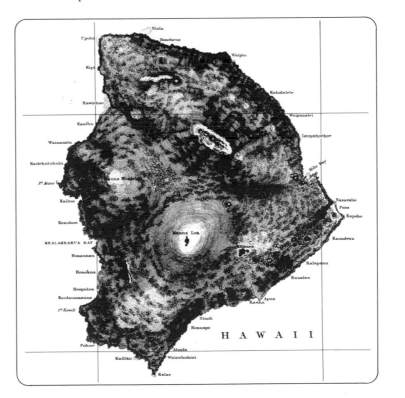

Island of Hawaii. Part of the Wilkes map of 1841 (see page 101).

Photograph by Robert P. Campbell

Arizona Memorial, Pearl Harbor.

Drawing by John A. Dixon

STATE GOVERNORS

William F. Quinn	1959–1962
John A. Burns	1962–1974
George R. Ariyoshi	1974–

elsewhere on Oahu or on any of the other islands. The resident population was 632,772 with citizens of Japanese ancestry the largest single ethnic component.

Federal spending (mainly defense), tourism, and agriculture (primarily sugar and pineapple) were central to the economy and responsible for revenues totalling $486 million, $131 million, and $150 million ($103 million from sugar and pineapple), respectively. Per capita income stood at $2,335, assessed real property values totalled $3 billion, and local tax collections produced $241 million. These and other activities generated a gross state product of $1.8 billion.

Twenty years later in 1980, Aloha Tower had disappeared amidst an array of glass and concrete towers stretching across the horizon from Pearl Harbor through central Honolulu to Waikiki. In conjuction with resort centers elsewhere throughout the State, these structures provided facilities for a burgeoning tourist industry which hosted 3,934,504 visitors, offices for a business community which had expanded and diversified, and housing for much of a resident population that had grown to 964,691. Of this total, citizens of white ancestry, due largely to heavy immigration after 1960, had become the largest single ethnic component.

Income from federal spending, tourism, and agriculture were still central to the economy, but at altered levels of significance. Federal spending remained the prime source of income with outlays of $3.3 billion. However, with revenues estimated at $3.0 billion, tourism had moved to a position of equal importance. Agriculture had fallen behind with production valued at less than $1 billion ($824 million from sugar and pineapple), while light manufacturing, construction, and other diversified economic activities had begun to make their presence felt. Per capita income had risen to $9,787, assess real property values had increased to $22 billion, and local tax collections had climbed to $1.3 billion. Reflecting these changes, the gross state product stood at an estimated $11.4 billion.

Although Hawaii enjoyed progress across a broad front during these years, events of the later 1970s demonstrated that it had not come unencumbered. Growing dependence on tourism rendered the economy subject to global trends largely immune to local control, a development that became painfully apparent when tourism peaked and then stagnated. Development to accommodate increasing numbers of tourists and residents changed Oahu and portions of Kauai, Maui, and Hawaii into densely populated, highrise urban centers, in the process consuming acres of once productive agricultural land. Ever-rising production costs made sugar and pineapple less competitive on world markets and threatened to drive them into extinction well in advance of the development of replacement crops. Declining employment opportunities and soaring housing costs forced many younger people to leave

the islands in search of opportunities. Worries about the increasingly Americanized physical and social environment caused resentment among native Hawaiian and other long-time local residents, and racial feeling—or at least its open expression—became more pronounced than at any time in the recent past. Hence, Hawaii's boom years came to be tempered by a remarkable degree of doubt and pessimism.

Political developments of this era paralleled the socioeconomic changes. After World War II, the long-dormant Democrats arose as a reform party to challenge the aging Republican oligarchy that had ruled almost since Annexation. Led by John A. Burns, they scored their first major victory in 1954, and by 1962, when Burns himself was elected Governor, they had taken almost total control of the State. Transformed by events into practical establishmentarians, they built a coalition of labor, capital, and ethnic groups which took the lead in promoting the post-statehood boom. However, as doubts about the course of this phenomenon arose in the 1970s, their resolve faltered. Internal factions developed, and the Republicans, purged of their territorial era perspectives and less hampered by doubts about an appropriate future, began serious planning for a comeback in the elections of the 1980s.

Hawaii thus entered its third decade of statehood evaluating both its past and its future. While the general outcome of this effort may be predictable, its more specific oscillations are not.

G.D.

was exceptionally high. There was also some out-migration, particularly among young men recruited by whaling captains.

Government and business leaders were deeply concerned about this rapid depopulation and took various steps to counteract it. A Board of Health was created in 1850, and the first large general hospital was built in 1859. The decline in the labor force was stemmed by importing plantation labor from abroad: Chinese beginning in 1852, Japanese from 1868, Portuguese starting in 1878, Puerto Ricans in 1901, Koreans in 1904, and Filipinos initially in 1907, as well as a number of smaller groups from other countries. This organized immigration, together with a growing number of foreigners arriving on an individual basis, became sufficient by the mid-1870s to counterbalance the natural decrease in population, and the total count began to rise.

Growth was rapid from 1876 until the end of World War II as birth rates rose, mortality dropped, and immigrants poured into the island chain. The population had increased to 80,578 in 1884, 154,001 in 1900, 255,881 in 1920, and 422,770 in 1940. War in the Pacific forced this curve sharply upward, and by mid-1944 there were an estimated 859,000 persons in the Territory, including 407,000 members of the armed forces and 65,000 civilian defense workers.

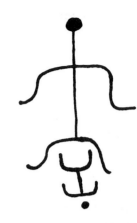

Petroglyph: birth scene, Kahaluu, Hawaii.

POPULATION

Number and Distribution of Inhabitants

The total resident population of Hawaii in 1980 was 964,691, according to final results of the decennial U.S. Census. This total was probably three or four times as large as the population two centuries earlier, on the eve of Captain Cook's arrival, and it was almost eighteen times the total in 1876, when Hawaii's population reached its lowest level in modern times.

Nobody knows the exact population of the Hawaiian Islands when they were first seen by Europeans. Captain James King, who completed Cook's account of the expedition after Cook's death, published an all-island estimate of 400,000, but one of his officers, Lt. William Bligh, guessed 242,200, and Captain George Dixon, a visitor in 1787, preferred a contact total of only 200,000. Most modern authorities have recommended estimates for 1778 ranging from 250,000 to 300,000.

Whatever the correct total at that time, it soon fell off precipitously and continued to decline for almost a century. In 1823 the newly arrived American missionaries estimated that there were about 140,000 inhabitants in the islands. They conducted actual censuses in 1831–1832 and 1835–1836, counting 130,313 the first time and 108,579 the second time. The first complete census taken by the Hawaiian government reported 84,165 in 1850. The low point was reached early in 1876, when only an estimated 53,900 persons lived in the Hawaiian Kingdom.

There were many reasons for this decline. The early navigators introduced gonorrhea, which caused sterility, and syphilis, which resulted in stillbirths. Many Hawaiians died in epidemics of previously unknown diseases, including *okuu* (probably cholera) in 1804, influenza in the 1820s, mumps in 1839, measles, whooping cough, and influenza in 1848–1849, and smallpox in 1853. Kamehameha's wars late in the eighteenth century resulted in battlefield deaths and famine. Fertility was surprisingly low, and infant mortality (some of it from infanticide)

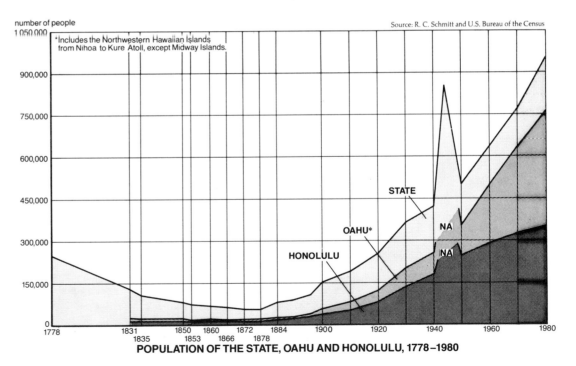

POPULATION OF THE STATE, OAHU AND HONOLULU, 1778–1980

Hawaiian arts and crafts: stamp design for clothing.
Bishop Museum drawing from Te Rangi Hiroa (1964:200)

The years following the end of World War II witnessed an initial period of decline followed by a resumption of past growth trends. Military cutbacks, extensive strikes in sugar, pineapple, and shipping industries, and the effects of a mainland recession triggered a sizeable net out-migration during the late 1940s and early 1950s, resulting in a postwar low of 498,000 reached in mid-1950. Increased military expenditures and burgeoning tourism reversed this net outflow after 1954, and the population increased from 505,000 in that year to 622,000 on the eve of statehood and 770,000 by 1970. The 1981 estimate was 981,000.

Recent totals appear even greater if the population is defined on a de facto basis. As indicated, the total resident population on April 1, 1980, was 964,691. This figure included 57,056 members of the armed forces (including many aboard Navy and Coast Guard ships home-ported in Hawaii), 64,023 civilian dependents of these island-based personnel, and 843,612 other civilians. It also included an estimated 9,635 Hawaii residents temporarily out of the State on business or vacation, but excluded an estimated 97,603 tourists and other visitors temporarily present. If the number of persons actually in the State on the census date is calculated, it comes to 1,052,659, or 9.1 percent more than the resident count.

Almost four-fifths of Hawaii's residents live on Oahu, an island which accounts for only 9.2 percent of the total land area of the State. This concentration has been building up for more than a century: Oahu had 22.9 percent of the all-island total in 1831, 38.0 percent in 1900, 61.0 percent in 1940, and 81.9 percent in 1970, before falling off to 79.0 percent in 1980. The population of the other islands until recently declined not only in relative terms but also in absolute terms. Their combined total reached a modern peak in 1930 with 165,413, and then, with mechanization of agriculture, fell quickly to 132,363 by 1960. Resort development sparked a resurgence of growth thereafter, and their 1980 population was 202,126. Long-term trends in some percentage distributions are as follows:

	1831	1878	1910	1940	1970	1980
Oahu	23%	35%	43%	61%	82%	79%
Honolulu	10	24	27	42	42	38
Rest of Oahu	13	11	16	19	40	41
Other islands	77	65	57	39	18	21
Urban	10	24	31	63	84	87
Rural	90	76	69	37	16	13

About half the current population of Oahu lives in Honolulu, the urban cluster officially described (for statistical purposes) as the area between Red Hill and Makapuu Point, between the crest of the Koolau Mountains and the southeastern shore of the island (page 126). The population of Honolulu proper has grown from 13,344 in 1831 to 39,306 in 1900, 179,358 in 1940, and 365,048 in 1980. The Honolulu Urbanized Area, a statistical entity defined for census purposes, consists of Honolulu itself and also the adjacent built-up area beyond Honolulu International Airport as far as Whitmore Village, Ewa, and Ewa Beach. The Urbanized Area, thus defined, had a 1980 population of 582,463. The Kailua-Kaneohe Urbanized Area, on the windward side of Nuuanu Pali, reported 105,712. The Honolulu Standard Metropolitan Statistical Area, another federally defined statistical unit, is the same as the City and County of Honolulu, and had 762,565 inhabitants in 1980.

Other urban places in the State are considerably less populous. In order of 1980 size they are: Pearl City, 42,575; Kailua, 35,812; Hilo (on Hawaii Island), 35,269; Aiea, 32,879; Kaneohe, 29,919; Waipahu, 29,139; and Mililani Town, 21,365. The twin cities of Wailuku and Kahului, Maui, had 10,260 and 12,978 residents, respectively. The largest towns on Kauai were Kapaa (4,467) and Lihue (4,000). Kaunakakai, Molokai, with 2,231, and Lanai City, Lanai, with 2,092, were the largest communities on those islands. Niihau is completely rural, and Kahoolawe is uninhabited. For the State as a whole, the urban population was 834,592 in 1980, or 86.5 percent of the total (page 126).

Population densities vary widely—from island to island and within major cities. For the State as a whole, the 1980 de facto density was 163.8 persons per square mile, or about the same as California, Michigan, or Florida. The City and County of Honolulu, however, had a density of 1,379.9, while the neighbor islands averaged only 39.6 and ranged from zero on Kahoolawe and 3.2 on Niihau to 105.5 on Maui. The 179 census tracts into which Oahu has been divided had 1980 resident densities as high as 71,067 in tract 62.02 (Kuhio Park Terrace) and 61,863 in tract 19.02 (Hobron Lane), and as low as 25.7 in tract 100 (Haleiwa-Kawailoa) and zero in tracts 68.03 (Mapunapuna) and 82 (Waipio Peninsula). These tract figures are resident densities rather than de facto densities, which would often be far higher. Waikiki, for example, had a 1980 resident population of 17,384 in its 628 acres, but this figure took no account of the 30,796 workers employed in the area (according to a 1975 survey), or the 43,000 or so nonresident guests in its 30,000 hotel rooms at peak times in 1980. The gross density of Waikiki could thus be given as either 17,721 or 93,000 per square mile, depending on the definition of "population."

R.C.S.

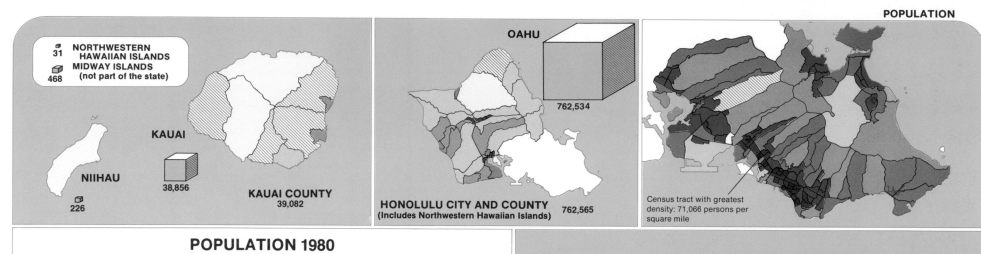

NORTHWESTERN HAWAIIAN ISLANDS 31
MIDWAY ISLANDS 468 (not part of the state)

NIIHAU
226

KAUAI
38,856

KAUAI COUNTY
39,082

OAHU
762,534

HONOLULU CITY AND COUNTY 762,565
(Includes Northwestern Hawaiian Islands)

Census tract with greatest density: 71,066 persons per square mile

POPULATION 1980
By Census Tracts for Oahu and Census Divisions for Other Islands

Persons Per Square Mile

25,000 or more	1500-4999	50-149
15,000-24,999	500-1499	11-49
5000-14,999	150-499	1-10

10   0   10   20   30 miles
10   0   10   20   30   40 kilometers

Source: U.S. Bureau of the Census

1980

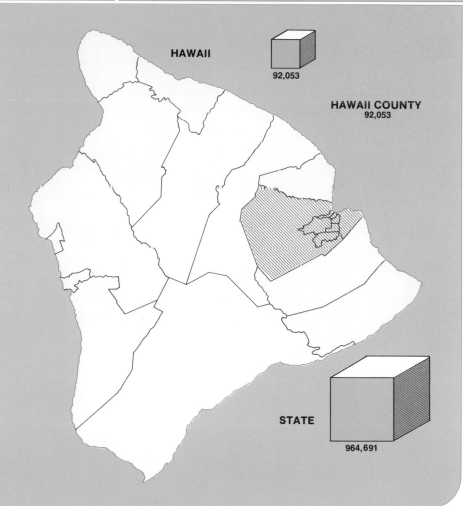

HAWAII
92,053

HAWAII COUNTY
92,053

STATE
964,691

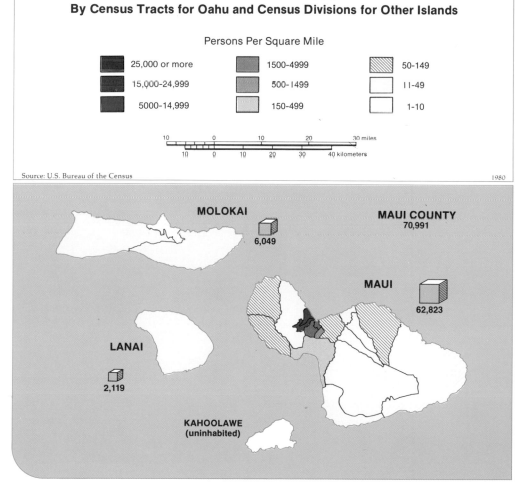

MOLOKAI
6,049

MAUI COUNTY
70,991

MAUI
62,823

LANAI
2,119

KAHOOLAWE
(uninhabited)

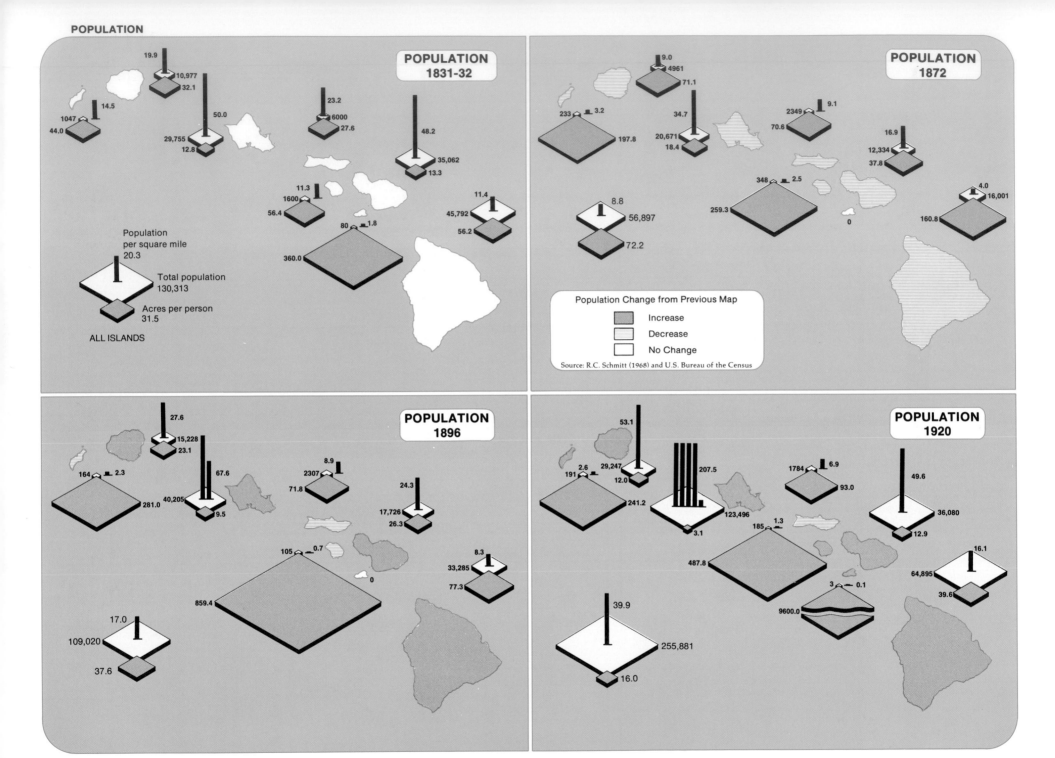

POPULATION
1831-32

Population
per square mile
20.3

Total population
130,313

Acres per person
31.5

ALL ISLANDS

POPULATION
1872

Population Change from Previous Map

Increase

Decrease

No Change

Source: R.C. Schmitt (1968) and U.S. Bureau of the Census

POPULATION
1896

POPULATION
1920

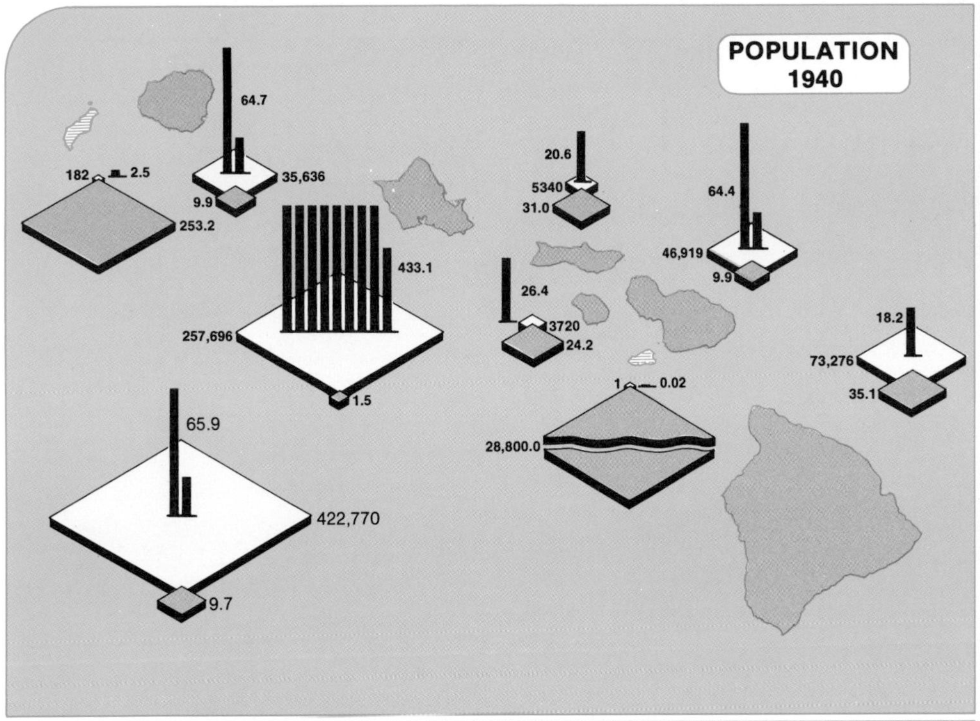

POPULATION
1940
64.7
182
2.5
35,636
9.9
253.2
20.6
5340
31.0
64.4
46,919
9.9
433.1
26.4
3720
24.2
257,696
18.2
73,276
35.1
1.5
1
0.02
65.9
28,800.0
422,770
9.7

Northwestern Hawaiian
Islands 15
POPULATION
1960
50.7
254
3.5
27,922
12.6
181.4
19.4
5023
33.0
49.1
35,717
13.0
841.0
15.0
2115
42.7
500,394
15.2
61,332
41.9
0
0.8
98.6
632,772
6.5

Northwestern Hawaiian
Islands 31
POPULATION
1970
53.6
29,524
237
3.3
11.9
194.4
20.3
5261
31.5
53.1
38,691
12.0
1059.7
15.6
2204
40.9
0
630,497
15.8
63,468
40.5
0.6
120.0
769,913
5.3

Northwestern Hawaiian
Islands 31
POPULATION
1980
70.2
226
3.1
38,856
9.0
197.1
23.2
6049
27.6
86.2
62,823
7.4
1286.5
762,534
15.2
2119
42.1
22.8
92,053
28.1
0.5
150.1
964,691
4.3

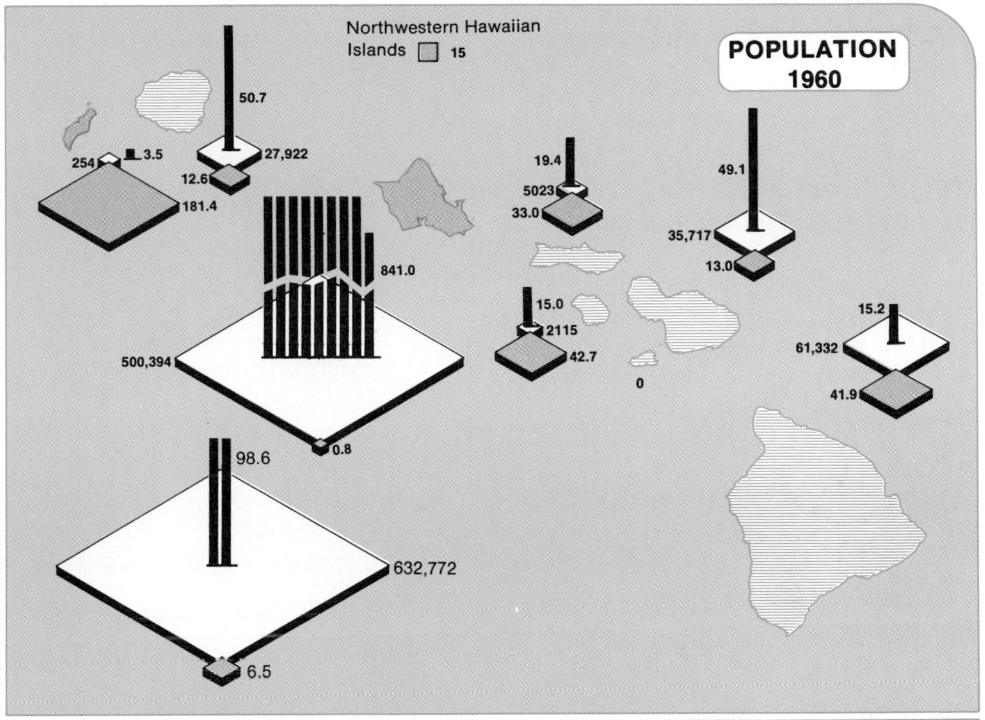

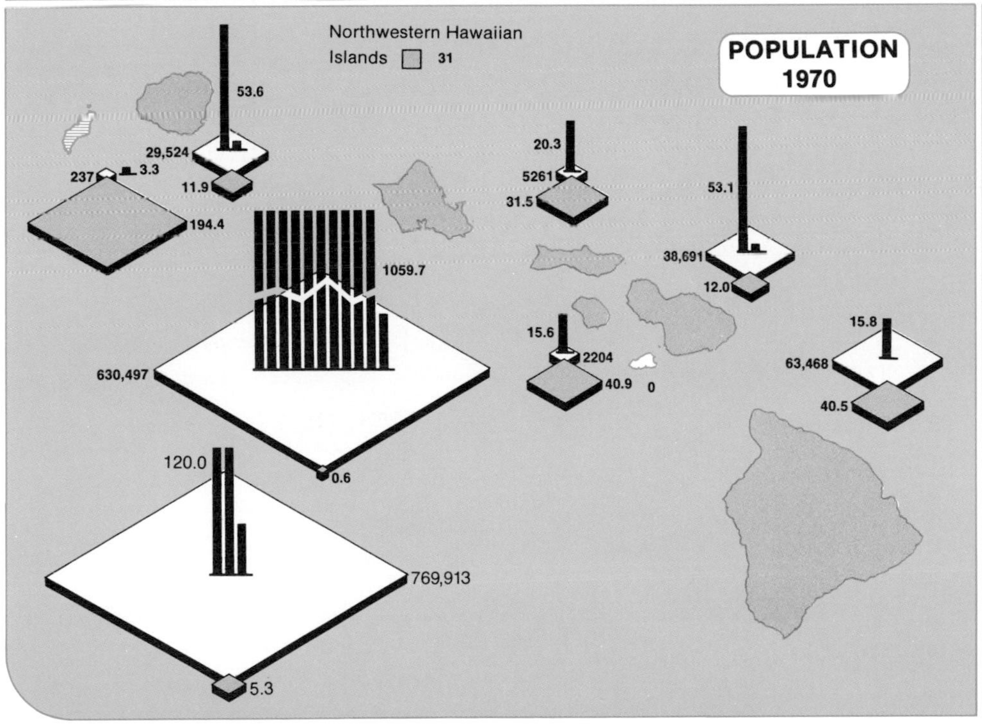

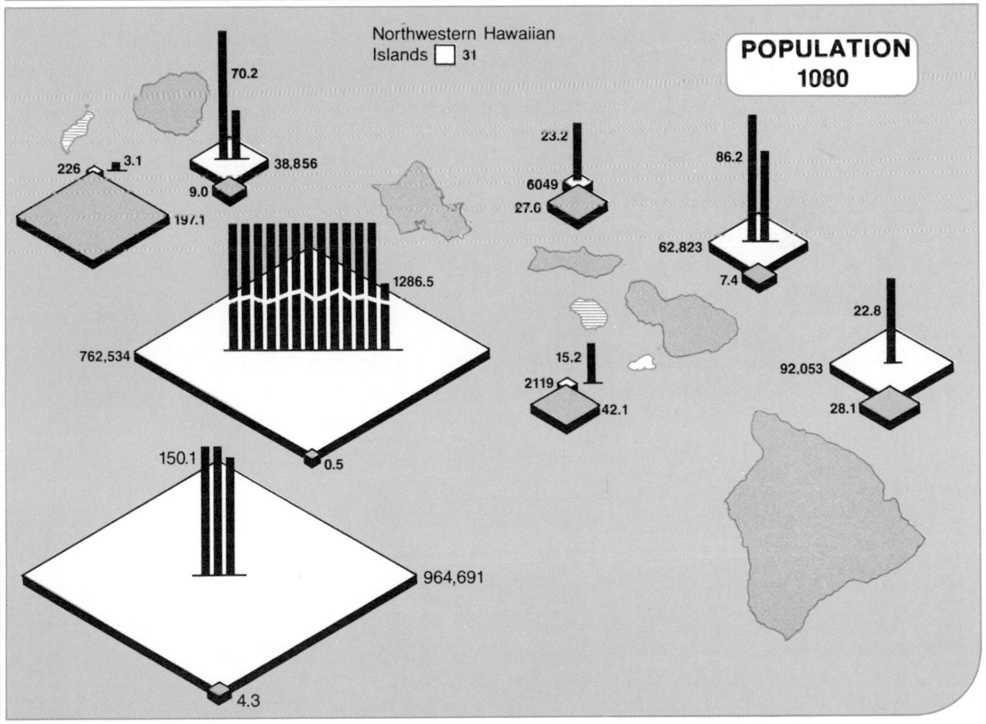

Demographic Characteristics

The population of Hawaii is relatively youthful; it has a surplus of males and includes a wide range of ethnic and national origins.

There were 105.2 males per 100 females in the 1980 resident total. The relative abundance of males was due in part to the large military population of the State and in part to the large number of older plantation workers who came to the islands as single men many years ago and never found wives.

Half of the residents in 1980 were under 28.3 years of age. Fully 28.6 percent were younger than 18, 63.5 percent were between 18 and 64, and only 7.9 percent were 65 years of age or older. The statewide median age rose from 21.7 years in 1930 to 23.2 in 1940 and 24.9 in 1950, dropped to 24.3 in 1960, and then increased to 25.0 in 1970 and 28.3 in 1980. It was 28.0 in the City and County of Honolulu, 29.4 in Hawaii County, 29.6 in Maui County, and 29.8 in Kauai County. In local areas, median ages ranged from 16.9 years in part of Schofield Barracks to 56.2 along the Waikiki shoreline and 58.1 at Kalaupapa Settlement.

The major ethnic groups are Caucasian and Japanese (pages 113 to 118). According to the results of a sample survey conducted by the Hawaii State Department of Health in 1980, approximately 26.3 percent of the non-barracks, non-institutional population was Caucasian (excluding Puerto Rican), 23.5 percent was Japanese, 17.9 percent was Part Hawaiian, 11.2 percent was Filipino, 9.4 percent was mixed other than Part Hawaiian, 5.1 percent was Chinese, 1.3 percent was Korean, 1.3 percent was Black, 1.2 percent was Samoan, 1.0 percent was unmixed Hawaiian, 0.7 percent was Puerto Rican, and 1.2 percent was other or unknown. These figures differ considerably from 1980 census totals, which arbitrarily combine all persons of mixed race (a fourth of the population and 47.8 percent of all births in 1980) with the race of the mother.

Ethnic distributions have changed greatly over the years. In 1853, 95.8 percent of the population was Hawaiian, 1.3 percent was Part Hawaiian, and 2.9 percent was non-Hawaiian. By 1910, only 13.6 percent was Hawaiian, 6.5 percent Part Hawaiian, and almost 80 percent non-Hawaiian, chiefly Japanese (41.5 percent) and Caucasian (23.0 percent). Growth since World War II has been greatest for the Caucasians, Filipinos, Koreans, Blacks, Samoans, and persons of mixed race.

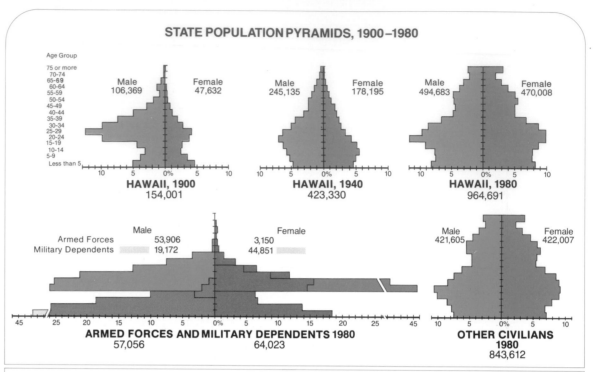

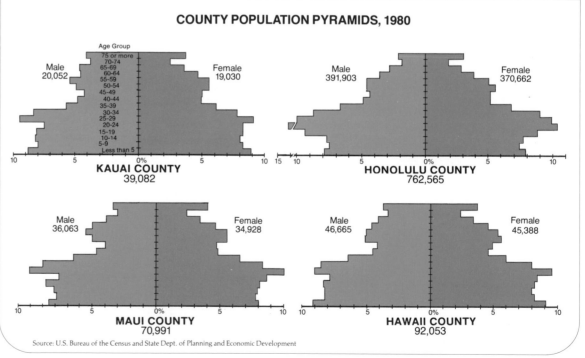

Source: U.S. Bureau of the Census and State Dept. of Planning and Economic Development

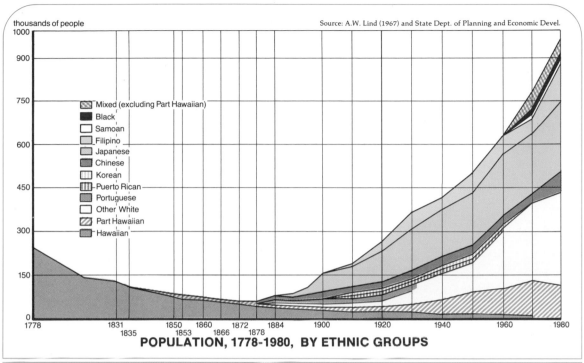

thousands of people

Source: A.W. Lind (1967) and State Dept. of Planning and Economic Devel.

Mixed (excluding Part Hawaiian)
Black
Samoan
Filipino
Japanese
Chinese
Korean
Puerto Rican
Portuguese
Other White
Part Hawaiian
Hawaiian

POPULATION, 1778-1980, BY ETHNIC GROUPS

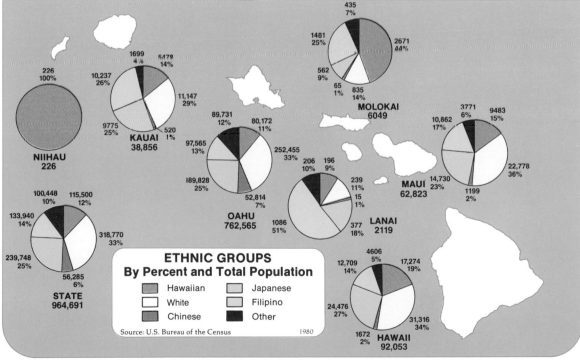

NIIHAU
226

226
100%

KAUAI
38,856

1699 4% 5479 14%
10,237 26%
11,147 29%
9775 25%
520 1%

OAHU
762,565

89,731 12% 80,172 11%
97,565 13%
252,455 33%
189,828 25%
52,814 7%

STATE
964,691

100,448 10% 115,500 12%
133,940 14%
318,770 33%
239,748 25%
56,285 6%

MOLOKAI
6049

435 7%
1481 25% 2671 44%
562 9%
65 1% 835 14%

LANAI
2119

206 10% 196 9%
239 11%
15 1%
1086 51% 377 18%

MAUI
62,823

3771 6% 9483 15%
10,862 17%
14,730 23%
22,778 36%
1199 2%

HAWAII
92,053

4606 5% 17,274 19%
12,709 14%
24,476 27%
31,316 34%
1672 2%

ETHNIC GROUPS
By Percent and Total Population

Hawaiian   Japanese
White   Filipino
Chinese   Other

Source: U.S. Bureau of the Census   1980

There are few ethnic enclaves in Hawaii. The best known are Niihau, a privately owned island populated entirely by Hawaiians and Part Hawaiians; Nanakuli, Waimanalo, and other communities under the jurisdiction of the Department of Hawaiian Home Lands, and thus given to concentrations of ethnic Hawaiians; and the large military bases on Oahu, with their clusters of mainland Caucasians and Blacks. The plantation "camps," once made up of single ethnic groups, have largely disappeared.

Most Hawaii residents were born in the islands, although a sizeable fraction is of mainland origin. The 1980 census reported that 57.8 percent were Hawaii-born, 25.8 percent were born elsewhere in the United States, and 16.4 percent foreign-born. Fifty years earlier, when the foreign-born were at their pre-1980 absolute peak at 121,209 (compared with 157,949 in 1980), they accounted for almost a third of the total:

	1872	1900	1930	1960	1980
Born in Hawaii	92.1%	38.3%	58.2%	66.6%	57.8%
Born on the mainland	1.6	2.8	8.2	22.6	25.8
Foreign born	6.4	58.9	32.9	10.9	16.4

The State had 294,052 households and 226,035 families in 1980 (page 126). Average household size was 3.15 individuals, compared with 3.59 in 1970, 3.87 in 1960, and 4.14 in 1950. Average household size ranged from 1.46 in Kalawao and 1.57 in downtown Honolulu to 5.51 on Niihau. Persons living in group quarters accounted for 4.1 percent of the State's population.

Among persons 15 years of age and over, 55.2 percent of the males and 56.8 percent of the females were currently married (and not separated) in 1980. These percentages have changed radically over the years with the changing balance of the sexes. In 1896, for example, only 34.4 percent of the males but 71.0 percent of the females were married. The number of unattached males per 1,000 unattached females rose from 1,919 in 1866 to 8,200 in 1900, then fell to 2,162 in 1940, 1,217 in 1970, and 1,101 in 1980.

113

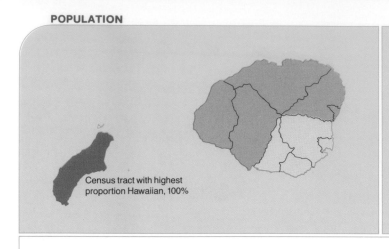

Census tract with highest
proportion Hawaiian, 100%

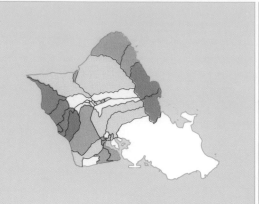

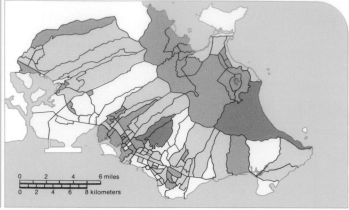

0   2   4   6 miles

0   2   4   6   8 kilometers

HAWAIIAN ETHNIC GROUP

Percent of Total Population in Each Census Tract

75 or more	10-24.9
50-74.9	5-9.9
25-49.9	0.1-4.9

0.0

10   0   10   20   30 miles

10   0   10   20   30   40 kilometers

Source: U.S. Bureau of the Census   1980

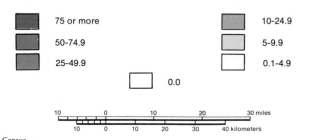

uninhabited

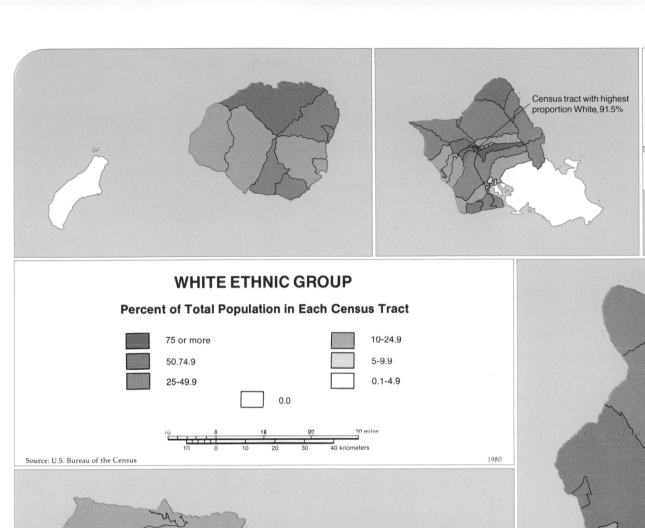

WHITE ETHNIC GROUP

Percent of Total Population in Each Census Tract

75 or more	10-24.9
50.74.9	5-9.9
25-49.9	0.1-4.9

0.0

Source: U.S. Bureau of the Census

1980

Census tract with highest proportion White, 91.5%

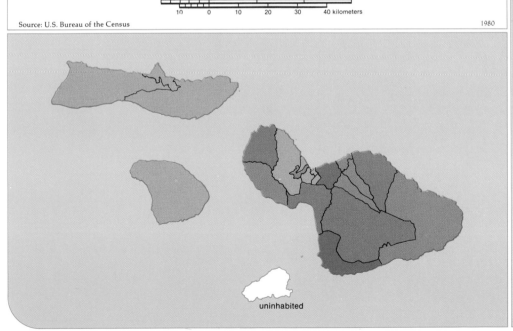

uninhabited

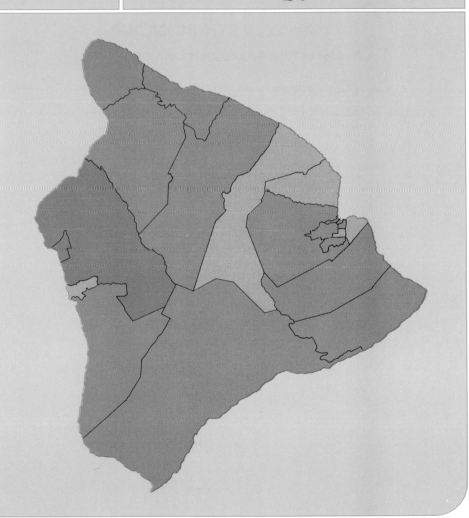

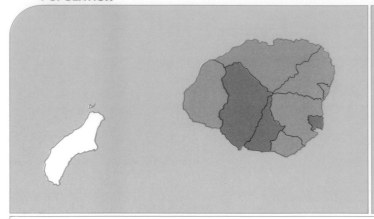

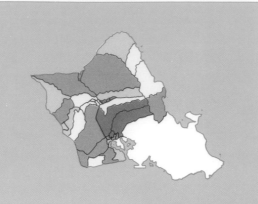

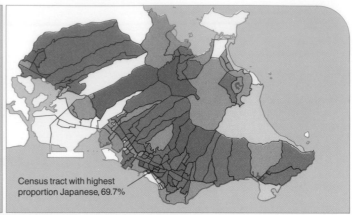

Census tract with highest
proportion Japanese, 69.7%

JAPANESE ETHNIC GROUP

Percent of Total Population in Each Census Tract

- 75 or more
- 50-74.9
- 25-49.9
- 10-24.9
- 5-9.9
- 0.1-4.9
- 0.0

10   0   10   20   30 miles
10   0   10   20   30   40 kilometers

Source: U.S. Bureau of the Census

1980

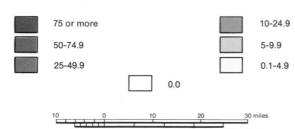

uninhabited

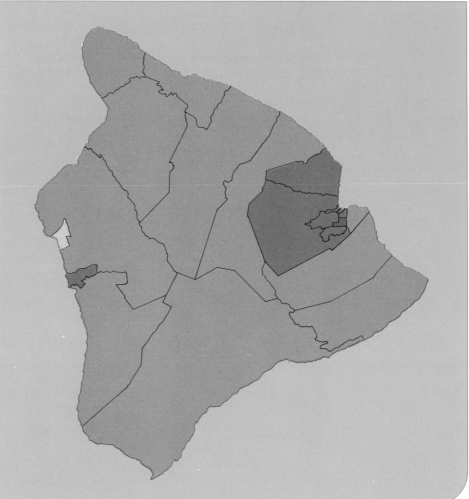

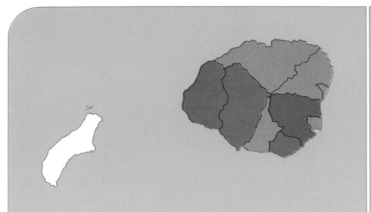

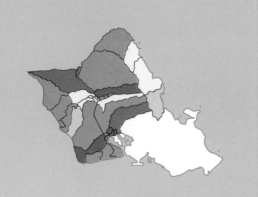

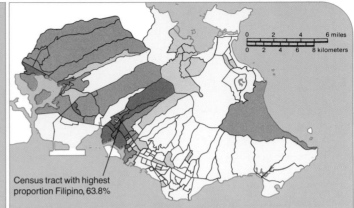

Census tract with highest proportion Filipino, 63.8%

FILIPINO ETHNIC GROUP

Percent of Total Population in Each Census Tract

75 or more	10-24.9
50-74.9	5-9.9
25-49.9	0.1-4.9

0.0

10   0   10   20   30 miles

10   0   10   20   30   40 kilometers

Source: U.S. Bureau of the Census

1980

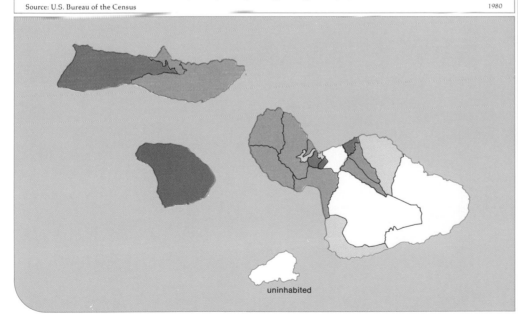

uninhabited

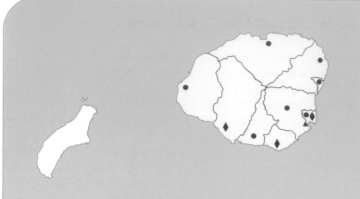

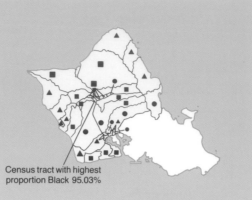

Census tract with highest
proportion Black 95.03%

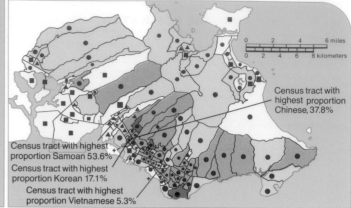

Census tract with
highest proportion
Chinese, 37.8%

Census tract with highest
proportion Samoan 53.6%

Census tract with highest
proportion Korean 17.1%

Census tract with highest
proportion Vietnamese 5.3%

CHINESE AND OTHER ETHNIC GROUPS
Percent of Total Population in Each Census Tract

Chinese

50-74.9	5-9.9
25-49.9	0.1-4.9
10-24.9	0.0

Other Ethnic Groups

Symbol appears in those tracts where
the group has the largest percentage
among the five minority groups

● Korean   ◆ American Indian
■ Black   ▲ Samoan
                  + Vietnamese

1980

Source: U.S. Bureau of the Census

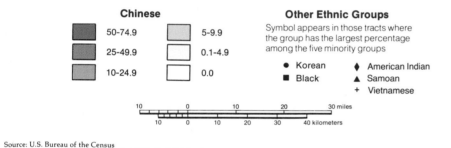

uninhabited

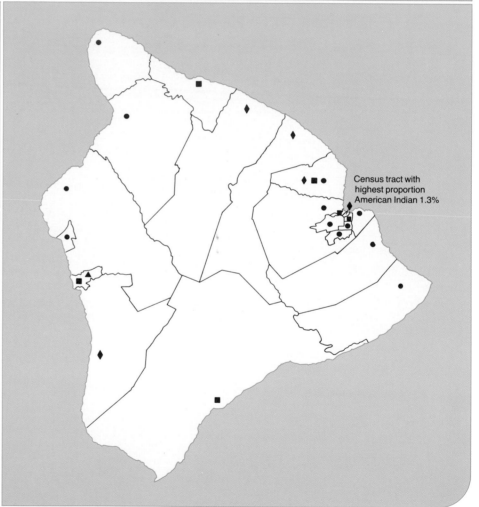

Census tract with
highest proportion
American Indian 1.3%

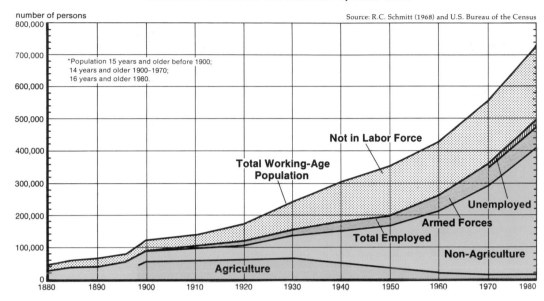

WORKING-AGE POPULATION, 1880–1980*; TOTAL EMPLOYED, 1880–1980; MILITARY STATUS OR ACTIVITY, 1900–1980

number of persons

Source: R.C. Schmitt (1968) and U.S. Bureau of the Census

*Population 15 years and older before 1900;
14 years and older 1900–1970;
16 years and older 1980.

Not in Labor Force

Total Working-Age Population

Unemployed

Armed Forces

Total Employed

Non-Agriculture

Agriculture

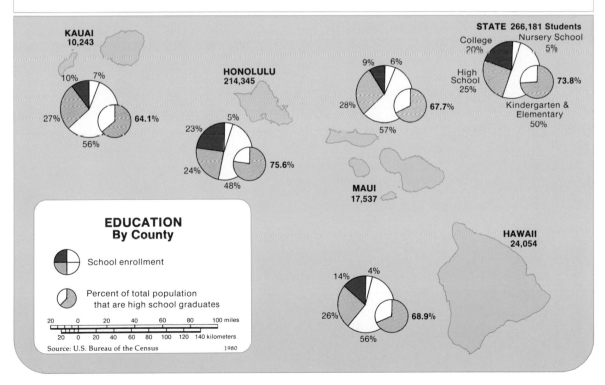

STATE 266,181 Students

KAUAI
10,243

HONOLULU
214,345

College 20%

Nursery School 5%

High School 25%

73.8%

Kindergarten & Elementary 50%

MAUI
17,537

HAWAII
24,054

**EDUCATION
By County**

School enrollment

Percent of total population
that are high school graduates

20 0 20 40 60 80 100 miles

20 0 20 40 60 80 100 120 140 kilometers

Source: U.S. Bureau of the Census   1980

Social and Economic Characteristics

Residents of Hawaii are in general characterized by relatively high educational attainment, by high rates of participation in the labor force, by concentration in government and service employment, and by high family incomes (pages 120 and 144).

According to census reports, more than 266,000 persons attended school in 1980—virtually everyone of school age in the islands. Among those in nursery, elementary, or high school, one out of five attended parochial or other private schools. Among persons 25 years old and over, 73.8 percent were high school graduates, with a range from 64.1 percent on Kauai to 75.6 percent on Oahu. Statewide, 20.3 percent of those 25 and over had completed at least four years of college (page 194).

Fully 57.8 percent of all females 16 years old and over were in the labor force in 1980. Among women with their own children under 6, the ratio was 51.5. Among males 16 and over, 78.3 percent were members of the labor force. Only 4.7 percent of the civilian labor force was unemployed at the time of the 1980 census.

The plantation economy of the past has given way to today's retailing-, service- and government-oriented economy. In 1900 agricultural workers outnumbered those in other civilian activities 57,125 to 32,802. The total in agriculture reached its peak in 1930 (at 63,478), then dropped, falling to 31,006 by 1950 and 14,793 in 1980. Nonagricultural employment meanwhile soared, to 74,317 in 1930, 135,765 in 1950, 274,527 in 1970, and 400,388 in 1980. By 1980, 19.9 percent of all employed persons were in retail trade, 55.5 percent had managerial, professional, technical, or sales occupations, 17.9 percent were in service occupations, and 21.8 percent worked for the federal, state, or country government (pages 120 and 146).

Family incomes were relatively high, with a median of $22,751 annually in 1979 compared with $11,554 in 1969, $6,366 in 1959, $3,568 in 1949, $742 in 1910, and about $50 in the 1840s. By counties, the 1979 median ranged from $19,132 in Hawaii County to $23,556 on Oahu. By census tracts, median incomes extended from $4,167 in part of Kakaako to $57,029 in the Diamond Head–Black Point area (page 120).

These measures of advancing prosperity must, however, be interpreted in the light of increased prices. The Honolulu consumer price index in 1980 was 100 percent above its 1970 level, 165 percent above 1960, 242 percent over 1950, and 464 percent greater than 1940. Living costs in Hololulu, moreover, were at least 23 percent above the mainland urban average in 1980, according to a survey by the U.S. Bureau of Labor Statisitics.

OCCUPATIONS
Total Employed in the State, 16 Years and Older

Males 54.3% Females 45.7%

percent

Occupation	Number
Managers and administrators	48,671
Professional specialty	48,935
Technical	11,982
Sales workers	47,475
Clerical workers	73,194
Precision production, craft, repair	48,198
Machine operators, assemblers	14,000
Transport operators	16,430
Handlers, cleaners, laborers	17,993
Farming, forestry, fishing	14,154
Service workers (food, cleaning, protective, etc.)	72,602
Private household workers	1,547

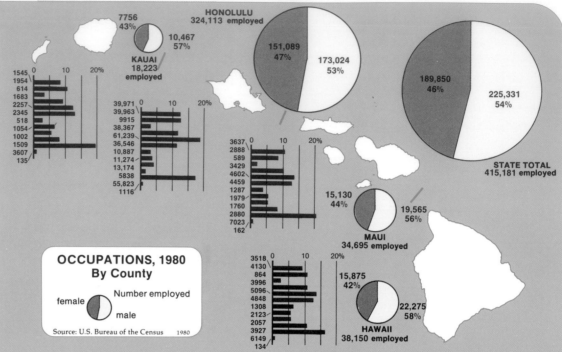

HONOLULU
324,113 employed

KAUAI
18,223 employed

7756 43% / 10,467 57%

151,089 47% / 173,024 53%

189,850 46% / 225,331 54%

STATE TOTAL
415,181 employed

MAUI
34,695 employed

15,130 44% / 19,565 56%

HAWAII
38,150 employed

15,875 42% / 22,275 58%

OCCUPATIONS, 1980
By County

female / male   Number employed

Source: U.S. Bureau of the Census   1980

FAMILY INCOMES AND
TOTAL FAMILIES IN THE STATE, 1979

percent

Income	Number
Less than $5000	11,533
$5000 to $7499	12,195
$7500 to $9999	15,068
$10,000 to $14,999	29,796
$15,000 to $24,999	56,963
$25,000 to $49,999	81,325
$50,000 or more	21,094

Median Family Income $22,751

	Number
Families with related children under 18 years of age	133,683
Female householder, no husband present	28,514
Householder 65 years and older	29,316
Families below poverty level	17,700

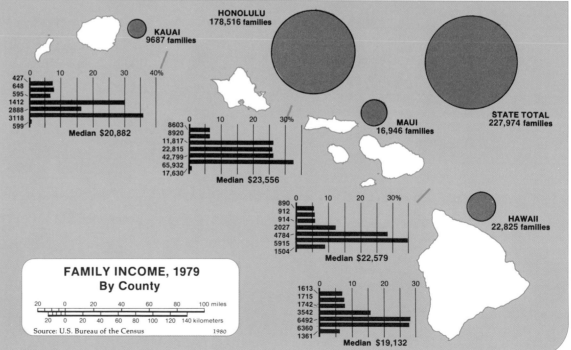

HONOLULU
178,516 families

KAUAI
9687 families

Median $20,882

Median $23,556

MAUI
16,946 families

STATE TOTAL
227,974 families

Median $22,579

HAWAII
22,825 families

Median $19,132

FAMILY INCOME, 1979
By County

20 0 20 40 60 80 100 miles
20 0 20 40 60 80 100 120 140 kilometers

Source: U.S. Bureau of the Census   1980

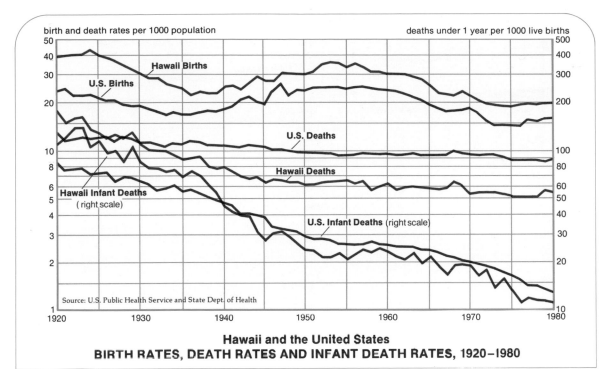

birth and death rates per 1000 population

deaths under 1 year per 1000 live births

Hawaii Births

U.S. Births

U.S. Deaths

Hawaii Deaths

Hawaii Infant Deaths
(right scale)

U.S. Infant Deaths (right scale)

Source: U.S. Public Health Service and State Dept. of Health

Hawaii and the United States
BIRTH RATES, DEATH RATES AND INFANT DEATH RATES, 1920–1980

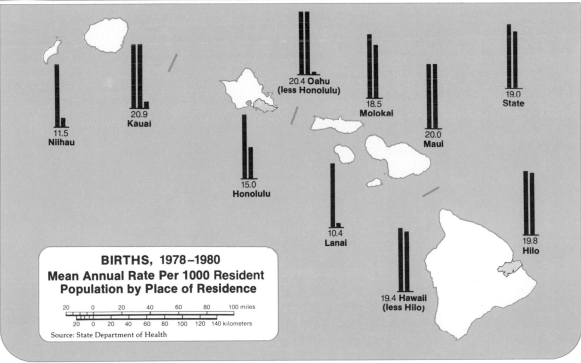

11.5
Niihau

20.9
Kauai

20.4 Oahu
(less Honolulu)

18.5
Molokai

19.0
State

15.0
Honolulu

20.0
Maui

10.4
Lanai

19.8
Hilo

19.4 Hawaii
(less Hilo)

BIRTHS, 1978–1980
Mean Annual Rate Per 1000 Resident
Population by Place of Residence

20   0   20   40   60   80   100 miles

20   0   20   40   60   80   100 120 140 kilometers

Source: State Department of Health

Vital Statistics

Birth and death rates have shifted significantly during Hawaii's two hundred years of recorded history. Fertility has fluctuated in response to new diseases, immigration patterns, war, depression and prosperity, and contraceptive procedures. A more consistent trend is seen in mortality rates during the last hundred years, as improved public health measures, medical discoveries, and better living conditions have gradually overcome the effects of introduced diseases and epidemics, high infant mortality, famine, and other conditions responsible for the high death rates of earlier periods.

Reproduction and survival were chancy matters in nineteenth-century Hawaii. Venereal diseases caused sterility or stillbirths. Some women resorted to abortion, using the crudest of procedures. There is also evidence of infanticide among Hawaiians, a practice that persisted until the middle of the nineteenth century. Early missionary doctors in the 1830s and 1840s estimated that more than half of all infants died before they were two years of age. Childhood diseases were common and far more severe among the previously unexposed Hawaiians. Epidemics killed perhaps 15,000 children and adults in 1804, 10,000 in 1848–1849, 5,000 or 6,000 in 1853, and 1,700 as late as 1918–1920. Crude birth rates before 1900 ranged from 16 to 41 per 1,000 inhabitants; crude death rates, from 19 to 105—with an unknown, but obviously high and variable, degree of underregistration. The average length of stay in The Queen's Hospital in 1877–1879 was 59 days, at an average daily cost of 61 cents. The average expectation of life at birth for babies born in Honolulu in 1878–1879 was only 21.9 years.

The crude birth rate rose during the first quarter of the twentieth century, in response as much to shifts in the age and sex distribution of the population as to any increase in completed fertility per married woman; the peak seems to have been 41.8 births per 1,000 inhabitants in 1924. Urbanization, increased knowledge of contraceptive techniques, and economic decline brought the rate down to 21.7 during the 1930s, but it recovered rapidly during and after World War II, reaching a postwar high of 32.0 in 1954. Partly because of the introduction of contraceptive pills in 1960 and legalized abortion in 1970, the rate again dropped, and by 1975 was only 17.8. Since then birth rates have more or less stabilized, standing at 18.6 in 1981.

Mortality rates in Hawaii declined sharply in the late nineteenth and early twentieth centuries, then began to level off (page 121). Whereas one of every three babies died before its first birthday during the first decade of the present century, in 1981 the infant death rate had dropped to an all-time low of 10.5 per 1,000 live births—one of the lowest rates in the United States and the Pacific (pages 121 and 199). Life expectancy at birth for males rose from 44.0 years in 1910 to 67.8 in 1950, and 74.8 in 1980; corresponding estimates for females were 43.8, 71.7, and 81.2. The 1981 crude death rate of 5.4 per 1,000 population was one of the lowest among the 50 states. A contributing factor is the larger proportion of young people in Hawaii compared with most states. The differences in death rates between islands are also partly due to age differences in island populations (page 112). The crude death rates used on these pages have not been adjusted statistically for age, sex, health, or other population differences, but they have the advantage of indicating the actual probability of death among their respective populations.

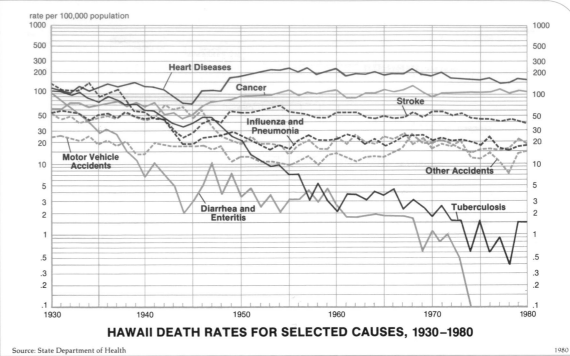

HAWAII DEATH RATES FOR SELECTED CAUSES, 1930–1980

Source: State Department of Health

1980

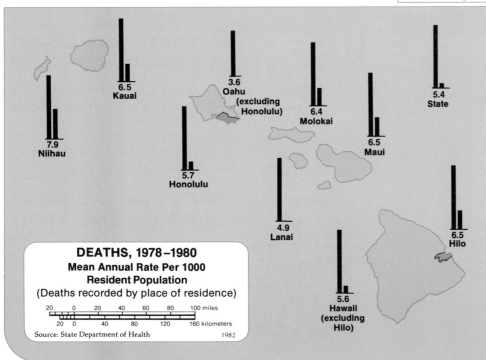

DEATHS, 1978–1980
Mean Annual Rate Per 1000
Resident Population
(Deaths recorded by place of residence)

Source: State Department of Health   1982

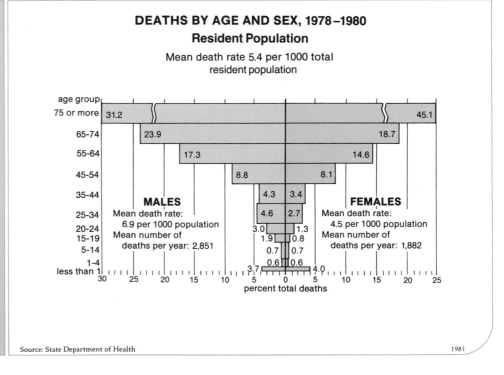

DEATHS BY AGE AND SEX, 1978–1980
Resident Population

Mean death rate 5.4 per 1000 total resident population

Source: State Department of Health

1981

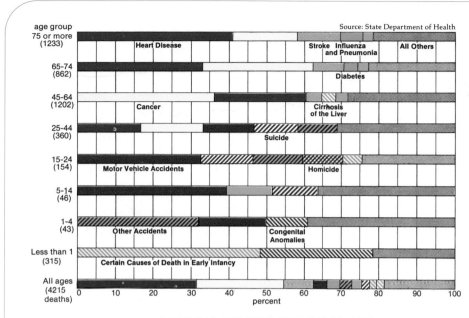

age group
75 or more (1233)
65-74 (862)
45-64 (1202)
25-44 (360)
15-24 (154)
5-14 (46)
1-4 (43)
Less than 1 (315)
All ages (4215 deaths)

Heart Disease
Stroke
Influenza and Pneumonia
All Others
Diabetes
Cancer
Cirrhosis of the Liver
Suicide
Motor Vehicle Accidents
Homicide
Other Accidents
Congenital Anomalies
Certain Causes of Death in Early Infancy

Source: State Department of Health

percent 0 10 20 30 40 50 60 70 80 90 100

LEADING CAUSES OF DEATH, 1980

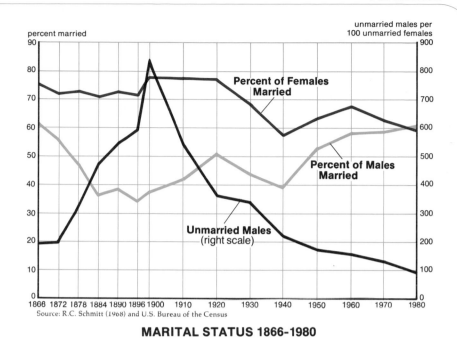

percent married

unmarried males per 100 unmarried females

Percent of Females Married
Percent of Males Married
Unmarried Males (right scale)

1866 1872 1878 1884 1890 1896 1900 1910 1920 1930 1940 1950 1960 1970 1980

Source: R.C. Schmitt (1968) and U.S. Bureau of the Census

MARITAL STATUS 1866-1980

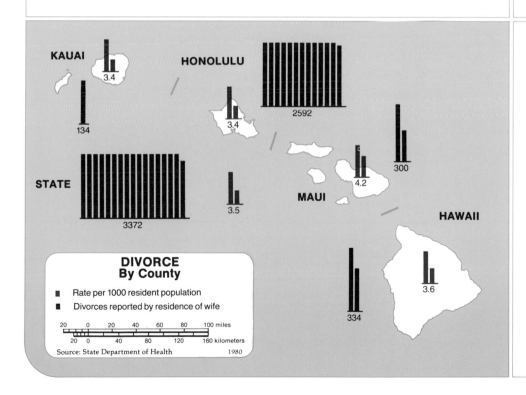

KAUAI 3.4
134

HONOLULU
3.4
2592

STATE
3.5
3372

MAUI
4.2
300

HAWAII
3.6
334

**DIVORCE
By County**

■ Rate per 1000 resident population
■ Divorces reported by residence of wife

20 0 20 40 60 80 100 miles
20 0 40 80 120 160 kilometers

Source: State Department of Health   1980

→ BRIDE
GROOM
Source: State Department of Health

White
Hawaiian
Part Hawaiian
Chinese
Filipino
Japanese
Puerto Rican
Korean
Samoan
Black
Portuguese
Other

5833
71
1465
442
1160
1675
117
140
187
428
56
262

STATE 11,856

25 20 15 10 5 0 percent

0 10 20 30 40 50 60 70 80 90 100 percent

MARRIAGES BY ETHNIC GROUPS, 1980

Migration

For more than a century migration has been a major factor in population growth and redistribution in Hawaii. As noted earlier, large numbers of workers were brought to Hawaii from China, Japan, Portugal, the Philippines, and other areas between 1852 and the 1930s as plantation laborers. After 1931 the mainland United States became the chief source of new residents, as well as the major destination of Hawaii's out-migrants.

In the decade between the 1970 and 1980 censuses, an estimated 234,000 persons (other than military personnel and their dependents) moved to Hawaii, while an estimated 129,000 civilians other than military dependents moved out of the State. Approximately 171,000 of the in-migrants came to Hawaii from the mainland, while 63,000 were migrants from abroad, chiefly the Philippines. Net in-migration averaged 10,500 annually. More than 400,000 military personnel and dependents moved to Hawaii during the decade, but they stayed on the average only two or three years. On leaving, they took with them most of the 3,700 babies born to military couples every year in the islands—about 23 percent of all babies born in Hawaii. Including military personnel and dependents, net in-migration averaged only 7,600 annually during the decade. Net in-migration thus accounted for 39.1 percent of overall growth for the decade when the armed forces and their dependents are included, but 55.3 percent when the analysis is limited to the civilian population.

Most of the civilians moving to Hawaii during the post-World War II period have been relatively young persons, usually less than 30 years of age; only a small number of retired and older persons have migrated to Hawaii, possibly because of high transportation and living costs, and many older persons already living in the islands have moved away upon reaching retirement age. The new residents have usually come from California and other western states, and many of them have been professional and technical workers. The out-migrants, in contrast, have included sizeable numbers of unskilled and semiskilled persons, along with young island-born persons who have left to attend school, enter the armed forces, or seek work on the mainland. The number of Hawaii-born persons living on the mainland increased from 588 in 1850 to 1,307 in 1900, 19,437 in 1930, 115,070 in 1960, 179,735 in 1970, and an estimated 250,000 in 1980.

R.C.S.

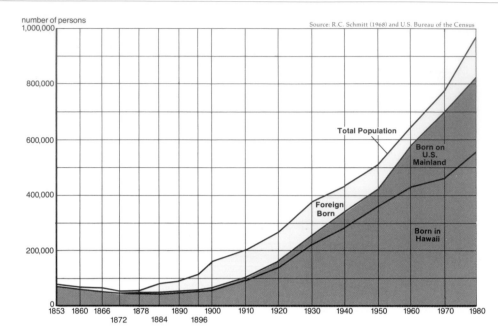

PLACE OF BIRTHS, 1853–1980

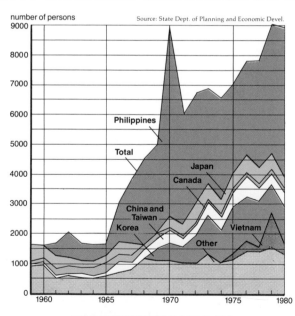

FOREIGN IMMIGRANTS BY COUNTRY OF BIRTH, 1959–1979

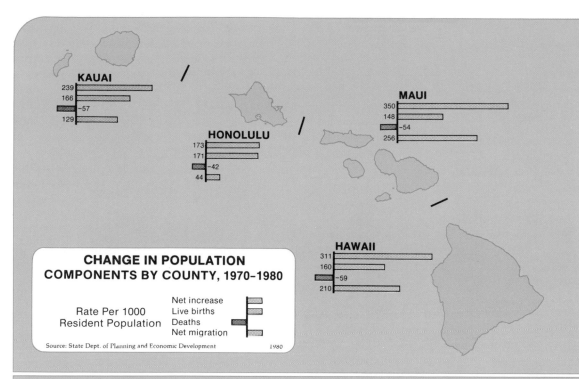

CHANGE IN POPULATION
COMPONENTS BY COUNTY, 1970–1980

Rate Per 1000
Resident Population

Net increase
Live births
Deaths
Net migration

Net increase

Source: State Dept. of Planning and Economic Development   1980

The graph below shows the Statewide rate of change for the resident population and for the military and military-dependent population, respectively, and the map to the left shows the total population by counties, in the major components of population change: births, deaths, and net migration. Births are additions to the population, deaths are subtractions. Net migration represents the difference between the number of people entering and leaving the State and counties. Between 1970 and 1980 net migration was positive for the armed forces and resident population, representing a gain, but negative—or a loss of population—for military dependents. The "net change" is a demographer's term which can be negative as well as positive. It is the combined effect of births, deaths, and migration. In all counties both the net change and net migration were positive. For the total population of the State (resident and military combined), there was a positive net change between 1970 and 1980 of 194,778 persons. This was comprised of 161,831 live births, 43,177 deaths, and a net in-migration of 76,124. Over the decade this represents a growth in the population of the State of 25.3 percent.

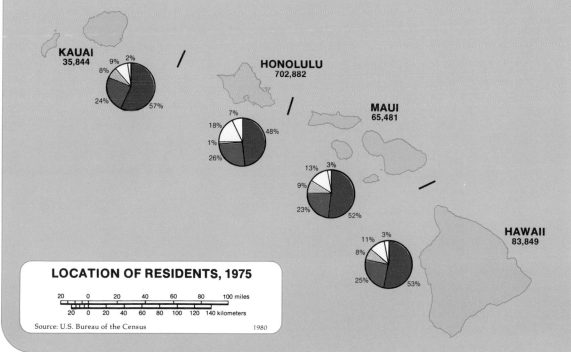

LOCATION OF RESIDENTS, 1975

20   0   20   40   60   80   100 miles

20   0   20   40   60   80   100   120   140 kilometers

Source: U.S. Bureau of the Census   1980

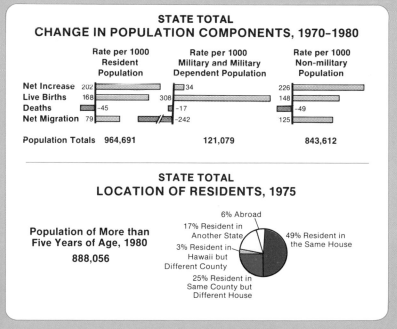

STATE TOTAL
CHANGE IN POPULATION COMPONENTS, 1970–1980

	Rate per 1000 Resident Population	Rate per 1000 Military and Military Dependent Population	Rate per 1000 Non-military Population
Net Increase	202	34	226
Live Births	168	308	148
Deaths	−45	−17	−49
Net Migration	79	−242	125
Population Totals	964,691	121,079	843,612

STATE TOTAL
LOCATION OF RESIDENTS, 1975

**Population of More than
Five Years of Age, 1980**

888,056

6% Abroad
17% Resident in Another State
3% Resident in Hawaii but Different County
49% Resident in the Same House
25% Resident in Same County but Different House

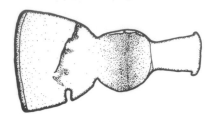

Post-contact iron hatchet head.

Drawing by T. Stell Newman

URBAN CENTERS

The 1980 census records important urban growth in the State, mainly, as in the 1960s, in the City and County of Honolulu (the island of Oahu). Whereas in 1970 there were nine centers of more than 10,000 population, eight of these on Oahu, there were fourteen in 1980, with eleven on Oahu. The three on neighbor islands were Hilo, the perennially leading town of the island of Hawaii, and Kahului and Wailuku on the island of Maui. However, in almost every respect, Honolulu is the state's only true city.

The total population of these fourteen places in 1980 made up 70.1 percent of the state's 964,691 residents. The city of Honolulu alone had 54.0 percent of all residents in all places of over 10,000, statewide, and 49.5 percent of all in those of over 5,000. The island of Oahu housed 79.1 percent of the state population compared with 81.9 percent in 1970, the nearly 3 percent difference stemming from the more rapid (largely urban) growth of certain of the other islands, chiefly Maui and Hawaii.

Differences in growth aside, the island of Oahu remained the urban heart of the state. Agriculture, though still important, tended to decline in the 1970s in favor of expanding urbanization. In addition, major population shifts within the City and County of Honolulu, augmented by domestic and foreign inmigration, have worked to change the manner of urbanization from one of simple expansion to more massive suburban and ex-urban development.

The spread of Honolulu eastward toward Hawaii Kai and Koko Crater and westward toward Aiea, Pearlridge, Waipahu, and Ewa, particularly northwestward toward Mililani Town, was paralleled somewhat by the growth of such former small, quiet places as Laie on the northern and Waianae on southern coasts of western Oahu, which grew by 51.0 and 96.8 percent, respectively. The most conspicuous increases, however, were in places closer to the city. The population of Hawaii Kai, for example, increased by 232.5 percent in the decade, and in the Ewa direction, the Red Hill residential area, close to the international airport and the Pearl Harbor naval complex, grew by nearly 600 percent. In the same direction, the Halawa Heights housing area grew by 274.5 percent; the Ewa Beach–Barbers Point industrial-residential areas by more than 160 percent.

The decade also saw the creation of new "dormitory" towns for commuters, the foremost of which is Mililani Town, mentioned above, sited in former pineapple fields south of the agro-military town of Wahiawa in central Oahu, which grew from 4,420 in 1970 to 24,860 in 1980, an increase of 462.5 percent. Another is Makakilo City, overlooking the leeward coast of southwest Oahu which, when taken together with the Ewa Beach–Barbers Point area adjoining it on the south, represents the rise of two communities of roughly 4,500 each in 1970 to a combined total of nearly 21,000 in 1980.

New highways, notably westward toward Waianae and Makaha on the leeward coast and Mililani Town on the Leilehua Plain, have helped provide access for the twice-daily rush of the horde of commuters to and from Honolulu, but environmental and economic concerns late in the 1970s have stymied like projects northward through the Koolau Range and eastward to Hawaii Kai and Koko Head.

These imposing gains in the urban periphery must be considered together with losses of population in some parts of the city and in some of the more elegant suburbs, mainly in the east (Kaimuki-Wilhelmina, Kahala, Diamond Head–Black Point, Aina Haina, and Niu). Hence, as seen in the 1980 data for census tracts, the city grew by only 12.4 percent, far less than the growth of the State (24.3 percent), of Oahu (21.0 percent), of the island of Hawaii (45.0 percent), or even of Kauai (31.6 percent).

Within Honolulu, losses may have resulted from increasing commercialization in certain tracts (the airport area, down 64.7 percent; the Sand Island and Sand Island Access areas, down 45.0 and 12.2 percent, respectively; and the Pearl City commercial tract along the highway, down 46.0 percent). Some of these losses were balanced by the construction of high-rise residences and new professional facilities, as in the Kukui, Kuwakini, and Harbor areas, but in general urban declines probably reflected rising interest and mortgage rates and taxes, along with the much higher cost of homes—all exacerbated in Hawaii by the so-called lease-hold system, by which much land is still owned by vast estates or corporations. By 1980, these great land-holders were only beginning to arrange conversion to "fee-simple" properties, but at costs that may force out present occupants. The maturing or disintegration of families has also fostered the conversion of older family homes to apartments, and, while zoning has generally checked high-rise growth in these neighborhoods, their nature is rapidly changing.

D.H.K.

KAUAI COUNTY
14,828

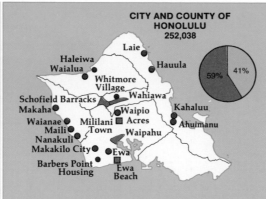

62% | 38%

Kapaa

Hanamaulu
Waimea
Wailua
Lihue
Kekaha
Kalaheo
Hanapepe
Koloa

CITY AND COUNTY OF HONOLULU
252,038

Laie

Haleiwa
Waialua
Hauula
Whitmore
Village
Wahiawa
Schofield Barracks
Makaha
Waipio
Kahaluu
Waianae
Mililani
Town
Acres
Ahuimanu
Maili
Waipahu
Nanakuli
Makakilo City
Ewa
Barbers Point
Housing
Ewa
Beach

59% | 41%

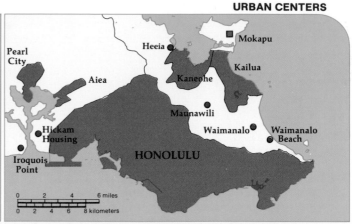

Pearl
City
Mokapu
Heeia
Kailua
Aiea
Kaneohe
Hickam
Housing
Maunawili
Waimanalo
Iroquois
Point
HONOLULU
Waimanalo
Beach

0 2 4 6 miles
0 2 4 6 8 kilometers

URBAN CENTERS, 1980

Place	Population	Households
State Total	964,691	294,052
Standard Metropolitan Statistical Area (Oahu)	762,565	230,214
Honolulu City	365,048	127,139
Other centers:	10,000 – 49,999	3000 – 15,000
	2500 – 9999	750 – 2999
	1000 – 2499	300 – 749

59% Renter
Occupied Vacant,
For Sale or
For Rent
41% Owner
Occupied

STATE TOTAL
HOUSING UNITS
334,235

10   0   10   20   30 miles
10   0   10   20   30   40 kilometers

Source: U.S. Bureau of the Census and State Dept. of Planning and Economic Development

HAWAII COUNTY
34,215

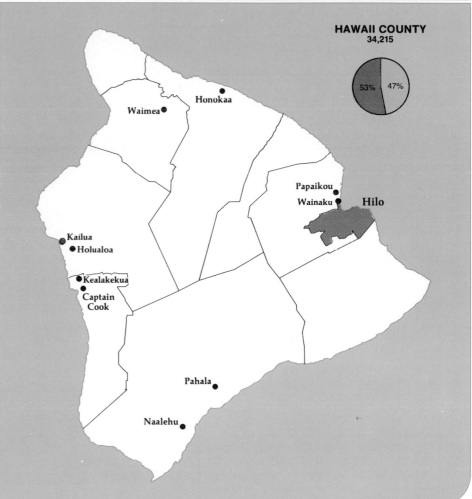

53% | 47%

Honokaa
Waimea
Papaikou
Wainaku
Hilo
Kailua
Holualoa
Kealakekua
Captain
Cook
Pahala
Naalehu

MAUI COUNTY
33,154

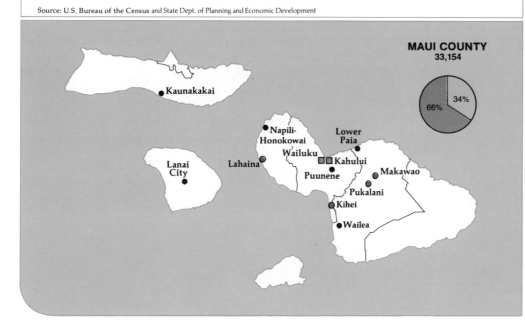

Kaunakakai

66% | 34%

Napili-
Honokowai
Lower
Paia
Wailuku
Lanai
City
Lahaina
Kahului
Puunene
Makawao
Pukalani
Kihei
Wailea

Housing

Between 1970 and 1980 in Hawaii as a whole there was an increase of 54.4 percent in the number of housing units, but among the counties, Maui registered an increase of 138.1 percent (349.3 for Lahaina, 135.6 for Makawao, 116.7 for Wailuku and 60.5 for Molokai), the numbers on Hawaii grew by 80.3 percent (150.1 for Puna, 146.4 for South Kohala, and 249.3 for North Kona), on Kauai by 64.4 percent, and in the City and County of Honolulu 44.3 percent.

Changes in number of housing units on Oahu (the City and County of Honolulu) were thus much less than on the other islands. Broken down by state housing districts, the city of Honolulu added 38.0 percent new housing units, the eastern windward coast (Koolaupoko) 35.7 percent, and the Waialua and Wahiawa districts 26.4 and 22.6 percent, respectively—the lowest among the districts on Oahu during the decade. Those districts showing the sharpest increases in the number of units were Koolauloa on the northern windward coast (which includes Punaluu, Hauula, Kahuku, and especially Laie), which grew by 72.0 percent, and the Waianae district on the western leeward coast of the island, which showed an increase of 81.8 percent. But the most important growth in housing is represented by the 70.7 percent increase in the large Ewa district, where the number of housing units rose from 29,454 in 1970 to 50,288 in 1980, chiefly because of new construction at Mililani Town, Makakilo City, and Ewa Beach.

The matter of ethnic neighborhoods bears mention here. In the past there was a tendency for people of like cultural leanings, mainly the Japanese and the Caucasian Americans (the more recent majority element) to dominate whole sections of Honolulu and its suburbs. However, with population shifts to new areas and the decline of older, often ethnic neighborhoods, coupled with the increase in numbers and affluence of other cultural groups and a general trend toward "standard" American ways, the newly built peripheral neighborhoods tend to be more mixed and thus typical of what is usually considered the general American scene.

A comparison of the four counties by characteristics of occupied housing units in the 1970s shows that Oahu has had a lower rate of one-family detached homes (only 57.7 percent) than has Maui (84.0 percent) or Hawaii (82.8 percent). This is also true to a lesser extent for owner-occupancy: on Oahu in 1975 owner-occupancy was 47.8 percent, compared with 53.8 percent on Kauai, 60.6 percent on Hawaii, and 65.9 percent on Maui. However, on Oahu there were wide variations in both characteristics. For example, the low figures for one-family detached homes, represented Waikiki, Makiki, or downtown commercial-industrial areas, while the high rates were found in affluent intra-urban or dormitory satellite areas. Monthly dollar costs for housing also varied by neighborhood, but on Oahu, rental costs were usually lower than for houses owned, whereas on other islands, the opposite was true. Oahu has a greater percentage of occupied units than the rest of the State, and although the average household size is only slightly larger, both the average median household size is only slightly larger, both the average median household and family incomes were higher, along with higher costs of monthly maintenance and utilities. The fast-rising price of housing on Oahu between 1970 and 1980 is shown on the accompanying map.

Government agencies owned or operated less than 8 percent of all housing units in 1980, of which 74 percent was military and 22 percent Hawaii State Housing Authority.

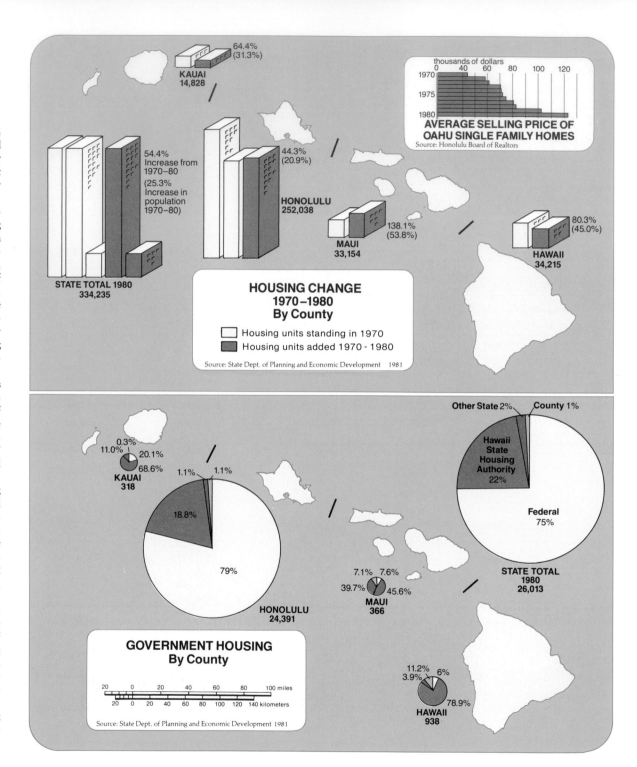

AVERAGE SELLING PRICE OF OAHU SINGLE FAMILY HOMES
Source: Honolulu Board of Realtors

KAUAI 14,828 — 64.4% (31.3%)

HONOLULU 252,038 — 44.3% (20.9%)

STATE TOTAL 1980 334,235 — 54.4% Increase from 1970–80 (25.3% Increase in population 1970–80)

MAUI 33,154 — 138.1% (53.8%)

HAWAII 34,215 — 80.3% (45.0%)

HOUSING CHANGE 1970–1980 By County

☐ Housing units standing in 1970
■ Housing units added 1970 - 1980

Source: State Dept. of Planning and Economic Development 1981

KAUAI 318 — 0.3% / 11.0% / 20.1% / 68.6%

HONOLULU 24,391 — 1.1% / 1.1% / 18.8% / 79%

MAUI 366 — 7.1% / 7.6% / 39.7% / 45.6%

HAWAII 938 — 11.2% / 3.9% / 6% / 78.9%

STATE TOTAL 1980 26,013 — Other State 2% / County 1% / Hawaii State Housing Authority 22% / Federal 75%

GOVERNMENT HOUSING By County

Source: State Dept. of Planning and Economic Development 1981

Honolulu, Oahu. Looking north toward the Pali. The downtown area is in the foreground, the State Capitol in the center with Punchbowl crater behind.

Waikiki, Oahu. Ala Moana Shopping Center and the Ala Wai boat harbor are in the left lower corner, the Ala Wai canal runs behind Waikiki toward Diamond Head crater (upper right).

Hilo, Hawaii. View south across Hilo Bay. The downtown area is in the right foreground, a shopping center and government buildings in the center, and hotel, airport, and light industrial areas to the left.

Wailuku (foreground) and Kahului, Maui. Looking south across the two towns toward Kihei. In the far distance is the island of Kahoolawe.

Photographs by R. M. Towill Corporation, Honolulu

State bird, *nene* (Hawaiian goose).

Source: Hawaii State Archives

LANGUAGES

Not every resident of Hawaii is multilingual, but many different languages and dialects are spoken in Hawaii. We single out for comment several languages, each of which has been the mother tongue of one of the ethnic groups who have resided in Hawaii since Captain Cook's arrival, at which time, of course, Hawaiian was the language of the islands.

English is the first language of the majority of residents and its use is widespread. It has been in competition with a variety of languages, among which are those of immigrants from several countries. Contacts between speakers of these languages became numerous in the last half of the nineteenth century and early decades of the present, and inevitably influenced the English spoken in the islands. Many factors favored the dominance of English, although this dominance has been checked to some degree by the recent liberalization of immigration laws, a marked increase in visitors from Japan, and a continuing awareness by many people in Hawaii of the values of a multicultural and multilingual society.

English in Hawaii assumes a variety of styles. Mainland English is a major influence, but many people speak a recognizably regional form of the language. Some speakers of this Hawaiian English shift from one to another of its various subtypes, which have been viewed as a continuum, encompassing utterances characteristic of an English-based Hawaiian pidgin, an English-based Hawaiian creole, nonstandard Hawaiian English, or standard Hawaiian English. Each of these subtypes has characteristic features, but individual speakers do not necessarily restrict themselves in range.

Tsuzaki (1971) illustrates varying ways of expressing a single idea. To the standard (Hawaiian) English "I am eating," correspond the possible equivalents in pidgin: "Me kaukau," "Me eat," "I kaukau," or "I eat"; in creole: "I stay eat," or "I stay kaukau"; and in nonstandard: "I stay eating," or "I eating." *Kaukau* is said to be a Hawaiianization of the Chinese pidgin English *chowchow*; thus the example illustrates both grammatical and vocabulary features. For differences in pronunciation, ready examples are at hand in such words as "ship" (rhyming with "sheep") or "pet" (rhyming with "pat").

Hawaiian is the home language of all residents of the island of Niihau and of individual families on the other islands. It is studied by other residents, and many outsiders learn at least a few words and display interest in Hawaiian songs, church services, and other aspects of the culture. Exemplifying the influence of languages with which it has been in contact are such Hawaiian loanwords as *Kalikimaka*, from English "Christmas"; *Pake*, "Chinese," attributed to Cantonese; *pakaliao*, "codfish," from Portuguese; *paniolo*, "cowboy," probably from Spanish; *popoki*, "cat," said to be from English "poor pussy."

Samoan, related to Hawaiian, has been introduced in this century. The language is used actively in homes and churches, even though most Samoans who come to Hawaii are familiar with English. The language is taught at Brigham Young University–Hawaii Campus, at Laie. Speakers of Samoan were recently the largest single group of non-English native speakers in Hawaii's public schools.

Philippine languages are likewise members of a group of languages designated as Austronesian, though not closely akin to Hawaiian or Samoan. The Filipinos comprise about one-tenth of the State's present population. They do not all share the same mother tongue. At the time of the first large migration (1907–1931), English had acquired official status, gradually supplanting Spanish. For the majority of the earlier immigrants, Ilocano, used in northern Luzon, was the mother tongue, though some immigrants spoke Visayan (Bisayan) or other Philippine languages. Today, Ilocano, heard on radio and television programs, is the dominant language of the local Filipinos. In recent decades, however, Tagalog, on which the national language of the Philippines is based, is ever more prevalent in Hawaii; perhaps one-third of the Ilocano speakers in the islands know Tagalog, reinforced by movies and other recent contacts.

Chinese were among the earliest immigrants to Hawaii; in 1876 there were already more than 2,000 in the islands, but the main migration took place between 1877 and 1898. Almost all were from Kwangtung province and spoke forms of Chinese used there: Hakka (a type of speech akin to northern Chinese) by perhaps 25 percent of the group; types of Cantonese by the vast majority of the rest. Mandarin, or Kuo Yü (the national language), based largely on the prestigious language of Beijing, is taught at the University of Hawaii. Cantonese, however, has been the language usually taught in the local Chinese language schools. No matter what type of Chinese they speak, literate Chinese share the ability to read material written in Chinese characters. The Chinese-language newspaper is evidence of the high regard for literacy held by Hawaii's Chinese (page 191).

Hawaii's Japanese population stems from periods of immigration which began in 1868 and were most active from 1885 to 1924. Not all the immigrants spoke standard Japanese, but churches, language schools, travel, radio, television, movies, and newspapers make it a familiar language in Hawaii. Stores and hotels in Waikiki have recently begun to use Japanese in dealing with increasing numbers of guests from Japan. The usual way of writing Japanese employs Chinese characters (kanji) together with hiragana or katakana, syllabic symbols to represent elements not provided by the characters: verb endings, prepositions, and the like, as well as foreign words.

Approximately two-thirds of Hawaii's Japanese population originated in the prefectures of Yamaguchi, Hiroshima, Kumamoto, and Okinawa. Representatives of the last-named prefecture first reached Hawaii in 1900, and their regional form of speech is not readily understood by speakers from the Naichi or main island prefectures, where regional languages are less divergent. Okinawans may account for about one-fifth of the total Japanese population, but their language is now rarely used except among the older members of the group. English is replacing Japanese for the younger generations; Hawaii's regional Japanese tends to resemble the dialects of western Japan, rather than Tokyo standard, and shows the influence of languages with which it has been in contact—English, Hawaiian, and others.

Koreans arrived chiefly in 1904 and 1905, speaking a language grammatically similar to Japanese. Like the latter, Korean has many words composed of Chinese elements. It has its own alphabet. Korean script, like the Japanese, may make use of Chinese characters together with the Korean letters, combined so as to indicate syllables. Regional variations of Korean do not present a great problem. The language is taught at the university, and in a language school. The Korean Christian churches have helped preserve the identity of the language, though English is gradually replacing it.

Most of the Portuguese immigrants to Hawaii arrived between 1878 and 1913 and acquired English with relative speed. Dialect variations between the speakers from Madeira and the Azores (including São Miguel) were leveled. At present the language is largely limited to occasional use by older members of the group. The language has been offered frequently at the university's Manoa campus and has been taught at the Hilo campus.

Spanish, closely related to Portuguese, was the language of the Puerto Rican immigrants, who arrived chiefly in 1901. Migrants from Spain came between 1907 and 1913. Some older Puerto Ricans still use Spanish at home and in connection with church and other organized activities. The word borinki, derived from Borinquén, the indigenous name of Puerto Rico, is sometimes applied to them locally.

The past decade has witnessed the immigration of hundreds of people from countries of Southeast Asia, with use by them in home and group situations of a variety of languages. Vietnam has been the country of origin of a fair number of these, some of whom speak French or Chinese besides Vietnamese.

In the table below are given the first five cardinal numbers as they occur in each of the major languages. This suggests cultural and linguistic similarities and differences between these competing forms of speech.

E.C.K.

English	Hawaiian	Samoan	Cantonese	Hakka	Japanese	Korean	Spanish	Portuguese	Ilocano	Tagalog
one	'ekahi	tasi	yat, 一	yit 一	hitotsu; ichi	hana 하나 il 일	uno	um	maysá; uno	isá; uno
two	'elua	lua	i̍ 二	nyì 二	futatsu; ni	tul 둘 i 이	dos	dous	duwá; dos	dalawá; dos
three	'ekolu	tolu	‚sám 三	sam 三	mittsu; san	set 셋 sam 삼	tres	três	talló; tres	tatló; tres
four	'ehā	fa	sz' 四	sì 四	yottsu; shi or yon	net 넷 sa 사	cuatro	quatro	uppát; kuwatro	ápat; kuwatro
five	'elima	lima	‛ng 五	ńg 五	itsutsu; go	tasŏt 다섯 o 오	cinco	cinco	limá; singko	limá; singko

The two sets of numerals in Ilocano, Tagalog, Japanese, and Korean show the retention of indigenous numerals as well as the use of borrowed ones. The second set for Ilocano and Tagalog reflect Spanish influence; that for Japanese and Korean reflect Chinese forms, which are represented directly by Cantonese and Hakka.

Indigenous Hawaiian

Shinto

Taoist

Buddhism

Christian

Judaism

MAJOR HAWAII RELIGIONS

RELIGIONS

The religious environment of Hawaii is unique on the American scene. While our statistics are not precise, they do demonstrate the remarkable variety of religious backgrounds and affiliations. Buddhism and Shinto are present as major religious communities. The "new religious movements" referred to in the tables are often combinations of Buddhist, Shinto, and Christian elements. These groups originated in Japan, some as early as the late 1800s, and several came to Hawaii in the 1920s. Their great growth, however, has taken place since 1945. Traditional Hawaiian faith and practices have influenced the development of Christianity in the islands, and ancient customs linger on. Hawaii is one of those cosmopolitan centers where one can become aware of the faith of other men.

However, a study of religious history reveals that geographical proximity does not assure understanding or harmony. Differences in faith may lead to intolerance and conflict. Religious bigotry may be more difficult to analyze and remedy than racial prejudice. For instance, the first Roman Catholic priests who arrived in Hawaii in 1827 were expelled by Protestant-influenced rulers. Catholics returned only after French authorities threatened the local government. The wartime experience of Buddhists in Hawaii is not reassuring: Buddhist temples and schools were closed; most priests were interned, and Buddhists were threatened with internment for persisting in holding "alien creeds."

Some aspects of religious expression in Hawaii show evidence that newcomers wanted to do things the "way they were done back home." The New England missionaries transplanted New England steeples and Protestant church music and theology. Most Buddhist churches use the Japanese language and art imported from Japan. These religious and cultural expressions can provide a creative base for exploration and for establishing identity, or they may be walls to defend one faith against others.

Perhaps it is no longer the American expectation that ethnic and religious distinctions need to be put into a "melting pot." We are increasingly aware that some distinctiveness of faith and identity is of value. Christians are uneasy in the knowledge that "Christianization" has often meant "Westernization," that Western clothes often went with the Christian religion. Christians are troubled because, though they may use Hawaiian traditions in worship, such as singing Queen Liliuokalani's prayer and giving leis to new members, Hawaiians have become a minority group whose identity is uncertain in an increasingly dominant "haole society." Buddhists are both hopeful and uncertain as to what "becoming Americanized" means. More recent immigrants—Samoan, Filipino, and Tongan—bring their own cultural and religious experiences.

The proportion of Protestants in the population is somewhat lower than the national average, but informal reports indicate that some Protestant and Pentecostal groups have grown more rapidly than any other religious denominations in Hawaii in the last ten years. Among Buddhist groups Nichiren Sho-shu has increased most rapidly in size. The traditional Buddhist denominations have generally increased in membership, but proportionally not as rapidly as the general population. The Christian churches came to the islands with varying experiences and philosophies of national or ethnic missionization. The Methodist church, for example, organized churches that served chiefly Korean or Japanese or Filipino persons. "Language" pastors were common. The United Church of Christ, the chief traditional Protestant denomination, on the other hand, did not organize congregations along ethnic or language lines. Ethnically, Buddhist congregations in Hawaii are almost entirely homogeneous. "English departments" have been organized in some temples, but they have not flourished. The socioreligious indigenization of Buddhism is undergoing a test in the present generation of young laymen and clergy.

Since Vatican II and other recent ecumenical events, we have hope that a new world of religious awareness is being discovered. Denominations and church councils are showing new openness and cooperation. Increasing numbers of university students throughout the country as well as in Hawaii are enrolling in courses in world religion. Our attitude toward religious and ethnic differences is more significant than the fact that such distinctions exist. The different faiths and traditions in Hawaii may be viewed on several levels: as an opportunity for personal and community enrichment, as a challenge to convert others, or, less seriously, as quaint customs which are interesting tourist attractions.

R.T.B.

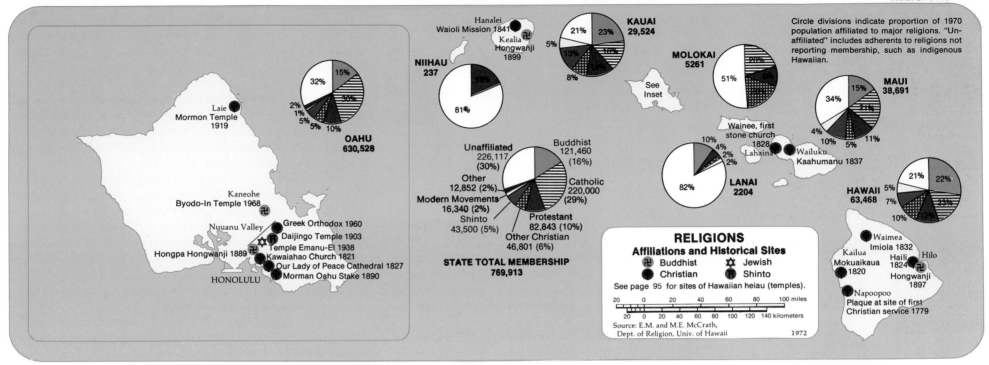

CHURCHES, CHURCH MEMBERSHIP AND CLERGY, 1982

Denomination	Members	Churches	Clergy
BUDDHIST			
Bodaiji	100	1	1
Buddhakaya Hawaii	800	1	1
Chinese Buddhist Assoc.	1,300	1	4
Chozenji	500	1	1
Dae-won-sa	1,000*	1	6
Diamond Sangha	100	2	†
Hawaii Chinese Buddhist Society	1,000	1	4
Hawaii Kyokai Bentenshu	40	1	1
Higashi Hongwanji	1,800	6	6
Honpa Hongwanji	21,500	36	40
Jodo Mission	2,000	21	14
Kagyu Theg Chen Ling (Tibetan Buddhist Dharma Center)	70	4	1
Kegonshu Todaiji	30,000[1]	1	2
Kuan-yin Temple	850	1	4
Nichiren	700	5	6
Nichiren Shoshu	NA	NA	NA
Shingon Mission	NA	NA	NA
Soto Mission	1,150	1	7
Tendai Mission	1,000	3	8
Vietnamese Buddhist Assoc. (Sacred Mt. Temple)	800	1	1
Yut Fut Temple	820	1	3

* Families
† Lay Leaders
‡ Local Assemblies
NA indicates not available
[1]Number receiving healing, blessing, or special amulet.

Denomination	Members	Churches	Clergy
CHRISTIAN			
Greek Orthodox (Eastern)	200*	1	1
Protestant			
American Baptist	687	4	7
Apostolic Faith Church	144,000[2]	7	27
Assembly of God	7,000	NA	NA
Assembly of God– Independent	NA	NA	NA
Church of Christ	NA	NA	NA
Church of God	1,251	17	23
Church of God Prophecy	125	4	8
Church of Jesus Christ of Latter-Day Saints	31,027	87	†
Church of the Living God	2,000	7	40
Conservative Baptist	NA	NA	NA
Disciples of Christ	500	4	7
Episcopal	10,541	40	85
Hoomana Naavao	NA	NA	NA
Hoomanaoke Akuole	NA	NA	NA
Jehovah's Witnesses	4,730	59	59
Korean Christian	NA	NA	NA
Lutheran	4,604	21	25
Missionary	NA	NA	NA
Nazarene	1,354	13	20
Peaceful Holiness Church	200	20	21
Pentecostal Church of the Pacific	150	1	2
Presbyterian	1,158	4	6

[2]Determined through Revelation 14:1.

Denomination	Members	Churches	Clergy
Reorganized Church of Jesus Christ of Latter-Day Saints	1,190	6	60
Salvation Army	2,032	13	28
Seventh-day Adventist	4,147	21	29
Southern Baptist	11,340	60	65
United Church of Christ	17,485	113	129
United Methodist Church	6,242	31	44
Roman Catholic	209,000	64	168
Other Christian			
Christian Science	NA	NA	NA
Religious Science	160	1	1
Society of Friends	95	1	†
Unity	3,000	1	3
INDIAN OR HINDU[3]			
Advaita Vedanta Institute (Shaivite)	15	1	1
Center for Spiritual Understanding (Ramananda)	15	1	1
Hare Krishna	1,300	2	25
Radha Soami Center	100	12	0
Ramakrishna Mission	30	1	0
Satya Sai Baba Center	20	1	0
Self Realization Fellowship	50	1	0
Siddha Yoga Dham	350	4	1
3 Ho (Kundalini Yoga)	NA	NA	NA

[3]Many groups with Indian background emphasizes a teacher rather than sectarian affiliation.

Denomination	Members	Churches	Clergy
JEWISH			
Congregation Sof Ma'arv	NA	NA	NA
Temple Emanu-El	442*	1	2
MUSLIM			
Muslim Student Assoc.	500	1	None
NEW RELIGIOUS MOVEMENTS			
Church of Perfect Liberty	280*	1	1
Church of World Messianity	3,000	6	1
Konko Kyo Mission	1,413	6	15
Rissho Kosei Kai Church	580*	1	1
Seicho No Ie	2,512	6	4
Tenrikyo	4,500	72	300
Tensho Kotai Jingyu Kyo	NA	NA	NA
SHINTO			
Daijingu Temple of Hawaii	7,500[1]	NA	NA
Inari Jinjya	NA	NA	NA
Ishizuchi Shrine	NA	NA	NA
Izumo Taishakyo Mission	NA	NA	NA
Kotohira Jinsha Mission	7,500[1]	NA	NA
OTHER RELIGIOUS FAITHS			
Baha'i	2,750	28‡	†
Scientology	3,400	2	None
Unification Church	NA	NA	NA
Unitarian	156	1	1

Source: Department of Religion, University of Hawaii, 1982.

Byodo-In Temple, Temple Valley, Oahu.
Drawing by John A. Dixon

LIBRARIES AND MUSEUMS

Hawaii has a wealth of libraries, ranging in scope from general public libraries to those that serve only the businesses that fund them. Furthermore, each public school and many private schools have libraries for the use of faculty and students.

The State Office of Library Services supervises a statewide system of public libraries; the system is divided into five districts—two on Oahu and one each on Kauai, Maui, and Hawaii. A microfilm catalog lists the holdings of the system, making the entire collection available to all the people of the State and facilitating the intralibrary loan system. The largest public library is the Hawaii State Library in Honolulu, with 377,304 volumes.

Each of the colleges and universities in the State has its own library. The largest of these is the Hamilton Library at the University of Hawaii, Honolulu, with 1.7 million volumes. It houses the main research collection for the university and several special holdings, such as the Asian, Government Documents, Hawaiian, Pacific, and Rare Books collections.

There are other important collections of Pacific and Hawaiian materials in the State. The Hawaii State Library has Hawaiian and Pacific holdings of 45,426 volumes, and State Archives houses documents of Hawaiian government and history, and books and copies of manuscript journals dealing with Cook's voyages in the Pacific. In addition, there are the B. P. Bishop Museum Library with the Fuller Collection of Pacific books and the Governor G. R. Carter Collection of Hawaiiana; the Hawaiian Historical Society Library with its holdings of early voyages in the Pacific; the Hawaiian Mission Children's Society Library, which houses material on early voyages and letters and reports of the Evangelical missionaries in Hawaii and Micronesia; and the Midkiff Learning Center on the campus of the Kamehameha Schools with 7,000 volumes of Hawaiiana available for reference use. On Kauai, the Regional Library's Hawaiiana collection also includes the Elsie H. and Mabel I. Wilcox rare books collection on Hawaii and the Pacific.

Military bases maintain both technical and general libraries. Hickam Air Force Base, Schofield Barracks, Wheeler Air Force Base, Pearl Harbor Naval Station, Fort Shafter, Camp Smith, Tripler Hospital, and Kaneohe Bay Marine Corps Air Station all have libraries for military personnel, Department of Defense employees, and their dependents. Many of these libraries participate in an interlibrary loan system.

There are also in the islands about 20 special libraries dealing with such subjects as history, art, medicine, law, engineering, and business. Among these are the National Marine Fisheries Service, specializing in marine biology and oceanography; the genealogical research library at Brigham Young University—Hawaii, at Laie; and the Mariska Aldrich Memorial Library with its extensive collection of recorded music.

Museums in Hawaii reflect natural environment, history, and culture. Bishop Museum is a major depository of Pacific and Polynesian research reports and artifacts; natural history collections, including the Herbarium Pacificum; and an entomological collection of more than 11 million specimens. The exhibits of Hawaiian artifacts, royal thrones, and the clothing worn by the people of the different cultures who have come to live in Hawaii are popular with visiting school children. Regular public lectures are offered at the Bishop Museum Planetarium.

Iolani Palace in Honolulu has recently been restored as a museum of the Kalakaua-Liliuokalani period of the Hawaiian monarchy. On the palace grounds are the barracks, still undergoing restoration, and the bandstand, erected for King Kalakaua's coronation in 1883. Also of note for those interested in the Hawaiian monarchy are Queen Emma's Summer Palace in Honolulu, and Hulihee Palace in Kailua-Kona.

The Mission Houses in Honolulu, exhibits in the Kauai Museum, the Waioli Mission House in Hanalei, and the Lyman Memorial Museum in Hilo depict missionary life in early nineteenth-century Hawaii. Life on the sugar plantations in the early days is shown at the Grove Farm Homestead on Kauai and the Waipahu Cultural Garden Park on Oahu.

Hawaii's maritime heritage is on display in Honolulu at the Aloha Tower Maritime Museum and at Pier 5, Honolulu Harbor, where the renovated *Falls of Clyde*, an early Matson ship, is docked; and at Lahaina Harbor on Maui is the *Carthaginian*, a reconstructed whaling vessel. There are a number of military museums on Oahu: the U.S.S. *Arizona* Memorial, Pacific Submarine Museum, the U.S.S. *Bowfin* (a World War II submarine), the U.S. Army Museum at Ft. DeRussy, and the Tropic Lightning Historical Center at Schofield Barracks. The T. A. Jaggar Memorial Museum at Hawaii Volcanoes National Park on the island of Hawaii has exhibits and collections demonstrating volcanic activity, and other natural history collections are found in small museums at Kokee State Park on Kauai and at Haleakala National Park on Maui.

S.W.M.

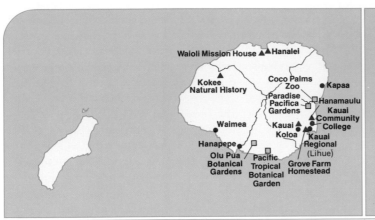

Waioli Mission House ▲ ▲ Hanalei

Kokee
Natural History ▲
Coco Palms
Zoo ▲
Paradise
Pacifica
Gardens ▲ ● Kapaa
□ Hanamaulu
Kauai ▲
Community
College
Kauai ▲ ●
Koloa
Kauai
Regional
(Lihue)
Grove Farm
Homestead
Olu Pua
Botanical
Gardens □
Pacific
Tropical
Botanical
Garden
● Waimea
Hanapepe ●

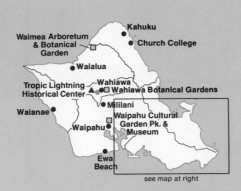

Waimea Arboretum
& Botanical
Garden □
● Kahuku
● Church College
● Waialua
Tropic Lightning ▲
Historical Center
● Wahiawa
□ Wahiawa Botanical Gardens
● Mililani
● Waipahu Cultural
Garden Pk. &
Museum
● Waianae
● Waipahu
● Ewa
Beach

see map at right

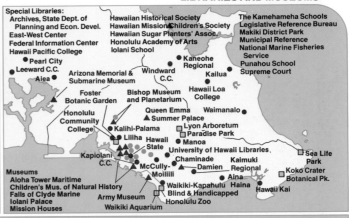

Special Libraries:
Archives, State Dept. of
Planning and Econ. Devel.
East-West Center
Federal Information Center
Hawaii Pacific College

Hawaiian Historical Society
Hawaiian Mission Children's Society
Hawaiian Sugar Planters' Assoc.
Honolulu Academy of Arts
Iolani School

The Kamehameha Schools
Legislative Reference Bureau
Makiki District Park
Municipal Reference
National Marine Fisheries
Service
Punahou School
Supreme Court

● Pearl City
● Leeward C.C.
● Aiea
Arizona Memorial &
Submarine Museum
Foster ▲
Botanic Garden
Honolulu ●
Community
College
● Kalihi-Palama
□ Liliha
Kapiolani
C.C.
● Kaneohe
Regional
● Windward
C.C.
Bishop Museum
and Planetarium
Queen Emma ●
▲ Summer Palace
Hawaii
State
● Manoa
University of Hawaii Libraries
● McCully-
Moiliili
● Chaminade
Damien ●
● Kailua
Hawaii Loa
College
Lyon Arboretum
□ Paradise Park
Waimanalo ●
Kaimuki
Regional
● Aina
● Haina
Sea Life
Park
Koko Crater
Botanical Pk.
Hawaii Kai ●

Museums
Aloha Tower Maritime
Children's Mus. of Natural History
Falls of Clyde Marine
Iolani Palace
Mission Houses
□ Waikiki-Kapahulu
□ Blind & Handicapped
Army Museum
Waikiki Aquarium
Honolulu Zoo

LIBRARIES AND MUSEUMS*

● Public library (Hawaii State
Library System)

● University or college library

● Special library (selected public
or private)

▲ Museum (public or private)

□ Botanical garden, aquarium
or zoo

10   0   10   20 miles
10   0   10   20   30 kilometers

Source: Hawaii Library Assn., and State Dept. of Planning and Economic Dev. 1981

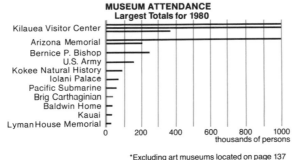

MUSEUM ATTENDANCE
Largest Totals for 1980

Kilauea Visitor Center
Arizona Memorial
Bernice P. Bishop
U.S. Army
Kokee Natural History
Iolani Palace
Pacific Submarine
Brig Carthaginian
Baldwin Home
Kauai
Lyman House Memorial

0   200   400   600   800   1000
thousands of persons

*Excluding art museums located on page 137

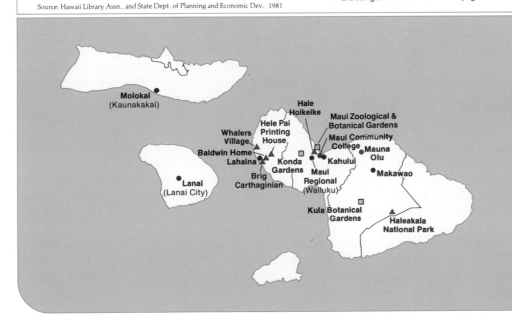

Molokai ●
(Kaunakakai)

Hale
Hoikeike
Whalers ▲
Village
Hele Pai
Printing
House
Maui Zoological &
Botanical Gardens
Baldwin Home ▲
Lahaina ▲
Maui Community
College
Mauna
Olu
Konda
Gardens
Brig
Carthaginian
Maui
Regional
(Wailuku)
Kahului
● Makawao

Lanai ●
(Lanai City)

Kula Botanical
Gardens □
Haleakala ▲
National Park

Bond Memorial ▲
(Kapaau)

Kamuela ▲
Museum
(Waiaka)
Thelma Parker
Memorial
(Waimea)
● Honokaa

● Laupahoehoe

Liliuokalani Gardens Park
Hilo Zoo
Hawaii Regional ●
Richardson
Ocean Center
Lyman House ●
Memorial
Hawaii Community College
Hilo College, University
of Hawaii
Panaewa Zoo &
Equestrian Center

Hulihee Palace ▲
(Kailua)
Kailua-Kona ▲
● Holualoa
● Keaau

● Kealakekua
● Mountain View

Puuhonua o ▲
Honaunau National
Historical Park
Kilauea Visitor Center
(Hawaii Volcanoes
National Park) ▲
● Pahoa

Wahaula Visitor Center ▲
(Hawaii Volcanoes
National Park)

● Pahala

Honolulu Academy of Arts.

Drawing by John A. Dixon

CENTERS FOR THE ARTS

Centers for the arts are those places and institutions where expression is given to beauty, pleasure, achievement, and other feelings in some artistic form. In Hawaii the centers reflect both the many ethnic groups that have settled in the Islands, in their particular Polynesian, Western, or Oriental forms, and an emerging cross-cultural form that is neo-Hawaiian, chiefly inspired by the environment of beauty seen in people, land, sea, and sky.

To the native Hawaiians the expressions of their artists were significant, but to subsequent immigrants intent on promoting Christianity and Western commerce, the Hawaiian expressions of art, and indeed the arts in general, were poorly understood and of minor importance. Traditional Hawaiian arts were ignored and at times repressed for 50 years, from 1830 to 1880. There was an important attempt to revive Hawaiian arts during the reigns of King Kalakaua and Queen Liliuokalani from 1874 to 1893, but with very few exceptions Western bourgeois values prevailed until the mid-twentieth century. Recently, several movements, local and national, have combined to raise interest in, and need for, art expressed in new ways. Most influential is a growing awareness that with increasing urbanization there is need to replace lost natural and cultural beauty with expressions of created art that can inspire us to appreciate more deeply and to foster "the spirit of Hawaii."

Since 1960 the government has made several major efforts to promote the arts: the State Foundation on Culture and the Arts, established in 1965; the passage of a law setting aside one percent of appropriations for new state buildings for purchasing works of art for those and other state buildings; the artist-in-the-schools program; and the expansion of the departments of art, architecture, dance, drama, and music at the several campuses of the University of Hawaii. Creative ideas in design of new buildings and in restoration of old ones, acquisition and display of works of art, and expansion of art institutions are some of the contributions of private firms and organizations. The community has pursued a variety of activities that have promoted music, dance, drama, painting, sculpture, ceramics, photography, flower work, and many other art forms. Part of this artistic endeavor is due to increased affluence and to government support, but most is due to a pronounced change in attitudes toward the arts by the majority of Hawaii's people. Of great significance is an accompanying strong movement among those of Hawaiian ancestry to revive and respect ancient Hawaiian arts.

The map on page 137 shows the location of those major centers for the arts that can be shown. Libraries and museums are treated on page 134, but also included here are such institutions as the B. P. Bishop Museum, which houses the most complete collection of Hawaiian arts and crafts in the world. Foremost among the centers is the Honolulu Academy of Arts, with its impressive collections of Oriental as well as of Western and local art. The Tennent Art Foundation Gallery is devoted to the drawings and paintings of Hawaiian people by Madge Tennent. Several churches, hotels, hospitals, and other buildings hold notable concentrations of paintings, murals, and sculpture. Commercial art galleries are located primarily in Honolulu, with smaller centers in Kailua, Kaneohe, and Haleiwa on Oahu, Lahaina on Maui, and Hilo, the Volcano area, and Kailua-Kona on Hawaii.

University, private, and military sponsored performing arts companies presented more than 100 productions in 1980, mostly on Oahu. Oriental drama—especially Peking Opera, Noh, and Kabuki—is presented frequently by local and visiting groups.

Presentations of Hawaiian hula and other dances, chants, and music are best seen at several annual events, such as the Merrie Monarch Festival in Hilo, Kamehameha Day, Aloha and Hula weeks throughout the islands. The Polynesian Cultural Center at Laie offers shows and displays of Polynesian dances, music, and crafts, principally for tourists, and some major hotels and visitor attractions also present traditional and modern Hawaiian dance and music by local companies. Oriental dances are a regular feature of traditional festivals, such as the widely attended Bon dances during mid-summer.

Modern Hawaiian music ranges in style from traditional to popular, including rock. A large number of orchestral and vocal groups perform in concerts, nightclubs, and on radio and television, but informal presentations occur everywhere. Of the many organizations for the cultivation of Western classical music, the most important is the Honolulu Symphony Orchestra, which gave 107 performances in the 1980–81 season to a total audience of 155,622.

Native Hawaiian architecture was modest and blended with the natural environment. Only the stone platforms and walls of some of the great heiaus (temples) survive. Memorable examples of Western and Oriental architecture appeared first in churches and temples. Iolani Palace, recently restored, is an excellent relic of the Victorian period. The State Capitol (1969) represents a genuine regional style that is exciting in concept. However, most modern urban architecture in Hawaii resembles that of any U.S. mainland city, although there are some interesting exceptions, such as the Grosvenor Center and restored older structures on Merchant Street in downtown Honolulu.

Staff

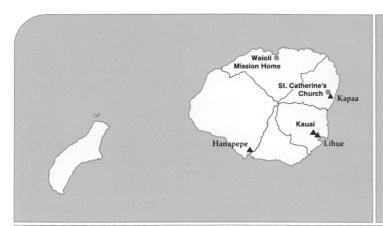

Waioli Mission Home

St. Catherine's Church

Kapaa

Kauai

Hanapepe

Lihue

Kahuku

Polynesian Cultural Center

Waianae

Waipahu

Pearl City

Kaneohe

Kailua

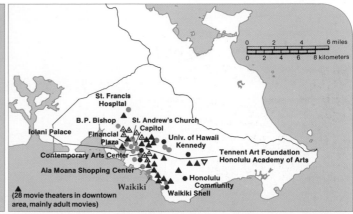

St. Francis Hospital

B.P. Bishop

St. Andrew's Church

Capitol

Iolani Palace

Financial Plaza

Univ. of Hawaii Kennedy

Contemporary Arts Center

Tennent Art Foundation
Honolulu Academy of Arts

Ala Moana Shopping Center

Honolulu Community

Waikiki

Waikiki Shell

(28 movie theaters in downtown area, mainly adult movies)

SELECTED CENTERS FOR THE ARTS

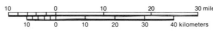

- ● Art concentration (murals, paintings, sculpture)

- ● Theater, concert and/or drama

Moving picture theater

- ▲ American films

- △ Predominantly Japanese, Chinese, Filipino

- ▽ Drive-In

Colleges and many high schools sponsor classical and folk dramatic arts, dance, and music. Most public buildings and churches feature art in the form of paintings, murals, sculpture or textile. The selection of art concentrations shown here represent only a small fraction of the art distributed throughout the islands.

```
10        0        10        20        30 miles
10   0    10   20   30        40 kilometers
```

Source: Atlas of Hawaii   1982

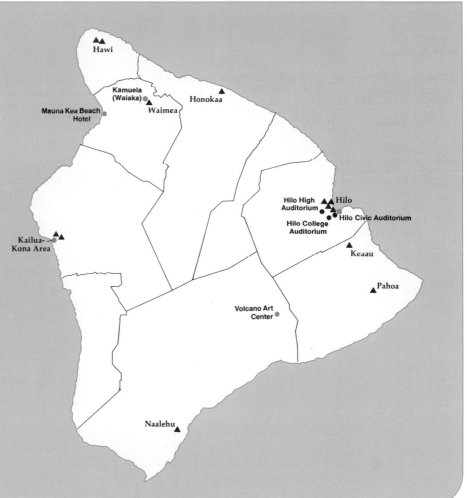

Hawi

Kamuela (Waiaka)

Honokaa

Mauna Kea Beach Hotel

Waimea

Hilo High Auditorium

Hilo

Hilo Civic Auditorium

Hilo College Auditorium

Kailua-Kona Area

Keaau

Pahoa

Volcano Art Center

Naalehu

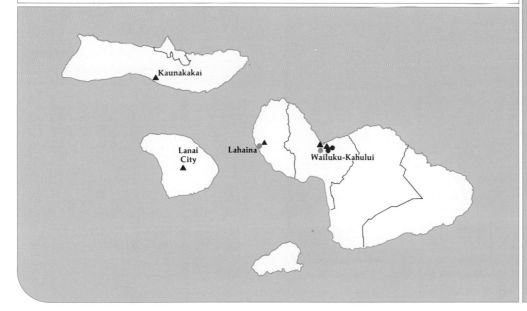

Kaunakakai

Lanai City

Lahaina

Wailuku-Kahului

Mele hula, traditional Hawaiian dance chant. The internationally recognized Hawaiian Dance Ensemble, University of Hawaii at Manoa, is a volunteer campus service organization committed to the study and performance of the mele hula traditions.

Photograph by Carl Hefner

Hoʻoulu Cambra, international performing artist, is Kumu Hula (Hula Master) of the mele hula traditions in the Department of Music, University of Hawaii at Manoa.

Photograph by Carl Hefner

The Honolulu Symphony led by Music Director Donald Johanos in a performance at the Neal S. Blaisdell Center Concert Hall.

Photograph by Tom Coffman Communications

Damien, written by Honolulu playwright Aldyth Morris and featuring actor Terence Knapp, received national acclaim when it was aired over 250 public television stations in January 1978. The 90-minute teledrama was produced and directed for Hawaii Public Television by Nino J. Martin.

Photograph by Joe F. Konno, Hawaii Public Television

THE SOCIAL ENVIRONMENT

State Capitol, Honolulu.

Drawing by John A. Dixon

GOVERNMENT AND POLITICS

The government of the State of Hawaii, in form and structure, is very similar to the governments of the 49 states that preceded Hawaii's admittance into the Union in 1959. This was also generally true of Hawaii's Territorial government that functioned from 1900 until 1959, when the "State" Constitution, drafted in 1950, in anticipation of statehood, went into effect.

Contemporary Hawaii governments is, however, more centralized than are the governments of the other states. Whereas the other states characteristically have several echelons of local government, such as counties, townships, cities, and school districts, Hawaii has only one level, namely counties (page 141). Each of the four counties, pursuant to provision of the State Constitution, functions within the framework of a locally adopted "home rule" charter.

Hawaii state government is more streamlined and compact than the other state governments. The legislature, which numbers 76 members, is below average in size, and only two administrative officers (governor and lieutenant governor) are elected. The Hawaii state legislature is bicameral in form, with a 51-member House of Representatives and a 25-member Senate. All members of the House (2-year terms) and approximately one-half of the Senate (4-year terms) are elected every two years. Until the election of 1982, Hawaii had used traditional multimember electoral districts based on the number of registered voters, but according to a court-ordered plan, representatives and senators are now elected from 76 single-member electorates based on population (pages 141 and 143). Each House district reflects a resident civilian population of approximately 17,300 persons, and each Senate district, a population of approximately 35,300 persons.

The Hawaii state legislature is assigned basic policy-making power, following the model established for Congress by the U.S. Constitution. Since 1954, the legislature has generally been a replica in miniature of Hawaii's several major ethnic groups. Annual legislative sessions convene on the third Wednesday of January and are scheduled to adjourn 90 legislative days later. Session extensions and special sessions are not uncommon. The taxing, appropriations, and confirmation (of executive appointees) powers and duties exercised by the legislature usually result in lively struggles and debates. Given the small land area of the State, legislators are subject to above-average public scrutiny.

The executive branch of Hawaii's state government is headed by a governor and a lieutenant governor, elected in tandem fashion on an at-large basis. Both serve four-year terms and cannot serve more than two consecutive full terms. The executive branch, which currently has 17 departments, is limited by the State Constitution to 20 departments. Heads of most of these departments are appointed by the governor (with approval by the Senate), and normally have tenure co-terminous with the governor. Most departments are headed by a single executive. They are organized along functional lines, such as education, transportation, and health, and serve the entire State. They are coordinated by an administrative director who serves at the pleasure of the governor.

The Department of Education, the University of Hawaii, and the Office of Hawaiian Affairs constitute notable exceptions to the concentration of administrative authority in that each agency is headed by a board. The Board of Education is elected on a non-partisan basis for four-year terms from two districts, ten members from Oahu, and three from the rest of the State. The board, in turn, appoints a superintendent to administer the department. The Board of Regents of the University of Hawaii is appointed by the governor, at least part of the membership representing geographical subdivisions of the State. The Board appoints the university president. The Board of Trustees of the Office of Hawaiian Affairs, established by constitutional mandate in 1979, is elected at large by qualified voters of Hawaiian extraction. Of its nine members, there must be at least one representative from each of the islands of Kauai, Oahu, Molokai, Maui, and Hawaii. The board appoints an executive officer to administer the office.

Hawaii's judiciary consists of a supreme court, an intermediate appellate court, four circuit courts, and 27 district courts. The supreme court, the smallest such court in the nation, has five justices. Supreme, appellate, and circuit court judges are appointed by the governor, with senatorial consent, for ten-year terms. District magistrates are appointed by the chief justice of the supreme court for six-year terms. Judges of circuit courts are appointed to serve in four judicial circuits (page 141). District courts and the 27 districts are shown on page 211. The supreme and intermediate appellate courts are courts of appeal. Circuit and district courts are courts of original jurisdiction.

D.W.T.

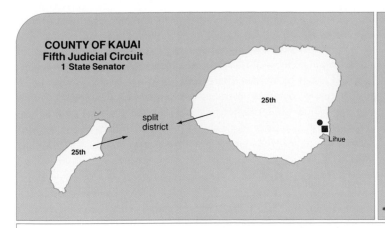

COUNTY OF KAUAI
Fifth Judicial Circuit
1 State Senator

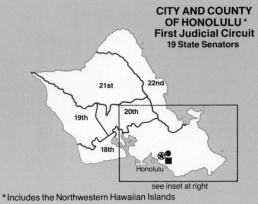

CITY AND COUNTY OF HONOLULU *
First Judicial Circuit
19 State Senators

*Includes the Northwestern Hawaiian Islands

see inset at right

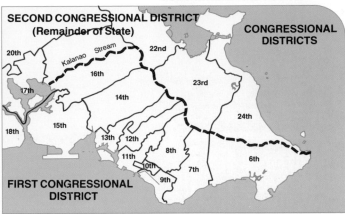

SECOND CONGRESSIONAL DISTRICT
(Remainder of State)

CONGRESSIONAL DISTRICTS

FIRST CONGRESSIONAL DISTRICT

CONGRESSIONAL AND STATE SENATORIAL DISTRICTS, COUNTIES, AND JUDICIAL CIRCUITS

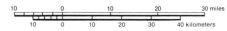

- - - Congressional district boundary

50th   State senatorial district boundary and number

⊛   State capital

●   County seat

■   Circuit courthouse

Note: The Fourth Judicial Circuit formerly comprised the districts of Hamakua, Hilo, and Puna on Hawaii. In 1943, it was merged with the Third Judicial Circuit (the other districts on the island). For district courts and district boundaries, see page 211.

10   0   10   20   30 miles
10 0 10 20 30 40 kilometers

Source: State Office of the Lieutenant Governor; The Judiciary

1982

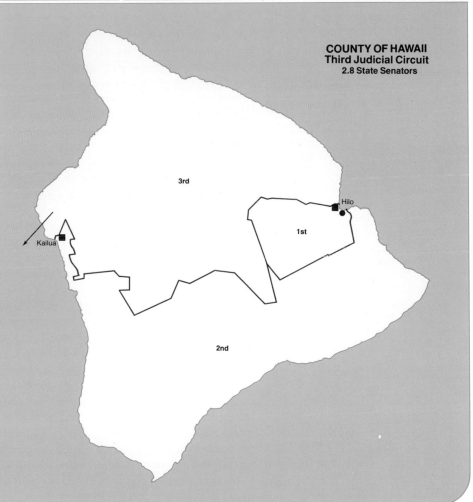

COUNTY OF HAWAII
Third Judicial Circuit
2.8 State Senators

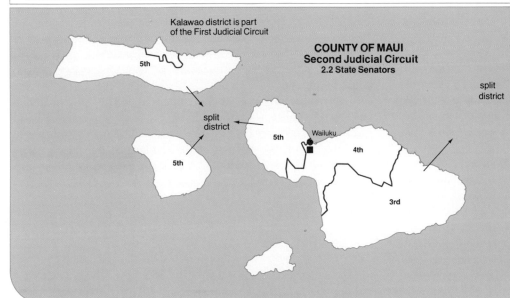

Kalawao district is part of the First Judicial Circuit

COUNTY OF MAUI
Second Judicial Circuit
2.2 State Senators

split district

split district

Iolani Bandstand, Palace Grounds, Honolulu.
Drawing by John A. Dixon

Politics

Hawaii's electoral system is similar to those found in the other 49 states. Political life is dynamic and generally competitive. All adult citizens, 18 years of age or older, may register and vote except those who are unpardoned felons, mentally incompetent, or illiterate. For many years, a system of permanent registration has been in effect. Once an elector registers, as long as he continues to vote, his name remains on the official rolls. Although registration percentage in Hawaii is close to the national average, voter turnout has usually been well above average. In the statehood election of 1959, 93 percent of registered voters voted. Since then, participation has declined, on the average, to about 80 percent. There were 402,792 persons registered to vote in 1980. Of these, 297,533, were registered on Oahu. In 1980, 78.9 percent of registered voters cast ballots.

Officials are elected to federal, state, and county positions at the general election, after having first succeeded in obtaining nomination at a primary election. Primary and general elections are held in even-numbered years, with the primary preceding the November general election by approximately six weeks. After a decade of experience with a closed partisan primary, Hawaii's primary law may now be classified as "open (secret choice of party)." Candidates are required to file periodic campaign expense statements and may, if they adhere to the specifics of spending limitations, share in public campaign funds collected through an income tax check-off system.

Most of the political life in Hawaii proceeds within the framework of political parties and pressure groups. Since 1900, the traditional American political parties have functioned in Hawaii. From 1900 to 1954, the Republican Party was dominant, with only occasional Democratic victories being recorded. Since 1954, the Democratic Party has prevailed and, since 1962, has been as successful as the Republican Party prior to 1954. Business, labor, professional, single-issue, and community-minded pressure groups have in recent years been more dynamic than the party organizations.

Hawaii's two major parties maintain private organizations that determine organizational structures and procedures and define and record membership. The organizational hierarchy for both parties includes precinct clubs, district (legislative) committees, county committees, and a state committee. Both parties hold annual state conventions, at which state committee members and members of national committees are selected. Conventions whose delegates are selected at the precinct level also draft election-year platforms. These often lengthy documents are less well utilized now than during the decades 1950 and 1960.

Inter-party competition, which was intense during the period 1954–1962, has become increasingly relaxed. Yet, even as this has occurred, intra-party Democratic competition has often been very dynamic and hard fought. Democratic strength has consistently been greater on all islands except Oahu. Areas of Republican strength include: the north coast of Kauai, the Kailua and Waikiki-Kahala areas on Oahu, the leeward coast of Maui, and the Kona Coast of the island of Hawaii. On the average, Democratic Party statewide strength in 1980, was 65 percent. Third parties have from time to time existed, but none has been a major factor in island politics since statehood.

There are at least 250 to 300 special interest organizations in a position to influence the direction of public policy in Hawaii. They exert their influence by lobbying in the legislative and executive branches of government. Those organizations that exert above-average influence include: the International Longshoremen's and Warehousemen's Union, the AFL-CIO, the Teamsters, the Hawaii Government Employees Association, the United Public Workers, the Tax Foundation of Hawaii, the Hawaii Visitors Bureau, the Chamber of Commerce of Hawaii, the Hawaii Sugar Planters Association, Common Cause, and the League of Women Voters. Most of these groups maintain statewide organizations with headquarters in Honolulu. Some of them play active roles in political campaigns.

Contemporary Hawaii political campaigns tend to revolve around individual candidates with interest group and party organizational backing. They are normally lively affairs that often involve strategic media programs, hand-held highway signs (billboards are illegal), mass meetings, and home coffee hours. A campaign for a major office, such as governor, usually means total expenditures in excess of $2 million.

D.W.T.

COUNTY OF KAUAI
2.3 Representatives

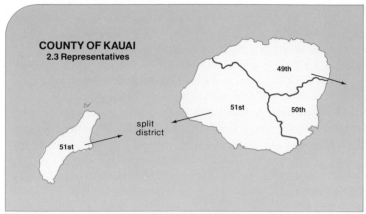

49th

51st

50th

split
district

51st

51st

CITY AND COUNTY
OF HONOLULU
39.7 Representatives

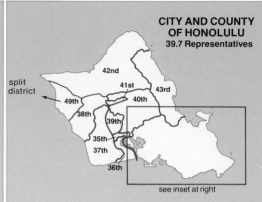

42nd

41st

43rd

split
district

49th

40th

38th

39th

35th

37th

36th

see inset at right

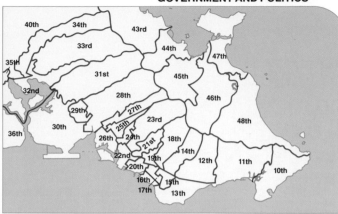

40th
34th
43rd
33rd
44th
47th
35th
31st
45th
32nd
28th
29th
27th
23rd
46th
30th
25th
24th
18th
48th
26th
21st
14th
22nd
19th
12th
11th
20th
16th
15th
13th
10th
17th

STATE REPRESENTATIVE DISTRICT
BOUNDARIES
1982

50th   Representative district boundary
       and number

10   0   10   20   30 miles
10   0   10   20   30   40 kilometers

Sources: State Office of the Lieutenant Governor: The Judiciary

1982

COUNTY OF HAWAII
5 Representatives

4th

3rd

5th

1st

2nd

COUNTY OF MAUI
4 Representatives

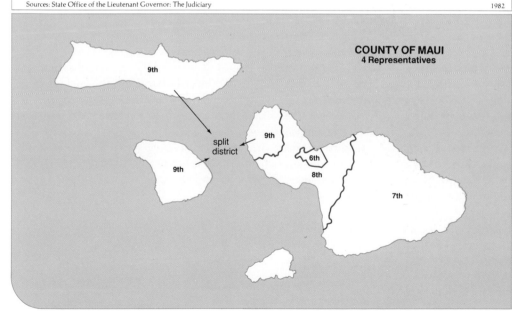

9th

9th

9th

6th

8th

9th

7th

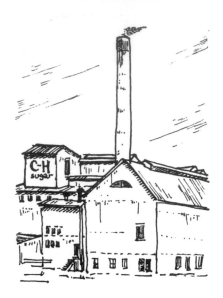

Sugar refinery, Aiea, Oahu.

Drawing by John A. Dixon

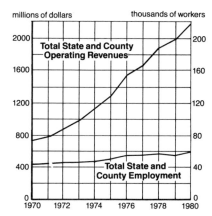

**TOTAL STATE AND COUNTY
REVENUES AND EMPLOYMENT**

THE ECONOMY

The rapid growth that has distinguished the Hawaiian economy since the end of World War II continued into the seventies, and by 1980 had raised Gross State Product (GSP) to more than $14 billion. In terms of per capita product, Hawaii ranked 14th among the 50 states, and well below the level of the Pacific Coast states. Much of this expansion, however, was the result of inflation, and after 1975 growth in real terms was modest. Yet the prolonged national recession following the great increase in oil prices in 1978/1979 did not have an overly severe impact, and unemployment remained below the national average. Despite the setback to the construction industry, the recession tended to confirm the pattern of structural change in the State economy, which is slowly becoming more varied and less dependent on the traditional activities of the past. Nevertheless, economic activity remains largely oriented toward services for tourists, for business visitors, and for the federal government, and is heavily concentrated on Oahu, which in 1980 accounted for nearly 79 percent of the State's total employment.

Tourism, which has long been the most vigorous force in the State's economic growth, received a set-back in 1980, which was the first year since 1949 to record a decrease in visitor arrivals over those of the previous years. Higher air fares and the depression in the automobile and related industries largely accounted for the decline, which was severely felt on Kauai and Hawaii islands, where the expansion of hotel facilities has been more rapid than on Oahu. Though growth has since resumed, the increase in tourist arrivals in the eighties will be on a more modest scale than in the past. In 1981 the approximately 3.9 million visitors spent more than $3 billion in the islands.

Federal government outlays maintain their position as the largest contributor to the State's economy, but by 1980 the margin over tourism was slender. Moreover, nondefense expenditure by the federal government, at $1.9 billion in 1981, substantially exceeded the $1.4 billion spent on defense purposes, a major break with the traditional pattern of federal expenditure in the State.

Manufacturing continues to make a larger contribution to GSP, and the range of manufactured goods produced in the islands is now very wide. In 1980, sales of diversified manufactured products—at almost 1.8 billion—were almost twice those of processed sugar and pineapple, for many years in the past the State's leading manufactures. Sugar and pineapples continue to dominate the agriculture sector, but here also their relative importance is slowly declining; with the single exception of 1979, every year between 1975 and 1981 recorded a drop in sugar output. Three sugar mills, one each on Kauai, Oahu, and Hawaii, ceased operations in the seventies, and because of the poor prospects for profitability, the Puna mill on Hawaii is to close by 1984. Yet the notorious instability of the world sugar market will undoubtedly result in periods of very high prices, as it has in the past, and the poor prognosis for the sugar industry may be premature. The scope for the expansion of other agricultural products appears limited, but macadamia nuts seem to have a bright future; large new plantings have been made, some on old sugar land.

Agriculture nevertheless contributes more to the State's economy than official figures indicate. The illegal cultivation of *pakalolo* (cannabis), an activity that embraces many forms of enterprise from substantial clearings in sugarcane fields, in State forests, and other public lands, to backyard and indoor pot plants, has a turnover that probably exceeds that of any other crop. Notwithstanding the depression in the sugar industry in the early eighties, many rural communities still wear a prosperous look, even in the areas where sugar cultivation has been terminated. For this situation *pakalolo* cultivation is probably an important contributory factor.

Hawaii has the most highly centralized local government structure of all fifty states; it has only four administrative units below the state level—the counties of Hawaii, Maui, and Kauai, and the City and County of Honolulu (page 140). State and local governments constitute the largest sources of employment in the islands, with over 59,000 employees in 1980. The school system operates under a single statewide school board. Hawaii is also unique in having a single state-wide telephone company, and the electricity supply also is virtually in the hands of a single utility undertaking. State and county revenue receipts and expenditure outlays appear on page 146.

D.W.F.

TOTAL RESIDENT POPULATION AS OF APRIL 1	1980	964,691	**CONSTRUCTION COMPLETED**	1980	$1.5 billion	
	1970	769,913		1970	$784 million	
EMPLOYMENT	1980	400,000	**RETAIL SALES**	1980	$6.4 billion	
	1970	335,450		1970	$2.0 billion	
PERSONAL INCOME	1980	$9.4 billion	**BANK DEBITS**	1980	$84.3 billion	
	1970	$3.4 billion		1970	$23.3 billion	
FEDERAL EXPENDITURES	1980	$3.3 billion	**REAL PROPERTY TAX BASE**	1980	$21.9 billion	
	1970	$1.1 billion		1970	$7.7 billion	
HOUSING INVENTORY	1980	334,364	**SUGAR PRODUCTION**	1980	$595 million	
	1970	216,774		1970	$198 million	
VISITOR ARRIVALS	1980	3,934,504	**PINEAPPLE PRODUCTION**	1980	$229 million	
	1970	1,746,970		1970	$135 million	
HOTEL ROOM INVENTORY	1980	56,769	**DIVERSIFIED AGRICULTURE**	1980	$172 million	
	1970	32,289		1970	$63 million	

Source: Bank of Hawaii, Dept. of Business Research

ECONOMIC PATTERN FOR THE STATE

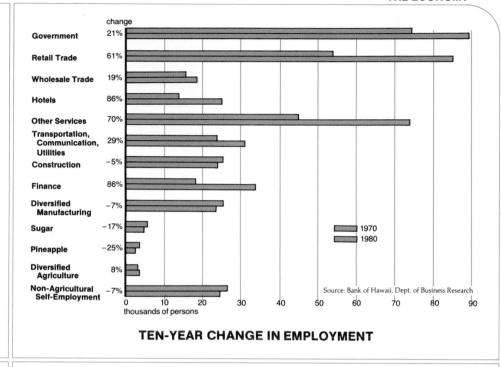

TEN-YEAR CHANGE IN EMPLOYMENT

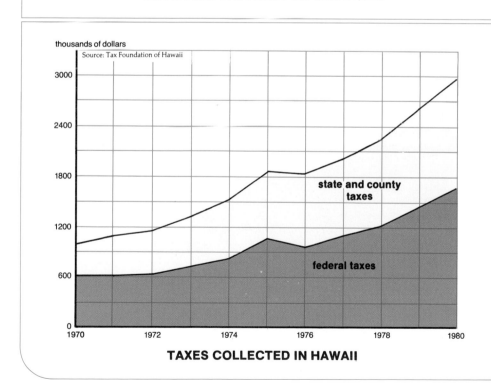

TAXES COLLECTED IN HAWAII

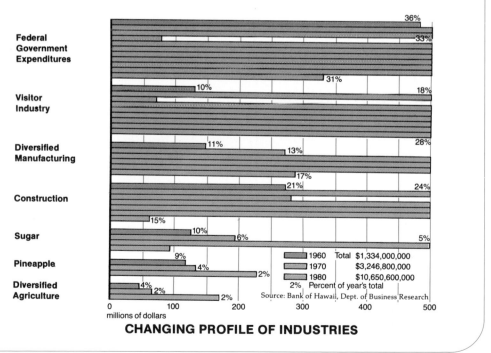

CHANGING PROFILE OF INDUSTRIES

STATE REVENUES AND EXPENDITURES

millions of dollars

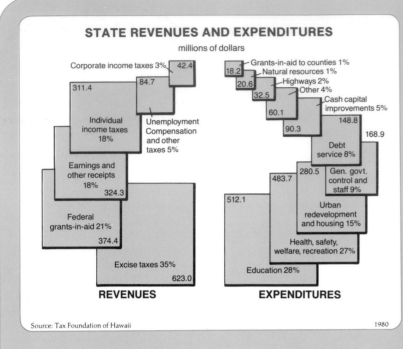

REVENUES

Corporate income taxes 3% — 42.4
84.7
311.4
Individual income taxes 18%
Unemployment Compensation and other taxes 5%
Earnings and other receipts 18%
324.3
Federal grants-in-aid 21%
374.4
Excise taxes 35%
623.0

EXPENDITURES

Grants-in-aid to counties 1% — 18.2
Natural resources 1% — 20.6
Highways 2% — 32.5
Other 4% — 60.1
Cash capital improvements 5% — 90.3
148.8
Debt service 8% — 168.9
Gen. govt. control and staff 9% — 280.5
Urban redevelopment and housing 15% — 483.7
Health, safety, welfare, recreation 27% — 512.1
Education 28%

Source: Tax Foundation of Hawaii   1980

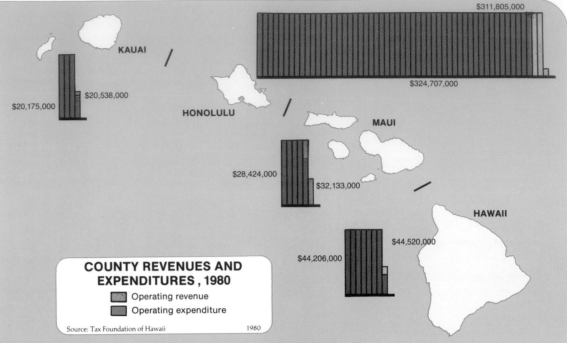

KAUAI
$20,175,000 $20,538,000

HONOLULU

$311,805,000

$324,707,000

MAUI
$28,424,000 $32,133,000

HAWAII
$44,206,000 $44,520,000

COUNTY REVENUES AND EXPENDITURES, 1980

Operating revenue
Operating expenditure

Source: Tax Foundation of Hawaii   1980

FEDERAL EXPENDITURES IN HAWAII

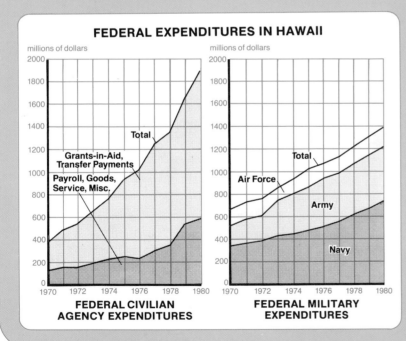

millions of dollars

FEDERAL CIVILIAN AGENCY EXPENDITURES

Total
Grants-in-Aid, Transfer Payments
Payroll, Goods, Service, Misc.

1970 1972 1974 1976 1978 1980

FEDERAL MILITARY EXPENDITURES

Total
Air Force
Army
Navy

1970 1972 1974 1976 1978 1980

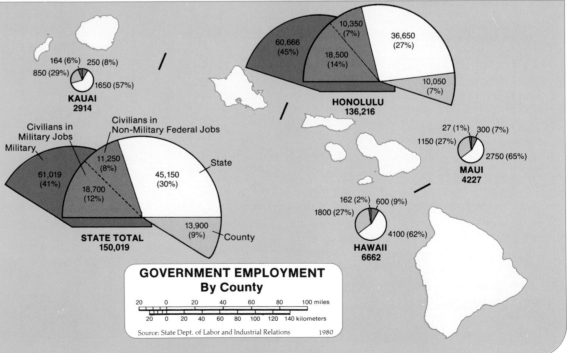

KAUAI 2914
164 (6%)   250 (8%)
850 (29%)   1650 (57%)

HONOLULU 136,216
60,666 (45%)   10,350 (7%)   36,650 (27%)
18,500 (14%)   10,050 (7%)

Civilians in Military Jobs
Military
Civilians in Non-Military Federal Jobs
State
County

STATE TOTAL 150,019
61,019 (41%)   11,250 (8%)   45,150 (30%)
18,700 (12%)   13,900 (9%)

MAUI 4227
27 (1%)   300 (7%)
1150 (27%)   2750 (65%)

HAWAII 6662
162 (2%)   600 (9%)
1800 (27%)   4100 (62%)

GOVERNMENT EMPLOYMENT
By County

20 0 20 40 60 80 100 miles
20 0 20 40 60 80 100 120 140 kilometers

Source: State Dept. of Labor and Industrial Relations   1980

LAND TENURE

The State of Hawaii has a small total land area, with a very limited supply of prime agricultural land and beautiful beach land—most of it, especially on the island of Oahu, under enormous pressure for residential and resort development. The need to identify the highest and best use of Hawaii's lands grows more urgent as the population continues to increase. And the process of land-use decision making becomes more complex as ecological, environmental, and open-space concerns grow.

There is growing competition for land for all uses. Of increasing importance is the demand for living space. To meet this need, land will have to be taken from the agricultural areas having highly productive soils. Such decisions regarding land use are essentially (economically) irreversible and therefore should be made only with a full awareness of the physical characteristics of the land involved, as well as the ecological, environmental, and socioeconomic consequences of the decision.

As larger segments of land are given over to urban pursuits, the likelihood and danger of costly mistakes in locating urban structures on soils ill-suited to the purpose will similarly grow. To minimize such mistakes, increasing attention must be given to matching the physical environment of an area to the requirements for specific uses; this is equally true for rural land uses.

The State of Hawaii consists of eight major islands and 124 minor islands with a combined total land area of 6,425 square miles. Ninety-eight percent, 4,050,176 acres, is on the six largest islands—Kauai, Oahu, Molokai, Lanai, Maui, and Hawaii. The island of Hawaii is 2,573,440 acres in size. A seventh island (Niihau) is owned in entirety by a private family and is occupied by native Hawaiians. The eighth (Kahoolawe) is now uninhabitable, principally because of the lack of water and current military use.

Not all the land area of the six largest islands is usable; 12 percent of the total is too steep for development or lacks productive capacity. Barren and steep land located within the national parks, game manage-ment areas, forest reserves, and military reservations throughout the State are accounted for in their respective uses.

About four-fifths of the usable area is devoted to extensive and intensive agricultural uses, of which about 75 percent is forest and grazing land. The acreage used for plantation agriculture is declining. This is particularly true of sugarcane, as costly and low-yielding plantations are taken out of production. Diversified agriculture is expanding to include macadamia nuts, papaya, guava, aquaculture, and foliage and nursery products.

Ownership of the usable land is highly concentrated. The state, county, and federal governments together are the biggest landowners, controlling about 47 percent of the total land area. About four-fifths of these public lands (including Hawaiian Home lands) belong to the State of Hawaii. These state lands constitute the bulk of the forest reserves or the conservation district set aside by the statewide zoning law. About one-fourth is leased, principally for pasture and sugarcane. The Department of Land and Natural Resources is the State's land management agency for state lands. This agency also manages Hawaii's natural area reserve system. This "reserve system" protects unique natural resources, such as volcanic and other geological features and distinctive marine and terrestrial plants and animals, many of which occur nowhere else in the world. Most of the federal acreage is in national parks on Hawaii and Maui and in military holdings on Oahu and Kauai.

Private ownership of land (53 percent of the total land area) is also highly concentrated; about 77 percent of this private land is in the hands of fewer than 40 owners, each with 5,000 acres or more. In addition to Lanai and Niihau, which are in effect 100-percent privately owned, large private landholders own 60 percent of the land on Molokai and 40 to 50 percent on Oahu, Hawaii, Kauai, and Maui. Agricultural uses, particularly for grazing and sugarcane, constitute the major application of the large private landholdings. A substantial acreage is unproductive and classified as conservation land. Only a small amount, about one percent of the large private landholdings, is in urban uses.

The last complete and systematic assessment of land use on an island-by-island and statewide basis was made by the Land Study Bureau in 1968. (See *Atlas of Hawaii*, 1st ed., 1973).

H.L.B.

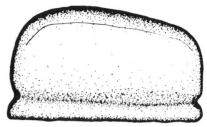

Hawaiian arts and crafts: stone weight for an octopus lure.

Drawing by T. Stell Newman

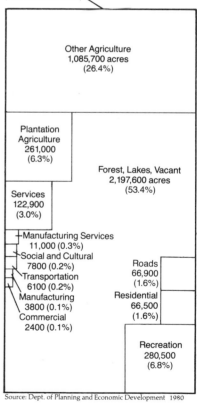

Total Area of State
4,112,200 acres
(1,664,146 hectares)

Other Agriculture
1,085,700 acres
(26.4%)

Plantation Agriculture
261,000
(6.3%)

Forest, Lakes, Vacant
2,197,600 acres
(53.4%)

Services
122,900
(3.0%)

Manufacturing Services
11,000 (0.3%)

Social and Cultural
7800 (0.2%)

Transportation
6100 (0.2%)

Manufacturing
3800 (0.1%)

Commercial
2400 (0.1%)

Roads
66,900
(1.6%)

Residential
66,500
(1.6%)

Recreation
280,500
(6.8%)

Source: Dept. of Planning and Economic Development 1980

STATE LAND USE

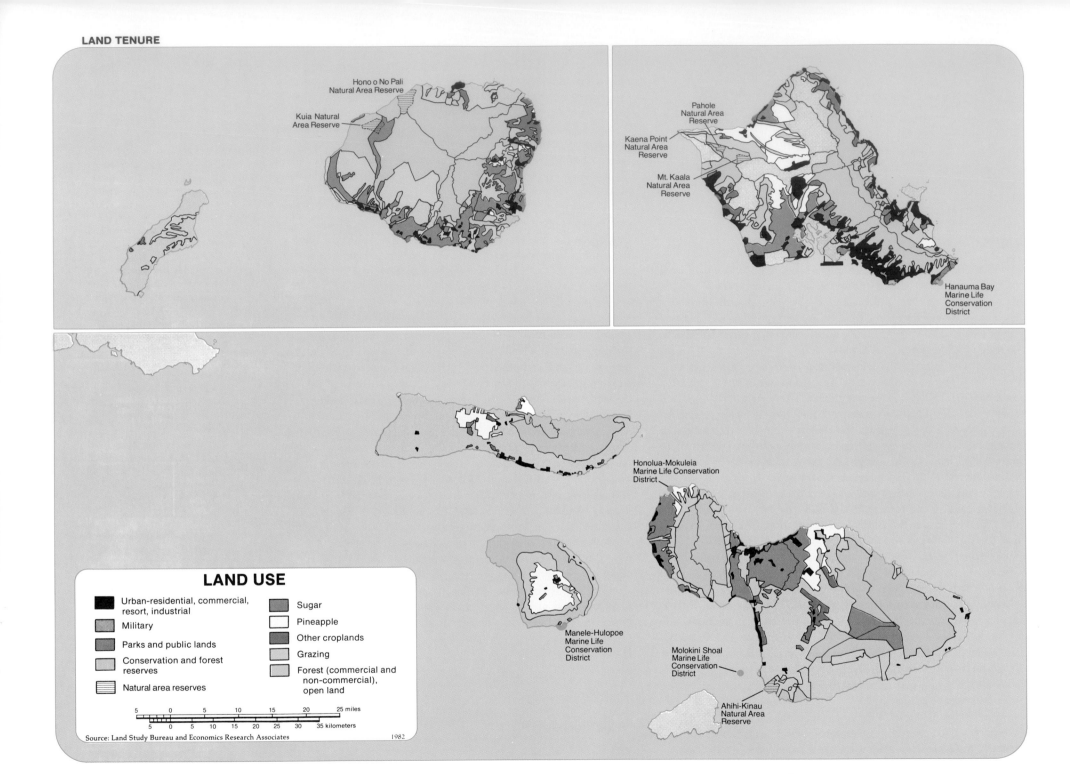

Hono o No Pali
Natural Area Reserve

Kuia Natural
Area Reserve

Pahole
Natural Area
Reserve

Kaena Point
Natural Area
Reserve

Mt. Kaala
Natural Area
Reserve

Hanauma Bay
Marine Life
Conservation
District

Honolua-Mokuleia
Marine Life Conservation
District

Manele-Hulopoe
Marine Life
Conservation
District

Molokini Shoal
Marine Life
Conservation
District

Ahihi-Kinau
Natural Area
Reserve

LAND USE

- Urban-residential, commercial, resort, industrial
- Military
- Parks and public lands
- Conservation and forest reserves
- Natural area reserves

- Sugar
- Pineapple
- Other croplands
- Grazing
- Forest (commercial and non-commercial), open land

5   0   5   10   15   20   25 miles
5   0   5   10   15   20   25   30   35 kilometers

Source: Land Study Bureau and Economics Research Associates   1982

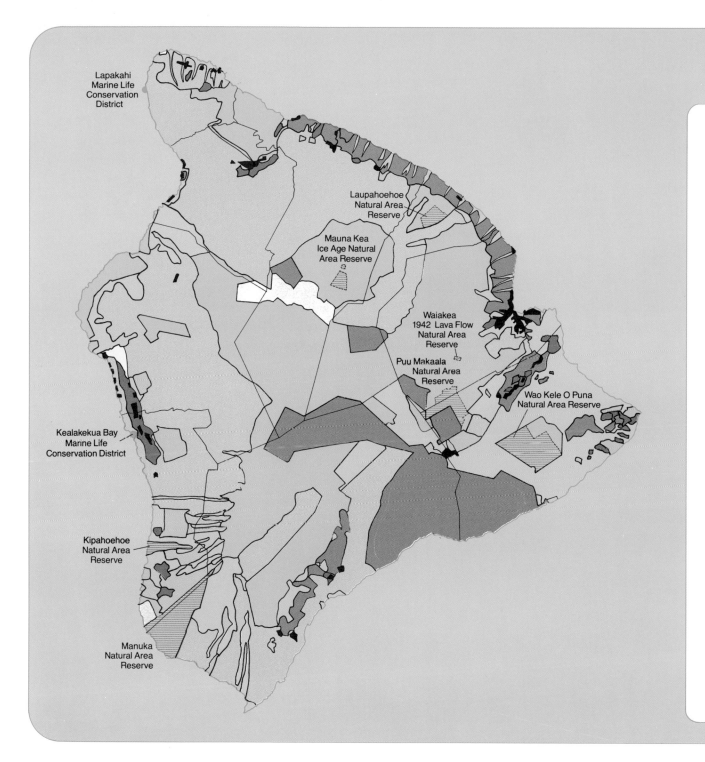

Lapakahi
Marine Life
Conservation
District

Laupahoehoe
Natural Area
Reserve

Mauna Kea
Ice Age Natural
Area Reserve

Waiakea
1942 Lava Flow
Natural Area
Reserve

Puu Makaala
Natural Area
Reserve

Wao Kele O Puna
Natural Area Reserve

Kealakekua Bay
Marine Life
Conservation District

Kipahoehoe
Natural Area
Reserve

Manuka
Natural Area
Reserve

Agriculture is the predominant land use in the Fiftieth State. About three-fourths of the total land area is used for forestry and grazing and for plantations and diversified agriculture. Forests and forest reserves account for about 50 percent of the area in this broad use category and embrace primarily those lands of importance for watershed protection. Grazing lands comprise more than one-third and generally include areas rated poor in overall agricultural productivity. Plantations use less than 10 percent of the total agricultural area, but this is more than three-fourths of the State's "prime" agricultural land. The acreage in sugarcane plantations is declining as operators seek to remove the most costly and lowest-yielding areas from production. Diversified crops, consisting primarily of orchard crops, flowers, foliage and nursery products, and vegetables, are produced on slightly more than one percent of the area in the broad agricultural land-use category. Most of the acreage in orchard crops is found on the island of Hawaii. Oahu has about the same area in vegetables as Hawaii and Maui but leads the major islands in area devoted to dairy, poultry, and swine enterprises.

Land classified as urban comprises about 4 percent of the total area of the State. The urban land acreage was not differentiated as to residential, commercial, and industrial uses. Military use occupies only about one percent of the total area, but this figure does not include the 17,600 acres in military housing and other urbanlike uses included under urban lands. Ninety-two percent of the military acreage is located on Oahu.

Pali and barren lands, that is, lands incapable of use because of steepness or lack of productive capacity, occupy about 12 percent of the total land area of the State.

Essentially all the remaining land is in national parks, game management reserves, and other recreational areas. The national parks are located on the islands of Hawaii and Maui, specifically the Hawaii Volcanoes and Haleakala National Parks. Hawaii has established a natural area reserves system (page 147), and marine life conservation districts. These are administered by the State Department of Land and Natural Resources and are intended to preserve natural resources, many of which occur nowhere else in the world. The location of the natural area reserves and marine life conservation districts is shown on the accompanying maps.

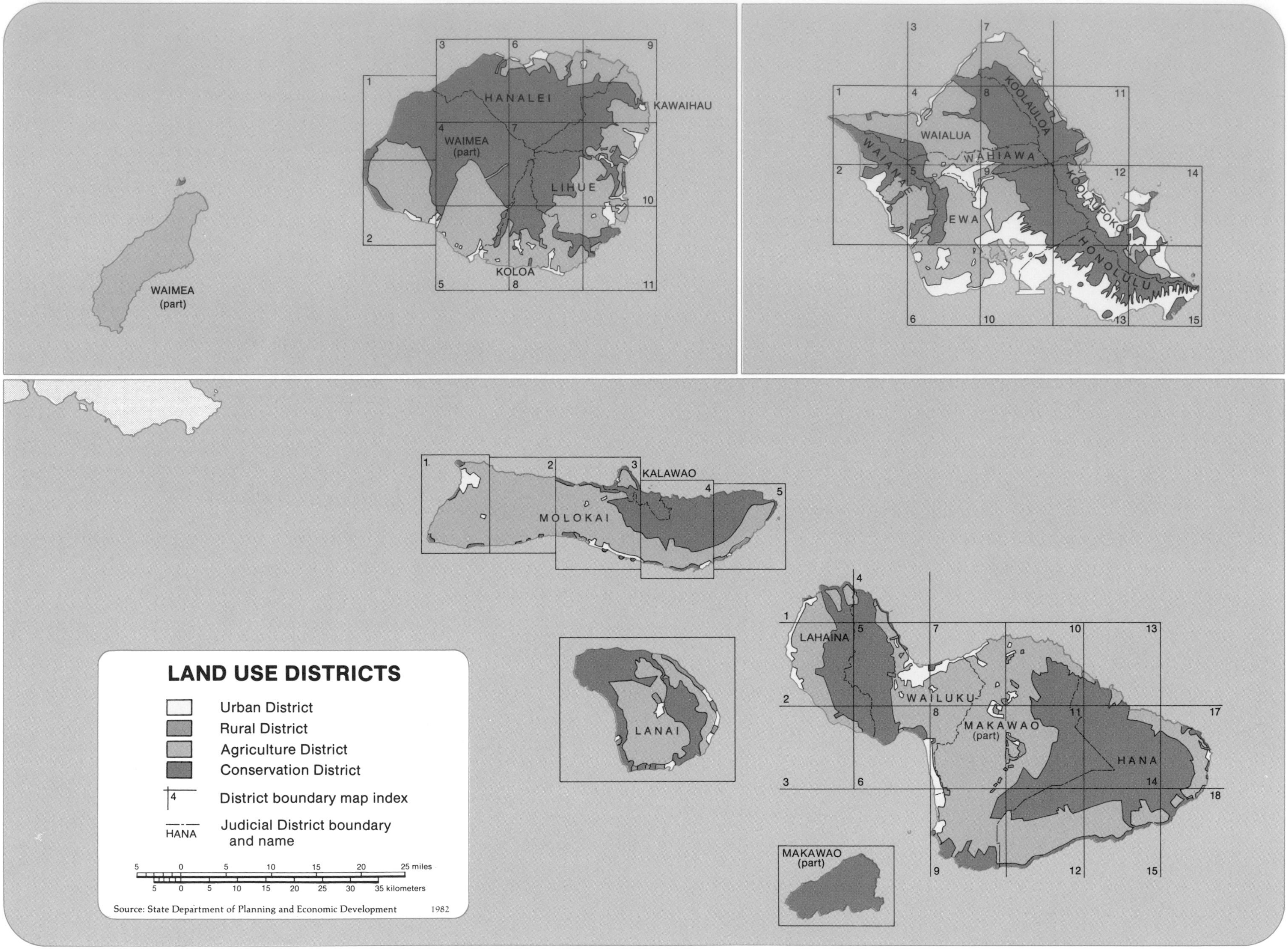

WAIMEA
(part)

3   6   9

1
HANALEI   KAWAIHAU

4   7
WAIMEA
(part)
LIHUE

2   10

5   8   11
KOLOA

3   7

1   4   8   11
KOOLAULOA
WAIALUA
WAIANAE   WAHIAWA

2   5   9   12   14
KOOLAUPOKO
EWA   HONOLULU

6   10   13   15

1.   2   3
KALAWAO
4   5
MOLOKAI

LAND USE DISTRICTS

Urban District

Rural District

Agriculture District

Conservation District

4   District boundary map index

HANA   Judicial District boundary
and name

5   0   5   10   15   20   25 miles

5   0   5   10   15   20   25   30   35 kilometers

Source: State Department of Planning and Economic Development   1982

LANAI

4

1   5   7   10   13
LAHAINA

2   WAILUKU   17
8
MAKAWAO   11
(part)
HANA

3   6   14   18

MAKAWAO
(part)

9   12   15

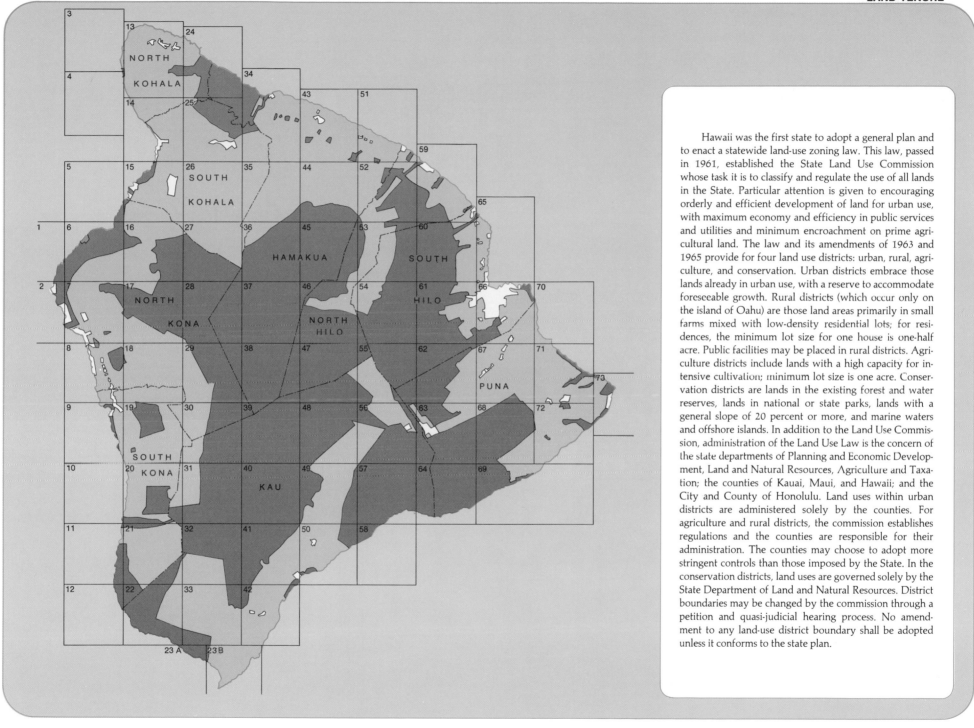

Hawaii was the first state to adopt a general plan and to enact a statewide land-use zoning law. This law, passed in 1961, established the State Land Use Commission whose task it is to classify and regulate the use of all lands in the State. Particular attention is given to encouraging orderly and efficient development of land for urban use, with maximum economy and efficiency in public services and utilities and minimum encroachment on prime agricultural land. The law and its amendments of 1963 and 1965 provide for four land use districts: urban, rural, agriculture, and conservation. Urban districts embrace those lands already in urban use, with a reserve to accommodate foreseeable growth. Rural districts (which occur only on the island of Oahu) are those land areas primarily in small farms mixed with low-density residential lots; for residences, the minimum lot size for one house is one-half acre. Public facilities may be placed in rural districts. Agriculture districts include lands with a high capacity for intensive cultivation; minimum lot size is one acre. Conservation districts are lands in the existing forest and water reserves, lands in national or state parks, lands with a general slope of 20 percent or more, and marine waters and offshore islands. In addition to the Land Use Commission, administration of the Land Use Law is the concern of the state departments of Planning and Economic Development, Land and Natural Resources, Agriculture and Taxation; the counties of Kauai, Maui, and Hawaii; and the City and County of Honolulu. Land uses within urban districts are administered solely by the counties. For agriculture and rural districts, the commission establishes regulations and the counties are responsible for their administration. The counties may choose to adopt more stringent controls than those imposed by the State. In the conservation districts, land uses are governed solely by the State Department of Land and Natural Resources. District boundaries may be changed by the commission through a petition and quasi-judicial hearing process. No amendment to any land-use district boundary shall be adopted unless it conforms to the state plan.

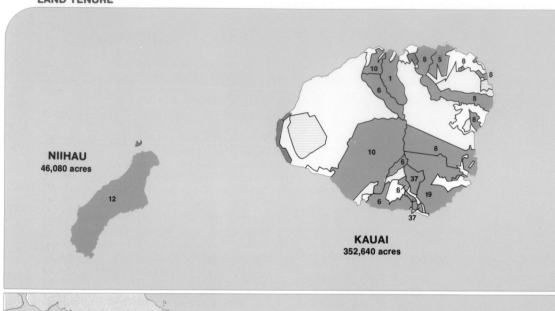

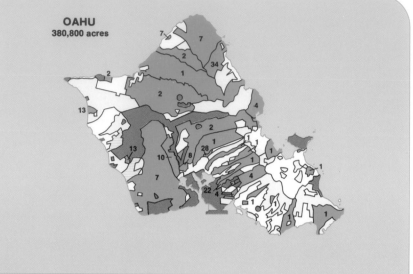

NIIHAU
46,080 acres

12

KAUAI
352,640 acres

10
1
6
8
5
8
8
8
8
10
8
6
37
6
19
6
37

OAHU
380,800 acres

7
7
2
34
2
1
13
2
2
4
13
1
28
10
8
1
7
22
4
1
1
1
1

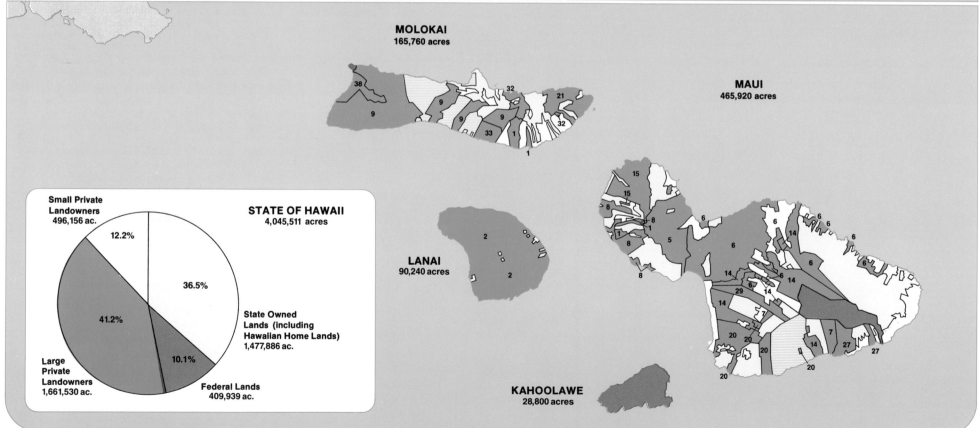

MOLOKAI
165,760 acres

38
9
32
21
9
9
9
32
33
1
1

MAUI
465,920 acres

15
15
8
8
8
6
6
6
6
1
6
5
6
14
6
8
6
6
14
6
14
29
6
14
14
7
7
7
20
20
14
27
20
27
20
20

LANAI
90,240 acres

2
2

KAHOOLAWE
28,800 acres

Small Private
Landowners
496,156 ac.

STATE OF HAWAII
4,045,511 acres

12.2%

36.5%

41.2%

10.1%

Large
Private
Landowners
1,661,530 ac.

Federal Lands
409,939 ac.

State Owned
Lands (including
Hawaiian Home Lands)
1,477,886 ac.

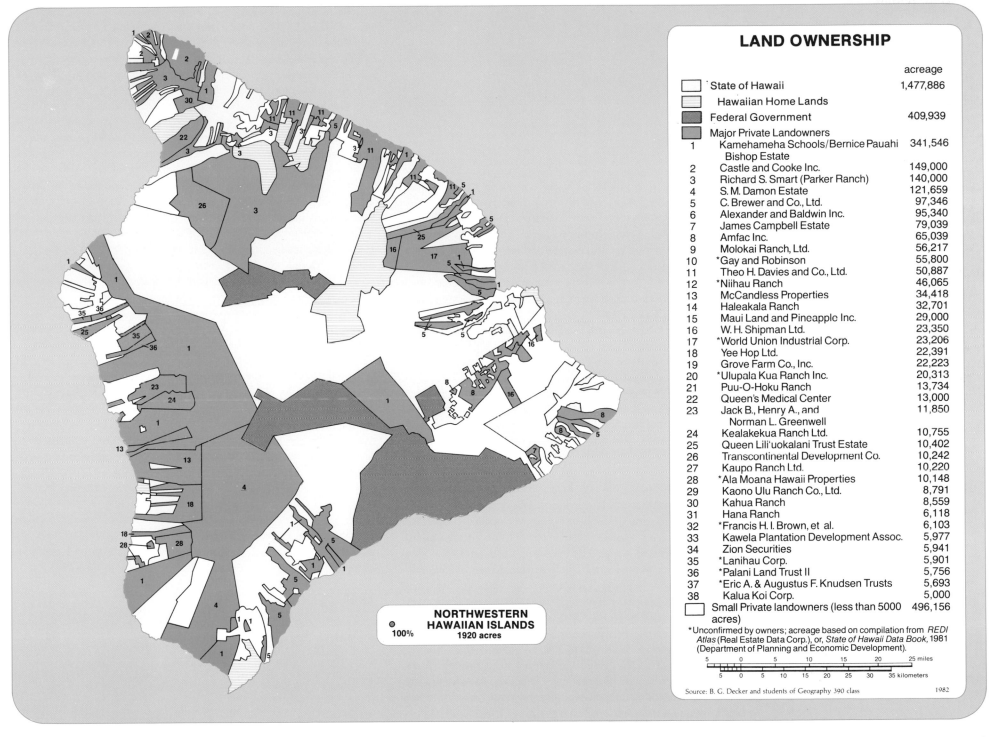

LAND OWNERSHIP

		acreage
☐	State of Hawaii	1,477,886
☐	Hawaiian Home Lands	
■	Federal Government	409,939
■	Major Private Landowners	
1	Kamehameha Schools/Bernice Pauahi Bishop Estate	341,546
2	Castle and Cooke Inc.	149,000
3	Richard S. Smart (Parker Ranch)	140,000
4	S. M. Damon Estate	121,659
5	C. Brewer and Co., Ltd.	97,346
6	Alexander and Baldwin Inc.	95,340
7	James Campbell Estate	79,039
8	Amfac Inc.	65,039
9	Molokai Ranch, Ltd.	56,217
10	*Gay and Robinson	55,800
11	Theo H. Davies and Co., Ltd.	50,887
12	*Niihau Ranch	46,065
13	McCandless Properties	34,418
14	Haleakala Ranch	32,701
15	Maui Land and Pineapple Inc.	29,000
16	W. H. Shipman Ltd.	23,350
17	*World Union Industrial Corp.	23,206
18	Yee Hop Ltd.	22,391
19	Grove Farm Co., Inc.	22,223
20	*Ulupala Kua Ranch Inc.	20,313
21	Puu-O-Hoku Ranch	13,734
22	Queen's Medical Center	13,000
23	Jack B., Henry A., and Norman L. Greenwell	11,850
24	Kealakekua Ranch Ltd.	10,755
25	Queen Lili'uokalani Trust Estate	10,402
26	Transcontinental Development Co.	10,242
27	Kaupo Ranch Ltd.	10,220
28	*Ala Moana Hawaii Properties	10,148
29	Kaono Ulu Ranch Co., Ltd.	8,791
30	Kahua Ranch	8,559
31	Hana Ranch	6,118
32	*Francis H. I. Brown, et al.	6,103
33	Kawela Plantation Development Assoc.	5,977
34	Zion Securities	5,941
35	*Lanihau Corp.	5,901
36	*Palani Land Trust II	5,756
37	*Eric A. & Augustus F. Knudsen Trusts	5,693
38	Kalua Koi Corp.	5,000
☐	Small Private landowners (less than 5000 acres)	496,156

*Unconfirmed by owners; acreage based on compilation from *REDI Atlas* (Real Estate Data Corp.), or, *State of Hawaii Data Book*, 1981 (Department of Planning and Economic Development).

5 0 5 10 15 20 25 miles
5 0 5 10 15 20 25 30 35 kilometers

Source: B. G. Decker and students of Geography 390 class   1982

NORTHWESTERN HAWAIIAN ISLANDS
100% 1920 acres

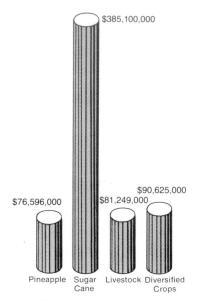

$385,100,000

$90,625,000
$81,249,000
$76,596,000

Pineapple Sugar   Livestock Diversified
          Cane   Crops

AGRICULTURAL SALES, 1980

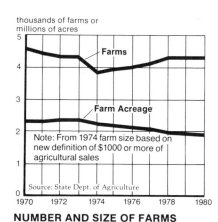

thousands of farms or
millions of acres

Farms

Farm Acreage

Note: From 1974 farm size based on
new definition of $1000 or more of
agricultural sales

Source: State Dept. of Agriculture

1970   1972   1974   1976   1978   1980

NUMBER AND SIZE OF FARMS

AGRICULTURE

Agriculture's importance to Hawaii was emphasized in 1981 by the publication of the State Agricultural Plan, which in great part focuses on the rapid changes taking place in the State that directly and indirectly affect the industry. Acreages, production volumes, and market values of agricultural products are going through a period of modification in all categories: plantation farming of sugarcane and pineapple, cattle ranching, fruit and nut farming, and diversified farming of small units by single farmer-operators. Evidence of this change is the general reduction in the number of farms, the overall increase in agricultural output, and the tendency toward an increase in the size of farms. Both geographic and economic factors have been at work in bringing about these alterations. In many areas prime agricultural land is being priced out of the market by land-use changes from agricultural to urban. Climate, soil, water supply, topographic conditions, and availability of land have been factors involved in closing down marginal operations, particularly in the plantation industries. Increasing foreign competition for mainland markets is also leading to unprofitable operations. In the past, agriculture in Hawaii has been dominated by the sugar and pineapple industries. Although these are still the major single crops, there has been a slow but steady growth of diversified agriculture. In 1980 the total value of diversified agriculture was $171.9 million as compared with $594.6 million for sugar and $229.2 million for pineapple.

From the first decade of this century the production of sugarcane has increased from about 5 tons per acre to over 11 tons per acre, giving the four sugar-producing islands (Hawaii, Maui, Oahu, and Kauai) the highest yield per acre in the world. The total land area in cane has fluctuated during the same period, but has slowly risen since a postwar low in 1948 of 206,550 acres to a 1968 high of 242,476 acres. Since then, cane acreage has begun to decrease, owing primarily to the closing of several of the major plantations. From 1975 to 1980 the number of sugarcane farms dropped from 520 to 330, and land in sugarcane decreased by 6,500 acres. The highly mechanized sugar plantations are located on coastal mountain slopes where rainfall can vary from 15 to 212 inches per year, depending on exposure and elevation. Almost half the total cane land is irrigated.

Pineapples are grown on all the major islands of the State except Hawaii Island. In 1980 there were 18 farms producing pineapple, but only three companies accounted for about 90 percent of the total value of pineapple sales (page 155). There has been a 32-percent decrease in pineapple acreage over the past decade and production has dropped from 916,000 tons in 1970 to 657,000 tons in 1980.

The production of livestock has contributed greatly to the diversification of agriculture in the State. Of these activities, cattle raising is by far the most important; grazing lands cover some 52 percent of the State's lands, 80 percent of it on Hawaii, 9 percent on Maui, 5 percent on Molokai, 3 percent on Kauai, and 3 percent on Oahu.

Before 1956, most of the State's papaya crop was grown on Oahu. The shift of major production to the Puna area of the island of Hawaii is attributed to urbanization and to virus disease afflicting papayas on Oahu, favorable growing conditions and low-cost land on Hawaii Island, and the inauguration of direct jet flights from Hilo to the U.S. mainland. During the decade 1960/1970, land planted to papayas increased from 500 to 1,700 acres, with 1,600 acres on Hawaii Island. By 1980 acreage harvested had increased to 1,950.

Besides pineapple and papaya, major fruits grown in the islands are banana, passion fruit, orange, tangerine, avocado, and guava. The most important of these is the banana, although this crop is decreasing in acreage harvested, with only 730 acres in 1980. Oahu produced most of the banana crop. Of lesser importance are lichee and mango.

Over half the vegetable production of the State is tomatoes, lettuce, head cabbages, and cucumbers. The number of vegetable farms decreased from 762 in 1961 to 488 in 1970, but by 1980 the trend was upward with 585 farms reported. Vegetable marketing volumes have increased over the past decade, and 70.7 million pounds were produced in 1980.

Other crops, such as macadamia nuts and flowers and nursery products are increasing in acreage and in production. In 1980 flowers and nursery products and macadamia nuts had sales of over $27 million and $24 million, respectively. However, coffee production in the Kona district of Hawaii Island has seen a decline from a high of 2.3 million pounds in 1977/1978 to a low of 1.4 million pounds in 1980/1981.

J.R.H.

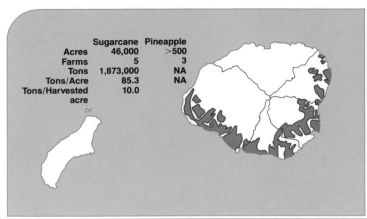

	Sugarcane	Pineapple
Acres	46,000	>500
Farms	5	3
Tons	1,873,000	NA
Tons/Acre	85.3	NA
Tons/Harvested acre	10.0	

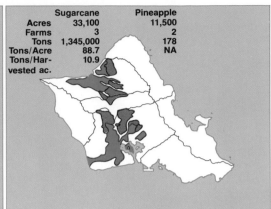

	Sugarcane	Pineapple
Acres	33,100	11,500
Farms	3	2
Tons	1,345,000	178
Tons/Acre	88.7	NA
Tons/Harvested ac.	10.9	

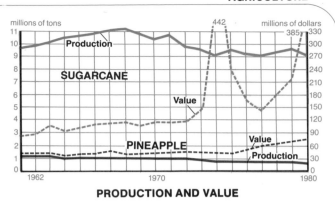

PRODUCTION AND VALUE

SUGARCANE AND PINEAPPLE

STATE TOTAL

	Sugarcane		Pineapple
Acres	217,700	Acres	43,000
Farms	330	Farms	18
Production in tons (unprocessed cane)	9,214,000	Production in tons	657,000
Average yield of cane (1978–1980) in tons per acre	94.5	Production not available by island	NA
Average yield of raw sugar (1978–1980) per harvested acre	10.5		

Source: State Dept. of Agriculture and Hawaiian Sugar Planters Assoc.

1982

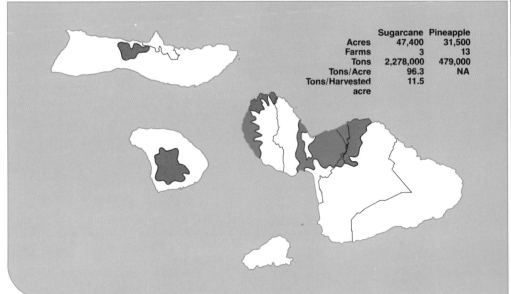

	Sugarcane	Pineapple
Acres	47,400	31,500
Farms	3	13
Tons	2,278,000	479,000
Tons/Acre	96.3	NA
Tons/Harvested acre	11.5	

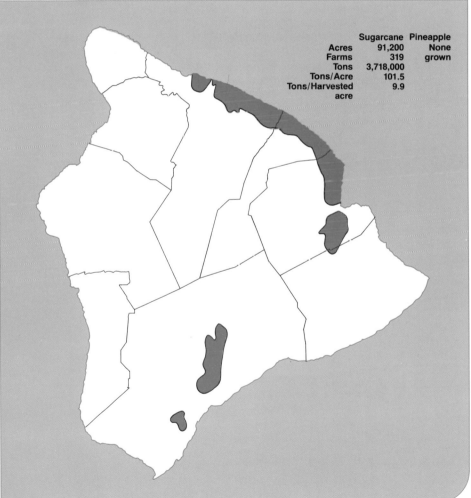

	Sugarcane	Pineapple
Acres	91,200	None grown
Farms	319	
Tons	3,718,000	
Tons/Acre	101.5	
Tons/Harvested acre	9.9	

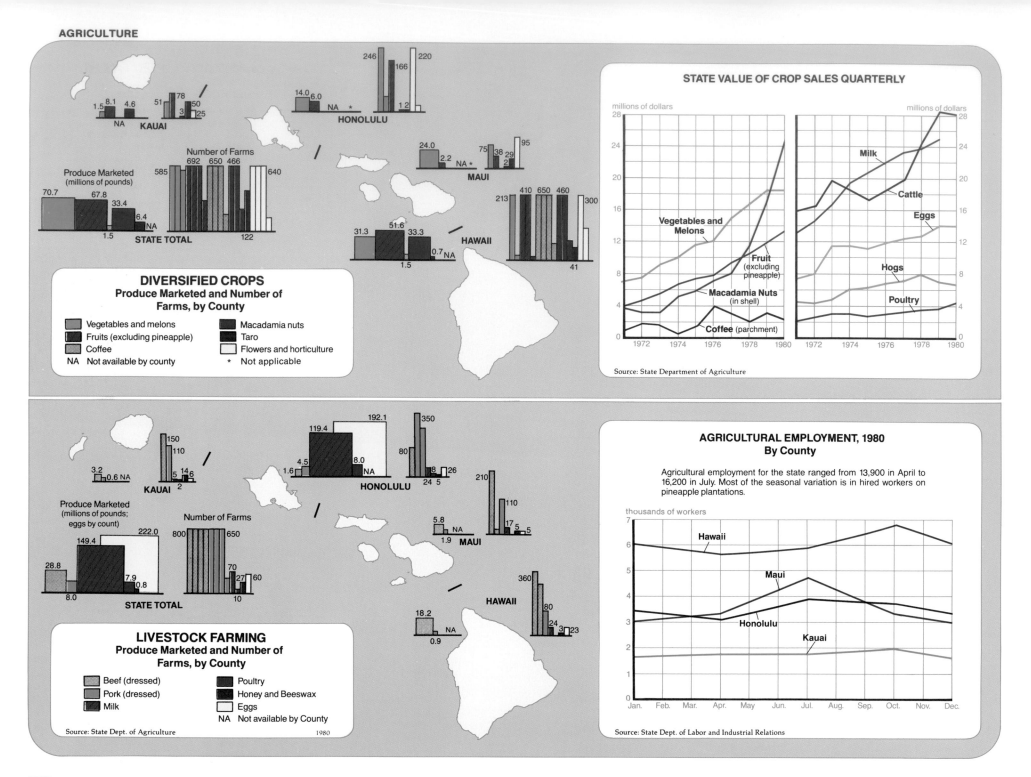

STATE VALUE OF CROP SALES QUARTERLY

millions of dollars

millions of dollars

Vegetables and Melons

Fruit (excluding pineapple)

Macadamia Nuts (in shell)

Coffee (parchment)

Milk

Cattle

Eggs

Hogs

Poultry

Source: State Department of Agriculture

KAUAI
1.5 8.1 4.6 NA

HONOLULU
14.0 6.0 NA *
246 166 220 1 2

MAUI
24.0 2.2 NA *
75 38 29 2 95

HAWAII
31.3 51.6 33.3 0.7 NA
1.5
213 410 650 460 300
41

STATE TOTAL
Produce Marketed (millions of pounds)
70.7 67.8 33.4 6.4 NA 1.5

Number of Farms
585 692 650 466 640
122

51 78 3 50 25

DIVERSIFIED CROPS
Produce Marketed and Number of Farms, by County

- Vegetables and melons
- Fruits (excluding pineapple)
- Coffee
- NA Not available by county
- Macadamia nuts
- Taro
- Flowers and horticulture
- * Not applicable

KAUAI
3.2 0.6 NA 2
150 110 5 14 6

HONOLULU
119.4 192.1 1.6 4.5 8.0 NA
80 350 24 5 8 26

MAUI
5.8 NA 1.9
210 110 17 5 5

HAWAII
18.2 NA 0.9
360 80 24 3 23

STATE TOTAL
Produce Marketed (millions of pounds; eggs by count)
28.8 149.4 7.9 0.8 8.0

Number of Farms
800 650 70 27 60 10

222.0

LIVESTOCK FARMING
Produce Marketed and Number of Farms, by County

- Beef (dressed)
- Pork (dressed)
- Milk
- Poultry
- Honey and Beeswax
- Eggs
- NA Not available by County

Source: State Dept. of Agriculture   1980

AGRICULTURAL EMPLOYMENT, 1980
By County

Agricultural employment for the state ranged from 13,900 in April to 16,200 in July. Most of the seasonal variation is in hired workers on pineapple plantations.

thousands of workers

Hawaii

Maui

Honolulu

Kauai

Jan. Feb. Mar. Apr. May Jun. Jul. Aug. Sep. Oct. Nov. Dec.

Source: State Dept. of Labor and Industrial Relations

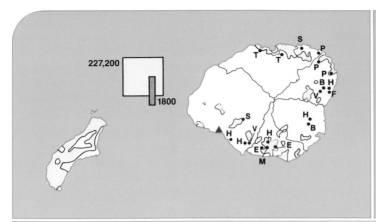

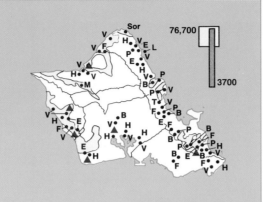

227,200
1800

Sor
76,700
3700

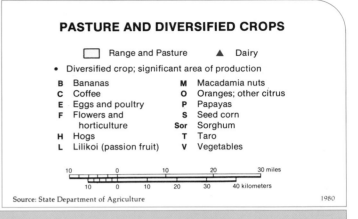

PASTURE AND DIVERSIFIED CROPS

☐ Range and Pasture ▲ Dairy

• Diversified crop; significant area of production

B	Bananas	M	Macadamia nuts
C	Coffee	O	Oranges; other citrus
E	Eggs and poultry	P	Papayas
F	Flowers and	S	Seed corn
	horticulture	Sor	Sorghum
H	Hogs	T	Taro
L	Lilikoi (passion fruit)	V	Vegetables

10 0 10 20 30 miles
10 0 10 20 30 40 kilometers

Source: State Department of Agriculture

1980

TRENDS IN PRODUCTION

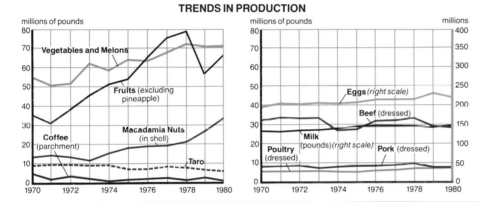

millions of pounds

Vegetables and Melons

Fruits (excluding pineapple)

Coffee (parchment)

Macadamia Nuts (in shell)

Taro

millions of pounds   millions
400

Eggs (right scale)

Beef (dressed)

Poultry (dressed)

Milk (pounds) (right scale)

Pork (dressed)

1970 1972 1974 1976 1978 1980

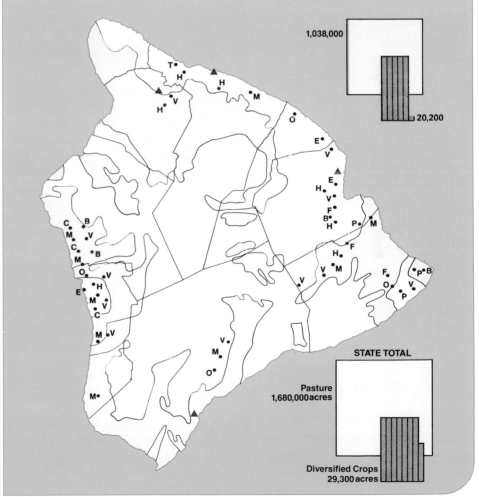

1,038,000
20,200

STATE TOTAL

Pasture
1,680,000 acres

Diversified Crops
29,300 acres

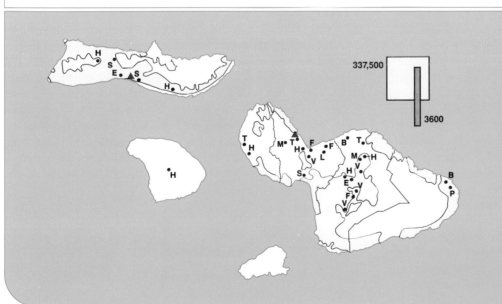

337,500
3600

Crack seed counter.

Drawing by John A. Dixon

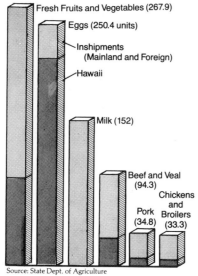

millions of pounds

Fresh Fruits and Vegetables (267.9)

Eggs (250.4 units)

Inshipments
(Mainland and Foreign)

Hawaii

Milk (152)

Beef and Veal
(94.3)

Chickens
and
Broilers
(33.3)

Pork
(34.8)

Source: State Dept. of Agriculture

**SOURCE OF FRESH FOOD
1980**

FOOD SOURCES

Hawaii's people have available a rich variety of foods from which to choose, and that they enjoy this abundance is shown in the high per capita consumption of food—at least as compared with most other countries and especially with other Pacific island groups. Most of this food is imported, and large quantities are needed to sustain a large resident and visiting population. Self-sufficiency is attained commercially in only one major item, milk; also almost 90 percent of the islands' eggs and 33 percent of their fresh vegetables and fruits are produced locally. Greater self-sufficiency could theoretically be attained, but for economic and social reasons it is unlikely that Hawaii will alter its present affluent, predominantly American-style diet. One reason is the need to cater to the tastes of over 2 million visitors from the U.S. mainland each year. Nevertheless, the present heavy dependence on imported food supplies is of concern in planning Hawaii's future.

Fifty years ago, Polynesian diets based on local taro and other vegetables, fruits, and fish, and Oriental diets based mostly on rice, vegetables, fish, and meats were predominant. A substantial proportion of these foods came from home gardens and from plants and animals in the forest. These patterns have now been greatly modified with increased use of American-style diets based on potatoes or rice, breads, meats, and dairy products. Most of these foodstuffs are imported and supplied through commercial brokers and retailers.

The most important foods produced in Hawaii are milk, eggs, meat, certain fresh vegetables and fruits (page 159), and local fish (page 160). Despite a 25-percent increase in population and over a doubling of visitors between 1970 and 1980, production of these local foods has generally kept pace with demand. The quantities of locally produced milk, eggs, and chickens show little change in relative contribution to total demand, while other items show modest decline in relative con-

tribution (page 159). Each of the main islands produces a variety of vegetable crops, including cabbage, lettuce, cucumbers, tomatoes, celery, and onions. Local commercially grown fruits include watermelons, bananas, oranges, papayas, and pineapples. Hawaii Island has the largest acreage and number of farms producing fresh vegetables and fruits (page 157). Home gardens also contribute an unknown amount to the supply of fresh produce. Hunting (for pigs, sheep, goats, and deer), fishing, and collection of wild fruits comprise minor sources of food supplies for some residents, mostly in rural areas.

The major source of all other food is the mainland United States; millions of pounds of fresh produce, grain, and packaged and frozen foods are shipped to Hawaii each year. Substantial imports of food are also received from other countries: beef from Australia, New Zealand, and Japan; butter from New Zealand; fresh fruits and vegetables from Canada, New Zealand, Mexico, and Japan; and canned food items from Japan, Taiwan, and Europe. Local processing of imported foods includes flour milling, preparation of bread and other baked goods, confections, and condiments, and considerable repackaging of bulk food imports.

Retail sale of food is done increasingly through supermarkets on all islands, while small grocery stores and markets become fewer in number. Bakeries, delicatessens, natural food shops, and wine and liquor stores are the more important specialty food shops in the larger towns.

A remarkable diversity of restaurants on all islands are patronized by residents as well as visitors. American-style restaurants predominate, in a wide variety of types from the most exclusive and unhurried to the practical fast-service drive-in, and, between these extremes, a full range of moderate-cost restaurants, coffee shops, and special food shops. Since 1970, fast-service food chain restaurants have shown a phenomenal increase in number and in patronage. Chinese and Japanese style restaurants are also numerous, with a similar range of high-, moderate-, and low-cost establishments. In Honolulu, as well as other main towns, there are Italian, Korean, Mexican, and Hawaiian style restaurants. Less numerous are those offering French, Filipino, Vietnamese, Samoan, Greek, Moslem, and Thai cuisines. Not counted in the accompanying table (page 159) are the many formal and informal Hawaiian luaus offering their own special foods to residents and visitors, or the numerous snack and ice cream shops, cocktail lounges, and bars which usually offer food.

Staff

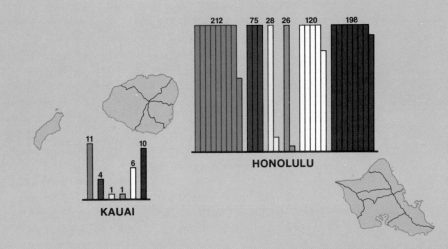

HONOLULU

212 75 28 26 120 198

KAUAI

11 4 1 1 6 10

MAUI

20 7 3 2 11 18

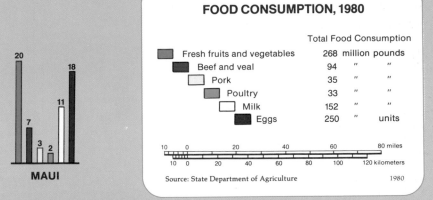

FOOD CONSUMPTION, 1980

Total Food Consumption

Fresh fruits and vegetables	268	million pounds
Beef and veal	94	" "
Pork	35	" "
Poultry	33	" "
Milk	152	" "
Eggs	250	" units

Source: State Department of Agriculture 1980

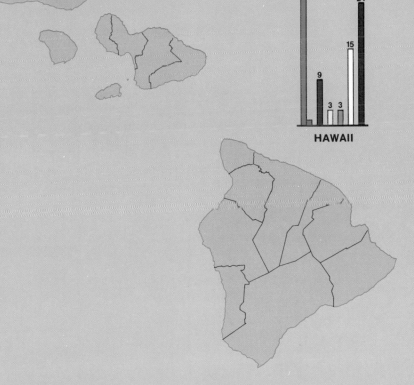

HAWAII

26 9 3 3 15 24

TREND IN FRESH FOOD SUPPLY:
Percentage Produced in Hawaii

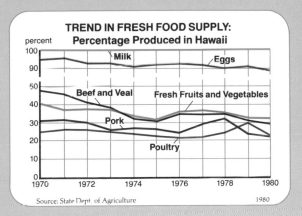

Milk Eggs
Beef and Veal Fresh Fruits and Vegetables
Pork
Poultry

Source: State Dept. of Agriculture 1980

RESTAURANTS

TYPE	KAUAI		OAHU		MOLOKAI		MAUI		LANAI		HAWAII	
American—standard	73	63%	541	47%	8	–	119	66%	2	–	101	59%
—fast service chain	6	6%	199	17%	–	–	14	8%	–	–	17	10%
Chinese	5	4%	110	9%	–	–	5	3%	–	–	14	8%
Japanese	2	2%	101	9%	1	–	12	7%	–	–	6	4%
Italian	7	6%	57	5%	–	–	8	4%	–	–	9	5%
Korean	–	–	35	3%	–	–	–	–	–	–	3	2%
Mexican	5	4%	32	3%	–	–	6	3%	–	–	3	2%
Hawaiian	7	6%	29	2%	1	–	5	3%	–	–	7	4%
French	–	–	9	1%	–	–	4	2%	–	–	1	–
Filipino	3	2%	6		–	–	–	–	–	–	–	–
Other and mixed	8	7%	42	4%	–	–	6	3%	–	–	9	5%
Total	116	100%	1161	100%	10	100%	179	100%	2	100%	170	100%

Oahu market, Honolulu.

Drawing by John A. Dixon

COMMERCIAL FISHING AND AQUACULTURE

Fish has always been an important staple in the Hawaiian diet. In the earliest reports by Captain Cook and other explorers, Hawaii was described as having a "fish and poi" economy. The sea was the major source of animal protein at that time.

Today, the commercial fishing industry is a small segment of the State's economy. The annual value of the commercial catch accounts for less than one percent of the value of the gross state product. This very low figure is not the result of an absolute decline in the value of commercial catch over the years, but to the rapid growth of other sectors of the economy.

The number of licensed commercial fishermen increased from 1,264 in 1970 to 2,577 in 1981. Many are part-time or recreational operators. In 1981, the fishing fleet was made up of 1,118 relatively small, old vessels, an increase of about 65 percent since 1970. Thirty-five of the fishing boats were equipped for high-sea fishing, that is, 15 tuna (aku) and 20 flagline vessels. There are 76 landing ports in the State, but in 1981 three major ports accounted for 70 percent of the total catch: Kewalo Basin (Oahu), 52 percent; Kailua-Honokohau

(Hawaii), 10 percent; and Maalaea (Maui), 8 percent.

Hawaiian fishery can be divided into three types: high sea or pelagic, inshore, and aquaculture. The high-sea fishery is engaged principally in tuna fishing, the most important species being skipjack tuna (aku). The number of aku vessels has declined from 32 in 1948 to 15 in 1981. Total catch has fluctuated between 9 and 20 million pounds, with no discernible trend. On the average, this fishery accounts for about 50 percent by weight of the State's total marine catch. Fishing trips are usually made within 20 miles off the coast. Primary fishing gear consists of a bamboo pole to which is attached a length of line bearing a hook and live bait. For bait, small anchovy is always used. This technique is called "pole-line and live-bait fishing." Skipjack tuna is the most important underexploited species in the Pacific Ocean, with a potential catch many times the level of the present catch.

Yellowfin and albacore tuna are other important species for high-sea fishing. These species are usually found in deep water and are caught with flagline (longline) techniques. The flagline is made up of a number of units of gear called baskets. Each basket of gear is composed of a main line from which branch lines are supported. Each branch line bears a single hook. The flagline is supported at the surface by glass or metal floats. Most of the flagline catches in Hawaii are consumed locally as sashimi (raw fish). Since 1978, the most significant change in Hawaii's high-sea fishery has been exploration of new fishing grounds, for example, the Northwestern Hawaiian Islands.

Inshore fisheries are of modest potential and therefore do not afford the basis for a major commercial fishing industry. An increasing proportion of the catchable stock is caught by sport fishermen.

Aquaculture formed an integral part of the Hawaiian culture in the past. There were approximately 360 fishponds in the islands prior to the arrival of Cook in 1778.

Early in this century, fish farming experienced a drastic decline due to such factors as natural erosion, lava inundation, destruction by tidal waves, and land-filling for shoreline expansion. Today only six of the old fishponds are being operated commercially. However, aquaculture has gradually gained a renewed significance since the late 1960s with the development of freshwater prawn (*Macrobrachium rosenbergii*) farming. Currently, there are 22 prawn farms with a total pond area of about 275 acres. In terms of technology, the State is regarded as the world leader in the culture of freshwater prawns. In addition, marine shrimp, oyster, catfish, mullet, tilapia, Chinese carps, and brine shrimp are also grown commercially. With Hawaii's year-round warm weather and advanced technology, aquaculture could again become an important industry.

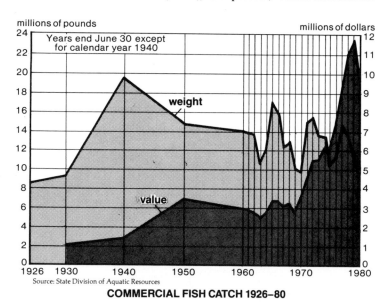

millions of pounds

millions of dollars

Years end June 30 except for calendar year 1940

weight

value

Source: State Division of Aquatic Resources

COMMERCIAL FISH CATCH 1926–80

Y.C.S.

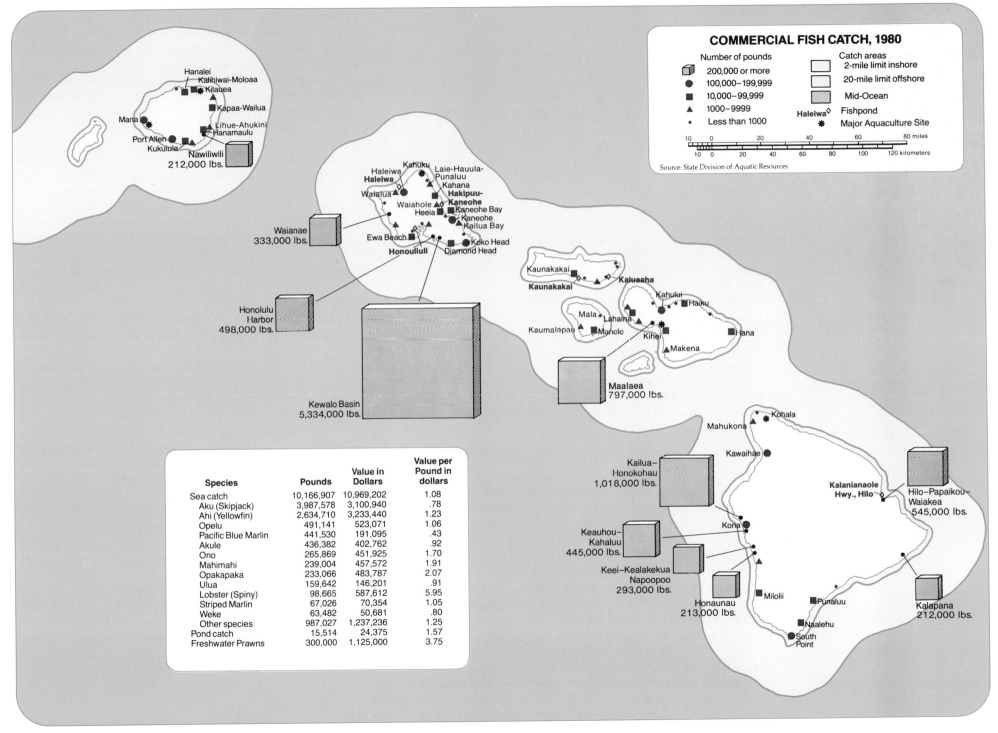

COMMERCIAL FISH CATCH, 1980

Number of pounds

- ◰ 200,000 or more
- ● 100,000–199,999
- ■ 10,000–99,999
- ▲ 1000–9999
- • Less than 1000

Catch areas
- 2-mile limit inshore
- 20-mile limit offshore
- Mid-Ocean

Haleiwa◇ Fishpond
✳ Major Aquaculture Site

10   0   20   40   60   80 miles
10   0   20   40   60   80   100   120 kilometers

Source: State Division of Aquatic Resources

Hanalei
Kalihiwai-Moloaa
Kilauea
Kapaa-Wailua
Mana
Lihue-Ahukini
Port Allen
Hanamaulu
Kukuiula
Nawiliwili
212,000 lbs.

Kahuku
Haleiwa
Haleiwa
Laie-Hauula-Punaluu
Kahana
Waialua
Hakipuu-Kaneohe
Waiahole
Kaneohe Bay
Heeia
Kaneohe
Kailua Bay
Waianae
333,000 lbs.
Ewa Beach
Koko Head
Honouliuli
Diamond Head

Honolulu
Harbor
498,000 lbs.

Kewalo Basin
5,334,000 lbs.

Kaunakakai
Kaluaaha
Kaunakakai
Mala
Lahaina
Kaumalapau
Manele
Kiei
Makena
Kahului
Haiku
Hana
Maalaea
797,000 lbs.

Kohala
Mahukona
Kawaihae
Kailua-
Honokohau
1,018,000 lbs.
Kalanianaole Hwy., Hilo
Hilo-Papaikou-Waiakea
545,000 lbs.
Kona
Keauhou-
Kahaluu
445,000 lbs.
Keei-Kealakekua
Napoopoo
293,000 lbs.
Milolii
Punaluu
Kalapana
212,000 lbs.
Honaunau
213,000 lbs.
Naalehu
South
Point

Species	Pounds	Value in Dollars	Value per Pound in dollars
Sea catch	10,166,907	10,969,202	1.08
Aku (Skipjack)	3,987,578	3,100,940	.78
Ahi (Yellowfin)	2,634,710	3,233,440	1.23
Opelu	491,141	523,071	1.06
Pacific Blue Marlin	441,530	191,095	.43
Akule	436,382	402,762	.92
Ono	265,869	451,925	1.70
Mahimahi	239,004	457,572	1.91
Opakapaka	233,066	483,787	2.07
Ulua	159,642	146,201	.91
Lobster (Spiny)	98,665	587,612	5.95
Striped Marlin	67,026	70,354	1.05
Weke	63,482	50,681	.80
Other species	987,027	1,237,236	1.25
Pond catch	15,514	24,375	1.57
Freshwater Prawns	300,000	1,125,000	3.75

Petroglyph: paddle man, Puako, Hawaii.

FORESTRY

Forestry is concerned with the understanding, managing, and protection of the forest ecosystem. Forests are the sole remaining habitat for many rare and endangered native plants, birds, insects, land snails, and other organisms that help make Hawaii such an extraordinary place. Forests give visual pleasure; they release oxygen into the air; they bind the soil to prevent erosion which would otherwise clog streams and pollute beaches and oceans; they facilitate infiltration of rain water into the soil and thus help to recharge the groundwater supply; they give shelter and food to wildlife; they provide attractive recreational settings for hikes and picnicking; they supply wood, fruits, and other products for the economy. In short, the diverse forest ecosystems help maintain environmental conditions essential for human and other life.

The discovery of fossilized shells and bones of organisms adapted to forest habitats in lowlands suggests that forests were much more extensive before human occupation. The original Hawaiians generally lived near the coast, but they were most likely responsible for the clearing of forest areas for agriculture, and for burning and cutting trees. The forests were valuable sources of logs, fiber, dyes, foods, and medicines, as well as bird feathers and plant materials for ceremonial use.

Not long after contact with Europeans in 1778, economic exploitation of the forests became a prime concern. Sandalwood was the first important item of commercial trade with the rest of the world. Although supplies of sandalwood were exhausted in the 1830s, Hawaii's forests became increasingly important to the foreigners for fuel wood, lumber, posts, poles, and railroad ties. Modification of the vegetation was greatly accelerated by the Europeans, who introduced many new plants and animals and cleared more land for crops and grazing.

Eventually, the need for reforestation was recognized. The first attempts were made in 1874, but it was not until 1904 that forest reserves were established on Oahu and Hawaii Island to protect watersheds. In an extensive replanting program more than 800 different species of trees were used, but the majority were exotics, chosen more for their rapid growth than for commercial value. These included *Eucalyptus* species, *Grevillea* (silk oak), *Casuarina* (ironwood), and *Melaleuca* (paperbark). The planting program was greatly expanded between 1935 and 1941 with the help of the Civilian Conservation Corps.

Hawaii now has nearly 2 million acres (8,094 sq. km.) of forest land—almost half the area of the State. About 1.2 million acres are held in 68 forest reserves, to protect forest and watershed from human activities. Most of the forest lies on mountain slopes between elevations of 2,000 and 6,000 feet (600–1,800 meters), where rainfall is generally more than 50 inches a year. Forest lands are classified as commercial (those capable of producing industrial wood) and noncommercial (lands where soil, climate, slope, or drainage do not permit growing sawtimber crops). Native trees, principally ohia (*Metrosideros collina*) and koa (*Acacia koa*), dominate on about 750,000 acres of commercial forest land and on nearly 250,000 acres of noncommercial forest land. Of current concern is the fact that ohia, the dominant forest tree, has died over extensive areas for reasons which are not fully understood. More than nine-tenths of the commercial ohia and koa forests are on the island of Hawaii. Introduced trees, principally eucalyptus, have been planted on less than 4 percent of the commercial forest land but comprise about 40 percent of the sawtimber volume in the islands. Young stands of exotic, planted trees average 8,000 board feet per acre; mature native stands, barely 500. Dominant in the noncommercial forest are tree associations such as kiawe, kukui, scrub ohia, and koa, and shrub associations such as mamani, pukiawe, and koa haole. The commercial forest land lies almost equally within and outside the forest reserves. Two-thirds of the forests are privately owned and concentrated in a few large holdings.

Harvesting of Hawaii's timber resources in recent years has been sporadic and on a small scale. Most processing is done on the island of Hawaii by portable mills from timber stands on private land. The most valuable species by far is the native koa which is highly prized for furniture, floors, paneling, and craft wood. Many species are cut for posts, including eucalyptus, ohia, and kiawe. The latter makes an excellent charcoal and is also in demand for fuel wood. Small amounts of milo (*Thespesia populnea*) and monkeypod (*Samanea saman*) are used for craft wood. The forests also yield other products, including bamboo, tree fern trunks, which are used in orchid cultivation, maile and other foliage, and flowers and seeds for lei making. Wood chips have been successfully used as fuel in boilers, and the production of biomass as an energy supply is currently under investigation. The unique Hawaiian biota, best preserved in the forest reserves, attracts amateur naturalists and professional scientists to the State and indirectly provides an additional source of revenue.

L.L.W.

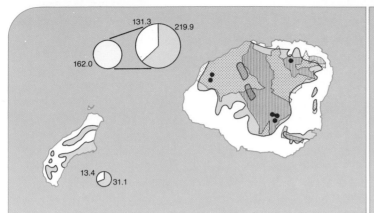

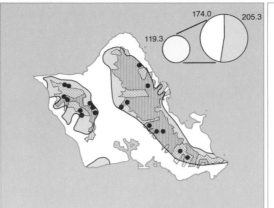

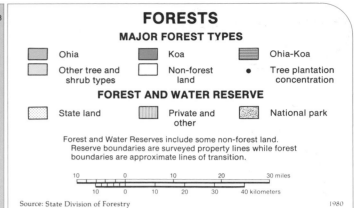

FORESTS

MAJOR FOREST TYPES

- Ohia
- Koa
- Ohia-Koa
- Other tree and shrub types
- Non-forest land
- • Tree plantation concentration

FOREST AND WATER RESERVE

- State land
- Private and other
- National park

Forest and Water Reserves include some non-forest land. Reserve boundaries are surveyed property lines while forest boundaries are approximate lines of transition.

10   0   10   20   30 miles
10   0   10   20   30   40 kilometers

Source: State Division of Forestry   1980

FOREST PRODUCTS HARVESTED, 1977

Product	Output/units	Unit Price	Value in Dollars
Logs for fiber	55,502 bone dry tons	$ 41.00	$2,310,500
Logs for lumber	2,750 thousand board feet	209.00	574,833
Logs for craftwood	299 cords (128 cubic feet)	224.00	51,330
Tree fern	95,000 cubic feet	1.42	135,000
Fuelwood from trees	4,191 cords	47.00	194,563
Fuelwood for charcoal	800 cords	34.00	26,820
Fuel from mill residue	5,000 tons	10.50	52,500
Round posts	32,700 posts	3.14	102,604
Split posts	3,525 posts	2.93	10,321
Driftwood	2 cords	300.00	600
Pallets	20 units	20.00	400
Bamboo	18,844 lineal feet	0.04	742
Kukui nuts	14 tons	362.00	5,020

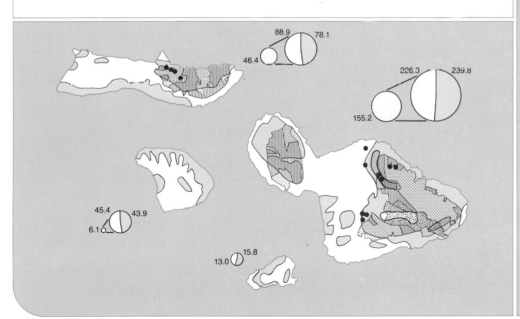

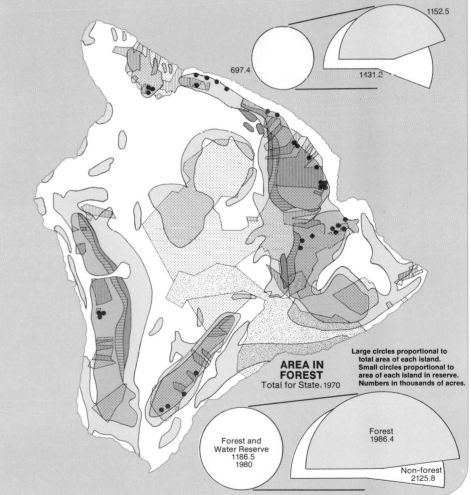

AREA IN FOREST
Total for State, 1970

Large circles proportional to total area of each island. Small circles proportional to area of each island in reserve. Numbers in thousands of acres.

Forest and Water Reserve 1186.5 1980

Forest 1986.4

Non-forest 2125.8

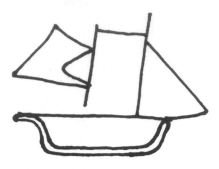

Petroglyph: ship, Kapalaoa, Hawaii.

ENERGY

During the decade 1970–1980, the supply and cost of energy became a major concern in Hawaii as it did in the rest of the nation. From 1959 Hawaii experienced rapid growth in its population and economy, but in 1978 the economy slowed while population growth and accompanying energy demand did not. With no fossil fuel reserves and near total dependence on imported oil for its energy supply, Hawaii could not counter the increasing prices of oil on the global market. At $42 per barrel, the cost of petroleum needed to produce 92 percent of the State's energy needs in 1980 amounted to over $1 billion.

During the seventies, the federal, state, and county governments, private industry, and independent research agencies combined resources to conduct research on alternative energy sources. The following is an outline of major projects begun before 1982.

Geothermal Energy. In 1972, the Hawaii Geothermal Project (HGP), a joint venture of federal, state and county governments, the University of Hawaii, and private interests, was established to develop energy supplies from active volcanoes. In 1975 drilling for the first geothermal well began on the east rift of Kilauea volcano, and the desired depth of 6,450 feet (1,970 meters) was reached in April 1976. With a temperature at the bottom of the well of 676°F (358°C), the well is reputedly the hottest in the United States. The project, now called HGP-A, has a 3-megawatt wellhead generator. Construction of the geothermal power plant itself began in 1980, and by mid-1981

Hawaii became the second state in the nation, after California, with on-line electric power generated from geothermal steam. As to the future, about 20 areas have been identified as having sufficient geothermal potential to warrant further study, as either high temperature or low temperature sites. The cutoff point is 400°F (204°C); wells with bottom temperatures below this would be exploited for other uses, mainly industrial. In addition to scientific and engineering requirements at each site, other issues such as land ownership, mineral rights, environmental effects, marketing conditions, and transmission have to be considered.

Ocean Energy. The ocean is a natural storage basin of thermal energy. Through the technique of ocean thermal energy conversion (OTEC), which is based on temperature differences of ocean water, energy can be generated to produce electricity. A sensitive working fluid such as ammonia can alternately be fluid or vapor in response to temperature changes, and in the vapor state can be made to drive a turbine-generator. A joint state government and private venture converted a Navy dump scow, 120 feet long by 34 feet in breadth, to an actual working model, named Mini-OTEC. On August 2, 1979, working off the Kona Coast of the island of Hawaii, using ammonia, warm surface and deep ocean cold water, Mini-OTEC generated 52 kilowatts of electricity. This was the world's first at-sea closed-cycle OTEC plant to produce net energy, an accomplishment which has stimulated worldwide interest. Plans have now been made to develop a 40-megawatt pilot plant off Kahe Point, Oahu (*OTEC for Oahu*, 1980). As a system, OTEC is amazingly simple—it requires no fuel, it releases nothing into the atmosphere, it has no byproducts, it does not involve any chemical or nuclear reactions, it requires no land and therefore no landscaping, and there are no waste products. Nevertheless, studies should be made to assess what impact, if any, OTEC has on the ocean environment.

Wind Energy. In 1974, the Hawaii Natural Energy Institute (HNEI) was established at the University of Hawaii to do research on wind energy conversion systems. In addition, wind towers have been installed throughout the islands by federal, state, county, and private agencies to obtain reliable data on wind speed and direction, and to test materials for corrosion potential. In 1978, Hawaiian Electric Company developed a 200-kilowatt wind turbine at Kahuku, Oahu, as part of the federal wind energy program. By the end of its first year of operation in 1980, this machine had outperformed all other similar wind turbines of the federal program, wherever located. In 1979, Hawaiian Electric Company agreed to purchase power from a private company (Windfarms, Ltd.), which will install a wind turbine farm at Kahuku capable of producing 80 megawatts. When completed in 1985, this operation will provide about 9 percent of Oahu's annual demand for electricity, which could reduce the annual imported oil requirement by as much as 600,000 barrels.

Direct Solar Energy. Hawaii's tropical latitude and clear atmosphere (pages 59 and 66), make it ideal for solar energy development. To be applied efficiently, solar energy must be collected and concentrated; current technology for this is expensive. Despite the cost, the use of solar energy in water heating systems, domestic and commercial, has been growing in recent years, due in part to tax incentives by the federal and state governments to offset equipment and installation costs to homeowners. By 1981 Hawaii had the highest per capita count of solar water heating systems in the nation. The most ambitious solar energy project in Hawaii so far is at G. N. Wilcox Memorial Hospital on Kauai. This system includes a combination of parabolic concentrators and silicon photovoltaic cells; the former track and direct the sun's rays for heating water, the latter produce electricity. In 1980 the U.S. Department of Energy funded the development of a solar thermal power installation at Palaau, Molokai, which is expected to generate 20 percent of Molokai's electricity, and a solar power tower at Pioneer Sugar Mill, Lahaina, Maui, that would generate enough electricity to replace 82 percent of the imported oil currently used in the mill's operation. In this instance 1,050 reflecting mirrors on the ground will focus the sun's rays to a receiver on a 300–400-foot (90–120-meter) tower to produce the needed energy.

Biomass Energy. Biomass includes any organic material, plant or animal. The most effective use of biomass for energy production at present in Hawaii is the burning of bagasse, the pithy remains of sugarcane after milling. In 1980 about 13 percent of the electricity sold as a utility commodity in the State was produced with bagasse as fuel. Two tree farms growing giant koa haole (*Leucaena*) and eucalyptus as a source of energy were planted in 1978 in a joint government and private project in the Hilo and Kau districts of the island of Hawaii. Plans to use the municipal waste collected by the City and County of Honolulu to produce electricity have been proposed since 1980 by way of a solid waste recovery system designed to handle from 1,200 to 1,800 tons per day. A suitable site has yet to be found for the installation. Besides its value as a solid fuel, biomass has potential as liquid fuel. Since 1978, research has been in progress on production of ethanol, protein, and potash from molasses, also a byproduct of sugar milling. Ethanol would be used to make gasohol for motor vehicle fuel. Two major canneries in Honolulu (Del Monte and Dole Co.), are now producing ethanol from pineapple juice to use as fuel and to manufacture vinegar.

The ultimate hope from all these different projects is to make Hawaii near self-sufficient in energy. Even if complete self-sufficiency is not attained, the present extreme dependence on imported petroleum should be greatly reduced by 1990.

A.P.

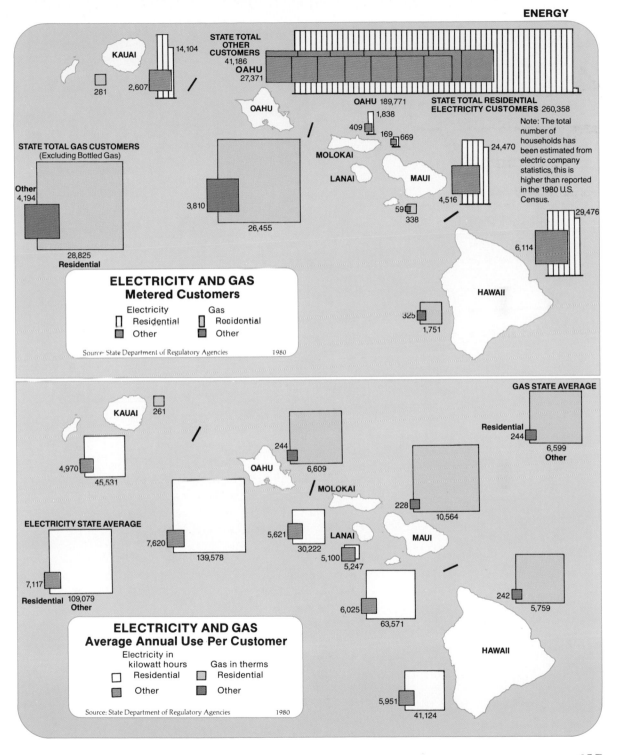

Note: Sugar company power houses on Kauai, Maui and Hawaii supply important amounts of electrical energy from time to time to community systems

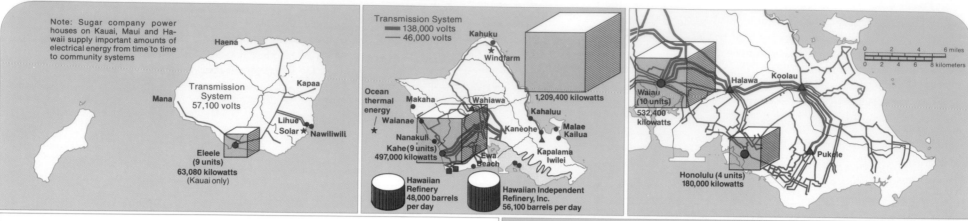

Transmission System
■ 138,000 volts
— 46,000 volts

Kahuku
Windfarm ★

1,209,400 kilowatts

Ocean thermal energy ★

Makaha
Wahiawa
Kahaluu

Waianae ★

Nanakuli
Kaneohe
Malae Kailua

Kahe (9 units)
497,000 kilowatts

Ewa Beach

Kapalama Iwilei

Hawaiian Refinery
48,000 barrels per day

Hawaiian Independent Refinery, Inc.
56,100 barrels per day

Waiau (10 units)
532,400 kilowatts

Halawa
Koolau

Pukele

Honolulu (4 units)
180,000 kilowatts

0 2 4 6 miles
0 2 4 6 8 kilometers

ELECTRICITY, GAS AND OIL

Electricity

● Power generating plant
▲ Major substation
▬ Transmission lines
⬛ Installed generating capacity
★ Alternative electricity sources (major developments only)

Gas

▨ Honolulu distribution area
● Local supply system

Total gas manufacturing capacity (Oahu, Maui, Hawaii Counties) 150,000 therms per day

Oil

■ Refinery

10   0   10   20   30 miles
10 0 10 20 30 40 kilometers

Source: Public Utilities Commission; Hawaiian Electric Co.; Gasco.

1980

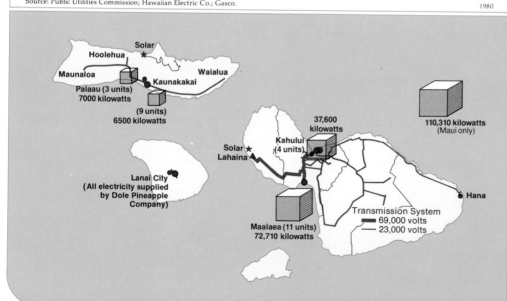

Haena
Kapaa
Mana

Transmission System
57,100 volts

Lihue
Solar ★ Nawiliwili

Eleele
(9 units)
63,080 kilowatts
(Kauai only)

Solar ★
Hoolehua
Maunaloa
Waialua
Palaau (3 units)
7000 kilowatts
Kaunakakai

(9 units)
6500 kilowatts

37,600 kilowatts

110,310 kilowatts
(Maui only)

Kahului
(4 units)

Solar ★
Lahaina

Lanai City
(All electricity supplied by Dole Pineapple Company)

Hana

Maalaea (11 units)
72,710 kilowatts

Transmission System
■ 69,000 volts
— 23,000 volts

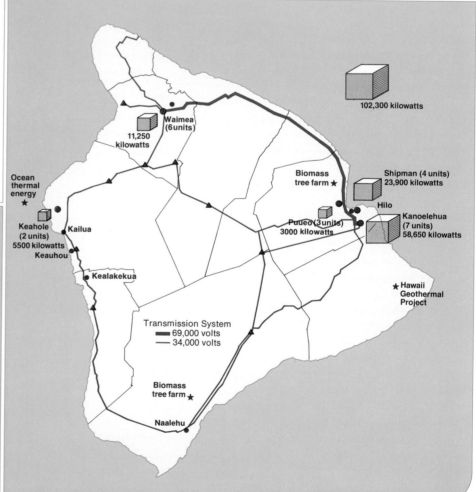

102,300 kilowatts

11,250 kilowatts
Waimea (6 units)

Biomass tree farm ★

Shipman (4 units)
23,900 kilowatts

Ocean thermal energy ★

Hilo

Keahole (2 units)
5500 kilowatts
Keauhou

Kailua

Puueo (3 units)
3000 kilowatts

Kanoelehua (7 units)
58,650 kilowatts

Kealakekua

Hawaii Geothermal Project ★

Transmission System
■ 69,000 volts
— 34,000 volts

Biomass tree farm ★

Naalehu

166

MANUFACTURING

In 1980 Hawaii's manufacturing industries achieved sales in excess of $2.4 billion and provided employment for some 24,000 workers. Traditionally the dominant manufacturing activities have been the processing of sugarcane and pineapples, activities solidly in the hands of a few large holding companies whose interests extend into many sectors of the economy, including transport, resort and real estate development, and wholesale and retail trade. But since the end of World War II diversified manufacturing (that is, all other types of manufacturing) has expanded greatly as new industrial enterprises, some launched by the nation's leading industrial corporations but many more by independents, have established themselves in Hawaii. By 1980 such activities accounted for 69 percent of total manufacturing sales.

Manufacturing in Hawaii faces many handicaps, such as physical isolation and a limited local market, limited local raw materials, and relatively high taxes and energy and transport costs. The earliest established industries depended either on natural protection, as in building material industries oriented to the local market or, alternatively, on some special local advantage, for example, textile and garment industries, which have now outgrown the links with the tourist trade and have a flourishing export business to the mainland and elsewhere. This latter pattern is also seen in petroleum refining, now Hawaii's largest industry by turnover, which capitalizes on the State's geographic position; in addition to meeting the demands of defense establishments, the industry profits from Hawaii's importance as a Pacific route center by helping to meet large demand for aviation jet fuel. Most newer industrial activities are of a "footloose" type, making articles of small bulk and high value and for whose manufacture the environment of Hawaii is ideal. As technological progress, especially in communications, steadily reduces the importance of traditional factors in determining location of industries and to increase that of a physically attractive environment, further industrial expansion in Hawaii seems assured. In electronics, perhaps the field with the greatest capacity for future growth, Hawaii had four companies in operation in 1981. A notable achievement was the State's selection as a location for the design and manufacture of the "daisy-wheel" printer for word processors and typewriters.

Diversified manufacturing is heavily concentrated on Oahu, and particularly in the vicinity of the port and airport of Honolulu, with a major outlier of heavier industry at the Campbell Industrial Park at Barbers Point in the southwesternmost area of the island. Here Hawaii's two petroleum refineries are located, one operated by Chevron and one by a subsidiary of Pacific Resources Inc. Campbell Park also accommodates a steel fabricating plant and cement and concrete product industries.

D.W.F.

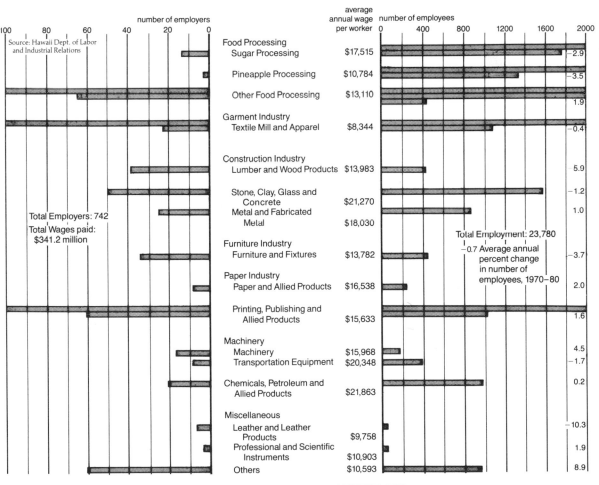

MANUFACTURERS AND EMPLOYMENT, 1980

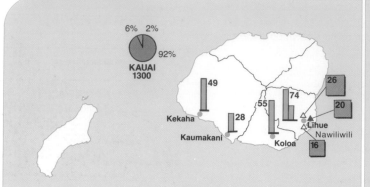

KAUAI
1300

6% 2%
92%

49
74
26
55
20
28
16
Kekaha
Kaumakani
Koloa
Lihue
Nawiliwili

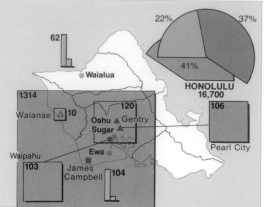

22% 37%
41%
HONOLULU
16,700

62
1314
120
106
Waialua
Waianae 10
Oahu Sugar Gentry
Waipahu
Ewa
James Campbell
103
104
Pearl City

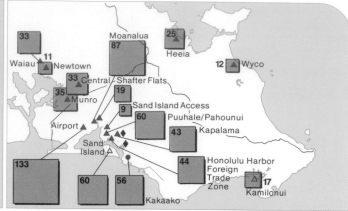

33
11
25
Heeia
12 Wyco
Waiau Newtown
Moanalua
87
33 Central Shafter Flats
35 Munro
19
9 Sand Island Access
60 Puuhale/Pahounui
43 Kapalama
Airport
Sand Island
44 Honolulu Harbor Foreign Trade Zone
133
60
56
17
Kakaako
Kamilonui

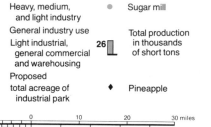

EMPLOYMENT IN MANUFACTURING, 1980

■ Heavy, medium, and light industry
● General industry use
▲ Light industrial, general commercial and warehousing
△ Proposed total acreage of industrial park
28
● Sugar mill
26 Total production in thousands of short tons
◆ Pineapple

10   0   10   20   30 miles
10   0   10   20   30   40 kilometers

STATE TOTAL EMPLOYEES

Textiles, apparel, printing and other nondurables 32%
Durable goods 18%
Food Processing 50%
23,500

Source: Dept. of Planning and Economic Development
1980

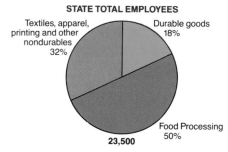

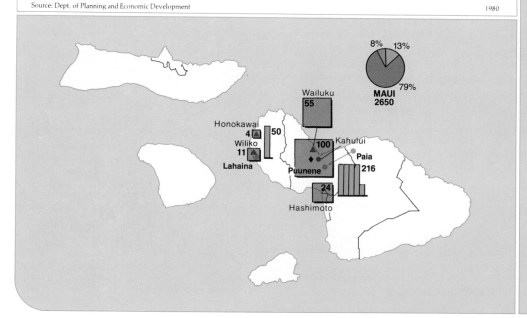

8% 13%
79%
MAUI
2650

Wailuku
55
Honokawai
4 50
Wiliko
11
Lahaina
100 Kahului
Paia
216
Puunene
24
Hashimoto

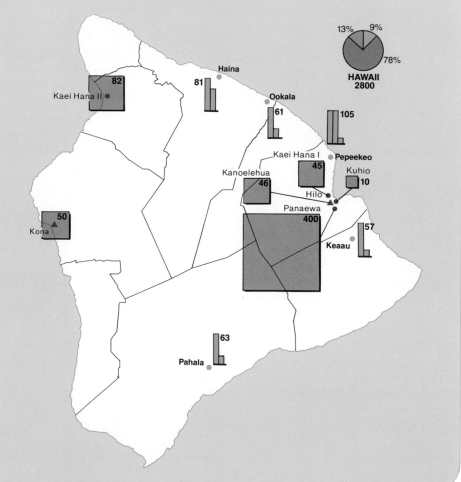

13% 9%
78%
HAWAII
2800

Haina
Kaei Hana II 82
81
61
Ookala
105
Kaei Hana I
Pepeekeo
45 Kuhio
Kanoelehua 46
10
Hilo
Panaewa
400
Kona 50
57
Keaau
63
Pahala

FINANCE AND TRADE

Hawaii's financial institutions comprise a great variety of enterprises and have played a major role in the State's economic growth. Many small institutions assist the larger commercial banks and insurance houses to mobilize local savings, but Hawaii's economy has long been capital deficient and continues to rely heavily on external resources for investment funds. Nearly all of Hawaii's major corporations have extensive operations on the mainland and some also in other countries, which contribute to the process of capital generation, but an important recent development has been increased direct foreign investment in Hawaii. Much of this has consisted of Japanese and Canadian investment in hotel and resort development or in retail trade, but capital from Hong Kong, Arab countries, Australia, and Europe has also been invested either directly or indirectly in the State. Such foreign investment is believed to exceed $1 billion.

Combined deposits of all financial institutions in Hawaii reached $9.0 billion at the end of 1981, which represented an average annual increase of a little more than 10 percent since 1970. Bank-held deposits amounted to some 53 percent of the total. Total loans of all financial institutions in 1980 exceeded $8.7 billion, of which bank advances accounted for some 40 percent.

Mortgage loans outstanding at the end of 1980 stood at more than $7 billion, a nearly four-fold increase over the level of 1970. The construction industry, however, experienced two sharp bouts of depression during the decade, resulting from the two international energy crises of 1970/1975 and 1978/1979, when the number of new mortgages contracted declined. In 1980 savings and loan associations held some 52 percent of mortgages outstanding and, with record high interest rates, faced a difficult period as the spread between receipts from outstanding conventional mortgages and outgoings, tended to enlarge. Most other outstanding mortgages in 1980 were held by banks, with 21 percent of the total, and by insurance companies with 19 percent.

Consumer loans, spurred on by the demands of consumers who believed that prices could only go higher in the future under the pressure of inflation, attained a total of $838 million in 1980. A significant change in the pattern of loans during the 1970s, like similar national trends, was a decline in the share of automobile loans and a sharp increase in loans for repairs and alterations to residences.

Hawaii's mid-Pacific location makes it dependent on fast, efficient transport connections with the U.S. mainland and foreign countries, and Hawaii's shipping companies have developed some of the most advanced containerized facilities—both surface and air—in the world. The imbalance between imports and exports, both with the mainland and foreign countries, has become progressively more unfavorable with economic growth, and there appears little likelihood of any substantial change in the foreseeable future. No detailed balance-of-payments accounting has been available since 1978, but in 1980 total trade with the U.S. mainland was estimated at more than $3 billion, of which nearly 80 percent represented imports; trade with foreign countries, estimated at some $2 billion showed a similar heavy preponderance of imports. Petroleum and petroleum products made up the largest proportion of foreign imports, and in the later 1970s represented more than half the value of all such imports, a virtual doubling of the share before the 1973 oil crisis.

In 1980 retail sales in the islands exceeded $6 billion, but the rate of growth in the later seventies did little more than keep up with the rate of inflation. Regional or planned unit shopping centers have continued to increase in numbers, and by 1982 Oahu will have four such centers, and at least one each on Kauai, Maui, and Hawaii.

D.W.F.

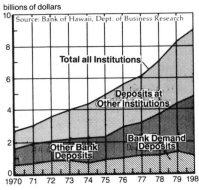

DEPOSITS OF ALL FINANCIAL INSTITUTIONS

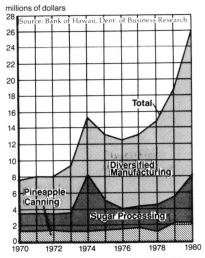

SALES OF MANUFACTURERS

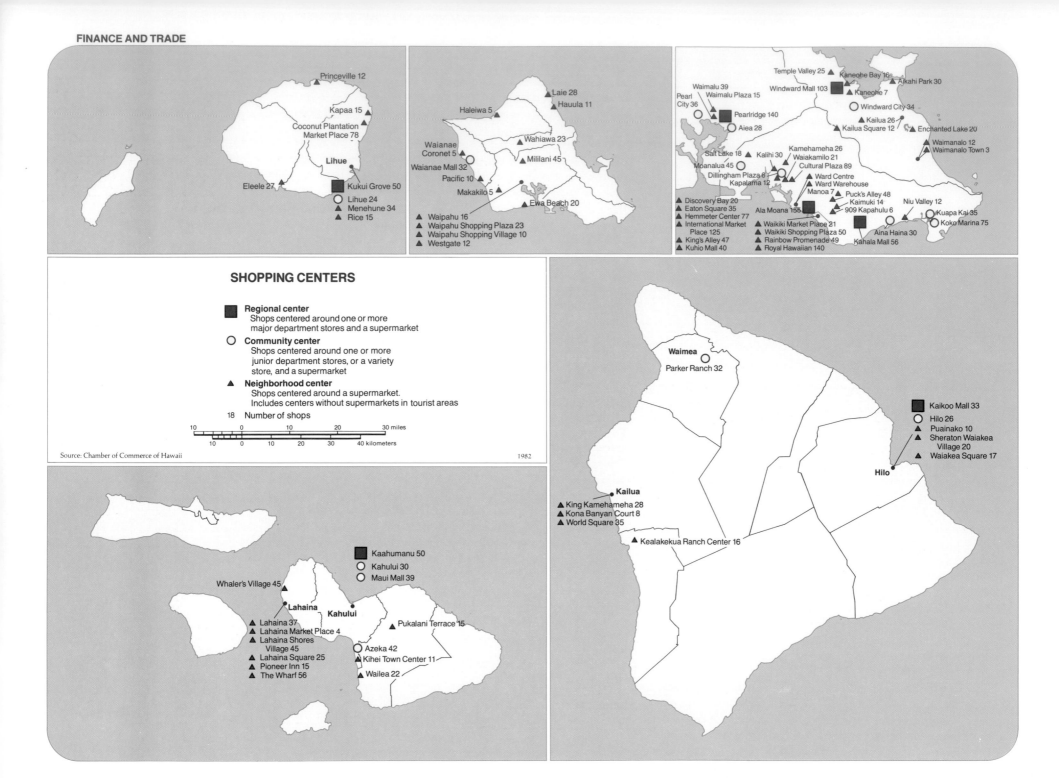

Princeville 12

Kapaa 15

Coconut Plantation
Market Place 78

Lihue

Eleele 27

Kukui Grove 50
○ Lihue 24
▲ Menehune 34
▲ Rice 15

Laie 28

Haleiwa 5
Hauula 11

Wahiawa 23

Waianae
Coronet 5
Waianae Mall 32
Mililani 45

Pacific 10

Makakilo 5

Ewa Beach 20

▲ Waipahu 16
▲ Waipahu Shopping Plaza 23
▲ Waipahu Shopping Village 10
▲ Westgate 12

Temple Valley 25   Kaneohe Bay 16   Akahi Park 30

Waimalu 39   Windward Mall 103   Kaneohe 7
Waimalu Plaza 15
Pearl
City 36   Pearlridge 140   ○ Windward City 34
○ Aiea 28   Kailua 26
Kailua Square 12   Enchanted Lake 20
Kamehameha 26   Waimanalo 12
Salt Lake 18   Kalihi 30   Waiakamilo 21   Waimanalo Town 3
Moanalua 45   Cultural Plaza 89
Dillingham Plaza 6   ▲ Ward Centre
Kapalama 12   ▲ Ward Warehouse
Manoa 7   Puck's Alley 48
▲ Discovery Bay 20   Kaimuki 14   Niu Valley 12
▲ Eaton Square 35   909 Kapahulu 6   Kuapa Kai 35
▲ Hemmeter Center 77   Koko Marina 75
▲ International Market   Ala Moana 155
Place 125   ▲ Waikiki Market Place 21   Aina Haina 30
▲ King's Alley 47   ▲ Waikiki Shopping Plaza 50   Kahala Mall 56
▲ Kuhio Mall 40   ▲ Rainbow Promenade 49
▲ Royal Hawaiian 140

SHOPPING CENTERS

■ **Regional center**
Shops centered around one or more
major department stores and a supermarket

○ **Community center**
Shops centered around one or more
junior department stores, or a variety
store, and a supermarket

▲ **Neighborhood center**
Shops centered around a supermarket.
Includes centers without supermarkets in tourist areas

18   Number of shops

10   20   30 miles
10   0   10   20   30   40 kilometers

Source: Chamber of Commerce of Hawaii   1982

Waimea
○
Parker Ranch 32

■ Kaikoo Mall 33
○ Hilo 26
▲ Puainako 10
▲ Sheraton Waiakea
Village 20
▲ Waiakea Square 17

Hilo

Kailua
▲ King Kamehameha 28
▲ Kona Banyan Court 8
▲ World Square 35

▲ Kealakekua Ranch Center 16

Whaler's Village 45

Lahaina   **Kahului**

■ Kaahumanu 50
○ Kahului 30
○ Maui Mall 39

▲ Lahaina 37
▲ Lahaina Market Place 4
▲ Lahaina Shores   Pukalani Terrace 15
Village 45
▲ Lahaina Square 25   ○ Azeka 42
▲ Pioneer Inn 15   Kihei Town Center 11
▲ The Wharf 56
Wailea 22

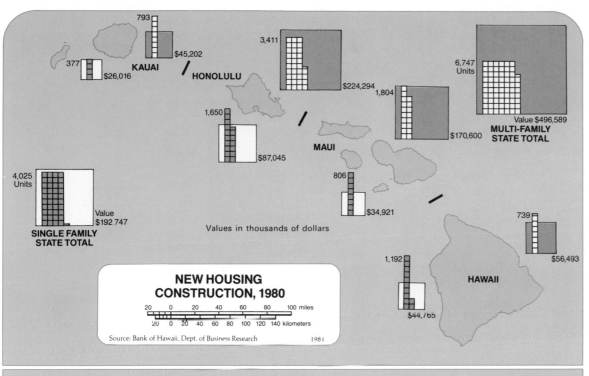

NEW HOUSING CONSTRUCTION, 1980

793
$45,202
KAUAI

377
$26,016

HONOLULU

3,411
$224,294

1,804
$170,600

6,747 Units
Value $496,589
MULTI-FAMILY STATE TOTAL

1,650
$87,045

MAUI

806
$34,921

739
$56,493

HAWAII

1,192
$44,765

4,025 Units
Value $192,747
SINGLE FAMILY STATE TOTAL

Values in thousands of dollars

20 0 20 40 60 80 100 miles
20 0 20 40 60 80 100 120 140 kilometers

Source: Bank of Hawaii, Dept. of Business Research   1981

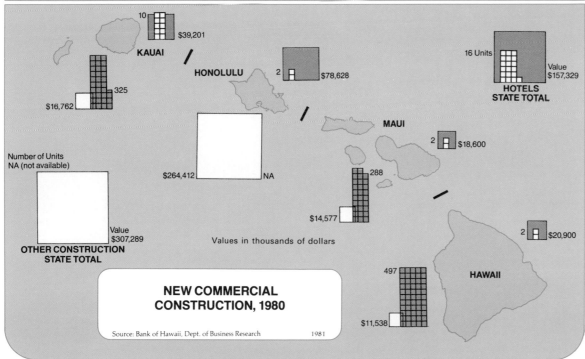

NEW COMMERCIAL CONSTRUCTION, 1980

10
$39,201
KAUAI

HONOLULU

325
$16,762

2
$78,628

16 Units
Value $157,329
HOTELS STATE TOTAL

MAUI

2
$18,600

288
$14,577

2
$20,900

497
$11,538

HAWAII

Number of Units
NA (not available)

$264,412   NA

Value $307,289
OTHER CONSTRUCTION STATE TOTAL

Values in thousands of dollars

Source: Bank of Hawaii, Dept. of Business Research   1981

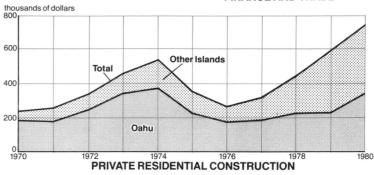

thousands of dollars

PRIVATE RESIDENTIAL CONSTRUCTION

Total   Other Islands

Oahu

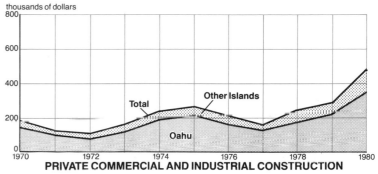

thousands of dollars

PRIVATE COMMERCIAL AND INDUSTRIAL CONSTRUCTION

Total   Other Islands

Oahu

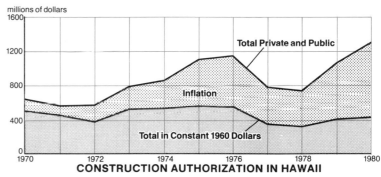

millions of dollars

CONSTRUCTION AUTHORIZATION IN HAWAII

Total Private and Public

Inflation

Total in Constant 1960 Dollars

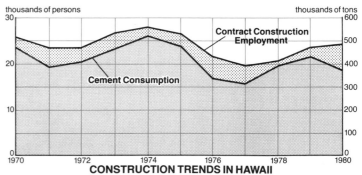

thousands of persons   thousands of tons

CONSTRUCTION TRENDS IN HAWAII

Contract Construction Employment

Cement Consumption

Source: Bank of Hawaii, Dept. of Business Research

171

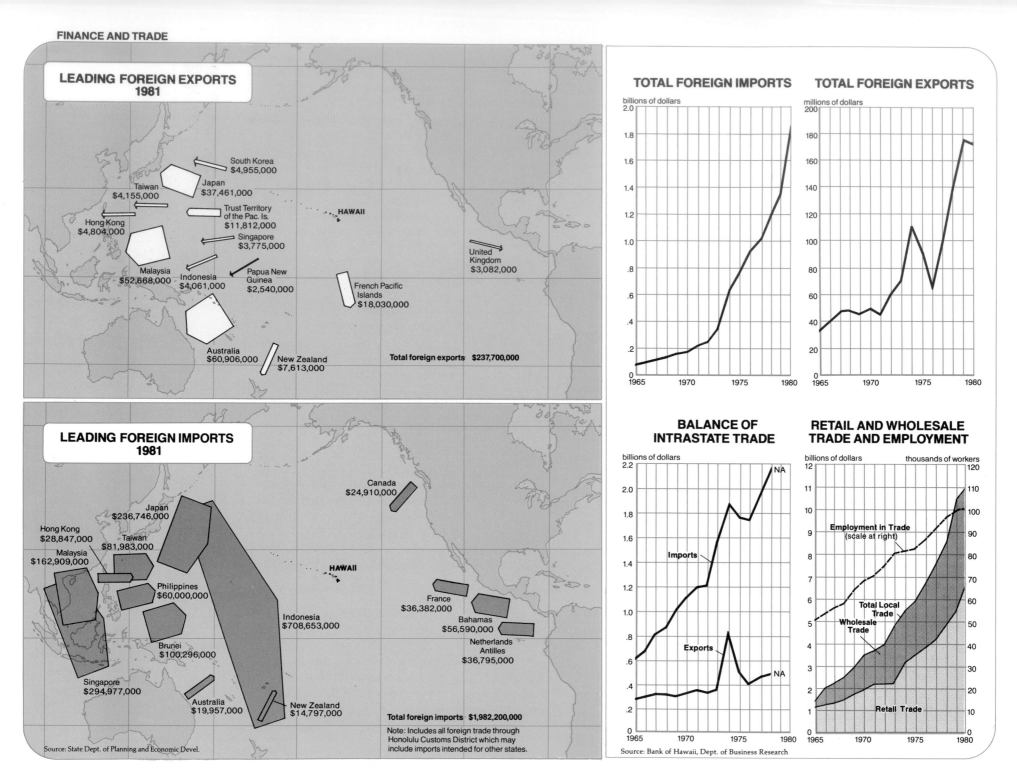

LEADING FOREIGN EXPORTS 1981

South Korea $4,955,000
Japan $37,461,000
Taiwan $4,155,000
Trust Territory of the Pac. Is. $11,812,000
Hong Kong $4,804,000
Singapore $3,775,000
Malaysia $52,668,000
Indonesia $4,061,000
Papua New Guinea $2,540,000
HAWAII
French Pacific Islands $18,030,000
United Kingdom $3,082,000
Australia $60,906,000
New Zealand $7,613,000

Total foreign exports $237,700,000

LEADING FOREIGN IMPORTS 1981

Canada $24,910,000
Japan $236,746,000
Hong Kong $28,847,000
Taiwan $81,983,000
Malaysia $162,909,000
Philippines $60,000,000
HAWAII
France $36,382,000
Indonesia $708,653,000
Bahamas $56,590,000
Brunei $100,296,000
Netherlands Antilles $36,795,000
Singapore $294,977,000
Australia $19,957,000
New Zealand $14,797,000

Total foreign imports $1,982,200,000

Note: Includes all foreign trade through Honolulu Customs District which may include imports intended for other states.

Source: State Dept. of Planning and Economic Devel.

TOTAL FOREIGN IMPORTS

billions of dollars

TOTAL FOREIGN EXPORTS

millions of dollars

BALANCE OF INTRASTATE TRADE

billions of dollars

Imports
Exports
NA
NA

RETAIL AND WHOLESALE TRADE AND EMPLOYMENT

billions of dollars   thousands of workers

Employment in Trade (scale at right)
Total Local Trade
Wholesale Trade
Retail Trade

Source: Bank of Hawaii, Dept. of Business Research

TOURISM

Tourism in Hawaii has grown rapidly since its modest nineteenth-century beginnings. In part this growth has resulted from continual improvements in transportation: the first regular steamship service from the mainland in 1867, interisland air service in 1929, a transpacific airline in 1936, and sharp (albeit temporary) reductions in air fares at irregular intervals. Another factor has been the stimulus provided by government and business through the efforts of the Hawaii Visitors Bureau, first established as the Hawaiian Promotion Committee in 1903. Constantly improving tourist accommodations have likewise played their part: notable developments include the first luxury hotel in Honolulu, the Hawaiian, in 1872; Waikiki's first large hotel, the Seaside Annex, in 1894; the Royal Hawaiian Hotel in 1927; on the island of Hawaii, the Volcano House in 1866 and the Kona Inn in 1928; and on Maui the Kaanapali complex in the early 1960s. State and county governments have made significant efforts in recent years to plan for and guide this growth.

Expansion has been especially rapid since World War II. Annual visitor arrivals increased from 2,040 in 1886 to 9,700 in 1922, 32,000 in 1941, 52,000 in 1951, 320,000 in 1961, 1,819,000 in 1971, and 3,935,000 in 1981. The average number of visitors present at any one time rose from 2,100 in 1941 to 12,000 in 1961, and 96,000 in 1981, and their annual expenditures (excluding transpacific travel) increased from $16.4 million to $3.2 billion during the same 40-year period. Hotel rooms numbered 1,572 at the end of 1946, 10,900 in 1962, and 58,000 in 1982.

Most of the visitors to Hawaii come from the western United States and other parts of the mainland, but a growing number are residents of Japan, Australia, and other countries of the Far East and South Pacific. In 1981, 76 percent of all visitors staying overnight or longer came on westbound flights or sailings, while 24 percent arrived on eastbound or northbound carriers. Among westbound visitors destined for Hawaii, 47 percent were residents of either the Pacific or Mountain states, and 30 percent were Californians. Foreign countries contributing the most visitors in 1981 were Japan (690,000), Canada (291,000), Australia (172,000), and the United Kingdom (96,000).

Hawaii Visitors Bureau surveys reveal the typical visitor to be a relatively affluent person of middle years. The median age of westbound visitors in 1981 was 40 years, and there were only 81 males for every 100 females. Sixty-one percent of all party heads reported themselves to be professional or technical workers or businessmen, managers, or officials. Median annual family income before taxes in 1980 was $33,400, approximately 59 percent above the national level.

Most westbound visitors came by air, stayed in hotels, and saw at least one island other than Oahu. Only a handful arrived by ship in 1981, compared with 43.6 percent in 1951. Twenty-nine percent arrived in June, July, or August, while 25 percent came during the winter months. More than 47 percent had made at least one earlier visit to Hawaii. Three fourths were on pleasure trips. The average intended length of stay in 1981 was 11.3 days, compared with 11.0 in 1971, 17.2 in 1961, and 25.0 in 1951. In 1981, 70 percent planned to stay in a hotel rather than in a rented comdominium or other apartment or with friends or relatives, and two-thirds planned to see at least two islands. The average expenditure per visitor day in 1980 was $185 for Japanese visitors and $71 for non-Japanese. The major expenditure items were gifts and souvenirs for the Japanese, and lodging for the non-Japanese.

An inventory of accommodations available in the islands as of February 1982 reported 417 hotels, apartment hotels, motels, and similar facilities, with a total of 57,968 rentable units: 33,492 on Oahu, 7,167 on the island of Hawaii, 11,596 on Maui, 5,147 on Kauai, 555 on Molokai, and 11 on Lanai. Major concentrations were in Waikiki and the adjacent Ala Moana area on Oahu, the Lahaina and Kihei-Wailea areas on Maui, Hilo and Kailua-Keauhou on Hawaii, and Wailua-Kapaa on Kauai. These data include 14,400 condominium units in rental pools for transient occupancy.

Although most of the interest in Hawaiian tourism centers on the mainlanders and foreigners visiting the islands, it should not be forgotten that the islanders themselves are frequent travelers. According to the National Travel Survey, Oahuans made 243,000 trips to other islands of Hawaii in 1977. A survey of travel during 1979 reported that 35 percent of all island adults vacationed outside the State in that year, making 355,000 round trips for that purpose, chiefly to California and Nevada.

R.C.S

Royal Hawaiian Hotel, Waikiki.

Drawing by John A. Dixon

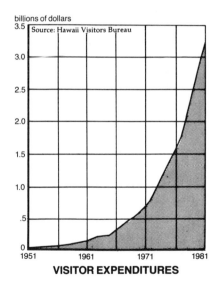

billions of dollars

Source: Hawaii Visitors Bureau

VISITOR EXPENDITURES

MAINLAND VISITORS TO HAWAII, 1981

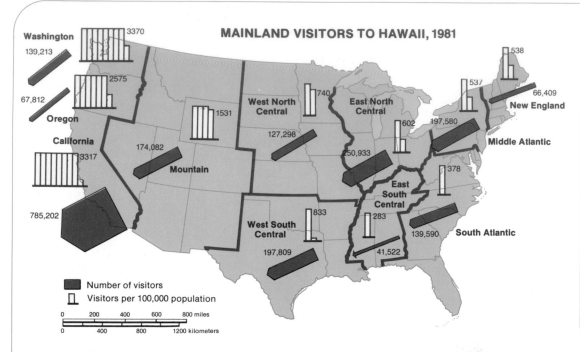

Washington
139,213
3370

Oregon
67,812
2575

California
3317
174,082
785,202

Mountain

West North Central
127,298
1531

East North Central
250,933
602

West South Central
197,809
833

East South Central
41,522
283

South Atlantic
139,590
378

Middle Atlantic
197,580
740

New England
66,409
538
537

■ Number of visitors
▯ Visitors per 100,000 population

0   200   400   600   800 miles
0   400   800   1200 kilometers

VISITOR CHARACTERISTICS
Westbound Only

percent   number of days

Staying in Hotels
Pleasure Trip
Intending to Visit Oahu and Other Islands
Repeat Visitors
Average Intended Stay
use scale at right

1961   1965   1970   1975   1980

Source: Hawaii Visitors Bureau

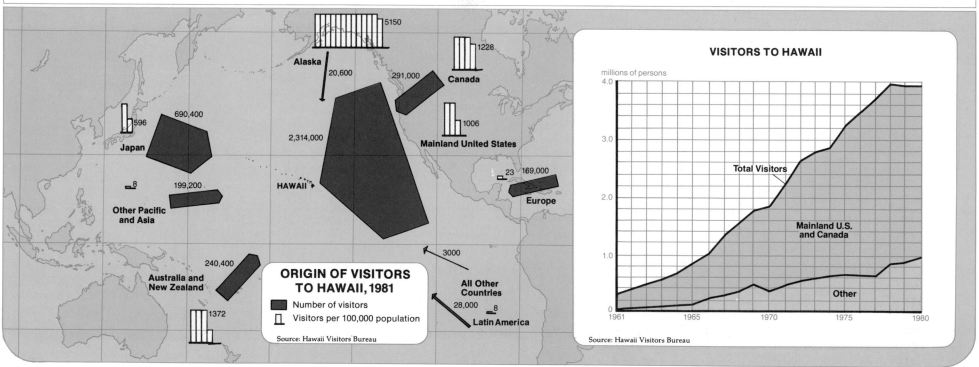

Alaska
20,600
5150

Canada
291,000
1228

Mainland United States
1006

Japan
690,400
596

Other Pacific and Asia
199,200
8

HAWAII →
2,314,000

Australia and New Zealand
240,400
1372

Europe
169,000
23

All Other Countries
3000

Latin America
28,000
8

ORIGIN OF VISITORS TO HAWAII, 1981

■ Number of visitors
▯ Visitors per 100,000 population

Source: Hawaii Visitors Bureau

VISITORS TO HAWAII

millions of persons

Total Visitors

Mainland U.S. and Canada

Other

1961   1965   1970   1975   1980

Source: Hawaii Visitors Bureau

MONTHLY VISITOR ARRIVALS

percent

1929

1940

1961

1971

1981

Jan Mar May Jul Sep Nov

Source: Hawaii Visitors Bureau

PASSENGER MODE OF TRAVEL TO HAWAII

millions of persons   thousands of persons

Air Travel

Surface Travel
(enlarged, use
right scale)

Surface Travel

1961   1971   1981

TRAVELLERS TO HAWAII AND VISITOR LENGTH OF STAY, 1981
By County

Visitor is defined as a person staying
overnight or longer
*Details on passengers not available

Source: Hawaii Visitors Bureau

6969

3.5

KAUAI

HONOLULU

South and Westbound
Arriving Travellers
3,780,383

Visitors to Hawaii 69%

Returning Residents 6%
Intending Residents 1%
Passing Through 24%

Average Visitors Census Per Day, 1981
HONOLULU 67,592

5.9

Honolulu

Hilo Airport
49,091 (1%)

Honolulu
Airport
5,256,718
(99%)

East and Northbound
Arriving Travellers*
1,525,426

Total Arriving
Passengers
5,305,809

15,210

4.1

MAUI

6324

HAWAII

Average Days
Visitors Stayed
3.6

Hilo

OUT-OF-STATE VACATION TRAVEL BY HAWAII RESIDENTS, 1979

To:
California	21.2%
Nevada	12%
Alaska	0.4%
Pacific Northwest	3.8%
Southwest States	1%
Rocky Mountain States	2%
Central States	3.8%
Southern States	3.2%
Eastern States	4.4%
Canada	2%
Mexico	0.8%
Caribbean	0.4%
South America	0%
Pacific Islands	0.2%
Australia/New Zealand	0.6%
Japan	1.6%
Philippines	1.4%
China, Korea	0.8%
Southeast Asia	0.6%
Indian Subcontinent	0.2%
Middle East	0.4%
Africa	0%
Europe	1.4%

35% of all adults vacationed outside Hawaii
28% of all adults never vacationed outside Hawaii
41% of all households vacationed outside Hawaii
2.08 was average size of vacation party
Length of vacation: median 12.8 nights,
    mean 17.2 nights (Time includes nonvacation
    purposes)
$2051 was average household expenditure
    per vacation trip

Source: State Dept. of Planning and Economic Development

DESTINATIONS OF WESTBOUND TRAVELLERS BEYOND HAWAII 1981

10   0   10   20   30 miles
10   0   10   20   30   40 kilometers

Source: Hawaii Visitors Bureau

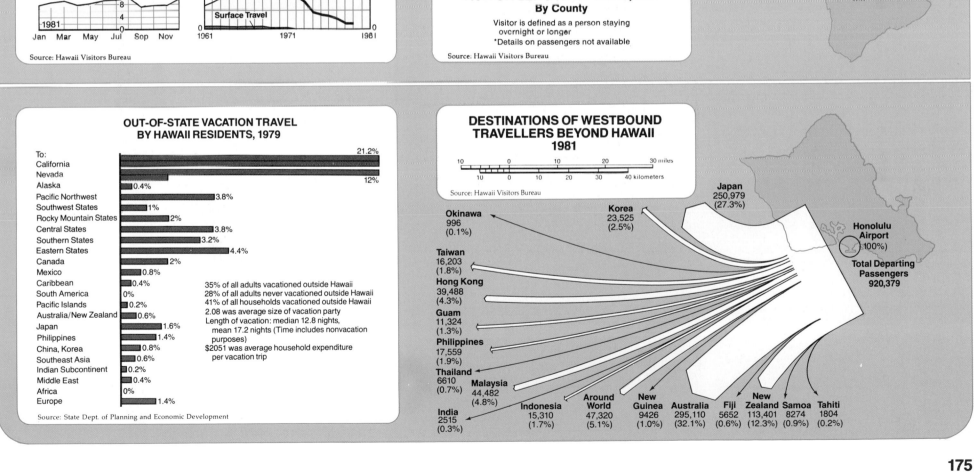

Japan
250,979
(27.3%)

Okinawa
996
(0.1%)

Korea
23,525
(2.5%)

Taiwan
16,203
(1.8%)

Hong Kong
39,488
(4.3%)

Guam
11,324
(1.3%)

Philippines
17,559
(1.9%)

Thailand
6610
(0.7%)

Malaysia
44,482
(4.8%)

India
2515
(0.3%)

Indonesia
15,310
(1.7%)

Around
World
47,320
(5.1%)

New
Guinea
9426
(1.0%)

Australia
295,110
(32.1%)

Fiji
5652
(0.6%)

New
Zealand
113,401
(12.3%)

Samoa
8274
(0.9%)

Tahiti
1804
(0.2%)

Honolulu
Airport
(100%)

Total Departing
Passengers
920,379

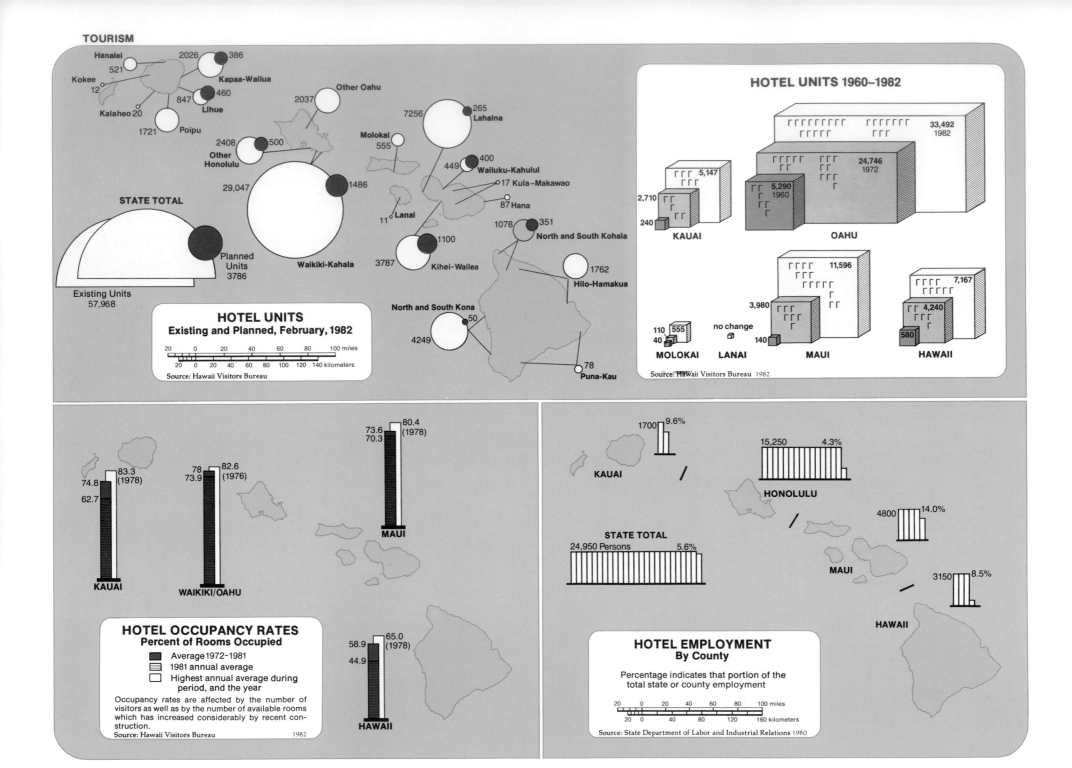

HOTEL UNITS
Existing and Planned, February, 1982

STATE TOTAL

Planned Units 3786

Existing Units 57,968

Hanalei 521 / 2026 / 386
Kokee 12
Kalaheo 20
847 / 460 Kapaa-Wailua
Lihue
1721 Poipu
2408 / 500
Other Honolulu
29,047 Waikiki-Kahala
Other Oahu 2037
7256 / 265 Lahaina
Molokai 555
449 / 400 Wailuku-Kahulul
17 Kula–Makawao
87 Hana
11 Lanai
1100
3787 Kihei-Wailea
1078 / 351 North and South Kohala
1762 Hilo-Hamakua
North and South Kona
50
4249
78 Puna-Kau

Source: Hawaii Visitors Bureau

HOTEL UNITS 1960–1982

KAUAI: 2,710 / 240 / 5,147
OAHU: 5,290 1960 / 24,746 1972 / 33,492 1982
MOLOKAI: 110 / 40 / 555
LANAI: no change
MAUI: 3,980 / 140 / 11,596
HAWAII: 580 / 4,240 / 7,167

Source: Hawaii Visitors Bureau 1982

HOTEL OCCUPANCY RATES
Percent of Rooms Occupied

KAUAI: 74.8 / 62.7 / 83.3 (1978)
WAIKIKI/OAHU: 78 / 73.9 / 82.6 (1976)
MAUI: 73.6 / 70.3 / 80.4 (1978)
HAWAII: 58.9 / 44.9 / 65.0 (1978)

▮ Average 1972-1981
▤ 1981 annual average
☐ Highest annual average during period, and the year

Occupancy rates are affected by the number of visitors as well as by the number of available rooms which has increased considerably by recent construction.

Source: Hawaii Visitors Bureau   1982

HOTEL EMPLOYMENT
By County

KAUAI: 1700 / 9.6%
HONOLULU: 15,250 / 4.3%
MAUI: 4800 / 14.0%
HAWAII: 3150 / 8.5%
STATE TOTAL: 24,950 Persons / 5.6%

Percentage indicates that portion of the total state or county employment

Source: State Department of Labor and Industrial Relations 1980

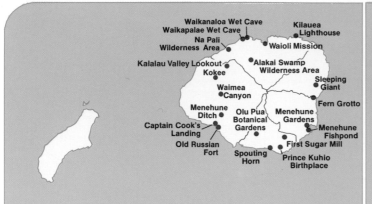

Waikanaloa Wet Cave
Waikapalae Wet Cave
Na Pali Wilderness Area
Kalalau Valley Lookout
Kokee
Waimea Canyon
Menehune Ditch
Captain Cook's Landing
Old Russian Fort
Olu Pua Botanical Gardens
Spouting Horn
First Sugar Mill
Menehune Gardens
Menehune Fishpond
Prince Kuhio Birthplace
Kilauea Lighthouse
Waioli Mission
Alakai Swamp Wilderness Area
Sleeping Giant
Fern Grotto

Washington Statue
Waimea Falls Park
Makua Dry Cave
Makaha Valley
Kukaniloko (birth stones)
Kolekole Pass
Wahiawa Botanical Garden
Polynesian Cultural Center
Crouching Lion
Old Sugar Mill
Chinaman's Hat Island

see map at right

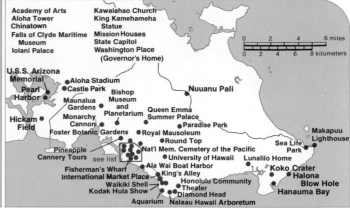

Academy of Arts
Aloha Tower
Chinatown
Falls of Clyde Maritime Museum
Iolani Palace
Kawaiahao Church
King Kamehameha Statue
Mission Houses
State Capitol
Washington Place (Governor's Home)

U.S.S. Arizona Memorial
Pearl Harbor
Hickam Field
Aloha Stadium
Castle Park
Maunalua Gardens
Monarchy Cannon
Foster Botanic Gardens
Pineapple Cannery Tours
see list
Fisherman's Wharf
International Market Place
Waikiki Shell
Kodak Hula Show
Bishop Museum and Planetarium
Queen Emma Summer Palace
Paradise Park
Royal Mausoleum
Round Top
Nat'l Mem. Cemetery of the Pacific
University of Hawaii
Ala Wai Boat Harbor
King's Alley
Honolulu Community Theater
Diamond Head
Nalaau Hawaii Arboretum
Aquarium
Nuuanu Pali
Sea Life Park
Makapuu Lighthouse
Lunalilo Home
Koko Crater
Halona
Blow Hole
Hanauma Bay

0 2 4 6 miles
0 2 4 6 8 kilometers

PLACES OF VISITOR INTEREST

Only a selection of the many places of interest in Hawaii to residents and visitors is indicated. Other places of interest, not shown here, appear elsewhere in the Atlas. For example, natural features are indicated on reference maps (pages 12–30), archaeological sites and heiau (page 95), churches (page 133), libraries and museums (page 135), centers of the arts (page 137) and parks and other recreation sites (pages 204–207).

10   10   20 miles
10 0 10 20 30 kilometers

Source: State Dept. of Planning and Econ. Devel. 1981

OAHU ATTRACTIONS, TEN LARGEST IN ATTENDANCE, 1981

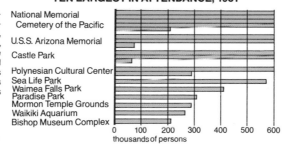

National Memorial Cemetery of the Pacific
U.S.S. Arizona Memorial
Castle Park
Polynesian Cultural Center
Sea Life Park
Waimea Falls Park
Paradise Park
Mormon Temple Grounds
Waikiki Aquarium
Bishop Museum Complex

0 100 200 300 400 500 600
thousands of persons

Start of Aloha Week Outrigger Race
Palaau Lookout
Father Damien's Church
Waikolu Valley
Wailau Valley
Halawa Valley
Kapuaiwa Coconut Grove
St. Joseph Church
Fishponds
Kahakuloa Village
Garden of the Gods
Keomoku Village
Hauola Gulch
Kaunolu Village Nat'l Historic Landmark
Lahaina, Kaanapali and Pacific Railroad
Iao Needle
Lahaina:
Baldwin House
Hale Aloha
Hale Paahao
Largest Banyan Tree
Pioneer Mill (1860)
Kanda Gardens
Maui Jinsha Shinto Shrine
Kanaha Bird Sanctuary
Kula Botanical Gardens
Polipoli Springs
Makee Sugar Mill (1878)
Kipahulu Mill (1890)
Huialoha Church
Hanawai Falls
Haleakala National Park
Keanae Peninsula
Queen Kaahumanu's Birthplace
Wailua Falls
Oheo Gulch (Seven Pools)
Charles Lindbergh Grave

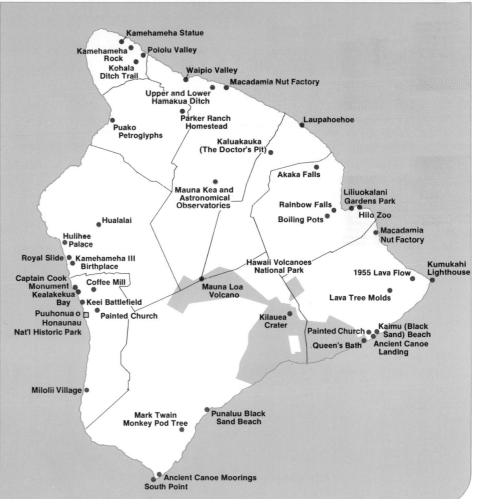

Kamehameha Statue
Kamehameha Rock
Kohala Ditch Trail
Pololu Valley
Waipio Valley
Macadamia Nut Factory
Upper and Lower Hamakua Ditch
Parker Ranch Homestead
Laupahoehoe
Puako Petroglyphs
Kaluakauka (The Doctor's Pit)
Akaka Falls
Mauna Kea and Astronomical Observatories
Rainbow Falls
Boiling Pots
Liliuokalani Gardens Park
Hilo Zoo
Hualalai
Hulihee Palace
Royal Slide
Kamehameha III Birthplace
Captain Cook Monument
Kealakekua Bay
Coffee Mill
Keei Battlefield
Puuhonua o Honaunau Nat'l Historic Park
Painted Church
Macadamia Nut Factory
Hawaii Volcanoes National Park
Mauna Loa Volcano
1955 Lava Flow
Lava Tree Molds
Kumukahi Lighthouse
Kilauea Crater
Painted Church
Queen's Bath
Kaimu (Black Sand) Beach
Ancient Canoe Landing
Milolii Village
Mark Twain Monkey Pod Tree
Punaluu Black Sand Beach
Ancient Canoe Moorings
South Point

THE MILITARY

The strategic position of Hawaii in the central Pacific makes it an ideal site for major commands of all five military services, including headquarters of the Commander in Chief, Pacific. Numerous permanent military installations provide support for land, sea, and air forces deployed throughout the Pacific. The Coast Guard, Navy, and Air Force operate a joint Rescue Coordination Center in Honolulu, which directs search and rescue operations throughout the central and eastern Pacific. The Navy has been established in the islands longer than the other services, having been granted the use of Pearl Harbor by the Kingdom of Hawaii in 1887, and it remains the dominant service today in terms of personnel and contributions to the local economy.

In 1981, a total of 61,521 service men and women were assigned to duty in Hawaii, distributed as follows: Air Force, 6,105; Army, 17,247; Coast Guard, 1,089; Marine Corps, 13,265; and Navy, 23,815. All but 450 were stationed on Oahu. Dependents of service personnel numbered 64,344 for a combined military and dependents total of 125,865, about 13 percent of the population of the State. Not included in these totals are personnel of the Hawaii National Guard (3,468) and Hawaii Air National Guard (1,910).

The armed forces employed an average of 19,200 civilians in technical and administrative support jobs in 1981, making them the largest single employer in the State. Sixty-four percent of all federal jobs were with the military. Military expenditures are a major element in the State's economy, having doubled in the decade ending in 1980, reaching a total in that year of $1.4 billion (page 144). By service, local expenditures were: Navy and Marine Corps, $734 million; Army, $470 million; Air Force, $141 million; and Coast Guard, $23 million. By major item of expenditure, 40 percent was for military pay, 32 percent for civilian pay, and 28 percent for supplies, equipment, and services.

The armed forces are among the largest landowners and land users in Hawaii (page 147). Some 100,000 acres (26 percent) of Oahu, a similar area on Hawaii (4 percent), all of Kahoolawe and Kure Atoll, but less than 1 percent of all the other islands is owned by or is under the control of the military services. Of the total, 71 percent is controlled by the Army and 25 percent by the Navy.

H.F.O.

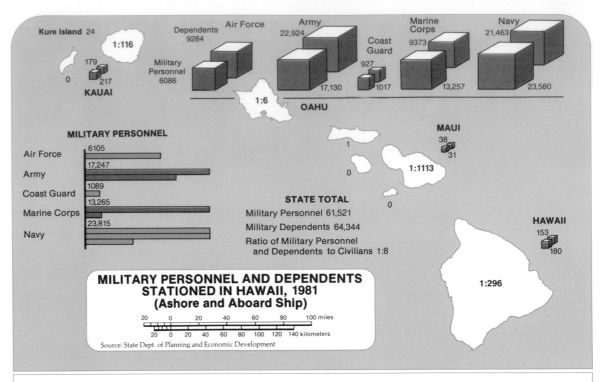

MILITARY PERSONNEL AND DEPENDENTS STATIONED IN HAWAII, 1981 (Ashore and Aboard Ship)

Source: State Dept. of Planning and Economic Development

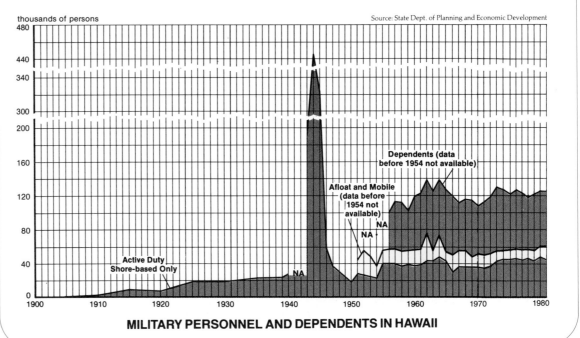

MILITARY PERSONNEL AND DEPENDENTS IN HAWAII

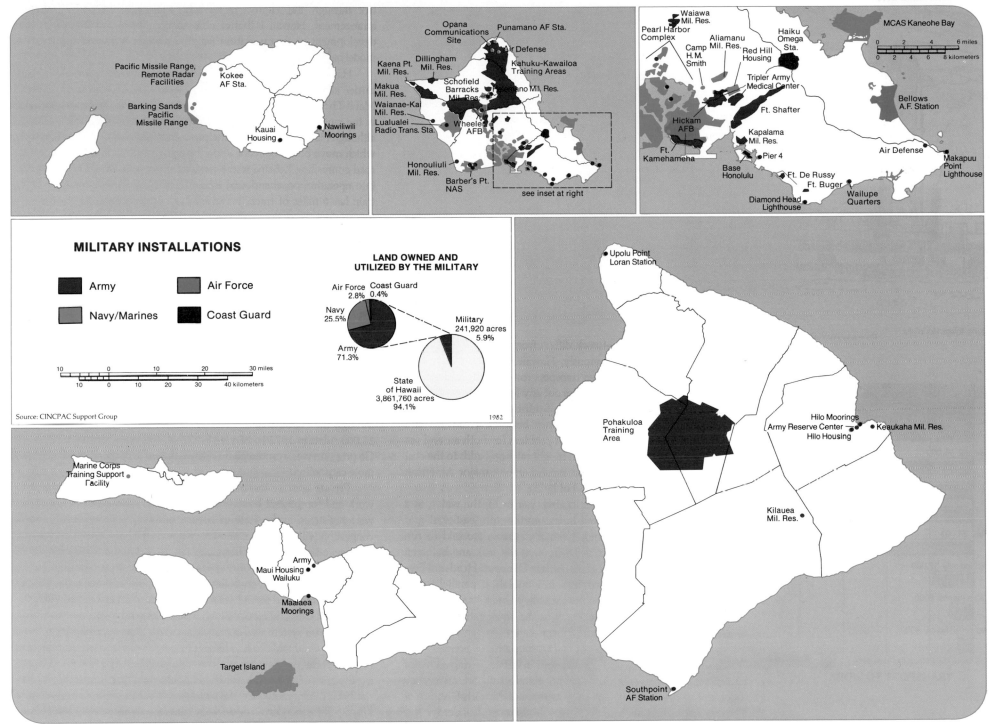

Kauai map (top left):
- Pacific Missile Range, Remote Radar Facilities
- Kokee AF Sta.
- Barking Sands Pacific Missile Range
- Kauai Housing
- Nawiliwili Moorings

Oahu map (top center):
- Opana Communications Site
- Punamano AF Sta.
- Air Defense
- Kaena Pt. Mil. Res.
- Dillingham Mil. Res.
- Kahuku-Kawailoa Training Areas
- Makua Mil. Res.
- Schofield Barracks Mil. Res.
- Helemano Mil. Res.
- Waianae-Kai Mil. Res.
- Wheeler AFB
- Lualualei Radio Trans. Sta.
- Honouliuli Mil. Res.
- Barber's Pt. NAS
- see inset at right

Oahu inset (top right): MCAS Kaneohe Bay
- Waiawa Mil. Res.
- Pearl Harbor Complex
- Camp H.M. Smith
- Aliamanu Mil. Res.
- Haiku Omega Sta.
- Red Hill Housing
- Tripler Army Medical Center
- Ft. Shafter
- Bellows A.F. Station
- Hickam AFB
- Kapalama Mil. Res.
- Ft. Kamehameha
- Pier 4
- Air Defense
- Base Honolulu
- Ft. De Russy
- Ft. Buger
- Makapuu Point Lighthouse
- Diamond Head Lighthouse
- Wailupe Quarters

Scale: 0 2 4 6 miles / 0 2 4 6 8 kilometers

MILITARY INSTALLATIONS

- ⬛ Army
- ◼ Air Force
- ◼ Navy/Marines
- ◼ Coast Guard

Scale: 10 0 10 20 30 miles / 10 0 10 20 30 40 kilometers

Source: CINCPAC Support Group

LAND OWNED AND UTILIZED BY THE MILITARY

- Air Force 2.8%
- Coast Guard 0.4%
- Navy 25.5%
- Army 71.3%
- Military 241,920 acres 5.9%
- State of Hawaii 3,861,760 acres 94.1%

1982

Maui / Molokai / Lanai / Kahoolawe map (bottom left):
- Marine Corps Training Support Facility
- Army
- Maui Housing Wailuku
- Maalaea Moorings
- Target Island

Hawaii (Big Island) map (right):
- Upolu Point Loran Station
- Pohakuloa Training Area
- Hilo Moorings
- Army Reserve Center
- Keaukaha Mil. Res.
- Hilo Housing
- Kilauea Mil. Res.
- Southpoint AF Station

Aloha Tower, Honolulu.   Drawing by John A. Dixon

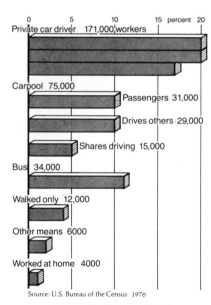

Source: U.S. Bureau of the Census 1976

TRANSPORT TO WORK

TRANSPORT

Hawaii's transportation network differs from that of the other 49 states in several ways. Most obviously, Hawaii is the only state that must rely entirely upon air and sea transport for exports and imports. The insular nature of the State also rules out any form of statewide land transportation. Hawaii's inability to be self-sufficient as an agricultural and/or industrial state creates an imbalance between westward and eastward trade, making a major backhaul problem for both air and sea transport. This imbalance is reflected in freight rates and adds to the cost of living in the State; Honolulu ranks second among major American metropolitan areas with respect to cost of living.

The major cities in Hawaii are located near or on the water; as a result, streets are often not laid out in the north-south, east-west grid systems common on the mainland. Normally, streets are said to run *mauka* (toward the mountains) or *makai* (toward the sea), and between major physical and/or geographic areas (such as Diamond Head and Ewa in Honolulu). The major traffic corridor in Honolulu is parallel to the coast, with feeder lines running up into the valleys and hills.

Hawaii also differs from other states in the organization it has set up to deal with the development of transportation. When Hawaii became a state in 1959, the Department of Transportation was established to replace existing divisions and commissions in administering all major ports, airports, and highways. All major ports and all airports are owned and operated by the State through the Harbors and Airports Division of the Department of Transportation, and the highways are under its con-

trol through the Highways Division. Through this organizational arrangement, Hawaii is better able to coordinate the financing and development of transportation facilities and services, and it has set a model to be emulated by other states.

Hawaii has had a total of seven railroads that have gained common carrier status—two each on Oahu, Hawaii, and Kauai, and one on Maui. The last of these went out of business in 1947, and today Hawaii is the only state in the Union without a common carrier railroad, although Hawaii does have some private freight transportation railroads which move bulk sugarcane and pineapple. In 1970 an amusement railroad connecting Lahaina and Kaanapali on the island of Maui was put into operation on abandoned tracks from an old sugarcane train. The train has 6 miles of track; it carried 111,600 passengers in 1980. With these minor exceptions, all passengers and freight carried on land in Hawaii are served by some form of motor transport.

Honolulu is the only city in the State with a major mass-transit system. This system has evolved from the horse-drawn cart of 1868 to the present diesel bus system. In 1971, the City bought its own fleet of buses and contracted with a private firm to run them. Until that time, the system was privately owned and operated. In 1981, the fleet consisted of 414 buses; it is expected that the number will increase to about 600 by 1990. In 1981 the transit system carried about 200,000 riders per day on 45 routes and had one of the highest per capita riderships in the United States.

The City has also inaugurated two additional mass-transit programs on Oahu. Service has been provided for the elderly and handicapped through the Handi-Van program, which has grown from 9 vans and 25,000 riders in 1977 to 22 vans with 240,000 riders in 1981. The Van-Go program was introduced in 1977 with 9 state-owned vehicles to promote carpooling.

Private cars are the major form of transportation for journeys to work and for general household activities; 514,669 passenger vehicles were registered in the State in 1980. Projections indicate future traffic congestion will seriously strain the city and state transportation system. Planners estimate that by the year 2000, 279,000 more people than at present will be traveling during peak times to work and school. Due to an anticipated half-billion-dollar cost, a proposal for a fixed-rail rapid transit system called HART (Honolulu Area Rapid Transit) running between Pearl City and Hawaii Kai has been deferred indefinitely. In 1981 the bus transit system was operating at capacity during peak commuting times and was unable to handle any more riders. The State Department of Transportation plans for widening Kalanianaole Highway and finishing the remaining 11 miles of the H-3 interstate highway on Oahu had not been implemented by 1981 because of community opposition and lawsuits. Present plans to deal with increased traffic congestion include

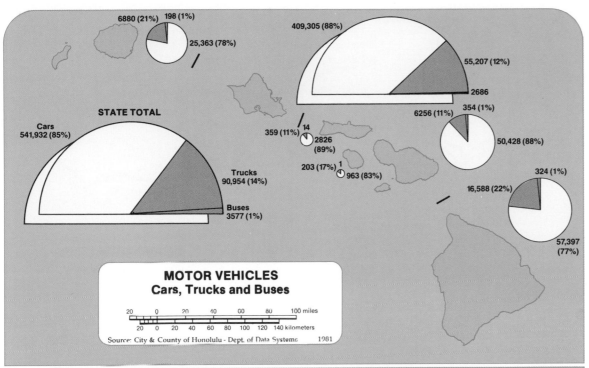

6880 (21%) 198 (1%)

25,363 (78%)

409,305 (88%)

55,207 (12%)

2686

STATE TOTAL

6256 (11%) 354 (1%)

Cars
541,932 (85%)

359 (11%) 14

50,428 (88%)

2826
(89%)

Trucks
90,954 (14%)

203 (17%) 1

963 (83%)

324 (1%)

16,588 (22%)

Buses
3577 (1%)

57,397
(77%)

MOTOR VEHICLES
Cars, Trucks and Buses

20   0   20   40   60   80   100 miles
20 0 20 40 60 80 100 120 140 kilometers

Source: City & County of Honolulu - Dept. of Data Systems   1981

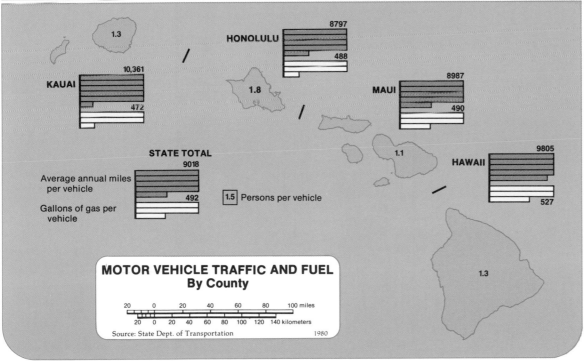

1.3

HONOLULU

8797

488

KAUAI

10,361

472

1.8

MAUI

8987

490

STATE TOTAL

9018

Average annual miles
per vehicle

492

1.5 Persons per vehicle

Gallons of gas per
vehicle

1.1

HAWAII

9805

527

1.3

MOTOR VEHICLE TRAFFIC AND FUEL
By County

20   0   20   40   60   80   100 miles
20 0 20 40 60 80 100 120 140 kilometers

Source: State Dept. of Transportation   1980

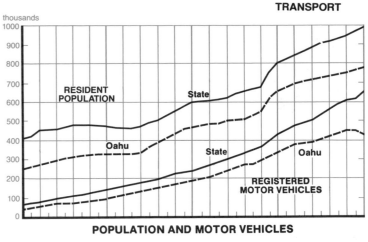

thousands

RESIDENT
POPULATION

State

Oahu

State

Oahu

REGISTERED
MOTOR VEHICLES

POPULATION AND MOTOR VEHICLES

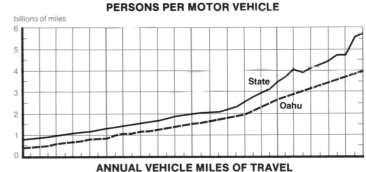

State

Oahu

PERSONS PER MOTOR VEHICLE

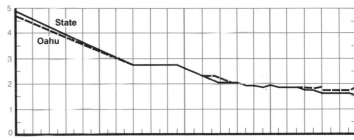

billions of miles

State

Oahu

ANNUAL VEHICLE MILES OF TRAVEL

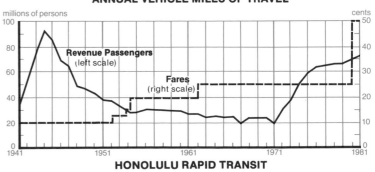

millions of persons   cents

Revenue Passengers
(left scale)

Fares
(right scale)

1941   1951   1961   1971   1981

HONOLULU RAPID TRANSIT

Source: City and County of Honolulu 1981

181

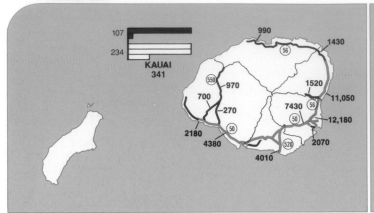

KAUAI
341

107
234

990
1430
1270
550
970
700
270
1520
11,050
7430
56
12,180
2180
50
4380
520
2070
4010

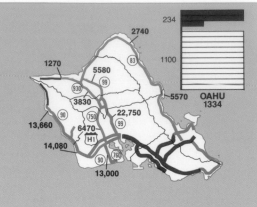

2740
5580
930
99
3830
22,750
90
750
6470
99
13,660
H1
14,080
90
760
13,000

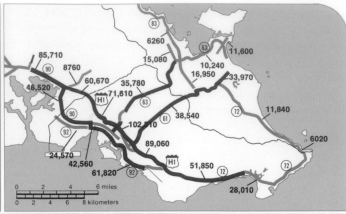

234
1100
5570

OAHU
1334

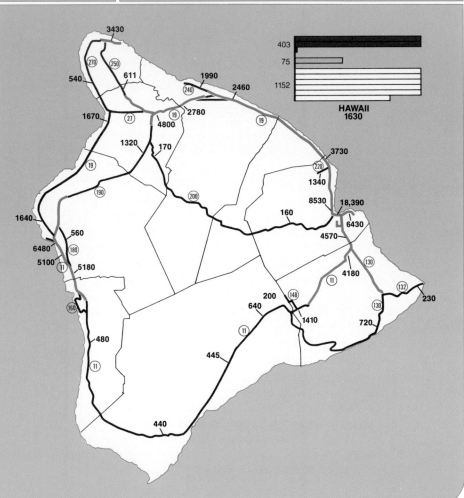

85,710
6260
63
11,600
15,080
8760
10,240
60,670
16,950
33,970
46,520
35,780
71,610
H1
63
38,540
102,570
72
11,840
92
89,060
24,570
H1
42,560
51,850
6020
61,820
92
72
28,010

0   2   4   6 miles
0   2   4   6   8 kilometers

403
75
1152

HAWAII
1630

TRAFFIC FLOW ON SELECTED HIGHWAYS, 1970

**STATE TOTAL
ROAD MILEAGE, 1981**

Vehicles per day
More than 70,000
30,001–70,000
10,001–30,000
2001–10,000
2000 or less

0000 Average traffic per day
at point indicated

63 State highway number

H1 Interstate highway

1016
75

2986

State Parks 49
Military Roads 23   **TOTAL 4147**   1981

10   0   10   20   30 miles
10   0   10   20   30   40 kilometers

Source: State Dept. of Transportation

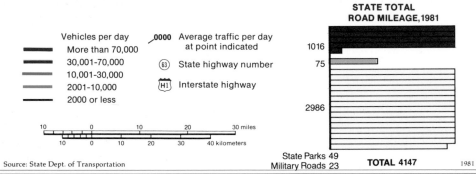

1170
650
540
460
470
460
2610
450
730
483

44
440
440

13
32
LANAI
45

53
73
MOLOKAI
126

206
14
395
MAUI
601

2700
340
500
1580
18,580
20,730
440
8670
30
4660
400
5080
37
4120
30
35
6100
377
420
1450
2470
680
360
31
2580
840
37
31
357

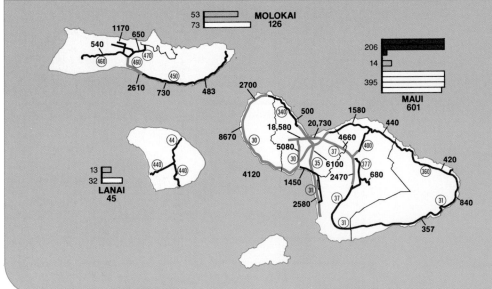

3430
270
250
1990
540
611
2460
240
1670
27
19
2780
1320
170
4800
19
19
220
3730
190
1340
200
160
8530
18,390
1640
6430
560
4570
6480
180
130
5100
11
5180
4180
200
148
640
130
720
11
1410
132
230
480
11
445
440

an enlarged bus fleet, an improved highway system with additional lanes, and possibly a toll system to encourage carpooling.

In 1980 Hawaii had a total of 89,755 trucks registered to carry freight. The typical truck fleet is small: 30 percent of the fleets have only one truck, 21 have two to five, and 49 percent have five trucks or more. The State Constitution of 1959 placed common and contract carriers under the economic regulatory control of the Public Utilities Commission. There were also, in 1980, 3,366 privately owned passenger buses distributed throughout Hawaii, most of them used as tour buses for visitors.

Overseas Shipping. The history of Hawaii and the development of shipping are inevitably connected. The arrival of the first people by canoe, the discovery of Hawaii by Captain Cook in 1778, the birth of today's dominant domestic carrier, Matson Lines, in 1882 all attest to this relationship. Today Hawaii is served by three scheduled ship operators, two of them American. Matson Lines carries 85 percent of the freight and the United States Line carries about 10 percent. Three barge companies, Sause Bros., Northland Marine Barge Service, and Hawaiian Marine Lines, account for the remaining 5 percent. In 1978 shipping accounted for 9.1 million tons of cargo. During the past 20 years, the number of passengers arriving by ship decreased from 54,000 in 1959 to 400 in 1980. No passenger liners have served Hawaii on a regular basis since service by the Pacific Far East Lines was terminated in early 1978. The *S.S. Queen Elizabeth II* generally stops in Hawaii once a year on its around-the-world cruise, as do other cruise liners.

Interisland Shipping. Although there were many small operators providing interisland service, the first major carrier to provide such services was the Inter-Island Steam Navigation Company, which commenced operations in 1883. After this firm merged with the Wilder Steamship Company in 1905, it was the only interisland operator until 1935, when Young Brothers began its tug and barge service. Inter-Island was forced to cease operations in 1950, and except for a two-year operation (1950–1952) by the Hilo Navigation Company using an old Inter-Island vessel, Young Brothers has been the only exclusively interisland water common carrier. Young Brothers provides a minimum of two round trips a week between Honolulu and Nawiliwili, Kaunakakai, Kahului, and Hilo, each round trip taking approximately two days. The only other significant carriers in the interisland trade are Matson Lines, carrying mainly transshipment cargo, and a tug and barge subsidiary of Dole Pineapple Company that mainly transports pineapple from Lanai to the cannery on Oahu. In 1978 the water carriers accounted for 6.6 million tons of interisland cargo.

There has been no significant interisland water passenger service since 1949 except for an attempt at interisland service using hydrofoils that was initiated in 1975 and then suspended in early 1978. In 1980 the

S.S. Independence, a passenger liner, began weekly cruises among the islands carrying an average of 750 passengers per week. In 1982 she was joined by her sister ship, the *S.S. Constitution.*

Overseas Air Carriers. The first scheduled air carrier operations to Hawaii commenced in 1936, and until 1969 the Hawaii-Mainland trade was plied by a maximum of three scheduled carriers—Pan American World Airways, United Airlines, and Northwest Orient Airlines. The Pacific air route awards of 1969 added five more airlines to this list. Federal decontrol of the airline industry led to a number of carriers entering and leaving the Hawaii-Mainland market. By 1981, there were 22 airlines serving Hawaii; 17 certified airlines and 5 supplemental carriers. During the past 20 years, airline arrivals have increased from 224,000 in 1959 to 4.3 million in 1980. In 1980 approximately 22 percent of the visitors were traveling eastbound and 78 percent westbound. Overseas air cargo amounted to 65,000 tons of freight.

Interisland Air Transportation. Scheduled air carrier service between the islands of Hawaii was inaugurated in 1929 by Hawaiian Airlines, which continued as the only approved scheduled carrier until Trans-Pacific Airlines (now Aloha Airlines) was granted permission to serve in this capacity in 1949. Mid-Pacific entered the field in 1981, with flights to Maui and Kauai and plans to provide service to Hawaii Island in 1982. There are also air taxi, air tour, and commuter air carriers that provide supplemental service. The Honolulu-Maui route is one of the busiest in the nation; with 2.5 million passengers in 1980, it ranks second to the New York-Washington, D.C. run. There were 5.8 million revenue passengers traveling interisland in 1981 with a predicted 4 percent growth for this market in 1982. At the end of 1981, Hawaiian Airlines had 44 percent of the total interisland business, Aloha 43 percent, and Mid-Pacific 13 percent. Interisland air cargo accounted for 69,000 tons of freight in 1980. All overseas and interisland traffic is under the regulatory control of the Federal Aviation Agency (FAA) and Civil Aeronautics Board (CAB).

H.D.B.

Nuuanu Pali tunnels, Oahu.

Drawing by John A. Dixon

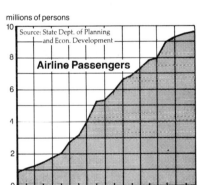

millions of persons

Source: State Dept. of Planning and Econ. Development

Airline Passengers

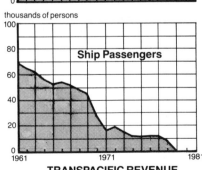

thousands of persons

Ship Passengers

1961   1971   1981

TRANSPACIFIC REVENUE PASSENGERS

There are seven deep-water ports in Hawaii: the Navy's Pearl Harbor on Oahu, and six State-owned commercial ports (Honolulu on Oahu, Hilo and Kawaihae on Hawaii, Kahului on Maui, and Nawiliwili and Port Allen on Kauai). There are also six commercial barge harbors: Kailua on Hawaii, Hana on Maui, Kamalapau (Lanai's only port), and Kaunakakai (Molokai's major port), Haleolono (source of bulk sand and cinders), and Kalaupapa on Molokai. All deep-water ports have a basin depth of 35 feet, heavy lift capacities, and transit shed facilities, but only Honolulu and Hilo have facilities for containerized cargo. Honolulu is by far the most important commercial port, accounting for over 50 percent of the overseas and interisland cargo tonnage. In addition it has the most extensive facilities for providing supplies, heavy lift, containerized cargo, and repairs. For repairs, there is a commercial floating drydock with a deadweight capacity of 2,800 tons and a marine railway with a capacity of 1,450 tons. The Navy facilities at Pearl Harbor have been used by commercial vessels in exceptional circumstances. Barbers Point is a privately owned anchorage and barge landing used primarily by oil tankers servicing the nearby refinery.

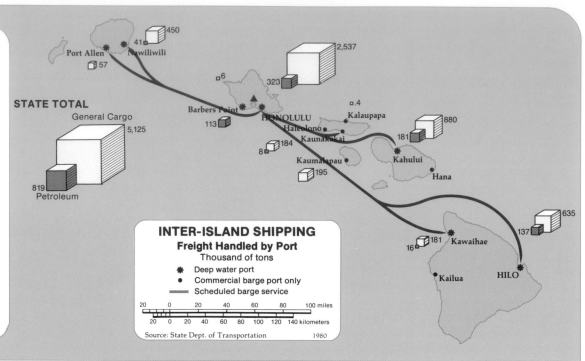

STATE TOTAL

General Cargo
5,125

819
Petroleum

INTER-ISLAND SHIPPING
Freight Handled by Port
Thousand of tons
✳ Deep water port
● Commercial barge port only
▬ Scheduled barge service

20   0   20   40   60   80   100 miles
20 0 20 40 60 80 100 120 140 kilometers

Source: State Dept. of Transportation   1980

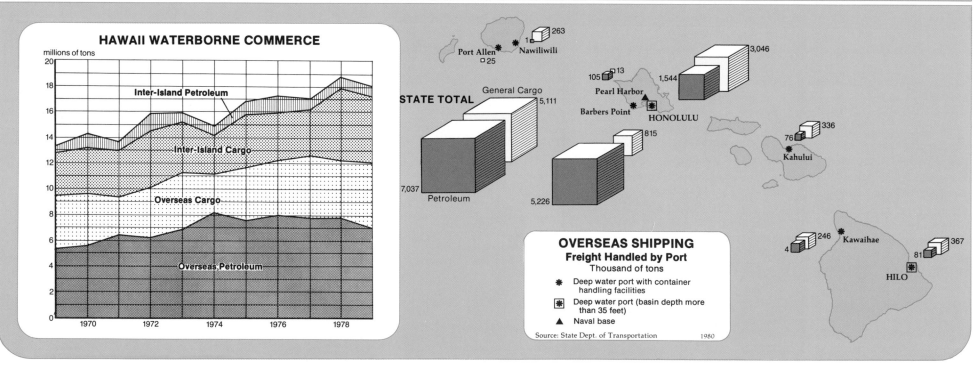

HAWAII WATERBORNE COMMERCE

millions of tons

Inter-Island Petroleum

Inter-Island Cargo

Overseas Cargo

Overseas Petroleum

1970   1972   1974   1976   1978

STATE TOTAL

General Cargo
5,111

7,037
Petroleum

815

5,226

OVERSEAS SHIPPING
Freight Handled by Port
Thousand of tons
✳ Deep water port with container handling facilities
✳ Deep water port (basin depth more than 35 feet)
▲ Naval base

Source: State Dept. of Transportation   1980

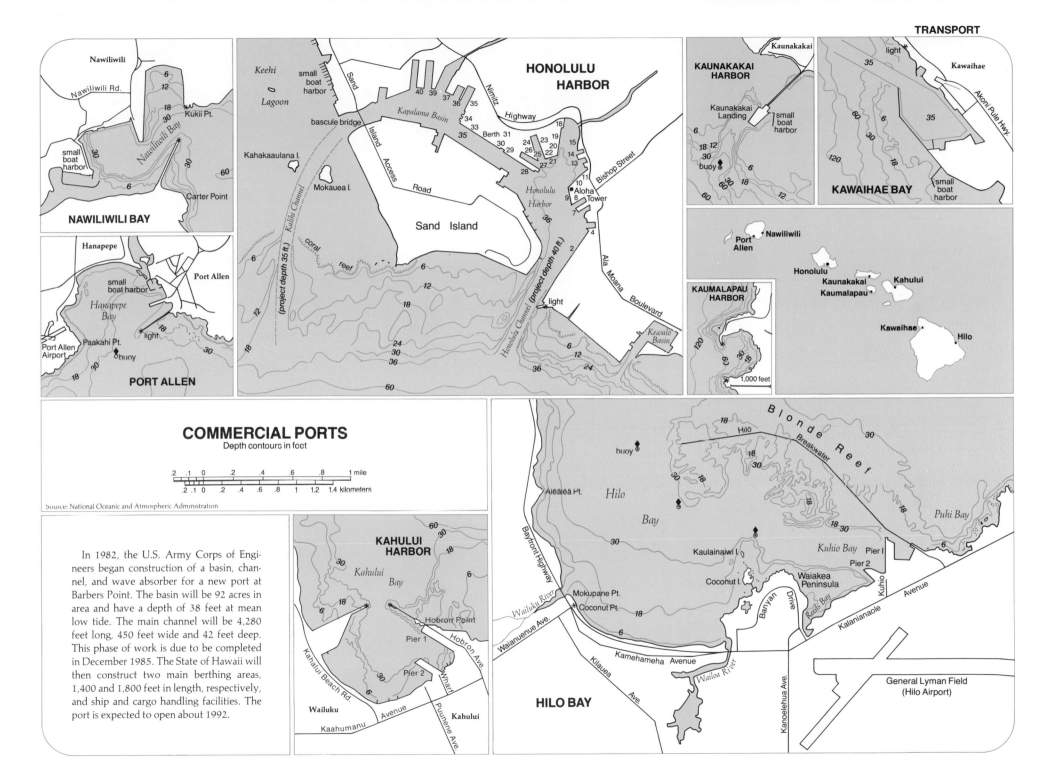

COMMERCIAL PORTS
Depth contours in feet

.2 .1 0   .2   .4   .6   .8   1 mile
.2 .1 0   .2 .4 .6   1   1.2 1.4 kilometers

Source: National Oceanic and Atmospheric Administration

In 1982, the U.S. Army Corps of Engineers began construction of a basin, channel, and wave absorber for a new port at Barbers Point. The basin will be 92 acres in area and have a depth of 38 feet at mean low tide. The main channel will be 4,280 feet long, 450 feet wide and 42 feet deep. This phase of work is due to be completed in December 1985. The State of Hawaii will then construct two main berthing areas, 1,400 and 1,800 feet in length, respectively, and ship and cargo handling facilities. The port is expected to open about 1992.

NAWILIWILI BAY

PORT ALLEN

HONOLULU HARBOR

KAUNAKAKAI HARBOR

KAWAIHAE BAY

KAUMALAPAU HARBOR

KAHULUI HARBOR

HILO BAY

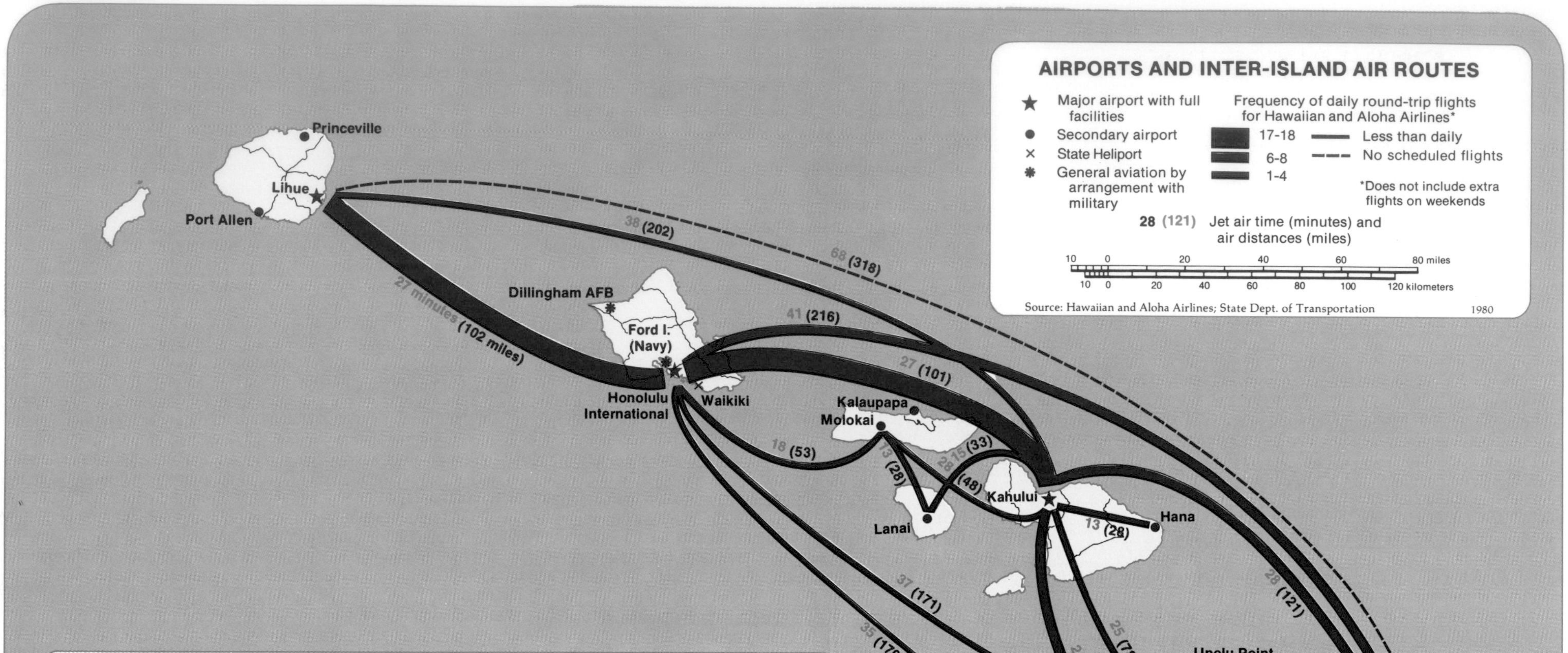

AIRPORTS AND INTER-ISLAND AIR ROUTES

Major airport with full facilities
Secondary airport
State Heliport
General aviation by arrangement with military

Frequency of daily round-trip flights for Hawaiian and Aloha Airlines*
17-18
6-8
1-4
Less than daily
No scheduled flights

*Does not include extra flights on weekends

28 (121) Jet air time (minutes) and air distances (miles)

10 0 20 40 60 80 miles
10 0 20 40 60 80 100 120 kilometers

Source: Hawaiian and Aloha Airlines; State Dept. of Transportation   1980

Princeville
Lihue
Port Allen
Dillingham AFB
Ford I. (Navy)
Honolulu International
Waikiki
Kalaupapa
Molokai
Lanai
Kahului
Hana
Upolu Point
Waimea-Kohala
Ke-ahole
General Lyman Field (Hilo)

38 (202)
68 (318)
27 minutes (102 miles)
41 (216)
27 (101)
18 (53)
13 (28)
15 (33)
28 (48)
13 (28)
28 (121)
37 (171)
35 (170)
24 (91)
25 (78)
25 (45)
15 (39)
23 (62)

INTER-ISLAND AND OVERSEAS PASSENGERS AND CARGO

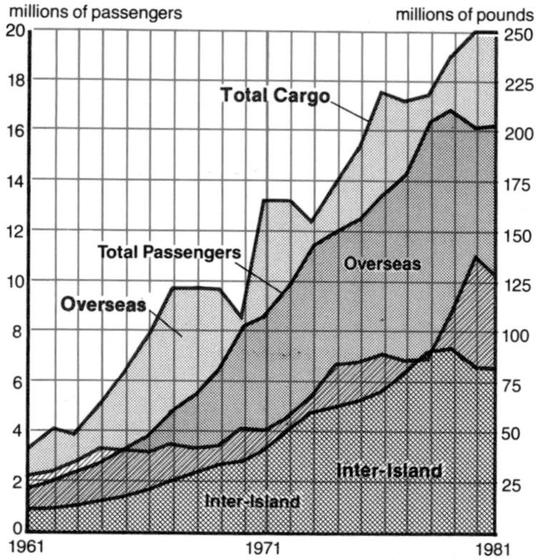

millions of passengers
millions of pounds

20 / 250
18 / 225
16 / 200
14 / 175
12 / 150
10 / 125
8 / 100
6 / 75
4 / 50
2 / 25
0 / 0

1961   1971   1981

Total Cargo
Total Passengers
Overseas
Overseas
Inter-Island
Inter-Island

The statewide system of airports consists of ten airports on six islands owned and operated by the State, four general aviation fields operated on special arrangements with the Navy and Air Force, and twelve heliports (2 State [commercial] and 10 semi-private). In addition there are some small private landing strips located on each island to serve agricultural or hotel ventures. Honolulu International Airport and General Lyman Field (Hilo) are the only two airports that handle overseas flights, and only Honolulu handles foreign flights. Honolulu, General Lyman, Kahului, Lihue, and Ke-ahole airports have substantial terminal buildings and offer fairly complete airport services. Honolulu airport also has maintenance and cargo facilities, in-flight kitchens and other facilities found at most major airports. Port Allen and Upolu airports provide only runways.

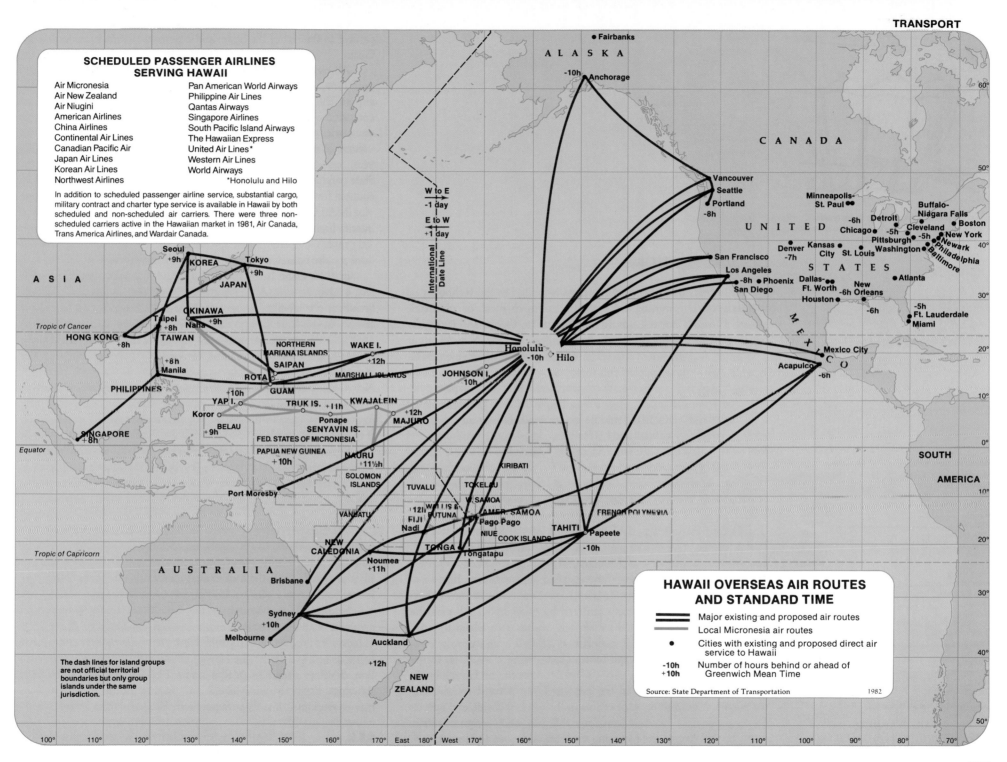

SCHEDULED PASSENGER AIRLINES SERVING HAWAII

Air Micronesia
Air New Zealand
Air Niugini
American Airlines
China Airlines
Continental Air Lines
Canadian Pacific Air
Japan Air Lines
Korean Air Lines
Northwest Airlines

Pan American World Airways
Philippine Air Lines
Qantas Airways
Singapore Airlines
South Pacific Island Airways
The Hawaiian Express
United Air Lines*
Western Air Lines
World Airways
*Honolulu and Hilo

In addition to scheduled passenger airline service, substantial cargo, military contract and charter type service is available in Hawaii by both scheduled and non-scheduled air carriers. There were three non-scheduled carriers active in the Hawaiian market in 1981, Air Canada, Trans America Airlines, and Wardair Canada.

The dash lines for island groups are not official territorial boundaries but only group islands under the same jurisdiction.

HAWAII OVERSEAS AIR ROUTES AND STANDARD TIME

Major existing and proposed air routes

Local Micronesia air routes

• Cities with existing and proposed direct air service to Hawaii

-10h
+10h   Number of hours behind or ahead of Greenwich Mean Time

Source: State Department of Transportation   1982

187

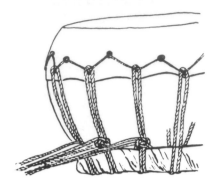

Hawaiian arts and crafts: knee drum (puniu).
Bishop Museum drawing from Te Rangi Hiroa (1964:404)

Hawaii to/from Locality	Number of Calls
Mainland United States	32,545,000
Canada	826,000
Japan	541,000
Alaska	301,000
Europe	239,000
Australia	136,000
Philippines	133,000
Other South Pacific Islands	120,000
Korea	109,000
Guam	91,000
Hong Kong	82,000
American Samoa	72,000
New Zealand	43,000
Taiwan	40,700
Mexico	24,800
Caribbean (West Indies)	24,000
South America	21,500
Tahiti	16,100
Fiji	12,000
Thailand	8,400
Midway/Wake	8,100
Africa	4,800
Central America	4,200

Source: Hawaiian Telephone Company

**PAID OVERSEAS
TELEPHONE (VOICE) CALLS, 1981**

COMMUNICATIONS

This discussion of communications is limited to the technological methods of transmitting information by mechanical or electronic means. Hawaii's isolated position in the Pacific Ocean and its insular nature give special importance to communications, and its multi-ethnic population and the use of several languages give a distinctive character to local newspapers, books, and radio and television programs. Some special emergency communications systems are dealt with on page 210.

The Hawaiian postal service was begun by foreign businessmen and missionaries who, in the middle of the nineteenth century, persuaded the king's privy council and his Hawaiian legislature to authorize and fund a mail linkage with the rest of the world. Hawaii's first stamps were hand typeset and hand printed by the king's press in Honolulu. Connections with the West Coast of the United States were through San Francisco, and with the East Coast via the Panama isthmus or Cape Horn.

Today, Hawaii is part of the Western Postal Region of the U.S. Postal Service, one of five regions in the nation. The Western region comprises all states west of Montana, Wyoming, Colorado, and New Mexico, and includes Alaska, American Samoa, and Guam. Because of its oceanic location and separate islands, postal services in Hawaii have some unique problems not encountered by other states. All mails between the islands are carried by air, and within each island by road. First-class mail from the U.S. mainland is airlifted from major gateway cities, while second, third, and fourth class—"surface mail"—is carried by ship. Twenty-nine percent of the mails originating in Honolulu city are destined for delivery in the city itself, 29 percent for the U.S. mainland, 37 percent for post offices in the rest of Hawaii, and approximately 5 percent for American Samoa, Guam, and foreign countries. Forty-five percent of the incoming mails are addressed to Honolulu, 53 percent to the rest of the State, and 2 percent to American Samoa and Guam.

All overseas mail passed through Honolulu International Airport until 1967, when direct flights to the U.S. mainland began from the Hilo airport. Hilo handled almost 257,000 pounds of overseas mail in 1974, compared with Honolulu's 36,250,000. However, there is now only one carrier providing this service from Hilo four times a week, and the volume of mail dispatched is down to approximately 50,000 pounds a year, consisting mostly of cut flowers. In 1980 the 76 post offices in the State handled 298 million pieces of mail originating in Hawaii, and accounted for postal receipts in excess of $58 million. Electronic mail service (MAILGRAM) to the U.S. mainland and Canada is operated on an interim basis by a group of carriers in cooperation with Western Union Telegraph Company. Telegraph, telex, record, and data communications are also operated by international organizations.

In 1982 Oahu had 9 FM and 17 AM radio stations, Hawaii 5 (1 FM, 4 AM), Kauai 2 (AM), Maui 5 (2 FM, 3 AM). Fifteen radio stations broadcast special ethnic programs (page 192). Hawaii's first live television show was broadcast on December 2, 1952, by station KGMB. By 1955 all three major national networks were established in Hawaii—KGMB (CBS), KHON (NBC), and KITV (ABC) (page 193). KHET (PBS), Hawaii Public Television (formerly the Hawaii Educational Television Network), made its debut in 1966 (page 192). KIKU, an independent station, appeared in 1967. Television has become one of the chief communications media in the islands for news, educational and entertainment programs, and local and national commercial advertising.

Educational and information films in 16mm are distributed by three major public film libraries. The State Department of Education library contains 15,057 prints of 5,170 film titles; the State Public Library, 1,660 film titles; and the University of Hawaii Library, 2,170 titles.

The Hawaii Visitor's Bureau, the State Department of Health, and some major airlines, tourist agencies, and local companies have small film collections relating directly to their own special activities. Military films are available at the audiovisual centers of the Army, Navy, Air Force, Tripler Army Medical Center, and Civil Defense.

Since 1965 Hawaii has been the scene of an increasing number of commercial and independent motion picture productions. The number of local film production companies has increased from only 2 in the early 1960s to 24 in 1982. The Hawaii Film Board, a non-profit organization, develops programs in film study, film training, and public film showings. Pacific Movie-Makers, an informal group of amateur filmmakers working primarily in Super 8mm film, was formed in 1974.

S.S.K.

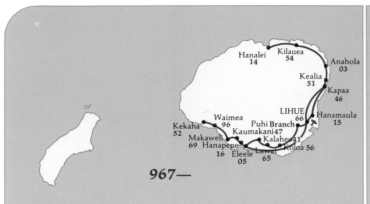

Hanalei 14
Kilauea 54
Anahola 03
Kealia 51
Kapaa 46
LIHUE 66
Hanamaula 15
Waimea 96
Puhi Branch
Kekaha 52
Kaumakani 47
Kalaheo 41
Makaweli 69
Hanapepe 16
Lawai
Koloa 56
Eleele 05
Kalaheo 65

967—

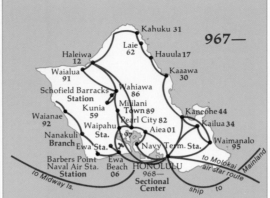

Kahuku 31
Laie 62
Hauula 17
Haleiwa 12
Kaaawa 30
Waialua 91
Wahiawa 86
Schofield Barracks Station
Mililani Town 89
Kaneohe 44
Kunia 59
Pearl City 82
Kailua 34
Waianae 92
Waipahu Sta.
Aiea 01
Nanakuli Branch
97
Waimanalo 95
Ewa Sta.
Navy Term. Sta.
Barbers Point Naval Air Sta. Station
Ewa Beach 06
HONOLULU 968— Sectional Center
to Molokai air star route
to Mainland
967—
to Midway Is.
ship to

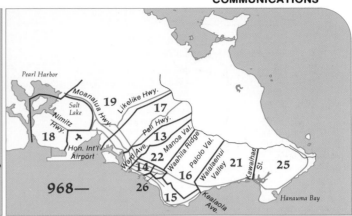

Pearl Harbor
Moanalua Hwy.
Likelike Hwy.
19
17
Nimitz Hwy.
Salt Lake
13
18
Hon. Int'l Airport
Ward Ave.
Pali Hwy.
Manoa Val.
22
Waahila Ridge
Paiolo Val.
14
16
21
25
26
15
Kealaola Ave.
Waialaenui Valley
Kawaihae St.
968—
Hanauma Bay

POSTAL SERVICE

Holualoa • Post office
——— Star (contract) route
⚓ Airstop point for inter-island mails
967— First three digits of ZIP code
25 Last two digits of ZIP code

10   0   10   20   30 miles
10   0   10   20   30   40 kilometers

Source: U.S. Postal Service   1982

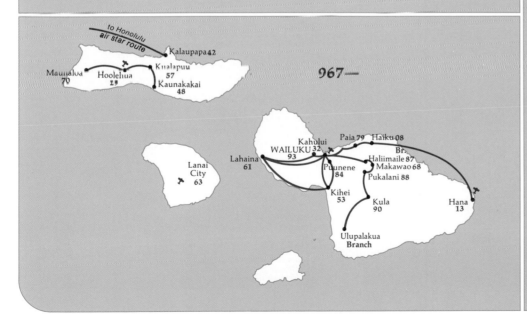

to Honolulu air star route
Kalaupapa 42
Maunaloa 70
Hoolehua 19
Kualapuu 57
Kaunakakai 48
967—

Paia 79
Haiku 08
Kahului
WAILUKU 32
Br.
Lahaina 61
93
Haliimaile 87
Puunene 84
Makawao 68
Lanai City 63
Pukalani 88
Kihei 53
Kula 90
Hana 13
Ulupalakua Branch

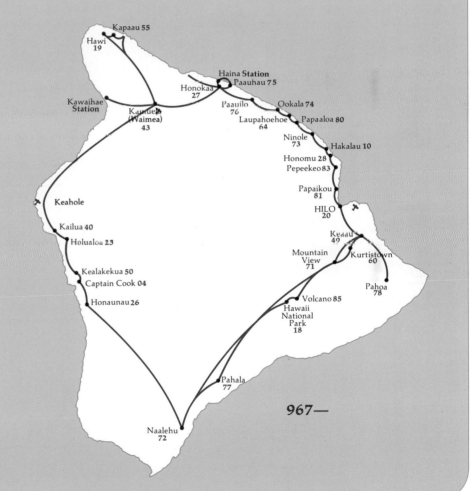

Kapaau 55
Hawi 19
Haina Station
Paauhau 75
Honokaa 27
Kawaihae Station
Kamuela (Waimea) 43
Paauilo 76
Ookala 74
Laupahoehoe 64
Papaaloa 80
Ninole 73
Hakalau 10
Honomu 28
Pepeekeo 83
Keahole
Papaikou 81
Kailua 40
HILO 20
Holualoa 23
Keaau 49
Kurtistown 60
Kealakekua 50
Mountain View 71
Captain Cook 04
Volcano 85
Pahoa 78
Honaunau 26
Hawaii National Park 18
Pahala 77
Naalehu 72
967—

PACIFIC SATELLITE AND CABLE COMMUNICATION

Satellite-earth station   1963 Date of cable installation

ANZCAN	Australia-New Zealand-Canada	**JASC**	Japan Soa Cable
ASEAN	Association of Southeast Asian Nations	**JK**	Japan-Korea
		LUHO	Luzon-Hong Kong
		OKITAI	Okinawa-Taiwan
APNG	Australia-Papua New Guinea	**OLUHO**	Okinawa-Luzon-Hong Kong
COMPAC	British Commonwealth Pacific Cable	**SEACOM**	S.E. Asia Commonwealth Cable
ECSC	East China Sea Cable	**TAIGU**	Taiwan-Guam
HAW	American Telephone and Telegraph and Hawaiian Telephone	**TAILU**	Taiwan-Luzon
		TASMAN	Australia-New Zealand
		TPC	Transpacific Cable

Source: Hawaiian Telephone Company   1982

— JASC (Naoetsu, Japan to Nakhodka, U.S.S.R.)

The Intelsat IV series of satellites provide international telecommunications circuits. The first was launched in 1972, the second in 1974.

The Dom Sat system provides telecommunications circuits to the Mainland. The first of three Comstar satellites went into service in 1976.

Communications from the world's telecommunications system, operated under Intelsat, the International Telecommunications Satellite Consortium, are fed into a satellite earth station at Paumalu, Oahu. This station complex has two antenna "dishes" and is one of the largest systems of its kind in the world. The GTE Satellite Corporation operates two domestic antennas at Sunset Beach, Oahu, which link Hawaii with the U.S. mainland via three Comstar satellites. The earth station complexes at Paumalu and Sunset are connected by microwave links to conventional networks serving Hawaii and process all forms of overseas communication—telephone calls, telegraph messages, data facsimile, and television. Since 1971, PEACESAT (Pan Pacific Education and Communication Experiments by Satellite), an experimental international educational satellite network, has interconnected institutions in eleven nations and jurisdictions in the Pacific Ocean area using the NASA ATS-1 satellite. The purpose is to demonstrate the benefits of currently available telecommunication technology when applied specifically to the needs of sparsely populated, less industrialized areas. Experiments include classroom instruction, professional seminars, community interaction, library networking, research project management, epidemic control, news networking, and administrative seminars.

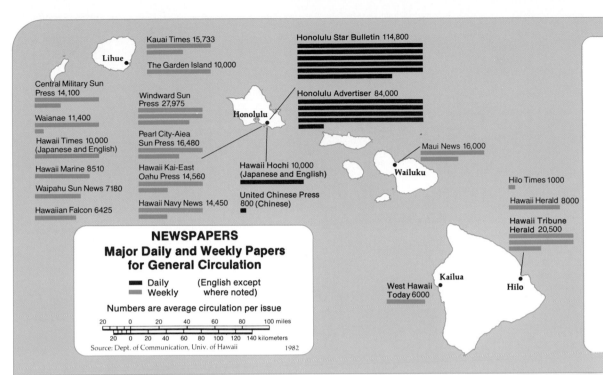

Kauai Times 15,733

The Garden Island 10,000

Lihue

Honolulu Star Bulletin 114,800

Central Military Sun Press 14,100

Waianae 11,400

Hawaii Times 10,000 (Japanese and English)

Hawaii Marine 8510

Waipahu Sun News 7180

Hawaiian Falcon 6425

Windward Sun Press 27,975

Honolulu

Honolulu Advertiser 84,000

Pearl City-Aiea Sun Press 16,480

Hawaii Kai-East Oahu Press 14,560

Hawaii Navy News 14,450

Hawaii Hochi 10,000 (Japanese and English)

United Chinese Press 800 (Chinese)

Maui News 16,000

Wailuku

Hilo Times 1000

Hawaii Herald 8000

Hawaii Tribune Herald 20,500

West Hawaii Today 6000

Kailua

Hilo

NEWSPAPERS
Major Daily and Weekly Papers for General Circulation

■ Daily   (English except where noted)
▬ Weekly

Numbers are average circulation per issue

20 0 20 40 60 80 100 miles
20 0 20 40 60 80 100 120 140 kilometers

Source: Dept. of Communication, Univ. of Hawaii   1982

There are two English-language daily newspapers in Hawaii and two foreign-language or bilingual dailies. Seventeen weekly newspapers are published in the State, including a group of six newspapers published by one firm for local communities on Oahu. There are many specialized newspapers and magazines mostly oriented toward business, tourist, school, church, and labor union readerships. Among 20 magazines published in Hawaii the principal general-interest publication is *Honolulu*, with a monthly circulation of 32,000. The main business publications are *Hawaii Business* and *Pacific Business News*, and for tourists, *Waikiki Beach Press*, *Discover Hawaii*, and *Aloha*. Other notable magazines include *Perspectives*, published by the East-West Center, and the Hawaii edition of *TV Guide*. University student newspapers are published on all campuses, the largest being *Ka Leo o Hawaii* from the University of Hawaii at Manoa in Honolulu. Scholarly journals with international circulations that are edited and published in Hawaii include *Journal of Medical Entomology*, *Pacific Science*, *Asian Perspectives*, *Oceanic Linguistics*, *Philosophy East and West*, and *Biography*. The major book publishers are Island Heritage, University of Hawaii Press, Bishop Museum Press, Press Pacifica, Petroglyph Press, and Topgallant Publishing Company.

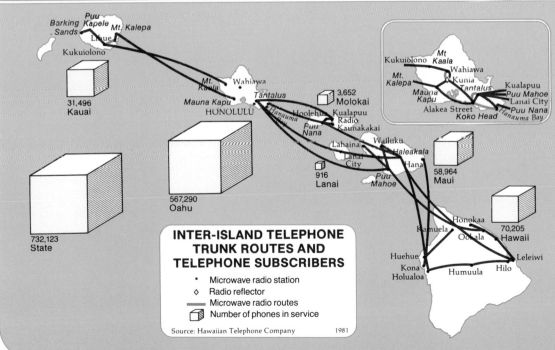

Puu Kapele
Barking Sands
Mt. Kalepa
Lihue
Kukuiolono

Mt. Kaala
Wahiawa
Mauna Kapu
Tantalus
HONOLULU
Hanauma

31,496 Kauai

3,652 Molokai
Hooleh
Kualapuu
Radio
Kaunakakai

Puu Nana

Lahaina
Lanai City

916 Lanai

Puu Mahoe

Wailuku
Haleakala
Hana

58,964 Maui

567,290 Oahu

732,123 State

Kukuiolono
Mt Kaala
Mt Kalepa
Wahiawa
Kunia
Mauna Kapu
Tantalus
Alakea Street
Koko Head
Kualapuu
Puu Mahoe
Lanai City
Puu Nana
Hanauma Bay

Kamuela
Honokaa
Ookala

70,205 Hawaii

Huehue
Kona
Holualoa
Humuula
Hilo
Leleiwi

INTER-ISLAND TELEPHONE TRUNK ROUTES AND TELEPHONE SUBSCRIBERS

•   Microwave radio station
◇   Radio reflector
—   Microwave radio routes
▱   Number of phones in service

Source: Hawaiian Telephone Company   1981

In 1880 Hawaii businessmen, frustrated by the slow communications systems of the time, invested in one of the first permanent telephone installations. By the end of 1881, the number of subscribers had tripled to 119, and by the end of 1882 there were 179. In 1981 there were 723,123 telephones in service statewide, and 98 percent of residences had telephones. It is projected that by the end of 1987, there will be 893,000 phones in service; to meet this continuing growth and improve service quality, Hawaiian Telephone Co. has since 1972 been converting to computer-driven electronic switching. By 1987 about 70 percent of all telephone lines will be serviced by these new electronic systems. Telephone communications within Hawaii are carried via the interisland microwave system, and outside the State by submarine cables and satellite systems. The first Pacific voice cable to link Hawaii with North America went into service in 1957, and with Tokyo in 1964. Today, direct circuits connect Hawaii with the U.S. mainland, West Germany, United Kingdom, Japan, Philippines, Australia, and 14 other points throughout the Pacific. Direct dialing is available from most parts of Hawaii to 70 countries around the globe.

National radio hookups are made through commercial telephone channels. Non-commercial FM radio stations are KHPR, Hawaii Public Radio affiliated with National Public Radio, and KTUH, University of Hawaii, Honolulu, both broadcasting music, drama, and public-service programs. Special ethnic radio programs are broadcast weekly by commercial stations as shown in the following table (time given in hours per week).

Station	Japanese	Hawaiian	Filipino	Korean	German	French
KIVM (Kauai)	124	–	10	–	–	–
KUAI (Kauai)	–	–	6	–	–	–
KCCN (Oahu)	–	168	–	–	–	–
KNDI (Oahu)	19	20	–	–	2	2
KZOO (Oahu)	100	–	–	–	–	–
KOHO (Oahu)	131	–	–	2	–	–
KLEI (Oahu)	–	42	–	–	–	–
KISA (Oahu)	–	–	119	–	–	–
KMVI (Maui)	13	–	7	–	–	–
KNUI (Maui)	–	–	11	–	–	–
KAOI FM (Maui)	–	14	2	–	–	–
KHLO (Hawaii)	8	–	5	–	–	–
KKON (Hawaii)	–	28	1	–	–	–
KPUA (Hawaii)	8	–	3	–	–	–
KIPA (Hawaii)	9	24	6	–	–	–
Total hours	412	296	170	2	2	2

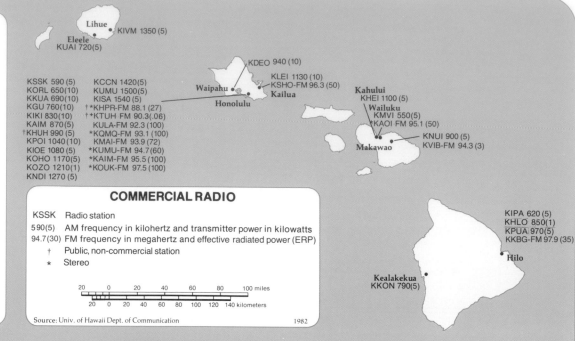

COMMERCIAL RADIO

KSSK   Radio station

590(5)   AM frequency in kilohertz and transmitter power in kilowatts

94.7(30) FM frequency in megahertz and effective radiated power (ERP)

†   Public, non-commercial station

✱   Stereo

20   0 20 40 60 80 100 miles

20 0 20 40 60 80 100 120 140 kilometers

Source: Univ. of Hawaii Dept. of Communication   1982

Concern for educational television in Hawaii began in the late 1950s with citizen groups stressing the need for an educational television system (ETV) in Hawaii. The University of Hawaii applied for a channel in 1962, and the Hawaii ETV Network (KHET) began broadcasting in April 1966. After a shift to public programming, Hawaii Education Television became Hawaii Public Television in 1973, and the license and management were transferred from the University of Hawaii to the Hawaii Public Broadcasting Authority. Hawaii Public Television is comprised of two standard broadcast transmitters and twelve UHF and VHF translators, low-power "transmitters" which receive the broadcast signal, translate it to another channel, and rebroadcast it to the immediate area. They also relay the signal to subsequent translators. Broadcasting time is approximately 100 hours per week and is devoted to two general areas—public and educational programming. Educational, in-school programs are broadcast for the State Department of Education from 8:00 A.M. to 3:00 P.M. weekdays during the school term. The programs are scheduled in the afternoons until 11:30 P.M. weekdays and from 7:30 A.M. to 10:30 P.M. Saturdays and Sundays. All programs are broadcast in color, either live or taped via the station's satellite earth receiver.

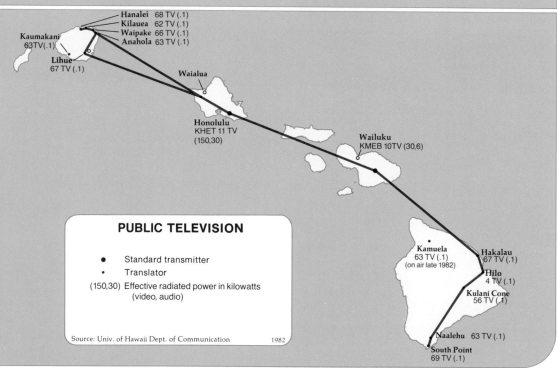

PUBLIC TELEVISION

●   Standard transmitter

○   Translator

(150,30) Effective radiated power in kilowatts (video, audio)

Source: Univ. of Hawaii Dept. of Communication   1982

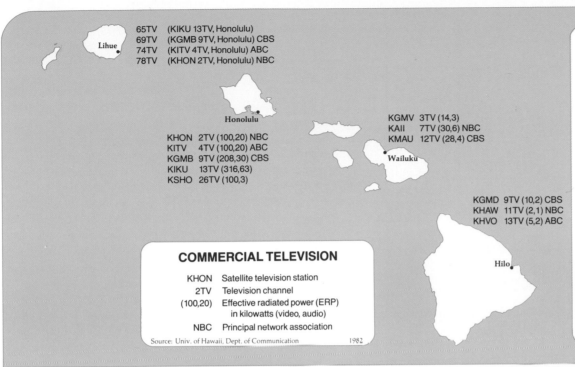

65TV (KIKU 13TV, Honolulu)
69TV (KGMB 9TV, Honolulu) CBS
74TV (KITV 4TV, Honolulu) ABC
78TV (KHON 2TV, Honolulu) NBC

Lihue

Honolulu

KHON 2TV (100,20) NBC
KITV 4TV (100,20) ABC
KGMB 9TV (208,30) CBS
KIKU 13TV (316,63)
KSHO 26TV (100,3)

KGMV 3TV (14,3)
KAII 7TV (30,6) NBC
KMAU 12TV (28,4) CBS

Wailuku

KGMD 9TV (10,2) CBS
KHAW 11TV (2,1) NBC
KHVO 13TV (5,2) ABC

Hilo

COMMERCIAL TELEVISION

KHON — Satellite television station
2TV — Television channel
(100,20) — Effective radiated power (ERP)
in kilowatts (video, audio)
NBC — Principal network association

Source: Univ. of Hawaii, Dept. of Communication   1982

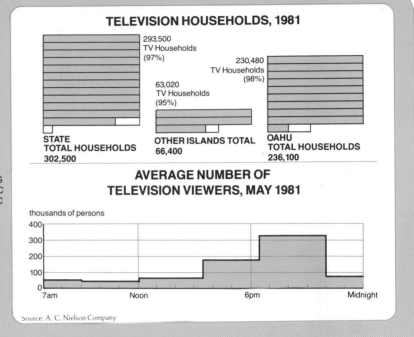

TELEVISION HOUSEHOLDS, 1981

293,500
TV Households
(97%)

230,480
TV Households
(98%)

63,020
TV Households
(95%)

STATE
TOTAL HOUSEHOLDS
302,500

OTHER ISLANDS TOTAL
66,400

OAHU
TOTAL HOUSEHOLDS
236,100

AVERAGE NUMBER OF
TELEVISION VIEWERS, MAY 1981

thousands of persons

400
300
200
100
0

7am   Noon   6pm   Midnight

Source: A. C. Nielson Company

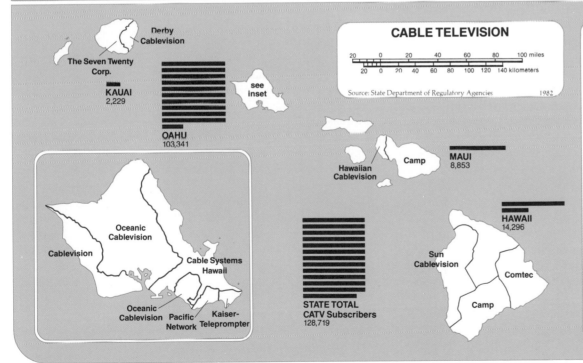

Derby
Cablevision

The Seven Twenty
Corp.

KAUAI
2,229

see
inset

CABLE TELEVISION

20 0   20   40   60   80   100 miles
20 0   20 40 60 80 100 120 140 kilometers

Source: State Department of Regulatory Agencies   1982

OAHU
103,341

Hawaiian
Cablevision

Camp

MAUI
8,853

Oceanic
Cablevision

Cablevision

Cable Systems
Hawaii

Oceanic
Cablevision   Pacific   Kaiser-
Network   Teleprompter

Sun
Cablevision

HAWAII
14,296

Comtec

STATE TOTAL
CATV Subscribers
128,719

Camp

Cable television (CATV) was first introduced in Hawaii in 1961 in the Kahala and Hawaii Kai districts of Oahu, initially to serve residences where TV antennas were banned for aesthetic reasons and to improve reception from local TV stations. By 1982, there were 11 cable television companies in operation: 5 on Oahu, 3 on the island of Hawaii, and 2 each on Kauai and Maui. One company served both Hawaii and Maui. Regulations for operation of cable franchises established in 1973 stipulate that companies must provide channels free-of-charge to develop public access, governmental access, and educational programming. In addition, cable companies were to operate their own "local origination" channel. These regulations are enforced and cable franchise operations are controlled through the State Department of Regulatory Agencies, CATV Division. Most cable subscribers now have access to six additional channels besides the five local broadcast channels. These offer news and sports originating from U.S. mainland cable networks, continuous and uninterrupted movies, education courses, and local community-service programs. In 1981, 44 percent of the 293,500 households with TV sets in Hawaii subscribed to CATV, compared with only 15 percent in 1972.

Center for Korean Studies,
University of Hawaii at Manoa.

Drawing by John A. Dixon

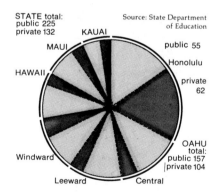

STATE total:
public 225
private 132

Source: State Department
of Education

KAUAI

public 55

MAUI

HAWAII

Honolulu

private
62

Windward

OAHU
total:
public 157
private 104

Leeward   Central

**NUMBER OF SCHOOLS,
KINDERGARTEN-12, BY DISTRICT,
SEPTEMBER, 1980**

EDUCATION

To capture its broadest meaning, education may be defined as the culture-referenced process through which the development of members of a given society takes place and a way of life is maintained from one generation to another. This definition both describes the historic role of education in the Hawaii of antiquity and gives us a preliminary insight into the centrality of education in the transformation of the traditional Polynesian and Asian cultures, through modernizing and Americanizing processes that were, and continue to be, carried to Hawaii through immigration. Teachers, in this usage, are cultural agents. The contemporary "Hawaiian Renaissance" and the strong thrusts in the direction of multi-cultural and multi-lingual education reveal the importance and tenacity of culture-referenced attitudes and values.

More recently, and with greater specificity, education has been defined as "the deliberate, systematic, and sustained effort to transmit, evoke, or acquire knowledge, attitudes, values, skills, or sensibilities, as well as any outcome of that effort, direct or indirect, intended or unintended" (Cremin, 1976). Here the emphasis is on the intentional and conscious purpose of education, a cultural characteristic of modern rationalism and technology carried to Hawaii, chiefly by Americans, in the late nineteenth and early twentieth centuries. This definition accompanies an historically based theory of education in which the family, the church or temple, the work and market place, the print and visual media, and such agencies as museums and art galleries in varied configuration with the schools also intentionally educate.

The education of Hawaii's people from early American missionary days was a part of the larger process of modernizing and transforming those of Hawaiian and Asian racial ancestry along the lines of the socio-linguistic order and cultural orientation of America. Schools alone did not educate although that was their specific intent. The re-education of members of the community of other than American heritage was the work of all major American institutions in Hawaii during the nineteenth century. But the "melting pot" metaphor has been only partially effec-

tive; not all ethnics melted.

Today's varied educational settings mirror more accurately the riches of languages, religions, and cultural traditions of Hawaii's people. Though the dominant cultural influence is American, the creation of a sense of community among Hawaii's people requires learning in a variety of cross-cultural and multi-lingual settings. Though the use of so-called culture-free metaphors in educational thought and practice is evident, this use is slowly becoming culturally grounded as the importance of the educational context is recognized and understood.

Island education today may be considered a process through which individuals are helped not only to become part of and identified with the primary or ethnic group into which they are born, through family and ethnic group efforts, but also to learn to avail themselves of the potential experiences beyond their immediate and primary community, and to integrate these experiences and thus become contributing members of the larger society, while carrying elements of their private community into the larger public community or culture.

During the two centuries that Hawaii has been in contact with the rest of the world, her people have experienced all the tensions, conflicts, and general heterogeneities which have marked Western civilization for the last two thousand years. Aristotle wrote that when we educate we aim at the good life, and since there is no universal agreement on the notion of the good life, neither is there agreement on the notion of education. Pluralism with dialog is recognition of Aristotle's wisdom applied to island education.

The two major public institutions of education are the State Department of Education and the University of Hawaii. The 230 public schools are organized by the Department of Education as a single, state-wide system, predominantly for youth 5 to 18 years of age, but including a system of community schools offering pre-collegiate studies for those 18 to 80. The University of Hawaii system consists of six community colleges, West Oahu College, the University of Hawaii at Hilo, and the University of Hawaii at Manoa. The academic work at Manoa is administered by seven colleges: Arts and Sciences, Business Administration, Continuing Education and Community Service, Education, Engineering, Health Sciences and Social Welfare, and Tropical Agriculture and Human Resources. Within this administrative frame are also found: the Hawaii Institute of Tropical Agriculture, the School of Travel Industry Management, the schools of Medicine, Nursing, Public Health, Social Work, Architecture, and Law, and the Graduate School of Library Studies.

Under private auspices are 141 primary and secondary schools ranging from those of national reputation to those struggling to survive. This class of schools is operated by religious and nonreligious organizations such as the Catholic Schools and the Kamehameha Schools for Hawaiian and part-Hawaiian youth. The French Catholic and English Anglican and Japanese Buddhist educational legacies of the nineteenth and early twentieth centuries have long since become Americanized and in combination with the American Protestant and Mormon legacies form an unusually strong island private school tradition.

Also under religious auspices are Chaminade University (Catholic), Brigham Young University—Hawaii Campus (Mormon), Hawaii Loa College (Protestant), and Hawaii Pacific College. In addition, there is another variety of private schools including the Chinese and Japanese language schools, a host of private trade and business schools and colleges, detention and rehabilitation schools, and schools for the severely physically and mentally handicapped.

Statements of mission and goals of lower and higher education are found in the Department of Education and University of Hawaii State Education Plan and State Higher Education Plan. These plans have their origin in the Hawaii State Plan which was enacted into law in 1978 as Act 100. These educational plans provide the governor and his cabinet the general perspective, institutional direction, priorities, and statistical data required for initiating legislation and budgeting, and with which to relate and coordinate lower and higher public education with government human and social services, the economy, and the State's total physical and socio-cultural environment.

Other major public agencies providing nonformal educational services include Public Television and Public Radio, the State Public Library System, the Office of Hawaiian Affairs and the Neal S. Blaisdell Center, and Aloha Stadium. It is well to single out the University's College of Continuing Education and Agricultural Extension for extending both formal and nonformal studies, organized from the total resources of the University, throughout the entire state community. The East-West Center, established in Hawaii by the U.S. Congress in 1960, promotes understanding among nations and peoples of Asia, the Pacific area, and the United States. This unique center adds greatly to the international and cross-cultural flavor of educational endeavor in Hawaii. It has access to University of Hawaii degree programs and facilities.

Finally, Hawaii's large military establishment maintains a great variety of formal and nonformal educational services, including overseas extension services of major mainland universities and colleges.

Other major private agencies providing essentially nonformal education services include the Honolulu Academy of Arts, the Bernice Pauahi Bishop Museum, temples and churches in abundance, and the Hawaiian Educational Council providing a great variety of courses, institutes, workshops and conferences for Hawaii's business community employees. Also found are agencies such as Boy and Girl Scouts. Young Men's and Young Women's Christian and Buddhist associations, camping and outdoor facilities, and Special Olympics.

The principal executive body of the Department of Education is an elected Board of Education. This board appoints a superintendent who supervises the seven school districts of the State and their respective district superintendents. For each district there is a governor-appointed School Advisory Council which advises the Board of Education. Also, each school has a community council advising the principal.

University of Hawaii governance is vested in a Board of Regents appointed by the governor. The board appoints the university president. Chief administrative officers serving under the president for the various campuses are provosts for the community colleges and chancellors for the remaining campuses.

The state legislature exercises fiscal control over all lower and higher public education. In 1980 the operating expenditures for public schools and universities were $306 million and $189 million, respectively, which together made up 27 percent of the state budget. The Board of Education has no taxing power, a feature unique to Hawaii and linked to the centralization of education as a government function extending back to the establishment of the Hawaiian Kingdom in 1840.

Hawaii's public school teachers are organized statewide for collective bargaining, as are University professors.

R.K.S.

Petroglyph: rainbow man, Nuuanu, Oahu.

Children of Hawaii.

Photograph by David Dinell

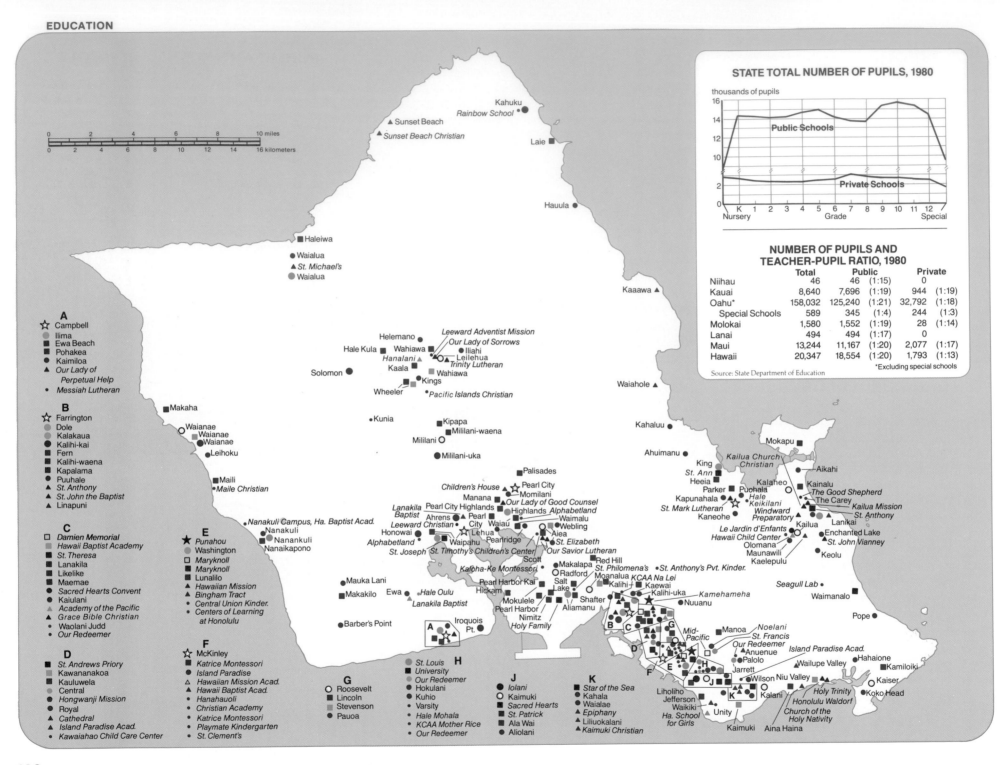

STATE TOTAL NUMBER OF PUPILS, 1980

thousands of pupils

Public Schools

Private Schools

Nursery · K 1 2 3 4 5 6 7 8 9 10 11 12 · Special

Grade

NUMBER OF PUPILS AND TEACHER-PUPIL RATIO, 1980

	Total	Public		Private	
Niihau	46	46	(1:15)	0	
Kauai	8,640	7,696	(1:19)	944	(1:19)
Oahu*	158,032	125,240	(1:21)	32,792	(1:18)
Special Schools	589	345	(1:4)	244	(1:3)
Molokai	1,580	1,552	(1:19)	28	(1:14)
Lanai	494	494	(1:17)	0	
Maui	13,244	11,167	(1:20)	2,077	(1:17)
Hawaii	20,347	18,554	(1:20)	1,793	(1:13)

Source: State Department of Education   *Excluding special schools

Map labels:

Kahuku
Rainbow School
Sunset Beach
Sunset Beach Christian
Laie
Hauula
Kaaawa
Waiahole
Kahaluu
Mokapu

Haleiwa
Waialua
St. Michael's
Waialua

Helemano
Leeward Adventist Mission
Our Lady of Sorrows
Hale Kula
Wahiawa
Iliahi
Hanalani
Leilehua
Kaala
Wahiawa
Trinity Lutheran
Solomon
Kings
Wheeler
Pacific Islands Christian

Kunia
Kipapa
Mililani-waena
Mililani
Mililani-uka

Makaha
Waianae
Waianae
Leihoku

Maili
Maile Christian

Nanakuli Campus, Ha. Baptist Acad.
Nanakuli
Nanankuli
Nanaikapono

Palisades
Children's House
Pearl City
Manana
Momilani
Our Lady of Good Counsel
Lanakila
Baptist
Pearl City Highlands
Highlands
Alphabetland
Leeward Christian
Ahrens
Pearl
City
Waiau
Waimalu
Webling
Honowai
Lehua
Pearlridge
Aiea
St. Elizabeth
Alphabetland
Waipahu
Our Savior Lutheran
St. Joseph
St. Timothy's Children's Center
Scott
Kaloha-Ke Montessori
Makalapa
St. Philomena's
St. Anthony's Pvt. Kinder.
Mauka Lani
Pearl Harbor Kai
Radford
Salt Lake
Moanalua
KCAA Na Lei
Makakilo
Ewa
Hale Oulu
Hickam
Mokulele
Kalihi
Kaewai
Kamehameha
Lanakila Baptist
Pearl Harbor
Shafter
Kalihi-uka
Barber's Point
Nimitz
Aliamanu
Nuuanu
Holy Family
Iroquois Pt.
Red Hill

King
St. Ann
Heeia
Parker
Puohala
Kapunahala
Hale Keikilani
Ahuimanu
Kailua Church Christian
Aikahi
Kalaheo
Kainalu
The Good Shepherd
St. Mark Lutheran
Windward Preparatory
The Carey
Kaneohe
Kailua Mission
Le Jardin d'Enfants
Kailua
St. Anthony
Hawaii Child Center
Lanikai
Olomana
Enchanted Lake
Maunawili
St. John Vianney
Kaelepulu
Keolu
Seagull Lab
Waimanalo
Pope

Manoa
Noelani
Mid-Pacific
St. Francis
Our Redeemer
Anuenue
Island Paradise Acad.
Palolo
Jarrett
Wailupe Valley
Hahaione
Kamiloiki
Liholiho
Jefferson
Wilson
Niu Valley
Waikiki
Kalani
Kaiser
Ha. School for Girls
Unity
Kaimuki
Aina Haina
Holy Trinity
Koko Head
Honolulu Waldorf
Church of the Holy Nativity

A
☆ Campbell
● Ilima
■ Ewa Beach
■ Pohakea
● Kaimiloa
▲ Our Lady of Perpetual Help
• Messiah Lutheran

B
☆ Farrington
○ Dole
● Kalakaua
● Kalihi-kai
■ Fern
■ Kalihi-waena
■ Kapalama
■ Puuhale
▲ St. Anthony
▲ St. John the Baptist
▲ Linapuni

C
□ Damien Memorial
■ Hawaii Baptist Academy
■ St. Theresa
■ Lanakila
■ Likelike
■ Maemae
■ Sacred Hearts Convent
■ Kaiulani
▲ Academy of the Pacific
▲ Grace Bible Christian
• Waolani Judd
• Our Redeemer

D
■ St. Andrews Priory
■ Kawananakoa
■ Kauluwela
● Central
■ Hongwanji Mission
■ Royal
■ Cathedral
▲ Island Paradise Acad.
• Kawaiahao Child Care Center

E
★ Punahou
● Washington
□ Maryknoll
■ Maryknoll
■ Lunalilo
▲ Hawaiian Mission
▲ Bingham Tract
• Central Union Kinder.
• Centers of Learning at Honolulu

F
☆ McKinley
■ Katrice Montessori
■ Island Paradise
△ Hawaiian Mission Acad.
▲ Hawaii Baptist Acad.
■ Hanahauoli
▲ Christian Academy
▲ Katrice Montessori
• Playmate Kindergarten
• St. Clement's

G
○ Roosevelt
■ Lincoln
■ Stevenson
● Pauoa

H
● St. Louis
■ University
● Our Redeemer
● Hokulani
● Kuhio
• Varsity
● Hale Mohala
• KCAA Mother Rice
• Our Redeemer

J
● Iolani
○ Kaimuki
■ Sacred Hearts
■ St. Patrick
● Ala Wai
● Aliolani

K
■ Star of the Sea
■ Kahala
■ Waialae
■ Epiphany
▲ Liliuokalani
▲ Kaimuki Christian

PUBLIC AND PRIVATE SCHOOLS

- ● Elementary (kindergarten-6th)
- ● Elementary and intermediate (kindergarten-7, 8 or 9th)
- ● Intermediate (7-9th)
- ● Intermediate and high school (7-12th)
- ○ High school (10th-12th, 9-12th)
- ● Elementary through high school (kindergarten-12th)

| Heeia | Public school |
| *Aloha* | Private school |

Enrollment
- • 5-100
- ▲ 101-300
- ● 301-500
- ■ 501-1000
- ● 1001-2000
- ★ 2001-3582

```
10        0        10       20       30 miles
10     0     10    20    30    40 kilometers
```

Source: State Department of Education

1982

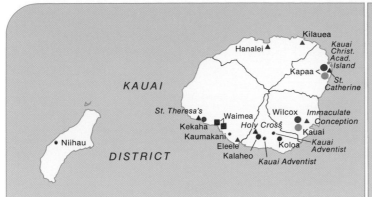

KAUAI

DISTRICT

Niihau

Kilauea
Hanalei
Kauai Christ. Acad. Island
Kapaa
St. Catherine
St. Theresa's
Waimea
Wilcox
Immaculate Conception
Kekaha
Holy Cross
Kauai
Kaumakani
Koloa
Kauai Adventist
Eleele
Kalaheo
Kauai Adventist

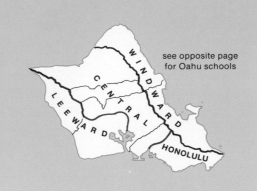

see opposite page for Oahu schools

WINDWARD
CENTRAL
LEEWARD
HONOLULU

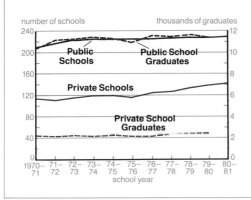

number of schools   thousands of graduates

240   12

200   10

Public Schools   Public School Graduates

160   8

Private Schools

120   6

80

Private School Graduates

40   2

1970- 71- 72- 73- 74- 75- 76- 77- 78- 79- 80-
71   72   73   74   75   76   77   78   79   80   81

school year

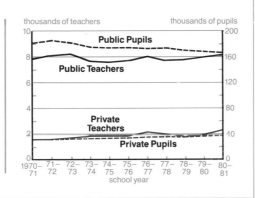

thousands of teachers   thousands of pupils

10   200

Public Pupils

8   160

Public Teachers

6   120

4   80

Private Teachers

2   40

Private Pupils

0   0

1970- 71- 72- 73- 74- 75- 76- 77- 78- 79- 80-
71   72   73   74   75   76   77   78   79   80   81

school year

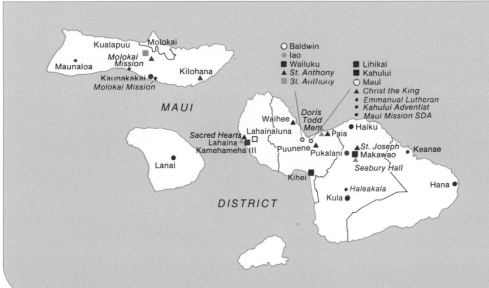

MAUI

DISTRICT

Kualapuu   Molokai
Maunaloa
Molokai Mission
Kaunakakai
Molokai Mission
Kilohana

Lanai

Baldwin
Iao
Wailuku
St. Anthony
St. Anthony
Lihikai
Kahului
Maui
Christ the King
Emmanual Lutheran
Kahului Adventist
Maui Mission SDA

Waihee
Doris Todd Mem.
Paia
Haiku
Keanae
Sacred Hearts
Lahainaluna
Lahaina
Kamehameha III
Puunene
Pukalani
St. Joseph
Makawao
Kihei
Seabury Hall
Haleakala
Kula
Hana

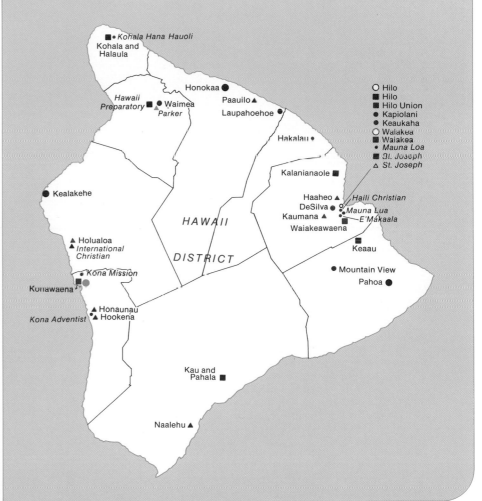

Kohala Hana Hauoli
Kohala and Halaula

Honokaa
Paauilo
Laupahoehoe
Hakalau

Hawaii Preparatory
Waimea Parker

○ Hilo
■ Hilo
■ Hilo Union
● Kapiolani
● Keaukaha
○ Waiakea
■ Waiakea
• Mauna Loa
■ St. Joseph
▲ St. Joseph

Kalanianaole

Haaheo   Haili Christian
DeSilva
Mauna Lua
Kaumana   E'Mákaala
Waiakeawaena

Kealakehe

Holualoa
International Christian

HAWAII

DISTRICT

Keaau

Kona Mission

Konawaena

Mountain View

Pahoa

Honaunau
Hookena
Kona Adventist

Kau and Pahala

Naalehu

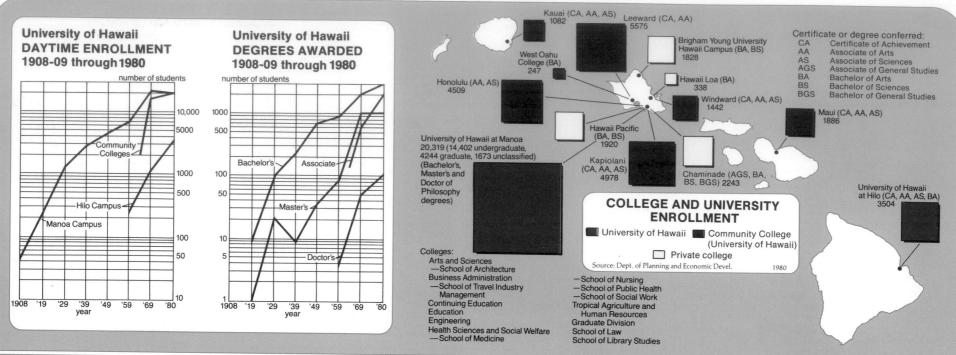

University of Hawaii DAYTIME ENROLLMENT 1908-09 through 1980

number of students

Community Colleges

Hilo Campus

Manoa Campus

10,000 / 5000 / 1000 / 500 / 100 / 50 / 10

1908 '19 '29 '39 '49 '59 '69 '80
year

University of Hawaii DEGREES AWARDED 1908-09 through 1980

number of students

Bachelor's · Associate

Master's

Doctor's

1000 / 500 / 100 / 50 / 10 / 5 / 1

1908 '19 '29 '39 '49 '59 '69 '80
year

Kauai (CA, AA, AS) 1082

Leeward (CA, AA) 5575

West Oahu College (BA) 247

Brigham Young University Hawaii Campus (BA, BS) 1828

Honolulu (AA, AS) 4509

Hawaii Loa (BA) 338

Windward (CA, AA, AS) 1442

Maui (CA, AA, AS) 1886

University of Hawaii at Manoa 20,319 (14,402 undergraduate, 4244 graduate, 1673 unclassified) (Bachelor's, Master's and Doctor of Philosophy degrees)

Hawaii Pacific (BA, BS) 1920

Kapiolani (CA, AA, AS) 4978

Chaminade (AGS, BA, BS, BGS) 2243

University of Hawaii at Hilo (CA, AA, AS, BA) 3504

Certificate or degree conferred:
CA   Certificate of Achievement
AA   Associate of Arts
AS   Associate of Sciences
AGS   Associate of General Studies
BA   Bachelor of Arts
BS   Bachelor of Sciences
BGS   Bachelor of General Studies

Colleges:
Arts and Sciences
—School of Architecture
Business Administration
—School of Travel Industry Management
Continuing Education
Education
Engineering
Health Sciences and Social Welfare
—School of Medicine
—School of Nursing
—School of Public Health
—School of Social Work
Tropical Agriculture and Human Resources
Graduate Division
School of Law
School of Library Studies

COLLEGE AND UNIVERSITY ENROLLMENT

■ University of Hawaii   ■ Community College (University of Hawaii)

□ Private college

Source: Dept. of Planning and Economic Devel.   1980

Public Adult Education Schools. Adult education centers, under the direction of the Department of Education of the State of Hawaii, provide educational opportunities for all adults in the community regardless of previous educational attainment. A statewide program is offered for adults who wish to improve their intellectual, cultural, and economic standing. Classes relating to adult basic education (grades 1-8), adult high school education, naturalization, home economics, and parent, civic, and avocational programs are provided tuition-free. Hobby classes designed to promote recreational, cultural, and leisure-time skills carry a tuition fee.

Private Trade, Vocational, or Technical Schools. A vital part of Hawaii's school system is its private trade, vocational, or technical schools. Licensing of these schools is based on the rules and regulations of the State Department of Education. In addition, schools must comply with state laws and city ordinances. A wide variety of instructional and specialized training programs are provided by these schools.

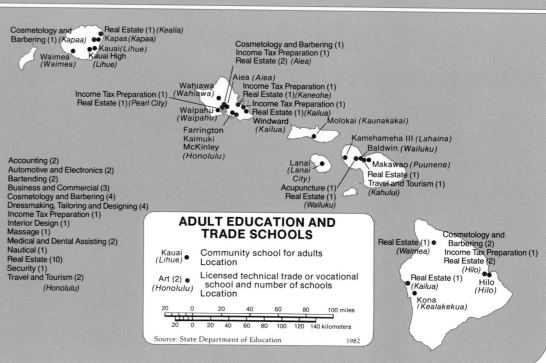

Cosmetology and Barbering (1) (Kapaa)

Real Estate (1) (Kealia)

Kapaa (Kapaa)

Kauai (Lihue)

Waimea (Waimea)

Kauai High (Lihue)

Cosmetology and Barbering (1)
Income Tax Preparation (1)
Real Estate (2) (Aiea)

Aiea (Aiea)
Income Tax Preparation (1)
Real Estate (1) (Kaneohe)

Income Tax Preparation (1)
Real Estate (1) (Kailua)

Wahiawa (Wahiawa)

Income Tax Preparation (1)
Real Estate (1) (Pearl City)

Waipahu (Waipahu)

Windward (Kailua)

Molokai (Kaunakakai)

Farrington
Kaimuki
McKinley
(Honolulu)

Kamehameha III (Lahaina)
Baldwin (Wailuku)

Makawao (Puunene)

Accounting (2)
Automotive and Electronics (2)
Bartending (2)
Business and Commercial (3)
Cosmetology and Barbering (4)
Dressmaking, Tailoring and Designing (4)
Income Tax Preparation (1)
Interior Design (1)
Massage (1)
Medical and Dental Assisting (2)
Nautical (1)
Real Estate (10)
Security (1)
Travel and Tourism (2)

(Honolulu)

Lanai (Lanai City)

Acupuncture (1)
Real Estate (1) (Wailuku)

Real Estate (1)
Travel and Tourism (1) (Kahului)

ADULT EDUCATION AND TRADE SCHOOLS

Kauai (Lihue) ● Community school for adults Location

Art (2) (Honolulu) ● Licensed technical trade or vocational school and number of schools Location

Real Estate (1) (Waimea)

Cosmetology and Barbering (2)
Income Tax Preparation (1)
Real Estate (2) (Hilo)

Real Estate (1) (Kailua)

Hilo (Hilo)

Kona (Kealakekua)

20 0 20 40 60 80 100 miles
20 0 20 40 60 80 100 120 140 kilometers

Source: State Department of Education   1982

HEALTH

By modern standards, the people of Hawaii are healthy. The health of the community compares favorably with the rest of the United States, as judged from both vital statistics (page 121) and from sickness and injury statistics (page 199). Life expectancy at birth in Hawaii is the same as that for the nation for women (77 years), and above the national average for men (74 versus 69 years). Hawaii probably enjoys the most advanced health conditions in the tropical world and among the best in the Pacific. One measure is provided by the international comparison of infant mortality rates (page 199).

The current situation has been achieved over a long period of time through improvements in diet, income, housing, hygiene, education, medical technology and services, and many other factors. For instance, strict animal quarantine rules have helped Hawaii remain one of the few places in the world that are free of rabies. Community immunization programs, especially for children entering school, keep diphtheria, pertussis, tetanus, mumps, measles, and poliomyelitis in check. Ninety-eight percent of elementary and more than 93 percent of secondary school children are adequately immunized. During the 1978–80 period, an average of 4,800 cases of scarlet fever and other streptococcal infections were reported each year, of gonorrhea, 4,055 cases annually, salmonellosis 432 cases, tuberculosis 243, shigellosis 128, infectious hepatitis 122, and leprosy 33. Seventy-eight percent of the tuberculosis cases and 90 percent of leprosy cases were among foreign-born immigrants. Leptospirosis persists in some rural areas, with 27 cases reported in 1980.

Mental illness affects about one percent of the State's population each year. In 1980, 6,328 patients utilized state mental health facilities of whom 5,886, or 93 percent, were treated as out-patients. The most prevalent chronic disease in Hawaii continues to be dental decay, with an average rate 30 percent above that of the nation. Other more serious chronic and degenerative diseases, such as arthritis, asthma, heart disease, cancer, and diabetes, have rates of incidence about the same, or less than, the national rate.

The chief risks to health in Hawaii today stem largely from culturally modified environments and from individual behaviors that expose people to potential health dangers. Motor vehicle accidents are the chief cause of death and serious injury to those under 35. As elsewhere, tobacco, alcohol, and other drugs are associated with degenerative and chronic diseases and accidents. The living conditions in some parts of the State are better than in others (page 199). In some areas on all islands poor housing, inadequate waste disposal, and social difficulties encountered by individuals contribute to the risk of ill-health. In Honolulu people experience the health risks associated with a large city—excessive noise, air pollution (page 67), and congested living space. Since 1970 there has been an increased community and individual awareness of health promotion through various health education agencies; through improved regulation of crime and violent behavior, environmental pollution and waste management, and the like; and through better personal health maintenance. These improvements combine to reduce risks to health throughout most of the life-span so that an increasing proportion of Hawaii's residents are reaching old age without having experienced a serious illness.

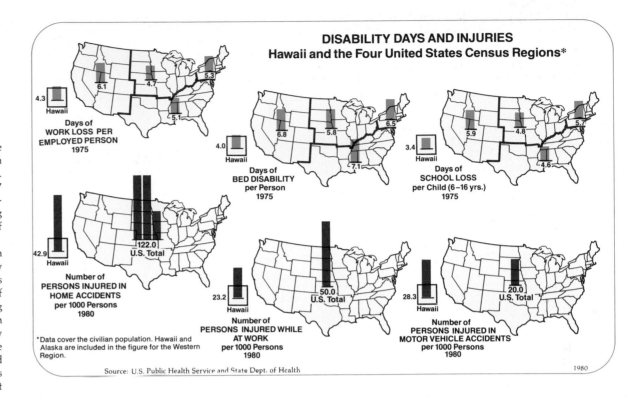

DISABILITY DAYS AND INJURIES
Hawaii and the Four United States Census Regions*

Days of WORK LOSS PER EMPLOYED PERSON 1975

Days of BED DISABILITY per Person 1975

Days of SCHOOL LOSS per Child (6–16 yrs.) 1975

Number of PERSONS INJURED IN HOME ACCIDENTS per 1000 Persons 1980

Number of PERSONS INJURED WHILE AT WORK per 1000 Persons 1980

Number of PERSONS INJURED IN MOTOR VEHICLE ACCIDENTS per 1000 Persons 1980

*Data cover the civilian population. Hawaii and Alaska are included in the figure for the Western Region.

Source: U.S. Public Health Service and State Dept. of Health

1980

Country Rankings				Country	Infant Death Rates*			
1965	1970	1975	1980		1965	1970	1975	1980
1.5	1	1	1	Japan	18	13	10	7
4	4	2	3	**Hawaii**	21	18	13	11
7	6.5	5	3	Canada	24	19	15	11
1.5	4	7	3	Australia	18	18	16	11
9	8	7	6	U.S.A.	25	20	16	12
13	11	3.5	6	Alaska	38	22	14	12
10	9	3.5	6	Singapore	26	21	14	12
3	2	7	8.5	N. Zealand	19	17	16	13
7	6.5	9	8.5	Hong Kong	24	19	17	13
12	13	10.5	10	Am. Samoa	34	25	20	15
11	11	10.5	11	Guam	32	22	20	16
5	4	13	12	Taiwan	22	18	26	24
15	15	14	13	Malaysia	50	41	33	31
7	11	12	14	Fiji	24	22	21	37
14	14	15	15	W. Samoa	43	40	40	40
17	16	17	16	Philippines	73	67	74	55
16	17	16	17.5	Mexico	61	69	66	56
18	18	18	17.5	Colombia	82	76	97	56
19	19	19	19	Papua New Guinea	200	170	159	104

* Rate of infant deaths under one year per 1000 live births

INFANT-MORTALITY IN THE PACIFIC AREA

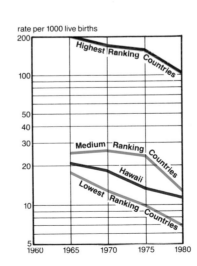

rate per 1000 live births

Highest Ranking Countries

Medium Ranking Countries

Hawaii

Lowest Ranking Countries

The infant mortality rates shown in the table and the condensed version in the graph are useful for indicating general trends. It will be noted that: (1) there has been a general decline in infant mortality in all countries; (2) decline has been greatest in certain countries that once showed high rates; (3) there are still great differences between countries; and, (4) Hawaii has gained rank in recent years and continues to have one of the lowest rates among Pacific countries. No analysis was attempted of the validity or actual comparability of the rates. Rates for single years from small populations (such as Samoa and Fiji) tend to be less reliable as indicators of average conditions than rates from large populations (such as the United States and Japan). Rate reliability is also influenced by such things as the completeness of reporting of infant deaths. Comparability of rates between countries may be affected, for example, by differences in the definition of an infant death versus a fetal death.

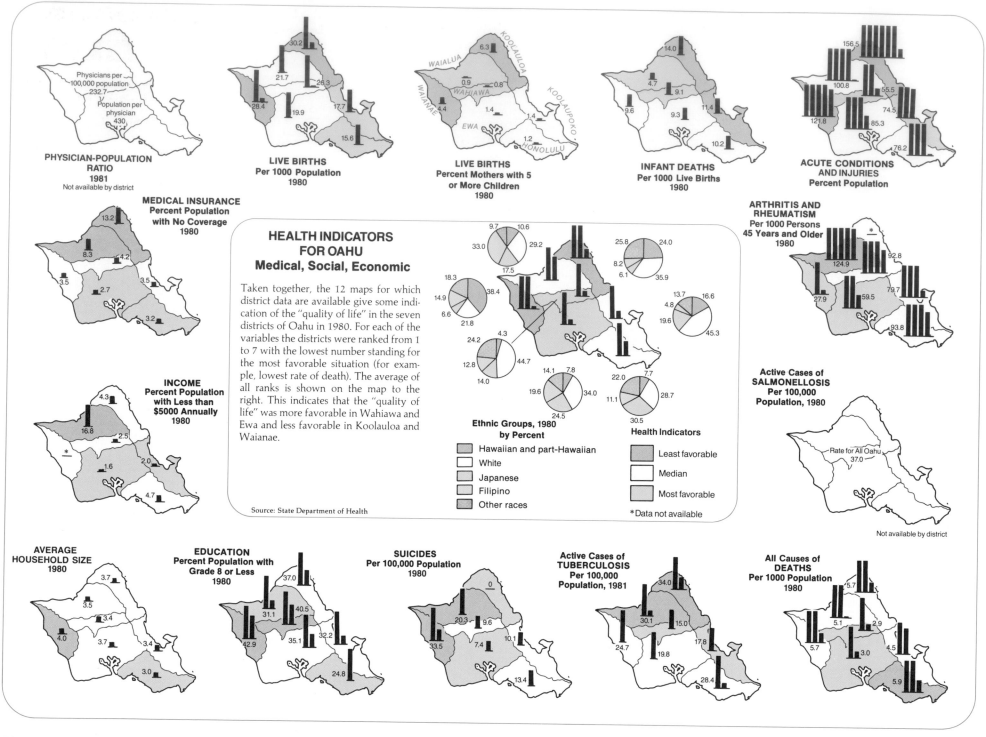

PHYSICIAN-POPULATION
RATIO
1981
Not available by district

Physicians per
100,000 population
232.7
Population per
physician
430

LIVE BIRTHS
Per 1000 Population
1980

30.2
21.7   26.3
28.4   19.9   17.7
15.6

LIVE BIRTHS
Percent Mothers with 5
or More Children
1980

WAIALUA   KOOLAULOA
6.3
WAIANAE   0.9   0.8
WAHIAWA
4.4   1.4   KOOLAUPOKO
1.4
EWA   1.2
HONOLULU

INFANT DEATHS
Per 1000 Live Births
1980

14.0
4.7   9.1
9.6   9.3   11.4
10.2

ACUTE CONDITIONS
AND INJURIES
Percent Population

156.5
100.8   55.5
121.8   74.5
85.3
76.2

MEDICAL INSURANCE
Percent Population
with No Coverage
1980

13.2
8.3   14.2
3.5   2.7   3.5
3.2

ARTHRITIS AND
RHEUMATISM
Per 1000 Persons
45 Years and Older
1980

*
124.9   92.8
27.9   79.7
59.5
93.8

**HEALTH INDICATORS
FOR OAHU
Medical, Social, Economic**

Taken together, the 12 maps for which
district data are available give some indication of the "quality of life" in the seven
districts of Oahu in 1980. For each of the
variables the districts were ranked from 1
to 7 with the lowest number standing for
the most favorable situation (for example, lowest rate of death). The average of
all ranks is shown on the map to the
right. This indicates that the "quality of
life" was more favorable in Wahiawa and
Ewa and less favorable in Koolauloa and
Waianae.

9.7   10.6   25.8   24.0
33.0   29.2   8.2   6.1   35.9
17.5
18.3   13.7   16.6
14.9   38.4   4.8   45.3
6.6   21.8   19.6
24.2   4.3
12.8   44.7   7.7
14.0   14.1   7.8   22.0   28.7
19.6   34.0   11.1
24.5   30.5

**Ethnic Groups, 1980
by Percent**   **Health Indicators**

Hawaiian and part-Hawaiian   Least favorable

White   Median

Japanese   Most favorable

Filipino

Other races   *Data not available

Source: State Department of Health

INCOME
Percent Population
with Less than
$5000 Annually
1980

4.3
16.8   2.5
*
1.6   2.0
4.7

Active Cases of
SALMONELLOSIS
Per 100,000
Population, 1980

Rate for All Oahu
37.0

Not available by district

AVERAGE
HOUSEHOLD SIZE
1980

3.7
3.5   3.4
4.0   3.7   3.4
3.0

EDUCATION
Percent Population with
Grade 8 or Less
1980

37.0
31.1   40.5
42.9   35.1   32.2
24.8

SUICIDES
Per 100,000 Population
1980

0
20.3   9.6
33.5   7.4   10.1
13.4

Active Cases of
TUBERCULOSIS
Per 100,000
Population, 1981

34.0
30.1   15.0
24.7   19.8   17.8
28.4

All Causes of
DEATHS
Per 1000 Population
1980

5.7
5.1   2.9
5.7   3.0   4.5
5.9

HEALTH SERVICES

Hawaii's system for health promotion and medical service is a complex blending of four factors: people, facilities and institutions, organizations, and money.

The People. More than 11,000 professional health and medical practitioners, technicians, and technologists, and a host of administrative, clerical, and vocational workers combine their skills to deliver needed health and medical care services to Hawaii's citizens. As an industry, the medical care system accounts for about 3 percent of the employed civilian labor force. The doctors, dentists, nurses, and others concerned with health service are generally concentrated relative to population distribution, with residents of Oahu enjoying immediate contact with the greatest number of specialized practitioners. While this proportional distribution of health manpower provides unequally for the full range of medical services for sparse population on neighbor islands, these skills and services are being made increasingly available to residents of semi-isolated areas through growing numbers of relocating specialists, visits of physician-specialists from Oahu, and, when necessary, rapid transport of patients to Honolulu. Even on Oahu, however, the great majority of health workers are found in Honolulu, where most of the hospitals and physicians' offices are located. A recent trend has been the erection of physician office buildings on the grounds of most major hospitals. Because most health workers are employed by hospitals and/or organizations and institutions, their distribution is controlled by the location of these employers. Physicians and dentists, however, most of them in private practice, decide the location of their own offices. A large number of self-employed physicians in Hawaii, about 27 percent, belong to group medical practices. This trend, which tends even more to concentrate physicians and their allied workers in large groupings, is more common in Hawaii than anywhere else in the world.

Although medical and health services are concentrated disproportionately in Honolulu, Hawaii has available all the professional and technical skills to be found anywhere, including even the skills and knowledge of the few remaining native healers, now probably numbering fewer than 100.

The Facilities. Hospitals, including many institutions providing bed care for acutely ill and long-term chronically ill or rehabilitating patients, though tending to be centrally located in Honolulu, are generally available to Hawaii's people wherever they live. Indeed, except for the semiskilled nursing care offered through care homes, the ratio of hospital and skilled nursing care beds to the population is less on Oahu than any other island. Hawaii's facilities for in-patient medical care include 29 hospitals of various types, including acute and long-term facilities, 16 skilled nursing facilities and intermediate care facilities, and 261 care homes.

The services offered through these institutions range from the most sophisticated organ transplant, cardiac surgery, and burn care capabilities to the least complicated custodial services. The more elaborate surgical procedures and therapeutic facilities, including the two specialized rehabilitation hospitals, are located in metropolitan Honolulu; these serve not only the dispersed outer island populations of Hawaii, but the more remote populations of outlying Pacific islands as well.

Eight acute care hospitals are operated directly by the state government and one by the federal government; 12 are nonprofit community hospitals. Most other medical institutions—skilled nursing facilities, intermediate care facilities, and care homes—are privately owned. In all, they provide 7,651 beds, or a ratio of more than 7.93 beds per 1,000 people. Hospital beds are available at a rate of 3.0 beds per 1,000 population, lower than the national rate of 6.03 per 1,000. Similarly, the number of long-term and nursing care beds is lower than the national average. Owing to this low ratio of hospital beds to population, Hawaii's citizens consume far fewer days of hospital service per year than does the general U.S. population (360 days/1,000 vs. 900/1,000). Nevertheless, Hawaii's population remains among the healthiest in the world.

One hospital, a private group medical clinic, and a proprietary firm provide home nursing services. On islands other than Oahu, these services are offered by staff members of the Department of Health.

Almost 400 drug stores and 26 hospital and clinic pharmacies provide a well-developed and generally well distributed system for dispensing drugs and medical appliances.

Hawaiian arts and crafts: stamp designs for clothing.
Bishop Museum drawing from Te Rangi Hiroa (1964:195)

Hawaiian arts and crafts: whale-tooth pendant.
Bishop Museum drawing from Te Rangi Hiroa (1964:535)

The laboratory needs of the system are met through hospital-based and free-standing clinical medical and dental laboratories. As is true of manpower and facilities, both laboratory and pharmacy services tend to be centralized in Honolulu.

The Organizations. A wide array of health and medical services are provided directly by government, and these fall almost entirely under state domain. From the highly centralized Kinau Hale (State Department of Health building) and its branch office in each county come the provision and coordination of 14 hospitals; various health centers, mental health clinics, and other clinics; and a large number of inspectorial, regulatory, and advisory activities designed to preserve, promote, and improve the health of Hawaii's citizens. The State Department of Health is responsible for (1) insuring purity of foods and drugs; (2) measurement and control of air, water, and noise pollution; (3) management of acute and long-term hospitals; (4) provision of the major part of emergency ambulance services on islands other than Oahu (page 211); (5) education of the public on health matters; (6) prevention and control of infectious and chronic diseases; (7) maintaining records of births, deaths, marriages, and other vital data.

Closely akin in their intent and purpose are a rich variety of nongovernmental health organizations having as their focus either education or service in prevention or treatment of illness, or in rehabilitation. Included are voluntary, nonprofit service agencies dealing specifically with cancer, heart disease, respiratory ailments, crippled children, arthritis, birth control and family planning, mental health, alcoholism, and many other human afflictions and problems. Most are state or regional affiliates of parent national organizations and rely heavily on contributions from the public for the funds making possible the services they provide. For the most part, the voluntary health organizations are represented in branch or local offices throughout the State.

Another set of organizations important to the control and design of Hawaii's health care system are the professional societies. More than 50 different professions and occupations in the health field are represented by individual professional associations, ranging from the full-time offices of the state medical, dental, hospital, and nursing associations to the part-time activities of many others. Each county in the State has its local counterpart of every major association. Most have the single function of representing and regulating the practices of their members and maintaining high standards of professional practice in their special fields. Some offer additional services such as dental insurance programs.

Professional and technical education and training needs are met largely through the University of Hawaii. Here, and through its system of community colleges, education is offered in medicine, nursing, public health, social work, medical technology, speech pathology and audiology, dental hygiene, dental assistance, and nutrition. Specialized programs for various technicians and assistants are conducted by many hospitals and medical clinics as well.

The Monies. Through governmental and private channels, Hawaii's citizens spend an estimated $600 million each year for health and medical services. Nearly 63 percent of this amount is accounted for by state expenditures of federal and state monies for the services provided by the Department of Health and for the medical assistance programs administered by the Department of Social Services and Housing. The remaining 37 percent is paid directly by the consumers of health service, in the form of insurance prepayments, charitable contributions, and out-of-pocket expenditures.

Both commercial and nonprofit health and medical insurance plans are offered in Hawaii, with the preponderance of prepaid care being handled by the Hawaii Medical Service Association (HMSA), Kaiser Foundation Health Plan, Health Plan Hawaii, and Island Health Care. Hawaii now boasts three federally qualified Health Maintenance Organizations and a fourth which is operated directly by the Hawaii Medical Service Association.

R.E.M.

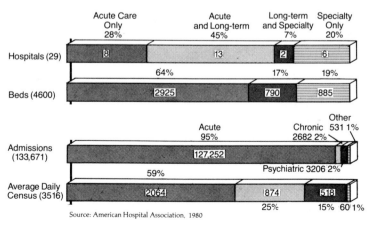

Source: American Hospital Association, 1980

HAWAII HOSPITAL STATISTICS, 1980

natural-resource areas and offer recreational opportunities as diverse as a wilderness experience on Kauai's Na Pali Coast and a club luau in Honolulu's Ala Moana Park. The public parks in Hawaii are under federal, state, and county jurisdiction. The national parks are designed to preserve natural and historic areas of outstanding national significance, the state parks include areas recognized by the State as worthy of preservation, and the county parks provide primarily for local recreation. In addition to state parks (20,835 acres), the State is responsible for over a million and a half acres of unimproved forest and hunting land.

The public park system in Hawaii had its beginning in 1843 (29 years before Yellowstone National Park was established), when King Kamehameha IV set aside Thomas Square in Honolulu as a public park. In 1858 a small park was created near Iolani Palace in honor of Queen Emma, and in 1874 Archibald Cleghorn, a prominent local citizen and unofficial father of Hawaii's parks, was directed to take charge of parks in Honolulu. King Kalakaua dedicated Kapiolani Park in 1877. Now, 140 years after the first park was established in Hawaii, there are almost 700 areas within the State that are administered by the national, state, and county park systems.

The National Park Service administers seven units in Hawaii with a combined area of 294,224 acres. In 1980 there were 3,497,797 visits to these national parks. Four of the units are on the island of Hawaii: Hawaii Volcanoes National Park, with the still active volcanoes Mauna Loa and Kilauea, and three sites of historical importance on the leeward coast of the island, Puuhonua O Honaunau National Historical Park, Puukohola Heiau National Historic Site, and Kaloko Honokohau National Cultural Park, which is not yet open to the public. Kalaupapa National Historical Park has recently been established on the island of Molokai, site of the historic leper colony. Haleakala National Park on Maui includes the summit and eastern slope of the dormant volcano and the habitat of several rare indigenous species, including the recently reintroduced nene or Hawaiian goose. On Oahu, the U.S.S. *Arizona* memorial, commemorating those who died in the attack on Pearl Harbor on December 7, 1941, is now under National Park jurisdiction.

The State Parks Division administers 71 areas, 15 designated as historical and archeological places and 56 as recreation parks. In 1980, 17,169,000 people used state park facilities. The most frequently visited parks include Kahana Valley State Park and Nuuanu Pali Wayside on Oahu; Iao Valley State Park on Maui; Wailua River State Park, Kokee State Park, and Waimea Canyon State Park on Kauai; and Wailuku River Recreation Area, Hapuna Beach State Park, and Akaka Falls State Park on Hawaii (page 208). The Aloha Stadium in Honolulu is also under the jurisdiction of the State Parks Division.

The 617 county parks in Hawaii comprise 8,187 acres. They are located primarily near beaches or within population centers. The fact that they account for only 0.5 percent of all the recreational land within the state belies their importance. They are heavily used and provide readily accessible recreational opportunities for all residents and visitors. The City and County of Honolulu, and the counties of Hawaii, Kauai, and Maui operate diverse recreational programs in conjunction with the county parks, including water safety programs, competitive sports events, craft programs, community gardens, and dance classes for senior citizens.

Camping is a popular activity in Hawaii; in 1980, 6,744 camp permits were issued on the island of Oahu alone. Of the 64 designated camping areas, 51 are beach sites. Camping areas are usually designated within parks, and campers use the general facilities rather than special campground services. In most parks, camping is by permit for a limited time period. Cabins for family and group camping are also available in some state parks.

Hunting for small deer, feral sheep, goats, and pigs, as well as some game birds is allowed on approximately one million acres within the state, although not all the areas are open for hunting at any one time. Between June 1980 and July 1981, 12,284 hunting licenses were issued.

N.D.L.

Petroglyph: incised fish, Keoneloa Beach, Kauai.

Soccer game, Hawaii Kai, 1982.

Photograph by David Dinell

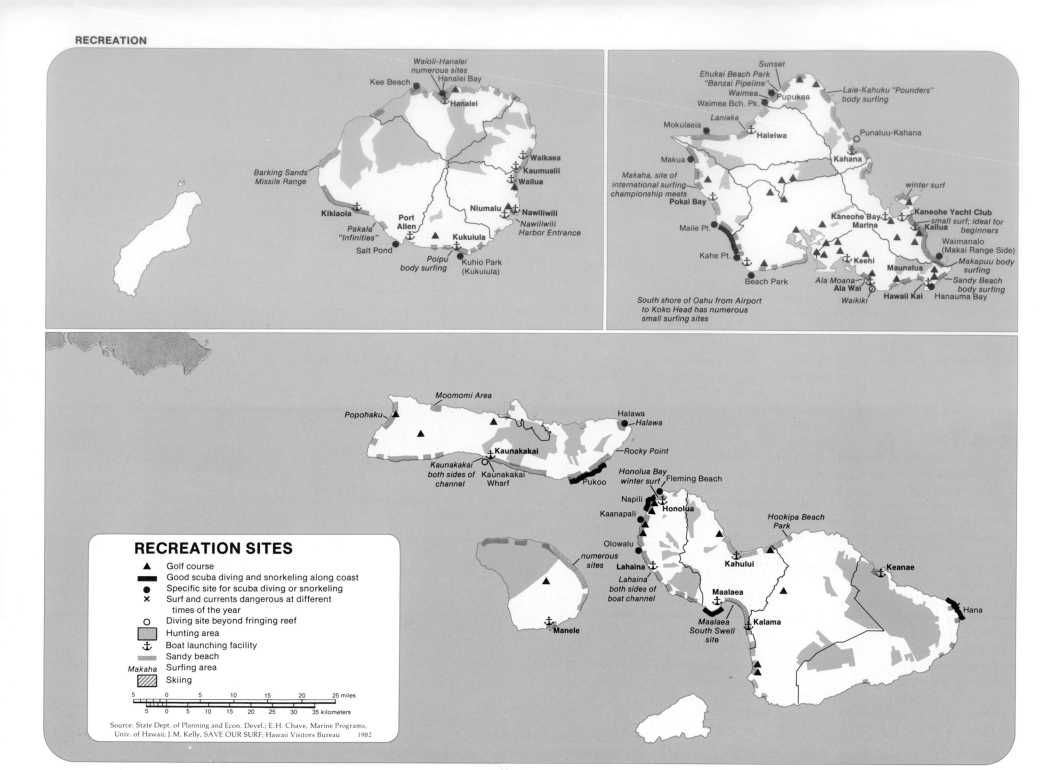

RECREATION SITES

▲ Golf course
▬ Good scuba diving and snorkeling along coast
● Specific site for scuba diving or snorkeling
✕ Surf and currents dangerous at different times of the year
○ Diving site beyond fringing reef
▨ Hunting area
⚓ Boat launching facility
〰 Sandy beach
Makaha Surfing area
▧ Skiing

Source: State Dept. of Planning and Econ. Devel.; E.H. Chave, Marine Programs, Univ. of Hawaii; J.M. Kelly, SAVE OUR SURF; Hawaii Visitors Bureau   1982

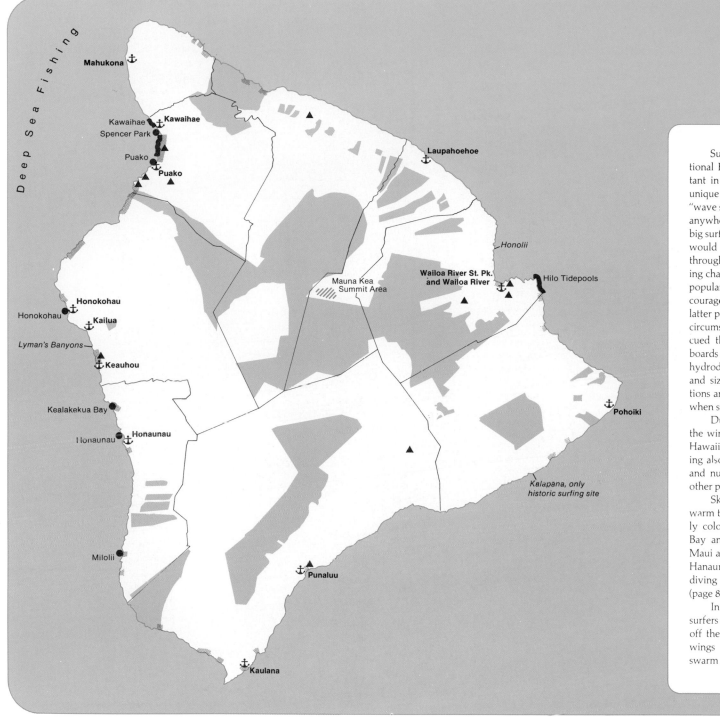

Deep Sea Fishing

Mahukona

Kawaihae
Kawaihae
Spencer Park
Puako
Puako

Laupahoehoe

Honolii

Wailoa River St. Pk.
and Wailoa River

Hilo Tidepools

Mauna Kea
Summit Area

Honokohau
Honokohau
Kailua

Lyman's Banyons

Keauhou

Kealakekua Bay

Pohoiki

Honaunau
Honaunau

*Kalapana, only
historic surfing site*

Milolii

Punaluu

Kaulana

Surfing and outrigger canoe racing are two traditional Hawaiian recreational pursuits that remain important in contemporary Hawaii. Board surfing is Hawaii's unique contribution to the world of recreation. *He'e nalu* or "wave sliding" was more highly developed in Hawaii than anywhere else in Polynesia. Perhaps having invoked the big surf with the chant quoted on page 204, a Hawaiian *alii* would take his heavy 18-foot *koa* board and swim out through the surf, hoping to catch the giant wave. The surfing champions of the old days used the same sites that are popular today, such as Pau Malu and Sunset Beach. Discouraged by missionaries, surfing was less popular in the latter part of the nineteenth century, but a combination of circumstances including the promotion of tourism, rescued the moribund art. The thick California redwood boards of the early 1900s have been replaced by modern, hydrodynamically designed boards in a variety of shapes and sizes. Most of the Hawaiian international competitions are held in winter (November–December) on Oahu, when surf is high on northern coasts.

During the summer the best swells are generated in the wintry Southern Hemisphere; then surfing is best on Hawaii's southern shores (page 54). Outrigger canoe racing also preserves a traditional Hawaiian athletic pursuit, and numerous clubs and teams from the mainland and other parts of the Pacific compete from June to October.

Skin and scuba diving enthusiasts are attracted by the warm tropical waters, infinitely varied coral, and brilliantly colored reef fish. Popular locations include Hulopoe Bay and Manele Bay on Lanai, off Molokini between Maui and Kahoolawe, and off the leeward shore of Maui. Hanauma Bay on Oahu has been set aside especially for diving because of its outstanding natural marine fauna (page 87).

In recent years the colorful sails of a myriad windsurfers have been added to the coastal scene, and, airborne off the cliffs of the windward coast of Oahu, the bright wings of hang-gliders. In winter, thousands of skiers swarm the slopes of snow-capped Mauna Kea.

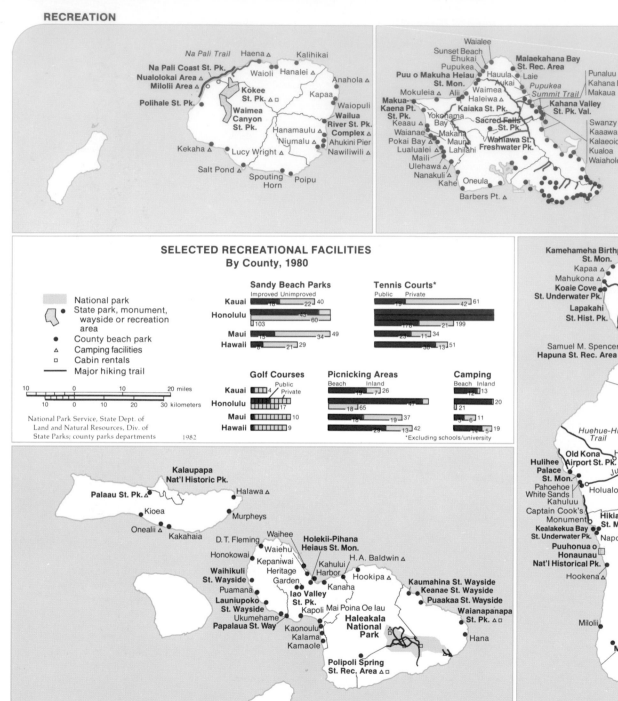

SELECTED RECREATIONAL FACILITIES
By County, 1980

National park
State park, monument, wayside or recreation area
County beach park
Camping facilities
Cabin rentals
Major hiking trail

National Park Service, State Dept. of Land and Natural Resources, Div. of State Parks; county parks departments
1982

*Excluding schools/university

SERVICES

District Courts. District courts are courts of record with limited jurisdiction in non-jury civil and criminal cases. Circuit courts are treated on pages 140–141. There are 25 district courthouses in Hawaii (page 211). In civil matters, district courts have exclusive original jurisdiction in small claims cases involving sums of less than $1,000. In criminal matters, district courts deal with traffic violations, petty criminal misdemeanors, and preliminary hearings in felony cases when an arrest is made without a grand jury indictment. In 1980/81, the Traffic Violations Bureau, a division of the district court, processed 630,697 traffic violations. About 72 percent were disposed of administratively. Revenues from traffic fines collected on Oahu totaled $3.7 million. Other divisions of the district court are the counseling service, which provides judges with alternatives to traditional punishment, and the office of the sheriff, responsible for serving civil processes and for the security of the courts.

Municipal Services. Emergency ambulance services (page 211) are provided by the State Department of Health on all islands except Oahu, where the City and County of Honolulu maintains the service under contract to the State. The U.S. Army also provides emergency helicopter ambulance service to civilians as part of its training operations. Fire departments are under the county governments, and services include special rescue facilities. On Oahu a helicopter is maintained for fire fighting and for ocean and mountain rescue operations. Police in Hawaii are organized by county, and unlike most states there is no state police force. (See page 210 for civil defense.) Lifeguard service is provided on 18 of Oahu's beaches by the City and County of Honolulu.

Water supplies are currently adequate on all populated islands (page 51). In 1980, fewer than one percent of households in the counties of Kauai, Honolulu, and Maui were not served by a public or private community water system (page 212). Ten percent of households in Hawaii County were not connected to a community water system but relied on individual sources such as wells, streams, and rain catchment tanks. Extension of public sewerage systems has not been as rapid as water service, especially in rural areas, but important extensions since

1972 have been made in the Kahuku district of Oahu and the Hanapepe-Eleele district of Kauai (page 212). Major improvements have been made since 1975 in the conversion of raw sewage outfalls to primary or secondary treatment facilities. Most important of these was the construction of the Sand Island sewage treatment plant to give advanced primary treatment to the bulk of Honolulu's sewage. The majority of the community sewage treatment plants in Hawaii now carry treatment to the secondary stage. In some small villages and in most rural areas, private septic tanks, cesspools, or lava tubes are used for sewage disposal.

Social Services. The provision of social services is undertaken by a large number of government, trade, and voluntary organizations. Federal agencies, such as the Social Security Administration and the Office of Employees Compensation, provide direct services, but federal funds also support state agencies such as the Department of Health, the Department of Social Services and Housing, and county agencies such as offices of human resources or concerns. (For a review of health services, see page 201).

The major responsibility for providing social services is borne by the State Department of Social Services and Housing. Between 1970 and 1980, economic assistance for welfare recipients increased 448 percent, owing in large part to a rise in unemployment, an increase in population (especially in-migrants), and rising costs. Public welfare expenditures by the department in 1980 amounted to $236 million, or 93 percent of its total budget of $255 million. Social welfare services include care of children in foster homes, arranging adoptions, licensing day-care centers, and family counseling. The Hawaii Housing Authority, a division of the department, maintained 5,190 living units in 1981 for elderly and low-income families. The department also provides vocational rehabilitation services, supervision of parolees, pardons, and criminal injuries compensation, and the maintenance of the State's correction facilities (page 211).

More than 400 voluntary, church, and other nonprofit organizations provide a wide range of social services in such areas as child care, safety, legal aid, labor relations, physical handicaps, care of the aged, drug abuse, suicide, and animal care. Financial support comes primarily from community donations, membership subscriptions, and government and philanthropic grants. Federated community funding for social services (United Way) is organized by county. The fund distributed $9.3 million among member organizations in 1980, chief recipients being the American Red Cross, the American Cancer Society, the Council on Social Work Education, and the YWCA and the YMCA.

Staff

Pineapple cannery water tower, Honolulu.

Drawing by John A. Dixon

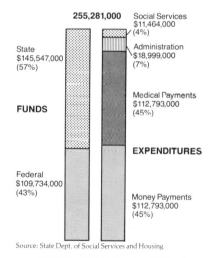

SOCIAL WELFARE SERVICES
1980

FUNDS

State $145,547,000 (57%)

Federal $109,734,000 (43%)

255,281,000

EXPENDITURES

Social Services $11,464,000 (4%)

Administration $18,999,000 (7%)

Medical Payments $112,793,000 (45%)

Money Payments $112,793,000 (45%)

Source: State Dept. of Social Services and Housing

Civil Defense

Civil defense in Hawaii is organized first at the county level of government to serve each island. The Civil Defense Division, State Department of Defense, coordinates plans, programs, and operations for the State and is responsible for dealing with major emergencies of disaster proportions. State civil defense also works with the Federal Emergency Management Agency as part of the national defense system.

The objective of civil defense is to minimize casualties, reduce property damage, and restore essential public services in the event of natural disaster. It also has the task of insuring maximum survival of the population in the event of nuclear war. Civil defense is government in time of emergency, but to be effective it must depend on considerable support from leaders in industry, agriculture, labor, finance, and from the community at large.

Most civil defense actions are initiated at the county level for local emergencies such as flood, drought, fire, earthquake, tsunami, and volcanic eruption. In turn the state and federal governments assume responsibility for funding and/or aid as the situation demands. State civil defense provides the organization, facilities, and equipment to meet emergencies both natural and man-made, such as tsunamis, severe weather, aircraft accidents, major fires, major marine pollution, and other catastrophes beyond the resources of the local jurisdictions. Three primary sources of warning are the National Weather Service for tsunamis, floods, and storms; the 326th Air Division, USAF, for enemy attack; and the National Warning System (NAWAS) for selective dissemination of warnings and emergency information nationwide. Other kinds of warnings could originate from a variety of community agencies or facilities.

Warnings are transmitted over the Hawaii Warning System (HAWAS) simultaneously to State Warning Point and to County Warning Points located in county police headquarters and State and County Emergency Operating Centers (EOCs). These warning points alert the public through siren signals and radio broadcast over Civ-Alert, the Emergency Broadcast System (EBS). Emergency Operating Centers are activated at state and county level. The diagram at the right shows the telecommunications network capable of use in an emergency. It includes the routine communications systems of county, state, and federal agencies, with links to the civil defense system on the mainland. Much of the system operates by cooperative agreement; for instance, the network can incorporate, when appropriate, the communications systems of commercial and public television, private industry, and amateur "ham" radio operators.

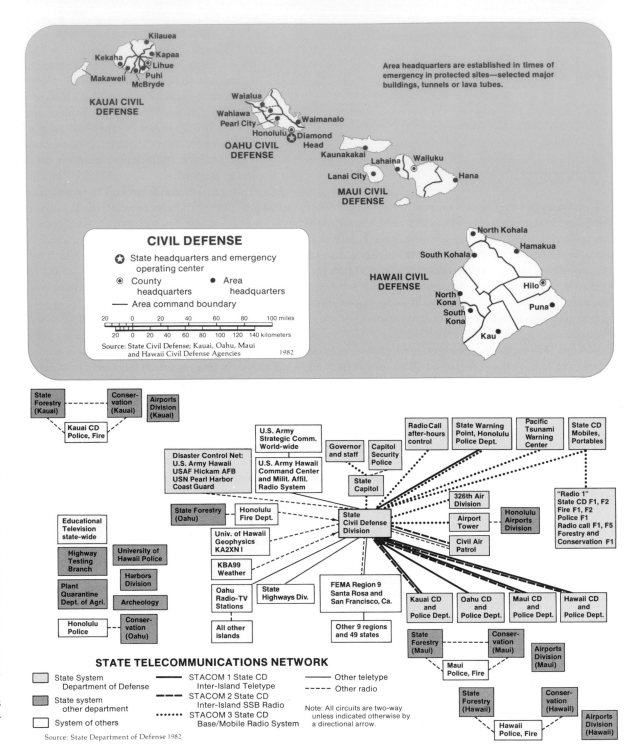

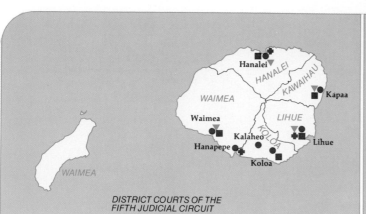

**DISTRICT COURTS OF THE
FIFTH JUDICIAL CIRCUIT**

Hanalei
HANALEI
KAWAIHAU
WAIMEA
WAIMEA
Kapaa
LIHUE
Waimea
LIHUE
Kalaheo
KOLOA
Lihue
Hanapepe
Koloa

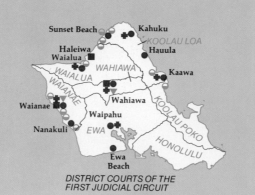

**DISTRICT COURTS OF THE
FIRST JUDICIAL CIRCUIT**

Sunset Beach
Kahuku
Haleiwa
KOOLAU LOA
Waialua
Hauula
WAHIAWA
WAIALUA
Kaawa
WAIANAE
Wahiawa
Waianae
Waipahu
EWA
Nanakuli
KOOLAU POKO
HONOLULU
Ewa
Beach

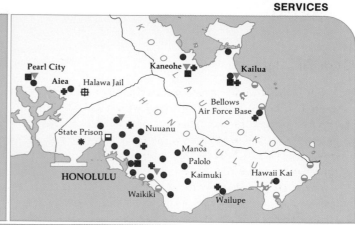

Pearl City
Kaneohe
Kailua
Aiea
Halawa Jail
Bellows
Air Force Base
State Prison
Nuuanu
Manoa
Palolo
Hawaii Kai
HONOLULU
Kaimuki
Waikiki
Wailupe

DISTRICT COURTS, FIRE, LAW ENFORCEMENT AND EMERGENCY AMBULANCE SERVICES

■ District courthouse
▼ Police station
⊞ County jail
▭ State correctional facilities

● Fire station
✳ Fire department helicopter unit
✚ Emergency ambulance station
◖ Beach lifeguard service

⎯⎯⎯ Judicial district boundary and name
(For Circuit Courts, see page 141)

10   0   20   30 miles
10   0   10   20   30   40 kilometers

Source: State Judiciary, City and County of Honolulu; counties of Kauai, Maui and Hawaii

1982

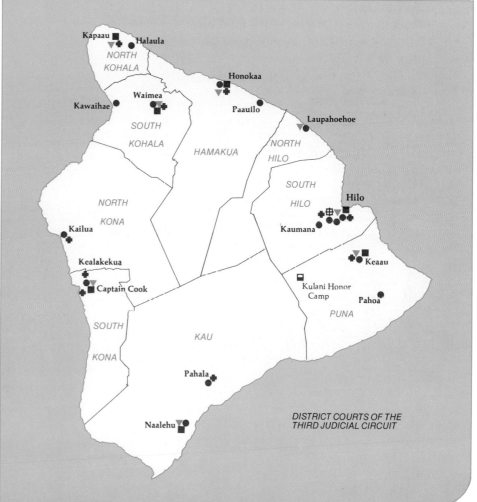

Kapaau
Halaula
NORTH
KOHALA
Honokaa
Waimea
Kawaihae
Paauilo
SOUTH
KOHALA
HAMAKUA
NORTH
HILO
Laupahoehoe
SOUTH
HILO
Hilo
NORTH
KONA
Kaumana
Kailua
Keaau
Kealakekua
Captain Cook
Kulani Honor
Camp
Pahoa
PUNA
SOUTH
KONA
KAU
Pahala
Naalehu

**DISTRICT COURTS OF THE
THIRD JUDICIAL CIRCUIT**

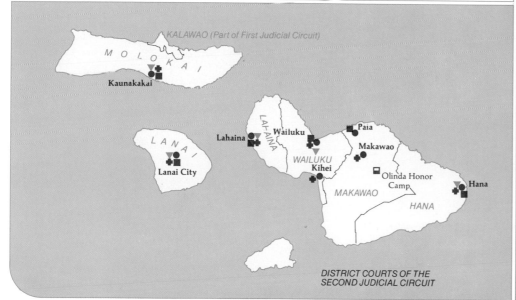

KALAWAO (Part of First Judicial Circuit)
MOLOKAI
Kaunakakai
LANAI
Lahaina
LAHAINA
Wailuku
Paia
WAILUKU
Makawao
Lanai City
Kihei
MAKAWAO
Olinda Honor
Camp
Hana
HANA

**DISTRICT COURTS OF THE
SECOND JUDICIAL CIRCUIT**

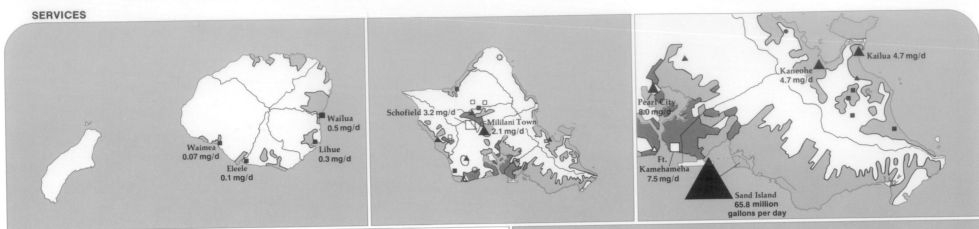

WATER AND SEWAGE SERVICES

Municipal Water Service Areas

County agency   Federal agency

Municipal Sewage Treatment Plants

County Federal

● ○ Raw sewage

▲ △ Primary treatment (screening and settling)

■ □ Secondary treatment (primary and biological reduction)

✿ Under construction

1969-70 flow data

● ▲ ■ Less than 500,000 gallons per day

● ▲ ■ 500,000–2,000,000 gallons per day

● ▲ ■ More than 2,000,000 gallons per day

30 miles
40 kilometers

Source: City and County of Honolulu; County of Kauai; State Department of Health

1980

Note: Counties of Maui and Hawaii 1972

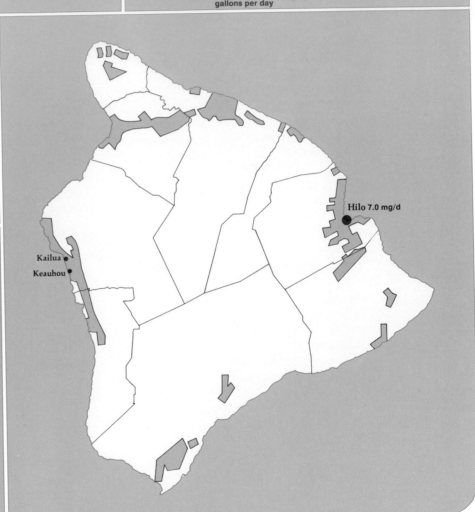

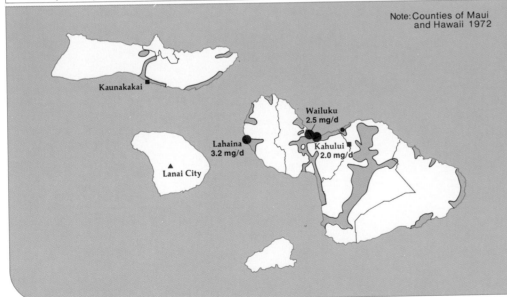

MAPPING AND GEODESY

The earliest maps of the Hawaiian Islands were the nautical charts produced by the British expedition commanded by Captain Cook. On his third and last voyage he constructed charts which depicted the coastlines of the islands he sighted with considerable accuracy and in impressive detail, considering the instruments available. In addition to a general coastal chart of the main islands, a chart of Kealakekua Bay was constructed. A reproduction of Cook's chart appears on page 99.

Twelve years after Cook's death, George Vancouver, who had been on board one of Cook's ships during the second expedition, commanded another British voyage during which additional charting of the islands and somewhat more detailed mapping of coastlines were accomplished. Additional contributions to nautical charting were made by La Pérouse, who visited the Hawaiian Islands a few years after Cook; by the Russian Mariner Lisianski; by Charles Malden, the marine surveyor aboard HMS *Blonde;* and by Charles Wilkes, who commanded the U.S. Exploring Expedition which visited Hawaii in 1841.

Topographic mapping of the islands came much later. It was not until the division of lands under King Kamehameha III, beginning in 1848 and known as the Great Mahele, that land maps were thought to be necessary. Part of the division required the survey of small parcels of land (*kuleana*) for distribution and grant of title to former tenants of the king and chiefs. These land parcels were usually irregular in shape, following natural features such as gulches, streams, ridges, and, in the case of the smaller features, actual occupancy. It soon became apparent that an accurate and coordinated land survey was needed to replace the many individual surveys being performed. In 1870 the Hawaiian Government Survey was formed under the direction of W. D. Alexander, then president of Oahu College (now Punahou School).

The first survey of the islands began in 1871 with measurement of a 4-mile baseline on the island of Maui. During 1871 and 1872 triangulation was extended from this baseline over central Maui. Surveying began on Oahu in 1872 with the measurement of a second baseline. By 1900 triangulation of all the individual islands was substantially complete.

When the Territory of Hawaii was organized in 1900, the islands came under the charting jurisdiction of the U.S. Coast and Geodetic Survey. Hydrographic surveys of the more important harbors and roadsteads were begun, followed by work in the deeper interisland and ocean waters. The earlier surveys were revised and additions were made to the previous triangulation. In 1928, after numerous unsuccessful attempts dating from 1910, a successful connection was made between the triangulation schemes of Oahu and Kauai, finally bridging the longest gap and tying the islands together geodetically. Improved signal lamps and favorable weather conditions were important factors in the effort.

Under the Hawaiian Government Survey there were six different standards of latitude and four of longitude. The hydrographic adjusted latitude was later calculated from the six original standards and 13 additional latitude determinations made at various points in the islands. In 1927 it was decided that a single datum for all the islands was necessary, since two or more of the islands were sometimes shown on the same nautical chart. The Old Hawaiian Datum was initially defined in terms of the coordinates of the Oahu baseline. The coordinates of Oahu west base were determined as:

Latitude: 21° 18' 13.89" North
Longitude: 157° 50' 55.79" West
Azimuth to Oahu east base: 291° 29' 36.0"

At the time of the Hawaiian Government Survey, uniform standards of accuracy had not been adopted, and so the accuracy of the older surveys cannot be determined. By today's standards, however, they were almost certainly inaccurate.

Modern equipment and improved procedures have greatly increased the accuracy of the Hawaiian survey. The latest horizontal control survey of Oahu, completed during 1969 by the U.S. Coast and Geodetic Survey (now the National Ocean Survey) and the State of Hawaii, consists of first order triangulation and second order traverse. On the accompanying map the locations of first, second, and third order stations are shown for the principal islands. First order triangulation is of the highest accuracy and precision and normally forms the basic network for national mapping surveys. Second order is somewhat less precise and accurate. Third order is the lowest that is suitable for use in topographic mapping.

J.R.M.

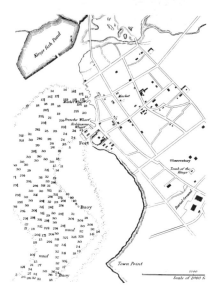

Honolulu Harbor in 1840
Reproduced from U.S. Exploring Expedition (1844)

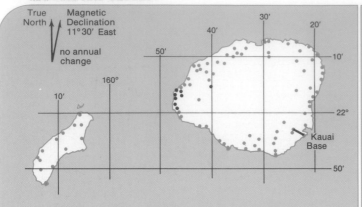

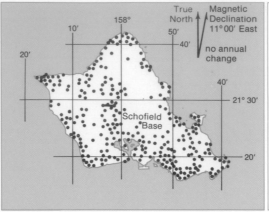

GEODETIC HORIZONTAL CONTROL AND COMPASS VARIATION

- • First order triangulation station
- • Second order triangulation station
- • Third order triangular station
  (selected within triangulation system)
- — Measured base line

Source: National Ocean Survey   1982

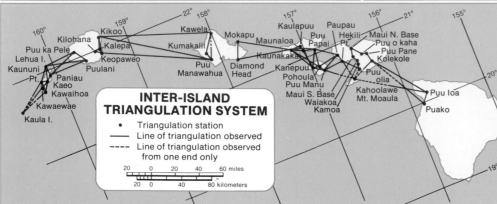

INTER-ISLAND TRIANGULATION SYSTEM

- • Triangulation station
- — Line of triangulation observed
- --- Line of triangulation observed from one end only

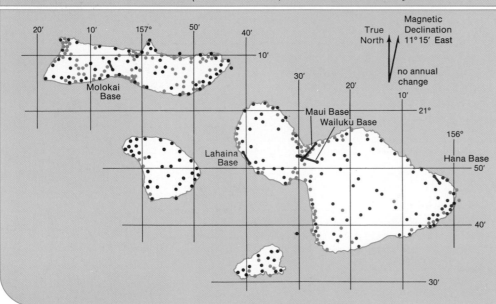

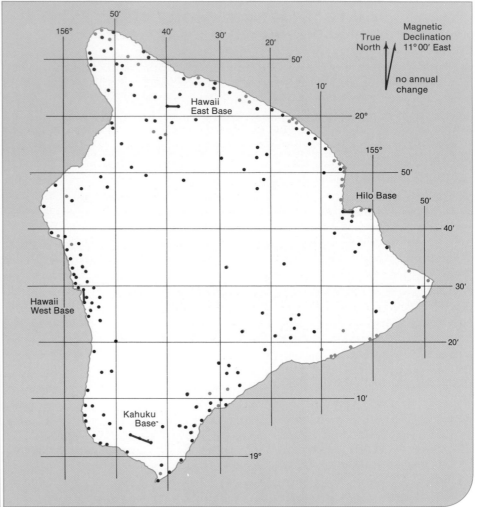

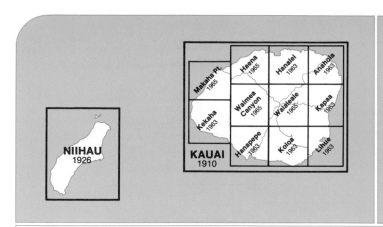

NIIHAU
1926

KAUAI
1910

Makaha Pt. 1965
Haena 1965
Hanalei 1963
Anahola 1963
Kekaha 1963
Waimea Canyon 1965
Waialeale 1965
Kapaa 1963
Hanapepe 1963
Koloa 1963
Lihue 1963

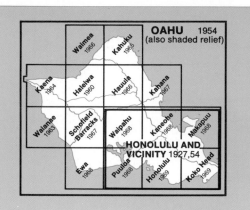

OAHU 1954
(also shaded relief)

Waimea 1966
Kahuku 1965
Kaena 1964
Haleiwa 1960
Hauula 1965
Kahana 1967
Waianae 1963
Schofield Barracks 1967
Waipahu 1968
Kaneohe 1968
Makapuu 1968
Ewa 1968
Puuloa 1968
Honolulu 1969
Koko Head 1969

HONOLULU AND VICINITY 1927,54

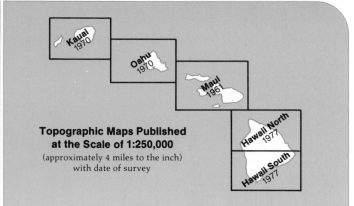

Kauai 1970

Oahu 1970

Maui 1961

Hawaii North 1977

Hawaii South 1977

Topographic Maps Published at the Scale of 1:250,000

(approximately 4 miles to the inch) with date of survey

UNITED STATES GEOLOGICAL SURVEY
TOPOGRAPHIC MAPS OF HAWAII

☐ Topographic map published at scale of 1:24,000 (approximately .4 mile to the inch or 7½ minute quadrangle) with date of survey. Also available as orthophotos (printed or blue diazo).

☐ Topographic map published at scale of 1:62,500 (approximately 1 mile to the inch or 15 minute quadrangle) with date of survey.

All topographic maps contain: elevation contour lines, water features, woodland (except for Niihau, Kauai, Lanai and Kahoolawe 1:62,500), roads and urban areas.

Maps may be purchased from the U.S.G.S. Washington Distribution Center, Reston VA 22092; U.S.G.S. Denver Distribution Center, Denver CO 80225; or from retail outlets in Honolulu.

Source: U.S. Geological Survey

1982

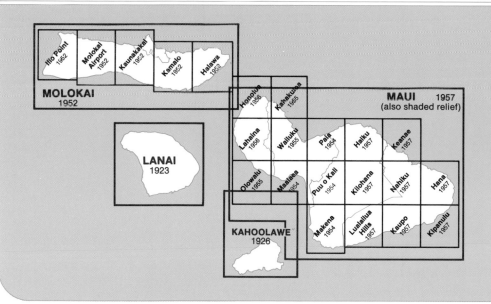

MOLOKAI
1952

Ilio Point 1962
Molokai Airport 1952
Kaunakakai 1952
Kamalo 1952
Halawa 1952

LANAI
1923

MAUI 1957
(also shaded relief)

Honolua 1956
Kahakuloa 1955
Lahaina 1956
Wailuku 1955
Paia 1954
Haiku 1957
Keanae 1957
Olowalu 1955
Maalaea 1954
Puu o Kali 1954
Kilohana 1957
Nahiku 1957
Hana 1957
Makena 1954
Luala Hills 1957
Kaupo 1957
Kipahulu 1957

KAHOOLAWE
1926

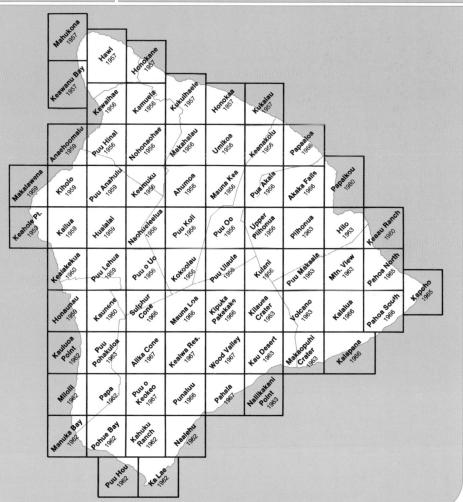

Mahukona 1957
Keawanu Bay 1957
Hawi 1957
Honokane 1957
Kawaihae 1956
Kamuela 1956
Kukuihaele 1957
Honokaa 1957
Kukaiau 1957
Anaehoomalu 1959
Puu Hinai 1956
Nohonaohae 1956
Makahalau 1956
Umikoa 1956
Keanakolu 1956
Papaaloa 1966
Makalawena 1959
Kiholo 1959
Puu Anahulu 1959
Keamuku 1956
Ahumoa 1956
Mauna Kea 1956
Puu Akala 1956
Akaka Falls 1966
Papaikou 1980
Keahole Pt. 1959
Kailua 1959
Hualalai 1959
Naohueleelua 1956
Puu Koli 1956
Puu Oo 1956
Upper Piihonua 1956
Piihonua 1963
Hilo 1963
Keaau Ranch 1980
Kealakekua 1960
Puu Lehua 1959
Puu o Uo 1956
Kokoolau 1956
Puu Ulaula 1956
Kulani 1956
Puu Makaala 1963
Mtn. View 1963
Pahoa North 1965
Honaunau 1959
Kaunene 1960
Sulphur Cone 1966
Mauna Loa 1966
Kipuka Pakekake 1966
Kilauea Crater 1963
Volcano 1963
Kalalua 1966
Pahoa South 1966
Kapoho 1965
Kauluoa Point 1962
Puu Pohakuloa 1963
Alika Cone 1967
Kealwa Res. 1967
Wood Valley 1967
Kau Desert 1963
Makaopuhi Crater 1963
Kalapana 1966
Milolii 1962
Papa 1962
Puu o Keokeo 1967
Punaluu 1966
Pahala 1967
Nalilikakani Point 1963
Manuka Bay 1962
Pohue Bay 1962
Kahuku Ranch 1962
Naalehu 1962
Puu Hou 1962
Ka Lae 1962

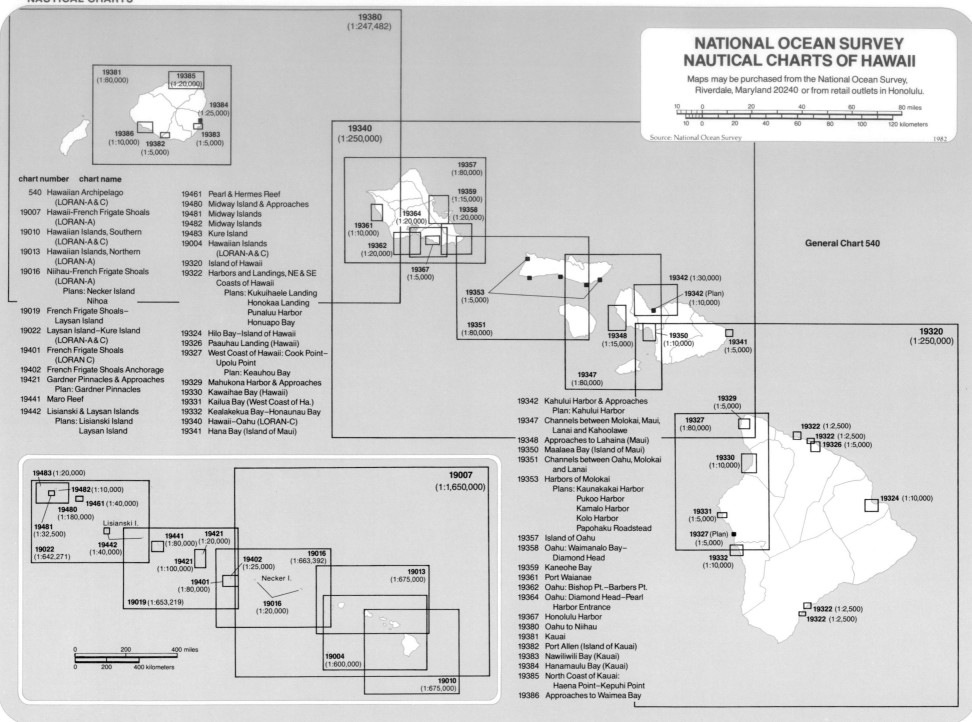

NATIONAL OCEAN SURVEY
NAUTICAL CHARTS OF HAWAII

Maps may be purchased from the National Ocean Survey, Riverdale, Maryland 20240 or from retail outlets in Honolulu.

Source: National Ocean Survey   1982

19380 (1:247,482)

19381 (1:80,000)

19385 (1:20,000)

19384 (1:25,000)

19386 (1:10,000)

19382 (1:5,000)

19383 (1:5,000)

chart number	chart name
540	Hawaiian Archipelago (LORAN-A & C)
19007	Hawaii–French Frigate Shoals (LORAN-A)
19010	Hawaiian Islands, Southern (LORAN-A & C)
19013	Hawaiian Islands, Northern (LORAN-A)
19016	Niihau–French Frigate Shoals (LORAN-A)
	Plans: Necker Island
	Nihoa
19019	French Frigate Shoals– Laysan Island
19022	Laysan Island–Kure Island (LORAN-A & C)
19401	French Frigate Shoals (LORAN C)
19402	French Frigate Shoals Anchorage
19421	Gardner Pinnacles & Approaches
	Plan: Gardner Pinnacles
19441	Maro Reef
19442	Lisianski & Laysan Islands
	Plans: Lisianski Island
	Laysan Island

19461	Pearl & Hermes Reef
19480	Midway Island & Approaches
19481	Midway Islands
19482	Midway Islands
19483	Kure Island
19004	Hawaiian Islands (LORAN-A & C)
19320	Island of Hawaii
19322	Harbors and Landings, NE & SE Coasts of Hawaii
	Plans: Kukuihaele Landing
	Honokaa Landing
	Punaluu Harbor
	Honuapo Bay
19324	Hilo Bay–Island of Hawaii
19326	Paauhau Landing (Hawaii)
19327	West Coast of Hawaii: Cook Point– Upolu Point
	Plan: Keauhou Bay
19329	Mahukona Harbor & Approaches
19330	Kawaihae Bay (Hawaii)
19331	Kailua Bay (West Coast of Ha.)
19332	Kealakekua Bay–Honaunau Bay
19340	Hawaii–Oahu (LORAN-C)
19341	Hana Bay (Island of Maui)

19340 (1:250,000)

19357 (1:80,000)

19359 (1:15,000)

19364 (1:20,000)

19358 (1:20,000)

19361 (1:10,000)

19362 (1:20,000)

19367 (1:5,000)

19353 (1:5,000)

19351 (1:80,000)

19347 (1:80,000)

19348 (1:15,000)

19350 (1:10,000)

19341 (1:5,000)

19342 (1:30,000)

19342 (Plan) (1:10,000)

General Chart 540

19320 (1:250,000)

19329 (1:5,000)

19327 (1:80,000)

19322 (1:2,500)

19322 (1:2,500)

19326 (1:5,000)

19330 (1:10,000)

19324 (1:10,000)

19331 (1:5,000)

19327 (Plan) (1:5,000)

19332 (1:10,000)

19322 (1:2,500)

19322 (1:2,500)

19342	Kahului Harbor & Approaches
	Plan: Kahului Harbor
19347	Channels between Molokai, Maui, Lanai and Kahoolawe
19348	Approaches to Lahaina (Maui)
19350	Maalaea Bay (Island of Maui)
19351	Channels between Oahu, Molokai and Lanai
19353	Harbors of Molokai
	Plans: Kaunakakai Harbor
	Pukoo Harbor
	Kamalo Harbor
	Kolo Harbor
	Papohaku Roadstead
19357	Island of Oahu
19358	Oahu: Waimanalo Bay– Diamond Head
19359	Kaneohe Bay
19361	Port Waianae
19362	Oahu: Bishop Pt.–Barbers Pt.
19364	Oahu: Diamond Head–Pearl Harbor Entrance
19367	Honolulu Harbor
19380	Oahu to Niihau
19381	Kauai
19382	Port Allen (Island of Kauai)
19383	Nawiliwili Bay (Kauai)
19384	Hanamaulu Bay (Kauai)
19385	North Coast of Kauai: Haena Point–Kepuhi Point
19386	Approaches to Waimea Bay

19483 (1:20,000)

19482 (1:10,000)

19461 (1:40,000)

19480 (1:180,000)

19481 (1:32,500)

Lisianski I.

19442 (1:40,000)

19022 (1:642,271)

19441 (1:80,000)

19421 (1:20,000)

19421 (1:100,000)

19402 (1:25,000)

19016 (1:663,392)

19401 (1:80,000)

Necker I.

19019 (1:653,219)

19016 (1:20,000)

19013 (1:675,000)

19007 (1:1,650,000)

19004 (1:600,000)

19010 (1:675,000)

0   200   400 miles

0   200   400 kilometers

APPENDICES

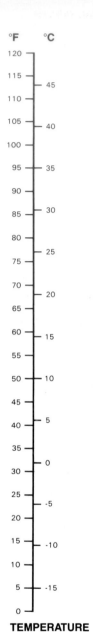

°F °C

120
115
    45
110
105
    40
100
95
    35
90
    30
85
80
    25
75
70
    20
65
60
    15
55
50
    10
45
40
    5
35
    0
30
25
    -5
20
15
    -10
10
5
    -15
0

**TEMPERATURE
SCALES**

STATISTICAL TABLES

Areas: State, Counties, and Islands

Place	Total Area		Inland Water
	Square kilometers	Square miles	Square miles
The State	16,706.5	6,450.4	25.0
Counties			
Hawaii	10,458.4	4,038.0	1.0
Honolulu	1,582.2	610.9	15.2
Kauai	1,624.2	627.1	8.0
Maui	3,041.6	1,174.4	0.8
Islands			
Hawaii	10,458.4	4,038.0	1.0
Maui	1,887.6	728.8	0.6
Oahu	1,573.9	607.7	15.0
Kauai	1,433.0	553.3	4.6
Molokai	676.2	261.1	0.2
Lanai	361.3	139.5	—
Niihau	189.1	73.0	3.4
Kahoolawe	116.5	45.0	—
Lehua	1.0	0.4	—
Kaula	1.1	0.4	—
Molokini	0.1	0.0	—
Northwestern Hawaiian Islands	8.2	3.2	0.2
Laysan Island	4.0	1.5	0.2
Lisianski Island	1.7	0.7	—
Kure Atoll	1.0	0.4	—
Nihoa	0.8	0.3	—
Pearl and Hermes Atoll (7 islets)	0.3	0.1	—
Necker Island	0.2	0.1	—
French Frigate Shoals (12 islets)	0.2	0.1	—
Gardner Pinnacles	0.0	0.0	—
Maro Reef	Awash	Awash	—
Other nearby islands (not in the State)			
Palmyra Islands	10.0	3.8	3.0
Midway Islands	5.2	2.0	—
Johnston Island	0.8	0.3	—
Kingman Reef	0.0	0.0	—

Major Mountains

Island and Mountain	Elevation	
	(feet)	(meters)
Hawaii:		
Mauna Kea[1]	13,796	4,205
Mauna Loa	13,677	4,169
Hualalai	8,271	2,521
Kohala	5,480	1,670
Kilauea (Uwekahuna)	4,093	1,248
Kilauea (Halemaumau Rim)	3,660	1,116
Kahoolawe:		
Lua Makika	1,477	450
Maui:		
Haleakala (Red Hill)	10,023	3,055
Haleakala (Kaupo Gap)	8,201	2,500
Puu Kukui	5,788	1,764
Iao Needle	2,250	686
Lanai:		
Lanaihale	3,370	1,027
Molokai:		
Kamakou	4,970	1,515
Puu Nana	1,381	421
Oahu:		
Kaala	4,020	1,225
Konahuanui[2]	3,150	960
Tantalus	2,013	614
Olomana	1,643	501
Diamond Head	760	232
Koko Head	642	196
Punchbowl	500	152
Kauai:		
Kawaikini	5,243	1,598
Waialeale	5,148	1,569
Niihau:		
Paniau	1,281	390
Lehua	702	214
Kaula	550	168
Nihoa	910	277
Necker Island	277	84
La Perouse Pinnacles	135	41
Gardner Pinnacles	190	58
Maro Reef	Awash	Awash
Laysan Island	35	11
Lisianski Island	20	6
Pearl and Hermes Atoll	10	3
Midway Islands[3]	12	4
Kure Atoll	20	6
Kingman Reef[3]	3	1
Palmyra Island[3]	6	2

1. Includes 19 cones over 11,000 feet, 5 of them over 13,000. The summit of Mauna Kea is between 29,400 and 30,600 feet above the ocean floor at the base of the Hawaiian chain.
2. Two distinct peaks. The lower has an elevation of 3,105 feet.
3. Not part of the State of Hawaii.

Major Streams

Island	Feature or Stream	Length or Avg. Discharge
Longest water feature (miles)		
Hawaii	Wailuku River	32.0
Maui	Kalialinui-Waiale Gulch	18.0
Kahoolawe	Ahupu Gulch	4.0
Lanai	Maunalei-Waialala Gulch	12.9
Molokai	Wailau-Pulena Stream	6.5
Oahu	Kaukonahua Stream (So. Fork)	33.0
Kauai	Waimea River-Poomau Stream	19.5
Niihau	Keanaulii-Puniopo Valley	5.9
Largest perennial stream (miles):		
Hawaii	Wailuku River	22.7
Maui	Palikea Stream	7.8
Molokai	Wailua-Pulena Stream	6.5
Oahu	Kaukonahua Stream	30.0
Kauai	Waimea River	19.7
Streams with greatest average discharge (million gal./day):		
Hawaii	Wailuku River	184.0
Maui	Iao Stream	54.1
Molokai	Pulena Stream	22.1
Oahu	Waikele Stream	25.7
Kauai	Hanalei River	151.0

Coastline

County or Island	General Coastline (miles)	General Coastline (km)	Tidal Shoreline (miles)	Tidal Shoreline (km)
The State[1]	750	1,207	1,052	1,693
Counties:				
Hawaii	266	428	313	504
Maui	210	338	343	552
Honolulu	137	220	234	377
Kauai	137	220	162	261
Islands:				
Hawaii	266	428	313	504
Maui[2]	120	193	149	240
Kahoolawe[2]	29	47	36	58
Lanai[2]	47	76	52	84
Molokai[2]	88	142	106	171
Oahu	112	180	209	336
Kauai	90	145	110	177
Niihau	45	72	50	80
Kaula	2	3	2	3
Northwestern Hawaiian Islands	25	40	25	40

1. Among the states and territories, Hawaii ranks fourth in general coastline and seventeenth in tidal shoreline.

2. The figures given here for the coastlines of the four islands of Maui County, totaling 284 miles, are not consistent with the official county total of 210 miles.

Channels

Channel	Approximate depth below sea level (feet)	Approximate depth below sea level (meters)	Width (statute miles)	Width (kilometers)	Adjacent Islands
Kaulakahi	3,570	1,088	17.2	27.7	Niihau and Kauai
Kauai	10,890	3,319	72.1	116.0	Kauai and Oahu
Kaiwi	2,202	671	25.8	41.5	Oahu and Molokai
Kalohi	540	165	9.0	14.8	Molokai and Lanai
Pailolo	846	258	8.8	14.2	Molokai and Maui
Kealaikahiki	1,086	331	17.8	28.6	Lanai and Kahoolawe
Alalakeiki	822	251	6.7	10.8	Maui and Kahoolawe
Alenuihaha	6,810	2,076	29.6	47.6	Maui and Hawaii

Largest Lakes

Island	Name of Largest Lake[1]	Category	Maximum Depth (feet)	Altitude (feet)	Area (acres)	Shoreline (miles)
Hawaii	Waiakea Pond	natural	(NA)[2]	sea level	27	2
Maui	Kanaha Pond	natural	(NA)	sea level	41	2
Kahoolawe	None					
Lanai	None					
Molokai	Meyer Lake	natural	5	2,021	6	1
Oahu	Wahiawa Reservoir	man-made	85	842	302	11
Kauai	Waita Reservoir	man-made	23	241	424	3
Niihau	Halulu Lake	natural	(NA)	sea level	182	3

1. Excludes shoreline fish ponds and areas filled only during floods. The largest intermittent lake is Halalii Lake, Niihau (840.7 acres). Other important lakes include Lake Waiau, Hawaii (1.28 acres), and Violet Lake, Maui (3.0 acres). Lake Waiau (elevation 13,020 feet) is the highest lake in the State and the third highest in the United States.

2. NA = Not available.

Conversion Factors

1 foot = 0.3048 meter

1 meter = 39.37 inches = 3.2808 feet

1 statute mile = 0.8684 nautical mile = 1.60934 kilometers = 5,280 feet

1 nautical mile = 1.152 statute miles = 1.852 kilometers

1 kilometer = 0.621372 statute mile = 0.5396 nautical mile

1 acre = 43,560 square feet = 0.404685 hectare

1 hectare = 2.47104 acres

1 square mile = 640 acres = 258.998 hectares = 2.58998 square kilometers

1 square kilometer = 247.106 acres = 100 hectares = 0.386103 square mile

1 fathom = 6 feet = 1.8288 meters

1 nautical mile = 1,000 fathoms

1 mile per hour = 1.467 feet per second = 0.447 meter per second = 1.6093 kilometers per hour = 0.868 knot

1 meter per second = 3.600 kilometers per hour = 1.940 knots

1 knot = 1.152 miles per hour = 1.854 kilometers per hour = 0.515 meter per second

1 pound (avoirdupois) = 0.453592 kilogram = 453.59237 grams

1 kilogram = 2.204623 pounds (avoirdupois)

1 ton (short) = 2,000 pounds = 907.18474 kilograms = 0.907184 tonne

1 tonne = 1000 kilograms = 2,204.623 pounds

1 gallon (U.S. liquid) = 3.785306 liter = 231 cubic inches = 0.0037854 cubic meter

1 liter = 0.264178 gallons (U.S. liquid)

1 cubic yard = 0.764559 cubic meter

1 inch mercury = 25.4 millimeters = 33.8640 millibars

1 millimeter mercury = 0.03937 inch = 1.3332 millibars

1 millibar = 0.02953 inch = 0.75006 millimeter

219

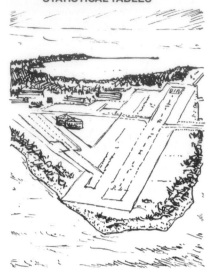

Midway Islands.

Drawing by John A. Dixon

Urban Areas (populations of 1,000 or more)

Town (by island)	Land Area (acres)	(hectares)	Population 1980	Town (by island)	Land Area (acres)	(hectares)	Population 1980
Kauai				**Oahu (cont.):**			
Hanamaulu	508	206	3,227	Waialua	784	317	4,051
Hanapepe	580	235	1,417	Waianae	2,194	888	7,941
Kalaheo	1,152	466	2,500	Waimanalo	255	103	3,562
Kapaa	2,415	977	4,467	Waimanalo Beach	973	394	4,161
Kekaha	646	261	3,260	Waipahu	1,815	734	29,139
Koloa	722	292	1,457	Waipio Acres	447	181	4,091
Lihue	3,959	1,602	4,000	Whitmore Village	470	190	2,318
Wailua	763	309	1,587				
Waimea	624	252	1,569	**Molokai**			
				Kaunakakai	1,289	522	2,231
Oahu							
Ahuimanu	1,646	666	6,238	**Lanai**			
Aiea	3,716	1,504	32,879	Lanai City	154	62	2,092
Barbers Point Housing	149	60	1,373				
Ewa	627	254	2,637	**Maui**			
Ewa Beach	882	357	14,369	Kahului	2,888	1,169	12,978
Haleiwa	1,207	488	2,412	Kihei	2,099	849	5,644
Hauula	1,006	407	2,997	Lahaina	1,150	465	6,095
Heeia	931	377	5,432	Lower Paia	626	253	1,500
Hickam Housing	776	314	4,425	Makawao	1,111	450	2,900
Honolulu	53,723	21,741	365,048	Napili-Honokowai	482	195	2,446
Iroquois Point	403	163	3,915	Pukalani	1,478	598	3,950
Kahaluu	841	340	2,925	Wailea	1,348	545	1,124
Kailua	4,470	1,809	35,812	Wailuku	2,283	924	10,260
Kaneohe	3,886	1,573	29,919				
Laie	781	316	4,643	**Hawaii**			
Maili	573	232	5,026	Captain Cook	4,800	1,942	2,008
Makaha	1,600	647	6,582	Hilo	35,929	14,540	35,269
Makakilo City	1,791	725	7,691	Holualoa	2,767	1,120	1,243
Maunawili	2,230	902	5,239	Honokaa	882	357	1,936
Mililani Town	2,354	953	21,365	Kailua	4,988	2,018	4,751
Mokapu	2,718	1,100	11,615	Kealakekua	1,327	537	1,033
Nanakuli	1,602	648	8,185	Naalehu	2,541	1,028	1,168
Pearl City	5,449	2,205	42,575	Pahala	637	258	1,619
Schofield Barracks	1,849	748	18,851	Papaikou	921	373	1,567
Wahiawa	1,492	604	16,911	Waimea	652	264	1,179
				Wainaku	275	111	1,045

Other Geographic Statistics

Island	Extreme Length (miles)	Extreme Width (miles)	Miles from Coast of Most Remote Point	Percentage of Area with Elevation: Less than 500 ft	2,000 ft or more	Percentage of Area with Slope: Less than 10 percent	10 to 19 percent	20 percent or more	Miles of Sea Cliffs with Heights of: 100 to 999 ft	1,000 ft or more
The State	—	—	28.5	20.8	50.9	63.5	19.5	17.0	145	33
Hawaii	93	76	28.5	12.0	68.4	76.0	20.0	4.0	50	4
Maui	48	26	10.6	24.9	41.4	38.5	25.5	36.0	29	—
Kahoolawe	11	6	2.4	38.9	0	60.0	31.0	9.0	14	—
Lanai	18	13	5.2	24.8	6.3	61.0	23.0	16.0	13	1
Molokai	38	10	3.9	37.3	17.8	53.0	21.0	26.0	15	14
Oahu	44	30	10.6	45.3	4.6	42.5	12.0	45.5	3	—
Kauai	33	25	10.8	35.6	24.0	33.5	16.0	50.5	14	11
Niihau	18	6	2.4	78.2	0	68.0	19.5	12.5	7	3

Source: State Department of Planning and Economic Development, 1982.

Highway Distances

Places	Statute Miles[1]	Kilometers[1]
Kauai		
Lihue—Haena	38.0	61.1
Lihue—Lihue Airport	2.0	3.2
Lihue—Poipu	11.8	19.0
Lihue—Mana	33.0	53.1
Lihue—Kalalau Lookout	41.5	66.8
Oahu		
Honolulu—Ala Moana Center	1.6	2.6
Honolulu—Waikiki (Kalakaua—Lewers)	3.0	4.8
Honolulu—Waimanalo, via Koko Head	21.2	34.1
Honolulu—Kailua, via Nuuanu	12.5	20.1
Honolulu—Kaneohe, via Kalihi	10.8	17.4
Honolulu—Kahuku, via Kaneohe	39.0	62.8
Honolulu—Kahuku, via Wahiawa	46.2	74.3
Honolulu—Kaena Point, via Wahiawa	42.3	68.1
Honolulu—Kaena Point, via Waianae	44.3	71.3
Honolulu—Wahiawa	19.6	31.5
Honolulu—Pearl Harbor Shipyard	6.5	10.5
Honolulu—Honolulu Airport	4.7	7.6
Waimanalo—Kahuku	36.2	58.2
Molokai		
Kaunakakai—Maunaloa	16.5	26.6
Kaunakakai—Hoolehua Airport	6.9	11.1
Kaunakakai—Halawa	27.5	44.2
Lanai		
Lanai City—Lanai Airport	3.3	5.3
Maui		
Wailuku—Kahului	2.3	3.7
Wailuku—Kahului Airport	5.3	8.5
Wailuku—Makena	17.4	28.0
Wailuku—Hana, via Kaupo	59.6	95.9
Wailuku—Hana, via Keanae	53.9	86.7
Wailuku—Haleakala Summit	39.4	63.4
Wailuku—Lahaina, via Kahakuloa	40.6	65.3
Wailuku—Lahaina, via Olowalu	20.8	33.5
Hawaii		
Hilo—General Lyman Airfield	1.8	2.9
Hilo—Kalapana	26.1	42.0
Hilo—Volcano House	31.0	49.9
Hilo—Kailua, via Naalehu	125.2	201.5
Hilo—Kailua, via Saddle Road	87.0	140.0
Hilo—Kailua, via Hamakua	92.9	149.5
Hilo—Waimea, via Saddle Road	60.0	96.6
Hilo—Waimea, via Hamakua	54.0	86.9
Hilo—Kawaihae, via Hamakua	66.0	106.2
Hilo—Upolu Point, via Hamakua	79.7	128.3
Kailua—Keahole Airport	7.2	11.6

1. Mileages (or kilometers) between towns represent distances between post office buildings.

Major Named Waterfalls

Island	Waterfall[1]	Height (feet) Sheer drop	Height (feet) Cascade	Horizontal Distance (feet)	Average Discharge (million gal./day)
Hawaii	Kaluahine	—	620	400	—
	Akaka	442	—	—	—
	Waiilikahi	320	—	—	6.6
	Hiilawe (3 falls)	—	300	200	—
	Rainbow	—	80	150	303.5
Maui	Honokohau	—	1,120	500	25.2
	Waihiumalu	—	400	150	—
	Waimoku	—	40	50	37.1
Molokai	Kahiwa	—	1,750	1,000	—
	Papalaua	—	1,200	500	—
	Wailele	—	500	150	—
	Haloku	—	500	200	—
	Hipuapua	—	500	300	—
	Oloupena	—	300	150	—
	Moaula	—	250	200	19.7
Oahu	Kaliuwaa (Sacred)[2]	80	1,520	3,000	—
	Waihee (Waimea)	40	—	—	6.8
	Manoa	—	200	250	2.4
Kauai	Waipoo (2 falls)	—	800	600	—
	Awini	—	480	500	—
	Hinalele	280	—	—	—
	Kapakanui	280	—	—	—
	Manawaipuna	280	—	—	—
	Wailua	80	—	—	—
	Opaekaa	40	—	—	—
	Puwainui	20	—	—	90.9

1. Includes the largest named waterfall on each major island, either in height or average discharge; all other named falls 250 feet high or higher; and well-known smaller falls. Many unnamed falls have sheer drops of 200 feet or more.
2. Sheer drop refers to northernmost fall of a cascade of six falls.

La Perouse Pinnacle,
Northwestern Hawaiian Islands.
Drawing by John A. Dixon

Lisianski Island, Northwestern Hawaiian Islands.

Drawing by John A. Dixon

Airline Distances (Great Circle Distances between Honolulu International Airport and Specified Places)

Place	Distance from Honolulu		Place	Distance from Honolulu	
	Statute miles	Kilometers		Statute miles	Kilometers
Hawaiian Islands:			Other Pacific locations (cont.):		
Cape Kumukahi, Hawaii[1]	236	380	Singapore	6,710	10,799
Hilo, Hawaii	214	344	Suva, Fiji	3,159	5,083
Ka Lae (South Cape), Hawaii	221	356	Sydney, Australia	5,070	8,158
Kailua, Kona, Hawaii	168	270	Taipei, Taiwan	5,046	8,120
Kahului, Maui	98	158	Tokyo, Japan	3,847	6,190
Lanai Airport	72	116	Vladivostok, U.S.S.R.	4,291	6,906
Molokai Airport	54	87	Wake Island	2,294	3,691
Lihue, Kauai	103	166	Wellington, N.Z.	4,738	7,625
Puuwai, Niihau	152	245			
Nihoa	283	455	North and South America:		
Necker Island	520	837	Anchorage, Alaska	2,781	4,475
French Frigate Shoals	556	895	Cape Horn, Chile	7,457	11,998
Gardner Pinnacles	688	1,107	Chicago, Illinois	4,179	6,724
Maro Reef	851	1,369	Cristobal, Canal Zone	5,214	8,389
Laysan Island	936	1,506	Lima, Peru	5,950	9,580
Lisianski Island	1,065	1,714	Los Angeles, California	2,557	4,114
Pearl and Hermes Atoll	1,208	1,944	Mexico City, Mexico	3,781	6,085
Midway Islands	1,309	2,106	Miami, Florida	4,856	7,813
Kure Atoll	1,367	2,200	Montreal, Quebec	4,910	7,902
			New York, New York	4,959	7,979
			Portland, Oregon	2,595	4,175
Other Pacific locations:			Rio de Janeiro, Brazil	8,190	13,180
Apra Harbor, Guam	3,806	6,124	San Diego, California	2,610	4,199
Auckland, N.Z.	4,393	7,068	San Francisco, California	2,397	3,857
Avarua, Rarotonga	2,950	4,750	Santiago, Chile	6,861	11,042
Brisbane, Australia	4,743	7,633	Seattle, Washington	2,679	4,311
Djakarta, Indonesia	6,807	10,955	Vancouver, B.C.	2,709	4,359
Funafuti, Tuvalu	2,550	4,106	Washington, D.C.	4,829	7,770
Hong Kong	5,541	8,915			
Johnston Island	820	1,319	Other world cities:		
Kingman Reef	1,073	1,726	Athens, Greece	8,277	13,320
Kolonia, Ponape Fed. States of Micronesia	3,087	4,967	Bangkok, Thailand	6,585	10,597
Koror, Belau	4,593	7,390	Bombay, India	8,010	12,890
Kwajalein, Marshall Islands	2,443	3,931	Cairo, Egypt	8,840	14,226
Manila, Philippines	5,293	8,516	Calcutta, India	7,037	11,325
Majuro, Marshall Islands	2,271	3,654	Cape Town, South Africa	11,532	18,559
Nuku'alofa, Tongatapu	3,165	5,096	Colombo, Sri Lanka	7,981	12,844
Nuku Hiva, Marquesas Islands	2,400	3,864	London, England	7,226	11,627
Pago Pago, American Samoa	2,606	4,193	Moscow, U.S.S.R.	7,033	11,318
Palmyra Island	1,101	1,772	Paris, France	7,434	11,964
Papeete, Tahiti	2,741	4,410	Peking, China	5,067	8,154
Saipan, Mariana Islands	3,704	5,960	Rome, Italy	8,022	12,910
Shanghai, China	4,934	7,940	Vienna, Austria	7,626	12,273

1. The great circle distance from Kure Atoll to Cape Kumukahi, Hawaii, is 1,523 statute miles. This distance represents the total length of the Hawaiian Archipelago.

SELECTED BIBLIOGRAPHY

Entries are grouped according to subject matter. The bibliography is intended only as a basic guide to source materials. No attempt is made to provide a comprehensive listing of the many public documents or serial publications available, such as annual reports and statistical studies. However, where beginning dates of publication are given, they are followed by a dash (–) to indicate that more recent information is still being published by that agency or author.

M.P.C.

General Reference

All About Hawaii: The Recognized Book of Authentic Information on Hawaii, Combined with Thrum's Hawaiian Annual and Standard Guide. 1875–.

Bell, J. E. 1970–1975. *A Selective Reading List of Hawaiian Books.* Hawaiian and Pacific Collection, University of Hawaii Library, Honolulu.

Conrad, A. 1974. *Genealogical Sources in Hawaii.* Honolulu: unpub.

Current Hawaiiana. 1944–. (Quarterly.)

Environmental Directory: Hawaii Region. 1982. Honolulu: Honolulu-Pacific Federal Executive Board and Office of Environmental Quality Control, State of Hawaii.

A Guide to Charitable Trusts and Foundations in the State of Hawaii. 1981. Honolulu: Alu Like.

Hawaii. 1981. Directed and designed by H. J. Hoefer. Hong Kong: APA Productions, Ltd.

Index to the Honolulu Advertiser and Honolulu Star-Bulletin, 1929–1967, 1968–. (Annual.)

Men and Women of Hawaii. 1954, 1962, 1972. Honolulu: Honolulu Star-Bulletin.

Men of Hawaii: A Biographical Reference Library, of the Men of Note and Substantial Achievement in the Hawaiian Islands, Vols. 1–5. 1917–1935. Honolulu: Honolulu Star-Bulletin.

Scott, R. L. *Encyclopedia of Hawaii.* 1980. Honolulu: Hawaii State Archives. 3 reels microfilm.

State of Hawaii, Department of Planning and Economic Development. 1967–. *The State of Hawaii Data Book: A Statistical Abstract.* Honolulu. (Annual.)

United States Exploring Expedition. 1844. *Atlas of Charts,* Vol. 2. From the Surveys of the Expedition during 1838–1841, Charles Wilkes, leader. Philadelphia: C. Sherman and Sons.

Geography

Amerson, A. B. 1971. *The Natural History of French Frigate Shoals, Northwestern Hawaiian Islands.* Atoll Research Bulletin, no. 150.

Amerson, A. B., Clapp, R. C., and Wirtz, W. O. 1974. *The Natural History of Pearl and Hermes Reef, Northwestern Hawaiian Islands.* Atoll Research Bulletin, no. 174.

Clapp, R. B., and Wirtz, W. O., II. 1975. *The Natural History of Lisianski Island, Northwestern Hawaiian Islands.* Atoll Research Bulletin, no. 186.

Ely, C. A., and Clapp, R. B. 1973. *The Natural History of Laysan Island, Northwestern Hawaiian Islands.* Atoll Research Bulletin, no. 171.

Kyselka, W., and Lanterman, R. 1980. *Maui: How It Came to Be.* Honolulu: The University Press of Hawaii.

Morgan, J. R. 1983. *Hawaii: A Geography.* Boulder, CO: Westview Press.

Morgan, J. R., and Street, J. 1978. *Oahu Environments.* Honolulu: Oriental Publishing Co.

Place Names

Alexander, W. D. 1903. *Hawaiian Geographic Names.* U.S. Coast and Geodetic Survey, Report for 1902, Appendix 7. Washington, D.C.

Coulter, J. W. 1935. *A Gazetteer of the Territory of Hawaii.* University of Hawaii Research Publications, 11. Honolulu.

Pukui, M., Elbert, S. H., and Mookini, E. T. 1974. *Place Names of Hawaii.* Honolulu: The University Press of Hawaii.

Sterling, E. P., and Summers, C. C. 1978. *The Sites of Oahu.* Honolulu: Department of Anthropology, Department of Education, Bernice P. Bishop Museum.

Summers, C. C. 1971. *Molokai: A Site Survey.* Bernice P. Bishop Museum, Pacific Anthropological Records, no. 14. Honolulu.

Thrum, T. G. 1922. "Hawaiian Place Names." In *A Dictionary of the Hawaiian Language* (by L. Andrews, revised by H. H. Parker), pp. 625–674. Honolulu: Board of Commissioners of the Public Archives of the Territory of Hawaii.

United States, Board on Geographic Names. 1954. *Decisions on Names in Hawaii.* Its Cumulative Decision List 5403. Washington, D.C.

Geology

Macdonald, G. A., and Kyselka, W. 1967. *Anatomy of an Island: A Geological History of Oahu.* Bernice P. Bishop Museum Special Publication 55. Honolulu.

Macdonald, G. A. 1972. *Volcanoes.* Englewood Cliffs, NJ: Prentice-Hall.

Macdonald, G. A., Abbott, A. T., and Peterson, F. L. 1983. *Volcanoes in the Sea: The Geology of Hawaii.* 2nd ed. Honolulu: University of Hawaii Press.

Macdonald, G. A., and Hubbard, D. H. 1973. *Volcanoes of the National Parks in Hawaii.* 6th ed. [n.p.]. Hawaii Natural History Association.

United States Geological Survey. 1959–1974. *Hawaii.* Washington, D.C. (Topographic maps.)

Earthquakes

Estill, R. E. 1979. *Seismotectonics and Velocity Structure of the Southeastern Hawaiian Ridge.* Ph.D. dissertation, University of Hawaii. Honolulu.

Macdonald, G. A., and Wentworth, C. K. 1952. "The Kona Earthquake of August 21, 1951, and Its Aftershocks." *Pacific Science* 6: 269–287.

Tilling, R. I., and others. 1976. *Earthquake and Related Catastrophic Events, Island of Hawaii. November 29, 1975,* U.S. Geological Survey Circular 740.

Wood, H. O. "On the Earthquakes of 1868 in Hawaii." 1914. *Bulletin of the Seismological Society of America* 4: 169–203.

Tsunamis

Eaton, J. P., Richter, D. H., and Ault, W. U. 1961. "The Tsunami of May 23, 1960, on the Island of Hawaii." *Bulletin of the Seismological Society of America* 51: 135–157.

Loomis, H. G. 1975. *The Tsunami of November 29, 1975 in Hawaii.* Honolulu: Hawaii Institute of Geophysics, University of Hawaii.

Macdonald, G. A., Shepard, F. P., and Cox, D. C. 1947. "The Tsunami of April 1, 1946, in the Hawaiian Islands." *Pacific Science* 1: 21–37.

Preisendorfer, R. W. 1971. *Recent Tsunami Theory.* Honolulu: Hawaii Institute of Geophysics, University of Hawaii.

Shepard, F. P., Macdonald, G. A., and Cox, D. C. 1950. "The Tsunami of April 1, 1946." *The Scripps Institution of Oceanography Bulletin* 5: 391–528.

Tsunami Reports. 1978–. Honolulu: International Tsunami Information Center.

Hawaiian arts and crafts: carved temple slab.
Bishop Museum drawing from Te Rangi Hiroa (1964:526)

SELECTED BIBLIOGRAPHY

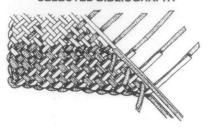

Hawaiian arts and crafts: detail of plaiting of a makaloa mat.
Bishop Museum drawing from Te Rangi Hiroa (1964:120)

Soils

State of Hawaii, State Conservation Needs Inventory Committee. 1972. *Hawaii Conservation Needs Inventory.* Portland, U.S. Dept. of Agriculture, Soil Conservation Service.

United States, Soil Conservation Service. 1960. *Soil Classification: A Comprehensive System, 7th Approximation.* Washington, D.C.

United States, Soil Conservation Service. 1973. *Soil Survey of Island of Hawaii, State of Hawaii,* by H. H. Sato and others. Washington, D.C.

United States, Soil Conservation Service. 1972. *Soil Survey of Islands of Kauai, Oahu, Maui, Molokai, and Lanai, State of Hawaii,* by D. E. Foote and others. Washington, D.C.

Water

Ekern, P. C., and others. 1971. "Hydrologic Systems in Hawaii." In *Systems Approach to Hydrology* (V. Yevjevic, ed.), pp. 186–200. Fort Collins, CO: Water Resources Publications.

Fujimura, F. N., and Chang, W. B. C. 1979. *Groundwater in Hawaii: A Century of Progress.* Honolulu: University of Hawaii at Manoa.

Hawaii Water Resources Regional Study. 1979. *Hawaii Water Resources Plan.* Honolulu.

State of Hawaii, Department of Land and Natural Resources. 1981. *State Water Resources Development Plan: A State Functional Plan.* Honolulu.

State of Hawaii, Department of Land and Natural Resources. 1981. *State Water Resources Development Plan: Technical Reference Document.* Honolulu.

State of Hawaii, State Water Commission. 1979. *Hawaii's Water Resources: Directions for the Future.* Honolulu.

Stearns, H. T. 1966a. *Geology of the State of Hawaii.* Palo Alto, CA: Pacific Books.

Stearns, H. T. 1966b. *Road Guide to Points of Geologic Interest in the Hawaiian Islands.* Palo Alto, CA: Pacific Books.

Stearns, H. T. 1967. *Geology of the Hawaiian Islands.* 2nd ed. Honolulu: Division of Water and Land Development, State of Hawaii. (Bulletin 8.)

Takasaki, K. J. 1978. *Summary Appraisals of the Nation's Groundwater Resources—Hawaii Region.* Geological Survey Professional Paper 813-M. Washington, D.C.

United States, Water Resources Council. 1978. *The Nation's Water Resources, 1975–2000. Vol. 4, Hawaii Region.* Washington, D.C.

The Ocean

Barkley, R. A. 1968. *Oceanographic Atlas of the Pacific Ocean.* Honolulu: University of Hawaii Press.

Chase, T. E., Menard, H. W., and Mammerickx, J. 1970. *Bathymetry of the North Pacific.* La Jolla, CA: Institute of Marine Resources, University of California, San Diego. (IMR technical report series TR3, 6–7, 9–15.)

Fan, P. F., and Grunwald, R. R. 1971. "Sediment Distribution in the Hawaiian Archipelago." *Pacific Science* 25: 484–488.

Malahoff, A., and Woollard, G. P. 1971. "Geophysical Studies of the Hawaiian Ridge and Murray Fracture Zone." In *The Sea,* Vol. 4 (A. E. Maxwell, ed.), pt. 2, pp. 73–131. New York: Wiley-Interscience.

Moberly, R., Jr. 1968. "Loss of Hawaiian Littoral Sand." *J. of Sedimentary Petrology* 38: 17–34.

Moberly, R., Jr., and McCoy, F. W. 1966. "The Sea Floor North of the Eastern Hawaiian Islands." *Marine Geology* 4: 21–48.

Ocean Resource Directory: Voyages Into Ocean Space. 1977. Honolulu(?).

Seckel, G. R. 1962. *Atlas of the Oceanographic Climate of the Hawaiian Islands.* Washington, D.C.: U.S. Fish and Wildlife Service. (Fishery Bulletin 193.)

Climate

American Meteorological Society. 1951. *On the Rainfall of Hawaii: A Group of Contributions.* Meterological Monographs, vol. 1, no. 3.

Blumenstock, D. I., and Price, S. 1967. *Climates of the States: Hawaii.* U.S. Environmental Data Service, Climatography of the United States, no. 60–51.

Ekern, P. C., and Worthley, L. E., comps. 1968. *Annotated Bibliography of Publications and Papers Relevant to Hawaiian Weather.* Honolulu: Hawaii Institute of Geophysics.

State of Hawaii, Division of Water and Land Development. 1961. *An Inventory of Basic Water Resources Data: Molokai.* (Report R15.) Honolulu.

State of Hawaii, Division of Water and Land Development. 1970. *An Inventory of Basic Water Resources Data: Island of Hawaii.* (Report R34.) Honolulu.

Taliaferro, W. J. 1959. *Rainfall of the Hawaiian Islands.* Hawaii Water Authority, Division of Water and Land Development. (Report R12.) Honolulu.

Taliaferro, W. J. 1961. *A Key to Climatological Observations in Hawaii.* Washington, D.C.: U.S. Weather Bureau. (Key to Meteorological Records Documentation 1.11.)

United States, Environmental Data Service. 1973–. *Climatological Data: Hawaii and Pacific.* Vol. 69–. (Monthly.)

United States, Weather Bureau. 1962. *Rainfall-frequency Atlas of the Hawaiian Islands.* Weather Bureau Technical Paper 43. Washington, D.C.

United States, Weather Bureau. 1963. *Probable Maximum Precipitation in the Hawaiian Islands.* Hydrometeorological Report 39. Washington, D.C.

Air Quality

Bach, W., and Lennon, K. 1972. "Air Pollution and Health at Ala Moana Shopping Center in Honolulu." *Hawaii Medical J.* 31: 104–113.

State of Hawaii, Air Sanitation Branch. 1972. *State of Hawaii Air Pollution Control Implementation Plan.* Honolulu.

State of Hawaii, Department of Health. 1937–. *Public Health Regulations.* See "Air Pollution Control," Chapter 43. Honolulu.

Plants

Carlquist, S. 1980. *Hawaii, a Natural History: Geology, Climate, Native Flora and Fauna Above the Shoreline.* 2nd ed. Lawai, Kauai, HI: Pacific Tropical Botanical Garden.

Degener, O. 1946. *Flora Hawaiiensis,* 2nd ed. Honolulu.

Degener, O. 1975. *Plants of Hawaii National Parks Illustrative of Plants and Customs of the South Seas.* Ann Arbor, MI: Braun-Brumfield.

Hillebrand, W. 1965. *Flora of the Hawaiian Islands.* Reprint. New York: Hafner Publishing Co. (First published in 1888.)

Kaaiakamanu, D. M. 1972. *Hawaiian Herbs of Medicinal Value Found Among the Mountains and Elsewhere in the Hawaiian Islands, and Known to the Hawaiians to Possess Curative and Palliative Properties Most Effective in Removing Physical Ailments.* Reprint. Honolulu: Pacific Book House. (First published in 1922.)

Kuchler, A. W. 1970. "Potential Natural Vegetation of Hawaii." In *The National Atlas of the United States of America* (U.S. Geological Survey), p. 92. Washington, D.C.

Neal, M. C. 1965. *In Gardens of Hawaii.* New and rev. ed. Bernice P. Bishop Museum Special Publication 50. Honolulu.

Ripperton, J. C., and Hosaka, E. Y. 1942. *Vegetation Zones of Hawaii.* University of Hawaii Agricultural Experiment Station Bulletin 89.

St. John, H. 1973. *List and Summary of the Flowering Plants in the Hawaiian Islands.* Lawai, Kauai, HI: Pacific Tropical Botanical Garden. Memoir 1.

Mammals

Atkinson, I. A. E. 1977. "A Reassessment of Factors, Particularly *Rattus rattus* L., that Influenced the Decline of Endemic Forest Birds in the Hawaiian Islands." *Pacific Science* 31: 109–133.

Balazs, G. H., and Whittow, G. C. 1978. *Bibliography of the Hawaiian Monk Seal.* Hawaii Institute of Marine Biology, Technical Report no. 35. Honolulu.

Halloran, A. F. 1972. *The Hawaiian Longhorn Story.* Hilo, HI: Petroglyph Press.

Herman, L. M. 1979. "Humpback Whales in Hawaiian Waters: A Study in Historical Ecology." *Pacific Science* 33: 1–15.

Kramer, R. J. 1971. *Hawaiian Land Mammals.* Rutland, VT: Charles E. Tuttle Co.

Payne, R. S. 1970. *Songs of the Humpback Whale.* Del Mar, CA: Communications Research Machines. (LP stereo recording, 2 sides.)

Shallenberger, E. W. 1981. *The Status of Hawaiian Cetaceans.* U.S. Marine Mammal Commission, National Technical Information Service, no. PB82-109398.

Titcomb, M. 1969. *Dog and Man in the Ancient Pacific.* Bernice P. Bishop Museum Special Publication 59. Honolulu.

Tomich, P. Q. 1969. *Mammals in Hawaii: A Synopsis and Notational Bibliography.* Bernice P. Bishop Museum Special Publication 57. Honolulu.

Wirtz, W. O., II. 1972. "Population Ecology of the Polynesian Rat, *Rattus exulans*, on Kure Atoll, Hawaii." *Pacific Science* 26: 433–465.

Birds

Alicata, J. E. 1969. *Parasites of Man and Animals in Hawaii.* New ed. Basel, New York: S. Karger.

Berger, A. J. 1975. "Hawaii's Dubious Distinction." *Defenders* 50: 491–496.

Berger, A. J. 1977. *The Exotic Birds of Hawaii.* Norfolk Island, Australia: Island Heritage.

Berger, A. J. 1977. "Nesting Seasons of Some Introduced Birds in Hawaii." *Elepaio* 38: 35–38.

Berger, A. J. 1980. "Longevity of Hawaiian Honeycreepers in Captivity." *Wilson Bulletin* 92: 263–264.

Berger, A. J. 1981. *Hawaiian Birdlife.* 2nd ed. Honolulu: The University Press of Hawaii.

Clapp, R. B., Kridler, E., and Fleet, R. R. 1977. "The Natural History of Nihoa Island, Northwestern Hawaiian Islands." *Atoll Research Bulletin*, no. 207.

Defenders. [Hawaii issue]. 1975. Washington, D.C.: Defenders of Wildlife, Vol. 50.

Ely, C. A., and Clapp, R. B. 1973. "The Natural History of Laysan Island, Northwestern Hawaiian Islands." *Atoll Research Bulletin*, no. 171.

Fisher, H. I. 1948. "The Question of Avian Introductions in Hawaii." *Pacific Science* 2: 59–64.

Hawaii Audubon Society. 1978. *Hawaii's Birds.* 2nd ed. Honolulu: The Hawaii Audubon Society.

Kear, J., and Berger, A. J. 1980. *The Hawaiian Goose: An Experiment in Conservation.* Vermillion, SD: Buteo Books.

Lewin, V. 1971. "Exotic Game Birds of the Puu Waawaa Ranch, Hawaii." *J. of Wildlife Management* 35: 141–155.

Medway, D. G. 1981. "The Contribution of Cook's Third Voyage to the Ornithology of the Hawaiian Islands." *Pacific Science* 35: 105–173.

Raikow, R. J. 1976. "The Origin and Evolution of the Hawaiian Honeycreepers (Drepanididae)." *Living Bird* 15: 95–117.

Richardson, F., and Bowles, J. 1964. *A Survey of the Birds of Kauai, Hawaii.* Bernice P. Bishop Museum Bulletin 227. Honolulu.

Rothschild, L. W. 1893–1900. *The Avifauna of Laysan and the Neighbouring Islands.* 2 vols. London: R. H. Porter.

Stearns, H. T. 1973. "Geologic Setting of the Fossil Goose Bones Found on Molokai Island, Hawaii." *Bernice P. Bishop Museum, Occasional Papers*, Vol. 24, no. 10. Honolulu.

Wilson, S. B., and Evans, A. H. 1974. *Aves Hawaiienses: The Birds of the Sandwich Islands.* Reprint. New York: Arno Press. (First published in 1890–1899.)

Insects

Carson, H. L., and others. 1970. "The Evolutionary Biology of the Hawaiian Drosophilidae." In *Essays in Evolution and Genetics in Honor of Theodosius Dobzhansky* (M. K. Hecht and W. C. Steere, eds.), pp. 437–543. New York: Appleton-Century-Crofts.

Howarth, F. G. 1980. "The Zoogeography of Specialized Cave Animals: A Bioclimatic Model." *Evolution* 34(2): 394–406.

Zimmerman, E. C., ed. 1948–. *Insects of Hawaii.* 14 vols. to date. Honolulu: University of Hawaii Press. (Vols. 1–8 by E. C. Zimmerman; vols. 10–14 by D. E. Hardy and others; vol. 9, pts. 1, 2 by E. C. Zimmerman.)

Land Snails

Hadfield, M. G., and Mountain, B. S. 1980. "A Field Study of a Vanishing Species, *Achatinella mustelina* (Gastropoda: Pulmonata), in the Waianae Mountains of Oahu." *Pacific Science* 34(4): 345–358.

Hart, A. D. 1978. "The Onslaught Against Hawaii's Tree Snails." *Natural History* 87(10): 46–57.

Meyen, F. J. F. 1981. *A Botanist's Visit to Oahu in 1831.* M. A. Pultz, ed. Honolulu: Press Pacifica.

Reef and Shore Communities

Devaney, D. M., and Eldredge, L. G. 1977. *Reef and Shore Fauna of Hawaii.* Section I: "Protozoa through Ctenophora." Bernice P. Bishop Museum Special Publication 64(1). Honolulu.

Gosline, W. A., and Brock, V. E. 1976. *Handbook of Hawaiian Fishes.* Honolulu: University of Hawaii Press.

Hobson, E. S., and Chave, E. H. 1972. *Hawaiian Reef Animals.* Honolulu: The University Press of Hawaii.

Kay, E. A., ed. 1972. *A Natural History of the Hawaiian Islands: Selected Readings.* Honolulu: The University Press of Hawaii.

Astronomy

Berman, L., and Evans, J. C. 1980. *Exploring the Cosmos.* Boston: Little, Brown and Co.

Bryan, E. H., Jr. 1977. *Stars Over Hawaii.* Hilo: Petroglyph Press.

Finney, B. R. 1977. "Voyaging Canoes and the Settlement of Polynesia." *Science* 196: 1277–1285.

Kyselka, W., and Lanterman, R. 1976. *North Star to Southern Cross.* Honolulu: The University Press of Hawaii.

Lindo, C. K., and Mower, N. A. 1980. *Polynesian Seafaring Heritage.* Honolulu: Kamehameha Schools and the Polynesian Voyaging Society.

Waldrop, M. M. 1981. "Mauna Kea (I): Halfway to Space." "Mauna Kea (II): Coming of Age." *Science* 214: pp. 1010–1013 (I), 1110–1114 (II).

Archaeology

Ancient Hawaiian Civilization: A Series of Lectures Delivered at the Kamehameha Schools. 1965. Rev. ed. Rutland, VT: Charles E. Tuttle Co.

Beckwith, M. 1940. *Hawaiian Mythology.* New Haven, CT: Yale University Press.

Hawaiian arts and crafts: detail of rafter and wall post in house construction.
Bishop Museum drawing from Te Rangi Hiroa (1964:87)

Hawaiian arts and crafts: stamp design for clothing.

Bishop Museum drawing

Buck, Sir P. H. 1975. *Arts and Crafts of Hawaii.* Honolulu: Bishop Museum Press.

Green, R. C., ed. 1980. *Makaha Before 1880, A.D.: Makaha Valley Historical Project: Summary Report, no. 5.* Bernice P. Bishop Museum, Pacific Anthropological Records, no. 31. Honolulu.

Handy, E. S. C., and Handy, E. G. 1972. *Native Planters in Old Hawaii: Their Life, Lore, and Environment.* Bernice P. Bishop Museum Bulletin no. 233. Honolulu.

Handy, E. S. C., and Pukui, M. K. 1972. *The Polynesian Family System in Ka'u.* New ed. Rutland, VT: Charles E. Tuttle Co.

Hawaii Library Association. 1976. *Hawaiian Legends Index.* Honolulu.

Hommon, R. J., and Barrera, W. M., Jr. 1971. *Archaeological Survey of Kahana Valley, Koolauloa District, Island of Oahu.* Bernice P. Bishop Museum, Dept. of Anthropology, Report 1971–1973. Honolulu.

Kamakau, S. M. 1964. *Ka Poe Kahiko: The People of Old.* Bernice P. Bishop Museum Special Publication no. 51. Honolulu.

Kamakau, S. M. 1961. *Ruling Chiefs of Hawaii.* Honolulu: Kamehameha Schools Press.

Kamakau, S. M. 1976. *The Works of the People of Old: Na Hana o Ka Poe Kahiko.* Bernice P. Bishop Museum Special Publication no. 61. Honolulu.

Kirch, P. V. 1979. *Marine Exploitation in Prehistoric Hawaii: Archaeological Investigations at Kalahuipua'a, Hawaii Island.* Bernice P. Bishop Museum, Pacific Anthropological Records, no. 29. Honolulu.

Johnson, R. K., ed. 1981–. *Kumulipo (Hawaiian Chant).* English and Hawaiian. Honolulu: Topgallant Pub. Co.

Leib, A. P., and Day, A. G. 1979. *Hawaiian Legends in English: An Annotated Bibliography.* 2nd ed. Honolulu: The University Press of Hawaii.

Malo, D. 1971. *Hawaiian Antiquities (Moolelo Hawaii).* 2nd ed. Honolulu: Bishop Museum Press. (First published in 1951.)

Newman, T. S., and others. 1970. *Hawaii Register of Historic Places: Bibliography of Hawaiiana.* Honolulu: Division of State Parks.

Newman, T. S. 1970. *Hawaiian Fishing and Farming on the Island of Hawaii in A.D. 1778.* Honolulu: Division of State Parks.

Polynesian Culture History: Essays in Honor of Kenneth P. Emory. 1967. Edited by G. A. Highland and others. Bernice P. Bishop Museum Special Publication no. 56. Honolulu.

Tuggle, H. D. 1973. *Lapakahi, Hawaii: Archaeological Studies.* Edited by H. D. Tuggle and P. B. Griffin. Honolulu: Social Science Research Institute, University of Hawaii.

Tuggle, H. D. 1979. "Hawaii." In *The Prehistory of Polynesia,* edited by J. D. Jennings. Cambridge, MA: Harvard University Press, pp. 167–199.

Tuggle, H. D., and Tomonari-Tuggle, M. J. 1980. "Prehistoric Agriculture in Kohala, Hawaii." *J. of Field Archaeology* 7: 297–312.

History

Anthony, J. G. 1955. *Hawaii Under Army Rule.* Stanford, CA: Stanford University Press.

Beaglehole, J. C., ed. 1955–1967. *The Journals of Captain James Cook on His Voyages of Discovery.* 3 vols. Cambridge, England: At the University Press (published for the Hakluyt Society).

Bradley, H. W. 1968. *American Frontier in Hawaii: The Pioneers, 1789–1843.* Gloucester, MA: P. Smith. (First published in 1942.)

Bushnell, O. A. 1975. *A Walk Thru Old Honolulu: An Illustrated Guide.* Honolulu: Kapa Associates.

Daws, G. 1974. *Shoal of Time: A History of the Hawaiian Islands.* Reprint. Honolulu: The University Press of Hawaii. (First published in 1968.)

Ellis, W. 1783. *An Authentic Narrative of a Voyage Performed by Captain Cook and Captain Clerke . . . in Search of a Northwest Passage Between the Continents of Asia and America.* Vol. 2. London: G. Robinson, J. Sewell and J. Debrett.

Feher, J. 1969. *Hawaii: A Pictorial History.* Bernice P. Bishop Museum Special Publication no. 58. Honolulu.

Fuchs, L. 1961. *Hawaii Pono: A Social History.* New York: Harcourt, Brace & World.

Hooper, P. F. 1979. *Elusive Destiny.* Honolulu: The University Press of Hawaii.

Kuykendall, R. S. 1938–1967. *The Hawaiian Kingdom.* 3 vols. Honolulu: University of Hawaii Press.

Pierce, R. A. 1976. *Russia's Hawaiian Adventure, 1815–1817.* Kingston, Ont.: Limestone Press.

Prange, G. W. 1981. *At Dawn We Slept: The Untold Story of Pearl Harbor.* New York: McGraw-Hill.

Schmitt, R. C. 1977. *Historical Statistics of Hawaii.* Honolulu: The University Press of Hawaii.

State of Hawaii, Department of Land and Natural Resources. 1981. *State Historic Preservation Plan: A State Functional Plan.* Honolulu.

State of Hawaii, Department of Land and Natural Resources. 1981. *State Historic Preservation Plan: Technical Reference Document.* Honolulu.

Population

Lind, A. W. 1980. *Hawaii's People.* 4th ed. Honolulu: The University Press of Hawaii.

Nordyke, E. C. 1977. *The Peopling of Hawaii.* Honolulu: published for the East-West Center by The University Press of Hawaii.

Schmitt, R. C. 1968. *Demographic Statistics of Hawaii: 1778–1965.* Honolulu: University of Hawaii Press.

Schmitt, R. C. 1981. "Early Hawaiian Statistics." *The American Statistician* 35(1): 1–3.

State of Hawaii, Department of Health. 1973–. *Population Report.* Honolulu.

United States, Bureau of the Census. 1900–. *Census.* Washington, D.C.: U.S. Govt. Print. Off. (Decennial.) (Census reports are available for Characteristics of the Population, Number of Inhabitants, Census Tracts, Housing, Race, and related topics.)

Ethnicity

Adams, R. 1933. *The Peoples of Hawaii.* Honolulu: Institute of Pacific Relations.

Burrows, E. G. 1970. *Hawaiian Americans: An Account of the Mingling of Japanese, Chinese, Polynesian, and American Cultures.* Hamden, CT: Archon Books.

Cross-Cultural Caring: A Handbook for Health Care Professionals in Hawaii. 1980. Transcultural Health Care Forum, John A. Burns School of Medicine, University of Hawaii. Honolulu.

Hiura, A., and Sumida, S. 1979. *Asian American Literature of Hawaii: An Annotated Bibliography.* Hawaii Ethnic Resources Center, Talk Story, Inc. Aiea, HI.

McDermott, J., Tseng, W., and Maretzki, T. eds. 1980. *People and Cultures of Hawaii.* Honolulu: The University Press of Hawaii.

Rubano, J. 1971. *Culture and Behavior in Hawaii: An Annotated Bibliography.* Honolulu: Social Science Research Institute, University of Hawaii. (Hawaii Series, no. 3.)

Social Process in Hawaii. 1935–1963. Vols. 1–26. Sociology Club, University of Hawaii. Honolulu.

Ethnic Groups

Alcantara, R. R. 1977. *The Filipinos in Hawaii: An Annotated Bibliography*. Honolulu: Social Science and Linguistics Institute, University of Hawaii. (Hawaii Series, no. 6.)

Char, T. Y., comp. 1975. *The Sandalwood Mountains: Readings and Stories of the Early Chinese in Hawaii*. Honolulu: The University Press of Hawaii.

DeFrancis, J. 1973. *Things Japanese in Hawaii*. Honolulu: The University Press of Hawaii.

Felix, J. H. 1978. *The Portuguese in Hawaii*. Honolulu: Felix, Senecal.

Gallimore, R. 1968. *Studies in a Hawaiian Community: Na Makamaka o Nanakuli*. Honolulu: Department of Anthropology, Bernice P. Bishop Museum.

Gardner, A. L. 1970. *The Koreans in Hawaii: An Annotated Bibliography*. Honolulu: Social Science and Linguistics Institute, University of Hawaii. (Hawaii Series, no. 2.)

Glick, C. 1980. *Sojourners and Settlers: Chinese Migrants in Hawaii*. Honolulu: The University Press of Hawaii.

Kamehameha Schools, Honolulu. 1971. *Aspects of Hawaiian Life and Environment*, 2nd ed. Honolulu.

Kim, H. C. 1974. *The Koreans in America, 1882–1974: A Chronology & Fact Book*. Dobbs Ferry, NY: Oceana Publications.

Kimura, Y. 1962. "Social-Historical Background of the Okinawans in Hawaii." Romanzo Adams Social Research Laboratory, University of Hawaii, Report no. 36. Honolulu.

Lo, C. H. 1972. *The Chinese in Hawaii: A Bibliographic Survey*. Taipei: China Printing.

Matsuda, M. 1975. *The Japanese in Hawaii: An Annotated Bibliography of Japanese Americans*. Revised by D. M. Ogawa and J. Y. Fujioka. Honolulu: Social Science and Linguistics Institute, University of Hawaii. (Hawaii Series, no. 5.)

Miller, C. D., Louis, L., and Yanazawa, K. 1946. *Foods Used by Filipinos in Hawaii*. University of Hawaii Agricultural Experiment Station, Bulletin 98. Honolulu.

Mitchell, D. D. 1972. *Resource Units in Hawaiian Culture: A Series of Studies Covering Sixteen Important Aspects of Hawaiian Culture*. Rev. ed. Honolulu: Kamehameha Schools.

Murphy, T. D. 1954. *Ambassadors in Arms: The Story of Hawaii's 100th Battalion*. Honolulu: University of Hawaii Press.

Ogawa, D. M. 1978. *Kodomo No Tame Ni: The Japanese American Experience in Hawaii*. Honolulu: The University Press of Hawaii.

Pukui, M. 1972–. *Nana I Ke Kumu. (Look to the Source)*. Vol. 1–. Honolulu: Hui Hanai.

Samoans in Hawaii: Selected Readings. 1977. Honolulu: General Assistance Center for the Pacific, College of Education, Educational Foundations, University of Hawaii.

State of Hawaii, Department of Planning and Economic Development. 1976. *The Portuguese Population of Hawaii*. Statistical Report no. 111, January 13, 1976. Honolulu.

State of Hawaii, Office of Hawaiian Affairs. 1981–. *Annual Report to the Governor and Legislature*. Honolulu.

Wakukawa, E. K. 1938. *A History of the Japanese People in Hawaii*. Honolulu: The Toyo Shoin.

Young, N. F. 1973. *Portuguese in Hawaii: A Resource Guide*. Honolulu: Ethnic Research and Resource Center.

Young, N. F. 1973. *The Chinese in Hawaii: An Annotated Bibliography*. Honolulu: Social Science Research Institute, University of Hawaii. (Hawaii Series, no. 4.)

Young, N. F. 1973. *The Samoans in Hawaii: A Resource Guide*. Honolulu: Ethnic Research and Resource Center.

Urban Centers

Baker, H. L., and Dill, H. W. 1969. "Urbanization of Agricultural Land in Hawaii." *J. of Soil and Water Conservation* 24: 98–100.

Hawaii Housing Authority. 1981. *State Housing Plan: A State Functional Plan*. Honolulu.

Hawaii Housing Authority. 1981. *State Housing Plan: Technical Reference Document*. Honolulu.

Kornhauser, D. H. 1969. "Possible Elements of Portent for Asian Metropolitan Growth: Some Examples from Honolulu." In *Modernization of the Pacific Region* (Report of the Malaysian Inter-congress Meeting of the Standing Committee on Geography, Pacific Science Congress, Kuala Lumpur, 1969), pp. 17–24.

State of Hawaii, Census Statistical Areas Committee. 1975–. *Statistics by Districts*. Honolulu. (Report CTC-30–.)

State of Hawaii, Department of Planning and Economic Development. Research and Economic Analysis Division. 1981. *Housing Unit Estimate for Hawaii, 1970–1981*. Honolulu. (Statistical Report 148.)

State of Hawaii, Department of Planning and Economic Development. Research and Economic Analysis Division. 1966–. *Population and Land Areas of Cities, Towns, and Villages in Hawaii*. Honolulu. (Report SB-A1–.) (Annual.)

State of Hawaii, Department of Planning and Economic Development. Research and Economic Analysis Division. 1963–. *The Population of Hawaii. 1980 Census Results*. Honolulu. (Statistical Report 1–.)

Vargha, L. A. 1962. *Urban Development on Oahu: 1946–1962*. Land Study Bureau, University of Hawaii, Bulletin 2. Honolulu.

Vargha, L. A. 1964. *Urban Development on Oahu, 1962–1963*. Land Study Bureau, University of Hawaii, Bulletin 2, supplement 1. Honolulu.

Languages

Aspinwall, D. B. 1960 "Languages in Hawaii." *Publications of the Modern Language Association* 75 (no. 4, pt. 2): 7–13.

Carr, E. B. 1972. *Da Kine Talk: From Pidgin to Standard English in Hawaii*. Honolulu: The University Press of Hawaii.

Hormann, B. L. 1960. "Hawaii's Linguistic Situation: A Sociological Interpretation in the New Key." *Social Process in Hawaii* 24: 6–31.

Pukui, M., and Elbert, S. H. 1971. *Hawaiian Dictionary: Hawaiian-English, and English-Hawaiian*. Honolulu: University of Hawaii Press.

Reinecke, J. E. 1969. *Language and Dialect in Hawaii: A Sociolinguistic History to 1935*. Honolulu: University of Hawaii Press.

Reinecke, J. E., with the collaboration of DeCamp, D.; Hancock, I.; Tsuzaki, S. M.; and Wood, R. E. 1975. *A Bibliography of Pidgin and Creole Languages*. Oceanic Linguistics Special Publications, no. 14, pp. 593–615. Honolulu: The University Press of Hawaii.

Tsuzaki, S. M., and Reinecke, J. E. 1966. *English in Hawaii: An Annotated Bibliography*. Honolulu: Pacific and Asian Linguistics Institute, University of Hawaii.

Tsuzaki, S. M. 1971. "Coexistent Systems of Language Variation: The Case of Hawaiian English." In *Pidginization and Creolization of Languages* (D. Hymes, ed.), pp. 327–340. Cambridge, England: Cambridge University Press.

Religions

Allen, G. E. 1969. *The Y.M.C.A. in Hawaii, 1869–1969*. Honolulu: Young Men's Christian Association.

Arrington, L. J., and Bitton, D. 1979. *The Mormon Experience: A History of the Latter-Day Saints*. New York: Knopf.

Hawaiian arts and crafts: sennit (cooking fiber cordage).

Drawing by T. Stell Newman

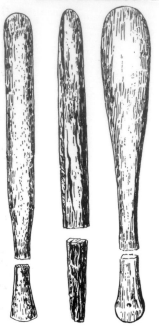

Hawaiian arts and crafts: sweet potato poi mixers.

Bishop Museum drawing from Te Rangi Hiroa (1964:25)

Gallagher, C. F. 1975. *Hawaii and Its Gods.* New York, Tokyo, and Honolulu: Weatherhill/Kapa.

Gulick, O. R., and Gulick, A. E. C. 1918. *The Pilgrims of Hawaii: Their Own Story of Their Pilgrimage from New England and Life Work in the Sandwich Islands, Now Known as Hawaii.* New York: Fleming H. Revell Co.

Hunter, L. H. 1971. *Buddhism in Hawaii: Its Impact on a Yankee Community.* Honolulu: The University Press of Hawaii.

Mulholland, J. F. 1970. *Hawaii's Religions.* Rutland, VT: Charles E. Tuttle Co.

Comstock, W. R. 1971. *Religion and Man.* New York: Harper and Row.

Schoofs, R. 1978. *Pioneers of the Faith: History of the Catholic Mission in Hawaii, 1827–1940.* Rev. ed. Waikane, HI: Boeynaems.

Yzendoorn, R. 1927. *History of the Catholic Mission in the Hawaiian Islands.* Honolulu: Honolulu Star-Bulletin.

Libraries and Museums

Fitzgerald, W. H., Force, R. W., and Kaeppler, A. L. 1969. *Directory of Asian-Pacific Museums.* Honolulu: Bishop Museum Press.

Luster, A. L., comp. 1981. *A Directory of Libraries and Information Sources in Hawaii and Pacific Islands.* 6th ed. Honolulu: Hawaii Library Association.

Official Museum Directory. 1971–. New York: American Association of Museums and National Register Publishing Co.

Wilcox, C. 1981. *The Kauai Album.* Kauai Historical Society.

Centers for the Arts

Abramson, J. 1976. *Photographers of Old Hawaii.* Norfolk Island, Australia: Island Heritage.

Charlot, J. 1958. *Choris and Kamehameha.* Honolulu: Bishop Museum Press.

Charlot, J. 1963. *Three Plays of Ancient Hawaii.* Honolulu: University of Hawaii Press.

Elbert, S. H., and Mahoe, N., eds. 1970. *Na Mele o Hawaii Nei: 101 Hawaiian Songs.* Honolulu: University of Hawaii Press.

Frankenstein, A. V. 1961. *Angels Over the Altar: Christian Folk Art in Hawaii and the South Seas.* Honolulu: University of Hawaii Press.

Haar, F., and Neogy, P. 1974. *Artists of Hawaii,* Vol. 1. Honolulu: The State Foundation on Culture and the Arts, and The University Press of Hawaii.

Haar, F., and Turnbull, M. 1977. *Artists of Hawaii,* Vol. 2. Honolulu: The State Foundation on Culture and the Arts, and The University Press of Hawaii.

Inouye, S. 1965. *The Arts of Shugen Inouye.* Kyoto, Japan: Hozokan.

Kanahele, G. S., ed. 1979. *Hawaiian Music and Musicians: An Illustrated History.* Honolulu: The University Press of Hawaii.

Martel, D. T. 1954. *The Honolulu Academy of Arts: Its Origins and Founder.* Master's thesis, University of Hawaii.

Morse, P. 1976. *Jean Charlot's Prints: A Catalogue Raissonné.* Honolulu: The University Press of Hawaii.

Neil, J. M. 1972. *Paradise Improved: Environmental Design in Hawaii.* Charlottesville, VA: University Press of Virginia, published for the American Association of Architectural Bibliographers. (Its Papers, vol. 8.)

Roberts, H. H. 1967. *Ancient Hawaiian Music.* New York: Dover Publications. (First published in 1926 as Bernice P. Bishop Museum Bulletin 29.)

Todaro, A. 1974. *The Golden Years of Hawaiian Entertainment: 1874–1974.* Honolulu: The Author.

Government and Politics

Directory of State, County, and Federal Officials; Supplement to *Guide to Government in Hawaii.* 1972–. Honolulu: Legislative Reference Bureau. (Annual.)

Guide to Government in Hawaii. 1973–. (Annual.)

Hawaii Documents: Cumulative Index. 1969–. Hawaii State Library, Hawaii Documents Center, Honolulu.

Hawaii Library Association, Hawaiiana Section. 1962. *Official Publications of the Territory of Hawaii, 1900–1959.* Public Archives, Department of Accounting and General Services, State of Hawaii. Honolulu.

State of Hawaii. 1976–. *Hawaii Revised Statutes: Comprising the Statutes of the State of Hawaii, Consolidated, Revised, and Annotated.* 1976 replacement. Honolulu.

Tax Foundation of Hawaii. 1957–. *Government in Hawaii: A Handbook of Financial Statistics.* (Annual.)

Wang, J. 1982. *Hawaii State and Local Politics.* Hilo: University of Hawaii at Hilo.

Who's Who in Government, State of Hawaii. 1957–. (Biennial.)

The Economy

Bank of Hawaii. 1956–. *Monthly Review.*

Bank of Hawaii. 1950–. *Economic Review.* (Annual.)

Economic Indicators: A Monthly Report on the Hawaiian Economy. 1961–. (Monthly.)

Hawaii Business Directory. 1981. Honolulu.

Morgan, T. 1948. *Hawaii. A Century of Economic Change, 1778–1876.* Cambridge, MA: Harvard University Press. (Harvard Economic Studies, vol. 83.)

Shang, Y. C., Albrecht, W. H., and Ifuku, G. 1970. *Hawaii's Income and Expenditure Accounts, 1958–1968.* Honolulu: Economic Research Center, University of Hawaii.

United States, Bureau of the Census. 1946–. *County Business Patterns: Hawaii.* Washington, D.C. (Annual.)

Land Tenure

Baker, H. L. 1979. *Agricultural Lands of Importance to the State of Hawaii.* Cooperative Extension Service, University of Hawaii, Circular 496.

Baker, H. L., and others. 1965–1973. *Detailed Land Classification—Island of Hawaii* [1965]; *—Island of Kauai* [1967]; *—Island of Lanai* [1967]; *—Island of Maui* [1967]; *—Island of Molokai* [1968]; *—Island of Oahu* [1973]. Land Study Bureau, University of Hawaii, Bulletins 6, 7, 8, 9, 10, 11.

Chinen, J. J. 1958. *The Great Mahele: Hawaii's Land Division of 1848.* Honolulu: University of Hawaii Press.

Ching, A. Y., and Sahara, T. 1969. *Land Use and Productivity Rating, State of Hawaii, 1968.* Land Study Bureau, University of Hawaii, Circular 15.

Eckbo, Dean, Austin & Williams. 1969. *State of Hawaii Land Use Districts and Regulations Review.* Prepared for the State of Hawaii Land Use Commission, Honolulu.

Economics Research Associates. 1969. *Hawaii Land Study: Study of Land Tenure, Land Cost and Future Land Use in Hawaii.* Los Angeles.

Furutani, G. Y. 1977. *The Hawaiian Land Use Law: Present Problems and Reform Alternatives.* Master's thesis, University of Hawaii.

Horwitz, R. H., and Meller, N. 1966. *Land and Politics in Hawaii.* 3rd ed. Honolulu: University of Hawaii Press.

Horwitz, R. H., and Finn, J. B. 1967. *Public Land Policy in Hawaii: Major Landowners.* Legislative Reference Bureau, University of Hawaii, Report, 1967, no. 3.

Real Estate Data, Inc. 1981. *Real Estate Atlas of the State of Hawaii.* 15th ed. Miami, FL: Real Estate Data, Inc. (Annual.)

State of Hawaii, Department of Hawaiian Home Lands. 1921/22–. *Report.* Honolulu. (Annual.)

State of Hawaii, Department of Land and Natural Resources. 1981. *Conservation Lands Plan: A State Functional Plan.* Honolulu.

State of Hawaii, Department of Land and Natural Resources. 1981. *Conservation Lands Plan: Technical Reference Document.* Honolulu.

State of Hawaii, Department of Land and Natural Resources. 1962–. *Report.* Honolulu. (Annual.)

Agriculture

Hawaiian Sugar Planters' Association. 1965?–. *Sugar Manual.* Honolulu. (Annual.)

State of Hawaii, Department of Agriculture. 1959/60–. *Report.* Honolulu. (Annual.)

State of Hawaii, Department of Agriculture. 1981. *State Agricultural Plan: A State Functional Plan.* Honolulu.

State of Hawaii, Department of Planning and Economic Development. 1969. *The Life of the Land; Agriculture in Hawaii: Its Background, Problems and Potential.* Honolulu.

State of Hawaii, Governor's Agriculture Coordinating Committee. 1970. *Opportunities for Hawaiian Agriculture. Agricultural Development Plan, State of Hawaii, 1970.* Honolulu: Department of Planning and Economic Development, State of Hawaii.

Statistics of Hawaiian Agriculture. 1975–. Honolulu: Hawaii Agriculture Reporting Service. (Annual.)

Food Sources

Miller, C. D. 1947. "Foods and Food Habits in the Hawaiian Islands." *American Dietetic Association J.* 23: 766–768.

Miller, C. D., Bazore, K., and Bartow, M. 1976. *Fruits of Hawaii.* 4th ed. Honolulu: The University Press of Hawaii.

Commercial Fishing and Aquaculture

Brock, V. E. 1965. *A Proposed Program for Hawaiian Fisheries.* Hawaii Marine Laboratory, University of Hawaii, Technical Report 6. Honolulu.

Shang, Y. C. 1981. *Freshwater Prawn Production in Hawaii: Practices and Economic Aquaculture Development Program, State of Hawaii.* University of Hawaii Seagrant Program UNIHI-Seagrant-MR-81-7. Honolulu.

Shang, Y. C. 1969. *The Skipjack Tuna Industry in Hawaii: Some Economic Aspects.* Honolulu: Economic Research Center, University of Hawaii.

State of Hawaii, Governor's Conference on Central Pacific Fishery Resources, 1966, Honolulu and Hilo. 1966. *Proceedings.* Edited and with an introduction by T. A. Manar. Honolulu.

State of Hawaii, Department of Land and Natural Resources. 1979. *Hawaii Fisheries Development Plan.* Honolulu.

State of Hawaii, Department of Planning and Economic Development. 1974. *Hawaii and the Sea.* Honolulu.

State of Hawaii, Department of Planning and Economic Development, Aquaculture Planning Program. 1978. *Aquaculture Development for Hawaii: Assessments and Recommendations.* Honolulu.

State of Hawaii, Division of Fish and Game. 1959–. *Commercial Fish Catch by Species.* Honolulu. (Monthly.)

Forestry

Burgan, R. E., and Wong, W. H. C., Jr. 1971. *Forest Products Harvested in Hawaii— 1969.* Berkeley, CA: Pacific Southwest Forest and Range Experiment Station.

Nelson, R. E. 1965. *A Record of Forest Plantings in Hawaii.* Berkeley, CA: Pacific Southwest Forest and Range Experiment Station. (U.S. Forest Service, Resource Bulletin PSW-1.)

Nelson, R. E., and Wheeler, P. R. 1963. *Forest Resources of Hawaii, 1961.* Honolulu: Forestry Division, Department of Land and Natural Resources, State of Hawaii, in cooperation with Pacific Southwest Forest and Range Experiment Station, Forest Service, U.S. Department of Agriculture.

Nelson, R. E. 1967. *Records and Maps of Forest Types in Hawaii.* Berkeley, CA: Pacific Southwest Forest and Range Experiment Station. Honolulu: State of Hawaii, Division of Forestry. (U.S. Forest Service, Resource Bulletin PSW-8.)

State of Hawaii, Division of Forestry. 1962. *A Multiple Use Program for the State Forest Lands of Hawaii.* Honolulu.

State of Hawaii, Department of Land and Natural Resources. 1961/62–. *Report to the Governor.* Honolulu. (Annual.)

State of Hawaii, Division of Forestry. 1977. *Hawaiian Forest Products.* Honolulu.

Energy

State of Hawaii, Department of Planning and Economic Development. 1981. *State Energy Plan: A State Functional Plan.* Honolulu.

State of Hawaii, Department of Planning and Economic Development. 1981. *State Energy Plan: Technical Reference Document.* Honolulu.

Manufacturing and Trade

Bank of Hawaii. 1967–. *Construction in Hawaii.* Honolulu. (Annual.)

Pineapple Growers Association of Hawaii. 1963–1973. *Pineapple Fact Book, Hawaii.* Honolulu.

United States, Bureau of the Census. 1980. *Census of Manufacturers: 1972. Area Series.* MC72(3)-12: Hawaii. Washington, D.C.

Tourism

Ghali, M., ed. 1980. *Tourism and Regional Growth: An Empirical Study of the Alternative Growth Paths for Hawaii.* Leiden: Martinus Nijhoff Social Sciences Division.

Hawaii Visitors Bureau, Research Department. 1948–. *Research Report.* Honolulu. (Annual.)

Hawaii Visitors Bureau, Research Department. 1962/1963–. *Visitor Reaction Survey.* Honolulu. (Annual.)

State of Hawaii, Department of Planning and Economic Development. 1981. *State Tourism Plan: A State Functional Plan.* Honolulu.

State of Hawaii, Department of Planning and Economic Development. 1981. *State Tourism Plan: A Technical Reference Document.* Honolulu.

State of Hawaii, Department of Planning and Economic Development, Office of Tourism. 1978. *Findings and Recommendations of the State Tourism Study.* Honolulu.

State of Hawaii, Department of Planning and Economic Development, Research and Economic Analysis Division. 1980. *Tourism and Hawaii's Economy: An Input-output Analysis.* Honolulu.

Tourism Research Project. 1978–1979. *Occasional Publication—Tourism Research Project,* no. 1–5. Honolulu.

The Military

United States, Department of Defense. 1972. *A Plan for Department of Defense Facilities, State of Hawaii.* Rev. ed. Washington, D.C.

United States, General Accounting Office. 1975. *Questionable Aspects of the Military's Study of Land Needs in Hawaii: Department of Defense.* Washington, D.C.

United States, Naval Facilities Engineering Command, Pacific Division. 1979. *Military Property Requirements in Hawaii (MILPRO-HI), State of Hawaii.* Pearl Harbor, HI.

Petroglyph: marchers, Puako, Hawaii.
Drawing by T. Stell Newman

SELECTED BIBLIOGRAPHY

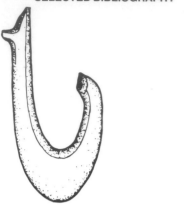

Hawaiian arts and crafts: bone fishhook.
Drawing by T. Stell Newman

Transport

State of Hawaii, Department of Transportation. 1981. *State Transportation Plan: A State Functional Plan.* Honolulu.

United States Army, Corps of Engineers. 1953–. *Waterborne Commerce of the United States. Part 4: Waterways and Harbors: Pacific Coast, Alaska and Hawaii.* U.S. Army Engineer District, San Francisco. (Annual.)

United States, Board of Engineers for Rivers and Harbors. 1971. *Ports of the Hawaiian Islands: Honolulu, Oahu; Hilo, Hawaii; Kawaihae, Hawaii; Kahului, Maui; Nawiliwili, Kauai; and Port Allen, Kauai.* Pt. 2. Port series, no. 50. Washington, D.C.

Communications

Broadcasting Publications, Inc. 1962–. *Yearbook.* Washington, D.C. (Annual.)

Diamont, L. 1978. *The Broadcast Communications Dictionary.* Rev. ed. New York: Hastings House.

Hawaii Media. 1974–. Vol. 1–. (Quarterly.)

Sterling, C. H., and Kittross, J. M. 1978. *Stay Tuned: A Concise History of American Broadcasting.* Belmont, CA: Wadsworth Pub. Co.

Education

American Council on Education. 1946. *Hawaiian Schools: A Curriculum Survey, 1944–45.* Washington, D.C.

Cremin, L. A. 1976. *Public Education.* New York: Basic Books, Inc. (The John Dewey Society, Lecture no. 15.)

Gallimore, R., Boggs, J., and Jordan, C. 1974. *Culture, Behavior and Education: A Study of Hawaiian Americans.* Beverly Hills: Sage Publications.

State of Hawaii, Department of Education. 1924/25–. *Educational Directory.* Honolulu. (Annual.)

State of Hawaii, Department of Education. 1981. *State Education Plan: A State Functional Plan.* Honolulu.

University of Hawaii, Land Grant Centennial Committee. 1962. *Land Grant College for the Pacific, 1907–1962.* Honolulu.

University of Hawaii at Manoa. 1981. *State Higher Education Plan: A State Functional Plan.* Honolulu.

University of Hawaii at Manoa, College of Education. 1981. *To Teach the Children: Historical Aspects of Education in Hawaii.* Honolulu.

Wist, B. O. 1940. *A Century of Public Education in Hawaii, October 15, 1840–October 15, 1940.* Honolulu: The Hawaii Educational Review.

Health

Burch, T. A. 1971. "Health Statistics as Socio-environmental Indicators." In *Proceedings of the Conference on Socio-environmental Indicators.* Honolulu: State of Hawaii, Department of Planning and Economic Development.

State of Hawaii, Department of Health. 1941–. *Hawaii Health Messenger.* Honolulu. (Bi-monthly.)

State of Hawaii, Department of Health. 1966–. *Report.* Honolulu. (Annual.)

State of Hawaii, Department of Health. 1981. *State Health Plan: A State Functional Plan.* Honolulu.

State of Hawaii, Department of Health, Research and Statistics Office. 1973–. *R and S Report.* Honolulu.

Schmitt, R. C. 1968. "Medical Costs in Hawaii, 1859–1967." *Hawaii Medical J.* 27: 236–239.

U.S. National Center for Health Statistics. 1981. *Hospitals. A County and Metropolitan Area Data Book, 1975–78.* DHHS Publications no. (PHS) 81–1223. Washington, D.C.

Recreation

Chisholm, C. 1975. *Hawaiian Hiking Trails.* Beaverton, OR: Touchstone Press.

Clark, J. R. K. 1980. *The Beaches of Maui County.* Honolulu: The University Press of Hawaii.

Clark, J. R. K. 1977. *The Beaches of Oahu.* Honolulu: The University Press of Hawaii.

Fast, A. W., and Seberg, G. 1981. *Cruising Guide for the Hawaiian Islands.* Honolulu: Pacific Writers' Corp.

Freund, G. 1969. *Skin Diver's Guide to Hawaii.* New ed. Honolulu. Distributed by Pacific Sports.

Grigg, R. W., and Church, R. 1963. *Surfer in Hawaii: A Guide to Surfing in the Hawaiian Islands.* Dana Point, CA: John Serverson Publications.

Filosa, G. F. R. 1977. *The Surfer's Almanac: An International Surfing Guide.* New York: Dutton.

Holmes, T. 1981. *The Hawaiian Canoe.* Hanalei, Kauai, HI: Editions Limited.

Immler, R. 1978. *Bicycling in Hawaii.* Berkeley, CA: Wilderness Press.

Kelley, J. M. 1965. *Surf and Sea.* New York: A. S. Barnes.

Kramer, R. J., and Walker, R. L. 1967. *Hunting in Hawaii.* Rev. ed. Honolulu: State of Hawaii, Division of Fish and Game, Department of Land and Natural Resources.

MacKellar, J. S. 1968. *Hawaii Goes Fishing.* Rutland, VT: Charles E. Tuttle Co.

Mitchell, D. D. K. 1976. *Recreation.* Honolulu: Hawaii Bicentennial Commission. (Books About Hawaii, no. 13.)

Morita, C. M. 1974. *Freshwater Fishing in Hawaii.* Honolulu: State of Hawaii, Division of Fish and Game, Department of Land and Natural Resources.

Murchie, N., and Ryan, P. 1981. *Hawaii, a Running Guide.* Honolulu: Oriental Pub. Co.

Rizzuto, J. 1977. *Modern Hawaiian Gamefishing.* Honolulu: The University Press of Hawaii.

Rizzuto, S. 1979. *Hawaiian Camping.* Berkeley, CA: Wilderness Press.

Smith, R. 1980. *Hiking Hawaii: The Big Isle.* Berkeley, CA: Wilderness Press.

Smith, R. 1977. *Hiking Kauai, the Garden Isle.* Berkeley, CA: Wilderness Press.

Smith, R. 1975. *Hiking Maui, the Valley Isle.* Pasadena, CA: Ward Ritchie Press.

Smith, R. 1978. *Hiking Oahu, the Capital Isle.* Berkeley, CA: Wilderness Press.

State of Hawaii, Department of Land and Natural Resources. 1981. *State Recreation Plan: A State Functional Plan.* Honolulu.

Sunset Editorial Staff. 1975. *Hawaii: A Guide to All the Islands.* Rev. ed. Menlo Park, CA: Lane Pub. Co.

Wallin, D. 1978. *Skin and Scuba Diving Guide for the Hawaiian Islands.* Honolulu: Worldwide Distributors.

Services

Catton, M. M. L. 1959. *Social Service in Hawaii.* Palo Alto, CA: Pacific Books.

Directory of Social Resources. 1981. Volunteer, Information and Referral Service. Honolulu.

State of Hawaii, Civil Defense Division. 1977–. *The State of Hawaii Plan for Emergency Preparedness.* New ed. Honolulu.

Mapping, Charting, and Geodesy

Bier, J. A. 1976–77–. *Reference Maps of the Islands of Hawaii.* Honolulu: The University Press of Hawaii.

Bryan, E. H. 1977–78–. *Bryan's Sectional Maps of Oahu, City and County of Honolulu.* (Annual.)

Mitchell, H. C. 1930. *Triangulation in Hawaii.* United States, Coast and Geodetic Survey, Special Publication 156. Washington, D.C.

GAZETTEER

Alphabetical listing of place names on the reference maps, pages 12 through 30.

The first number to the right of each entry identifies the page where the entry appears. The letter and number refer to the index of letters (along the left margins) and numbers (along the top margins) of each reference map. For example, Diamond Head, Oahu . . . 16 F7 means that on page 16, Diamond Head can be found by looking in the square formed where F intersects with 7.

Island abbreviations after each entry are as follows: Ha. = Hawaii, Ka. = Kauai, Kah. = Kahoolawe, Lan. = Lanai, Maui = Maui, Mid. = Midway Islands, Mol. = Molokai, Ni. = Niihau, NWHI = Northwestern Hawaiian Islands, Oahu = Oahu. The Midway Islands, although not part of the State of Hawaii, are included in the Gazetteer.

A place name enclosed in parentheses is less preferred than the accompanying name without parentheses; for example, (Kamuela) Waimea, Ha. For cities, towns and villages for which statistical boundaries have been defined, the 1980 U.S. census population is given in parentheses after the place name; for example, Hawi (795).

The following system for geographic labels was developed for the *Reference Maps of the Islands of Hawaii* series of sheet maps (University of Hawaii Press) by James A. Bier, and is used here. A geographic label in small letters following a place name and a comma identifies the name but is not commonly used as part of the name; for example, Kokomo, hill. When the Hawaiian word for a geographic label is incorporated in the Hawaiian name for a place or feature, the English equivalent for the label is added after the name in small letters and in parentheses; for example Pu'u 'Eu (hill). In such cases, it is not strictly correct to add the English geographic label since the Hawaiian term is included in the name.

Pronunciation of Hawaiian names is aided by the use of a reversed apostrophe, ', to indicate the glottal stop, a stopping of sound, as between the vowel sounds in *oh-oh!* in English; and by macrons over vowels—ā, ē, ī, ō, ū—which denote long stress. An asterisk preceding a place name indicates that pronunciation of the name is uncertain.

A

'A'ahoaka, hill, Ka. . . . 13 C6
'A'ahuwela, cone, Ha. . . . 25 G9
'A'aka Ridge, Ha. . . . 13 D3
'A'akahi Stream, Ha. . . . 24 D6
'A'akaki'i Gulch, Oahu . . . 16 B5
'A'akukui Valley, Ka. . . . 13 D3
'A'āwela, peak, Ka. . . . 13 D4
Adams Bay, NWHI . . . 30 C4
'Ahihi Bay, Maui . . . 20 F9
'Ahihi Point, Ha. . . . 13 B7
Ahole Rock, Maui . . . 21 F14
*Ahua'eliku, peak, Ka. . . . 13 D4
'Āhualoa, Ha. . . . 24 D8
'Āhuimanu (6238), Oahu . . . 16 D6
Ahukini Point, Ka. . . . 13 D6
'Ahulili, peak, Maui . . . 21 E13
Ahuloa, Ha. . . . 28 P3
Ahumoa, cone, Ha. . . . 24 C4
Ahumoa, cone, Ha. . . . 26 G6
Ahu o Laka Islet, Oahu . . . 16 D7
Ahūpu, Kah. . . . 21 G15
Ahūpu Bay, Kah. . . . 21 G15
Ahūpu Gulch, Kah. . . . 21 G15
Ahūpūiki Gulch, Kah. . . . 21 G15
Aiea (32,879), Oahu . . . 16 E5
Aiea Heights, Oahu . . . 16 E5
Aiea Stream, Oahu . . . 16 E6
Aiea Stream, Oahu . . . 17 A2
Aikahi Park, subdivision, Oahu . . . 17 E3
'Āina Haina, subdivision, Oahu . . . 16 F7
'Āinahou, land division, Ha. . . . 26 H8
'Āinahou, lava flat, Ha. . . . 24 C6
'Āinakoa, subdivision, Oahu . . . 17 C8
'Āinaloa Estates, subdivision, Ha. . . . 27 K14
'Āina Moana State Recreation Area (Magic Island), Oahu . . . 17 D6
'Āinaola Road, Ha. . . . 25 J12
'Āinapō, Ha. . . . 26 M8
'Āinapō Trail, Ha. . . . 26 L7
'Akahipu'u (cone), Ha. . . . 26 G2
'Akahukaimu, Ha. . . . 13 E3
'Akaka Falls, Ha. . . . 25 F12
Akasaki Camp, Ha. . . . 25 D10
'Ako'ako'a Point, Ha. . . . 24 B5

'Akōlea Road, Ha. . . . 25 H12
'Alae, peak, Mol. . . . 19 A5
Alaeloa Point, Maui. . . . 20 B6
Alahaka Bay, Ha. . . . 26 M3
Alakaha, Ha. . . . 28 Q7
Alakaha Point, Ka. . . . 25 D10
Alakahi Stream, Ha. . . . 24 D6
Alaka'i Swamp, Ka. . . . 13 B4
Alakoko (Menehune) Fishpond, Ka. . . . 13 D6
Alakukui Point, Ka. . . . 13 C7
'Alalā Lava Flow, Ha. . . . 26 M6
'Alala Point, Oahu . . . 16 E8
'Alalākeiki Channel, Maui . . . 20 G9
Ala Moana Beach, Oahu . . . 17 D6
Alanahihi Point, Ha. . . . 24 A4
Alapi'i Point, Ha. . . . 13 B7
'Alau Island, Maui . . . 21 E15
'Ale'ale, Ka. . . . 21 G15
'Āle'ale'a Point, Ha. . . . 25 H12
'Alele Stream, Maui . . . 21 E14
Alenaio Stream, Ha. . . . 25 D14
*Alenaio Stream, Ha. . . . 25 H12
'Alenuihāhā Channel, Maui . . . 21 F14
'Ālewa Heights, neighborhood, Oahu . . . 17 B5
Alexander Reservoir, Ka. . . . 13 D4
'Ālia Point, Ha. . . . 25 F12
'Ālia Stream, Ha. . . . 25 F12
Āliaiki Lake, Ni. . . . 12 C1
Āliamanu Crater, Oahu . . . 16 E6
(Āliapa'aka) Salt Lake, neighborhood, Oahu . . . 16 E6
Ali'i Fishpond, Mol. . . . 19 C5
Ali'i Shores, neighborhood, Oahu . . . 17 F1
'Ālika Bay, Ha. . . . 28 O3
'Ālika Cone, Ha. . . . 28 N5
'Ālika Lava Flow, Ha. . . . 28 N4
Aluea Banks, Maui . . . 21 C13
'Amikopala, hill, Mol. . . . 19 B2
'Anaeho'omalu, Ha. . . . 24 E3
'Anaeho'omalu Bay, Ha. . . . 24 E3
'Anaeho'omalu Point, Ha. . . . 24 E3
Anahaki Gulch, Mol. . . . 19 A3
Anahola (915), Ka. . . . 13 B7
Anahola Bay, Ka. . . . 13 B7
Anahola Mountains, Ka. . . . 13 B6
Anahola Stream, Ka. . . . 13 B6
Anahulu River, Oahu . . . 16 B4
Anakaluahine Gulch, Maui . . . 20 B7

Ananoio (cave), Mol. . . . 19 A6
*Anapalau Point, Ka. . . . 13 B7
Anapuka (cave), Mol. . . . 19 A2
Ana Puka (cave), Maui . . . 21 H14
Anapuka (cave), Ha. . . . 25 F12
Andrade, Ha. . . . 25 F12
Anianikeha, coast, Mol. . . . 19 A4
Anianinui Ridge, Oahu . . . 17 H15
'Anini Beach, Ka. . . . 13 A5
'Anini Stream, Ka. . . . 13 A5
Anipe'ahi, upland, Ha. . . . 26 M7
Annexation Hill, NWHI . . . 30 D3
('Ānuenue) Sand Island, Oahu . . . 16 F6
'Apakuie, cone, Ha. . . . 25 E8
'Āpana Valley, Ni. . . . 12 C2
*Apole Point, Maui . . . 21 F12
'Apua, Ha. . . . 24 B5
'Āpua Point, Ha. . . . 27 N11
Arched Rock, Ha. . . . 28 O3
'Auwae, Ha. . . . 27 J14
'Au'au Channel, Lan. . . . 19 E4
'Auwaiakeakua Gulch, Ha. . . . 24 E4
'Āwehi, coast, Lan. . . . 19 F4
'Āwehi Gulch, Lan. . . . 19 F4
'Āwehi Stream, Ha. . . . 25 G11
'Āwili Point, Ha. . . . 28 Q3
'Awini Falls, Ka. . . . 13 B3

B

Baldwin Avenue, Maui. . . . 21 C10
Barbers Point (Kalaeloa), Oahu . . . 16 F3
Barbers Point Housing (1373), Oahu . . . 16 F4
Barbers Point Naval Air Station, Oahu . . . 16 F4
Bare Island, NWHI . . . 30 B3
Barking Sands, Oahu . . . 16 C2
Barking Sands, beach, Ka. . . . 13 C1
Barking Sands Pacific Missile Range, Ka. . . . 13 C1
Bellows Air Force Station, Oahu . . . 16 E8
Big Hill Camp, Ha. . . . 26 M4
Bird Island, NWHI . . . 30 D1
(Bird Park) Kīpuka Puaulu, Ha. . . . 27 L10

(Black) Kūpikipikiō Point, Oahu . . . 16 F7
(Black Sand Beach) Kaimū Beach County Park, Ha. . . . 27 M14
Blonde Reef, Ha. . . . 25 C15
Blowhole, Hālona, Oahu . . . 16 F8
Brooks Shoal, NWHI . . . 30 C3

C

Camp H. M. Smith Naval Reserve, Oahu . . . 17 A2
Captain Cook (2008), Ha. . . . 26 L2
Carter Point, Ka. . . . 13 D6
Chain of Craters, Ha. . . . 27 M11
Chain of Craters Road, Ha. . . . 27 M11
(Chinaman's Hat) Mokoli'i Island, Oahu . . . 16 C7
(City of Refuge) Pu'uhonua o Hōnaunau National Historical Park, Ha. . . . 26 M3
(Coconut Island) Moku o Lo'e, Oahu . . . 16 D7
Cook Point, Ka. . . . 26 L2
Crater Hill, Ha. . . . 13 A6
Crater Reservoir, Maui . . . 20 C6
Crater Rim Drive, Ha. . . . 27 M10
Crestview, Oahu . . . 16 E5
(Crouching Lion) Kauhi'imakaokalani, rock formation, Oahu . . . 16 C6
Crown Terrace, neighborhood, Oahu . . . 17 F1

D

Devil Country, Ha. . . . 26 J4
Dewey Cone, Ha. . . . 26 K7
Diamond Head, Oahu . . . 16 F7
Dillingham Air Force Base, Oahu . . . 16 C2
Disappearing Island, NWHI . . . 30 B4
(Disappearing Sands) White Sands Beach County Park, Ha. . . . 26 J2
Dowsett Highlands, neighborhood, Oahu . . . 17 A6
Dowsett Reef, NWHI . . . 30 B3

E

East Loch, Pearl Harbor, Oahu . . . 16 E5
Eastern Island, Mid. . . . 30 C1
'Ekahanui Gulch, Oahu . . . 16 D4
'Eke Crater, Maui . . . 20 B8
'Eke, hill, Ha. . . . 24 D5
'Ekuakapua'a, Ha. . . . 28 R6
'Eleao Peak, Maui . . . 20 D6
'Ele'ele (580), Ka. . . . 13 E3
'Elehaha Stream, Ha. . . . 16 B4
'Eleuweuwe, hill, Mol. . . . 19 A4
Flevenmile Homestead, Ha. . . . 27 J13
Enchanted Lake, subdivision, Oahu . . . 17 F5
'Enuhe Ridge, Ha. . . . 28 O7
'Ewa (2637), Oahu . . . 16 E4
'Ewa Beach (14,369), Oahu . . . 16 F4
'Ewa District, Oahu . . . 16 E4

F

Farrington Highway, Oahu . . . 16 D2
Fern Forest Vacation Estates, subdivision, Ha. . . . 27 L12
Fern Grotto, Ka. . . . 13 C6
Fernandez Village, Oahu . . . 16 E4
(Fleming's) Kapalua Beach, Maui . . . 20 A6
Ford Island, Oahu . . . 16 E5
Ft. Ruger Military Reserve, Oahu . . . 17 D8
Ft. De Russy Military Reserve, Oahu . . . 17 D7
Foster Village, Oahu . . . 17 B2
French Frigate Shoals, NWHI . . . 30 B4
Frigate Point, Mid. . . . 30 C1

G

Gambia Shoal, NWHI . . . 30 B1
Garden of the Gods, Lan. . . . 19 E2
Gardner Pinnacles, NWHI . . . 30 B3
Gaspar's Dairy, Ha. . . . 26 L4
General Lyman Field (Hilo Airport), Ha. . . . 25 H13
Gin Island, NWHI . . . 30 B4
Glenwood, Ha. . . . 27 L12
Glenwood Road, Ha. . . . 27 L12
(Goat Island) Moku Auia, Oahu . . . 16 B5
Gooney Spit Island, Mid. . . . 30 C1

Grass Island, NWHI . . . 30 D1
Great Crack, Ha. . . . 28 O8
Green Island, NWHI . . . 30 B1
Green Lake, Ha. . . . 27 K15

H

Ha'akoa Stream, Ha. . . . 25 E11
Hā'ao Valley, Ni. . . . 12 C2
Hā'ele'ele Ridge, Ka. . . . 13 B2
Hā'ele'ele Valley, Ka. . . . 13 B2
Hā'ena, Ka. . . . 13 A4
Hā'ena, Ha. . . . 24 B3
Hā'ena, Ha. . . . 25 J14
Hā'ena Point, Ka. . . . 13 A4
Hā'ena Point, Ha. . . . 24 B3
Haha'ione Valley, Oahu . . . 17 E9
Hāhākea Gulch, Maui . . . 20 C7
Hāhālawe Gulch, Maui. . . . 21 E14
Ha'ikū (619), Maui . . . 21 B11
Ha'ikū Point, Maui . . . 25 E11
Ha'ikū Valley, Oahu . . . 16 E6
Haina, Ha. . . . 24 C8
Hainoa Crater, Ha. . . . 26 H3
Hainoa Hill, Ha. . . . 26 G4
Haipua'ena Stream, Maui . . . 21 C12
*Hāka'a'ano, flat, Mol. . . . 19 A7
Hakalau (250), Ha. . . . 25 F12
Hakalau Bay, Ha. . . . 25 F12
Hakalau Stream, Ha. . . . 25 G10
Hakina Gulch, Mol. . . . 19 B1
Hakioawa, Kah. . . . 21 F16
Hakuhe'e Point, Maui . . . 20 B8
*Hakuma Point, Ha. . . . 27 M14
Hala Point, coast, Maui . . . 21 E12
Hālāli'i, Ni. . . . 12 C1
Hālāli'i Lake, Ni. . . . 12 C1
Halapē Shelter, Ha. . . . 27 N10
Halapē Trail, Ha. . . . 27 N10
Hala'ula, Ha. . . . 24 B4
Hālawa, Ha. . . . 19 A8
Hālawa, Mol. . . . 24 B4
Hālawa, Ha. . . . 19 B8
Hālawa, cape, Ha. . . . 19 B8
Hālawa Bay, Mol. . . . 19 A8
Hālawa Heights, Oahu . . . 16 E5
Hālawa Stream, Mol. . . . 19 B7
Hālawa Stream, North, Oahu . . . 16 E6
Hālawa Stream, South, Oahu . . . 16 E6
*Halawela, Ni. . . . 21 E12
Haleakalā peak, Maui . . . 21 E12
Haleakalā Crater, Maui. . . . 21 E12
Haleakalā Crater Road, Maui . . . 21 D11
Haleakalā Highway, Maui . . . 21 D11
Haleakalā National Park, Maui . . . 21 E12
Hale'au'au Gulch, Oahu . . . 16 C3
Halehaku Point, Maui . . . 21 B11
Hale Ho'omaha, Ha. . . . 13 A4
*Haleiele Valley, Ka. . . . 13 C2
Hale'iwa (2412), Oahu . . . 16 B3
Halekamahina, cone, Ha. . . . 27 K15
Halekou Pond, Oahu . . . 17 G2
Halekua Stream, Ha. . . . 13 C4
Halekula, ridge, Ha. . . . 26 G3
Halelā'au, Ha. . . . 26 J4
Halemanu, peak, Ha. . . . 13 B2
Halema'uma'u Crater, Ha. . . . 27 M10
Hālena, Ha. . . . 19 B2
Hālena Gulch, Mol. . . . 19 B2
Halenānahu Reservoir, Ka. . . . 13 D5
Hale o Kāne, Ha. . . . 28 Q7
Hale o Lolo, Lan. . . . 19 D1
Hale o Lono Harbor, Mol. . . . 19 B1
Haleone, hill, Ha. . . . 13 B5
Halepalaoa Landing, Lan. . . . 19 F4
Halepili, Ha. . . . 26 J3
Halepiula, Ha. . . . 25 E9
Halepiula Road, Ha. . . . 28 O4
Halepōhaku, peak, Maui . . . 26 C7
Halepōhaku Section, Mauna Kea State Park, Ha. . . . 26 G8
Hāli'i Falls, Ka. . . . 13 C5
Hāli'i Stream, Ka. . . . 13 C5
Hāli'imaile (741), Maui . . . 21 C10
Hāli'ipalala, Ha. . . . 28 Q4
Hāloa, hill, Ha. . . . 24 D6
Hāloa Point, Maui . . . 20 E9
Hālona Blowhole, Oahu . . . 16 F8
Halulu Lake, Ni. . . . 12 C1

I

K

GAZETTEER